Frommer's®
San Francisco 2013

by Matthew Poole & Erika Lenkert

WILEY

John Wiley & Sons, Inc.

Published by:
JOHN WILEY & SONS, INC.
111 River St.
Hoboken, NJ 07030-5774

ISBN 978-1-118-28866-5 (paper); ISBN 978-1-118-33387-7 (ebk), ISBN 978-1-118-33500-0 (ebk), ISBN 978-1-118-33170-5 (ebk)

Editor: Stephen Bassman
Production Editor: Lindsay Conner
Cartographer: Andrew Dolan
Photo Editor: Richard Fox
Design and Layout by Vertigo Design
Graphics and Prepress by Wiley Indianapolis Composition Services

Front cover photo: The Powell-Hyde cable car climbs Hyde Street. ©Brian Jannsen / Alamy Images
Back cover photos: *Left:* Muir Woods ©Sean DuFrene. *Middle:* Biking towards the Golden Gate Bridge ©Sean DuFrene. *Right:* Belden Place restaurant row ©Sean DuFrene.

For information on our other products and services or to obtain technical support, please contact our Customer Care Department within the U.S. at 877/762-2974, outside the U.S. at 317/572-3993 or fax 317/572-4002.

Wiley also publishes its books in a variety of electronic formats. Some content that appears in print may not be available in electronic formats.

Manufactured in China

5   4   3   2   1

CONTENTS

5 WHERE TO EAT 102

6 EXPLORING SAN FRANCISCO 167

7 CITY STROLLS 224

LIST OF MAPS

ABOUT THE AUTHORS

Matthew Poole, a native Californian and San Francisco resident, has authored more than two dozen travel guides to California, Hawaii, and abroad, and is a regular contributor to radio and television travel programs. Before becoming a full-time travel writer and photographer, he worked as an English tutor in Prague, a ski instructor in the Swiss Alps, and a scuba instructor in Maui and Thailand. His other titles include *Frommer's California*, *Frommer's Irreverent Guide to San Francisco*, *Frommer's San Francisco Day by Day*, and *Frommer's San Francisco Free & Dirt Cheap*. You can follow Matthew's weekly blog posts about travel adventures in Northern California at LocalGetaways.com.

A native San Franciscan, **Erika Lenkert** divides her time between San Francisco and Napa Valley, where she is forever seeking the next best restaurant, hotel room, and fun way to savor the region. She frequently writes *Every Day with Rachael Ray* party guides and offers up tasty local tips for other various magazines. In her spare time she tours the region with her husband, Colie, and daughter, Viva, and authors books such as *The Last-Minute Party Girl: Fashionable, Fearless, and Foolishly Simple Entertaining; The Real Deal Guide to Pregnancy;* and *Healthy Eating During Pregnancy.*

ACKNOWLEDGMENTS

I would like to acknowledge the following people for their time and effort in helping me complete this 2013 edition: Kristi Wilson, Michele Mandell, David Lytle, Molly Blaisdell, Kathryn Connor, Erika Lenkert, Yigit Pura, Heklina, Eugenio Jardim, and my unflappable editor, Stephen Bassman.

—Matthew Poole

HOW TO CONTACT US

In researching this book, we discovered many wonderful places—hotels, restaurants, shops, and more. We're sure you'll find others. Please tell us about them, so we can share the information with your fellow travelers in upcoming editions. If you were disappointed with a recommendation, we'd love to know that, too. Please write to:

Frommer's San Francisco 2013
John Wiley & Sons, Inc. • 111 River St. • Hoboken, NJ 07030-5774
frommersfeedback@wiley.com

AN ADDITIONAL NOTE

Please be advised that travel information is subject to change at any time—and this is especially true of prices. We therefore suggest that you write or call ahead for confirmation when making your travel plans. The authors, editors, and publisher cannot be held responsible for the experiences of readers while traveling. Your safety is important to us, however, so we encourage you to stay alert and be aware of your surroundings. Keep a close eye on cameras, purses, and wallets, all favorite targets of thieves and pickpockets.

FROMMER'S STAR RATINGS, ICONS & ABBREVIATIONS

Every hotel, restaurant, and attraction listing in this guide has been ranked for quality, value, service, amenities, and special features using a **star-rating system.** In country, state, and regional guides, we also rate towns and regions to help you narrow down your choices and budget your time accordingly. Hotels and restaurants are rated on a scale of zero (recommended) to three stars (exceptional). Attractions, shopping, nightlife, towns, and regions are rated according to the following scale: zero stars (recommended), one star (highly recommended), two stars (very highly recommended), and three stars (must-see).

In addition to the star-rating system, we also use **seven feature icons** that point you to the great deals, in-the-know advice, and unique experiences that separate travelers from tourists. Throughout the book, look for:

Special finds—those places only insiders know about

Fun facts—details that make travelers more informed and their trips more fun

Kids—best bets for kids and advice for the whole family

Special moments—those experiences that memories are made of

Overrated—places or experiences not worth your time or money

Insider tips—great ways to save time and money

Great values—where to get the best deals

The following **abbreviations** are used for credit cards:

AE	American Express	**DISC**	Discover	**V**	Visa
DC	Diners Club	**MC**	MasterCard		

TRAVEL RESOURCES AT FROMMERS.COM

Frommer's travel resources don't end with this guide. Frommer's website, **www. frommers.com**, has travel information on more than 4,000 destinations. We update features regularly, giving you access to the most current trip-planning information and the best airfare, lodging, and car-rental bargains. You can also listen to podcasts, connect with other Frommers.com members through our active-reader forums, share your travel photos, read blogs from guidebook editors and fellow travelers, and much more.

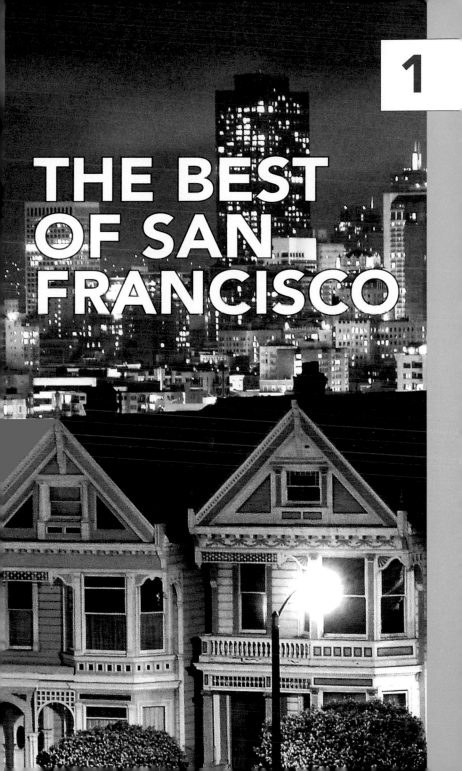

THE BEST OF SAN FRANCISCO

1

Span Francisco's reputation as a rollicking city where almost anything goes dates back to the boom-or-bust days of the California gold rush. It's always been this way: This city is so beautiful, exciting, diverse, and cosmopolitan that you can always find something new to see and do no matter if it's your 1st or 50th visit. Oh, and bring a warm jacket: Bob Hope once remarked that San Francisco is the city of four seasons—every day.

Things to Do   Consistently ranked as America's Favorite City, San Francisco never ceases to entertain. Enjoy the cool blast of salty air as you stroll across the **Golden Gate.** Stuff yourself with dim sum in **Chinatown.** Browse the second-hand shops along **Haight Street.** Recite poetry in a **North Beach** coffeehouse. Stroll **Ocean Beach,** skate through **Golden Gate Park,** ride the **cable cars** to **Fisherman's Wharf,** tour a **Victorian mansion,** explore **Alcatraz Island,** go to a **Giants** ball game—the list is endless.

Shopping   Oh baby, start polishing that credit card. Some of our favorites include strolling the hip boutiques in **Hayes Valley,** gourmet delicacies at the **Ferry Building Marketplace,** the wow factor of **Union Square** and **West-field San Francisco Centre,** real vinyl at **Amoeba Records** on Haight Street, and the weird-to-wonderful shopping bazaar that is **Chinatown.**

Nightlife & Entertainment   It's true: San Francisco sells more theater tickets per capita than any other major city in America. We love to watch our recycled Broadway musicals at the **A.C.T.** and transgender tragedies at **Theatre Rhinoceros.** The San Francisco **Symphony, Opera,** and **Ballet** are three great reasons to dress up. Sundays are a Drag (show) at **Harry Denton's Starlight Room,** while anything goes down at the **Endup.** Maceo Parker's playing at **Yoshi's,** Stanton Moore is at the **Boom Boom Room,** and Tainted Love is sold out at **Bimbo's 365 Club.** Let's end the night with a Golden Gate Martini at **Top of the Mark.**

Restaurants & Dining   With more than 3,500 restaurants in San Francisco, you could eat at a different restaurant every night for 10 years and still not visit them all. Try **Afghan, Burmese, Cambodian, Cajun, Moroccan, Persian, Ethiopian**—or better yet, follow the **street food craze** at roaminghunger.com/sf in search of **Sam's Chowdermobile, Chairman Bao,** and **Waffle Mania** food trucks.

THE best ONLY-IN–SAN FRANCISCO EXPERIENCES

- **A Powell–Hyde Cable Car Ride:** Skip the less-scenic California line and take the Powell–Hyde cable car down to Fisherman's Wharf—the ride is worth the wait. When you reach the top of Nob Hill, grab the rail with one hand and hold your camera with the other, because you're about to see a view of the bay that'll make you all weepy. See p. 172.

A world-class bike ride.

The Powell–Hyde cable car.

o **An Adventure at Alcatraz:** Even if you loathe tourist attractions, you'll dig Alcatraz. Just looking at the Rock from across the bay is enough to give you the heebie-jeebies—and the park rangers have put together an excellent audio tour with narration by former inmates and guards. Heck, even the boat ride across the bay is worth the price. See p. 168.

o **A Walk or Bike Ride Across the Golden Gate Bridge:** Don your wind-breaker and walking shoes and prepare for a wind-blasted, exhilarating journey across San Francisco's most famous landmark. It's simply one of those things you have to do at least once in your life. See p. 178.

o **A Stroll Through Chinatown:** Chinatown is a trip—about as close to experiencing Asia as you can get without a passport. Skip the ersatz camera and

Alcatraz Island.

luggage stores and head straight for the food markets, where a cornucopia of critters that you'll never see at Safeway sit in boxes waiting for the wok. (Is that an armadillo?) Better yet, take one of Shirley Fong-Torres's Wok Wiz tours of Chinatown (p. 194).

o **A San Francisco Giants Game at AT&T Park:** If it's baseball season, then you *must* spend an afternoon or evening watching the National League's Giants at one of the finest ballparks in America. For only $10, you can buy a bleacher seat on the day of a game. Even if the season's over, you can still take a guided tour of the stadium. See p. 222.

THE best SPLURGE HOTELS

o The **Ritz-Carlton San Francisco,** 600 Stockton St., Nob Hill (𝄡 800/241-3333 or 415/296-7465; www.ritzcarlton.com), is the sine qua non of luxury hotels, offering near-perfect service and every possible amenity. Even if you can't afford a guest room, come for the mind-blowing Sunday brunch. See p. 77.

o **Four Seasons Hotel San Francisco,** 757 Market St., south of Market Street (SoMa; 𝄡 800/819-5053 or 415/633-3000; www. fourseasons.com), is the perfect combination of opulence, hipness, and class. We can't afford it either, but we sure love to hang out at the bar and pretend. See p. 80.

o The **Mandarin Oriental,** 222 Sansome St., Financial District (𝄡 800/622-0404 or 415/276-9888; www.mandarinoriental.com/sanfrancisco), is perched so high

The Ritz-Carlton lobby.

above the city that the fog rolls in *below* you. Take in the view from your glass-wall bathtub. Maybe we really did die and go to heaven? See p. 85.

o The **St. Regis Hotel,** 125 Third St., SoMa (𝄡 877/787-3447 or 415/284-4000; www.stregis.com/sanfrancisco), has these touch-screen remote controls that let you operate everything in your room—without leaving your bed. Add a destination restaurant and a fabulous two-floor spa, and why would you ever want to leave? See p. 82.

THE best MODERATELY PRICED HOTELS

o The **Golden Gate Hotel,** 775 Bush St., Union Square (𝄡 800/835-1118 or 415/392-3702; www.goldengatehotel.com), receives nothing but kudos from satisfied returning guests. Just 2 blocks from Union Square, this 1913 Edwardian hotel is a charmer and a fantastic value. See p. 74.

A room at the Hotel Union Square.

- **Hotel Adagio,** 550 Geary St., Union Square (© **800/228-8830** or 415/775-5000; www.thehoteladagio.com), is far more chic and hip than its category counterparts. The 1929 Spanish Revival building has sexy streamlined rooms swathed in rich spice and earth tones. See p. 65

- The **Hotel Bohème,** 444 Columbus Ave., Nob Hill (© **415/433-9111;** www.hotelboheme.com), is the perfect mixture of art, style, class, romance, and location—just steps from the sidewalk cafes of North Beach. If Bette Davis were alive today, this is where she'd stay. See p. 89.

- **Hotel Union Square,** 114 Powell St., Union Square (© **415/397-3000;** www.hotelunionsquare.com), is an updated classic in an ideal location. A $5-million renovation in 2008 melded contemporary elements with historical San Francisco features dating back to 1915. See p. 70

- **Laurel Inn,** 444 Presidio Ave., Pacific Heights (© **800/552-8735** or 415/567-8467; www.thelaurelinn.com), may be off the beaten track, but it's one of the best affordable, fashionable hotels in the city. Just outside of the southern entrance to the Presidio in the midst of residential Presidio Heights, it's a chic motel with soothing, contemporary decor and equally calming prices. See p. 91.

THE best DINING EXPERIENCES

- **The Best of the City's Fine Dining: La Folie,** 2316 Polk St., Russian Hill (© **415/776-5577**), has been the place to go for cuisine at its finest since 1988. Celebrity chef Roland Passot never fails to offer his guests a delightfully long, lavish meal. And then there's **Restaurant Gary Danko,** 800 North Point St., Fisherman's Wharf (© **415/749-2060;** p. 136), always a sure bet for a perfect contemporary French meal complete with polished service and flambéed finales.

- **Best Classic San Francisco Dining Experience:** The lovable loudmouths working behind the narrow counter of **Swan Oyster Depot,** 1517 Polk St. (© **415/673-1101**), have been satisfying patrons with fresh crab, shrimp, oysters, and clam chowder since 1912. The father of this guide's author,

A vendor at Fisherman's Wharf.

Swan Oyster Depot.

Matthew Poole, doesn't care much for visiting San Francisco ("Too crowded!"), but he loves having lunch at this beloved seafood institution. See p. 127.

○ **Best Dining on Dungeness Crab:** Eating fresh Dungeness crabmeat straight from Fisherman's Wharf seafood vendors' boiling pots at the corner of Jefferson and Taylor streets may be touristy, but it's the quintessential San Francisco experience. See p. 176. Locals are more apt to go to **Swan Oyster Depot.** See p. 127.

○ **Best Dim Sum Feast:** If you like Chinese food in bite-size portions, you'll love dim sum. At **Ton Kiang,** 5821 Geary Blvd., the Richmond (© 415/387-8273; p. 165), you'll be wowed by the variety of dumplings and mysterious dishes. Don't worry about the language barrier; just point at what looks good and it will be delivered. For downtown dim sum, the venerable **Yank Sing,** 101 Spear St. (© 415/957-9300; p. 119), offers an exotic edible surprise on every cart that's wheeled to your table.

○ **Best Breakfast:** We have a tie: **Dottie's True Blue Café,** 28 Sixth St. (© 415/885-2767; p. 125), has taken the classic American breakfast to a new level—maybe the best we've ever had. **Ella's,** 500 Presidio Ave. (© 415/441-5669; p. 142), is far more yuppie, equally divine, and in a much better neighborhood, but it's so popular that the wait on weekend mornings is brutal.

o **Best Funky Atmosphere:** That's an easy one: **Tommy's Joynt,** 1101 Geary Blvd. (© **415/775-4216**). The interior looks like a Buffalo Bill museum that imploded, the exterior paint job looks like a circus tent on acid, and the huge trays of *hofbrau* classics will make your arteries harden just by looking at them. See p. 149.

o **Best Family-Style Restaurant:** Giant platters of classic Italian food and carafes filled with table wine are placed on long wooden tables by motherly waitresses while Sinatra classics play to the festive crowd of contented diners. Welcome to North Beach–style family dining at **Capp's Corner,** 1600 Powell St. (© **415/989-2589**). See p. 132.

o **Best Surreal Dining Experience:** This has to be sitting cross-legged on a pillow, shoes off, smoking apricot tobacco out of a hookah, eating baba ghanouj, and drinking spiced wine in an exotic Middle Eastern setting while beautiful, sensuous belly dancers glide across the dining room. Unwind your mind at **Kan Zaman,** 1793 Haight St. (© **415/751-9656**). See p. 161.

o **Best Wine Country Dining:** If you're a foodie, you already know that one of the top restaurants in the world, the **French Laundry,** 6640 Washington St. (© **707/944-2380;** p. 357), is about 1½ hours north of the city in the Wine Country's tiny town of Yountville. Only die-hard diners need apply: You'll need to fight for a reservation 2 months in advance. A more relaxed alternative is **Terra,** 1345 Railroad Ave., St. Helena (© **707/963-8931;** p. 361), where award-winning chef Hiro Sone shows his culinary creativity and mastery of French, Italian, and Japanese cuisine within a historic fieldstone split dining room.

THE best THINGS TO DO FOR FREE (OR ALMOST)

o **Meander Along the Marina's Golden Gate Promenade and Crissy Field.** There's something about strolling the promenade that just feels right. The combination of beach, bay, boats, Golden Gate views, and clean, cool breezes is good for the soul. Don't miss snacks at the Warming Hut. See p. 202.

o **Wake up with North Beach Coffee.** One of the most pleasurable smells of San Francisco is the aroma of roasted coffee beans wafting down Columbus Avenue in the early morning. Start the day with a cup of Viennese on a sidewalk table at **Caffè Greco,** 423 Columbus Ave. (© **415/397-6261**), followed by a walk down Columbus Avenue to the bay.

o **Browse the Haight.** Though the power of the flower has wilted, the Haight is still, more or less, the Haight: a sort of resting home for aging hippies, exDeadheads, skate punks, and an eclectic assortment of young panhandlers. Think of it as a people zoo as you walk down the rows of used-clothing stores, hip boutiques, and leather shops. End the tour with a pitcher of sangria and a plate of mussels at **Cha Cha Cha** (p. 161), one of our favorite restaurants that's a bargain to boot.

10 free & dirt-cheap **SECRETS**

You'll find more frugal tips in *Frommer's San Francisco Free & Dirt Cheap* (John Wiley & Sons, Inc.):

1. Tickets to the **de Young Museum** (p. 184; pictured at right) ain't cheap, but you can climb to the top of the museum's 144-foot observation tower for free. And if you can time it right, admission is free the first Tuesday of each month.

2. The **Boudin Demonstration Bakery** (p. 172; pictured below) at the Wharf has a nifty little free museum hidden upstairs that explains the symbiotic relationship between San Francisco and its unique sourdough loaf. The story and science behind the "mother dough" is fascinating, as are

their demonstrations. Bakery visitors can watch the entire baking process from a 30-foot observation window along Jefferson Street.

3. Hard to find, but worth the effort, is a funky little bar in North Beach called **Specs'** (p. 280). It looks like a maritime museum that imploded, with walls featuring historically eclectic seafaring oddities brought back by long-dead sailors who dropped in between voyages (dried whale penis, anyone?).

4. If you log onto www.calacademy.org/webcams/penguins, you can see what the California Academy of Sciences' penguins are up to via their **PenguinCams,** which offer three real-time views of the new penguin exhibit. It's mesmerizing.

5. If you want to watch a Giants game for free, you can join the "knothole gang" at the **Portwalk** (located behind right field) to catch a free glimpse of the game through cut-out portholes into the ballpark. In the

For a better view, of our bakery, and to learn more about Boudin San Francisco's oldest business visit the information desk in the lobby for tickets to the Boudin Museum and Bakery Tour.

o **Pretend to be a guest at the Palace or Fairmont Hotels.** You may not be staying the night, but you can certainly feel like a million bucks in the public spaces at the **Palace Hotel** (p. 81). The extravagant creation of banker "Bonanza King" Will Ralston in 1875, the Palace Hotel has one of the grandest rooms in the city: the **Garden Court,** where you can have high tea under a stained-glass dome. Running a close second is the magnificent lobby at Nob Hill's **Fairmont San Francisco** (p. 76).

o **Sip a cocktail in the clouds.** One of the greatest ways to view the city is from a top-floor lounge in hotels such as the **Sir Francis Drake** (p. 67), the **Grand Hyatt San Francisco** (p. 62), and the venerable **InterContinental Mark Hopkins** (p. 77). Drinks aren't cheap, but considering you're not paying for the view, it almost seems like a bargain.

spirit of sharing, Portwalk peekers are encouraged to take in only an inning or two before giving way to fellow fans.

6. Free steak sandwiches! Well, kinda free. Every Monday through Friday, **Morton's Steakhouse** (400 Post St. at Powell St.; (📞 **415/986-5830**) hosts a happy hour at their BAR 12•21, where you can stuff yourself on four Petite Filet Mignon Sandwiches at the bar for only $7.

7. Every second Thursday of the month, you can watch **free movies in Dolores Park,** located at 20th and Dolores streets. Bring a blanket and even your dog if you'd like, as well as a little cash to buy the world's best tamales from the Tamale Lady.

8. The **Good Vibrations** sex-toy shop (p. 256) on Valencia Street is worth visiting just to see their Antique Vibrator Museum. Who knew that vibrators have been around since 1869 and were prescribed by physicians to treat "hysteria"? Fascinating.

9. If you're looking for a buddy to ride bikes with, the **511 Bike Buddy Ridematch Service** will pair you up with someone at your skill level at no cost. Log onto www.ridematch.511. org, click on "Bicycling," then click on "Bike Buddy Matching."

10. If city life is stressing you out, take some **free tai chi lessons.** Log onto www.sfnpc.org/tai-chi-in-the-parks for a list of places and times that the free lessons are offered. There's no need to register; just show up and dress comfortably.

THE best OUTDOOR ACTIVITIES

o **A Day in Golden Gate Park:** Exploring Golden Gate Park is an essential part of the San Francisco experience. Its arboreal paths stretch from the Haight all the way to Ocean Beach, offering dozens of fun things to do along the way. Top sights are the Conservatory of Flowers, the Japanese Tea Garden, the fabulous **de Young Museum** (p. 184), and its eco-fabulous cross-concourse neighbor, the **California Academy of Sciences** (p. 182). The best time to go is Sunday, when main roads in the park are closed to traffic (rent a bike for the full effect). Toward the end of the day, head west to the beach and watch the sunset. See p. 204.

o **A Walk Along the Coastal Trail:** Stroll the forested Coastal Trail from Cliff House to the Golden Gate Bridge, and you'll see why San Franciscans put up

The Coastal Trail is steps from the beach.

with living on a fault line. Start at the parking lot just above Cliff House and head north. On a clear day, you'll have incredible views of the Marin Headlands, but even on foggy days, it's worth the trek to scamper over old bunkers and relish the cool, salty air (dress warmly). See "The Presidio & Golden Gate National Recreation Area," beginning on p. 199, for more on this area.

o **A Wine Country Excursion:** It'll take you about an hour to get there, but once you arrive you'll want to hopscotch from one winery to the next, perhaps picnic in the vineyards, or have an alfresco lunch somewhere atmospheric like Tra Vigne. And consider this: When the city is fogged in and cold, Napa and Sonoma are almost always sunny and warm. See chapter 11 for more information.

> ### The Best Activities for Families
>
> For a list of San Francisco attractions that appeal to kids of all ages, see the "Especially for Kids" box on p. 211 of chapter 6.

o **A Climb up or down the Filbert Street Steps:** San Francisco is a city of stairways, and the crème de la crème of scenic steps is Filbert Street between Sansome Street and the east side of Telegraph Hill, where steep Filbert Street becomes Filbert Steps, a 377-stair descent that wends its way through flower gardens and some of the city's oldest and most varied housing. It's a beautiful walk down from Coit Tower, and great exercise going up.

THE best OFFBEAT TRAVEL EXPERIENCES

o **A Soul-Stirring Sunday Morning Service at Glide Memorial Church:** Every city has churches, but only San Francisco has the Glide. An hour or so with Reverend Cecil Williams and his exuberant gospel choir will surely shake your soul and let the glory out. No matter what your religious beliefs may be—everybody leaves this Tenderloin church spiritually uplifted and slightly misty-eyed. See p. 206.

○ **A Cruise Through the Castro:** The most populated and festive street in the city is not just for gays and lesbians (though the best cruising in town *is* right here). Great shops and cafes aside, the best reason to come here is for the people-watching. If you have time, catch a flick and a live organ performance at the beautiful 1930s Spanish colonial movie palace, the Castro Theatre (p. 291). See "Neighborhoods Worth a Visit," beginning on p. 192, for more info.

The Castro Theatre.

○ **Skating Through Golden Gate Park on a Weekend:** C'mon, when's the last time you went rollerblading? If you've never tried skating before, there's no better place to learn than on the wide, flat main street through Golden Gate Park, which is closed to vehicles on Sundays.

Glide Memorial Church.

10 PLACES TO spot locals IN THEIR NATURAL HABITATS

Here's your guide to some of the city's most curious (and beloved) characters:

o Eccentric Oakland resident **Frank Chu** is like the Waldo of San Francisco protests, if easier to spot: At any protest on Market Street, look for an Asian-American man holding a sign lambasting the "12 Galaxies." Frank believes the galaxies and U.S. presidents owe his family $20 billion. He's spread this message daily since the early 1990s, and his persistence has made him a legend, a meme, the subject of a Yelp.com page, and the inspiration for a bar, Twelve Galaxies. The back of his sign is now sponsored by LaughingSquid.com.

various degrees of hunkiness (and nakedness) and lots of religious irreverence.

o Spotting a **graffiti artist at work** is rare; you may have more luck finding a **muralist at work** in the Mission district. Contact **Precita Eyes** (p. 199), which oversees much of the mural painting, for more information, and ask if they'll clue you in on their painting schedule.

o You'll find a crowd of older Chinese men smoking up a storm and playing **mah-jongg** and cards in Portsmouth Square in Chinatown. Try www.sanfranciscochinatown.com.

o Strictly devout Christians don't always find this amusing, but every Easter brings the **Hunky Jesus Contest** to Dolores Park, which combines men of

o More nudity (there's no shortage of it here if you know where to look): The **World Naked Bike Ride** (pictured above) takes place around the world twice a year (partially to bring attention to the dangers of gas emissions); the Northern Hemisphere date is in mid-March, and the Southern Hemisphere date is in mid-June. San Francisco now participates in both, naturally. Visit www.sfbikeride.org for specific dates, routes, and more.

o Head to Golden Gate Park (p. 204) on a weekend to find **lawn-bowlers** and occasionally an impromptu **drum circle.**

o **Catching Big Air in Your Car:** Relive *Bullitt* or *The Streets of San Francisco* as you careen down the center lane of Gough Street between Ellis and Eddy streets, screaming out "Wooooeee!" Feel the pull of gravity leave you momentarily, followed by the thump of the car suspension bottoming out. Wimpier folk can settle for driving down the steepest street in San Francisco: Filbert Street, between Leavenworth and Hyde streets.

- Head to Ocean Beach (p. 217) to watch **surfers in action,** especially on weekends. You may hear surfer lingo similar to this comment posted on www.wannasurf.com: "48 F, cold and scary . . . but tubed every once in a while . . . ice-cream headaches every duck dive . . . what an awesome break, though."

- David Johnson, aka the **Bush Man,** has been popping out from behind his faux bush at Pier 39 since 1980, when he decided to give up his robot act for something more unique. His former collaborator, Gregory Jacobs, is now a rival competitor. Watch video of startled tourists at http://bit.ly/dArD58.

- You'll meet some of the city's friendliest foodies at the Saturday morning **Farmers' Market at the Ferry Building** (p. 175). Nosh on free samples while you chat up the vendors. Visit Cap'n Mike & Sally in the outdoor market area for fantastic smoked fish; you can take smoked fish with you back on a plane as a treat for yourself or as a gift for your housesitter. Visit www.holysmoked salmon.com.

- The **Sisters of Perpetual Indulgence** (www.thesisters.org; pictured at left) appear at almost every public event to give their blessing—though these "sisters" have Adam's apples and sometimes beards. What started in 1976 as a group of gay men performing *The Sound of Music* then morphed into nuns carrying fake machine guns and cigars in local parades; now the satirical act is also a charity that is devoted to "community service, ministry and outreach to those on the edges, and to promoting human rights, respect for diversity and spiritual enlightenment."

- **AsiaSF:** The gender-bending waitresses—mostly Asian men dressed *very* convincingly as hot-to-trot women—will blow your mind with their performance of lip-synched show tunes, which takes place every night. Bring the parents—they'll love it. See p. 125.

2

SAN FRANCISCO IN DEPTH

U nlike most American cities that have evolved in a more measured fashion, San Francisco has been molded politically, socially, and physically by a variety of (literally) earth-shaking events. In this chapter, we give you a little rundown on the history of the City by the Bay along with some other useful background on local views and customs.

SAN FRANCISCO TODAY

Shaken but not stirred by the Loma Prieta earthquake in 1989, San Francisco has witnessed a spectacular rebound ever since. The seaside Embarcadero, once plagued by a horrendously ugly freeway overpass, was revitalized in the early 1990s by a multimillion-dollar face-lift, complete with palm trees, a new trolley line, and wide cobblestone walkways. SoMa, the once industrial neighborhood south of Market Street, exploded with new development, including the beautiful Yerba Buena arts district, the sleek lofts of Mission Bay, and a slew of hip new clubs and cafes. South Beach is the darling of young professionals living the condo-in-the-city life, and in the past decade, the spectacular California Academy of Sciences and de Young Museum have given even the locals two more reasons to visit Golden Gate Park.

All that glitters is not the Golden Gate, however. At the end of World War II, San Francisco was the largest and wealthiest city on the West Coast. Since then, it has been demoted to the fourth-largest city in California, home to only 825,000 people in 2012, less than 5% of the state's total. The industrial heart of

Occupy Oakland protesters take to the streets in fall of 2011. FACING PAGE: **November 8, 1977: Harvey Milk celebrates his election victory as a San Francisco supervisor and California's first openly gay elected official.**

15

the city has been knocked out and shipped off to less costly locations such as Oakland and Los Angeles, and increasingly San Francisco has had to fall back on tourism as a major source of revenue. The Occupy SF movement, itself part of Occupy Wall Street, brought the city's economic struggles front and center in the fall of 2011, as hundreds camped out and protested in San Francisco, Oakland, and throughout the Bay Area. (The scene that went global—the image of Lt. John Pike pepper-spraying peaceful protesters—happened at University of California, Davis.) A legitimate question we heard from the encampment in Justin Herman Plaza: *Why can't everyone who works in San Francisco afford housing in or near San Francisco?* Some worry we may someday become another Las Vegas, whose only raison d'être will be pleasing its visitors like one vast Fisherman's Wharf—a frightening premonition. Then, of course, there are the typical big-city problems: Crime is up along with drug use, and despite efforts to curb the ubiquitous problem of homelessness, it's still a thorny issue.

San Franciscans enjoy an excuse to wear a costume—including Easter in Dolores Park.

But the spirit of San Francisco is still alive and well. The Giants are still riding high after a 2010 World Series win. Gay couples may finally get closure on the Proposition 8 case against gay marriage, which is poised to go to the Supreme Court as we go to print. Dot.com companies seem to be staging a comeback, this time around with an actual plan to make money (in 2012, Facebook bought the locally based app company Instagram for $1 billion). Despite the recession blues, San Franciscans are finding ways to have fun—lining up for hot, new restaurants and nightspots, packing theaters and film festivals, and crowding into Apple Stores to get their hands on the latest iPhone. Though it may never relive its heady days as the king of the West Coast, San Francisco will undoubtedly retain the title as everyone's favorite California city.

LOOKING BACK AT SAN FRANCISCO

Born as an out-of-the-way backwater of colonial Spain and blessed with a harbor that would have been the envy of any of the great cities of Europe, San Francisco boasts a story that is as varied as the millions of people who have passed through its Golden Gate.

THE AGE OF DISCOVERY After the "discovery" of the New World by Columbus in 1492, legends of the fertile land of California were discussed in the universities and taverns of Europe, even though no one really understood where the mythical land was. (Some evidence of arrivals in California by Chinese merchants hundreds of years before Columbus's landing has been unearthed, although few scholars are willing to draw definite conclusions.) The first documented visit by a European to northern California, however, was by the Portuguese explorer João Cabrilho, who circumnavigated the southern tip of South America and traveled as far north as the Russian River in 1542. Nearly 40 years later, in 1579, Sir Francis Drake landed on the northern California coast, stopping for a time to repair his ships and to claim the territory for Queen Elizabeth I of England. He was followed several years later by another Portuguese, Sebastian Cermeño, "discoverer" of Punta de los Reyes (King's Point) in the mid-1590s. Ironically, all three adventurers completely missed the narrow entrance to San Francisco Bay, either because it was enshrouded in fog or, more likely, because they simply weren't looking for it. Believe it or not, the bay's entrance is nearly impossible to see from the open ocean. It would be another 2 centuries before a European actually saw the bay that would later extend Spain's influence over much of the American West. Gaspar de Portolá, a soldier sent from Spain to meddle in a rather ugly conflict between the Jesuits and the Franciscans, accidentally stumbled upon the bay in 1769, en route to somewhere else, but then stoically plodded on to his original destination, Monterey Bay, more than 100 miles to the south. Six years later, Juan Ayala, while on a mapping expedition for the Spanish, actually sailed into San Francisco Bay and immediately realized the enormous strategic importance of his find.

Colonization quickly followed. Juan Bautista de Anza and around 30 Spanish-speaking families marched through the deserts from Sonora, Mexico, arriving after many hardships at the northern tip of modern-day San Francisco in June 1776. They immediately claimed the peninsula for Spain. (Ironically, their claim of allegiance to Spain occurred only about a week before the 13 English-speaking colonies of North America's eastern seaboard, a continent away, declared their independence from Britain.) Their headquarters was an adobe fortress, the Presidio, built on the site of today's park with the same name. The settlers' church, built a mile to the south, was the first of five Spanish missions later developed around the edges of San Francisco Bay. Although the name of the church was officially Nuestra Señora de Dolores, it was dedicated to St. Francis of Assisi and nicknamed San Francisco by the Franciscan priests. Later, the name was applied to the entire bay.

In 1821, Mexico broke away from Spain, secularized the Spanish missions, and abandoned all interest in the Indian natives. Freed of Spanish restrictions, California's ports were suddenly opened to trade. The region around San Francisco Bay supplied large numbers of hides and tallow for transport around Cape Horn to the tanneries and factories of New England and New York. The prospects for prosperity persuaded an English-born sailor, William Richardson, to jump ship in 1822 and settle on the site of what is now San Francisco. To impress the commandant of the Presidio, whose daughter he loved, Richardson converted to Catholicism and established the beginnings of what would soon became a thriving trading post and colony. Richard named his trading post Yerba Buena (or "good herb"), because of a species of wild mint that grew there, near the site of today's Montgomery Street. (The city's original name was recalled with endless mirth 120 years later during San Francisco's hippie era.) He conducted a profitable hide-trading business and eventually became harbor master and the city's first merchant prince. By 1839, the place was a veritable town, with a mostly English-speaking populace and a saloon of dubious virtue.

Throughout the 19th century, armed hostilities between English-speaking settlers from the eastern seaboard and the Spanish-speaking colonies of Spain and Mexico erupted in places as widely scattered as Texas, Puerto Rico, and along the frequently shifting U.S.–Mexico border. In

Miners pan for gold.

1846, a group of U.S. Marines from the warship *Portsmouth* seized the sleepy main plaza of Yerba Buena, ran the U.S. flag up a pole, and declared California an American territory. The Presidio (occupied by about a dozen unmotivated Mexican soldiers) surrendered without a fuss. The first move the new, mostly Yankee citizenry made was to officially adopt the name of the bay as the name of their town.

THE GOLD RUSH   The year 1848 was one of the most pivotal years in European history, with unrest sweeping through Europe, horrendous poverty in Ireland, and widespread disillusionment about the hopes for prosperity throughout Europe and the eastern coast of the United States. Stories about the golden port of San Francisco and the agrarian wealth of the American West filtered slowly east, attracting slow-moving groups of settlers. Ex-sailor Richard Henry Dana extolled the virtues of California in his best-selling

DATELINE

1542 Juan Cabrillo sails up the California coast.

1579 Sir Francis Drake lands near San Francisco, missing the entrance to the bay.

1769 Members of the Spanish expedition led by Gaspar de Portolá become the first Europeans to see San Francisco Bay.

1775 The *San Carlos* is the first European ship to sail into San Francisco Bay.

1776 Captain Juan Bautista de Anza establishes a presidio (military fort); San Francisco de Asís Mission opens.

1821 Mexico wins independence from Spain and annexes California.

1835 The town of Yerba Buena develops around the port; the United States tries unsuccessfully to purchase San Francisco Bay from Mexico.

1846 Mexican-American War.

novel *Two Years Before the Mast* and helped fire the public's imagination about the territory's bounty, particularly that of the Bay Area.

The first overland party crossed the Sierra and arrived in California in 1841. San Francisco grew steadily, reaching a population of approximately 900 by April 1848, but nothing hinted at the population explosion that was to follow. Historian Barry Parr has referred to the California gold rush as the most extraordinary event to ever befall an American city in peacetime. In time, San Francisco's winning combination of raw materials, healthful climate, and freedom would have attracted thousands of settlers even without the lure of gold. But the gleam of the soft metal is said to have compressed 50 years of normal growth into less than 6 months. In 1848, the year gold was first discovered, the population of San Francisco jumped from under 1,000 to 26,000 in less than 6 months. As many as 100,000 more passed through San Francisco in the space of less than a year on their way to the rocky hinterlands where the gold was rumored to be.

If not for the discovery of some small particles of gold at a sawmill that he owned, Swiss-born John Augustus Sutter's legacy would have been far less flamboyant. Despite Sutter's wish to keep the discovery quiet, his employee John Marshall leaked word of the discovery to friends. It eventually appeared in local papers, and smart investors on the East Coast took immediate heed. The rush did not start, however, until Sam Brannan, a Mormon preacher and famous charlatan, ran through the streets of San Francisco shouting, "Gold! Gold in the American River!" (Brannan, incidentally, bought up all the harborfront real estate he could get and cornered the market on shovels, pickaxes, and canned food, just before making the announcement that was heard around the world.)

A world on the brink of change responded almost frantically. The gold rush was on. Shop owners hung GONE TO THE DIGGINGS signs in their windows. Flotillas of ships set sail from ports throughout Europe, South America, Australia, and the East Coast, sometimes nearly sinking with the weight

continues

of mining equipment. Townspeople from the Midwest headed overland, and the social fabric of a nation was transformed almost overnight. Not since the Crusades of the Middle Ages had so many people been mobilized in so short a period of time. Daily business stopped; ships arrived in San Francisco and were almost immediately deserted by their crews. News of the gold strike spread like a plague through every discontented hamlet in the known world. Although other settlements were closer to the gold strike, San Francisco was the famous name, and therefore, where the gold-diggers disembarked. Tent cities sprung up, demand for virtually everything sky-rocketed, and although some miners actually found gold, smart merchants quickly discovered that more enduring hopes lay in servicing the needs of the thousands of miners who arrived ill-equipped and ignorant of the lay of the land. Prices soared. Miners, faced with staggeringly inflated prices for goods and services, barely scraped a profit after expenses. Most prospectors failed, many died of hardship, others committed suicide at the alarming rate of 1,000 a year. Yet despite the tragedies, graft, and vice associated with the gold rush, within mere months San Francisco was forever transformed from a tranquil Spanish settlement into a roaring, boisterous boomtown.

BOOMTOWN FEVER   By 1855, most of California's surface gold had already been panned out, leaving only the richer but deeper veins of ore, which individual miners couldn't retrieve without massive capital investments. Despite that, San Francisco had evolved into a vast commercial magnet, sucking into its warehouses and banks the staggering riches that overworked newcomers had dragged, ripped, and distilled from the rocks, fields, and forests of western North America.

   Investment funds were being lavished on more than mining, however. Speculation on the newly established San Francisco stock exchange could make or destroy an investor in a single day, and several noteworthy writers (including Mark Twain) were among the young men forever influenced by the boomtown spirit. The American Civil War left California firmly in the

1950 The Beat Generation moves into the bars and cafes of North Beach.

1967 A free concert in Golden Gate Park attracts 20,000 people, ushering in the Summer of Love and the hippie era.

1974 BART's high-speed transit system opens the tunnel linking San Francisco with the East Bay.

1978 Harvey Milk, a city supervisor and America's first openly gay politician, is assassinated, along with Mayor George Moscone, by political rival Dan White.

1989 An earthquake registering 7.1 on the Richter scale hits San Francisco during a World Series baseball game, as 100 million watch on TV; the city quickly rebuilds.

1991 Fire rages through the Berkeley/Oakland hills, destroying 2,800 homes.

1993 Yerba Buena Center for the Arts opens.

1995 New San Francisco Museum of Modern Art opens.

1996 Former Assembly Speaker Willie Brown elected mayor of San Francisco.

Union camp, ready, willing, and able to receive hordes of disillusioned soldiers fed up with the internecine war-mongering of the eastern seaboard. In 1869, the transcontinental railway linked the eastern and western seaboards of the United States, ensuring the fortunes of the barons who controlled it. The railways, however, also shifted economic power bases as cheap manufactured goods from the east undercut the high prices hitherto charged for goods that sailed or steamed their way around the tip of South America. Ownership of the newly formed Central Pacific and Southern Pacific railroads was almost completely controlled by the "Big Four," all iron-willed capitalists—Leland Stanford, Mark Hopkins, Collis P. Huntington, and Charles Crocker—whose ruthlessness was legendary. (Much of the bone-crushing labor for their railway was executed by low-paid Chinese newcomers, most of whom arrived in overcrowded ships at San Francisco ports.) As the 19th century came to a close, civil unrest became more frequent as the monopolistic grip of the railways and robber barons became more obvious. Adding to the discontent were the uncounted thousands of Chinese immigrants, who fled starvation and unrest in Asia at rates rivaling those of the Italians, Poles, Irish, and British.

During the 1870s, the flood of profits from the Comstock Lode in western Nevada diminished to a trickle, a cycle of droughts wiped out part of California's agricultural bounty, and local industry struggled to survive against the flood of manufactured goods imported via railway from the well-established factories of the East Coast and Midwest. Often, discontented workers blamed their woes on the now-unwanted hordes of Chinese workers, who by preference and for mutual protection had congregated into teeming all-Asian communities.

Despite these downward cycles, the city enjoyed other bouts of prosperity around the turn of the 20th century, thanks to the Klondike gold rush in Alaska and the Spanish-American War. Long accustomed to making a buck off gold fever, San Francisco managed to position itself as a point of

---

2000 Pacific Bell Park (now AT&T Park), the new home to the San Francisco Giants, opens.

2002 The San Francisco Giants make it to the World Series but lose to the Anaheim Angels in Game 7.

2004 Thirty-six-year-old supervisor Gavin Newsom becomes the city's 42nd mayor and quickly makes headlines by authorizing City Hall to issue marriage licenses to same-sex couples. Six months later, the state supreme court invalidates 3,955 gay marriages.

2005 The new, seismically correct $202-million de Young Museum opens in Golden Gate Park.

2006 The 100-year anniversary of the Great Earthquake and fire of 1906 is commemorated, the greatest disaster ever to befall an American metropolis.

2007 A tiger escapes from its pen at the San Francisco Zoo, killing one man and injuring two others before the police shoot and kill it.

continues

embarkation for supplies bound for Alaska. Also during this time emerged the Bank of America, which eventually evolved into the largest bank in the world. Founded in North Beach in 1904, Bank of America was the brain-child of Italian-born A. P. Giannini, who later funded part of the construc-tion for a bridge that many critics said was preposterous: the Golden Gate.

THE GREAT FIRE   On the morning of April 18, 1906, San Francisco changed for all time. The city has never experienced an earthquake as destructive as the one that hit at 5:13am. (Scientists estimate its strength at 8.1 on the Richter scale.) All but a handful of the city's 400,000 inhabitants lay fast asleep when the ground beneath the city went into a series of convulsions. As one eyewit-ness put it, "The earth was shaking . . . it was undulating, rolling like an ocean breaker." The quake ruptured every water main in the city, and simultaneously started a chain of fires that rapidly fused into one gigantic conflagration. The fire brigades were helpless, and for 3 days, San Francisco burned.

Militia troops finally stopped the flames from advancing by dynamiting entire city blocks, but not before more than 28,000 buildings lay in ruins. Minor tremors lasted another 3 days. The final damage stretched across a path of destruction 450 miles long and 50 miles wide. In all, 497 city blocks were razed, or about one-third of the city. As Jack London wrote in a heart-rending newspaper dispatch, "The city of San Francisco is no more." The earthquake and subsequent fire so decisively changed the city that post-1906 San Francisco bears little resemblance to the town before the quake. Out of the ashes rose a bigger, healthier, and more beautiful town, though latter-day urbanologists regret that the rebuilding that followed the San Francisco earthquake did not follow a more enlightened plan. So eager was the city to rebuild that the old, somewhat unimaginative gridiron plan was reinstated, despite the opportunities for more daring visions that the after-math of the quake afforded.

In 1915, in celebration of the opening of the Panama Canal and to prove to the world that San Francisco was restored to its full glory, the city

2008 The California Supreme Court overturns the ban on same-sex marriage, touching off short-lived celebrations at San Francisco City Hall. The ban is reinstated in an election later that year, added to the ballot as "Proposition 8."

2009 The economic downturn has San Francisco in a financial tailspin, but amazingly, tourism dollars keep pouring in. After a dismal start, hotel occupancies resurge. Small businesses continue to struggle, however, battling high rents and a cash-strapped public.

2010 The San Francisco Giants baseball team wins the World Series against the Texas Rangers; thou-sands of fans fill Civic Center Plaza for the parade and celebration.

2011 Ed Lee is elected San Francisco's 43rd mayor.

2012 The new eastern span of the Bay Bridge nears completion at an estimated cost of $6.3 billion.

2013 San Francisco hosts the America's Cup sailing race, injecting more than $1.4 billion into the regional economy.

hosted the Panama Pacific International Exhibition, a world's fair that exposed hundreds of thousands of visitors to the city's unique charms. The general frenzy of civic boosterism, however, reached its peak during the years just before World War I, when investments and civic pride might have reached an all-time high. Despite Prohibition, speak-easies did a thriving business in and around the city, and building sprees were as high-blown and lavish as the profits on the San Francisco stock exchange.

The earthquake of April 18, 1906, led to the Great Fire, which forever changed the city's landscape.

WORLD WAR II The Japanese attack on Pearl Harbor on December 7, 1941, mobilized the United States into a massive war machine, with many shipyards strategically positioned along the Pacific Coast, including San Francisco. Within less than a year, several shipyards were producing up to one new warship per day, employing hundreds of thousands of people working in 24-hour shifts. (The largest, Kaiser Shipyards in Richmond, employed more than 100,000 workers alone.) In search of work and the excitement of life away from their villages and cornfields, workers flooded into the city from virtually everywhere, forcing an enormous boom in housing. Hundreds found themselves separated from their small towns for the first time in their lives and reveled in their newfound freedom.

After the hostilities ended, many soldiers remembered San Francisco as the site of their finest hours and returned to live there permanently. The economic prosperity of the postwar years enabled massive enlargements of the city, including freeways, housing developments, a booming financial

A view of the Golden Gate Bridge mid-construction in 1936.

district, and pockets of counterculture enthusiasts such as the beatniks, gays, and hippies.

THE 1950S: THE BEATS   San Francisco's reputation as a rollicking place where anything goes dates from the Barbary Coast days when gang warfare, prostitution, gambling, and drinking were major city pursuits, and citizens took law and order into their own hands. Its more modern role as a catalyst for social change and the avant-garde began in the 1950s when a group of young writers, philosophers, and poets challenged the materialism and conformity of American society by embracing anarchy and Eastern philosophy, expressing their notions in poetry. They adopted a uniform of jeans, sweaters, sandals, and berets, called themselves Beats, and hung out in North Beach where rents were low and cheap wine was plentiful. *San Francisco Chronicle* columnist Herb Caen, to whom they were totally alien, dubbed them *beatniks* in his column.

Allen Ginsberg, Gregory Corso, and Jack Kerouac had begun writing at Columbia University in New York, but it wasn't until they came west and hooked up with Lawrence Ferlinghetti, Kenneth Rexroth, Gary Snyder, and others that the movement gained national attention. The bible of the Beats was Ginsberg's "Howl," which he first read at the Six Gallery on October 13, 1955. By the time he finished reading, Ginsberg was crying, the audience was chanting, and his fellow poets were announcing the arrival of an epic bard. Ferlinghetti published *Howl*, which was deemed obscene, in 1956. A trial followed, but the court found that the book had redeeming social value, thereby reaffirming the right of free expression. The other major work, Jack Kerouac's *On the Road*, was published in 1957, instantly becoming a bestseller. (He had written it as one long paragraph in 20 days in 1951.) The freedom and sense of possibility that this book conveyed became the bellwether for a generation.

While the Beats gave poetry readings and generated controversy, two clubs in North Beach were making waves, notably the

A copy of Allen Ginsberg's *Howl* at the Beat Museum in North Beach.

You can still visit Jack Kerouac's former home—where he wrote *On the Road*—at 29 Russell Street, in Russian Hill.

Three Haight-Ashbury icons: Hendrix, Joplin, and Garcia.

hungry i and the Purple Onion, where everyone who was anyone or became anyone on the entertainment scene appeared—Mort Sahl, Dick Gregory, Lenny Bruce, Barbra Streisand, and Woody Allen all worked here. Maya Angelou appeared as a singer and dancer at the Purple Onion. The cafes of North Beach were the center of bohemian life in the '50s: the Black Cat, Vesuvio, Caffe Trieste and Tosca Cafe, and Enrico's Sidewalk Café. When the tour buses started rolling in, rents went up, and Broadway turned into strip club row in the early 1960s. Thus ended an era, and the Beats moved on. The alternative scene shifted to Berkeley and the Haight.

THE 1960S: THE HAIGHT   The torch of freedom had been passed from the Beats and North Beach to Haight-Ashbury and the hippies, but it was a radically different torch. The hippies replaced the Beats' angst, anarchy, negativism, nihilism, alcohol, and poetry with love, communalism, openness, drugs, rock music, and a back-to-nature philosophy. Although the scent of marijuana wafted everywhere—on the streets, in the cafes, in Golden Gate Park—the real drugs of choice were LSD (a tab of good acid cost $5) and other hallucinogens. Timothy Leary experimented with its effects and exhorted youth to turn on, tune in, and drop out. Instead of hanging out in coffeehouses, the hippies went to concerts at the Fillmore or the Avalon Ballroom to dance.

The first Family Dog Rock 'n' Roll Dance and Concert, "A Tribute to Dr. Strange," was given at the Longshoreman's Hall in fall 1965, featuring Jefferson Airplane, the Marbles, the Great Society, and the Charlatans. At this event, the first major happening of the 1960s, Ginsberg led a snake dance through the crowd. In January 1966, the 3-day Trips Festival, organized by rock promoter Bill Graham, was also held at the Longshoreman's Hall. The climax came with Ken Kesey and the Merry Pranksters Acid Test show, which used five movie screens, psychedelic visions, and the sounds of the Grateful Dead and Big Brother and the Holding Company. The "be-in" followed in the summer of 1966 at the polo grounds in Golden Gate Park, when an estimated 20,000 heard Jefferson Airplane perform and Ginsberg chant, while the Hell's Angels acted as

Haight Street today: Funky shops, still-thriving bars and restaurants, and panhandlers.

unofficial police. It was followed by the Summer of Love in 1967 as thousands of young people streamed into the city in search of drugs and free love.

The '60s Haight scene was very different from the '50s Beat scene. The hippies were much younger than the Beats had been, constituting the first youth movement to take over the nation. Ironically, they also became the first generation of young, independent, and moneyed consumers to be courted by corporations. Ultimately, the Haight and the hippie movement deteriorated from love and flowers into drugs and crime, drawing a fringe of crazies like Charles Manson and leaving only a legacy of sex, drugs, violence, and consumerism. As early as October 1967, the "Diggers," who had opened a free shop and soup kitchen in the Haight, symbolically buried the dream in a clay casket in Buena Vista Park.

The end of the Vietnam War and the resignation of President Nixon took the edge off politics. The last fling of the mentality that had driven the 1960s occurred in 1974 when Patty Hearst was kidnapped from her Berkeley apartment by the Symbionese Liberation Army and participated in their bank-robbing spree before surrendering in San Francisco in 1975.

THE 1970S: GAY RIGHTS The homosexual community in San Francisco was essentially founded at the end of World War II, when thousands of military personnel were discharged back to the United States via San Francisco. A substantial number of those men were homosexual and decided to stay on in San Francisco. A gay community grew up along Polk Street between Sutter and California streets. Later, the larger community moved into the Castro, where it remains today.

The modern-day gay political movement is usually traced to the 1969 Stonewall raid and riots in Greenwich Village. Although the political movement started in New York, California had already given birth to two major organizations for gay rights: the Mattachine Society, founded in 1951 by Henry Hay in Los Angeles, and the Daughters of Bilitis, a lesbian organization founded in 1955 in San Francisco.

After Stonewall, the Committee for Homosexual Freedom was created in spring 1969 in San Francisco; a Gay Liberation Front chapter was organized at Berkeley. In fall 1969, Robert Patterson, a columnist for the *San Francisco Examiner*, referred to homosexuals as "semi males, drag darlings," and "women who aren't exactly women." On October 31 at noon, a group began a peaceful picket of the *Examiner*. Peace reigned until someone threw a bag of printer's ink from an *Examiner* window. Someone wrote "Fuck the Examiner" on the wall, and the police moved in to clear the crowd, clubbing them as they went. The remaining pickets retreated to

Harvey Milk's message lives on in this wheatpaste by artist Jeremy Novy.

Glide Methodist Church and then marched on City Hall. Unfortunately, the mayor was away. Unable to air their grievances, they started a sit-in that lasted until 5pm, when they were ordered to leave. Most did, but three remained and were arrested.

Later that year, an anti-Thanksgiving rally was staged at which gays protested against several national and local businesses: Western and Delta airlines, the former for firing lesbian flight attendants, the latter for refusing to sell a ticket to a young man wearing a Gay Power button; KFOG, for its anti-homosexual broadcasting; and also some local gay bars for exploitation. On May 14, 1970, a group of gay and women's liberationists invaded the convention of the American Psychiatric Association in San Francisco to protest the reading of a paper on aversion therapy for homosexuals, forcing the meeting to adjourn.

The rage against intolerance was appearing on all fronts. At the National Gay Liberation conference held in August 1970 in the city, Charles Thorp, chairman of the San Francisco State Liberation Front, called for militancy and issued a challenge to come out with a rallying cry of "Blatant is beautiful." He also argued for the use of what he felt was the more positive, celebratory term *gay* instead of *homosexual,* and decried the fact that homosexuals were kept in their place at the three B's: the bars, the beaches, and the baths. As the movement grew in size and power, debates on strategy and tactics occurred, most dramatically between those who wanted to withdraw into separate ghettos and those who wanted to enter mainstream society. The most extreme proposal was made in California by Don Jackson, who proposed establishing a gay territory in California's Alpine County, about 10 miles south of Lake Tahoe. It would have had a totally gay administration, civil service, university, museum—everything. The residents of Alpine County were not pleased with the proposal. But before the situation turned really ugly, Jackson's idea was abandoned because of lack of support in the gay community. In the end, the movement would concentrate on integration and civil rights, not separatism. They would elect politicians who were sympathetic to their cause and celebrate their new identity by establishing National Gay Celebration Day and Gay Pride Week, the first of which was celebrated in June 1970 when 1,000 to 2,000 marched in New York, 1,000 in Los Angeles, and a few hundred in San Francisco.

By the mid-1970s, the gay community craved a more central role in San Francisco politics. Harvey Milk, owner of a camera store in the Castro, decided to run as an openly gay man for the board of supervisors. He won, becoming the first openly gay person to hold a major public office. He and liberal mayor George Moscone developed a gay rights agenda, but in 1978 both were killed by former supervisor Dan White, who shot them after Moscone refused White's request for reinstatement. White, a Catholic and former police officer, had consistently opposed Milk's and Moscone's more liberal policies. At his trial, White successfully pleaded temporary insanity caused by additives in his fast-food diet. The media dubbed it the "Twinkie defense," but it worked, and the murder charges against White were reduced to manslaughter. That day, angry and grieving, the gay community rioted, overturning and burning police cars in a night of rage. To this day, a candlelight memorial parade is held each year on the anniversary of Milk's death, and Milk's martyrdom remains both a political and a practical inspiration to gay candidates across the country.

The emphasis in the gay movement shifted abruptly in the 1980s when the AIDS epidemic struck the gay community. AIDS has had a dramatic impact on the Castro. While it's still a thriving and lively community, it's no longer the constant party that it once was. The hedonistic lifestyle that had played out in the discos, bars, baths, and streets changed as the seriousness of the epidemic sunk in and the number of deaths increased. Political efforts have shifted away from enfran-

A lesbian couple weds in 2008 before the passage of Proposition 8. The case is poised to go to the Supreme Court.

chisement and toward demanding money for social services and research money to deal with the AIDS crisis. The gay community has developed its own organizations, such as Project Inform and Gay Men's Health Crisis, to publicize information about the disease, treatments available, and safe sex. Though new cases of AIDS within the gay community are on the decline in San Francisco, it still remains a serious problem.

THE 1980S: THE BIG ONE, PART TWO   The '80s may have arrived in San Francisco with a whimper (compared to previous generations), but they went out with quite a bang. At 5:04pm on Tuesday, October 17, 1989, as more than 62,000 fans filled Candlestick Park for the third game of the World Series—and the San Francisco Bay Area commute moved into its heaviest flow—an earthquake of magnitude 7.1 struck. Within the next 20 seconds, 63 lives would be lost, $10 billion in damage would occur, and the entire Bay Area community would be reminded of its humble insignificance. Centered about 60 miles south of San Francisco within the Forest of Nisene Marks, the deadly temblor was felt as far away as San Diego and Nevada.

Though scientists had predicted an earthquake would hit on this section of the San Andreas Fault, certain structures that were built to withstand such an earthquake failed miserably. The most catastrophic event was the collapse of the elevated Cypress Street section of I-880 in Oakland, where the upper level of the freeway literally pancaked the lower level, crushing everything with such force that cars were reduced to inches. Other structures heavily damaged included the San Francisco–Oakland Bay Bridge, shut down for months when a section of the roadbed collapsed; San Francisco's Marina district, where several multimillion-dollar homes collapsed on their weak, shifting bases of landfill and sand; and the Pacific Garden Mall in Santa Cruz, which was completely devastated.

President George H. W. Bush declared a disaster area for the seven hardest-hit counties, where 63 people died, at least 3,700 people were reported injured, and more than 12,000 were displaced. More than 18,000 homes were damaged and 963 others destroyed. Although fire raged within the city and water supply systems were damaged, the major fires sparked within the Marina district were brought under control within 3 hours, due

A highway decimated by the 1989 earthquake.

mostly to the heroic efforts of San Francisco's firefighters.

After the rubble had finally settled, it was unanimously agreed that San Francisco and the Bay Area had pulled through miraculously well—particularly when compared to the more recent earthquake in northeast Japan, which killed thousands. After the San Francisco quake, a feeling of esprit de corps swept the city as neighbors helped each other rebuild and donations poured in from all over the world. Though it's been 2 decades since, the city is still feeling the effects of the quake, most noticeably during rush hour as commuters slog across the approaches to the Bay Bridge, the second leg of which is still under construction. That another "big one" will strike is inevitable: It's the price you pay for living on a fault line. But if there is ever a city that is prepared for a major shakedown, it's San Francisco.

THE 1990S: THE DOT.COM BUBBLE During the 1990s, the nationwide recession influenced the beginning of the decade, while the quiet rumblings of the new frontier in Silicon Valley escaped much notice. By the middle of the decade, San Francisco and the surrounding areas were the site of a new kind of gold rush—the birth of the Internet industry.

Not unlike the gold fever of the 1800s, people flocked to the western shores to strike it rich—and they did. In 1999, the local media reported that each day 64 Bay Area residents were gaining millionaire status. Long before the last year of the millennium, real estate prices went into the stratosphere, and the city's gentrification financially squeezed out many of those residents who didn't mean big business (read: alternative and artistic types, seniors, and minorities who made the city colorful). New business popped up everywhere—especially in SoMa, where start-up companies jammed warehouse spaces to the rafters.

As the most popular post-education destination for MBAs and the leader in the media of the future, San Francisco no longer opened its Golden Gate to everyone looking for the legendary alternative lifestyle—unless he or she could afford a $1,000 studio apartment and $20-per-day fees to park the car.

The new millennium was christened with bubbly in hand, foie gras and caviar on the linen tablecloth, and seemingly everyone in the money. New restaurants charging $35 per entree were all the rage, hotels were renovated, the new bayfront ballpark was packed, and stock market tips were as plentiful as million-dollar SoMa condos and lofts. Though there were whispers of a stock market correction, and inklings that venture capital might dry up, San Franciscans were too busy raking in the dough to heed the writing on the wall.

THE MILLENNIUM When the city woke up from the dot.com party, San Franciscans found themselves suffering from a major new millennium hangover. In the early 2000s, dot.coms became "dot.bombs" faster than you could say "worthless stock options," with companies shuttering at a rate of several per day. The crash of the Internet economy brought with it a real estate exodus, and scads of empty live-work lofts sprouted up in SoMa. But from the ashes of the collapse grew the seeds of innovation, and by mid-decade, San Francisco was back on the cutting edge with a little search engine that could, called Google. Wikipedia, YouTube, and new skyscrapers followed, holding steady even as Wall Street and big banks fell around their feet in 2008. It's an undeniable testament to the resilience and mettle of San Franciscans, who always seem to have an ace in the hole, even when things seem at their worst.

SAN FRANCISCO IN POPULAR CULTURE: BOOKS, FILMS & MUSIC

Getting acquainted with San Francisco through the work of authors and filmmakers will provide an extra dimension to your trip and perhaps some added excitement when you happen upon a location you recognize from a favorite cinematic moment or literary passage. San Francisco's own Chronicle Books publishes a great variety of material on the city, for children, cooks, art and architecture students, and readers of memoirs and fiction. One of Chronicle's best books to stimulate your interest and curiosity is *San Francisco Stories: Great Writers on the City,* edited by John Miller. This collection of short pieces covers the personal and the political as recalled by acclaimed authors including Mark Twain, Jack Kerouac, Tom Wolfe, and Amy Tan. To find out about a smaller, more intimate city, check out *Good Life in Hard Times: San Francisco in the '20s and '30s,* by former journalist and San Francisco native Jerry Flamm (published by Chronicle Books). *Season of the Witch: Enchantment, Terror and Deliverance in the City of Love,* by David Talbot (Free Press), brilliantly covers the city's turbulent era from 1967 to 1982 and looks at the formation of "San Francisco values." Charles Manson, Patty Hearst, Harvey Milk, Joe Montana and the Super Bowl 49ers are all covered.

One of the more famous and beloved pieces of modern fiction based in San Francisco is Armistead Maupin's *Tales of the City* (published by Perennial). Maupin's 1970s soap opera covers the residents of 28 Barbary Lane (Macondry Lane on Russian Hill was the inspiration), melding sex, drugs, and growing self-awareness with enormous warmth and humor.

A work of fiction featuring San Francisco during the gold rush is *Daughter of Fortune,* by acclaimed novelist and Marin County resident Isabel Allende (published by HarperTorch).

As one of the loveliest spots on the planet, San Francisco has been a favorite of location scouts since the beginning of the film industry. It may be difficult to locate at your local video store, but the 1936 Clark Gable/Jeanette MacDonald romance, *San Francisco,* is lauded for its dramatic reenactment of the 1906 earthquake and for MacDonald's rendition of the song of the same name. *The Maltese Falcon* (1941), Dashiell Hammett's classic detective story, with Humphrey Bogart starring as Sam Spade, includes shots of the Bay Bridge, the Ferry Building, and Burrit Alley (above the Stockton Tunnel). John's Grill, mentioned in the novel, continues to flog its association with Hammett's hero from its location at 63 Ellis St. (btw. Stockton and Powell sts.).

A film still from *Vertigo* (1958): Jimmy Stewart pulls Kim Novak from the bay at Fort Point.

Alfred Hitchcock's *Vertigo* (1958), starring James Stewart and Kim Novak, is admittedly an obvious choice on the list of great San Francisco films, but it's always worth viewing. Stewart plays a former detective hired to tail the wife of an old college friend, but the woman's identity is less than clear-cut. In the meantime, Stewart becomes obsessed with his prey as they make their way around the Palace of the Legion of Honor, Fort Point, Mission Dolores, and the detective's apartment at 900 Lombard St. The city also fared well in the 1968 thriller *Bullitt*, starring a young Steve McQueen. Along with the hair-raising car chase over many hills, you'll see the Bay Bridge from a recognizable point on the Embarcadero, Mason Street heading north next to the Fairmont Hotel, the front of the Mark Hopkins Hotel, Grace Cathedral, and the fairly unchanged Enrico's Sidewalk Café.

For a change of pace and no tragic law-enforcement characters, screen the romantic comedy *What's Up, Doc?* (1972) with Barbra Streisand and Ryan O'Neal. Along with being very funny, it's got one of cinema's all-time classic car chase scenes, with shots of Lombard Street, Chinatown, and Alta Plaza Park in Pacific Heights. If you have kids to rev up, the 1993 comedy *Mrs. Doubtfire*, starring Sally Field and the city's favorite son, Robin Williams, shows San Francisco under blue skies and cable cars with plenty of room. The house where the character's estranged wife and children live is located in Pacific Heights at 2640 Steiner St. (at Broadway St.), in case you care to gawk.

Finally, *24 Hours on Craigslist* is a documentary that covers a day in the life of the Internet community bulletin-board phenom. The filmmaker posted an ad on Craigslist, followed up with a handful of volunteers—an Ethel Merman impersonator seeking a Led Zeppelin cover band; a couple looking for others to join a support group for diabetic cats; a single, older woman needing a sperm donor—and sent film crews to cover their stories. Unlike other films that show the physical splendors of San Francisco, *24 Hours on Craigslist* will give you a sense of the city's psyche, or at least offer an explanation of why non–San Franciscans think the place is populated with . . . um . . . unusual types.

Sounds of the '60s

During its heyday in the 1950s and 1960s, San Francisco was the place to be for anyone who eschewed the conventional American lifestyle. From moody beatniks to political firebrands, the city was a vortex for poets, writers, actors, and a bewildering assortment of free thinkers and activists. Drawn by the city's already liberal views on life, liberty, and the pursuit of happiness, thousands of the country's youth—including some of America's most talented musicians—headed west to join the party. What culminated in the 1960s was San Francisco's hat trick of rock legends: It was able to lay claim to three of the rock era's most influential bands—the Grateful Dead, Big Brother and the Holding Company and Janis Joplin, and Jefferson Airplane.

THE GRATEFUL DEAD   Easily the most influential band to be spawned from the psychedelic movement of the 1960s, the Grateful Dead was San Francisco's own music guru. Described as the "house band for the famous acid tests that transformed the City by the Bay into one endless freak-out," the Dead's music was played simultaneously on so many stereo systems (and at such high volumes) that the group almost seemed to have set the tone for one enormous, citywide jam session.

Though the group disbanded in 1995 after the death of its charismatic lead vocalist, Jerry Garcia, the group's devoted fans had already elevated the Grateful Dead to cult empire status. Tie-dyed "Deadheads" (many of whom followed the band on tour for decades) can still be found tripping within the Haight, reminiscing about the good old days when the group never traveled with a sound system weighing less than 23 tons. In fact, more than any other band produced during the 1960s, the Grateful Dead were best appreciated during live concerts, partly because of the love-in mood that frequently percolated through the acidic audiences. Many rock critics remember with nostalgia that the band's most cerebral and psychedelic music was produced in the 1960s in San Francisco, but in the 1980s and 1990s, permutations of their themes were marketed in repetitive, less threatening forms that delighted their aficionados and often baffled or bored virtually everyone else.

For better or for worse, the Grateful Dead was a musical benchmark, expressing in new ways the mood of San Francisco during one of its drug-infused and most creatively fertile periods. But the days of the Dancing Bear and peanut butter sandwiches will never be quite over: Working from a proven formula, thousands of bands around the world continue to propagate the Dead's rhythmical standards, and several of the band's original members still tour in various incarnations.

But reading about the Grateful Dead is like dancing to architecture: If you're looking for an album whose title best expresses the changing artistic premises of San Francisco and the ironies of

Visit the former home of the Grateful Dead, at 710 Ashbury.

the pop culture that developed here, look for its award-winning retrospective *What a Long Strange Trip It's Been* at any of the city's record stores.

BIG BROTHER AND THE HOLDING COMPANY AND JANIS JOPLIN The wide-open moral and musical landscape of San Francisco was almost unnervingly fertile during the 1960s. Despite competition from endless numbers of less talented singers, Texas-born Janis Joplin formulated much of her vocal technique before audiences in San Francisco. Her breakthrough style was first acknowledged at the Monterey Jazz Festival in 1967. Audiences reached out to embrace a singer whose rasping, gravely, shrieking voice expressed the generational angst of thousands of onlookers. *Billboard* magazine characterized her sound as composed of equal portions of honey, Southern Comfort, and gall. She was backed up during her earliest years by Big Brother and the Holding Company, a group she eventually outgrew.

Warned by specialists that her vocal technique would ruin her larynx before she was 30, Janis wailed, gasped, growled, and staggered over a blues repertoire judged as the most raw and vivid ever performed. Promoters frantically struggled to market (and protect) Janis and her voice for future artistic endeavors but, alas, her talent was simply too huge for her to handle, the time and place too destructive for her raw-edged psyche. Her style is best described as "the desperate blues," partly because it never attained the emotional nonchalance of such other blues singers as Bessie Smith or Billie Holiday.

Parts of Janis's life were the subject of such lurid books as *Going Down with Janis*, and stories of her substance abuse, sexual escapades, and general raunchiness litter the emotional landscape of modern-day San Francisco. The star died of a heroin overdose at the age of 27, a tragedy still mourned by her thousands of fans, who continue to refer to her by her nickname, "Pearl." Contemporary photographs taken shortly before her death show a ravaged body and a face partially concealed behind aviator's goggles, long hair, and a tough but brittle facade. Described as omnisexual—and completely comfortable with both male and female partners—she once (unexpectedly) announced to a group of nightclub guests her evaluation of the sexual performance of two of the era's most visible male icons: Joe Namath (not particularly memorable) and Dick Cavett (absolutely fantastic). The audience (like audiences in concert halls around California) drank in the anecdotes that followed as "Gospel According to Janis."

JEFFERSON AIRPLANE In the San Francisco suburbs of the late 1960s, hundreds of suburban bands dreamed of attaining stardom. Of the few that succeeded, none expressed the love-in ethic of that time in San Francisco better than the soaring vocals and ferocious guitar-playing of Jefferson Airplane. Singers Grace Slick and Marty Balin—as well as bass guitar player Jack Casady—were considered at the top of their profession by their peers and highly melodic even by orchestral standards. Most importantly, all members of the band, especially Paul Kantner and Jorma Kaukonen, were songwriters. Their fertile mix of musical styles and creative energies led to songs that still reverberate in the minds of anyone who owned an AM radio during the late 1960s. The intense and lonely songs such as "Somebody to Love" and "White Rabbit" became the musical anthems of at least one summer, as American youth emerged into a highly psychedelic kind of consciousness within the creatively catalytic setting of San Francisco.

Although in 1989 the group reassembled its scattered members for a swan song as Jefferson Starship, the output was considered a banal repetition of earlier themes, and the energy of those long-faded summers of San Francisco in the late 1960s was never recovered. But despite its decline in its later years, Jefferson Airplane is still considered a band inextricably linked to the Bay Area's historic and epoch-changing Summer of Love.

WHEN TO GO

If you're dreaming of convertibles, Frisbee on the beach, and tank-topped evenings, change your reservations and head to Los Angeles. Contrary to California's sunshine-and-bikini image, San Francisco's weather is "mild" (to put it nicely) and can often be downright bone-chilling because of the wet, foggy air and cool winds—it's really nothing like Southern California. Summer, the most popular time to visit, is often the coldest time of year, with damp, foggy days; cold, windy nights; and crowded tourist destinations. A good bet is to visit in spring or, better yet, autumn. Just about every September, right about the time San Franciscans mourn being cheated (or fogged) out of another summer, something wonderful happens: The thermometer rises, the skies clear, and the locals call in sick to work and head for the beach. It's what residents call "Indian summer." The city is also delightful during winter, when the opera and ballet seasons are in full swing; there are fewer tourists, many hotel prices are lower, and downtown bustles with holiday cheer.

> ## 🔖 Travel Attire
>
> Even if it's sunny out, don't forget to bring a jacket and dress in layers; the weather can change almost instantly from sunny and warm to windy and cold—especially as you move between microclimates.

San Francisco's temperate, marine climate usually means relatively mild weather year-round. In summer, chilling fog rolls in most mornings and evenings, and if temperatures top 70°F (21°C), the city is ready to throw a celebration. Even when autumn's heat occasionally stretches into the 80s (upper 20s Celsius) and 90s (lower 30s Celsius), you should still dress in layers, or by early evening you'll learn firsthand why sweatshirt sales are a great business at Fisherman's Wharf. In winter, the mercury seldom falls below freezing and snow is almost unheard of, but that doesn't mean you won't be whimpering if you forget your coat. Still, compared to most of the state's weather conditions, San Francisco's are consistently pleasant, and even if it's damp and chilly, head north, east, or south 15 minutes and you can usually find sun again.

The coastal fog is caused by a rare combination of water, wind, and topography. The fog lies off the coast, and rising air currents pull it in when the land heats up. Held back by coastal mountains along a 600-mile front, the low clouds seek out any passage they can find. The easiest access is the slot where the Pacific Ocean penetrates the continental wall—the Golden Gate.

San Francisco's Average Temperatures (°F/°C)

	JAN	FEB	MAR	APR	MAY	JUNE	JULY	AUG	SEPT	OCT	NOV	DEC
AVG. HIGH	56/13	59/15	61/16	64/18	67/19	70/21	71/22	72/22	73/23	70/21	62/17	56/13
AVG. LOW	43/6	46/8	47/8	48/9	51/11	53/12	55/13	56/13	55/13	52/11	48/9	43/6

Holidays

Banks, government offices, post offices, and many stores, restaurants, and museums are closed on the following legal national holidays: January 1 (New Year's Day), the third Monday in January (Martin Luther King, Jr., Day), the third Monday in February (Presidents' Day), the last Monday in May (Memorial Day), July 4 (Independence Day), the first Monday in September (Labor Day), the second Monday in October (Columbus Day), November 11 (Veterans Day/Armistice Day), the fourth Thursday in November (Thanksgiving Day), and December 25 (Christmas). The Tuesday after the first Monday in November is Election Day, a federal government holiday in presidential-election years (held every 4 years).

San Francisco–Area Calendar of Events

For more information on San Francisco events, visit www.onlyinsanfrancisco.com for an annual calendar of local events, as well as http://events.frommers.com, where you'll find a searchable, up-to-the-minute roster of what's happening in cities all over the world.

FEBRUARY

Chinese New Year, Chinatown. Public celebrations spill onto every street in Chinatown, beginning with the "Miss Chinatown USA" pageant parade, and climaxing a week later with a celebratory parade of marching bands, rolling floats, barrages of fireworks, and a block-long dragon writhing in and out of the crowds. The action starts at Market and Second streets and ends at Kearny Street. Arrive early for a good viewing spot on Kearny Street. You can purchase bleacher seats online starting in December. Make your hotel reservations early. For dates and information, call ☏ **415/982-3000** or visit www.chineseparade.com.

MARCH

St. Patrick's Day Parade, Union Square and Civic Center. Everyone's an honorary Irish person at this festive affair, which starts at 11:30am at Market and Second streets and continues to City Hall. But the party doesn't stop there. Head down to the Civic Center for the post-party, or venture to the Embarcadero's Harrington's Bar & Grill (245 Front St.) and celebrate with hundreds of the Irish-for-a-day yuppies as they gallivant around the closed-off streets and numerous pubs. For information, call ☏ **415/675-9885** or visit www.sfstpatricksdayparade.com. Sunday before March 17.

APRIL

Cherry Blossom Festival, Japantown. Meander through the arts-and-crafts and food booths lining the blocked-off streets around Japan Center and watch traditional drumming, flower arranging, origami making, and a parade celebrating the cherry blossoms and Japanese culture. Call ☏ **415/563-2313** for information. Mid- to late April.

San Francisco International Film Festival, around San Francisco with screenings at the Sundance Kabuki Cinemas (Fillmore and Post sts.), and at many other locations. Begun in 1957, this is America's oldest film festival. It features close to 200 films and videos from more than 50 countries. Tickets are relatively inexpensive, and screenings are accessible to the public. Entries include new films by beginning and established directors, and star-studded tributes. For a schedule or information, call ☏ **415/561-5000** or visit www.sffs.org. Mid-April to early May.

MAY

Cinco de Mayo Festival, Mission District. This is when the Latino community celebrates the victory of the Mexicans over the French at Puebla in 1862; mariachi bands, dancers, food, and revelers fill the streets of the Mission. The celebration is usually in Dolores Park (Dolores St. btw. 18th and 20th sts.). Contact the

Mission Neighborhood Center for more information at ☎ **415/206-0577** or www.sfcincodemayo.com.

Zazzle Bay to Breakers Foot Race, the Embarcadero through Golden Gate Park to Ocean Beach. Even if you don't participate, you can't avoid this giant, moving costume party (which celebrated its 100th year in 2011) that goes from downtown to Ocean Beach. More than 75,000 entrants gather—many dressed in wacky, innovative, and sometimes X-rated costumes—for the approximately 7.5-mile run. If you don't want to run, join the throng of spectators who line the route. Sidewalk parties, bands, and cheerleaders of all ages provide a good dose of true San Francisco fun. For recorded information, call ☎ **415/359-2800,** or check their website, www.baytobreakers.com. Third Sunday of May.

Carnaval Festival, Harrison Street between 16th and 23rd streets. The Mission District's largest annual event, held from 9:30am to 6pm, is a day of festivities that includes food, music, dance, arts and crafts, and a parade that's as sultry and energetic as the Latin American and Caribbean people behind it. For one of San Franciscans' favorite events, more than half a million spectators line the parade route, and samba musicians and dancers continue to entertain on 14th Street, near Harrison, at the end of the march, where you'll find food and craft booths, music, and more revelry. Call the hot line at ☎ **415/920-0125** for information. Celebrations are held Saturday and Sunday of Memorial Day weekend, but the parade is on Sunday morning only. See www.carnaval.com/sf/sf_carn.htm for more information.

JUNE

Union Street Art Festival, Pacific Heights, along Union Street from Steiner to Gough streets. This outdoor fair celebrates San Francisco with themes, gourmet food booths, music, entertainment, and a juried art show featuring works by more than 250 artists. It's a great time and a chance

to see the city's young well-to-dos partying it up. Call the **Union Street Association** (☎ **415/441-7055**) for more information or see www.unionstreetfestival.com. First weekend of June.

Haight-Ashbury Street Fair, Haight-Ashbury. A far cry from the froufrou Union Street Fair, this grittier fair features alternative crafts, ethnic foods, rock bands, and a healthy number of hippies and street kids whooping it up and slamming beers in front of the blaring rock-'n'-roll stage. The fair usually extends along Haight Street between Stanyan and Ashbury streets. For details, call ☎ **415/863-3489** or visit www.haightashburystreetfair.org. Second Sunday of June.

North Beach Festival, Grant Avenue, North Beach. In 2009, this party celebrated its 55th anniversary; organizers claim it's the oldest urban street fair in the country. Close to 100,000 city folk meander along Grant Avenue, between Vallejo and Union streets, to eat, drink, and browse the arts-and-crafts booths, poetry readings, swing-dancing venue, and *arte di gesso* (sidewalk chalk art). But the most enjoyable parts of the event are listening to music and people-watching. Call ☎ **415/989-2220** for details. Usually Father's Day weekend, but call to confirm.

Stern Grove Music Festival, Sunset District. Pack a picnic and head out early to join the thousands who come here to lie in the grass and enjoy classical, jazz, and ethnic music and dance in the grove, at 19th Avenue and Sloat Boulevard. Celebrating its 75th season, the free concerts take place every Sunday at 2pm between mid-June and August. Show up with a lawn chair or blanket. There are food booths if you forget snacks, but you'll be dying to leave if you don't bring warm clothes—the Sunset District can be one of the coldest parts of the city. Call ☎ **415/252-6252** for listings or go to www.sterngrove.org. Sundays, mid-June through August.

San Francisco Lesbian, Gay, Bisexual, Transgender Pride Parade & Celebration, downtown's Market Street. This prideful event draws up to one million participants who celebrate all of the above—and then some. The parade proceeds west on Market Street until it gets to the Civic Center, where hundreds of food, art, and information booths are set up around several soundstages. Call ℂ **415/864-3733** or visit www.sfpride.org for information. Usually the third or last weekend of June.

JULY

Fillmore Jazz Festival, Pacific Heights. July starts with a bang, when the upscale portion of Fillmore closes to traffic and the blocks between Jackson and Eddy streets are filled with arts and crafts, gourmet food, and live jazz from 10am to 6pm. Call ℂ **510/970-3217** for more information or visit www.fillmorejazz festival.com. First weekend in July.

Fourth of July Celebration & Fireworks, Fisherman's Wharf. This event can be something of a joke—more often than not, fog comes into the city, like everyone else, to join in the festivities. Sometimes it's almost impossible to view the million-dollar pyrotechnics from Pier 39 on the northern waterfront. Still, it's a party, and if the skies are clear, it's a darn good show.

San Francisco Marathon, San Francisco and beyond. This is one of the largest marathons in the world. It starts and ends at the Ferry Building at the base of Market Street, winds 26-plus miles through virtually every neighborhood in the city, and crosses the Golden Gate Bridge. For entry information, visit www. thesfmarathon.com. Usually the last weekend in July.

SEPTEMBER

Sausalito Art Festival, Sausalito. A juried exhibit of more than 20,000 original works of art, this festival includes music—provided by jazz, rock, and blues performers from the Bay Area and beyond—and international cuisine, enhanced by wines from some 50 Napa and Sonoma producers.

Parking is impossible; take the **Blue & Gold Fleet ferry** (ℂ **415/705-5555**) from Fisherman's Wharf to the festival site. For more information, call ℂ **415/332-3555** or log on to www.sausalitoartfestival.org. Labor Day weekend.

Opera in the Park, usually in Sharon Meadow, Golden Gate Park. Each year, the San Francisco Opera launches its season with a free concert featuring a selection of arias. Call ℂ **415/861-4008** to confirm the location and date. Usually the Sunday after Labor Day.

Folsom Street Fair, along Folsom Street between 7th and 12th streets, the area south of Market Street (SoMa), from 11am to 6pm. This is a local favorite for its kinky, outrageous, leather-and-skin gay-centric blowout celebration. It's hard-core, so only open minded and adventurous types need head into the partially dressed or nude, paddle-wielding crowd. For info call ℂ **415/861-3247** or visit www.folsom streetfair.org. Last Sunday of September.

OCTOBER

Fleet Week, Marina and Fisherman's Wharf. Residents gather along the Marina Green, the Embarcadero, Fisherman's Wharf, and other vantage points to watch incredible (and loud!) aerial performances by the Blue Angels and other daring stunt pilots, as well as the annual parade of ships. Call ℂ **650/599-5057** or visit www.fleetweek.us for details and dates.

Artspan Open Studios, various San Francisco locations. Find an original piece of art to commemorate your trip, or just see what local artists are up to by grabbing a map to over 800 artists' studios that are open to the public during weekends in October and May. Call ℂ **415/ 861-9838** or visit www.artspan.org for more information.

Castro Street Fair, the Castro. Celebrate life in the city's most famous gay neighborhood. Call ℂ **415/841-1824** or visit www. castrostreetfair.org for information. First Sunday in October, from 11am to 6pm.

The Treasure Island Music Festival rocks in October, with East Bay views of the city.

Italian Heritage Parade, North Beach and Fisherman's Wharf. The city's Italian community leads the festivities around Fisherman's Wharf, celebrating Columbus's landing in America with a parade along Columbus Avenue. But for the most part, it's a great excuse to hang out in North Beach and people-watch. For information, call ✆ **415/587-8282** or visit www.sfcolumbusday.org. Observed the Sunday before Columbus Day.

Halloween, Citywide. Once a huge street party in the Castro, Halloween has been tamed down by city officials in recent years to curb violence and overcrowding. The city still whoops it up with extravagant costumes, but the party has shifted off the streets and into the bars and clubs. October 31.

San Francisco Jazz Festival, various San Francisco locations. This festival presents eclectic programming in an array of fabulous jazz venues throughout the city. With close to 3 weeks of nightly entertainment and dozens of performers, the jazz festival is a hot ticket. Past events have featured Herbie Hancock, Dave Brubeck, the Modern Jazz Quartet, Wayne Shorter, and Bill Frisell. For information, call ✆ **800/850-SFJF** (7353) or 415/788-7353 or visit www.sfjazz.org. Also check the website

for other events throughout the year. Late October and early November.

Treasure Island Music Festival, Treasure Island. Bands and crowds take over this East Bay landfill island (and former U.S. Navy base) for the weekend. Free shuttle from AT&T Park. Visit www.treasureislandfestival.com. Mid-October.

DECEMBER

The Nutcracker, War Memorial Opera House, Civic Center. The **San Francisco Ballet** (✆ **415/865-2000**) performs this Tchaikovsky classic annually. (It was actually the first ballet company in America to do so.) Order tickets to this holiday tradition well in advance. Visit www.sfballet.org for information.

SantaCon, various San Francisco locations. Get into the holiday spirit and join thousands as they booze their way across the city. Dress up as Santa, Mrs. Clause, an elf, or your own interpretation for a full day of drinking, singing, and being merry. This is an adults-only pub-crawl that, true to San Francisco style, includes nudity. The time, date, and location change annually and the details are released only a few days before the event, so follow SantaCon on twitter or check out the website at www.santacon.info/San_Francisco-CA.

3

SAN FRANCISCO NEIGHBORHOODS & SUGGESTED ITINERARIES

f you've left your brain at the office and want someone else to make all the tough decisions during your vacation, you'll love this chapter. It's where we tell you what *we* think you should see and do during your vacation in San Francisco. It's broken down into 1-day, 2-day, and 3-day sections, depending on how long you're in town. If you've already made your way through "The Best of San Francisco in 1 Day," the 2-day tour starts where the 1-day schedule left off, and so on. But if you really want to enjoy even a fraction of what San Francisco has to offer, you should plan on staying at least 3 days, preferably a week. And because renting a car in the city is an expensive hassle (and driving in the city is insane), we're going to do all our transportation via foot, bus, and bike. Right, then: Let's get started.

CITY LAYOUT

San Francisco occupies the tip of a 32-mile peninsula between San Francisco Bay and the Pacific Ocean. Its land area measures about 46 square miles, although the city is often referred to as being 7 square miles. At more than 900 feet high, towering Twin Peaks (which are, in fact, two neighboring peaks), mark the geographic center of the city and make a great place to take in a vista of San Francisco.

With lots of one-way streets, San Francisco might seem confusing at first, but it will quickly become easy to navigate. The city's downtown streets are arranged in a simple grid pattern, with the exceptions of Market Street and Columbus Avenue, which cut across the grid at right angles to each other. Hills appear to distort this pattern, however, and can disorient you. As you learn your way around, the hills will become your landmarks and reference points.

MAIN ARTERIES & STREETS **Market Street** is San Francisco's main thorough-fare. Most of the city's buses travel this route on their way to the Financial District from the outer neighborhoods to the west and south. The tall office buildings clustered downtown are at the northeast end of Market; 1 block beyond lies the Embarcadero and the bay.

The **Embarcadero ★**—an excellent strolling, skating, and biking route (thanks to recent renovations)—curves along San Francisco Bay from south of the Bay Bridge to the northeast perimeter of the city. It terminates at Fisherman's Wharf, the famous tourist-oriented pier. Aquatic Park, Fort Mason, and Golden Gate National Recreation Area are on the northern-most point of the peninsula.

From the eastern perimeter of Fort Mason, **Van Ness Avenue** runs due south, back to Market Street. The area just described forms a rough triangle, with Market Street as its southeastern boundary, the waterfront as

PREVIOUS PAGE: **The Powell–Market cable car travels between Fisherman's Wharf and Powell and Market streets.**

its northern boundary, and Van Ness Avenue as its western boundary. Within this triangle lie most of the city's main tourist sights.

FINDING AN ADDRESS Because most of the city's streets are laid out in a grid pattern, finding an address is easy when you know the nearest cross street. Numbers start with 1 at the beginning of the street and proceed at the rate of 100 per block. When asking for directions, find out the nearest cross street and your destination's neighborhood, but be careful not to confuse numerical avenues with numerical streets. Numerical avenues (Third Ave. and so on) are in the Richmond and Sunset districts in the western part of the city. Numerical streets (Third St. and so on) are south of Market Street in the east and south parts of town.

Neighborhoods in Brief

For further discussion of some of the neighborhoods below, see the "Neighborhoods Worth a Visit" section of chapter 6, beginning on p. 192. Also see the "San Francisco Neighborhoods" map on p. 42.

UNION SQUARE Union Square is the commercial hub of San Francisco. Most major hotels and department stores are crammed into the area surrounding the actual square, which was named for a series of violent pro-union rallies staged here on the eve of the Civil War. A plethora of upscale boutiques, restaurants, and galleries occupy the spaces tucked between the larger buildings. A few blocks west is the **Tenderloin** neighborhood, a patch of poverty and blight where you should keep your wits about you. The **Theater District** is 3 blocks west of Union Square.

THE FINANCIAL DISTRICT East of Union Square, this area, bordered by the Embarcadero and by Market, Third, Kearny, and Washington streets, is the city's business district and the stomping grounds for many major corporations. The pointy Transamerica Pyramid, at Montgomery and Clay streets,

Lombard Street, famous for its steep slope and hairpin turns, offers a staircase for pedestrians.

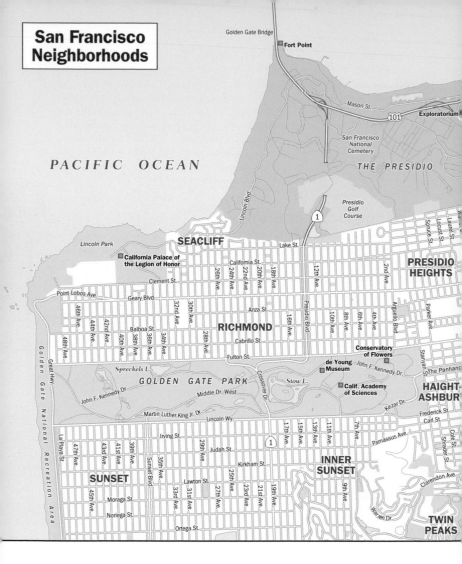

San Francisco Neighborhoods

PACIFIC OCEAN

is one of the district's most conspicuous architectural features. To its east sprawls the Embarcadero Center, an 8½-acre complex housing offices, shops, and restaurants. Farther east still is the old Ferry Building, the city's prebridge transportation hub. Ferries to Sausalito and Larkspur still leave from this point. However, in 2003, the building became an attraction all its own when it was completely renovated, jampacked with outstanding restaurants and gourmet food- and wine-related shops, and surrounded by a farmers' market a few days a week, making it a favorite place of San Francisco's residents seeking to stock their kitchens.

NOB HILL & RUSSIAN HILL Bounded by Bush, Larkin, Pacific, and Stockton streets, Nob Hill is a genteel, well-heeled district still occupied by the city's major power brokers and the neighborhood businesses they frequent.

Russian Hill extends from Pacific to Bay streets and from Polk to Mason streets. It contains steep streets, lush gardens, and high-rises occupied by both the moneyed and the bohemian.

CHINATOWN A large red-and-green gate on Grant Avenue at Bush Street marks the official entrance to Chinatown. Beyond lies a 24-block labyrinth, bordered by Broadway, Bush, Kearny, and Stockton streets, filled with restaurants, markets, temples, shops, and, of course, a substantial percentage of San Francisco's Chinese residents. Chinatown is a great place for exploration all along Grant and Stockton streets, Portsmouth Square, and the alleys that lead off them, like Ross and Waverly. This district has a maddening combination of incessant traffic and horrible drivers, so don't even think about driving around here.

NORTH BEACH This Italian neighborhood, which stretches from Montgomery and Jackson streets to Bay Street, is one of the best places in the city to grab a coffee, pull up a cafe chair, and do some serious people-watching. Night-life is equally happening in North Beach; restaurants, bars, and clubs along Columbus and Grant avenues attract folks from all over the Bay Area, who fight for a parking place and romp through the festive neighborhood. Down Columbus Avenue toward the Financial District are the remains of the city's Beat Generation landmarks, including Ferlinghetti's City Lights Booksellers and Vesuvio's Bar. Broadway Street—a short strip of sex joints—cuts through the heart of the district. **Telegraph Hill** looms over the east side of North Beach, topped by Coit Tower, one of San Francisco's best vantage points.

FISHERMAN'S WHARF North Beach runs into Fisherman's Wharf, which was once the busy heart of the city's great harbor and waterfront industries. Today it's a kitschy and mildly entertaining tourist area with little, if any, authentic waterfront life, except for a small fleet of fishing boats and some lethargic sea lions. What it does have going for it are activities for the whole family, with honky-tonk attractions and museums, restaurants, trinket shops, and beautiful views everywhere you look.

THE MARINA DISTRICT Created on landfill for the Panama Pacific Exposition of 1915, the Marina District boasts some of the best views of the Golden Gate, as well as plenty of grassy fields alongside San Francisco Bay. Elegant Mediterranean-style homes and apartments, inhabited by the city's well-to-do singles and wealthy families, line the streets. Here, too, are the Palace of Fine Arts, the Exploratorium, Fort Mason, and Crissy Field. The main street is Chestnut, between Franklin and Lyon streets, which abounds with shops, cafes, and boutiques. Because of its landfill foundation, the Marina was one of the hardest-hit districts in the 1989 quake.

The seals of Pier 39.

The Peace Pagoda, a gift from Osaka, Japan, is located at the heart of Japantown, at Post and Buchanan streets.

COW HOLLOW Located west of Van Ness Avenue, between Russian Hill and the Presidio, this flat, grazable area supported 30 dairy farms in 1861. Today, Cow Hollow is largely residential and largely yuppie. Its two primary commercial thoroughfares are Lombard Street, known for its many relatively inexpensive motels, and Union Street, an upscale shopping sector filled with restaurants, pubs, cafes, and boutiques.

PACIFIC HEIGHTS The ultra-elite, such as the Gettys and Danielle Steel—and those lucky enough to buy before the real-estate boom—reside in the mansions and homes in this neighborhood. When the rich meander out of their fortresses, they wander down to Fillmore or Union Street and join the pretty people who frequent the chic boutiques and lively neighborhood restaurants, cafes, and bars.

JAPANTOWN Bounded by Octavia, Fillmore, California, and Geary streets, Japantown shelters only a small percentage of the city's Japanese population, but exploring the Japanese knickknack shops and noodle restaurants inside the Japantown Center is a whole day's cultural experience. Duck inside one of the photo booths and take home a dozen Hello Kitty stickers as a souvenir.

CIVIC CENTER Although millions of dollars have gone toward brick sidewalks, ornate lampposts, and elaborate street plantings, the southwestern section of Market Street can still feel a little sketchy due to the large number of homeless who wander the area. The Civic Center at the "bottom" of Market Street, however, is a stunning beacon of culture and refinement. This large complex of buildings includes the domed and dapper City Hall, the Opera House, Davies Symphony Hall, and the Asian Art Museum. The landscaped plaza connecting the buildings is the staging area for San Francisco's frequent demonstrations for or against just about everything.

SOMA No part of San Francisco has been more affected by recent development than the area south of Market Street (dubbed "SoMa"), the area within the triangle of the Embarcadero, Hwy. 101, and Market Street. Until a decade ago it was a district of old warehouses and industrial spaces, with a few scattered underground nightclubs, restaurants, and shoddy residential areas. But when it became the hub of dot.commercialization and half-million-dollar-plus lofts, its fate changed forever. Today, though dot.coms don't occupy much of the commercial space, the area is jumping thanks to fancy high-rise residences, AT&T Park (the Giants' baseball stadium), a bevy of new businesses, restaurants, and nightclubs, and cultural institutions that include the Museum of Modern Art, Yerba Buena Gardens, the Jewish and African Diaspora museums, and Metreon. Though still gritty in some areas, it's growing more glittery by the year, as big-bucks hotels and residence towers dominate over what's left of the industrial zone.

MISSION DISTRICT This is another area that was greatly affected by the city's Internet gold rush. Mexican and Latin American populations make this area home, with their cuisine, traditions, and art creating a vibrant cultural area. Some parts of the neighborhood are still poor and sprinkled with the homeless, gangs, and drug addicts, but young urbanites have also settled here, attracted by its "reasonably" (a relative term) priced rentals and endless oh-so-hot restaurants and bars that stretch from 16th and Valencia streets to 25th and Mission streets. Less adventurous tourists may just want to duck into Mission Dolores (San Francisco's oldest building), cruise past a few of the 200-plus amazing murals, and head back downtown. But anyone who's interested in hanging with the hipsters and experiencing the hottest restaurant and bar nightlife should definitely beeline it here.

THE CASTRO One of the liveliest districts in town, the Castro is practically synonymous with San Francisco's gay community, who moved here back in the 1970s, turning this once Irish working-class neighborhood into a bustling hotbed of shops, bars, and restaurants. Located at the top of Market Street, between 17th and 18th streets, the Castro offers a thoroughly entertaining dose of street theater, and while most businesses cater to the gay community, it's more than welcoming to open-minded straight people.

HAIGHT-ASHBURY Part trendy, part nostalgic, part funky, the Haight, as it's most commonly known, was the soul of the psychedelic free-loving 1960s and the center of the counterculture movement. Today, the gritty neighborhood straddling upper Haight Street on the eastern border of Golden Gate Park is more gentrified, but the commercial area still harbors all walks of life. Leftover aging hippies mingle with grungy, begging street kids outside Ben & Jerry's Ice Cream Store (where they might still be talking about Jerry Garcia, or was that Cherry Garcia), nondescript marijuana dealers whisper "Buds" as shoppers pass, and many people walking down the street have Day-Glo hair. But you don't need to be a freak or wear tie-dye to enjoy the Haight—the ethnic food, trendy shops, and bars cover all tastes. From Haight Street, walk south on Cole Street for a more peaceful and quaint neighborhood experience.

RICHMOND & SUNSET DISTRICTS San Francisco's suburbs of sorts, these are the city's largest and most populous neighborhoods, consisting mainly of small homes, shops, cafes, and neighborhood restaurants. Although they border Golden Gate Park and Ocean Beach, few tourists venture into "the

A mural by Ray Patlan on the side of the Leonard R. Flynn Elementary School in the Mission.

The famous legs above Piedmont Boutique in Haight-Ashbury.

Avenues," as these areas are referred to locally, unless they're on their way to the Cliff House, zoo, beach, or Palace of the Legion of Honor Museum.

THE BEST OF SAN FRANCISCO IN 1 DAY

If you've got only 1 day to explore the city, put on your walking shoes and start early. You've got a lot of ground to cover just to get to the must secs, but luckily, condensed geography (and hopefully weather) are in your favor. The whirlwind tour starts with a scenic ride on a cable car followed by a tour of Alcatraz Island. Next you'll hoof it up to two of the city's most colorful neighborhoods—Chinatown and North Beach—for lunch, shopping, browsing, cocktails, dinner, and cappuccino. Get an early start, because you're about to have a long yet wonderful day in the City by the Bay. ***Start:*** *Bus no. 2, 3, 30, 45, or 76 to Union Square.*

1 Union Square

Union Square—which was named for a series of pro-union mass demonstrations staged here on the eve of the Civil War—isn't an attraction in itself, but it's the epicenter of the city's shopping district. Macy's, Saks, Tiffany's, Barneys, and company are located here and are surrounded by blocks crammed with hundreds of other high-end boutiques. There are very few shopping bargains here, but it's fun to play lookey-loo. Just 3 blocks down, at Powell and Market streets, is the cable car turnaround where you'll embark on a ride on the nation's only moving National Historic Landmark. See p. 41.

2 Cable Cars & Lombard Street ★★★

Don't be intimidated by the line of people at the cable car turnaround at Market and Powell streets—the ride is worth the wait. The $5 thrill ride starts with a steep climb up Nob Hill, and then passes through Chinatown and Russian Hill before plummeting down Hyde Street to Fisherman's Wharf. It's an experience you'll never forget. (***Note:*** If you want to check out the famous winding stretch of Lombard Street, hop off the cable car at the intersection of Hyde and Lombard streets and, when you've seen enough, either walk the rest of the way down to Fisherman's Wharf or take the next

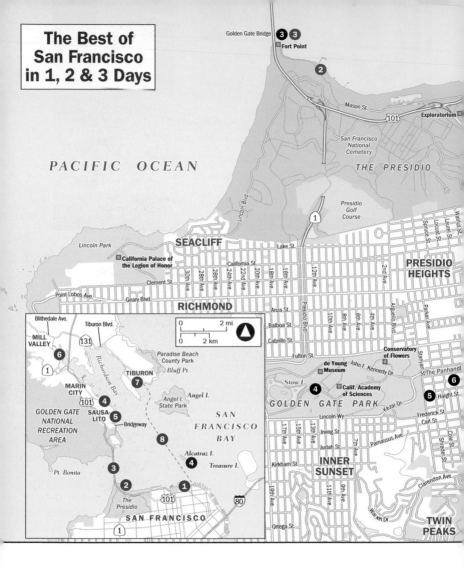

The Best of San Francisco in 1, 2 & 3 Days

Golden Gate Bridge **3** **3**
◻ Fort Point
2

Mason St.
101
Exploratorium ◻

PACIFIC OCEAN

San Francisco
National
Cemetery

THE PRESIDIO

Lincoln Blvd.

Presidio
Golf
Course

1

Lincoln Park

SEACLIFF

Lake St.

PRESIDIO
HEIGHTS

◻ California Palace of
the Legion of Honor

California St.

Clement St.

Point Lobos Ave.
Geary Blvd.

Anza St.

RICHMOND

Balboa St.

Cabrillo St.

Conservatory
of Flowers

Fulton St.

de Young ◻ John F. Kennedy Dr.
Museum

The Panhandl

6

Stow L.

4

◻ Calif. Academy
of Sciences

5 Haight St.

GOLDEN GATE PARK

Kezar Dr.

Frederick St.
Carl St.

Lincoln Wy.

Irving St.

Judah St.

Parnassus Ave.

INNER
SUNSET

Kirkham St.

Clarendon Ave.

Ortega St.

Warren Dr.

TWIN
PEAKS

Inset map

Blithedale Ave.

Tiburon Blvd.

0   2 mi
0   2 km

MILL
VALLEY

131

6

1

Richardson Bay

Paradise Beach
County Park

Bluff Pt.

MARIN
CITY

TIBURON

7

101

4

Angel I.
State Park

Angel I.

SAN
FRANCISCO
BAY

SAUSA-
LITO

5

Bridgeway

GOLDEN GATE
NATIONAL
RECREATION
AREA

8

Alcatraz I.

4

Treasure I.

Pt. Bonita

3

2

The
Presidio

101

1

1

SAN FRANCISCO

---

cable car that comes along.) For maximum thrill, stand on the running
boards during the ride and hold on Doris Day style. See p. 172 and 179.

3   Buena Vista Café 🍴
After you've completed your first Powell–Hyde cable car ride, it's a San Francisco tradition to celebrate with an Irish coffee at the Buena Vista Café, located
at 2765 Hyde St. across from the cable car turnaround (✆ **415/474-5044**). The
first Irish coffees served in America were mixed here in 1952, and they're still
the best in the Bay Area. See p. 279.

BEST IN 1 DAY	BEST IN 2 DAYS	BEST IN 3 DAYS
1 Union Square	1 Marina District	1 Blazing Saddles
2 Cable Cars & Lombard Street	2 The Grove 🍽	2 The Warming Hut 🍽
3 Buena Vista Café 🍽	3 Golden Gate Bridge	3 Golden Gate Bridge
4 Alcatraz Tour	4 Golden Gate Park	4 Sausalito
5 Chinatown	5 Cha Cha Cha 🍽	5 Horizons 🍽
6 House of Dim Sum 🍽	6 Haight-Ashbury	6 North Bay
7 North Beach	7 Isa	7 Sam's Anchor Cafe 🍽
8 Mario's Bohemian Cigar Store 🍽		8 Ferry to San Francisco
9 Capp's Corner		
10 Caffè Greco 🍽		

4   Alcatraz Tour ★★★

To tour "the Rock," the Bay Area's famous abandoned prison on its own
island, you must first get there, and that's half the fun. The brief but beautiful ferry ride offers captivating views of the Golden Gate Bridge, the Marin
Headlands, and the city. Once inside, an excellent audio tour guides you
through cellblocks and offers a colorful look at the prison's historic past as
well as its most infamous inmates. Book well in advance because these
tours consistently sell out in the summer. Bring snacks and beverages—the
ferry's pickings are slim and expensive, and nothing is available on the
island. See p. 168.

A cable car whips down Powell Street.

The Buena Vista Café.

5 Chinatown ★★

One block from North Beach is a whole other world: Chinatown. San Francisco has one of the largest communities of Chinese people in the United States, with more than 80,000 people condensed into the blocks around Grant Avenue and Stockton Street. Although frequented by tourists, the area caters mostly to Chinese, who crowd the vegetable and herb markets, restaurants, and shops carrying those ubiquitous pink plastic bags. It's worth a peek if only to see the Stockton Street markets hawking live frogs, armadillos, turtles, and odd sea creatures destined for tonight's dinner table. *Tip:* The dozens of knickknack shops are a great source of cheap souvenirs. See p. 194.

6 House of Dim Sum 🍵

You can't visit Chinatown and not sample dim sum. Walk to 735 Jackson St. to the House of Dim Sum (ℂ **415/399-0888**) and order shrimp dumplings, pork dumplings, sweet buns, turnip cake, and the sweet rice with chicken wrapped in a lotus leaf. Find an empty table, pour a side of soy sauce, and dig in.

7 North Beach ★★★

One of the best ways to get the San Francisco vibe is to mingle with the locals, and one of our favorite places to do so is in San Francisco's "Little Italy." Dozens of Italian restaurants and coffeehouses continue to flourish in what is still the center of the city's Italian community. A stroll along Columbus Avenue will take you past eclectic little cafes, delis, bookstores, bakeries, and coffee shops that give North Beach its Italian-bohemian character. See p. 194.

Tip: Be sure to see chapter 7, "City Strolls," for highlights of North Beach and Chinatown.

8 Mario's Bohemian
Cigar Store
Okay, so the menu's limited to coffee drinks and a few sandwiches (the meatball is our favorite), but the convivial atmosphere and large windows that are perfect for people-watching make this tiny, pie-shaped cafe a favorite even with locals. It's at 566 Columbus Ave. (✆ **415/362-0536**). See p. 133.

9 Dinner at Capp's Corner ★

The best thing about North Beach is its old-school restaurants—those dusty, frumpy, loud, and over-sauced bastions of red sauce

Depiction of an artist's cell at Alcatraz. Prisoners could also bide their time by volunteering as gardeners (check the site's website for garden tour times).

and chianti. **Capp's Corner** (1600 Powell St.; ✆ **415/989-2589**) is one of our favorites, where patrons sit at long tables and dine family style via huge platters of Italian comfort food served by brusque waitresses, while Frank Sinatra croons his classics on the jukebox. See p. 132.

10 Caffè Greco  ★
By now you should be stuffed and exhausted. Good. End the night with a cappuccino at Caffè Greco (423 Columbus Ave.; ✆ **415/397-6261**). Sit at one of the sidewalk tables and reminisce on what a great day you had in San Francisco.

THE BEST OF SAN FRANCISCO IN 2 DAYS

On your second day, get familiar with other famous landmarks around the city. Start with breakfast, a science lesson, and a pleasant bayside stroll in the Marina District. Next, cross the famed Golden Gate Bridge on foot; then take a bus to Golden Gate Park. After a stroll through the city's beloved park, it's time for lunch and power shopping on Haight Street, followed by dinner and cocktails back in the Marina District. Smashing. ***Start:*** *Bus no. 22, 28, 30, 30X, 43, 76, or 82X.*

1 Good Morning Marina District

The area that became famous for its scenes of destruction after the 1989 earthquake has long been one of the most picturesque and coveted patches of local real estate. Here, along the northern edge of the city, multimillion-dollar homes back up to the bayfront **Marina,** where flotillas of sailboats and the mighty Golden Gate Bridge make for a magnificent backdrop on a morning stroll.

Start the day with a good cup of coffee on Chestnut Street (see "The Grove," below); then walk to the **Palace of Fine Arts,** built for the Panama Pacific Exhibition of 1915 and home to the **Exploratorium** (p. 185). Spend a few hours on sensory overload at the "best science museum in the world" (kids *love* this place), and then walk over to **Crissy Field** (p. 202), where restored wetlands and a beachfront path lead to historic **Fort Point** (p. 202) and to the southern underside end of the **Golden Gate Bridge.**

A mini-tornado at the Palace of Fine Arts' Exploratorium.

2 The Grove 🍵

If you can't jump-start your brain properly without a good cup of coffee, then begin your day at the Grove (2250 Chestnut St.; ☏ **415/474-4843**), located in the Marina District—it's as cozy as an old leather couch. See p. 144.

3 The Golden Gate Bridge ★★★

It's one of those things you have to do at least once in your life—walk across the fabled Golden Gate Bridge, the most photographed man-made structure in the world (p. 178). As you would expect, the views along the span are spectacular and the wind a wee bit chilly, so bring a jacket. It takes at least an hour to walk northward to the vista point and back. When you return to the southern end, board either Muni bus no. 28 or 29 (be sure to ask the driver whether the bus is headed toward Golden Gate Park).

4 Golden Gate Park ★★★

Stretching from the middle of the city to the Pacific Ocean and comprising 1,017 acres, Golden Gate Park is one of the city's greatest attributes. Since its development in the late 1880s, it has provided San Franciscans with respite from urban life—offering dozens of well-tended gardens, museums, a buffalo paddock, a Victorian greenhouse, and great grassy expanses prime for picnicking, lounging, or tossing a Frisbee.

Have the bus driver drop you off near John F. Kennedy Drive. Walking eastward on JFK Drive, you'll pass three of the park's most popular attractions: Stow Lake, the de Young Museum, and the wonderful Conservatory of Flowers (a must-visit). See p. 204.

5 Cha Cha Cha 🍵 ★★

By now you're probably starving, so walk out of the park and into the Haight to Cha Cha Cha (1801 Haight St.; ☏ **415/386-7670;** p. 161), one of our favorite restaurants in the city. Order plenty of dishes from the tapas-style menu and dine family style. Oh, and don't forget a pitcher of sangria—you've earned it.

The Best of San Francisco in 2 Days

NEIGHBORHOODS & ITINERARIES

Cha Cha Cha restaurant.

6 Exploring the Haight-Ashbury District ★★★

Ah, the Haight. Birthplace of the Summer of Love and Flower Power, shrine to the Grateful Dead, and the place where America's nonconformists still congregate over beers, bongos, and buds. Spend at least an hour strolling up Haight Street (p. 198), browsing the cornucopia of used-clothes stores, leather shops, head shops, and poster stores. There are some great bargains to be found here, especially for vintage clothing. When you get to the intersection of Haight and Masonic streets, catch the Muni no. 43 bus heading north, which will take you through the Presidio and back to the Marina District.

7 Dinner & Drinks

You've had a full day, my friend, so rest your weary bones at the back patio at **Isa** (3324 Steiner St.; ℂ **415/567-9588;** p. 142), a fantastic and surprisingly affordable French restaurant in the Marina. If there's still gas in your tank after dinner, walk over to the **Balboa Café** (3199 Fillmore St., ℂ **415/921-3944**) and practice your pickup lines among the young and restless who practically live here.

THE BEST OF SAN FRANCISCO IN 3 DAYS

This is one of our all-time favorite things to do on a day off—ride a bike from Fisherman's Wharf to Sam's Anchor Café in Tiburon (that small peninsula just north of Alcatraz Island). The beautiful and exhilarating ride takes you over the Golden Gate Bridge, through the heart of Sausalito, and along the scenic North Bay bike path, ending with a frosty beer and lunch at the best outdoor cafe in the Bay Area. And here's the best part: You don't have to bike back. After lunch, you can take the passenger ferry across the bay to Fisherman's Wharf—right to your starting point. Brilliant. *Start: Powell–Hyde cable car line. Bus no. 19, 30, or 47.*

1 Rent a Bicycle

Walk, take a bus, or ride the Powell–Hyde cable car (which goes right by it) to **Blazing Saddles** bicycle rental shop at 2715 Hyde St., between Beach and North Point streets near Ghirardelli Square (ℂ **415/202-8888;** p. 218). Rent a single or tandem bike for a full day, and be sure to ask for: 1) a free map pointing out the route to Sam's in Tiburon, 2) ferry tickets, 3) a bicycle lock, and 4) a bottle of water. Bring your own sunscreen, a hat (for the deck at Sam's), and a light jacket—no matter how warm it is right now, the weather can change in minutes. Each bike has a small pouch hooked to the handlebars where you can stuff your stuff.

Fun tip: While you're here, ask about the GoCar rentals—they're a blast to drive and a great way to explore the city. Also, they talk to you. (See the GoCar sidebar on p. 180 for more info.)

Start pedaling along the map route to Golden Gate Bridge. You'll encounter one short, steep hill right from the start at Aquatic Park, but it's okay to walk your bike (hey, you haven't had your coffee fix yet). Keep riding westward through Fort Point and the Marina Green to Crissy Field.

2 The Warming Hut ☕

At the west end of Crissy Field, alongside the bike path, is the Warming Hut (✆ **415/561-3040**), a barnlike building where you can fuel up with a light (organic, sustainable) snack and coffee drinks.

3 Biking the Golden Gate

After your break, there's another steep hill up to the bridge. If the bridge's *east* lane is open to bikes, take it. Once you cross the bridge, stay to the right and you'll enjoy a downhill ride to Sausalito. If you take the bridge's *west* side lane, you'll veer left after you cross, down the path that winds under Hwy. 101, then up one more hill (last one, we promise) to Sausalito. See http://goldengatebridge.org for east and west lane hours.

4 Exploring Sausalito

You'll love Sausalito (p. 313). Cruising down Bridgeway is like being transported to one of those seaside towns on the French Riviera. Lock the bikes and mosey around on foot for a while.

Biking across an icon.

5 Horizons ☕

If you're thirsty, ask for a table on the bayside deck at **Horizons** (558 Bridge-way; ℂ **415/331-3232**) and order a bloody mary, but don't eat yet. See p. 317.

6 North Bay Tour

Back on the bike, head north again on the bike path as it winds along the bay. When you reach the Mill Valley Car Wash at the end of the bike path, turn right onto East Blithedale Avenue, which will cross Hwy. 101 and turn into Tiburon Boulevard. (This is the only sucky part of the ride where you'll encounter traffic.) About a mile past Hwy. 101, you'll enter a small park called Blackie's Pasture. (Look for the life-size bronze statue erected in 1995 to honor Tiburon's beloved "mascot," Blackie the horse.) Now it's an easy cruise on the bike path all the way to Sam's.

7 Sam's Anchor Café ☕

Ride your bike all the way to the south end of Tiburon Boulevard and lock your bike at the bike rack near the ferry dock. Walk over to the ferry loading dock and check the ferry departure schedule for "Tiburon to Pier 39/Fisherman's Wharf." Then walk over to Sam's Anchor Café (27 Main St.; ℂ **415/435-4527**; p. 313), request a table on the back patio overlooking the harbor, and relax with a cool drink. Sweet.

8 Ferry Ride Back to San Francisco

When it's time to leave, board the ferry with your bike (bike riders board first, so don't stand in line) and enjoy the ride from Tiburon to San Francisco, with a short stop at Angel Island State Park. From Pier 39, it's a short ride back to the rental shop.

After all this adventuring, it's time to reenergize your body and soul with another Irish whiskey at the **Buena Vista Café** (2765 Hyde St.; ℂ **415/474-5044**; across from the cable car turnaround), a short walk from the bike rental shop. After libations, take the cable car back to your hotel for some rest and a shower; then spend the rest of the evening enjoying dinner.

If this isn't one of the best days you've had on your vacation, send us this book, and we'll eat it.

Cap off your bike ride with some oysters and a bloody mary. You earned it.

WHERE TO STAY

4

Whether you want a room with a view or just a room, San Francisco is more than accommodating to its 15.7 million annual guests. Most of the city's 200-plus hotels cluster near Union Square, but some smaller independent gems are scattered around town. It's the savvy San Francisco traveler who avoids the heavily touristed areas such as Union Square and Fisherman's Wharf, and instead hangs his or her hat at the city's outlying (and quieter) districts such as the Marina and walks or takes a bus into city central.

WHAT YOU'LL REALLY PAY

When reading over your options, keep in mind that prices listed are "rack" (published) rates. At big, upscale hotels almost no one actually pays them, and there are always deals to be had. Therefore, you should always ask for special discounts or, even better, vacation packages. It's often possible to get the room you want for $100 less than what is quoted here, except when the hotels are packed (usually during summer and due to conventions) and bargaining is close to impossible. Use the rates listed here for the big hotels as guidelines for comparison only; prices for inexpensive choices and smaller B&Bs are closer to reality, however.

THE BEST HOTEL BETS

o **Best for Families:** Kids like the **Westin St. Francis** because upon arrival, children 11 and under get the travel-themed Westin Kids Club backpack filled with a make-your-own postcard kit, colored pencils, a travelogue, a map of the world, and a safari hat. Parents with babies get a rubber duck, a night light, and an emergency kit. At the nautically themed **Argonaut,** kids get to pick a toy out of the "treasure chest," and parents will appreciate the free cribs and strollers. But the place kids will probably love the most is the **Hotel Del Sol** with its "Kids are VIPs" program that includes a lending library of books, toys, and videos; evening cookies and milk; and a plethora of toys to use by the heated outdoor pool. Parents will love the bonded babysitting services and the three baby-proofed rooms, among many other perks for families. See p. 62, 88, and 91, respectively.

o **Best Bang for Your Buck:** We've received nothing but glowing reviews from readers who've stayed at the **Golden Gate Hotel.** The hotel offers individually decorated rooms with handsome antique furnishings, quilted bedspreads, fresh flowers, afternoon tea, and free Wi-Fi, and it's only 2 blocks north of Union Square—starting at $95 a night. See p. 74.

o **Best Splurge:** Custom-made mattresses and pillows, beautiful works of art, and huge luxury marble bathrooms with deep tubs and L'Occitane toiletries:

PREVIOUS PAGE: **A lounge area at the Clift Hotel.**

If only we could afford to live in an Executive Suite at the **Four Seasons Hotel San Francisco.** See p. 80.

o **Best Elevator Ride:** Sometimes getting there is half the fun. No need for Disneyland: Take a ride in a glass elevator at the **Westin St. Francis** to get your thrills. See p. 62.

o **Best City Views:** Preview heaven on the 48th floor of the **Mandarin Oriental,** particularly when the fog rolls in . . . below you. Enjoy the best views of the city from your Japanese soaking tub. See p. 85.

o **Best for Business Travelers:** If you have to do business, why not do it in a centrally located replica of Giorgio Armani's villa in Milan, complete with double-paned soundproof windows, private screening room, work desks, and spa tubs? That would be the **Hotel Milano.** See p. 70.

o **Most Romantic:** Oozing with bohemian romance is the **Hotel Bohème** in North Beach. Gauze-draped canopy beds, Beat-era jazz images, and ornate parasols shading ceiling lights set a romantic mood. See p. 89.

o **Best Public Space in a Historic Hotel:** The **Palace Hotel,** the extravagant creation of banker "Bonanza King" Will Ralston in 1875, has one of the grandest rooms in the city: the Garden Court. Equally eye-catching is the magnificent lobby at Nob Hill's the **Fairmont San Francisco.** See p. 81 and 76, respectively.

o **Best Trendy Scene:** If you want to shack up with the tragically hip, head to **Clift Hotel,** which promises upscale flirting at its bar, the Redwood Room. See p. 59. A close second and far less douchey is the **W San Francisco Hotel** in SoMa. See p. 82. Those with shallower pockets can opt for the **Phoenix Hotel,** where guests lounge poolside or hang at the too-cool Chambers Eat + Drink. See p. 95.

o **Best Service:** As usual, the **Ritz-Carlton** corners the market in ultimate luxury, from its stunning ground-floor bathrooms to its fabulous restaurant to everything in between. Of course such pampering comes at a cost, but if you can afford it, it's worth the splurge. See p. 77. While it doesn't have quite the number of perks that the Ritz has, the **St. Regis Hotel** is a fabulous place to stay. From its state-of-the-art rooms swathed in browns and creams to

---

Price Categories

Very Expensive: $250 and up
Expensive: $200–$249
Moderate: $150–$199
Inexpensive: Under $150

---

its huge spa, gym, hopping bar scene, and destination-restaurant Ame—not to mention its location next to the Museum of Modern Art. See p. 82.

UNION SQUARE

This area is the Times Square of San Francisco and a shopper's delight: Macy's, Nordstrom, Neiman Marcus, Tiffany, and more.

Best For: Travelers who enjoy the hustle and bustle of a big city, walking everywhere, shopping, and riding the cable cars.

Drawbacks: Noisy, crowded, difficult street parking, outrageous hotel garage rates, panhandlers, and premium-location hotel rates.

Very Expensive

Taj Campton Place ★★   This luxury boutique hotel offers some of the most exclusive accommodations in town—not to mention the most expensive. Rooms are compact but comfy, with limestone, pear wood, and Italian-modern decor. The two executive suites and one luxury suite push the haute envelope to even more sumptuous heights. Discriminating returning guests will still find superlative service, including California king-size beds, exquisite bathrooms, bathrobes, top-notch toiletries, slippers, and every other necessity and extra that's made Campton Place a favored temporary address. A recent change in ownership also brought a new chef to the restaurant, which now offers local California cuisine with Mediterranean and Indian inspirations. The bar/bistro in front is a chic clubby spot for a dry martini.

340 Stockton St. (btw. Post and Sutter sts.), San Francisco, CA 94108. www.tajhotels.com. ℂ **866/332-1670** or 415/781-5555. Fax 415/955-5536. 110 units. $250–$685 double; $490–$3,000 suite. American breakfast $18. AE, DC, MC, V. Valet parking $45. Bus: 2, 3, 30, 38, or 45. Cable car: Powell–Hyde or Powell–Mason line (1 block west). BART: Market St. **Amenities:** Restaurant; concierge; outdoor fitness terrace; room service. *In room:* A/C, TV w/pay movies, hair dryer, minibar, Wi-Fi ($13 per day).

Clift Hotel ★   Ian Schrager, king of such ultrahip hotels as New York's Royalton and Paramount, L.A.'s Mondrian, and Miami's Delano, renovated this classic old luxury property a few years back. Young trendsetters now flock here for overpriced monochrome lavender streamlined rooms with often minuscule bathrooms, glamorous atmosphere, and a heavy dose of attitude. Its best attribute is the renovated historic Redwood Room, complete with sexy redwood walls (all made from one tree!), Deco lighting from 1933, and a luxurious (though rather uncomfortable) interior designed by Philippe Starck. The equally trendy, expensive, and mediocre Asia de Cuba restaurant adjoins the swank lounge. The only reason to pay the high prices here is if you'd like to be surrounded by the young and hip. Otherwise, you'll find better rooms around town at a similar or lower price.

495 Geary St. (at Taylor St.), San Francisco, CA 94102. www.clifthotel.com. ℂ **800/697-1791** or 415/775-4700. Fax 415/441-4621. 366 units. $215–$275 double; from $600–$900 studio suite; from $650–$1,200 deluxe suite. AE, DC, DISC, MC, V. Valet parking $50. Bus: 2, 3, 30, 38, or 45. Cable car: Powell–Hyde or Powell–Mason line (2 blocks east). **Amenities:** Restaurant; bar; concierge; exercise room, room service. *In room:* TV/DVD, hair dryer, minibar, Wi-Fi ($15 per day).

Inflation at the Clift

When it first opened in 1915, the Clift Hotel charged a mere $2 per night.

Prescott Hotel ★★   It may be small and lack common areas, but the boutique Prescott Hotel has some big things going for it. The staff treats you like royalty, rooms are attractively unfrilly and masculine, the location (just a block from Union Square) is perfect, and limited room service is provided by the in-house restaurant, Postrio. Ralph Lauren fabrics in dark tones of green, plum, and burgundy and crisp white Italian linens blend well with the cherrywood furnishings in each of the soundproof rooms; the view, alas, isn't so pleasant. The very small bathrooms contain terry robes and Aveda products, and the suites have Jacuzzi bathtubs. Concierge-level guests are pampered with a free continental breakfast and evening cocktails and hors d'oeuvres.

0   1/2 mi
0   1/2 km

☐ **Exploratorium**

MARINA

Marina Green
Marina Blvd.
Cervantes Blvd.

North Point St.

Fort
Mason

Bay St.

Francisco St.

⑫

Moscone
Rec. Ctr.

Chestnut St.

Mason St.

101

Richardson Ave.

San Francisco
National
Cemetery

THE PRESIDIO

Lincoln Blvd.

②

Presidio
Golf
Course

Divisadero St.

Pierce St.

Avila St.

Lombard St.

⑤   ⑥   ⑦   ⑨

Greenwich St.

COW HOLLOW

Filbert St.

Union St.

⑧

Green St.

Fillmore St.

Vallejo St.

Broadway

Pacific Ave.

⑩

Lyon St.

Broderick St.

④

Scott St.

Jackson St.

Alta
Plaza

**PACIFIC
HEIGHTS**

Washington St.

Clay St.

Sacramento St.

Laguna St.

Buchanan St.

Octavia St.

Gough St.

Franklin St.

⑪

101

Lafayette
Park

**PRESIDIO
HEIGHTS**

Locust St.

Laurel St.

Walnut St.

③

Baker St.

California St.

Pine St.

Bush St.

㉞   ㉜

Lake St.

5th Ave.

Cornwall St.

Maple St.

Cherry St.

Commonwealth Ave.

Parker Ave.

Jordan Ave.

Spruce St.

Collins St.

Wood St.

Presidio Ave.

Lyon St.

Sutter St.

Euclid Ave.

Post St.

Japan Center ☐

㉝

Hamilton Sq.

Geary Blvd.

**WESTERN
ADDITION**

Clement St.

←①

O'Farrell St.

Ellis St.

Steiner St.

Eddy St.

Jefferson
Square

Anza St.

6th Ave.

4th Ave.

3rd Ave.

2nd Ave.

Arguello Blvd.

Palm Ave.

**UNIVERSITY OF
SAN FRANCISCO**

Turk Blvd.

Golden Gate Ave.

Webster St.

RICHMOND

Balboa St.

Masonic Ave.

McAllister St.

Fulton St.

Cabrillo St.

U.S.F.

Alamo
Square

Willard St.

Central Ave.

Divisadero St.

Fell St.

Fulton St.

Grove St.

Hayes St.

**HAYES
VALLEY**

☐ **Conservatory
of Flowers**

Stanyan St.

Cole St.

Lyon St.

Oak St.

Pierce St.

Fillmore St.

Laguna St.

Octavia

John F. Kennedy Dr.

Shrader St.

Clayton St.

The Panhandle

**HAIGHT-
ASHBURY**

Page St.

Haight St.

Waller St.

Hermann St.

Ashbury St.

Duboce
Park

Duboce Ave.

⑳⑦

GOLDEN GATE PARK

㉟   ㊱

Kezar Dr.

☐ **Kezar
Stadium**

Frederick St.

Downey St.

Buena
Vista
Park

Alpine Terr.

Buena Vista Ave.

14th St.

Noe St.

Sanchez St.

Lincoln Wy.

Hugo St.

Carl St.

Belvedere St.

Cole St.

15th St.

Corona
Heights
Park

States St.

Castro St.

㊳

16th St.

Church St.

Dolores St.

**Mission
Dolores** ☐

**INNER
SUNSET**

6th Ave.

5th Ave.

Parnassus Ave.

㊲

17th St.

CASTRO

㊴

☐ **Castro Theatre**

㊵

Guerrero St.

**UNIVERSITY OF
CALIFORNIA–
SAN FRANCISCO**

Carmel St.

Market St.

18th St.

Dolores
Park

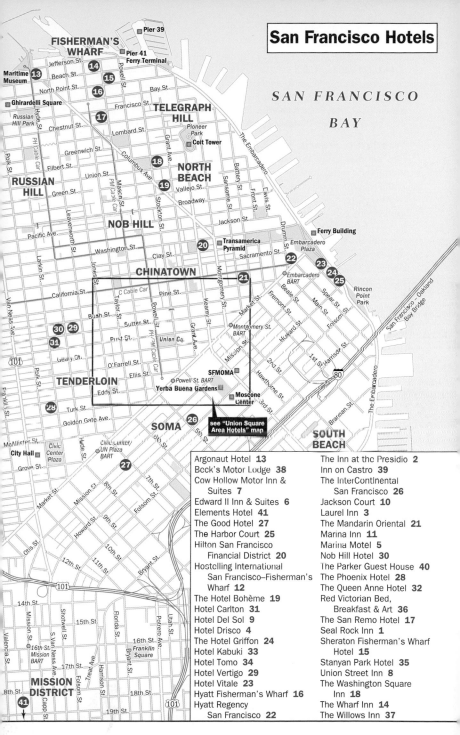

San Francisco Hotels

Pier 39

FISHERMAN'S WHARF

Jefferson St.
Beach St.
North Point St.

Maritime Museum ⑬

⑭

Pier 41 Ferry Terminal

⑮
Powell St.
⑯
Bay St.

Ghirardelli Square

Russian Hill Park
Chestnut St.

Francisco St.

TELEGRAPH HILL

⑰

Lombard St.
Greenwich St.
Filbert St.

Pioneer Park
Coit Tower

RUSSIAN HILL

Union St.
Green St.

⑱
NORTH BEACH
⑲ Vallejo St.
Broadway

NOB HILL

Jackson St.

Pacific Ave.
Washington St.
Clay St.

⑳ **Transamerica Pyramid**

Ferry Building

Embarcadero Plaza

CHINATOWN

California St.

㉑

Sacramento St.

㉒

Embarcadero BART

㉓
㉔
㉕

Rincon Point Park

Pine St.
Bush St.
Sutter St.
Post St.

Beale St.
Fremont St.
Main St.
Spear St.
Folsom St.

San Francisco–Oakland Bay Bridge

㉚ ㉙
㉛

Union Sq.

Geary St.

Montgomery St. BART

O'Farrell St.
Ellis St.

TENDERLOIN

㉘

Turk St.
Golden Gate Ave.

Eddy St.

SFMOMA
Powell St. BART
Yerba Buena Gardens

Moscone Center

2nd St.
Hawthorne St.
Harrison St.

80

SOMA
㉖
see "Union Square Area Hotels" map

Brannan St.

SOUTH BEACH

McAllister St.
City Hall

Civic Center Plaza

Civic Center/ UN Plaza BART

Grove St.

㉗

Market St.

MISSION DISTRICT

㊶

Argonaut Hotel **13**	The Inn at the Presidio **2**
Beck's Motor Lodge **38**	Inn on Castro **39**
Cow Hollow Motor Inn & Suites **7**	The InterContinental San Francisco **26**
Edward II Inn & Suites **6**	Jackson Court **10**
Elements Hotel **41**	Laurel Inn **3**
The Good Hotel **27**	The Mandarin Oriental **21**
The Harbor Court **25**	Marina Inn **11**
Hilton San Francisco Financial District **20**	Marina Motel **5**
	Nob Hill Hotel **30**
Hostelling International San Francisco–Fisherman's Wharf **12**	The Parker Guest House **40**
	The Phoenix Hotel **28**
	The Queen Anne Hotel **32**
The Hotel Bohème **19**	Red Victorian Bed, Breakfast & Art **36**
Hotel Carlton **31**	The San Remo Hotel **17**
Hotel Del Sol **9**	Seal Rock Inn **1**
Hotel Drisco **4**	Sheraton Fisherman's Wharf Hotel **15**
The Hotel Griffon **24**	
Hotel Kabuki **33**	Stanyan Park Hotel **35**
Hotel Tomo **34**	Union Street Inn **8**
Hotel Vertigo **29**	The Washington Square Inn **18**
Hotel Vitale **23**	
Hyatt Fisherman's Wharf **16**	The Wharf Inn **14**
Hyatt Regency San Francisco **22**	The Willows Inn **37**

545 Post St. (btw. Mason and Taylor sts.), San Francisco, CA 94102. www.prescotthotel.com. ℂ **866/271-3632** or 415/563-0303. Fax 415/563-6831. 164 units. $245–$350 double; $280 concierge-level double (including breakfast and evening cocktail reception); from $365 suite. AE, DC, DISC, MC, V. Valet parking $40. Bus: 2, 3, 30, 38, or 45. Cable car: Powell–Hyde or Powell–Mason line (1 block east). **Amenities:** Restaurant; bar; concierge; small exercise room; limited room service. *In room:* TV w/pay movies, hair dryer, minibar, free Wi-Fi.

Westin St. Francis ★★ ☺ At the turn of the 20th century, Charles T. Crocker and a few of his wealthy buddies decided that San Francisco needed a world-class hotel, and up went the St. Francis. Hordes of VIPs have hung their hats and hosiery here, including Emperor Hirohito of Japan, Queen Elizabeth II, Mother Teresa, King Juan Carlos of Spain, the shah of Iran, and the U.S. presidents from Taft through Clinton.

The hotel has done massive renovations, costing $185 million over the past decade, the most recent being a $40-million upgrade that was completed mid-2009—$12 million of which was delegated to the Main Building. The older rooms of the Main Building vary in size and have more old-world charm than the newer rooms, but the Tower is remarkable for its great views of the city from above the 18th floor. If you can swing a room in the Main Building overlooking Union Square, it's worth it. Although the St. Francis is too massive to offer the personal service you get at the smaller hotels on Nob Hill, few other hotels in San Francisco can match its majestic aura.

335 Powell St. (btw. Geary and Post sts.), San Francisco, CA 94102. www.westinstfrancis.com. ℂ **866/937-8461** or 415/397-7000. Fax 415/774-0124. 1,195 units. $229–$529 Main Building double; $179–$559 Tower (Grand View) double; from $650 suite (in either building). Extra person $30. Continental breakfast $15–$18. AE, DC, DISC, MC, V. Valet parking $42. Bus: 2, 3, 30, 38, 45, or 76. Cable car: Powell–Hyde or Powell–Mason line (direct stop). Pets under 40 lb. accepted (dog beds available on request). **Amenities:** 2 restaurants; concierge; elaborate health club and spa; room service. *In room:* A/C, TV, fridge (some rooms), hair dryer, minibar, Wi-Fi ($9.95 per day).

Expensive

The Donatello ★ 🗲 If you're not looking for trendy lodgings or an anonymous business hotel but want old-world elegance, book a room here. The Donatello is, in a word, dignified. The lobby is classy, with Italian marble and a serious staff. The airy, contemporary Art Nouveau rooms, which are some of the largest in the city (an average of 400 sq. ft.), were overhauled in 2012 with new bedding, carpet, and furniture, and feature original art, king-size mattresses, and textiles. Unfortunately, most of the extra-large windows lack great views, but if it's fresh air you're after, the fifth floor has seven terrace rooms.

501 Post St. (at Mason St.), San Francisco, CA 94102. www.shellhospitality.com/en/The-Donattelo. ℂ **888/732-8021** or 415/441-7100. Fax 415/885-8842. 94 units. $109–$300 double; $300 presidential suite. Children 11 and under stay free in parent's room. AE, DC, DISC, MC, V. Valet parking $28. Bus: 2, 3, 30, 38, or 45. Cable car: Powell–Hyde or Powell–Mason line (1 block west). **Amenities:** Restaurant; bar; concierge; exercise room; limited room service. *In room:* A/C, TV w/pay movies, CD player, fridge, hair dryer, free Wi-Fi.

Grand Hyatt San Francisco ★ If the thought of a 10-second walk to Saks Fifth Avenue makes your pulse race, this high-rise luxury hotel is the place for you. The Grand Hyatt sits amid all the downtown shopping while also boasting some of the best views in the area. The lobby is indeed grand, with Chinese artifacts and enormous ceramic vases. Thankfully, the well-kept rooms were recently

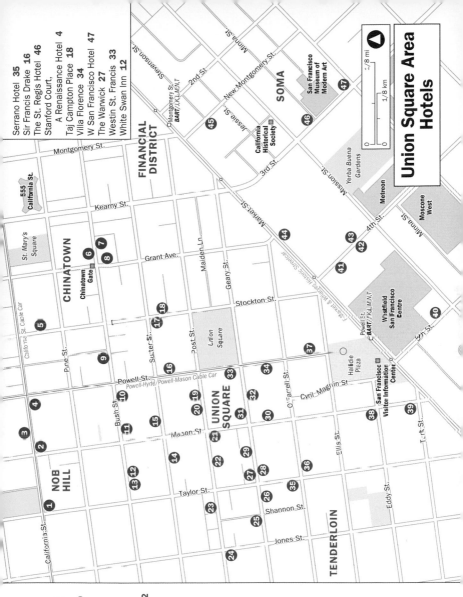

Union Square Area Hotels

The Andrews Hotel **23**
Beresford Hotel **14**
Beresford Arms Hotel **25**
Clift Hotel **28**
The Cornell Hotel de France **10**
The Donatello **21**
Executive Hotel Vintage Court **9**
The Fairmont San Francisco **3**
Four Seasons Hotel
    San Francisco **44**
The Golden Gate Hotel **11**
Grand Hyatt San Francisco **17**
Handlery Union Square Hotel **32**
Hilton San Francisco **36**
Hotel Adagio **25**
Hotel Bijou **38**
Hotel des Arts **7**
Hotel Diva **29**
Hotel Frank **31**
Hotel Metropolis **39**
Hotel Milano **40**
Hotel Monaco **26**
Hotel Palomar **41**
Historical Rex **15**
Hotel Triton **8**
Hotel Union Square **37**
The Huntington Hotel **1**
The Inn at Union Square **19**
InterContinental
    Mark Hopkins **2**
Kensington Park Hotel **20**
King George Hotel **30**
The Mosser **42**
The Orchard Garden Hotel **6**
The Palace Hotel **45**
Petite Auberge **13**
Prescott Hotel **22**
The Ritz-Carlton,
    San Francisco **5**
San Francisco Marriott **43**

Serrano Hotel **35**
Sir Francis Drake **16**
The St. Regis Hotel **46**
Stanford Court,
    A Renaissance Hotel **4**
Taj Campton Place **18**
Villa Florence **34**
W San Francisco Hotel **47**
The Warwick **27**
Westin St. Francis **33**
White Swan Inn **12**

renovated and they also added 23 "Pure" rooms for guests with allergies (specially treated to remove bacteria and viruses; $25 extra). Overall, rooms are swankier than they used to be and now feature the Hyatt's signature Grand Bed with pillow-top mattresses, ultraplush pillows and down (or down alternative) duvets. Each room has a lounge chair as well as a small desk and sitting area. Views from most of the 36 floors are truly spectacular.

345 Stockton St. (btw. Post and Sutter sts.), San Francisco, CA 94108. www.sanfrancisco.grand. hyatt.com. ℂ **888/591-1234** or 415/398-1234. Fax 415/391-1780. 685 units. $199–$379 double; Regency Club $50 additional. AE, DC, DISC, MC, V. Valet parking $44. Bus: 2, 3, 30, 38, or 45. Cable car: Powell–Hyde or Powell–Mason line (2 blocks west). **Amenities:** Restaurant; bar; concierge; health club; limited room service; free Wi-Fi in public areas. *In room:* A/C, TV w/pay movies, hair dryer, high-speed Internet access ($9.95 per day), minibar.

Handlery Union Square Hotel ★ ☺ A mere half-block from Union Square, the family-owned Handlery was already a good deal frequented by European travelers before the 1908 building underwent a complete overhaul a few years ago. Now you'll find every amenity you could possibly need, plus lots of extras, in the extremely tasteful and modern (although sedate and a little dark) rooms. Literally everything was replaced: mattresses, alarm radios, refrigerators, light fixtures, paint, carpets, and furnishings. Perks include adjoining L.A.-based chain restaurant the Daily Grill (which is unfortunately not as good as its sister restaurants down south) and club-level options (all in the newer building) that include larger rooms, a complimentary morning newspaper, a bathroom scale, robes, two 2-line phones, and adjoining doors that make the units great choices for families. Downsides? Not a lot of direct light, no grand feeling in the lobby, and lots of trekking if you want to go to and from the adjoining buildings that make up the hotel.

351 Geary St. (btw. Mason and Powell sts.), San Francisco, CA 94102. www.handlery.com. ℂ **800/995-4874** or 415/781-7800. Fax 415/781-0216. 377 units. $115–$229 double; club section $188–$269 double; suite $315–$529. Extra person $10. AE, DC, DISC, MC, V. Parking $32. Bus: 2, 3, 30, 38, or 45. Cable car: Powell–Hyde or Powell–Mason line (direct stop). **Amenities:** Restaurant; babysitting; access to nearby health club ($10 per day); heated outdoor pool; room service; sauna. *In room:* A/C, TV w/Nintendo and pay movies, fridge, hair dryer, free Wi-Fi.

Hilton San Francisco Complete with bustling conventioneers and a line to register that resembles an airport check-in, the Hilton's lobby is so enormous and busy that it feels more like a convention hall than a hotel. The three connecting buildings (the original 19-story main structure, a 46-story tower topped by a panoramic restaurant, and a 23-story landmark with 386 luxurious rooms and suites) bring swarms of visitors. Even during quieter times, the sheer enormity of the place makes the Hilton somewhat overwhelming.

After you get past the sweeping grand lobby, jump on an elevator, and wind through endless corridors to your room, you're likely to find the mystique ends with clean but run-of-the-mill standard-size corporate accommodations. That said, some of the views from the floor-to-ceiling windows in the main tower's rooms are memorable. All rooms have bathrooms with walk-in showers (no tubs), Serta Suite Dreams beds, and a pillow menu that ensures you get a pillow that suits your firmness preference.

333 O'Farrell St. (btw. Mason and Taylor sts.), San Francisco, CA 94102. www.hiltonsanfrancisco hotel.com. ℂ **800/445-8667** or 415/771-1400. Fax 415/771-6807. 1,908 units. $149–$239 double; $214–$359 suite. Children stay free in parent's room. AE, DC, DISC, MC, V. Parking $52–$56

(some oversize vehicles cannot be accommodated, depending on height). Bus: 2, 3, 9, 21, 27, 30, 38, 45, or 71. Cable car: Powell–Hyde or Powell–Mason line (1 block east). **Amenities:** 2 restaurants; bar; concierge; health club; outdoor whirlpool; outdoor pool; room service; sauna; spa. *In room:* A/C, flatscreen TV, hair dryer, free high-speed Internet access, minibar.

Hotel Adagio ★★ ✦ Undergoing a complete renovation in 2012, the Hotel Adagio revamped every one of this 1929 Spanish Revival hotel's 171 guest rooms. The large guest rooms feature calming neutral browns set against hip splashes of vibrant color. Other pluses include firm mattresses, double-paned windows that open, quiet surroundings, MP3 docking stations, Wi-Fi, and flatscreen TVs. Executive floors (7–16) also come with robes, upscale amenities, makeup mirrors, and stereos with iPod ports. Bathrooms are old but spotless and have resurfaced tubs. Feel like splurging? Go for one of the two penthouse-level suites; one has lovely terraces with a New York vibe. Adjacent Bar Adagio is a hip spot for cocktails, wines by the glass, and pizzettas, panini, and burgers. *Tip:* Rooms above the eighth floor have good, but not great, views of the city.

550 Geary St., San Francisco, CA 94102. www.thehoteladagio.com. *✆* **800/228-8830** or 415/775-5000. Fax 415/775-9388. 171 units. $139–$349 double. AE, DISC, MC, V. Valet parking $39. **Amenities:** Restaurant; bar; concierge; fitness center; room service. *In room:* TV w/Nintendo and pay movies, CD player and/or MP3 docking station, fridge, hair dryer, free high-speed Internet, minibar.

Hotel Diva ★ ☺ A showbiz darling when it opened in 1985, the well-priced Diva is so sleek and ultramodern it won "Best Hotel Design" from *Interiors* magazine not long after it opened and is still as svelte as ever. A profusion of curvaceous glass, marble, and steel marks the lobby, and the minimalist rooms are spotless and neat, with cobalt blue carpets and Euro-chic furnishings of monochromatic colors, silver accents, and rolled steel. Each room is equipped with 36-inch flatscreen TVs, iPod alarm clocks, and blond-wood desks. The downside is that the rooms have views that make you want to keep the chic curtains closed. Services abound, ranging from fitness and business centers to four themed Diva Lounges for business (including 24-hr. free use of a computer) and pleasure. Families should inquire about their two-room Little Divas Suite designed for kids that can accommodate a family of four. A nice touch for music lovers, iPods are available at the front desk for $10 to $15 per day, complete with special Diva music mixes.

440 Geary St. (btw. Mason and Taylor sts.), San Francisco, CA 94102. www.hoteldiva.com *✆* **800/553-1900** or 415/885-0200. Fax 415/346-6613. 116 units. $159–$359 double; $199–$799 suite. AE, DC, DISC, MC, V. Valet parking $35–$40. Bus: 38 or 38L. Cable car: Powell–Mason line. **Amenities:** Concierge; exercise room; free Wi-Fi. *In room:* A/C, TV/DVD/CD, hair dryer.

Hotel Monaco ★★ This remodeled 1910 Beaux Arts building has plenty of atmosphere, thanks to a whimsically ethereal lobby with a two-story French inglenook fireplace. The guest rooms, which were upgraded in 2006, follow suit, with canopy beds, Asian-inspired armoires, bamboo writing desks, lively stripes, and vibrant color. Everything is bold but tasteful, and as playful as it is serious, with nifty extras like flatscreen TVs and complimentary Wi-Fi. The decor, combined with the truly grand neighboring Grand Café restaurant that's ideal for cocktails and mingling (but also serves breakfast and lunch), would put this place on our top-10 list if it weren't for rooms that tend to be too small (especially for the price) and the lack of a sizable gym. Your stay also includes a complimentary wine and cheese tasting accompanied by shoulder and neck massages. *Tip:* If you were/are a big fan of Jefferson Airplane, inquire about their Grace Slick Shrine Suite.

501 Geary St. (at Taylor St.), San Francisco, CA 94102. www.monaco-sf.com. ℃ **866/622-5284** or 415/292-0100. Fax 415/292-0111. 201 units. $139–$279 double; $279–$539 suite. Rates include evening wine and cheese tasting. Call for discounted rates. AE, DC, DISC, MC, V. Valet parking $49. Bus: 2, 3, 27, or 38. Pets accepted. **Amenities:** Restaurant; concierge; exercise room; Jacuzzi; room service; sauna; spa. *In room:* A/C, TV, CD player, hair dryer, minibar, free Wi-Fi.

Hotel Rex ★   Joie de Vivre (JDV), the most creative hotel group in the city, is the brains behind this cleverly restored historic building, a restoration that was inspired by the San Francisco art and literary salons of the 1920s and 1930s. JDV kept some of the imported furnishings and the European boutique hotel ambience, but gave the lobby and rooms a major face-lift, adding the decorative flair that makes its hotels among the most popular in town. The clublike lobby lounge is modeled after a 1920s literary salon and is, like all the group's properties, cleverly stylish. (They even host jazz artists Fri 6–8pm.) The guest rooms are above average in size, decorated with custom wall coverings, hand-painted lampshades, and works by local artists. If you have one of the rooms in the back, you'll look out over a shady, peaceful courtyard. It's also in a great location, situated near several fine galleries, theaters, and restaurants.

562 Sutter St. (btw. Powell and Mason sts.), San Francisco, CA 94102. www.thehotelrex.com. ℃ **800/433-4434** or 415/433-4434. Fax 415/433-3695. 94 units. $139–$269 double; $400 suite. AE, DC, DISC, MC, V. Valet parking $36. Bus: 2, 3, 30, 38, or 45. Cable car: Powell–Hyde or Powell–Mason line (1 block east). **Amenities:** Concierge; access to nearby health club; room service. *In room:* TV w/pay movies, CD player, hair dryer, minibar, free Wi-Fi.

Hotel Triton ★   Described as vogue, chic, retro-futuristic, and even neo-baroque, this Kimpton Group property is whimsy at its boutique-hotel best. The completely renovated lobby features a 360-degree mural by emerging artist Kari Pei (yes, from *that* Pei family—she's I. M. Pei's daughter-in-law) that relates the history of San Francisco and Triton. The funky-fun (if not a wee bit too small) designer suites named after musicians and artists like Jerry Garcia, Wyland (the ocean artist), and Santana, along with all the other rooms, are eco-friendly, featuring filtered water and air, all-natural linens, recycling trash cans, and water conservation fixtures. Even the cleaning products used in the hotel are environmentally sensitive to please the tree-hugger in all of us. All the rooms include modern touches like armoires hiding Sony flatscreen TVs and iPod docking stations that double as clock radios. Not to be outdone, the fitness center touts DirecTV in the cardio machines.

342 Grant Ave. (at Bush St.), San Francisco, CA 94108. www.hoteltriton.com. ℃ **800/800-1299** or 415/394-0500. Fax 415/394-0555. 140 units. $95–$269 double; $329–$369 suite. AE, DC, DISC, MC, V. Parking $38, oversize vehicles an additional $2. Cable car: Powell–Hyde or Powell–Mason line (2 blocks west). Pets stay free with conditional agreement. **Amenities:** Cafe; fitness center; room service. *In room:* A/C, flatscreen TV, Web TV, hair dryer, minibar, free Wi-Fi.

The Inn at Union Square ★★   As narrow as an Amsterdam canal house, the Inn at Union Square is the antithesis of the big, impersonal hotels that surround Union Square. If you need plenty of elbowroom, skip this one. But if you're looking for an inn whose staff knows each guest's name, read on. One-half block west of the square, this six-story inn makes up for its small stature by spoiling guests with a pile of perks. Mornings start with a continental breakfast served in lounges stocked with daily newspapers, and evening emerges with appetizers of wine, cheese, fruit, and chocolates served in sweet little fireplace lounges at the end of each hall. There's also unlimited use of a nearby full-service health club with heated lap pool. The handsome rooms are individually decorated with Georgian reproductions, goose-down pillows, and floral fabrics, and they are smaller than average but infinitely more appreciated than the cookie-cutter rooms of most larger hotels. Smoking is not allowed anywhere in the hotel.

440 Post St. (btw. Mason and Powell sts.), San Francisco, CA 94102. www.unionsquare.com. © **800/288-4346** or 415/397-3510. Fax 415/989-0529. 30 units. $171–$224 double; from $219–$379 suite. Rates include continental breakfast, all-day tea and cider, afternoon wine and hors d'oeuvres, and evening cookies. AE, DC, DISC, MC, V. Valet parking $36. Bus: 2, 3, 30, 38, or 45; all Market St. buses. Cable car: Powell–Hyde or Powell–Mason line. **Amenities:** Concierge; access to nearby health club (for a nominal fee). *In room:* TV, hair dryer, free Wi-Fi.

The Orchard Garden Hotel ★★ If Al Gore were a hotelier, this would be his hotel. The Orchard Garden is California's first generation of truly "green" hotels and the only hotel in the state that was built to the nationally accepted standards for green buildings developed by the U.S. Green Building Council (USGBC). It's the first hotel in the city to use the European-style keycard system that turns power off each time you leave, saving about 20% in energy consumption. But going green doesn't mean you have to cut back on comfort—yes, that's Egyptian cotton linen on the king-size bed, real feather down in the pillows, Aveda bath products, and plush spa-style robes in the closet. Rooms are superinsulated (and very quiet). The hotel also has a pleasant rooftop garden and **Roots Restaurant,** serving contemporary American cuisine made from locally sourced organic products. *Note:* If the hotel is booked, inquire about its sister property—the Orchard Hotel—up the street.

466 Bush St. (at Grant Ave.), San Francisco, CA 94108. www.theorchardgardenhotel.com. © **888/717-2881** or 415/399-9807. Fax 415/393-9917. 86 units. $169–$499 double. AE, DC, DISC, MC, V. Valet parking $40. Cable car: Powell–Hyde or Powell–Mason line. **Amenities:** Restaurant; concierge; fitness center (and $15 passes to Club One). *In room:* A/C, flatscreen HDTV, free DVD library available, hair dryer, minibar, MP3 docking station, free Wi-Fi.

Sir Francis Drake ★★ This landmark hotel is one of San Francisco's grand dames, operating continuously since 1928 in the heart of Union Square. The Kimpton Hotel company has done a wonderful job renovating the hotel (which has been sorely needed), giving this elegant lady a much-needed makeover. It's always a pleasure to have Tom Sweeny, the ebullient (and legendary) Beefeater doorman, handle your bags as you enter the elegant, captivating lobby, with its gilded high ceilings, glittering crystal chandeliers, and massive marble staircase that leads to a mezzanine overlooking bustling Powell Street.

Scala's Bistro (p. 113), one of the most festive restaurants downtown, serves good Mediterranean cuisine in a stylish setting on the first floor; the speakeasy-styled **Bar Drake** offers a variety of cocktails for guests while relaxing in the lobby. **Harry Denton's Starlight Room** (p. 276), on the 21st floor, offers cocktails, entertainment, and dancing nightly with a panoramic view of the city.

450 Powell St. (at Sutter St.), San Francisco, CA 94102. www.sirfrancisdrake.com. © **800/795-7129** or 415/392-7755. Fax 415/391-8719. 416 units. $183–$303 double; from $5,200 suite. AE, DC, DISC, MC, V. Valet parking $44. Bus: 2, 3, 45, or 76. Cable car: Powell–Hyde or Powell–Mason line (direct stop). Pets welcome. **Amenities:** 2 restaurants, including Scala's Bistro (review, p. 113); bar; concierge; exercise room; room service. *In room:* A/C, TV w/movies on demand, hair dryer, minibar, free Wi-Fi.

White Swan Inn ★★ From the moment you're buzzed into this well-secured inn, you'll know you're not in a generic bed-and-breakfast. The romantically homey rooms are warm and cozy—the perfect place to snuggle up with a good book. They're also quite big, with hardwood entryways, rich dark-wood furniture, working fireplaces, and an assortment of books tucked in nooks. The decor is English elegance at its best, if not to excess (floral prints and ceramic bric-a-brac abound). The luxury king suites are not much better than regular rooms, just a wee bit bigger, and feature perks like evening turndown, bathrobes, and a wet bar stocked with complimentary beverages. Each morning, a breakfast buffet is served in a common room just off a tiny garden. Afternoon reception, consisting of hors d'oeuvres, sherry, wine, and home-baked pastries, can be enjoyed in front of the fireplace while you browse through the books in the library or in the parlor.

845 Bush St. (btw. Taylor and Mason sts.), San Francisco, CA 94108. www.whiteswaninnsf.com. ℂ **800/999-9570** or 415/775-1755. Fax 415/775-5717. 26 units. $159–$229 double; $269 luxury king suite; $319 2-room suite. Extra person $20. Rates include breakfast and afternoon wine and hors d'oeuvres. AE, DC, DISC, MC, V. Valet parking $32. Bus: 1, 2, 3, 27, or 45. Cable car: Powell–Hyde line (1 block north). **Amenities:** Concierge; small exercise room. *In room:* TV, fridge w/free beverages, hair dryer, Wi-Fi ($7.95 per day).

Moderate

Beresford Arms Hotel 🗝 The bargain prices are the main reason to recommend this dependable, if unfashionable, hotel. On the plus side, suites have bidets, whirlpool bathtubs, and a wet bar or fully equipped kitchenette—an advantage for families—and a continental breakfast is included in the price of all rooms. All accommodations include plenty of in-room perks, including an afternoon "Social Hour" with wine, tea, and snacks. The location, between the Theater District and Union Square, in a quieter section of San Francisco, is ideal for visitors without cars, and the price for what you get is hard to beat. *Tip:* Rooms

You can't miss the Sir Francis Drake hotel's Tom Sweeney in his $1,400 Beefeater duds. The head doorman has shaken hands with every U.S. president since Jerry Ford.

that face Post Street might be a bit noisier than others, but they're also larger and sunnier, and some have window seats.

701 Post St. (at Jones St.), San Francisco, CA 94109. www.beresford.com. ☎ **800/533-6533** or 415/673-2600. Fax 415/929-1535. 95 units. $99–$289 double. Extra person $10. Children 11 and under stay free in parent's room. Rates include pastry, coffee, afternoon wine and tea. Senior and AAA discounts available. AE, DC, DISC, MC, V. Valet parking $20. Bus: 2, 3, 27, or 38. Cable car: Powell–Hyde line (3 blocks east). **Amenities:** Access to nearby health club ($10 per day); free Internet access in lobby. *In room:* TV, hair dryer upon request, minibar.

Executive Hotel Vintage Court ★ ✦ Consistent personal service and great value attract a loyal clientele at this European-style hotel 2 blocks north of Union Square. The chocolate-brown lobby, accented with comfy couches, is welcoming enough to actually spend a little time in, especially when California wines are being poured each evening from 5 to 6pm free of charge. (Each week a local vintner is on hand to do the pouring.)

But the varietals don't stop at ground level. Each tidy, quiet, and comfortable room is named after a winery and boasts a modern country look (think Pottery Barn meets Napa Valley), where greens and earth tones reign supreme, with cream duvets and lovely mahogany-slat blinds. Niebaum-Coppola Penthouse Suite (named after the movie maverick's winery, now called Rubicon Estate), the deluxe two-room penthouse suite, has an original 1912 stained-glass skylight, wood-burning fireplace, whirlpool tub, complete entertainment center, and panoramic views of the city.

Masa's, one of the city's more upscale restaurants, serves very expensive contemporary French dinners here.

650 Bush St. (btw. Powell and Stockton sts.), San Francisco, CA 94108. www.executivehotels.net/ vintagecourt. ☎ **888/388-3932** or 415/392-4666. Fax 415/433-4065. 107 units. $105–$329 double; $325–$395 penthouse suite. Rates include continental breakfast and evening wine reception. AE, DC, DISC, MC, V. Valet parking $37; self-parking $27. Bus: 2, 3, 30, 45, or 76. Cable car: Powell–Hyde or Powell–Mason line (direct stop). Pets accepted. **Amenities:** Restaurant; concierge; access to off-premises health club ($11 per day). *In room:* A/C, TV w/Nintendo and pay movies, hair dryer, minibar, free Wi-Fi.

Hotel Frank ★★ Only a block from Union Square, this former Maxwell Hotel is the new darling among hip business travelers and serious shoppers. A major renovation was finished in the spring of 2009, bringing the hotel to an even more upscale, boutique-hotel standard. A clever interior makeover by one of the country's most cutting-edge designers incorporates a blend of popular design trends through the decades; check out the Art Deco light fixtures and bold color scheme throughout. The guest rooms exude a custom-designed look: houndstooth-patterned carpeting, elongated emerald green headboards in crocodile-patterned leather, sleek white leather couches, vintage 1930s artwork. Even the bathrooms are outfitted in floor-to-ceiling Carrara marble. The hotel's 28 roomy junior suites offer excellent value despite the slightly audible elevator noise, but best of all are the pair of one-bedroom penthouses that offer separate living rooms and exceptional views of the city.

386 Geary St. (at Mason St.), San Francisco, CA 94102. www.hotelfranksf.com. ☎ **877/828-4478** or 415/986-2000. 153 units. $169–$399 double; $209–$469 junior suite; from $699 penthouse suite. AE, DC, DISC, MC, V. Valet parking $35, an additional $5 for oversize cars. Bus: 2, 3, 30, 38, or 45. Cable car: Powell–Hyde or Powell–Mason lines (1 block east). **Amenities:** Concierge; room service. *In room:* A/C, flatscreen TV w/pay movies, hair dryer, minibar, MP3 docking station, free Wi-Fi.

Hotel Metropolis ★ ☺ 🎁   On a slightly sketchy block just off of Market Street, a few blocks from Union Square, the Hotel Metropolis is ideal for people who dread staying at a boring, corporate McHotel. As with most downtown hotels, the rooms are on the small side, but all are vibrant and cheery, with vivid colors, custom African Limba-wood furnishings, and comfy beds with wave-shaped headboards with portholes. The six Executive Rooms on the 10th floor are upgraded with feather beds and pillows, iPod alarm clocks, and robes, while the three-room Urban Explorers Kids Suite, which sleeps up to six adults and three children, is filled with pint-size furniture, bunk beds, a computer, a chalk-board wall, toys, and rubber ducky decor in the bathroom.

25 Mason St. (at Turk and Market sts.), San Francisco, CA 94102. www.hotelmetropolis.com. ✆ **877/628-4412** or 415/775-4600. 105 units. $99–$289 double; $159–$369 suite. AE, DC, DISC, MC, V. Valet parking $30. Bus: All Market St. buses. Streetcar: Powell St. station. **Amenities:** Exercise room; room service. *In room:* TV w/pay per view, hair dryer, free Wi-Fi.

Hotel Milano ★   Neoclassical Italian design patterned after Giorgio Armani's villa in Milan, elegantly streamlined rooms (with double-paned soundproof windows), moderate prices, and a central location next to the San Francisco Centre make Hotel Milano a popular choice for tourists and businesspeople alike. The hotel also has a film-production facility and private screening room to entice media types. Corporate travelers come for the spacious guest rooms, which feature everything an executive could want, from Wi-Fi to video game systems and work desks. Suites have spa tubs and bidets.

55 Fifth St. (btw. Market and Mission sts.), San Francisco, CA 94103. www.hotelmilanosf.com. ✆ **415/543-8555.** Fax 415/543-5885. 108 units. $109–$199 double. Extra person $20. AE, DC, DISC, MC, V. Valet parking $45. Bus: All Market St. buses. **Amenities:** Concierge; fitness room; sauna; spa. *In room:* A/C, TV w/video games, fridge, hair dryer, Wi-Fi ($9.95 per day).

Hotel Union Square ★★   The Hotel Union Square has achieved that rare hat trick of history, location, and style. It's San Francisco's first boutique hotel, built in 1913 for the 1915 Pan Pacific Exposition, and it's only a half-block from Union Square, in the heart of the city with the cable cars passing by your window. Its 2008 renovation has juxtaposed contemporary and classic San Francisco with original 1915 Egyptian mosaic murals and opulent moldings contrasted by sleek furnishings and state-of-the-art technology. The guest rooms are like urban apartments, each outfitted with platform beds with custom-made leather headboards, velvety chaise longues, and flatscreen televisions. Many have an open, loftlike layout with exposed brick walls and floating ceiling installations, while the two rooftop penthouses are the ultimate in chic, with expansive redwood decks with city views. There's also a custom Kids Suite, a Dashiell Hammett–themed suite, and "Sleep and Soak" rooms on each floor that feature spalike bathrooms.

114 Powell St. (btw. O'Farrell and Ellis sts.), San Francisco, CA 94102. www.hotelunionsquare. com. ✆ **800/553-1900** or 415/397-3000. 131 units. $149–$349 double; $199–$499 suite; $229–$799 penthouse suite. Rates include morning coffee and tea and weekday wine reception. AE, DC, DISC, MC, V. Valet parking $30. Bus: 2, 3, 30, 38, 45, or 76. Cable car: Powell–Hyde or Powell–Mason line. Streetcar: Powell St. station. **Amenities:** Fitness center access; room service (from the adjacent Tad's Steakhouse). *In room:* TV w/pay per view, hair dryer, free Wi-Fi.

Hotel Vertigo ★★   Formerly the York Hotel, the Hotel Vertigo opened its doors in fall 2008 to much pressure after being dubbed *the* hot new place to stay and play in San Francisco by more than one jaded San Francisco critic (this writer included). The good news: It lived up to the buzz, and its new stylistic design will undoubtedly attract tourists and business travelers looking for an alternative to the W San Francisco Hotel. There's even some colorful history involved as well—the hotel occupies the former site of the Empire Hotel made famous in Alfred Hitchcock's *Vertigo,* hence the name. The movie plays 24/7 in the lobby and is available for free viewings in each room as well. Guest rooms feature playful, eclectic design features such as white tufted-leather headboards, custom wingback chairs in vibrant orange, and crocodile-patterned tiles in the bathrooms.

940 Sutter St. (btw. Leavenworth and Hyde sts.), San Francisco, CA 94109. www.hotelvertigosf. com. **☎ 888/444-4605** or 415/885-6800. 102 units. $169–$399 double; $350–$495 suite. Rates include morning beverages in lobby. AE, DISC, MC, V. Valet parking $35. Bus: 2 or 3. Pets under 40 lb. accepted for a $25 cleaning fee. **Amenities:** Concierge. *In room:* TV w/pay movies, hair dryer, MP3 docking station, free Wi-Fi.

Kensington Park Hotel ★   Housed in a stately 1925 Moorish/Gothic-style building that also houses the Post Street Theatre and Farallon restaurant (p. 108), the Kensington underwent a $1.5-million renovation in the spring of '08 and is now one of the best midpriced lodging deals near Union Square. Exuding old-school San Francisco charm, the lobby features hand-painted ceilings, mosaic tile, and classic Queen Anne antiques accented by crystal chandeliers and palm trees. Large guest rooms on the 5th through 12th floors have a mix of classic and contemporary furnishings such as 36-inch flatscreen TVs and iPod alarm clocks, and the bathrooms, though small, are sweetly appointed in brass and marble. If you want the royal treatment, book the Royal Suite, which features a canopy bed, formal dining room, living room, whirlpool bath, two fireplaces, and wonderful views of Union Square. The hotel lacks a fitness center, but guests have complimentary use of the adjacent Hotel Diva fitness center.

450 Post St. (btw. Powell and Mason sts.), San Francisco, CA 94102. www.kensingtonparkhotel. com. **☎ 800/553-1900** or 415/788-6400. Fax 415/399-9404. 92 units. $97–$209 double; from $399 suite. Rates include morning coffee and tea and afternoon tea and sherry. AE, DC, DISC, MC, V. Valet parking $35; extra charge for oversize cars. Cable car: Powell–Hyde or Powell–Mason line (½ block east). **Amenities:** Restaurant, Farallon (review, p. 108); concierge. *In room:* TV w/pay movies, hair dryer, free Wi-Fi.

King George Hotel ★ 🦆   Built in 1914 for the Panama Pacific Exhibition (when rooms went for $1 per night), the boutique King George has fared well over the years with its mostly European clientele. The location—surrounded by cable car lines, the Theater District, Union Square, and dozens of restaurants—is superb, and the rooms are surprisingly quiet for such a busy spot (sadly, the interior noise is definitely audible through thin, old walls). The guest rooms can be very small (in the smallest rooms it can be difficult for two people to maneuver at the same time), but they still manage to find room for writing desks, private bathrooms, and king- or queen-size pillow-top beds with down comforters. A big hit since it started a few years back is the hotel's English afternoon tea, served in the Windsor Tea Room Saturday, Sunday, and holidays from 1 to 4pm. Recent additions include a pub, a 24-hour business center, and an upgraded "executive" level.

334 Mason St. (btw. Geary and O'Farrell sts.), San Francisco, CA 94102. www.kinggeorge.com. **☎ 800/288-6005** or 415/781-5050. Fax 415/835-5991. 153 units. $66–$188 double; $195 suite. Breakfast $9.95–$13. Special-value packages available seasonally. AE, DC, DISC, MC, V. Valet

4

WHERE TO STAY

Union Square

parking $26; self-parking $23. Bus: 1, 2, 3, 5, 30, 38, 45, or 71. Cable car: Powell–Hyde or Powell–Mason line (1 block west). **Amenities:** Tearoom; evening lounge/bar; concierge; $12 access to health club ½ block away; room service. In room: TV w/video games and pay movies, hair dryer, free Wi-Fi.

Petite Auberge ★★   Nobody does French Provincial like Petite Auberge: handcrafted armoires, delicate sheer curtains, cozy little fireplaces in most rooms, and an adorable array of antiques and knickknacks. Honeymooners should splurge on the petite suite, which has a private entrance, deck, and spa tub. Guests turn up in robes for the bountiful breakfast in the sunny breakfast room, with its mural of a country market scene, terra-cotta tile floors, cheerful tablecloths, and garden patio. California wines, tea, and hors d'oeuvres (included in the room rates) are served each afternoon, and guests have free rein of the fridge stocked with soft drinks. Bathers take note: Eight rooms have showers only, while others also have tubs.

863 Bush St. (btw. Taylor and Mason sts.), San Francisco, CA 94102. www.petiteaubergesf.com. ✆ **800/365-3004** or 415/928-6000. Fax 415/673-7214. 26 units. $119–$269 double; $269 petite suite. Rates include full breakfast and afternoon reception. AE, DC, DISC, MC, V. Parking $32. Bus: 2, 3, 30, 38, or 45. Cable car: Powell–Hyde or Powell–Mason line. **Amenities:** Babysitting; concierge; access to small exercise room available at sister hotel next door, the **White Swan Inn** (p. 68). In room: TV, hair dryer, Wi-Fi ($7.95 per day).

Serrano Hotel ★   Los Angeles designer Cheryl Rowley (who also designed the Hotel Monaco; p. 65) swathed this 17-story 1920s hotel in her trademark vibrant red and added a playful dash of Moroccan flair while preserving the building's Spanish Revival integrity. Original architectural elements dot the colorful lobby, with its whimsically painted beams, high ceilings, large ornate fireplace, and dramatic colonnade. Equally vibrant guest rooms (sometimes small) have oversize windows and high ceilings, cherrywood headboards, terry robes, and theater-themed artwork. Guests can borrow puzzles and board games from the hotel's large game library. The hotel is in the heart of the Theater District, right off Union Square, and is pet friendly.

405 Taylor St. (at O'Farrell St.), San Francisco, CA 94102. www.serranohotel.com. ✆ **866/289-6561** or 415/885-2500. Fax 415/474-4879. 236 units. From $128 double; from $300 suite. Rates include morning coffee and tea service and afternoon beverages. AE, DC, DISC, MC, V. Valet parking $40. Bus: 2, 3, 27, or 38. Cable car: Powell–Market. Pets accepted. **Amenities:** Restaurant/bar; babysitting by referral; concierge; exercise room; limited room service; sauna. In room: A/C, TV w/pay movies, hair dryer, minibar, free Wi-Fi.

Villa Florence ★★   Located a half-block south of Union Square, fronting the Powell Street cable car line, this seven-story hotel is in one of the liveliest sections of the city (no need to drive, 'cause you're already here). The Villa Florence provides guests with a taste of contemporary Italian decor with cherrywood furniture, plantation shutters, windows that actually open, and perks such as flatscreen TVs with DVD players and CD players. In late 2008, a major remodel was completed, which translated to an upgrade in amenities for all rooms and suites. You'll like the large, comfortable beds draped in down comforters with FeatherBorne Bed dressings, as well as such luxury touches as L'Occitane bath products and Frette bathrobes. The hotel's ground-floor restaurant, Kuleto's (p. 112), is one of downtown's most bustling and stylish Italian restaurants. That and Bar Norcini wine bar help make the hotel a worthy contender among Union

Square's boutique inns—as if the location alone weren't reason enough to book a room.

225 Powell St. (btw. Geary and O'Farrell sts.), San Francisco, CA 94102. www.villaflorence.com. **© 866/553-4411** or 415/397-7700. Fax 415/397-1006. 182 units. $117–$159 double; $249–$299 studio suite. Rates include evening wine. AE, DC, DISC, MC, V. Valet parking $40, plus an extra $10–$15 per day for oversize vehicles and SUVs. Bus: 2, 3, 30, 38, or 45. Cable car: Powell–Hyde or Powell–Mason line (direct stop). **Amenities:** Restaurant, Kuleto's (review, p. 112); babysitting on request; concierge; access to nearby health club ($15 per day). *In room:* A/C, ceiling fan, flatscreen TV w/pay movies, CD player, fridge, hair dryer, minibar, free Wi-Fi.

The Warwick ★★ ♠ Louis XVI might have been a rotten monarch, but he certainly had taste. Fashioned in the style of pre-Revolutionary France, the Warwick is awash with French and English antiques, Italian marble, chandeliers, four-poster beds, hand-carved headboards, and the like. The result is an expensive-looking hotel that, for all its pleasantries and perks, is surprisingly affordable when compared to its Union Square contemporaries. Rooms can be on the small side; nonetheless, they're some of the city's most charming. Honeymooners should splurge on the fireplace rooms with four-poster beds—ooh la la! Adjoining the lobby is La Scene Restaurant and Bar, a beautiful place to start your day with a latte and end it with a nightcap.

490 Geary St. (btw. Mason and Taylor sts.), San Francisco, CA 94102. www.warwicksf.com. **© 800/203-3232** or 415/928-7900. Fax 415/441-8788. 74 units. $84–$204 double; from $114 suite. AE, DC, DISC, MC, V. Parking $35. Bus: 2, 3, 27, or 38. Cable car: Powell–Hyde or Powell–Mason line. **Amenities:** Restaurant; babysitting; concierge; access to nearby health club ($15 per day), room service. *In room:* TV, hair dryer, minibar, free Wi-Fi.

Inexpensive

The Andrews Hotel For the location, price, and service, the Andrews is a safe bet for an enjoyable stay in San Francisco. Two blocks west of Union Square, the Andrews was a Turkish bath before its conversion in 1981. As is typical in Euro-style hotels, the rooms are small but well maintained and comfortable, with nice touches like white lace curtains and fresh flowers. Continued upgrades help keep things fresh, but large-bathroom lovers beware—the facilities here are tiny. A bonus is the adjoining Fino Bar and Ristorante, which offers respectable Italian fare and free wine to hotel guests in the evening.

624 Post St. (btw. Jones and Taylor sts.), San Francisco, CA 94109. www.andrewshotel.com. **© 800/926-3739** or 415/563-6877. Fax 415/928-6919. 48 units, some with shower only. From $59 double; from $139 suite. Rates include continental breakfast, coffee in lobby, and evening wine. AE, DC, MC, V. Valet parking $25. Bus: 2, 3, 30, 38, or 45. Cable car: Powell–Hyde or Powell–Mason line (3 blocks east). **Amenities:** Restaurant; babysitting; concierge; access to nearby health club; room service. *In room:* TV/VCR w/video library, CD player in suites only, fridge, hair dryer on request, free Wi-Fi.

The Cornell Hotel de France It's the quirks that make this small French-style family-owned hotel more charming than many others in its price range. Pass the office, where a few faces will glance in your direction and smile, stop to pet the resident golden retriever, and embark on a ride in the old-fashioned elevator (we're talking turn of the 20th century here) to get to your basic room. Each floor is dedicated to a French painter and decorated with reproductions. Rooms are all plain and comfortable, with desks and chairs, and are individually and simply decorated. Smoking is not allowed. The full American breakfast included in the rate is served in the cool cavernlike provincial basement restaurant, Jeanne d'Arc. Union Square is just a few blocks away.

715 Bush St. (btw. Powell and Mason sts.), San Francisco, CA 94108. www.cornellhotel.com. ℂ **800/232-9698** or 415/421-3154. Fax 415/399-1442. 55 units. $80–$180 double. Rates include full American breakfast. AE, DC, DISC, MC, V. Parking across the street $17. Bus: 2, 3, 30, or 45. Cable car: Powell–Hyde or Powell–Mason line. **Amenities:** Restaurant. *In room:* TV, hair dryer, free Wi-Fi.

The Golden Gate Hotel ★ ✦   San Francisco's stock of small hotels in historic turn-of-the-20th-century buildings includes some real gems—the Golden Gate Hotel is one of them. It's 2 blocks north of Union Square and 2 blocks down (literally) from the crest of Nob Hill, with cable car stops at the corner for easy access to Fisherman's Wharf and Chinatown. The city's theaters and restaurants are also within walking distance. But the best thing about the 1913 Edwardian hotel is that it's family run: John and Renate Kenaston and daughter Gabriele are hospitable innkeepers who take obvious pleasure in making their guests comfortable. Each individually decorated room has been repainted and carpeted and has handsome antique furnishings from the early 1900s, quilted bedspreads, and fresh flowers. Request a room with a claw-foot tub if you enjoy a good, hot soak. Afternoon tea is served daily from 4 to 7pm, and guests are welcome to use the house fax and computer with Wi-Fi free of charge.

775 Bush St. (btw. Powell and Mason sts.), San Francisco, CA 94108. www.goldengatehotel.com. ℂ **800/835-1118** or 415/392-3702. Fax 415/392-6202. 25 units, 14 with bathroom. $95–$105 double without bathroom; $150–$165 double with bathroom. Rates include continental breakfast and afternoon tea. AE, DC, MC, V. Self-parking $25. Bus: 2, 30, 38, or 45. Cable car: Powell–Hyde or Powell–Mason line (1 block east). BART: Powell and Market. **Amenities:** Access to health club 1 block away. *In room:* TV, hair dryer upon request, free Wi-Fi.

Beresford Hotel   The small, less expensive sister property of the Hotel Beresford Arms (see earlier), the seven-floor Hotel Beresford is another decent, moderately priced choice near Union Square. Perks are the same: satellite TV, phone, radio, private bathrooms with either a tub or shower, and stocked fridges. The guest rooms are decorated in Victorian style and very well kept, with plenty of personal touches you don't often find in a budget hotel. Rates even include continental breakfast. The on-site **White Horse Tavern,** a quaint replica of an old English pub, serves dinner Tuesday through Saturday and is a favorite for folks who like less trendy hullabaloo with their meal.

635 Sutter St. (near Mason St.), San Francisco, CA 94102. www.beresford.com. ℂ **800/533-6533** or 415/673-9900. Fax 415/474-0449. 114 units. $89–$165 double. Extra person $10. Rates include continental breakfast. Children 11 and under stay free in parent's room. AE, DC, DISC, MC, V. Valet parking $20. Bus: 2, 3, 30, 38, or 45. Cable car: Powell–Hyde line (1 block east). **Amenities:** Restaurant/pub; access to nearby health club ($10 per day); free high-speed Internet access in kiosk in lobby. *In room:* TV, hair dryer upon request, minibar.

Hotel Bijou ★ ✦   Although it's on the periphery of the gritty Tenderloin (just 3 blocks off Union Square), once inside this gussied-up 1911 hotel, all's cheery, bright, and perfect for budget travelers who want a little style with their savings. Joie de Vivre hotel group disguised the hotel's age with lively decor, a Deco theater theme, and a heck of a lot of vibrant paint. To the left of the small lobby is a "theater" where guests can watch San Francisco–based double features nightly (it has cute old-fashioned theater seating, though it's just a basic TV showing videos). Upstairs, rooms named after locally made films are small, clean, and colorful (think buttercup, burgundy, and purple) and have tiny bathrooms (one of which is so small you have to close the door to access the toilet). Alas, a few mattresses could be firmer, and the single elevator is small and slow. But considering the price, and perks like the continental breakfast and friendly service, you can't go wrong here.

111 Mason St., San Francisco, CA 94102. www.hotelbijou.com. ℭ **800/771-1022** or 415/771-1200. Fax 415/346-3196. 65 units. $99–$159 double. Rates include continental breakfast. AE, DC, DISC, MC, V. Valet parking $32. Bus: All Market St. buses. Streetcar: Powell St. station. **Amenities:** Concierge; room service. *In room:* TV, hair dryer, Wi-Fi ($7.95 per day).

Hotel Carlton ★ ✦ If you're looking for wonderfully cheap, attractive, and clean accommodations and don't mind being in the gritty center of the city, book a room here. The Joie de Vivre hotel group is behind this 163-room hotel that was built in 1927 and revamped in May 2004 with "global vintage" decor and LEED-certified standards. (It was the first hotel in the U.S. to receive the eco-friendly LEED gold rating.) The interior design is worldly eclectic, with travel photographs from the American Himalayan Foundation, tribal figurines, Oriental rugs, a vibrant sarilike color scheme, imported hand-painted Moroccan tables, and cool Lucite-beaded table lamps in the guest rooms. Another good reason to book here: Outside, the neighborhood is drab, but it's only a 7-block walk to Union Square, and with doubles starting at a mere $93, you can splurge for a taxi with the money saved. Or stick nearby and try **Saha,** their Arabian-fusion restaurant (think hummus, pizza, Yemenese meatballs, and seared scallops), which serves breakfast and dinner. Heck, they even throw in a complimentary evening wine hour in the lobby.

1075 Sutter St. (btw. Larkin and Hyde sts.), San Francisco, CA 94109. www.jdvhotels.com/carlton. ℭ **800/922-7586** or 415/673-0242. Fax 415/673-4904. 161 units. $89–$199 double. Rates include evening wine reception. AE, MC, V. Valet parking $30; self-parking $25. Bus: 2, 3, 19, or 76. **Amenities:** Restaurant; concierge. *In room:* TV, hair dryer, free Wi-Fi.

Hotel des Arts ★★ ✦ While this bargain find has the same small lobby, narrow hallways, and cramped rooms as San Francisco's numerous other Euro-style hotels, the des Arts distances itself from the competition by including a visually stimulating dose of artistic license. The lobby, for example, hosts a rotating art gallery featuring contemporary works by emerging local artists and is outfitted with groovy furnishings. You'll love the lively location as well: right across the street from the entrance to Chinatown and 2 blocks from Union Square. There's even a French brasserie right downstairs. Considering the price (rooms with a very clean shared bathroom start at $59), quality, and location, it's quite possibly the best budget hotel in the city. One suite can sleep up to four persons at no additional charge. *Tip:* Log on to the hotel's website to check out the "Painted Rooms" designed by local artists, and then call the hotel directly to book your favorite.

447 Bush St. (at Grant St.), San Francisco, CA 94108. www.sfhoteldesarts.com. ℭ **800/956-4322** or 415/956-3232. Fax 415/956-0399. 51 units, 26 with private bathroom. $79–$159 double with bathroom; $59–$79 double without bathroom. Rates include continental breakfast. AE, DC, MC, V. Nearby parking $18. Cable car: Powell–Hyde or Powell–Mason line. **Amenities:** Concierge. *In room:* TV, minifridge in many rooms, hair dryer, free Wi-Fi.

A room designed by artist Damon Soule at the Hotel des Arts.

NOB HILL

Most of the city's finest hotels are perched here. Nob Hill is where San Francisco's railroad and mining barons once lived and modern barons stay during their visits.

Best For: Wealthy travelers who prefer luxury accommodations. Easy access to cable cars.

Drawbacks: Very expensive hotels, steep hills (good luck in heels), and heavy traffic on California Street.

Very Expensive

The Fairmont San Francisco ★★★ ☺   The granddaddy of Nob Hill's elite cadre of ritzy hotels, the century-old Fairmont is a must-visit if only to marvel at the incredibly glamorous lobby with its vaulted ceilings, Corinthian columns, a spectacular spiral staircase, and rococo furniture. Such decadence carries to the guest rooms, where luxuries abound: oversize marble bathrooms, thick down blankets, goose-down king pillows, extra-long mattresses, and large walk-in closets. Its perch atop Nob Hill affords spectacular city views from every room—though the panoramic views from the Tower Suites are the best. It's fun to indulge in afternoon tea (daily 2:30–4:30pm) in the ornate **Laurel Court** restaurant and lounge, which serves as the hotel's centerpiece. A local institution is the hotel's **Tonga Room,** a Disneyland-like tropical bar and restaurant where happy hour hops with bands playing on a floating island in a pool, and there's a "rain storm" every 30 minutes.

950 Mason St. (at California St.), San Francisco, CA 94108. www.fairmont.com/sanfrancisco. ✆ **866/540-4491** or 415/772-5000. Fax 415/772-5013. 591 units. Main building $229–$349 double, from $500 suite; Tower $289–$469 double, from $750 suite; penthouse $12,500. Extra person $30. AE, DC, DISC, MC, V. Parking $50. Cable car: California St. line (direct stop). **Amenities:** 2 restaurants/bars; babysitting; concierge; health club (free for Fairmont President's Club

members; $15 per day or $20 per 2 days, nonmembers); room service. *In room:* A/C, TV w/pay movies and video games available, hair dryer, high-speed Internet, kitchenette in some units, minibar.

The Huntington Hotel ★★   One of the kings of Nob Hill, the stately Huntington Hotel has long been a favorite retreat for Hollywood stars and political VIPs who desire privacy and security. Family owned since 1924—an extreme rarity among large hotels—the Huntington eschews pomp and circumstance; absolute privacy and unobtrusive service are its mainstays. Although the lobby, decorated in grand 19th-century style, is rather petite compared to its Nob Hill neighbors, the guest rooms are like spacious apartments; they feature Brunschwig & Fils fabrics and bed coverings, antique French furnishings, and dreamy views of the city. Be warned, however, and the sprinkled with downscale items; one room had motel-quality doorknobs and a tiny, plain bathroom. Where they make up for the room deficiencies is a genuinely gracious staff and the celestial **Nob Hill Spa** (one of the city's best).

1075 California St. (btw. Mason and Taylor sts.), San Francisco, CA 94108. www.huntingtonhotel. com. ☎ **800/227-4683** or 415/474-5400. Fax 415/474-6227. 136 units. $350–$500 single or double; $600–$1,350 suite. Continental breakfast $14. Special packages available. AE, DC, DISC, MC, V. Valet parking $29. Bus: 1. Cable car: California St. line (direct stop). **Amenities:** Restaurant; lounge; babysitting; concierge; health club; Jacuzzi; indoor heated pool (ages 16 and up); sauna; spa. *In room:* A/C, TV w/pay movies, hair dryer, kitchenettes in some units, minibar, Wi-Fi ($9.95 per day).

InterContinental Mark Hopkins ★★★   Built in 1926 on the spot where railroad millionaire Mark Hopkins's turreted mansion once stood, the 19-story Mark Hopkins gained fame during World War II as the kiss-and-cry spot for Pacific-bound servicemen toasting their goodbyes at the Top of the Mark cocktail lounge. Nowadays, this grand hotel caters mostly to convention-bound corporate executives, since its prices often require corporate charge accounts. Each neoclassical room is exceedingly comfortable and comes with all the fancy amenities you'd expect from a world-class hotel, including custom furniture, plush fabrics, sumptuous bathrooms, Frette bathrobes, and extraordinary views of the city. The luxury suites are twice the size of most San Francisco apartments and cost close to a month's rent per night. A minor caveat: The hotel has only three guest elevators, making a quick trip to your room difficult during busy periods. Be sure and head up to the **Top of the Mark** (p. 283) for a twilight cocktail and some of the best views in the city.

1 Nob Hill (at California and Mason sts.), San Francisco, CA 94108. www.markhopkins.net. ☎ **888/424-6835** or 415/392-3434. Fax 415/421-3302. 380 units. $399–$599 double; from $650 suite; from $3,000 luxury suite. Breakfast $17 for juice, coffee, and pastry to $23 for full buffet. AE, DC, DISC, MC, V. Valet parking $54, some oversize vehicles prohibited. Bus: 1. Cable car: California St. or Powell–Market line (direct stop). **Amenities:** 2 restaurants; bar; babysitting; concierge; exercise room; room service. *In room:* A/C, TV w/pay movies, VCR/DVD in suites only, hair dryer, minibar, Wi-Fi ($13 per day).

The Ritz-Carlton, San Francisco ★★★   The Ritz-Carlton San Francisco has been the benchmark for the city's luxury hotels since it opened in 1991 in the former Metropolitan Insurance headquarters. The interior was restored with fine furnishings, fabrics, and artwork, including a pair of Louis XVI blue marble urns with gilt mountings, and 19th-century Waterford candelabras. Club rooms, on

The Mark as Movie Star

One of the city's most architecturally impressive hotels, the Mark has starred in numerous films. In Steve McQueen's famous cop thriller *Bullitt*, a suspect is spotted in the hotel's marble lobby. In Alfred Hitchcock's *Vertigo*, Jimmy Stewart can be spotted at the hotel's grand *porte-cochere* entrance (but vertigo prevents him from going to the Top of the Mark). The Mark also makes a cameo in Clint Eastwood's *Sudden Impact*. The Mark occasionally screens these films for free on its rooftop in the summer. Check www.markhopkins.net for details.

the top floors, have a dedicated concierge, separate elevator-key access, and complimentary small plates throughout the day. With the opening of **Parallel 37** in 2012, happily gone is the stuffy, formal Dining Room, replaced by a gorgeous, modern restaurant, lounge, and bar where famed chef Ron Siegel (a veteran of French Laundry and Charles Nob Hill, and one of the only non-Japanese chefs to win the Iron Chef competition) serves contemporary American cuisine in a lively, sexy setting. Also enjoying a recent makeover is the **Lounge at the Ritz-Carlton**, serving small plates in a sophisticated yet relaxed setting. (The Chacuterie and Cheese Tasting plates are superb.)

600 Stockton St. (btw. Pine and California sts.), San Francisco, CA 94108. www.ritzcarlton.com. ℂ **800/241-3333** or 415/296-7465. Fax 415/291-0288. 336 units. $445–$480 double; $499–$629 club-level double; from $579–$699 executive suite. Buffet breakfast $32; Sun champagne brunch $65. Weekend discounts and packages available. AE, DC, DISC, MC, V. Parking $62. Cable car: California St. cable car line (direct stop). **Amenities:** 2 restaurants; 3 bars; concierge; outstanding fitness center; Jacuzzi; indoor pool; room service. *In room:* A/C, TV w/pay movies, hair dryer, minibar, Wi-Fi ($13 per day).

Moderate

Nob Hill Hotel ✦   The Nob Hill Hotel is an amazing deal for such an over-the-top Victorian inn, with rates around $130 in peak season (and often less). Located in a quiet area between the Tenderloin and Nob Hill (aka Tendernob), it was built in 1906 and fully restored in 1998, and whoever renovated the lobby did a smashing job restoring it to its original "Old San Francisco Victorian" splendor, complete with original marble flooring, high ceilings with decorative moldings, and stained-glass panels and alabaster dating from about 1892. Though the rooms are small, they are all handsomely decorated with old-fashioned furnishings such as Victorian antique armoires, rich carpeting, marble bathrooms, brass beds with comforters, and carved-wood nightstands. A pleasant oxymoron: All the rooms are equipped with a plethora of high-tech amenities such as Internet access and personal voice mail. Complimentary pastries and coffee are served each morning, and there's even free evening wine tasting. The adjacent **Colombini** restaurant is a good place to refuel on regional Italian cuisine (specialty: risotto) before venturing down the street to Union Square.

835 Hyde St. (btw. Bush and Sutter sts.), San Francisco, CA 94109. www.nobhillhotel.com. ℂ **877/662-4455** or 415/885-2987. Fax 415/921-1648. 53 units. $89–$150 double. Rates include continental breakfast. DC, DISC, MC, V. Parking $34. Bus: 2 or 3. **Amenities:** Adjoining restaurant (Italian); 24-hr. fitness passes available. *In room:* TV w/pay movies, CD/radio alarm clocks, fax, hair dryer, free Wi-Fi.

Stanford Court, A Renaissance Hotel ★★   The Stanford Court has maintained a long and discreet reputation as one of San Francisco's most exclusive hotels. Keeping company with the Ritz, Fairmont, Mark Hopkins, and Huntington hotels atop Nob Hill, it's frequented mostly by corporate execs. The foundation was originally the mansion of Leland Stanford, whose legacy lives on in the many portraits and biographies that adorn the rooms. At first, the guest rooms come across as austere and antiquated compared to those at most other top-dollar business hotels, but the quality and comfort of the furnishings are so superior that you're forced to admit there's little room for improvement. The Stanford Court also prides itself on its impeccable service. The lobby, furnished in 19th-century style with Baccarat chandeliers, French antiques, and a gorgeous stained-glass dome, makes for a grand entrance. A thoughtful perk: There is no charge for toll-free or credit card calls made from your room, and complimentary coffee and tea are available with a wake-up call request.

905 California St. (at Powell St.), San Francisco, CA 94108. www.stanfordcourt.com. (C) **415/989-3500.** Fax 415/391-0513. 393 units. $169–$189 double; from $209 suite. Continental breakfast $17–$22; American breakfast $21–$26. AE, DC, DISC, MC, V. Valet parking $45. Bus: 1. Cable car: Powell–Hyde, Powell–Mason, or California–Van Ness line (direct stop). **Amenities:** Restaurant; lounge; concierge; 24-hr. fitness center; room service. *In room:* A/C, TV w/pay movies and Web TV, hair dryer, high-speed Internet access ($13).

SOMA

SoMa offers an eclectic mix of lodgings, from the Four Seasons to budget motels. It's home to the Moscone convention center, MOMA, and Yerba Buena Center for the Arts.

Best For: Conventioneers, W Hotel types, foodies, clubbers, business travelers, and anyone with an affinity for the arts.

Drawbacks: Beware of seemingly great deals to hotels in sketchy areas. Long blocks mean long walks.

ACCOMMODATIONS WITH free parking

Despite our exhortations to leave the driving to locals and use the public transportation system to get around, some of you will still want to drive the crazy streets of San Francisco, or at least arrive by car. But with parking fees averaging $45 to $55 a night at most hotels, the extra charges can add up for visitors with wheels. So if you're going to rent a car or bring your own, you might want to consider staying at one of these hotels that offers free parking:

o **Beck's Motor Lodge,** the Castro, p. 96

o **Cow Hollow Motor Inn & Suites,** Marina District/Cow Hollow, p. 92

o **Hostelling International San Francisco,** Fisherman's Wharf, p. 93

o **Hotel Del Sol,** Marina District/Cow Hollow, p. 91

o **Marina Motel,** Marina District/Cow Hollow, p. 93

o **The Phoenix Hotel,** Civic Center, p. 95

o **Seal Rock Inn,** Richmond District, p. 88

o **The Wharf Inn,** North Beach/Fisherman's Wharf, p. 90

Very Expensive

Four Seasons Hotel San Francisco ★★★ What makes this über-luxury hotel one of our favorites is its perfect combination of elegance, trendiness, and modern luxury. The entrance, either off Market or through a narrow alley off Third Street, is deceptively underwhelming, although it does tip you off to the hotel's overall discreetness. Many of the oversize rooms (starting at 460 sq. ft. and including 46 suites) overlook Yerba Buena Gardens. Not too trendy, not too traditional, they're just right, with custom-made mattresses and pillows, beautiful works of art, and huge luxury marble bathrooms with deep tubs and L'Occitane toiletries. Adding to the perks are free access to the building's huge Sports Club L.A. (the best hotel gym in the city), a 2-block walk to Union Square, and a vibe that combines sophistication with a hipness far more refined than the W or the Clift. Its only contender in that department is the St. Regis.

757 Market St. (btw. Third and Fourth sts.), San Francisco, CA 94103. www.fourseasons.com/sanfrancisco. ✆ **800/819-5053** or 415/633-3000. Fax 415/633-3001. 277 units. $355–$855 double; $750 executive suite. AE, DC, DISC, MC, V. Parking $50. Bus: All Market St. buses. Streetcar: F, and all underground streetcars. BART: All trains. **Amenities:** Restaurant; bar; concierge; huge fitness center; room service; spa. *In room:* A/C, TV w/pay movies, hair dryer, high-speed Internet ($15 per day), minibar.

Hotel Palomar ★★ The Kimpton Group's most refined downtown property occupies the top five floors of a refurbished 1907 landmark office building, where fashion models and musicians mingle freely with ordinary folks. The Art Deco–inspired interior designed by Cheryl Rowley features rooms with an updated twist on 1930s modern design—artful, understated textural elements such as emerald-tone velvets, fine woods, and raffia. Tailored lines and rich textures throughout lend a sophisticated, fresh aspect to the overall air of elegance. Rooms, however, can range from very cozy (read: small) to soothingly spacious (try for a corner room overlooking Market St.). There's not much in the way of public spaces, but the hotel makes up for it with a delicious air of exclusivity (there's even a private back entrance for celebrities). Its dining room, the **Fifth Floor Restaurant,** is one of the most well-regarded restaurants in town. If you want the full-blown luxury hotel experience, however, you're better off with one of the Nob Hill or Union Square big boys.

12 Fourth St. (at Market St.), San Francisco, CA 94103. www.hotelpalomar-sf.com. ✆ **866/373-4941** or 415/348-1111. Fax 415/348-0302. 198 units. $179–$429 double; from $379–$679 suite. Continental breakfast $22. Rates include a nightly hosted wine reception. AE, DC, DISC, MC, V. Parking $42. Streetcar: F, and all underground streetcars. BART: All trains. Pets welcome. **Amenities:** Restaurant; babysitting; concierge; fitness center; room service. *In room:* A/C, TV, CD player, fridge, hair dryer, minibar, MP3 docking station, free Wi-Fi.

Hotel Vitale ★★ Perched at the foot of the Embarcadero with outstanding waterfront and Bay Bridge views from east-facing rooms, this 199-unit hotel opened in early 2005 to instant popularity. In addition to its prime location across from the Ferry Building Marketplace (p. 174), Hotel Vitale looks pretty darn chic, from the clean-lined lobby, lounge, and **Americano** restaurant (with a hopping after-work bar scene), to the modern and masculine rooms armed with contemporary perks like flatscreen TVs, CD players with groovy compilations, gourmet minibars, huge bathrooms with walk-in showers (in some), and nature-themed pop art. Despite excellent service from the well-trained staff, a few subtleties separate Vitale from true luxury-hotel status: For example, the fitness room is pretty basic. However, they offer complimentary access to the nearby fancy YMCA, which has all the workout essentials, including a full-size pool—and the penthouse spa with outdoor soaking tubs makes up for a lot. If you can live with a few quirks, it's a very attractive place to stay, especially if you book one of the suites with 270-degree San Francisco views.

8 Mission St. (at Embarcadero), San Francisco, CA 94105. www.hotelvitale.com. ℭ **888/890-8868** or 415/278-3700. Fax 415/278-3750. 199 units. $299–$499 double; from $799 suite. Rates include morning paper, free morning yoga, and free courtesy car to downtown locations on weekdays. AE, DC, DISC, MC, V. Valet parking $48. Bus: 2, 14, 21, 71, or 71L. **Amenities:** Restaurant; concierge; exercise room; spa. *In room:* A/C, TV w/pay movies, MP3/CD player, hair dryer, minibar, free Wi-Fi.

The Palace Hotel ★ The original 1875 Palace was one of the world's largest and most luxurious hotels, and every time you walk through the doors here, you'll be reminded how incredibly majestic old luxury really is. Rebuilt after the 1906 quake, its most spectacular attributes remain the regal lobby and the Garden Court, a San Francisco landmark restaurant that was restored to its original 1909 grandeur. A double row of massive Italian-marble Ionic columns flank the court, and 10 huge chandeliers dangle above. The real heart-stopper, however, is the 80,000-pane stained-glass ceiling. (Good special effects made Michael Douglas look like he fell through it in the movie *The Game*.) Regrettably, the rooms aren't *quite* as grand. But they're vastly improved and emulate yesteryear's refinement with mahogany beds, warm gold paint and upholstery, and tasteful artwork.

The **Garden Court** is famous for its high tea, and an elaborate brunch on special holidays (scaled-down on regular weekends).

2 New Montgomery St. (at Market St.), San Francisco, CA 94105. www.sfpalace.com. ℭ **888/627-7196** or 415/512-1111. Fax 415/543-0671. 553 units. $199–$399 double; from $775 suite. Extra person $40. Children 17 and under sharing existing bedding stay free in parent's room. Weekend rates and packages available. AE, DC, DISC, MC, V. Parking $40. Bus: All Market St. buses.

The Garden Court at the Palace Hotel. In 1884 Andrew Carnegie wrote, "The court of the Grand at Paris is poor compared to that of the Palace."

Streetcar: All Market St. streetcars. **Amenities:** 4 restaurants; bar; concierge; health club w/ skylight-covered, heated lap pool; Jacuzzi; room service; sauna; spa; free Wi-Fi in lobby and conference rooms. *In room:* A/C, TV w/pay movies, hair dryer, high-speed Internet access ($16 per day), minibar.

The St. Regis Hotel ★★★   The latest in full-blown high-tech luxury is yours at this über-chic 40-story SoMa tower. Strategically near the Museum of Modern Art and Yerba Buena Gardens, this shrine to urban luxury welcomes guests (and residents willing to pay upward of $2 million for an apartment) with a 16-foot-long gas fireplace and streamlined lobby bar that's frequented by city socialites. A "personal butler" takes you to your room and shows you how to use its touch-screen control panel that works everything, from the temperature to the lights. Decor is minimalist, with sexy touches like Barcelona benches, 42-inch plasma TVs, and leather walls. Bathrooms beckon with deep soaking tubs, 13-inch LCD TVs, rainfall shower heads, and fancy toiletries, but definitely leave your room for an afternoon at the posh two-floor **Remède Spa,** the huge pool and fitness center, and restaurant **Ame,** where chef Hiro Sone, who also owns Terra in Napa Valley, presides over an Asian-influenced menu.

125 Third St. (at Mission St.), San Francisco, CA 94103. www.stregis.com/sanfrancisco. ℭ **877/ 787-3447** or 415/284-4000. Fax 415/284-4100. 260 units. $459–$679 double; $750–$8,500 suite. AE, DC, DISC, MC, V. Parking $45 per day. Bus: 30 or 45. Streetcar: J, K, L, or M to Montgomery. **Amenities:** 2 restaurants, including Ame (review, p. 119); bar; concierge; whirlpool; health club w/heated lap pool; room service; sauna; giant spa; Wi-Fi ($15 per day). *In room:* A/C, 2 TVs w/ pay movies, hair dryer, high-speed Internet access ($15 per day), minibar.

W San Francisco Hotel ★★   As modern and hip as its fashionable clientele, this 31-story property suits its neighbors, which include the Museum of Modern Art, the Moscone Center, and the Metreon entertainment center. The trendy, urban style extends to the guest rooms, which contain a feather bed with a goose-down comforter and pillows, an upholstered chaise longue, and louvered blinds that open to (usually) great city views. Bathrooms are super-sleek and stocked with Bliss products. Whimsical touches like kaleidoscopes and mini-Buddha statues make the place all the more homey. The W's new restaurant, Trace, has a theme of traceable, local foods. The W boasts a 5,000-square-foot outpost of NYC's **Bliss Spa,** and pets are allowed in guest rooms (in fact, they offer dog-walking and grooming services, as well as litter boxes, beds, bowls, and gifts; a $100 cleaning fee applies). All in all, this is one of the top places to stay in San Francisco, particularly if you enjoy the nightlife scene, which quite literally begins at the W's doorstep.

181 Third St. (btw. Mission and Howard sts.), San Francisco, CA 94103. www.wsanfrancisco.com. ℭ **877/822-0000** or 415/777-5300. Fax 415/817-7823. 410 units. From $359 double; $1,800– $2,500 suite. AE, DC, DISC, MC, V. Valet parking $49. Bus: 30 or 45. Streetcar: J, K, L, or M to Montgomery. Pets accepted for $100 fee. **Amenities:** Restaurant; 2 bars; concierge; fitness center; heated atrium pool and Jacuzzi; room service; spa. *In room:* A/C, TV w/pay movies, CD/DVD player, hair dryer, minibar, free Wi-Fi.

Expensive

The Harbor Court ★★   When the Embarcadero Freeway was torn down after the Big One in 1989, one of the major benefactors was the "wellness-themed" Harbor Court hotel: The 1926 landmark building's backyard view went from a wall of cement to a dazzling vista of the Bay Bridge (be sure to request a bay-view room, for an extra fee). Just off the Embarcadero at the edge of the Financial District and a few blocks from AT&T Park, this former YMCA books a lot of corporate travelers, but anyone who seeks stylish, high-quality accommodations—half-canopy beds, large armoires, soundproof windows, and 27-inch LCD TVs—with a superb view and lively scene will be perfectly content here. A major bonus is the free use of the adjoining fitness club, a top-quality YMCA facility with a giant indoor swimming pool. Two more reasons to stay here are the daily hosted evening wine reception and the adjacent **Ozumo Sushi Bar and Robata Grill,** which has a hugely popular happy hour, a cool vibe, and wonderful cuisine.

165 Steuart St. (btw. Mission and Howard sts.), San Francisco, CA 94105. www.harborcourthotel. com. ⓒ **866/792-6283** or 415/882-1300. Fax 415/882-1313. 131 units. $87–$295 double; from $519 suite. Continental breakfast $10. AE, DC, DISC, MC, V. Parking $40. Bus: 14 or 80X. Street-car: Embarcadero. Pets accepted. **Amenities:** Access to adjoining health club and large, heated indoor pool; room service. *In room:* A/C, TV, hair dryer, minibar, free Wi-Fi.

The Hotel Griffon ★★   Among San Francisco's small boutique hotels, this is a top contender. Ideally situated on the historic waterfront and steps from the heart of the Financial District and Ferry Building Marketplace (p. 174), the Griffon is impeccably outfitted with a soothing design sensibility. Completely renovated in 2007, it boasts contemporary features such as 32-inch flatscreen TVs, lofty ceilings, marble vanities, Aveda bath products, cozy window seats, and plush bedding (really, this place is smooth). Be sure to request a bay-view room overlooking the Bay Bridge—the added perks and view make it well worth the extra cost. Smokers, book a room elsewhere—there's no puffing allowed here. Another big bonus: It's attached to an upscale outpost of the classic American eatery, **Perry's**—the restaurant made famous in Armistead Maupin's *Tales of the City* books.

155 Steuart St. (btw. Mission and Howard sts.), San Francisco, CA 94105. www.hotelgriffon.com. ⓒ **800/321-2201** or 415/495-2100. Fax 415/495-3522. 62 units. $166–$259 double; from $339 suite. Rates include extended continental breakfast and newspaper and free Mon–Fri morning town car service within the Financial District. AE, DC, DISC, MC, V. Parking $40. All Market St. buses and streetcars, BART, and ferries. **Amenities:** Restaurant; concierge; access to large health club and pool next door (for a fee), limited room service. *In room:* TV, hair dryer, minibar, free Wi-Fi.

The InterContinental San Francisco ★★   You can't enter San Francisco from the south without wondering what the odd-but-pretty facade vaguely resembling a cross between a test tube and a larger-than-life aquarium looming in the distance is. But fear not: It's just the second InterContinental property to nab a San Francisco zip code. When the InterContinental began welcoming guests in February 2008, it was the first new lodging to open in the city in 3 whole years. Common spaces have a more neo-Japanese feel, but rooms are quite classic—ask for one on a top floor. Spanning 32 levels, it's hard to find a better view of the city this side of Market Street. One of the hotel's highlights is its posh lobby lounge, **Bar 888,** where the house specialty grappa is dispensed generously, and the adjoining restaurant, **Luce,** already the recipient of a Michelin star. Another is the luxe **I-Spa,** comprising a state-of-the-art gym and sky-lit lap pool. The InterContinental isn't the most unique place to stay in town—amenities are pretty much the same stuff you'd expect from any five-star—but it's still every bit as nice, and often cheaper, than its neighboring competitors.

888 Howard St. (at Fifth St.), San Francisco, CA 94105. www.intercontinentalsanfrancisco.com. ℭ **888/811-4273.** Fax 415/616-6501. 500 units. $139–$399 double; from $500 suite. AE, DC, DISC, MC, V. Valet parking $46. Bus: 6, 9, 19, 21, 27, 30, 31, 45, or 71. BART: Civic Center or Powell St. **Amenities:** Restaurant; concierge; fitness center; pool; room service; spa. *In room:* A/C, TV w/pay movies, CD player, hair dryer, minibar, MP3 docking station, Wi-Fi ($15 per day).

San Francisco Marriott ★★ Some call it a masterpiece; others liken it to the world's biggest parking meter. In either case, the Marriott is one of the largest buildings in the city, making it a popular stop for conventiongoers and those looking for a room with a view. Fortunately, the controversy does not extend to the rooms, which are pleasant, vibrant, and contemporary with large bathrooms and exceptional city vistas. *Tip:* Upon arrival, enter from Fourth Street, between Market and Mission streets, to avoid a long trek to the registration area.

55 Fourth St. (btw. Market and Mission sts.), San Francisco, CA 94103. www.marriott.com/sfodt. ℭ **888/575-8934** or 415/896-1600. Fax 415/486-8101. 1,598 units. $199–$349 double; $269–$3,250 suite. AE, DC, DISC, MC, V. Parking $56. Bus: All Market St. buses. Streetcar: All Market St. streetcars. Cable car: Powell–Hyde or Powell–Mason line (3 blocks west). **Amenities:** 2 restaurants; 2 bars; health club; indoor pool; free Wi-Fi in select areas. *In room:* A/C, TV w/pay movies, hair dryer, high-speed Internet ($13 per day).

Moderate

The Good Hotel ★ In 2008, this "socially conscious" budget hotel became an affordable alternative to SoMa's traditionally pricey lineup of hotels. With an eco-friendly take on things—hybrid car drivers, for example, get free parking—the hotel is designed to give back to the environment. But the hotel definitely doesn't take itself too seriously. There's a fun-for-all photo booth in the lobby, where your photo outtake lives a long life as part of the hotel's wallpaper scheme, and you'll glimpse the glow-in-the-dark GOOD NIGHT sticker pasted on the ceiling only when you turn the lights off. The sometimes-tongue-in-cheek "Be Good" mantra is scribbled throughout the establishment even in the most unnecessary of places (such as the bedroom). The hotel has a yummy pizzeria on tap, too, **Good Pizza,** serving up artisan thin-crust pies with fresh, local ingredients. *Note:* The neighborhood is one of San Francisco's more interesting (to put it delicately). While residents don't think twice about patrolling the Seventh Street corridor solo, visitors are often a bit more reluctant.

112 Seventh St. (btw. Minna and Mission sts.), San Francisco, CA 94103. www.thegoodhotel. com. ℭ **800/444-5819** or 415/621-7001. Fax 415/621-4069. 117 units. $89–$139 double. AE, DC, DISC, MC, V. Parking free for hybrid cars, $20 for nonhybrids. Bus: 6, 9, 19, 21, 27, 31, or 71. BART: Civic Center or Powell St. Cable car: Powell–Hyde or Powell–Mason line (2 blocks west). **Amenities:** Restaurant; access to heated pool across the street. *In room:* TV, hair dryer, MP3 docking station, free Wi-Fi.

The Mosser ★ 🖋 "Hip on the Cheap" might best sum up the Mosser, a highly atypical budget hotel that incorporates Victorian architecture with modern interior design. It originally opened in 1913 as a luxury hotel, only to be dwarfed by the far more modern sky-rise hotels that surround it. But a major multimillion-dollar renovation a few years back transformed this aging charmer into a sophisticated, stylish, and surprisingly affordable SoMa lodging. Guest rooms are replete with original Victorian flourishes—bay windows and hand-carved moldings—that juxtapose well with the contemporary custom-designed furnishings, granite showers, stainless-steel fixtures, ceiling fans, Frette linens, double-paned

Elements: A Hip Mission District Hotel

Bad credit? No problem. There's finally a place for the perpetually young and broke to stay and play in the heart of the Mission District. The **Elements Hotel** is sort of a cross between a boutique hotel and a hostel, offering both private rooms and shared dorms, all with private bathrooms. Add to that Wi-Fi access throughout the hotel, a free Internet lounge, rooftop parties, free movie nights, lockers, free continental breakfast, luggage storage and laundry facilities, free linens, TVs (in private rooms), a lively restaurant and lounge called Medjool, and a plethora of inexpensive ethnic cafes in the neighborhood, and, baby, you've got it made. The hotel is at 2516 Mission St., between 21st and 22nd streets (www.elementssf.com; *℗* **866/327-8407** or 415/647-4100). Rates per person are between $80 and $90; expect higher rates and minimum stays during holidays.

windows, and modern electronics. The least expensive rooms are quite small and share a bathroom, but are an incredible deal for such a central location—3 blocks from Union Square, 2 blocks from the MOMA, and half a block from the cable car turnaround. It also borders on a "sketchy" street, but so do most hotels a few blocks west of Union Square. The hotel's restaurant, **Annabelle's Bar & Bistro,** serves lunch and dinner.

54 Fourth St. (at Market St.), San Francisco, CA 94103. www.themosser.com. *℗* **800/227-3804** or 415/986-4400. Fax 415/495-7653. 166 units, 112 with bathroom. $79–$209 double with bathroom; $47–$119 double without bathroom; $143–$359 suite. Rates include safe-deposit boxes at front desk. AE, DC, DISC, MC, V. Parking $29, plus $8 for oversize vehicles. Streetcar: F, and all underground Muni. BART: All trains. **Amenities:** Restaurant; bar; concierge. *In room:* Ceiling fan, TV, AM/FM stereo w/CD player, hair dryer, Wi Fi ($9.95 per day).

THE FINANCIAL DISTRICT

This is where the captains of industry and their underlings gather on weekdays in those tall buildings. It's an area worth considering if you can score a weekday discount.

Best For: Business travelers, discount weekend rates at business hotels, and a central location for people who love to explore on foot. Lively après-work scene at the bars.

Drawbacks: Very noisy and crowded Monday to Friday 7am to 7pm, minimal nightlife scene, zero street parking during the day.

Very Expensive

The Mandarin Oriental ★★★   No hotel combines better ultraluxury digs with incredible views than this gem. Heaven begins after a rocketing ride on the elevators to the rooms, located between the 38th and 48th floors of a high-rise. The opulent rooms feature contemporary Asian-influenced decor, but the best details by far are the huge windows with superb city views, particularly when the fog rolls in. Not all rooms have bathtub-side views (incredible and standard with the signature rooms), but every one does have a luxurious marble bathroom stocked with terry and cotton cloth robes, a makeup mirror, and silk slippers. The 2,000-square-foot Taipan suite—which has a kitchenette, living room, dining area, bedroom, roomy bathroom, and bay-view balcony half the size of a football

THE best FAMILY-FRIENDLY HOTELS

Argonaut Hotel (p. 88)   Not only is it near all the funky kid fun of Fisherman's Wharf and the National Maritime Museum, but this bayside hotel, a winner for the whole family, also has kid-friendly perks like the opportunity for each child to grab a gift from the hotel's "treasure chest."

Cow Hollow Motor Inn & Suites (p. 92) Two-bedroom suites allow kids to shack up in style instead of camping on the pullout couch.

Hotel Diva (p. 65)   The sleek, mod Diva has all sorts of fun kid-friendly perks. Check out SF's version of the Walk of Fame right outside the door, and definitely ask about their two-room Little Divas Suite, with bunk beds, drawing tables, and a TV loaded with kids' movies.

The Fairmont San Francisco (p. 76) While the glamorous lobby and spectacular city views will please parents, kids will be thrilled by the hotel's **Tonga Room,** a fantastically kitsch Disneyland-like tropical bar and restaurant where "rain" falls every 30 minutes.

Handlery Union Square Hotel (p. 64) Never mind that it's been completely renovated. The real kid-friendly kickers here are the adjoining rooms in the "newer" addition; a heated, clean, outdoor pool; and the adjoining restaurant, the Daily Grill, which offers the gamut of American favorites.

Hotel Del Sol (p. 91)   It's colorful enough to represent a Crayola selection, but tots are more likely to be impressed by the "Kids are VIPs" program that includes a lending library, toys and videos, evening cookies and milk, and accouterments for the heated pool (think sunglasses, visors, beach balls). Parental perks include access to a bonded babysitting service, three baby-proofed rooms, and a family suite (three adjoining rooms).

Hotel Metropolis (p. 70)   The lobby walls at this playful yet serene hotel are covered with more than 80 works of colorful (and curiously abstract) art created by children. The three-room Urban Explorers Kids Suite, which sleeps up to six adults and three children, is filled with pint-size furniture, bunk beds, a computer, a chalkboard wall, toys, and rubber ducky decor in the bathroom.

Stanyan Park Hotel (p. 97)   Plenty of elbowroom and a half-block walk to Golden Gate Park's Children's Playground make this a prime spot for crashing family style. But the biggest bonuses are the suites, which come with one or two bedrooms, a full kitchen, and a dining area.

Westin St. Francis (p. 62)   A classic San Francisco hotel down to its hospitality, the Westin welcomes the little ones with fun gifts and free drink refills at its restaurants.

field—is twice as big as our entire house. An added bonus: The restaurant, **Silks,** has a kitchen crew working wonders with the Asian-influenced menu, though the dining room can be awkwardly empty.

222 Sansome St. (btw. Pine and California sts.), San Francisco, CA 94104. www.mandarinoriental. com/sanfrancisco. ☏ **800/622-0404** or 415/276-9888. Fax 415/276-9304. 158 units. $395–$640 double; from $875 suite. Continental breakfast $21; American breakfast $32. AE, DC, DISC, MC, V. Valet parking $36. Bus: All Market St. buses. Streetcar: J, K, L, or M to Montgomery. **Amenities:** Restaurant; bar; concierge; fitness center; room service. *In room:* A/C, TV w/pay movies, CD player, hair dryer, minibar, Wi-Fi ($13 per day).

Expensive

Hilton San Francisco Financial District ★ Finally there's a good reason to stay in Chinatown. Having recently undergone a $55-million renovation, this upscale hotel geared toward the needs of the business traveler is a good choice for anyone seeking a convenient downtown location perfect for forays into Chinatown, North Beach, and beyond. All of the comfortably modern rooms feature either city or bay views, so you really can't go wrong. The panoramic bay views of Coit Tower, Telegraph Hill, and Alcatraz are wholly unobstructed as you look straight down the Columbus Avenue thoroughfare to Ghirardelli Square. The in-room contemporary decor includes dark muted earth-tone carpets, warm honey-colored wood, and lush, pristine palette beds with crisp white linens and feather beds swathed in masculine dusty blue, tan, and slate-gray pillows and accents. The seven suites have bamboo floors, fireplaces, balconies, and large luxurious bathrooms, some with nice touches like sleek yours-and-mine sinks. For concierge-floor guests, a complimentary breakfast is served in a private lounge.

750 Kearny St. (at Washington St.), San Francisco, CA 94108. www.sanfranciscofinancialdistrict. hilton.com. ☏ **800/HILTONS** (445-8667) or 415/433-6600. Fax 415/765-7891. 549 units. $199–$429 double; $989–$1,200 suite. AE, DC, DISC, MC, V. Valet parking $42. Bus: 1. Cable car: California. **Amenities:** Restaurant; bar; coffee bar; concierge; fitness room; room service; spa. In room: A/C, TV w/pay movies, hair dryer, minibar, Wi-Fi ($9.95 per day).

Hyatt Regency San Francisco ★ The Hyatt Regency, a convention favorite, rises from the edge of the Embarcadero Center at the foot of Market Street. The gray concrete structure, with a 1970s, bunkerlike facade, is shaped like a vertical triangle, serrated with long rows of jutting balconies. The 17-story atrium lobby, illuminated by museum-quality theater lighting, has a waterway flowing through it. (Be sure to ride the glass elevators to the top floor for a great indoor view.)

Rooms are furnished in "contemporary decor" a la corporate hotel fashion. Bonuses include ergonomic workstation chairs; textiles in shades of gold, charcoal gray, and celadon; and coffeemakers. Definitely not a standout choice for shacking up. The Eclipse Café serves breakfast and lunch daily; during the evening it becomes A Cut Above steakhouse. The 13-Views Lounge serves cocktails and bar food for dinner.

5 Embarcadero Center, San Francisco, CA 94111. www.sanfranciscoregency.hyatt.com. ☏ **888/591-1234** or 415/788-1234. Fax 415/398-2567. 802 units. $159–$299 double. Continental breakfast $18. AE, DC, DISC, MC, V. Valet parking $50. Bus: All Market St. buses. Streetcar: All Market St. streetcars. **Amenities:** Restaurant; cafe; bar; concierge; fitness center. In room: A/C, TV w/pay movies, hair dryer, minibar, Wi-Fi ($9.95 per day).

NORTH BEACH/FISHERMAN'S WHARF

This area is the birthplace of the Beat Generation, where Little Italy meets and mixes with Big China. It's home to boutique hotels, family-run restaurants, and a lively nightlife scene.

Best For: Hopeless romantics, foodies, wannabe novelists, coffee lovers, and peripatetic insomniacs.

Drawbacks: Tough parking, few hotel bargains, rowdy out-of-towners on weekend nights, and (family alert) plenty of porn on Broadway.

🎁 SLEEPING seaside

You would think that a city surrounded on three sides by water would have a slew of seaside hotels. Oddly enough, it has very few, one of which is the **Seal Rock Inn.** It's about as far from Union Square and Fisherman's Wharf as you can place a hotel in San Francisco, but that just makes it all the more unique. The motel fronts Sutro Heights Park, which faces Ocean Beach. Most rooms in the four-story structure have at least partial views of the ocean; at night, the sounds of the surf and distant foghorns lull guests to sleep. The rooms, although large and clean, are old and basic, with rose and teal floral accents. Only some rooms have kitchenettes, but phones, TVs, fridges, covered parking, and use of the enclosed patio and pool area are standard. On the ground floor of the inn is a small old-fashioned restaurant serving breakfast and lunch. Golden Gate Park and the Presidio are both nearby, and the Geary bus—which snails its way to Union Square and Market Street—stops right out front and takes at least a half-hour to get downtown.

The Seal Rock Inn (www.sealrockinn.com; ✆ **888/732-5762** or 415/752-8000; fax 415/752-6034) is at 545 Point Lobos Ave. (at 48th Ave.), San Francisco, CA 94121. Double rooms range from $114 to $152.

Expensive

Argonaut Hotel ★★ ☺ The four-story timber-and-brick landmark building that houses the Argonaut Hotel was originally built in 1908 as a warehouse for the California Fruit Canners Association. Its rooms are whimsically decorated to emulate a luxury cruise ship in cheerful nautical colors (though evidence of its modest past appears in original brick walls, large timbers, and steel warehouse doors). Suites have wonderful views and come fully loaded with telescopes and spa tubs, and "view" rooms overlook the wharf or bay (some offer fabulous views of Alcatraz and the Golden Gate Bridge). The friendly staff goes out of their way to make little ones feel at home and allows each pint-size guest to pick a new plaything from the hotel's "treasure chest." The hotel is attached to the **Blue Mermaid Chowder House & Bar,** a friendly casual eatery. *Tip:* The concierge seems to be able to work wonders when you need tickets to Alcatraz—even when the trips are officially sold out.

495 Jefferson St. (at Hyde St.), San Francisco, CA 94109. www.argonauthotel.com. ✆ **800/790-1415** or 415/563-0800. Fax 415/563-2800. 252 units. $189–$389 double; $489–$1,089 suite. Rates include evening wine in the lobby, daily newspaper, and kid-friendly perks like cribs and strollers. AE, DC, DISC, MC, V. Parking $39. Bus: 30 or 47. Streetcar: F. Cable car: Powell–Hyde line. **Amenities:** Restaurant; bar; concierge; fitness center. *In room:* A/C, flatscreen TV w/Nintendo and pay movies, Web TV, DVD and CD players, hair dryer, free high-speed Internet access, minibar.

Sheraton Fisherman's Wharf Hotel Built in the mid-1970s, this contemporary, four-story hotel offers the reliable comforts of a Sheraton in San Francisco's most popular tourist area. In other words, the clean, modern rooms are comfortable and well equipped but nothing unique to the city. On the bright side, they have a heated outdoor pool (a rarity in San Francisco) and just underwent a $33-million renovation, meaning most of the rooms are decked out in bright colors like pinks, yellows, and aquamarines and are outfitted with brand-new furnishings as well. A corporate floor caters exclusively to business travelers.

2500 Mason St. (btw. Beach and North Point sts.), San Francisco, CA 94133. www.sheratonatthewharf.com. ✆ **888/627-7024** or 415/362-5500. Fax 415/956-5275. 529 units. $119–$279 double; $550–$1,000 suite. Extra person $20. Continental breakfast $13. AE, DC, DISC, MC, V. Valet parking $49. Bus: 47. Streetcar: F. Cable car: Powell–Mason line (1 block east, 2 blocks south). **Amenities:** Restaurant; bar; concierge; exercise room; outdoor heated pool; limited room service. *In room:* A/C, TV, fax (in suites only), hair dryer, high-speed Internet ($9.95 per day).

The Washington Square Inn ★   This small, comely, European-style bed-and-breakfast is ideal for older couples who prefer a quieter, more subdued environment than the commotion of downtown San Francisco. It's across from Washington Square in North Beach—a coffee-craver's haven—and within walking distance of Fisherman's Wharf and Chinatown. All rooms feature European antiques, ceiling fans, flatscreen TVs, and private bathrooms, while some have fireplaces or sitting areas in bay windows. A light breakfast is served in your room or the lobby, and in the evening hors d'oeuvres are served with wine.

1660 Stockton St. (btw. Filbert and Union sts.), San Francisco, CA 94133. www.wsisf.com. © **800/ 388-0220** or 415/981-4220. Fax 415/397-7242. 15 units. $209–$329 double. Rates include continental breakfast and afternoon tea, wine, and hors d'oeuvres. AE, DISC, MC, V. Valet parking $35; self-parking $20. Bus: 30, 41, or 45. **Amenities:** Limited room service. *In room:* Flatscreen TV, CD player, hair dryer, free Wi-Fi.

Moderate

Best Western Tuscan Inn at Fisherman's Wharf ★★   Like an island of respectability in a sea of touristy schlock, this boutique Best Western is one of the best midrange hotels at Fisherman's Wharf. It continues to exude a level of style and comfort far beyond that of its neighboring competitors. For example, every evening in the plush lobby warmed by a grand fireplace, a wine reception is hosted by the manager, and the adjoining **Café Pescatore** serves wonderful pizzas and grilled meats from their wood-burning oven. The rooms are a definite cut above competing Fisherman's Wharf hotels: All are handsomely decorated and have writing desks and armchairs. The only caveat is the lack of scenic views—a small price to pay for a good hotel in a prime location.

425 North Point St. (at Mason St.), San Francisco, CA 94133. www.tuscaninn.com. © **800/648- 4626** or 415/561-1100. Fax 415/561-1199. 221 units. $149–$269. Rates include coffee, tea, and evening wine reception. AE, DC, DISC, MC, V. Parking $42. Bus: 47. Cable car: Powell–Mason line. Pets welcome for $50. **Amenities:** Concierge; access to nearby gym; room service. *In room:* A/C, TV w/video games and pay movies, hair dryer, minibar, free Wi-Fi.

The Hotel Bohème ★★ 🛏   Romance awaits at the intimate Hotel Bohème. Although it's on the busiest avenue in North Beach, once you climb the staircase to this narrow second-floor boutique hotel, you'll discover a style and demeanor reminiscent of a home on Russian Hill. Beat-era jazz photos decorate the hallways and, while there are no common areas other than a little booth for check-in and concierge, rooms are truly sweet, with gauze-draped canopies, stylish decor such as ornate parasols shading ceiling lights, and dramatically colored walls. Although the bathrooms are spiffy, they're tiny and have showers only. The staff is ultra-hospitable, and bonuses include sherry in the lobby each afternoon. Some fabulous cafes, restaurants, bars, and shops along Columbus Avenue are just a few steps away, and Chinatown and Union Square are within easy walking distance. *Tip:* Request a room off the street side, which is quieter.

444 Columbus Ave. (btw. Vallejo and Green sts.), San Francisco, CA 94133. www.hotelboheme. com. © **415/433-9111.** Fax 415/362-6292. 15 units. $174–$214 double. Rates include afternoon sherry. AE, DC, DISC, MC, V. Parking $12–$31 at nearby public garages. Bus: 12, 30, 41, or 45. Cable car: Powell–Mason line. **Amenities:** Concierge. *In room:* TV, hair dryer, free Wi-Fi.

Inexpensive

The San Remo Hotel ★ 🐾   This small, European-style *pensione* is one of the best budget hotels in San Francisco. In a quiet North Beach neighborhood, within walking distance of Fisherman's Wharf, the Italianate Victorian structure originally served as a boardinghouse for dockworkers displaced by the fires that followed the 1906 earthquake. As a result, the rooms are small and bathrooms are shared, but all is forgiven when it comes time to pay the bill. Rooms are decorated in cozy country style, with brass and iron beds; oak, maple, or pine armoires; and wicker furnishings. The immaculate shared bathrooms feature tubs and brass pull-chain toilets with oak tanks and brass fixtures. If the penthouse—which has its own bathroom, TV, fridge, and patio—is available, book it: You won't find a more romantic place to stay in San Francisco for so little money.

2237 Mason St. (at Chestnut St.), San Francisco, CA 94133. www.sanremohotel.com. Ⓒ **800/352-7366** or 415/776-8688. Fax 415/776-2811. 62 units, 61 with shared bathroom. $75–$99 double; $175–$185 penthouse suite. AE, DC, MC, V. Self-parking $13–$14. Bus: 30 or 47. Streetcar: F. Cable car: Powell–Mason line. **Amenities:** Access to nearby health club; Internet kiosk in lobby. *In room:* Ceiling fan.

The Wharf Inn 🐾   This is our top choice for good-value/great-location lodging at Fisherman's Wharf. The Wharf Inn offers your standard no-frills motel accommodations, but it's the location—right next to one of the most popular tourist attractions in the world—that counts. The rooms are done in pleasant tones of earth, muted greens, and burnt orange, but more importantly, they are situated smack-dab in the middle of the wharf, a mere 2 blocks from Pier 39 and the cable car turnaround, and within walking distance of the Embarcadero and North Beach. The inn is ideal for car-bound families because parking is free (that saves at least $30 a day right off the bat).

2601 Mason St. (at Beach St.), San Francisco, CA 94133. www.wharfinn.com. Ⓒ **877/275-7889** or 415/673-7411. Fax 415/776-2181. 51 units. $125–$159 double; $299–$439 penthouse. Rates include coffee/tea and newspapers. AE, DC, DISC, MC, V. Free parking. Bus: 39 or 47. Streetcar: F. Cable car: Powell–Mason or Powell–Hyde line. **Amenities:** Access to nearby health club ($10 per day). *In room:* TV, hair dryer on request, free Wi-Fi.

THE MARINA/PACIFIC HEIGHTS/ COW HOLLOW

This is where the college Greek crowd ends up after graduating. It's our top pick for staying at a reasonably priced hotel or motel. Opening in the Presidio as we go to print is the **Inn at the Presidio,** an historic military quarters now a 22-room inn, at 42 Moraga Avenue (**www.innatthepresidio.com; Ⓒ 415/800-7356**).

Best For: Eye candy, shopping, kid-friendly lodging, lively restaurant and bar scene, nonhill strolling, beach access.

Drawbacks: Few sightseeing attractions, and you'll need to take a taxi or bus (or a very long walk) to the city center.

Expensive

Hotel Drisco ★★ 🎁   On one of the most sought-after blocks of residential property in all of San Francisco, the Drisco, built in 1903, is one of the city's best small hotels. Refinements are evident, from the welcoming lobby to the calming ambience of the cream, yellow, and light green guest rooms. As in the neighboring mansions, traditional custom-made furnishings and thick, luxurious fabrics abound here. The hotel's comfy beds will make you want to loll late into the morning before primping in the large marble bathrooms, complete with robes and slippers, and then enjoying a leisurely breakfast in the newly redecorated dining room. Each suite has a couch that unfolds into a bed (although you would never guess from the looks of it), two HDTVs, and superior views. A 24-hour coffee and tea service is available in the sitting room just off the lobby. Street parking is at no cost, and the hotel's staff will help you find a convenient spot.

2901 Pacific Ave. (at Broderick St.), San Francisco, CA 94115. www.hoteldrisco.com. (€) **800/634-7277** or 415/346-2880. Fax 415/567-5537. 48 units. $169–$259 deluxe king; $351–$519 suite. Rates include gourmet continental breakfast and evening wine and cheese. AE, DC, DISC, MC, V. Street parking available. Bus: 3 or 24. **Amenities:** Concierge; exercise room and free pass to YMCA; room service. *In room:* TV/DVD, CD player, fridge, hair dryer, free high-speed DSL Internet, minibar.

Moderate

Hotel Del Sol ★★ ☺ ✦   The cheeriest motel in town is just 2 blocks off the Marina District's bustling section of Lombard. Three-level Hotel Del Sol is all about festive flair: The sunshine theme extends from the Miami Beach–style use of vibrant color, as in the yellow, red, orange, and blue exterior, to the heated courtyard pool, which beckons the youngish clientele as they head for their cars parked (for free!—unheard of in San Francisco) in cabana-like spaces. This is also one of the most family-friendly places to stay, with a "Kids are VIPs" program, including a family suite (with bunks and toys); a library of books, toys, and videos; childproofing kits; rooms that have been baby-proofed; bonded babysitting services; evening cookies and milk; pool toys; and kids' sunglasses and visors.

3100 Webster St. (at Greenwich St.), San Francisco, CA 94123. www.thehoteldelsol.com. (€) **877/433-5765** or 415/921-5520. Fax 415/931-4137. 57 units. $139–$199 double; $179–$239 suite. Rates include continental breakfast and free newspapers in the lobby. AE, DC, DISC, MC, V. Free parking. Bus: 22, 28, 41, 43, 45, or 76. **Amenities:** Heated outdoor pool. *In room:* TV/VCR, CD player, fridge and DVD in suites only, kitchenette in 3 units, Wi-Fi ($7.95 per day).

Jackson Court ★★   The Jackson Court, a stately three-story brownstone Victorian mansion, is in one of San Francisco's most exclusive neighborhoods, Pacific Heights. Its only fault—that it's far from the action—is also its blessing: If you crave a blissfully quiet vacation in elegant surroundings, this is the place. The rooms are individually furnished with superior-quality antique furnishings; two have wood-burning fireplaces (whose use is de rigueur in the winter) and two have gas fireplaces. The Blue Room features an inviting window seat; the Garden Court Suite has handcrafted wood paneling, a king-size bed, and a large picture window looking onto the private garden patio. After a continental breakfast of muffins, scones, croissants, oatmeal, juice, and fruit, spend the day browsing the shops along nearby Union and Fillmore streets and return in time for afternoon tea.

2198 Jackson St. (at Buchanan St.), San Francisco, CA 94115. www.jacksoncourt.com. (€) **415/929-7670.** Fax 415/929-1405. 12 units. $160–$225 double. Rates include continental breakfast and afternoon tea. AE, MC, V. Parking on street only. Bus: 1, 3, or 22. **Amenities:** Concierge. *In room:* TV, hair dryer, high-speed Internet access.

Laurel Inn ★★ ✦   If you don't mind being out of the downtown area, this hip hotel is one of the most tranquil and affordably high-style places to rest your head. Tucked just beyond the southernmost tip of the Presidio and Pacific Heights, the outside is nothing impressive—just another motor inn. Then the Joie de Vivre group got a hold of it, giving it a hip new life with modern decor and Zen-like influences (think W San Francisco Hotel at half the price). The rooms, some of which have excellent city views, are smartly designed and decorated in the style of a contemporary studio apartment. The continental breakfast is fine, but why bother when you're across the street from **Ella's** (p. 142), which serves San Francisco's best breakfast? Other thoughtful touches: 24-hour coffee and tea service, pet-friendly rooms, a CD and video lending library, and indoor parking. There's also great shopping a block away at Sacramento Street; and the groovy downstairs **Swank Cocktail Club,** which serves sultry libations and a surprisingly active slice of glamorous young Pacific Heights nightlife.

444 Presidio Ave. (at California Ave.), San Francisco, CA 94115. www.thelaurelinn.com. ℂ **800/ 552-8735** or 415/567-8467. Fax 415/928-1866. 49 units. $159–$209 double. Rates include continental breakfast and afternoon lemonade and cookies. AE, DC, DISC, MC, V. Free parking. Bus: 1, 3, or 43. Pets accepted. **Amenities:** Adjoining bar; concierge; access to the enormous JCC gym across the street at $10 per day. *In room:* TV/VCR, CD player, hair dryer, kitchenette in some units, free Wi-Fi.

Union Street Inn ★★   Who would have guessed that one of the most delightful B&Bs in California would be in San Francisco? This two-story 1903 Edwardian fronts perpetually busy (and trendy shopping and barhopping stop) Union Street, but is as quiet as a church on the inside. The individually decorated rooms are furnished with down comforters, fresh flowers, fruit baskets, and bay windows (beg for one with a view of the garden). A few even have Jacuzzi tubs for two. An extended full breakfast is served in the parlor, in your room, or on an outdoor terrace overlooking a lovely English garden. The ultimate honeymoon retreat is the private carriage house behind the inn, but any room at this warm, friendly inn is guaranteed to please.

2229 Union St. (btw. Fillmore and Steiner sts.), San Francisco, CA 94123. www.unionstreetinn. com. ℂ **415/346-0424.** Fax 415/922-8046. 5 units, 1 cottage. $199–$329 double. Rates include breakfast, hors d'oeuvres, and evening beverages. AE, DISC, MC, V. Nearby parking $15. Bus: 22, 41, or 45. *In room:* TV, CD/DVD player, free Wi-Fi.

Inexpensive

Cow Hollow Motor Inn & Suites ☺   If you're less interested in being downtown than in playing in and around the beautiful bayfront Marina, check out this modest brick hotel on busy Lombard Street. There's no fancy theme, but each room has cable TV, free local phone calls, free covered parking, and a coffeemaker. Families will appreciate the one- and two-bedroom suites, which have full kitchens and dining areas as well as antique furnishings and surprisingly tasteful decor.

2190 Lombard St. (btw. Steiner and Fillmore sts.), San Francisco, CA 94123. www.cowhollow motorinn.com. ℂ **415/921-5800.** Fax 415/922-8515. 129 units. $82–$150 double. Extra person $10. AE, DC, MC, V. Free parking. Bus: 28, 30, 43, or 76. **Amenities:** Restaurant. *In room:* A/C, TV, hair dryer, full kitchens in suites only, free Wi-Fi.

Edward II Inn & Suites ★   This three-story "English country" inn has a room for almost anyone's budget, ranging from *pensione* units with shared bathrooms to luxuriously appointed suites and cottages with whirlpool bathtubs and fireplaces. Originally built to house guests who attended the 1915 Pan Pacific Exposition, it's still a good place to stay in spotless and comfortably appointed rooms with cozy antique furnishings. They've recently added a small fitness center and there's a decent seafood restaurant next door, as well as a seasonal English pub. Room prices even include a full continental breakfast. Nearby Chestnut and Union streets offer some of the best shopping and dining in the city. The only caveat is that the hotel's Lombard Street location is usually congested with traffic.

3155 Scott St. (at Lombard St.), San Francisco, CA 94123. www.edwardii.com. (℃ **800/473-2846** or 415/922-3000. Fax 415/931-5784. 31 units, 21 with bathroom. $69 double with shared bathroom; $99–$139 double with private bathroom; $150–$200 junior suite. Extra person $25. Rates include continental breakfast and evening sherry. AE, DISC, MC, V. Self-parking $12 1 block away. Bus: 28, 30, 43, or 76. **Amenities:** Pub; fitness center ($10 per day); computer station (for nominal fee). *In room:* TV, hair dryer available on request, free Wi-Fi.

Hostelling International San Francisco—Fisherman's Wharf 🛏

Unbelievable but true—you can get front-row bay views for a mere $26 a night. This hostel, on a prime piece of national park property in Fort Mason, provides dorm-style accommodations and offers easy access to the Marina's shops and restaurants. Rooms sleep 2 to 12 people and there are 10 private rooms available; communal space includes a fireplace, kitchen, dining room, coffee bar, pool table, and foosball. The breakfast alone practically makes it worth the price. Make reservations well in advance.

Fort Mason, Bldg. 240, San Francisco, CA 94123. www.sfhostels.com. (℃ **415/771-7277.** Fax 415/771-1468. 150 beds. $24 per person per night; $65 private rooms. Rates include breakfast. MC, V. Free limited parking. Bus: 28, 30, 47, or 49. **Amenities:** Computer kiosks for small fee; free Wi-Fi.

Marina Inn ★ 🦆

Marina Inn is one of the best low-priced hotels in San Francisco. How it offers so much for so little is mystifying. Each guest room in the 1924 four-story Victorian looks like something from a country furnishings catalog, complete with rustic pinewood furniture, a four-poster bed with silky-soft comforter, pretty wallpaper, and soothing tones of rose, hunter green, and pale yellow. You also get remote-control televisions discreetly hidden in pine cabinetry all for as little as $60 a night. Combined with continental breakfast, friendly service, free Wi-Fi, and an armada of shops and restaurants within easy walking distance, it is one of our top choices for best overall value. *Note:* Traffic can be a bit noisy here, so the hotel added double panes on windows facing the street.

3110 Octavia St. (at Lombard St.), San Francisco, CA 94123. www.marinainn.com. (℃ **800/274-1420** or 415/928-1000. Fax 415/928-5909. 40 units. $59–$69 double. Rates include continental breakfast. AE, DC, DISC, MC, V. Bus: 28, 30, 43, or 76. *In room:* TV, hair dryer (upon request), free Wi-Fi.

Marina Motel

Established in 1939, the Marina Motel is one of San Francisco's first motels, built for the opening of the Golden Gate Bridge. The same family has owned this peach-colored, Spanish-style stucco building for three generations, and they've taken exquisite care of it. All rooms look out onto an inner courtyard, which is awash with beautiful flowering plants and wall paintings by local artists. Though the rooms show minor signs of wear and tear, they're all quite clean, bright, quiet, and pleasantly decorated with framed lithographs of old San Francisco. Two-bedroom suites come with fully equipped kitchens. The Presidio and Marina Green are mere blocks away, and you can easily catch a bus downtown. The only downside is the street noise, which is likely to burden light sleepers. *Bonus:* All rooms include a breakfast coupon valid for two entrees for the price of one at nearby **Judy's Cafe.**

2576 Lombard St. (btw. Divisadero and Broderick sts.), San Francisco, CA 94123. www.marinamotel.com. (℃ **800/346-6118** or 415/921-9406. Fax 415/921-0364. 38 units. $75–$165 double;

4

WHERE TO STAY

The Marina/Pacific Heights/Cow Hollow

$109–$199 suite. Lower rates in winter. Rates include 2-for-1 breakfast coupon at nearby cafe. AE, DISC, MC, V. Free covered parking. Bus: 28, 30, 43, 45, or 76. Dogs accepted for a $10 nightly fee. *In room:* Fridge, hair dryer.

JAPANTOWN & ENVIRONS

If you're staying in or near Japantown, it's because you found a lodging deal you couldn't pass up. If you have kids, try **Hotel Tomo,** 1800 Sutter Street (**www. jdvhotels.com/tomo;** ⓒ **415/921-4000**), a Best Western property given an anime (Japanese cartoon) makeover by hotel group Joie de Vivre.

Best For: Central location for exploring the entire city, Japanese culture, quiet lodgings.

Drawbacks: Limited nightlife and dining, far from city center.

Moderate

Hotel Kabuki ★★ If you want accommodations a little east of center, and you don't mind being out of the downtown loop, the Kabuki is a solid choice. Located in the heart of Japantown, steps from the shops and yummy noodle houses of the Japan Center, and just up the street from Robert Redford's Sundance movie theater complex, the Hotel Kabuki is an underdiscovered gem of a luxury hotel. Designed in serene Japonesque style, with koi ponds, shoji screens, Zen gardens, and Japanese artwork throughout, the Kabuki has a grace, style, and quiet elegance that you don't find in a lot of Western hotels (certainly nowhere else in San Francisco). Guest rooms feature high-thread-count linens, flatscreen TVs, MP3 docking stations, bathrobes, Asian tea kettles, and Japanese snacks in the honor bar. Many rooms have deep soaking tubs, some suites have dry saunas, but if yours doesn't, the hotel offers complimentary passes to the communal baths at nearby **Kabuki Springs & Spa** (p. 197; make your reservation online). The in-house restaurant, O Izakaya Lounge, sports a J-Pop baseball theme and offers a great bar-snack menu with more than 20 different kinds of sake.

1625 Post St. (btw. Gough and Octavia sts.), San Francisco, CA 94109. www.jdvhotels.com/hotels/kabuki. ⓒ **800/533-4567** or 415/922-3200. Fax 415/614-5498. 218 units. $99–$224 double; $219–$249 suite. Extra person $10. Breakfast buffet $16. AE, DC, DISC, MC, V. Parking $35. Bus: 2 or 3. **Amenities:** Restaurant; concierge; 24-hr. fitness room. *In room:* TV, hair dryer, MP3 docking station, free Wi-Fi.

The Queen Anne Hotel ★★ ✦ This majestic 1890 Victorian charmer was once a grooming school for upper-class young women. Restored in 1980 and renovated in early 2006, the four-story building recalls San Francisco's golden days. Walk under rich red draperies to the lavish "grand salon" lobby replete with English oak wainscoting and period antiques, and it feels like a different era. Guest rooms also contain a profusion of antiques—armoires, marble-top dressers, and other Victorian-era pieces. Some have corner turret bay windows that look out on tree-lined streets, as well as separate parlor areas and wet bars; others have cozy reading nooks and fireplaces. All rooms have phones and nice bath amenities in their marble-tiled bathrooms. Guests can relax in the parlor, with two fireplaces, or in the hotel library. If you don't mind staying outside the downtown area, this hotel is highly recommended and very classic San Francisco.

1590 Sutter St. (btw. Laguna and Webster sts.), San Francisco, CA 94115. www.queenanne.com. ⓒ **800/277-3970** or 415/441-2828. Fax 415/775-5212. 48 units. $110–$199 double; $169–$350 suite. Extra person $10. Rates include continental breakfast on weekday mornings, afternoon tea and sherry, and morning newspaper. AE, DC, DISC, MC, V. Parking $14. Bus: 2 or 3. **Amenities:** Concierge; access to nearby health club for $10. *In room:* TV, hair dryer, free Wi-Fi.

CIVIC CENTER

Gritty and unpretty, the Civic Center area's only fan base is clubbers looking to stay at the Phoenix Hotel.

Best For: Playing wannabe rock star at the Phoenix Hotel.

Drawbacks: Not the nicest part of town. Expect panhandlers, and take taxis after dark.

Moderate

The Phoenix Hotel ★★   If you'd like to tell your friends you stayed in the same hotel as David Bowie, Keanu Reeves, Moby, Franz Ferdinand, and Interpol, this is the place to go. On the fringes of San Francisco's aromatic Tenderloin District (rife with the homeless and addicts), this well-sheltered retro 1950s-style hotel is a gathering place for visiting rock musicians, writers, and filmmakers who crave a dose of Southern California—hence the palm trees and pastel colors. The focal point of the Palm Springs–style hotel is a small, heated outdoor pool adorned with a mural by artist Francis Forlenza and ensconced in a modern sculpture garden. Rooms are more pop than plush, with bright island-inspired furnishings and original local art; each faces the pool. If you want luxury and quiet, stay elsewhere, but if you're looking for a great scene, head to the Phoenix.

601 Eddy St (at Larkin St.), San Francisco, CA 94109. www.thephoenixhotel.com ℰ **800/248-9466** or 415/776-1380. Fax 415/885-3109. 44 units. $119–$149 double; $219–$399 suite. Rates include continental breakfast and free passes to Kabuki Springs & Spa. AE, DC, MC, V. Free parking. Bus: 19, 31, 38, or 47. **Amenities:** Bar; concierge; heated outdoor pool. *In room:* TV, VCR (upon request), fridge (some rooms), hair dryer, free Wi-Fi.

THE CASTRO

It's the Castro, so most accommodations (usually converted homes) cater to LGBT customers. But even breeders can have a lot of fun in this lively neighborhood.

Best For: Excellent nightlife and dining scene, great for people-watching and augmenting your sex toy collection.

Drawbacks: Minimal selection of hotel choices, far from city center, noise and crowds on Pride and holiday weekends.

Moderate

The Parker Guest House ★★   This is the best B&B option in the Castro, and one of the best in the entire city. In fact, even some of the better hotels could learn a thing or two from this fashionable, gay-friendly, 5,000-square-foot, 1909 beautifully restored Edwardian home and adjacent annex a few blocks from the heart of the Castro's action. Within the bright, cheery urban compound, period antiques abound. But thankfully, the spacious guest rooms are wonderfully updated with smart patterned furnishings, voice mail, robes, and spotless private bathrooms (plus amenities) en suite or, in two cases, across the hall. A fire burns nightly in the cozy living room, and guests are also welcome to make themselves at home in the wood-paneled common library (with fireplace and piano), sunny breakfast room overlooking the garden, and spacious garden with fountains and a steam room. Animal lovers will appreciate the companionship of the house pugs Porter and Pasty.

520 Church St. (btw. 17th and 18th sts.), San Francisco, CA 94114. www.parkerguesthouse.com. ℂ **888/520-7275** or 415/621-3??? Fax 415/621-4139. 21 units. $129–$199 double; $219 junior suite. Rates include extended continental breakfast and evening wine and cheese. AE, DISC, MC, V. Self-parking $17. Bus: 22 or 33. Streetcar: J Church. **Amenities:** Concierge; access to nearby health club. *In room:* TV, hair dryer, free Wi-Fi.

Inexpensive

Beck's Motor Lodge   In a town where DINK (double income, no kids) tourists happily spend fistfuls of money, you'd think someone would create a gay luxury hotel—or even a moderate hotel, for that matter. But absurdly, the most commercial and modern accommodations in the touristy Castro are in this run-of-the-mill motel. Standard but contemporary, the ultra-tidy rooms include low-Levitz furnishings, a sun deck overlooking upper Market Street's action, and free parking. ***But be warned:*** This is a party spot, popular with late-night party people and cruisers, and the staff can be brusque.

2222 Market St. (at 15th St.), San Francisco, CA 94114. www.becksmotorlodgesf.com. ℂ **800/ 227-4360** in the U.S., except CA, 800/955-2325 within CA or 415/621-8212. Fax 415/241-0435. 58 units. $93–$151 double. AE, DC, DISC, MC, V. Free parking. Bus: 37. Streetcar: F. *In room:* TV, fridge, free Wi-Fi.

Inn on Castro ★   One of the better choices in the Castro, half a block from all the action, this Edwardian-style inn is decorated with contemporary furnishings, original modern art, and fresh flowers throughout. It definitely feels more like a home than an inn, so if you like less commercial abodes, this place is for you. Most rooms share a small back patio, and the suite has a private entrance and outdoor sitting area. The inn also offers access to six individual nearby apartments ($155–$250) with complete kitchens. Note that rates include a full breakfast, and that the least expensive rooms share a bathroom.

321 Castro St. (at Market St.), San Francisco, CA 94114. www.innoncastro.com. ℂ **415/861-0321.** Fax 415/861-0321. 8 units, 2 with bathroom across the hall; 6 apts. $115–$185 double. Rates include full breakfast, evening brandy, and hall fridges stocked with free sodas and water. AE, DC, MC, V. Streetcar: F, K, L, or M. *In room:* Flatscreen TV, DVD/CD, hair dryer, free Wi-Fi.

The Willows Inn ★   Right in the heart of the Castro, the all-nonsmoking Willows Inn employs a staff eager to greet and attend to their mostly gay and lesbian guests. The country and antique willow furnishings don't strictly suit a 1903 Edwardian home, but everything's quite comfortable—especially considering the extras, which include an expanded continental breakfast (fresh fruit, yogurt, baked goods, gourmet coffee, eggs, and orange juice), the morning paper, nightly cocktails, a sitting room (with a DVD player), and a pantry with limited kitchen facilities. The homey rooms vary in size from large (queen-size bed) to smaller (double bed) and are priced accordingly. Each room has a vanity sink, and all the rooms share eight water closets and shower rooms.

710 14th St. (near Church and Market sts.), San Francisco, CA 94114. www.willowssf.com. ℂ **800/431-0277** or 415/431-4770. Fax 415/431-5295. 12 units, none with bathroom. $99–$140 double; $160 suite. Rates include continental breakfast. AE, DC, DISC, MC, V. Bus: 22 or 37. Streetcar: Church St. station (across the street) or F. *In room:* TV/VCR, fridge, free Wi-Fi.

HAIGHT-ASHBURY

San Francisco's summers of love are long gone, but open-minded folk who eschew touristy schlock and embrace eccentricity will dig the Haight.

Best For: Finding your inner hippie, eclectic array of shops and restaurants with plenty of visual stimulation, close to Golden Gate Park.

Drawbacks: "Got change?" Young squatters begging for change on Haight Street get old real fast.

Moderate

Red Victorian Bed, Breakfast & Art ★ 🎁   Still having flashbacks from the 1960s? Or want to? No problem. A room at the Red Vic, in the heart of the Haight, will throw you right back into the Summer of Love (minus, of course, the free-flowing LSD). Owner/artist Sami Sunchild has re-created this historic hotel and "Peace Center" as a living museum honoring the bygone era. The rooms are inspired by San Francisco's sights and history, and are decorated accordingly. The Flower Child Room has a sun on the ceiling and a rainbow on the wall, while the bed sports a hand-crocheted shawl headboard. The Peacock Suite, though pricey, is one funky room, with red beads, a canopy bed, and multicolored patterns throughout. The clincher is its bedroom bathtub, which has a circular pass-through looking into the sitting area. Four guest rooms have private bathrooms; the rest share four bathrooms down the hall. In general, the rooms and bathrooms are clean and the furnishings lighthearted. Rates for longer stays are a great deal. A family-style continental breakfast is a gathering place for a worldly array of guests, and there's a gift shop called the Meditation Room and Peace Center. Be sure to check out Sami's website to get a sneak peek at the weird and wonderful guest rooms.

1665 Haight St. (btw. Cole and Belvedere sts.), San Francisco, CA 94117. www.redvic.com. 📞 **415/864-1978.** Fax 415/863-3293. 18 units, 4 with private bathroom. $89–$99 double with shared bathroom; $129–$149 double with private bathroom; $229 suite. Rates include continental breakfast and afternoon tea. Lower rates for stays of 3 days or more. AE, DISC, MC, V. Guarded parking lot nearby. Metro: N line. Bus: 66 or 71. **Amenities:** Cafe.

Stanyan Park Hotel ★★ ☺ 🐾   The only real hotel on the east end of Golden Gate Park and the west end of funky-chic Haight Street, this small inn offers classic San Francisco–style living at a very affordable price. The Victorian structure, which has operated as a hotel under a variety of names since the turn of the 20th century and is on the National Register of Historic Places, offers good-size rooms all done in period decor. Its three stories are decorated with antique furnishings, Victorian wallpaper, and pastel quilts, curtains, and carpets. Families will appreciate the six one- and two-bedroom suites, each of which has a full kitchen and formal dining and living rooms and can sleep up to six comfortably. Tea is served each afternoon from 4 to 6pm. Continental breakfast is served in the dining room off the lobby from 6 to 10am. All rooms are nonsmoking.

750 Stanyan St. (at Waller St.), San Francisco, CA 94117. www.stanyanpark.com. 📞 **415/751-1000.** Fax 415/668-5454. 36 units. $139–$225 double; $275–$350 suite. Rates include continental breakfast and afternoon and evening tea service. Rollaway $20; cribs free. AE, DISC, MC, V. Off-site parking $14. Bus: 33, 43, 66, or 71. Streetcar: N. *In room:* TV, hair dryer, kitchen (in suites only), free Wi-Fi.

NEAR SAN FRANCISCO INTERNATIONAL AIRPORT

My grandmother always stayed at an airport hotel the night before she flew, and grandmothers always know best.

Best For: Business travelers or anyone with an early flight.

Drawbacks: A 30-minute BART ride away from the city center, with few dining options and zero nightlife.

Moderate

Embassy Suites ★   If you've stayed at an Embassy Suites before, you know the drill. But this hotel is one of the best airport options, if only for the fact that every room is a suite. But there is more: The property has an indoor pool, whirlpool, courtyard with fountain, palm trees, and bar/restaurant. Each tastefully decorated two-room suite has comfy linens and mattresses and nice additions such as two TVs. Additionally, a complimentary breakfast of your choice is available before you're whisked to the airport on the free shuttle—all that and the price is still right.

250 Gateway Blvd., South San Francisco, CA 94080. www.embassysuites.com. ⓒ **800/362-2779** or 650/589-3400. Fax 650/876-0305. 312 units. $139–$199 double. Rates include breakfast and free evening beverages. AE, DC, MC, V. Parking $15. **Amenities:** Restaurant; bar; free airport shuttle; Jacuzzi; indoor pool. *In room:* A/C, TV, fridge, hair dryer, Wi-Fi ($9.95 per day).

PRACTICAL INFORMATION
The Big Picture

Hunting for hotels in San Francisco can be a tricky business, particularly if you're not a seasoned traveler. What you don't know—and the reservations agent may not tell you—could very well ruin your vacation, so keep the following pointers in mind when it comes time to book a room:

- Prices listed in this chapter do not include state and city taxes, which together total 14%. Other hidden extras include parking fees, which can be up to $50 per day (also subject to 14% tax!), and hefty surcharges—up to $1 per local call—for telephone use.

- San Francisco is Convention City, so if you want a room at a particular hotel during high season (summer, for example), book well in advance.

- Be sure to have a credit card in hand when making a reservation, and know that you may be asked to pay for at least 1 night in advance. (This doesn't happen often, though.)

- Hotels usually hold reservations until 6pm. If you don't tell the staff you're arriving late, you might lose your room.

- Almost every hotel in San Francisco requires a credit card imprint for "incidentals" (and to prevent walkouts). If you don't have a credit card, be sure to make special arrangements with the management before you hang up the phone, and make a note of the name of the person with whom you spoke.

- When you check in, if your room isn't up to snuff, politely inform the front desk of your dissatisfaction and ask for another. If the hotel can accommodate you, they almost always will—and sometimes will even upgrade you!

Getting the Best Deal

Many hotels offer rooms at rates above and below the price category that applies to most of the units. If you like the sound of a place that's a bit over your budget, it never hurts to call and ask a few questions. Also note that these reviews do not list single rates. Some hotels, particularly more affordable choices, do charge lower rates for singles, so inquire about them if you are traveling alone.

San Francisco is a popular destination year-round, so although there are bargains available, rooms here will still seem expensive compared to those in many other U.S. destinations. Still, you should always ask about weekend discounts, corporate rates, and family plans. Most larger hotels, and many smaller ones, offer them, but many reservations agents don't mention them unless you ask about them specifically.

You'll find nonsmoking rooms available in all larger hotels and many smaller hotels; reviews indicate establishments that are entirely nonsmoking. Nowadays, the best advice for smokers is to confirm a smoking-permitted room in advance, and if there's a special cleaning charge per night.

Although you'll find that most accommodations have an abundance of amenities (including phones, unless otherwise noted), don't be alarmed by the lack of air-conditioned guest rooms. San Francisco's weather is so mild, you'll hardly ever need it.

Most larger hotels can accommodate guests who use wheelchairs and those who have other special needs. Ask when you make a reservation to ensure that your hotel can accommodate your needs, especially if you are interested in a bed-and-breakfast.

When booking a room in a chain hotel, call the hotel's local line and the toll-free number and see where you get the best deal. A hotel makes nothing on a room that stays empty. The clerk who runs the place is more likely to know about vacancies than someone from the toll-free number and will often grant deep discounts in order to fill up rooms.

Reservation Services

Having reservations about your reservations? Leave it up to the pros: **San Francisco Reservations** (✆ **800/677-1570**; www.hotelres.com) arranges reservations for more than 150 of San Francisco's hotels and often offers discounted rates. Their website allows Internet users to make reservations online. Another great local source for discounted rates is **LocalGetaways.com**.

The **San Francisco Convention & Visitors Bureau** also provides an online source for booking hotels, tickets, and packages at www.onlyinsanfrancisco.com.

Alternative Accommodations

An alternative to booking a room at a hotel is to swap homes or apartments. House/apartment-swapping is becoming a more popular and viable means of travel; you stay in their place, they stay in yours, and you both get an authentic and personal view of the area, the opposite of the escapist retreat that many hotels offer. It's usually done by online classified ads at such sites as **HomeExchange.com**, **HomeLink** (Homelink.org), and **Craigslist.org** (www.sfbay.craigslist.org/swp).

Hostels

Though you sometimes get what you pay for at a hostel, at their best they can be homey places where you meet nice people, get great information, and get a free or very inexpensive breakfast.

If you haven't stayed at a hostel, here's what you can expect: Most offer shared rooms (either same sex or mixed; HI hostels have only single-sex dorm rooms) with shared bathrooms, usually for less than (sometimes a *lot* less than) $50 a night; prices can vary by season. Some hostels offer private rooms for one, two, or three people, or en-suite bathrooms, with the price going up accordingly, though top end for private rooms is still usually well under $100.

HI hostels offer free breakfast; the **Green Tortoise** (*©* **415/834-1000;** www.greentortoise.com) offers free breakfast and free dinner 3 nights a week. Most hostels have a communal kitchen/dining area, free Wi-Fi, a lounge, lockers or other locked storage, and free or low-cost organized activities, ranging from local tours, movies, and pub-crawls, to day or overnight trips. The staff members are usually pretty good at helping you plan individual activities based on your interests. Many hostels also offer free or discount airport/train station/bus station pickup, if you're arriving without a car.

There are several recommendable (and *non*-recommendable) places in San Francisco, both HI hostels, and private hostels or "backpackers." You can count on clean, safe, and well-managed properties with a Hostelling International hostel, all of which are part of an international nonprofit that "promote[s] international understanding of the world and its people through hostelling." You don't have to be a member of HI to stay, but you do get a slight discount if you are a member.

There are three HI hostels in San Francisco proper (in city center, downtown, and Fisherman's Wharf), and several more within public transit or driving distance if you're looking for a cheap overnight trip.

For information on how to join **Hostelling International USA** (which also gives you membership in all international HI hostels), visit www.hiusa.org. Membership is free if you're 17 or under, $28 annually for people 18 to 54. As a member, you can make prepaid reservations at HI hostels, and you're eligible for a lot of discounts, from long-distance calling to bus travel to organized tours.

Private hostels can be just as inexpensive, and sometimes more laid-back than HI places. You may stay in a coed dorm room, find a bar on the premises, or see a bulletin board offering rides or temp jobs. You may find a noisier, more partying crowd at a backpacker, which could be a plus or minus, depending on what you're looking for.

You'll find a comprehensive listing of hostels, both HI and backpacker (as well as budget hotels and guesthouses), at www.hostels.com, which claims to list "every hostel, everywhere." The website gives properties a "satisfaction rating," based on user reviews (which you can read). Granted, like most Internet reviews, they can be artificially inflated, but you can at least get an idea of what to expect, and if you like it, make reservations through that website, or go directly to the hostel's site.

In addition to the hostels listed in this chapter (HI and Green Tortoise, above, as well as Elements, p. 85), some of the other top-rated hostels in the San Francisco area at press time include:

- **Pacific Tradewinds Backpacker Hostel,** 680 Sacramento St. (www.pac tradewinds.com; *©* **888/SFHOSTEL** [734-6783]), was selected as the number-one hostel in the USA by Hostelworld.com in 2007. Prices start at $26 per night ($23 if booked online), in coed dorms. BART: Montgomery Street; Bus: 1, 10, or 41.

o **USA Hostels San Francisco,** 711 Post St. (www.usahostels.com; ℂ **877/ 483-2950**), features an "all you can make" pancake breakfast daily, a game room, and an on-site laundry. Rates start from $25 ($24 if booked online) for single-sex and coed dorms, and they also offer private rooms with bathroom starting at $75 ($72 online). BART: Powell Street.

o The **Dakota Hostel,** 606 Post St. (ℂ **415/931-7475**), and the **Adelaide Hostel and Hotel,** 5 Isadora Duncan Lane, at Post and Taylor streets (www. adelaidehostel.com; ℂ **877/359-1915**), are owned by the same management and located near each other, though the Dakota gets warmer reviews on Hostels.com. In a landmark 1914 building, the Dakota's rooms all have private bathrooms, with rates ranging from $28 and up for a four-bed room, to $75 and up for a single room. The Adelaide offers both single-sex and coed dorm rooms from $23, and single, twin, and double en-suite rooms starting from $45 to $75. BART: Powell Street.

4

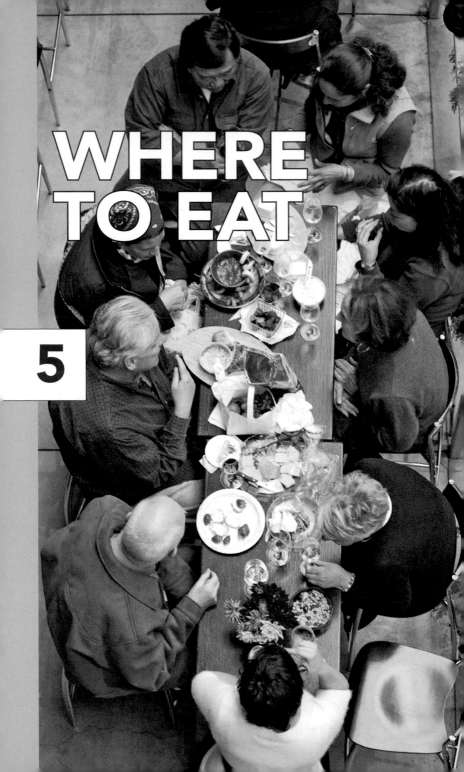

WHERE TO EAT

5

For more than a decade, the readers of *Bon Appétit* magazine have named San Francisco their top city for dining out. And for good reason—with more than 3,500 restaurants offering cuisines from around the globe, San Francisco has more restaurants per capita than any other city in the United States.

San Francisco also attracts some of the world's most talented chefs, drawn not only to the creative freedom that has always defined San Francisco's culinary scene, but also to the year round access to Northern California's unparalleled abundance of organic produce, seafood, free-range meats, and wine.

Afghan, Cajun, Burmese, Moroccan, Persian, Cambodian, Basque, vegan—whatever you're in the mood for, this town has it covered, which is why more San Franciscans eat out than any other city's residents in the U.S. All you need to join America's largest dinner party is an adventurous palate, because half the fun of visiting San Francisco is sampling a dish you've never heard of, from a country you've never been to—and then doing it all over again.

THE BEST RESTAURANT BETS

o **Best Hotel Restaurant: Ame,** 689 Mission St. (© 415/284-4040), located in the swank St. Regis Hotel, means "rain" in Japanese. But the only drops you'll see coming down here are tears of joy from local foodies who no longer have to drive to St. Helena to enjoy a meal by Hiro Sone, James Beard Award winner and master of Japanese, French, and Italian cuisine. See p. 119.

o **Best for Impressing Clients:** Show your business associates you've got class—and know what's hip with the foodies these days—by reserving a table at the Financial District's **Wayfare Tavern,** 558 Sacramento St. (© 415/772-9060). See p. 117.

o **Best Romantic Spot:** Anyone who loves classic French cooking will be seduced at **Fleur de Lys,** 777 Sutter St. (© 415/673-7779), under the rich burgundy-tented canopy that swathes the elegant room in romance. There's lots of question-popping here, too. See p. 108.

o **Best for a Celebration:** Great food, a full bar, and a lively atmosphere are the key ingredients that make **Boulevard,** 1 Mission St. (© 415/543-6084), the place to celebrate. See p. 120. Or celebrate Latino-style with pitchers of sangria at Haight-Ashbury's **Cha Cha Cha,** 1801 Haight St. (© 415/386-7670). See p. 161.

o **Best Decor:** Celeb restaurant designer Pat Kuleto spent a week sketching sea life at the Monterey Bay Aquarium before applying his genius to whimsical **Farallon,** 450 Post St. (© 415/956-6969). See p. 108. A glass "caviar" chandelier sets the tone for Kuleto's equally spectacular **Waterbar,** 399 Embarcadero (© 415/284-9922), and at **Grand Café,** 501 Geary St. (© 415/292-0101), he marries old-world European elegance with Art Nouveau glamour. See p. 122 and 109.

PREVIOUS PAGE: **The Ferry Building offers terrific dining options in addition to its food stalls and Farmers' Markets.**

Price Categories

The restaurants listed below are classified first by area, then by price, using the following categories: **Very Expensive,** dinner from $75 per person; **Expensive,** dinner from $50 per person; **Moderate,** dinner from $35 per person; and **Inexpensive,** dinner less than $35 per person. These categories reflect prices for an appetizer, main course, dessert, and glass of wine.

---

o **Best Dim Sum:** Downtown and Chinatown dim sum restaurants may be more centrally located, but that's all they've got on **Ton Kiang,** 5821 Geary Blvd. (☏ **415/387-8273**), where carts bring the best Chinese dumplings and other dim sum delicacies to your table. See p. 165.

o **Best Vegetarian Food:** For excellent farm-fresh food and an equally stunning view of the Golden Gate, go to **Greens,** Building A, Fort Mason Center (☏ **415/771-6222**). See p. 142. Also check out **Millennium,** 580 Geary St. (☏ **415/345-3900**), which makes vegan seem positively decadent. See p. 112.

o **Best Cafe:** If you want to know what life was like before Starbucks, spend some time at North Beach's beloved **Mario's Bohemian Cigar Store,** 566 Columbus Ave. (☏ **415/362-0536**), and **Caffe Trieste,** 601 Vallejo St. (☏ **415/392-6739**). See p. 186.

o **Best Food Truck Sampling:** Food truck fans, we have found your Utopia, and it is called **Off the Grid,** a daily roving food court of trucks. Go to http://offthegridsf.com for locations and participants. On Most Fridays you can sample nearly 30 vendors, 5 to 10pm at Fort Mason Center.

UNION SQUARE

For a map of restaurants in this section, see the "Union Square Area Restaurants" map on p. 109.

Very Expensive

Bourbon Steak ★★★ STEAKHOUSE Michael Mina's eponymous restaurant moved out of the Westin St. Francis and up the road a few blocks (and eventually closed in 2010), and the first California outpost of his famous steakhouse brand moved in. The new restaurant is more casual and less stuffy than before (with the same great service and cuisine) and also boasts a roomy lounge for those just wanting to stop in for a cocktail and dessert. All diners are treated to a complimentary tray of three kinds of duck fat fries served with three dipping sauces once they order. As expected, the steak options will knock your socks

Fine dining on the sidewalk at Market and Sutter streets. Find this cart and nearly 30 other food trucks Friday nights at Off the Grid, Fort Mason Center.

DINING ONLINE RESOURCES

- Want to book your reservations online? Go to **Open Table** (www.opentable.com), where you can reserve seats in real time.

- For local food blogs, Grub Street (http://sanfrancisco.grubstreet.com) posts daily updates, and Marcia Gagliardi's **Tablehopper** (www.tablehopper.com) posts smart, gourmand observations every Tuesday and Friday.

- While Los Angeles has It celebrities, San Francisco has It restaurants; to see what's hot during your visit (it may or may not stay hot), check **SF Eater's Heatmap** (http:sf.eater.com/tags/heat-map), updated monthly by popularity. A few of the restaurants that are listed as we go to print: **Plum**; **Commonwealth**; **Sons & Daughters**; **Locanda**, 557 Valencia Street (✆ 415/863-6800; www.locandasf.com); and **Nojo**, at 231 Franklin St. (✆ 415/896-4587; www.nojosf.com).

- For an epic culinary scavenger hunt, or simply more dining ideas, see **7x7 Magazine's "The Big Eat 2012: 100 Things To Try Before You Die"** (www.7x7.com/eat-drink/big-eat-2012-list). The list singles out specific dishes like Soft Garlic Pretzel bites ($8) at **Absinthe** (p. 147); the Salt Cod Fried Rice ($10) at wildly popular **Mission Chinese Food**, at 2234 Mission St. (✆ 415/863-2800; www.missionchinesefood.com); a few

tasting-menu-only items like the Faux Shark's Fin Soup (course 16 of 18 on an extravagant $180 tasting menu) at **Benu**, at 22 Hawthorne St. in SOMA (✆ 415/685-4860; www.benusf.com); and a few items with limited availability like the Duck and Sausage Jambalaya, only served Thursdays at **Boxing Room**, at 399 Grove St. (✆ 415/430-6590; www.boxingroomsf.com).

- If you really want to nosh like a tech-savvy local, download the **Foodspotting** mobile app (www.foodspotting.com), which lets you photograph and tag your favorite foods. Look for 7x7's "Big Eat" list (and other lists within the app), and tag their recommended items as you eat them. You can also search for dishes others have tagged at restaurants near you to see what looks appetizing.

- For food trucks, your best bet is **Off the Grid**, a daily gathering of a half dozen or so trucks, usually 11am to 2pm, occasionally with live music. Check www.offthegrid.com for locations. Otherwise, **Roaming Hunger** (http://roaminghunger.com) lists locations of food trucks, based on their Twitter feeds.

- Vegetarians and won't have trouble finding dishes on a typical menu here, and you'll find restaurants marked "vegetarian" throughout this chapter. For vegan eats, consult **Vegansaurus** (http://vegansaurus.com).

off, from the 14-ounce New York strip to the 8-ounce Snake Rivers Farms Rib Cap, the highest ticketed item on the menu. If steak isn't your thing, try the cioppino, a San Francisco specialty, or the classic lobster potpie. Sides are served family style; you'd do yourself a favor to try the black truffle mac and cheese or hubbard squash risotto. Be sure and save room for Mina's signature dessert, though: The root beer float features homemade sassafras ice cream and root beer sorbet sipped out of chocolate straws, with fresh-baked cookies served on the side.

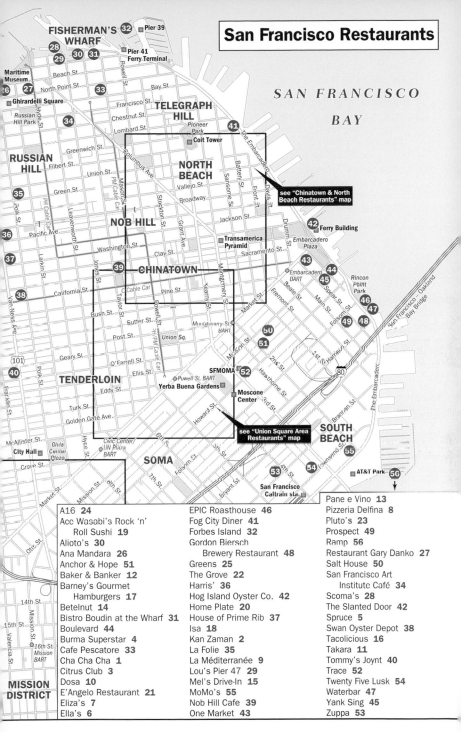

San Francisco Restaurants

FISHERMAN'S WHARF **32** ■ Pier 39

■ Pier 41 Ferry Terminal

28
29 **30** **31**

Maritime Museum

6 **27** North Point St.

Beach St.

Bay St.

33

■ Ghirardelli Square

Russian Hill Park

34

Francisco St.

Chestnut St.

Lombard St.

TELEGRAPH HILL

Pioneer Park

■ Coit Tower

41

SAN FRANCISCO

BAY

RUSSIAN HILL

Greenwich St.

Filbert St.

Union St.

35

Green St.

NORTH BEACH

Vallejo St.

Broadway

see "Chinatown & North Beach Restaurants" map

NOB HILL

Jackson St.

36

Pacific Ave.

■ Transamerica Pyramid

42 ■ Ferry Building

37

Washington St.

Clay St.

Sacramento St.

Embarcadero Plaza

43

California St.

39 CHINATOWN

● Embarcadero BART

44 Rincon Point Park

45

38

Pine St.

46

47

Bush St.

Sutter St.

Montgomery St. BART

Post St.

Union Sq.

49 **48**

50

51

SFMOMA **52**

Geary St.

O'Farrell St.

Ellis St.

● Powell St. BART

TENDERLOIN

Eddy St.

Yerba Buena Gardens ■

Moscone Center

(101)

40

Turk St.

Golden Gate Ave.

see "Union Square Area Restaurants" map

SOUTH BEACH

55

McAllister St.

Civic Center/
UN Plaza
BART

City Hall Civic Center Plaza

Grove St.

SOMA

53 **54** Townsend St.

■ AT&T Park **56**

San Francisco Caltrain sta.

MISSION DISTRICT

335 Powell St. (at Geary St.). ℂ **415/397-3003.** www.michaelmina.net. Reservations recommended. Main courses $16–$72. AE, DC, DISC, MC, V. Sun–Thurs 5:30–10pm; Fri–Sat 5:30–10:30pm. Bus: 6, 9, 21, 30, 31, 45, 71, or 91. Streetcar: F. BART: Powell.

Farallon ★ SEAFOOD   Although this seafood restaurant is hands-down the most whimsical with its stunning oceanic fantasy decor, the high price tag, and fine, but not mind-blowing, food make it a better cocktail-and-appetizer stop than dinner choice. The multimillion-dollar attraction's outrageous decor follows the "coastal" cuisine theme; handblown jellyfish lamps, kelp bedlike backlit columns, glass clamshells, sea-urchin light fixtures, a sea-life mosaic floor, and a tentacle-encircled bar set the scene. (Thankfully, designer Pat Kuleto's impressive renovation of the 1924 building left the original Gothic arches intact.)

Executive chef Mark Franz, who opened the once-famous restaurant Stars with Jeremiah Tower, orchestrates the cuisine. He offers starters ranging from the expected (a variety of very expensive oysters) to the more ambitious (grilled Quinault River steelhead with seared squid, cannellini beans, and house-made chorizo)—with a few meat and game items stuck in for good measure. The whimsy-meets-sophistication extends only as far as the food—the service and wine lists (more than 400 by the bottle; 30 by the glass) are seriously professional. Personally, I prefer a bite and a drink at the bar. Go for their "Six Until Seven" happy hour, 4:30 to 7pm, for $6 plates: 6 oysters, crab cakes, truffle fries, and more.

450 Post St. (btw. Mason and Powell sts., adjoining the Kensington Park Hotel). ℂ **415/956-6969.** www.farallonrestaurant.com. Reservations recommended. Pretheater 3-course prix-fixe dinner menu $45; main courses $35–$42 dinner. AE, DC, DISC, MC, V. Mon–Thurs 5:30–9:30pm; Fri–Sat 5:30–10pm; Sun 5–9:30pm. Valet parking $12. Bus: 2, 3, or 38.

Fleur de Lys ★★ FRENCH   Fleur de Lys is the city's most traditional and formal classic French affair. Draped in 900 yards of rich patterned fabric mood-lit with dim French candelabras and accented with an extraordinary sculptural floral centerpiece, this restaurant is a romantic spot, so long as your way of wooing includes donning a dinner jacket, which is "appreciated" but not required. Equally formal is the cuisine of chef Hubert Keller (former president Clinton's first guest chef at the White House), who manages to divide his time between here and his operation in Las Vegas, while simultaneously writing cookbooks and starring in PBS television shows. Three-, four-, and five-course tasting menus allow diners to sample a variety of items. Best bet is to start with the "Symphony" appetizer, a culinary medley with bite-size samplings of roasted beet and anchovies, pistachio-crusted foie gras, Maine lobster tartare, and butternut squash vichyssoise. Other sure things include radicchio-wrapped salmon with cannellini beans and Banyuls vinegar and

You'll feast first with your eyes at Fleur de Lys.

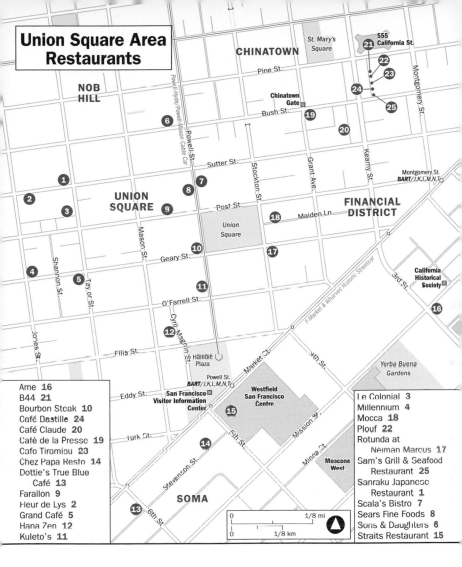

Union Square Area Restaurants

CHINATOWN

St. Mary's Square

555 California St.

NOB HILL

Chinatown Gate

UNION SQUARE

Union Square

FINANCIAL DISTRICT

Montgomery St.
BART/J,K,L,M,N,T

Powell-Hyde/Powell-Mason Cable Car

California Historical Society

F-Market & Wharves Historic Streetcar

Hallidie Plaza

Powell St.
BART/J,K,L,M,N,T

San Francisco Visitor Information Center

Westfield San Francisco Centre

Yerba Buena Gardens

SOMA

Moscone West

Ame **16**
B44 **21**
Bourbon Steak **10**
Café Bastille **24**
Café Claude **20**
Café de la Presse **19**
Café Tiramisu **23**
Chez Papa Resto **14**
Dottie's True Blue Café **13**
Farallon **9**
Fleur de Lys **2**
Grand Café **5**
Hana Zen **12**
Kuleto's **11**

Le Colonial **3**
Millennium **4**
Mocca **18**
Plouf **22**
Rotunda at Neiman Marcus **17**
Sam's Grill & Seafood Restaurant **25**
Sanraku Japanese Restaurant **1**
Scala's Bistro **7**
Sears Fine Foods **8**
Sons & Daughters **6**
Straits Restaurant **15**

0   1/8 mi
0   1/8 km

olive oil; and lamb loin with roasted potato stew, whole-grain mustard, and honey and red-wine reduction. The selection of some 700 French, California, and Northwestern wines is also impressive.

777 Sutter St. (at Jones St.). ☎ **415/673-7779.** www.fleurdelyssf.com. Reservations required. 3-course menu $70; 4-course $77; 5-course $88; vegetarian tasting menu $68. Vegan option available with advance notice. AE, DC, MC, V. Tues–Thurs 6–9:30pm; Fri 5:30–10pm; Sat 5–10pm. Valet parking $13. Bus: 2, 3, 27, or 38.

Expensive

Grand Café ★ FRENCH   If you aren't interested in exploring restaurants beyond those in Union Square and want a huge dose of atmosphere with your seared salmon, Grand Café is your best bet. Its claims to fame? The grandest dining room in San Francisco, an enormous 156-seat, turn-of-the-20th-century ballroomlike dining oasis that combines the sensibilities of Art Nouveau with a Parisian train station. To match the surroundings, the menu features such extravagant French-inspired California dishes as *carre d'agneau á la forestiere* (Sonoma rack of lamb crusted with herbed mixed vegetable *tian,* in wild mushroom and pearl onion sauce) or *cassolette de la mer* (lobster tail, prawns, sea bass, mussels, little neck clams, and savoy cabbage in tomato Pastis lobster broth). You can also drop by for a lighter meal or an après-theater drink in the more casual bar, which offers similar dishes for about half the price. There's also a wonderful selection of small-batch American whiskeys and single-malt Scotches.

501 Geary St. (at Taylor St., adjacent to the Hotel Monaco). ✆ **415/292-0101.** www.grandcafe-sf. com. Reservations recommended. Main courses $18–$33. AE, DC, DISC, MC, V. Mon–Fri 7–10:30am and 11:30am–2:30pm; Sat–Sun 8am–2:30pm; Fri–Sat 5:30–11pm; Sun–Thurs 5:30–10pm. Valet parking free at brunch, $15 for 3 hr. at dinner, $3 each additional half-hour. Bus: 2, 3, 27, or 38.

Le Colonial ★ VIETNAMESE   Viet-chic environs and quality French Vietnamese food make this an excellent choice for folks who want to nosh at one of the sexiest restaurants in town. Picture slowly spinning ceiling fans, tropical plants, rattan furniture, and French colonial decor. The upstairs lounge (which opens at 4:30pm) is where romance reigns, with cozy couches, seductive surroundings, and a well-dressed cocktail crowd of post-work professionals who nosh on coconut-crusted crab cakes and Vietnamese spring rolls. In the tiled downstairs dining room and along the stunning heated front patio, guests savor the vibrant flavors of coconut curry with black tiger prawns, mangos, eggplant, and Asian basil and tender wok-seared beef tenderloin with watercress onion salad.

20 Cosmo Place (off Taylor St., btw. Post and Sutter sts.). ✆ **415/931-3600.** www.lecolonialsf. com. Reservations recommended. Main courses $20–$38. AE, DC, MC, V. Sun–Wed 5:30–10pm; Thurs–Sat 5:30–11pm; brunch Sat–Sun 11:30am–2:30pm. Public valet parking $10 1st 3 hr., $2 each additional half-hour. Bus: 2, 3, or 27.

Perbacco ★★ ITALIAN   Stockholm native Staffan Terje makes some of the best Italian food in town, and he's not afraid to push the limits for what cuts of meat he puts on his outstanding, oft-changing menu. You'll find better known traditional items such as braised beef short ribs, whole-roasted rabbit and a variety of well-prepared seafood, but the more adventurous can explore poached veal tongue, blood sausage, and sweetbreads. (Terje is committed to using the whole animal.) The menu is wide and varying; be sure to start with something from the lengthy selection of house-made salumis and cured meats, small plates of delicate pastas, or the outstanding *fritto misto* with shrimp, fennel, and olives—all great for sharing. Finish it all off with a selection of cheeses, some hazelnut cookies, and a glass of grappa. For a more casual (and less expensive) meal, visit the newly opened trattoria **Barbacco** (see below) right next door.

230 California St. (btw. Battery and Front sts.). ✆ **415/955-0663.** www.perbaccosf.com. Reservations recommended. Main courses $15–$28. AE, DC, DISC, MC, V. Mon–Fri 11:30am–10pm; Sat 5:30–10pm. Valet parking $10. Train: F, J, K, L, M, or N to Embarcadero. See map p. 129.

Moderate

Barbacco ★★ ITALIAN   If the much-touted Perbacco (see above) is out of your price range, drop into this more casual cousin of the popular Italian eatery.

Barbacco is all about small plates—lots of 'em—with an emphasis on flavor-packed house-made cured meats, bruschette, pastas, salads, and sandwiches. Favorites include *ascolane* (pork-stuffed fried olives), farm eggs (so fresh, their yolks are brilliant orange) broiled in a skillet with *nduja* and *rapini,* and *polpette* (perfect little pork meatballs with raisins, pine nuts, and chard). It's inspired by the urban street food scene in cities throughout Italy, so think portability. Hours for calling in for carry-out are 8am to 2pm. *Tip:* Enjoy a most excellent picnic lunch or a private dinner in your hotel room—without the exorbitant cost of room service. See map p. 129.

220 California St. (btw. Battery and Front sts.). ℂ **415/955-1919.** www.barbaccosf.com. Reservations recommended. Small plates $3–$14. AE, DC, DISC, MC, V. Mon–Fri 11:30am–3pm; Mon–Sat 5–10pm. Carry-out available. Valet parking $10. Train: F, K, L, M, J, or N to Embarcadero.

Bocadillos ★★ 🏫 SPANISH/BASQUE TAPAS   The sister to Piperade (p. 131) is flat-out fabulous if you're in the mood for tapas or Spanish-influenced small plates and a seat at the communal table. Executive chef Gerald Hirigoyen celebrates his Basque roots with outstanding offerings such as warm octopus with confit potatoes and piquillos, scallops *"mole cortado"* with sherry and orange, cold poached foie gras with calamari and grape *salpicon,* and astounding warm chocolate cake with sautéed bananas. Just watch your budget—at up to $12 per plate the tab can creep up on you. You might also want to check out their breakfast, which includes baked eggs with chorizo and manchego cheese. Don't come anticipating a formal dining environment or a cocktail: This small Financial District space is cafe-casual and serves beer and wine only.

710 Montgomery St. (at Washington St.). ℂ **415/982-2622.** www.bocasf.com. Breakfast items $2–$6; lunch and dinner small items $7–$15. AE, DC, DISC, MC, V. Mon–Fri 7am–10pm; Sat 5–10pm. Closed Sun. Bus. 30X or 41. See map p. 129.

Café Claude ★ FRENCH   Euro transplants love Café Claude, a crowded and lively restaurant tucked into a narrow (and very European-feeling) side street near Union Square. Seemingly everything—every table, spoon, saltshaker, waiter—is imported from France (on my last visit they even imported some of that famous French *l'attitude*). With prices topping out at about $27 (and most dishes well under that), the bistro features classics like steak tartare; steamed mussels; duck confit; escargot; coq au vin; and the always-fashionable croque-monsieur and -madame. There's live jazz on Thursdays, Fridays, and Saturdays from 7:30 to 10:30pm, and atmospheric sidewalk seating is available when the weather permits.

7 Claude Lane (off Sutter St.). ℂ **415/392-3505.** www.cafeclaude.com. Reservations recommended. Main courses $8–$12 lunch; $14–$27 dinner. AE, DC, DISC, MC, V. Mon–Sat 11:30am–10:30pm; Sun 5:30–10:30pm. Bus: 30. Cable car: Powell–Mason line.

Hana Zen ★ 🏫 JAPANESE   Even most locals don't know about this Japanese restaurant, mistaking it for just another touristy sushi bar. Sure, they serve good sushi, but what makes this place special is the yakitori bar, which cranks out savory skewered and grilled meats and veggies cooked over 500-degree charcoal that we can never seem to get enough of. It's all prepared Benihana style, with acrobatic chefs whirling knives around and making lots of *"hai!,"* "ahhh," and "ooohh" sounds. Our favorite dishes are the asparagus spears wrapped in thinly sliced pork, and the grilled marinated shiitake mushrooms. A few tables are perched beside windows overlooking downtown, but the best seats are at the long, arched yakitori bar, where deft chefs spear together nearly 30 versions of the meal on a stick. You can order either one pair at a time if you like the show, or all at once for a feast; about a half-dozen make a meal. The terminally indecisive can opt for the Yakitori Dinner Set for $32, which makes an interesting meal for two.

115 Cyril Magnin St. (at Ellis St.). ✆ **415/421-2101.** www.hanazenrestaurant.com. Sushi/yakitori items $5–$10. AE, DC, MC, V. Daily 11:30am–4:30pm; Sun–Thurs 5pm–midnight; Fri–Sat 5pm–1am. Bus: 27 or 38.

Kuleto's ★ ITALIAN   Kuleto's is one of downtown's Italian darlings. Muscle your way into a seat at the antipasto bar or at the chef's counter overlooking the kitchen and fill up on Italian specialties and selections from the wine list featuring 30 by-the-glass options. Partake in the likes of penne pasta drenched in tangy lamb-sausage marinara sauce, clam linguine (generously overloaded with fresh clams), or any of the grilled fresh-fish specials in the casually refined dining room. If you don't arrive by 6pm, expect to wait—this place fills up fast. Not to worry, though; you can always cross the hotel lobby to the wine bar, which also serves the full menu and is open from 6 to 10pm daily.

In the Villa Florence Hotel, 221 Powell St. (btw. Geary and O'Farrell sts.). ✆ **415/397-7720.** www.kuletos.com. Reservations recommended. Breakfast $5–$15; main courses $16–$37. AE, DC, DISC, MC, V. Mon–Fri 7–10:30am; Sat–Sun 8–10:30am; Sun–Thurs 11:30am–10:30pm; Fri–Sat 11:30am–11pm. Bus: 2, 3, or 38. Streetcar: All streetcars. Cable car: Powell–Mason or Powell–Hyde line.

Millennium ★★ VEGAN   Chef Eric Tucker and his band of merry waiters led the charge on the sustainable, farm-to-table food movement and proved early on that a meatless menu doesn't mean you have to sacrifice taste. In a narrow, handsome, Parisian-style dining room with checkered tile flooring, French windows, and sponge-painted walls, Millennium has had nothing but favorable reviews for its egg-, butter-, and dairy-free creations since the day it opened. Favorites include Balinese-style salt-and-pepper-crusted oyster mushrooms with blood orange chili jam, and main courses such as truffled potato Wellington stuffed with shiitake mushroom *duxelles* served with spring onion and lentil *sugo,* seared asparagus, blood orange, and capers; or *masala dosa,* a lentil rice crepe with South Indian chickpea and red chard curry, sweet and spicy papaya chutney, and mint *raita.* All the wine selections are organic.

In the Hotel California, 580 Geary St. (at Jones St.). ✆ **415/345-3900.** www.millennium restaurant.com. Reservations recommended. Main courses $20–$24. AE, DC, DISC, MC, V. Sun–Thurs 5:30–9:30pm; Fri–Sat 5:30–10pm. Bus: 38. Streetcar: All Muni lines. BART: Powell St.

Rotunda at Neiman Marcus ★ AMERICAN   For decades, this has been *the* hobnobbing spot for ladies who lunch and the men who shlep along with them. Set in the round beneath the stained-glass dome inside Neiman Marcus, the restaurant affords splendid views of Union Square and downtown, and offers such fashionable favorites as lobster club sandwiches, classic chicken salad, and wild mushroom tart. Bring your white gloves for Afternoon Tea, an elaborate affair involving cookies, finger sandwiches, and scones with Devonshire cream and jam.

150 Stockton St. (at Geary St.). ✆ **415/249-2720.** Reservations accepted. Main courses $16–$28. AE, MC, V. Mon–Thurs 11am–4pm; Fri–Sat 11am–5pm; Sun noon–4pm. Bus: All Union Square buses.

Scala's Bistro ★★ FRENCH/ITALIAN   Firmly entrenched at the base of the refurbished Sir Francis Drake hotel, this downtown favorite blends Italian bistro and old-world atmosphere with jovial and bustling results. Offering just the right balance of elegance and informality, this is a perfect place to stop in for a late-night bite. Of the tempting array of Italian and French dishes, it's de rigueur to start with the "Earth and Surf" calamari appetizer with grilled portobello mushrooms. Golden beet salad and garlic cream mussels are also good bets. Generous portions of moist, rich duck-leg confit will satisfy hungry appetites, but if you can order only one thing, make it Scala's signature dish: seared salmon. Resting on a bed of creamy buttermilk mashed potatoes and accented with a tomato, chive, and white-wine sauce, it's downright delicious. Finish with Bostini cream pie, a dreamy combo of vanilla custard and orange chiffon cake with a warm chocolate glaze.

In the Sir Francis Drake hotel, 432 Powell St. (at Sutter St.). ✆ **415/395-8555.** www.scalasbistro. com. Reservations recommended. Breakfast $7–$10; main courses $12–$30 lunch and dinner. AE, DC, DISC, MC, V. Daily 8–10:30am and 11:30am–midnight. Bus: 2, 3, 30, 45, or 76. Cable car: Powell–Hyde line.

Straits Restaurant ★ SINGAPOREAN   Straits is the place to go if you're in the mood for an adventure in Asian-inspired dining. We're huge fans of chef Chris Yeo's spicy Malaysian-Indian-Chinese offerings, such as *murtabak* (stuffed Indian bread), chili crab, basil chicken, *nonya daging rendang* (beef simmered in lime leaves), *ikan panggang* (banana leaf–wrapped barbecued salmon with chili paste), and, hottest of all, his green curry (prawns, scallops, and mussels simmered in a jalapeño-based curry). The stylish restaurant—practically glowing with its profusion of polished woods, stainless-steel accents, and gleaming open kitchen—is located on the fourth floor of the fancy Westfield Centre (right above Bloomingdale's, in fact), so you can squeeze in an afternoon of power shopping before your culinary adventure begins.

Westfield San Francisco Centre, 845 Market St., Ste. 597. ✆ **415/668-1783.** www.straits restaurants.com. Reservations recommended. Main courses $10–$34. AE, DC, MC, V. Sun–Thurs 11am–9pm; Fri–Sat 11am–10pm. Bus: 2, 3, or 38.

Inexpensive

Café de la Presse FRENCH/AMERICAN   Parisians will find this 1930s-style French bistro and international newsstand comfortingly familiar. But you needn't hail from across the pond to enjoy freshly baked pastries, coffee drinks, sidewalk seating, and a French-speaking staff. Its location, directly across from the Chinatown gates, makes it one of the best places in the Union Square area to sit and enjoy the busy downtown vibe. The menu offers light fare for breakfast—at somewhat inflated prices—and meatier bistro-style entrees such as duck leg confit and braised beef stew for lunch and dinner. But the main reason to come here isn't to indulge your appetite; it's to browse the foreign magazine and newspaper racks for a bit, then rest your weary feet, nurse a cappuccino, nibble on a pastry, and soak up the street-side scene.

352 Grant Ave. (at Bush St.). ✆ **415/398-2680.** www.cafedelapresse.com. Breakfast $6.25–$10; lunch and dinner main courses (other than fish and meat) $9–$13; fish and meat main courses $15–$20. AE, DC, DISC, MC, V. Mon–Fri 7:30–10am; Sat–Sun 8–11:30am; Mon–Fri 11:30am–2:30pm; Mon–Thurs 5:30–9:30pm; Fri–Sun 5:30–10pm; brunch Sat–Sun 11:30am–4pm. Bus: 9X, 15, 30, or 45.

Mocca ★ ITALIAN If you're like us and can't be bothered with a long lunch when there's serious shopping to be done, head to this classic Italian deli on pedestrian-only Maiden Lane. Here it's counter service and cash only for sandwiches, *caprese* (Italian tomato and mozzarella salad), and big leafy salads. You can enjoy them at the few indoor tables or the umbrella-shaded tables on the street front that looks onto Union Square.

175 Maiden Lane (at Stockton St.). ✆ **415/956-1188.** Reservations not accepted. Main courses $7–$13. No credit cards. Daily 10:30am–5:30pm. Bus: All Union Square buses.

Sanraku Japanese Restaurant ★ 🗡 JAPANESE/SUSHI A perfect combination of great cooked dishes and sushi at bargain prices makes this straightforward, bright, and busy restaurant the best choice in the area for Japanese food. The friendly, hardworking staff does its best to keep up with diners' demands, but the restaurant gets quite busy during lunch, when a special box lunch containing a California roll, soup, salad, deep-fried salmon roll, and beef with noodles with steamed rice comes at a very digestible $11. The main menu, which is always available, features great sesame chicken with teriyaki sauce and rice; tempura; a vast selection of *nigiri* (raw fish sushi) and rolls; and delicious combination plates of sushi, sashimi, and teriyaki. Dinner sees brisk business, too, but a table always seems to be available.

704 Sutter St. (at Taylor St.). ✆ **415/771-0803.** www.sanraku.com. Main courses $7–$13 lunch, $10–$26 dinner; 7-course fixed-price dinner $55. AE, DC, DISC, MC, V. Mon–Sat 11am–10pm; Sun 4–10pm. Bus: 2, 3, 27, or 38. Cable car: Powell–Mason line.

Sears Fine Foods ★ ☺ AMERICAN Sears is not just another downtown diner—it's an old-fashioned institution, famous for its crispy, dark-brown waffles; light sourdough French toast served with house-made strawberry preserves; and silver dollar–size Swedish pancakes (18 per serving!). As the story goes, Ben Sears, a retired clown, founded the diner in 1938. His Swedish wife, Hilbur, was responsible for the legendary pancakes, which, although the restaurant is under new ownership, are still whipped up according to her family's secret recipe. Sears also offers classic lunch and dinner fare—try the Reuben for lunch and codfish and chips for dinner, followed by a big slice of pie for dessert. Breakfast is served until 3pm every day, and plan on a brief wait to be seated on weekends.

439 Powell St. (btw. Post and Sutter sts.). ✆ **415/986-0700.** www.searsfinefood.com. Reservations accepted for parties of 6 or more. Breakfast $3–$12; salads and soups $3–$8; main courses $14–$29. AE, DC, MC, V. Daily 6:30am–10pm (breakfast until 3pm). Bus: 2, 3, or 38. Cable car: Powell–Mason or Powell–Hyde line.

FINANCIAL DISTRICT

For a map of restaurants in this section, see the "Chinatown & North Beach Restaurants" map on p. 129.

Expensive

Kokkari ★★★ GREEK/MEDITERRANEAN The funny thing is, I've been to Athens, and the food there wasn't nearly as good as what they're serving at Kokkari (Ko-*kar*-ee), one of my favorite restaurants in the city. My love affair starts with the setting: a beautifully rustic dining area with a commanding fireplace and oversize furnishings. Past the tiny bar, the other main room is pure rustic revelry, with exposed wood beams, pretty standing lamps, and a view of the glass-enclosed private dining room. Then there are the wonderful, traditional Aegean dishes. A must-order appetizer is the *Marithes Tiganites,* a beautiful platter of whole crispy smelts enhanced with garlic-potato *skordalia* (a traditional Greek dip) and lemon. Other favorites are the *pikilia* (a sampling of traditional Greek spreads served with dolmades and house-made pitas) and the fabulous mesquite-grilled octopus salad. Try not to overindulge before the main courses, which include grilled whole petrale sole with lemon, olive oil, and braised greens; to-die-for moussaka (eggplant, lamb, potato, and béchamel); and lamb chops with oven-roasted lemon-oregano potatoes. Also consider the rotisserie specialties such as roasted pork loin.

200 Jackson St. (at Front St.). *C* **415/981-0983.** www.kokkari.com. Reservations recommended. Main courses $14–$23 lunch, $19–$39 dinner. AE, DC, DISC, MC, V. Mon–Fri 11:30am–2:30pm; bar menu 2:30–5:30pm; Mon–Thurs 5:30–10pm; Fri 5:30–11pm; Sat 5–11pm, Sun 5-10pm. Valet parking (dinner only) $8. Bus: 12 or 41.

One Market ★★ CALIFORNIAN This top-notch Embarcadero restaurant has remained popular with San Francisco's notoriously fickle dining public since it opened in 1993. Amid the airy main dining room with its open exhibition kitchen, cozy banquettes, mahogany trim, and slate flooring, a sea of diners feast from a farm-fresh menu put together by chef Mark Dommen, who has a passion for impeccably fresh local ingredients. One Market was one of the early supporters of Ferry Plaza Farmers' Market—and Dommen shops there regularly to create his highly original dishes. During my last visit, my table was wowed by the truly divine beet carpaccio, shellfish, and seafood sampler (*not* your everyday platter), and a superb crispy skin pork saddle with fava beans and chorizo broth. Whatever you choose, you're bound to find a perfect accompanying wine from the "cellar," which has over 500 selections of American vintages. Arrive early to mingle with the spirited corporate crowd that convenes from 4:30 to 7pm for happy hour at the bar—it's a fun scene.

1 Market St. (at Steuart St., across from Justin Herman Plaza). *C* **415/777-5577.** www.onemarket. com. Reservations recommended. Lunch $16–$23; dinner $19–$29; chef's tasting menu $79 per person. AE, DC, DISC, MC, V. Mon–Fri 11:30am–2pm; daily 5:30–9pm. Valet parking $12 for lunch, $10 for dinner. Bus: All Market St. buses. BART. All BART trains. See map p. 106.

Quince ★★ CALIFORNIAN/ITALIAN In its new expansive location in the Financial District, fans of Quince no longer have to book a month in advance to savor chef Michael Tusk's nightly changing Italian-inspired menu. Tusk honed his chops at Chez Panisse and his cooking style reflects it: simple food that honors a few high-quality, just-picked organic ingredients. Quince-ophiles might start with a pillowy spring garlic soufflé or white asparagus with a lightly fried egg and brown butter, but no true fan skips the pasta course—garganelli with English peas and prosciutto, tagliatelle with crab, agnolotti stuffed with veal, pork, and rabbit. Meat and fish selections don't fall short either, with delicately prepared mixed grill plates, sweetbreads with shaved black truffles, and juicy lamb with fennel and olives. For desserts, the choices are a tad limited, but really, why would you need anything more than butternut squash fondant with brown-butter ice-cream and caramelized honey?

You won't find lunch at Quince—for that, head next door to the less formal but equally sophisticated and fresh **Cotogna** (Italian for "quince," naturally), 490 Pacific Ave. (*C* **415/775-8508;** www.cotognasf.com), open Monday to Friday 11:30am to 2:30pm and 5:30 to 11pm (midnight on Fri.), and Saturdays from 11am to 3pm and 5:30 to midnight. On our last visit, a $24 fixed-price lunch

This town works magic with vegetables: try roasted wild carrots with honey and anise seed at Cotogna.

menu included chilled asparagus soup with Olio Nuovo, tagliatelle with pork and red dandelion ragu, and a milk chocolate and almond milk budino.

470 Pacific Ave. (at Montgomery St.). (℡) **415/ 775-8500.** www.quincerestaurant.com. Reservations required. Main courses $16–$29. AE, MC, V. Mon–Thurs 5:30–10pm; Fri–Sun 5–10pm. Valet parking $8. Bus: 12, 15, 41, or 83.

The Slanted Door ★★ VIETNAMESE What started in 1995 as an obscure little family-run restaurant in the Mission District has become one of the most popular and written-about restaurants in the city. Due to its meteoric rise—helped along by celebrity fans such as Mick Jagger, Keith Richards, and Quentin Tarantino—it's been relocated within a beautiful bay-inspired, custom-designed space at the Ferry Building Marketplace. What hasn't changed is a menu filled with incredibly fresh and flavorful Vietnamese dishes from chef Charles Phan, including catfish clay-pot flavored with cilantro, ginger, and Thai chilies; an amazing green papaya salad with roasted peanuts; and fragrant peppercorn duck served with apples and watercress. If the cellophane noodles with fresh Dungeness crabmeat are on the menu, *definitely* order them. Be sure to start the feast with a pot of tea from their eclectic collection. If you're just looking to grab something on the go, stop by **Out the Door,** the Slanted Door's more casual—but still tasty—little sister, on the bottom floor of

THE sun on your face AT BELDEN PLACE

San Francisco has always been woefully lacking in the alfresco dining department, which may or may not have something to do with the Arctic summer fog. But **Belden Place**—an adorable little brick alley in the heart of the Financial District—defies that convention. A skinny walkway open only to foot traffic, it's a little bit of Paris just off Pine Street. Restaurants line the alley sporting big umbrellas, tables, and chairs, and, when the weather is agreeable, diners linger long after the lunch hour.

A handful of cafes line Belden Place and offer a variety of cuisines at moderate prices. There's **Cafe Bastille,** 22 Belden Place ((℡) **415/986-5673**), a classic French bistro with a boho basement that serves excellent crepes, mussels, and French onion soup; it offers live jazz on Fridays. **Cafe Tiramisu,** 28 Belden Place ((℡) **415/ 421-7044**), is a stylish Italian hot spot serving addictive risottos and gnocchi. **Plouf,** 40 Belden Place ((℡) **415/986-6491**), specializes in big bowls of mussels slathered in your choice of seven sauces, as well as fresh seafood. **B44,** 44 Belden Place ((℡) **415/986-6287**), serves up a side order of Spain alongside its revered paella and other seriously zesty Spanish dishes.

At night, Belden Place takes on a Euro-speak-easy vibe—perfect for sipping aperitifs and nibbling on frites.

Oysters, a decadently creamy oyster stew, some bread to sop it up, and a beer at Hog Island Oyster Co. at the Ferry Building.

the Westfield Centre. It has both seating and a pickup window. Phan's latest creation, **Heaven's Dog** (Mission and Seventh sts.), offers noodles, soups, and classic Northern Chinese dishes.

1 Ferry Plaza (at the Embarcadero and Market). ℂ **415/861-8032.** www.slanteddoor.com. Reservations recommended. Lunch main courses $6–$17; dinner dishes $10–$34; 7-item fixed-price dinner $45 (parties of 7 or more only). AE, MC, V. Daily 11am–2:30pm (until 3pm on Sun); Daily 5:30–10pm. Bus: All Market St. buses. Streetcar: F line. See map p. 106.

Tommy Toy's ★ CHINESE   If you want romantic, extravagant Chinese, come to Tommy's. Fashioned after the 19th-century quarters of the Empress Dowager's sitting room and replete with mood-lit candelabras and antique paintings, it's perhaps the only Chinese restaurant in the city where dressing up is apropos. Most evenings, the dining room is filled mostly with tourists and traveling business types, while locals are more likely to come for the fixed-price lunches. (The multicourse "Executive Luncheon" is a bargain at $25.) Not much changes on the expensive, French-influenced Chinese menu, but that's fine with the loyalists who return year after year for such beautifully presented dishes as minced squab in leaves of lettuce; sautéed lobster with mushrooms, chives, and angel-hair crystal noodles; and puff-pastry-topped creamy lobster bisque. The gracious and convivial Tommy passed away in 2008, but the food remains steady, with substantial portions and a pleasing, if slightly opulent decor.

655 Montgomery St. (at Clay and Washington sts.). ℂ **415/397-4888.** www.tommytoys.com. Reservations recommended. Main courses $17–$23; fixed-price lunch $38; fixed-price dinner $48 (4 courses). AE, DC, DISC, MC, V. Mon–Fri 11:30am–2:30pm; daily 5:30–9:30pm. Valet parking (dinner only) $8. Bus: 9AX, 9BX, 12, 15, or 41.

Wayfare Tavern ★★ AMERICAN   One of Food Network celebrity chef Tyler Florence's three new offerings in the Bay Area, Wayfare Tavern was the most buzzed about dining spot to open in 2010. With upscale pub grub in a hunting lodge–like environment—animal heads adorn the walls, the color palette sticks to hues of khaki and black—this intimate experience added some much-needed juice to the Financial District's somewhat tired food scene.

Florence puts his own creative spin on classic comfort foods like mac and cheese, pot roast, and grits. The Wayfare Burger "Le Grand" may very well be the most popular item on the menu: a hunk of grass-fed proprietary grind, with local Mt. Tam cheese, roasted onion, and smoked bacon on brioche (with the option to add a Petaluma egg, sunny side up). More inventive fare like chicken liver mousse with pomelo marmalade and toasted brioche, or *poutine* (that Canadian favorite of french fries with mozzarella curd), braised short rib, and truffle gravy, round out the menu, and if you like fried chicken you have to try Tyler's version. The portion sizes are pretty generous, and the free popovers are addictive. The best way to understand what Wayfare Tavern is all about is to order a combination of dishes for the table to share.

558 Sacramento St. (at Leidesdorff Alley). ✆ **415/772-9060.** www.wayfaretavern.com. Reservations recommended. Main courses $22–$28. AE, DC, DISC, MC, V. Mon–Sat 11am–11pm; Sun 5–11pm. Bus: 1, 10, 12, 30X, 41, or 82X.

Moderate

Hog Island Oyster Co. ★ SEAFOOD   Fans of fresh, local oysters will be in slurping nirvana at this smart little seafood spot inside the Ferry Plaza Marketplace. Belly up to the bar overlooking the ferry dock for a dozen Sweetwaters or Kumamotos from Hog Island's Tomales Bay farm, or branch out with baked oysters casino, oyster stew, or a steaming bowl of clam chowder. Prices are a tad steep, but on weekdays there's a happy hour featuring $1 oysters and $3.50 pints of beer. Even if you're not a big oyster fan, it's worth a stop just to watch the expert shuckers strut their stuff.

Ferry Building Marketplace, 1 Ferry Building, no. 11–1 (at Embarcadero and Market St.). ✆ **415/391-7117.** www.hogislandoysters.com. Reservations not accepted. Oysters $12–$17 for half-dozen; other items $6–$14. AE, MC, V. Mon–Fri 11:30am–8pm; Sat–Sun 11am–6pm. Bus: All Market St. buses. Streetcar: F or N-Judah line. See map p. 106.

Sam's Grill & Seafood Restaurant ★ 🎒 SEAFOOD   Power-lunching at Sam's is a San Francisco tradition, and Sam's has done a brisk business with Financial District suits since—get this—1867. Even if you're not carrying a briefcase, this is the place to come for time-capsule dining at its most classically San Francisco. Pass the crowded entrance and small bar to get to the main dining room—packed with virtually all men—kick back and bask in yesteryear. (Or conversely, slide into a curtained booth and see nothing but your dining companion.) Tuxedo-clad waiters race around, doling out big crusty cuts of sourdough bread and distributing salads overflowing with fresh crab and Roquefort vinaigrette, towering plates of seafood pasta with marinara, charbroiled fish, roasted chicken, and old-school standbys like calves' liver with bacon and onions or Salisbury steak. Don't worry—they didn't forget classic creamed spinach. The restaurant's mildly salty service and good old-fashioned character make everything on the menu taste that much better.

374 Bush St. (btw. Montgomery and Kearny sts.). ✆ **415/421-0594.** www.belden-place.com/samsgrill. Reservations recommended for dinner and for 6 or more at lunch. Main courses $12–$29. AE, DC, DISC, MC, V. Mon–Fri 11am–9pm; Sat 5–9pm. Bus: 45 or 76. See map p. 109.

Tadich Grill ★ SEAFOOD   Not that the veteran restaurant needed more adulation, but the city's ongoing loss of local institutions makes 164-year-old Tadich the last of a revered dying breed. This business began as a coffee stand during the 1849 gold rush and claims to be the very first to broil seafood over mesquite charcoal back in the early 1920s. An old-fashioned power-dining restaurant to its core, Tadich boasts its original mahogany bar, which extends the length of the restaurant, and seven booths for private powwows. Big plates of sourdough bread top the tables.

You won't find fancy California cuisine here. The novella-like menu features a slew of classic salads such as sliced tomato with Dungeness crab or prawn Louis, meats and fish from the charcoal broiler, and even casseroles. The seafood cioppino is a specialty, as is the baked casserole of stuffed turbot with crab and shrimp a la Newburg, and the petrale sole with butter sauce. Everything comes with a heaping side of fries, but if you crave something green, order the creamed spinach.

240 California St. (btw. Battery and Front sts.). ✆ **415/391-1849.** www.tadichgrill.com. Reservations not accepted. Main courses $14–$20. MC, V. Mon–Fri 11am–9:30pm; Sat 11:30am–9:30pm. Bus: All Market St. buses. Streetcar: All Market St. streetcars. BART: Embarcadero.

Financial District

WHERE TO EAT

Food Trucks, Food Courts & Other Moveable Feasts

If you're looking for a quick, inexpensive meal, you don't have to sacrifice quality or variety—if you know where to go. The crown for gourmet inexpensive noshing goes to, hands down, the **Ferry Building Marketplace**—see our complete run-down of eats on p. 253 and 254. Your options here multiply during the Farmers' Market on Thursdays 10am to 2pm and Saturdays 8am to 2pm, when you'll find plenty of vendors and food trucks. Trucks also gather daily at **Off the Grid** events, occasionally with bands. Look up locations at http://offthegrid.com. Live music, artisanal truck food, and hopefully some sun on your face—this is the kind of lunch we San Franciscans treat ourselves to. Food *courts* are less exciting, but you'll find some respectable options. The **Rincon Center's Food Court** at the corner of Spear and Mission streets has about a dozen to-go places running the gastronomic gamut: Korean, American, Mexican, pizza, coffee and cookies, Indian, Thai, sandwiches, Middle Eastern, and Chinese. Most of the restaurants are open Monday through Friday from 11am to 3pm, but some until early evening. Similar inexpensive eats can be found at the basement food courts of the **Westfield San Francisco Centre** (www.westfield.com), on Market and 5th streets, and **Macy's** (www.macys.com), on the south end of Union Square. If you're near the Financial District, the **Crocker Galleria** offers decent lunch options including Indian, Japanese, Mexican, and coffee and pastry shops—all open until 2pm, closed Sundays.

Yank Sing ★★ CHINESE/DIM SUM   Loosely translated as "a delight of the heart," Yank Sing is widely regarded as the best dim sum restaurant in the downtown area. The servers are good at guessing your gastric threshold as they wheel stainless-steel carts carrying small plates of exotic dishes around the vast dining room; if they whiz right by your table, there's probably a good reason. If you're new to dim sum (which, translated, means "to touch the heart"), stick with the safe, recognizable classics such as spare ribs, stuffed crab claws, scallion pancakes, shrimp balls, pork buns, and steamed dumplings filled with delicious concoctions of pork, beef, fish, or vegetables. A second location, open Monday through Friday from 11am to 3pm, is at 49 Stevenson St., off First Street (© **415/541-4949**) in SoMa, and has outdoor seating for fair-weather dining.

101 Spear St. (at Mission St. at Rincon Center). © **415/781-1111.** www.yanksing.com. Dim sum $3.65–$10 for 2–6 pieces. AE, DC, MC, V. Mon–Fri 11am–3pm; Sat–Sun and holidays 10am–4pm. Validated parking in Rincon Center Garage. Bus: 1, 12, 14, or 41. Streetcar: F. Cable car: California St. line. BART: Embarcadero. See map p. 106.

SOMA

For a map of restaurants in this section, see the "San Francisco Restaurants" map on p. 107.

Very Expensive

Ame ★★★ NEW AMERICAN   Restaurateurs Hiro Sone and Lissa Doumani, the owners of the sensational Napa Valley restaurant Terra, have blessed us foodies with an equally fantastic restaurant in the city. On the ground level of the *très* chic St. Regis Hotel, the L-shaped dining room with its mesquite flooring, red accents, and long striped curtains fits right in with the hotel's minimalist theme. Sone, a master of Japanese, French, and Italian cuisines, offers an array of exotic selections that are utterly tempting: ragout of sweetbreads with salsify and forest mushrooms; Japanese egg custard with lobster and urchin; mushroom risotto topped with foie gras; grilled Wagyu beef with fried Miyagi oysters and rémoulade sauce. If you can't figure out where to start on a menu where everything looks wonderful, opt for Sone's A Taste of Ame, an $89 five-course tasting menu that, for an additional $65, is paired with a bevy of wines by the glass. After dinner, be sure to enjoy an aperitif at the hotel's swank bar where the city's elite congregate nightly.

689 Mission St. (at Third St.). ℭ **415/284-4040.** www.amerestaurant.com. Reservations recommended. Main courses $22–$38. AE, DC, DISC, MC, V. Daily 5:30–10pm. Valet parking $15 for the 1st 3 hr. Bus: 30 or 45. Streetcar: J, K, L, or M to Montgomery. See map p. 109.

Boulevard ★★ AMERICAN   Master restaurant designer Pat Kuleto and chef Nancy Oakes are behind one of San Francisco's most beloved restaurants. Inside, the historic Belle Epoque interior with its vaulted brick ceilings, floral banquettes, mosaic floor, and tulip-shaped lamps sets the stage for Oakes's equally impressive sculptural and mouthwatering upscale American dishes. Starters alone could make a perfect meal, especially if you indulge in pan-seared day boat sea scallops with sautéed fresh hearts of palm, pomelo, basil, toasted shallots, and macadamia nuts, or the pan-seared foie gras with rhubarb syrup on whole-grain toast. The nine or so main courses are equally creative and might include grilled Pacific sea bass with fresh gulf prawns, grilled artichoke, spring asparagus, and green garlic purée; or fire-roasted Angus filet with crispy Yukon gold potatoes, béarnaise sauce, spinach, crimini mushrooms, and red wine *jus.* Finish with warm chocolate cake with a chocolate caramel center, caramel corn, and butterscotch ice cream. Three levels of formality—bar, open kitchen, and main dining room—keep things from getting too snobby. Although steep prices prevent most from making Boulevard a regular gig, you'd be hard-pressed to find a better place for a special, fun-filled occasion.

1 Mission St. (btw. Embarcadero and Steuart sts.). ℭ **415/543-6084.** www.boulevardrestaurant. com. Reservations recommended. Main courses $14–$22 lunch, $29–$39 dinner. AE, DC, DISC, MC, V. Mon–Fri 11:30am–2pm; Mon–Thurs 5:30–10pm; Fri–Sat 5:30–10:30pm. Valet parking $12 lunch, $10 dinner. Bus: 12, 30, or 41. BART: Embarcadero.

EPIC Roasthouse ★★ STEAKHOUSE   Location is everything, and the EPIC Roasthouse and its adjoining sister restaurant, Waterbar (see below), were both built from the ground up on perhaps the most prime piece of real estate in the city, with spectacular, glittering views of the Bay Bridge, Treasure Island, and city skyline. At EPIC, it's all about steak—you'd be unwise to order anything but. Renowned chef and co-owner Jan Birnbaum, a New Orleans man who knows his meat, runs the show in his huge exhibition kitchen, overseeing the wood-fired hearth to make sure your $84 rib-eye for two is cooked to your specs. The restaurant's Pat Kuleto–designed interior makes for a grand entrance: Only when you're done marveling at the bold industrial elements of leather, stone, mahogany, and massive cast iron gears do you notice the phenomenal view of the Bay Bridge from the two-story-tall wall of windows. Perhaps the only thing prettier than the scenery is Birnbaum's sizzling 26-ounce bone-in porterhouse on your plate ("Every steak comes with a handle," claims Jan). If you don't have a reservation, the upstairs Quiver Bar serves both bar and full menus, but the crowd often consists of obnoxious businessmen and Gucci-toting gold-diggers from across the bridge. *Tip:* On sunny days, beg the hostess for a table on the bay-view patio.

Anchor & Hope.

369 Embarcadero (at Harrison St.). ℂ **415/369-9955.** www.epicroasthousesf.com. Reservations recommended. Main courses $19–$42. AE, DC, DISC, MC, V. Thurs–Fri 11:30am–2pm; Sun–Thurs 5–9:30pm; Fri–Sat 5–10:30pm; brunch Sat–Sun 11am–3pm. Valet parking $12 lunch, $10 dinner. Bus: 1, 12, 14, or 41. Streetcar: F, N, or T. BART: Embarcadero.

Prospect ★★★ AMERICAN   From the genius team behind award-winning Boulevard, Prospect was perhaps San Francisco's hottest new opening of 2010. And it well lived up to its hype, too with its loftlike space made comfortable by its earth tones and reclaimed wood, while keeping stylish with unique details, including wrought-iron chandeliers. Stop by any night of the week when the workday is drawing to a close and the spacious building will be packed with businessmen (and women) who drop by after working hours (and often during, too, as happy hour starts daily at 4pm). Co executive chefs Nancy Oakes and Pamela Mazzola use their culinary expertise to dish up contemporary American cuisine. Entrees might be braised goat ragu with slow-roasted tomatoes and cerignola olives or Sonoma quail stuffed with bacon and apple butter, caramelized Fuji apples, and parsnip puttee braised red Russian kale. More unique items rounding out the menu include crispy pig trotters (Don't worry: They're far better than they may sound.) Wine is a subject in which Prospect excels as well, with quite the selection of bottles from around the world and more than a dozen available by the glass.

300 Spear St. (at Folsom St.). ℂ **415/247-7770.** www.prospectsf.com. Reservations recommended. Main courses $25–$43. AE, DC, DISC, MC, V. Mon–Thurs 5:30–10pm; Fri–Sat 5:30–10:30pm; Sun 11am–2:30pm and 5:30–9:30pm. Bus: 2, 6, 21, or 31. Streetcar: F or N. BART: Embarcadero.

Trace ★★ NEW AMERICAN   While its mission is to fuse the vibrant, local personality of the Bay Area with a dedication to socially responsible food," Trace does something more impressive: It offers surprisingly good food for a hotel dining room. Echoing its très-hip W Hotel surroundings, the room (which is sadly often under attended) is city chic and modern (read: stark)—a perfect place to drift into for a bite after downing a cocktail or two at the equally suave lobby bar. The seasonal menu forgoes expected fare for fantastic starters such as braised pork with crisp gnocchi, hen of the woods mushroom, and pecorino (a must order!) and gem lettuce salad with Fuji apples, dates, candied pecans, and cheddar dressing. In fact, you could easily nosh the night away on appetizers. But entrees satisfy, too, be they poached cod with braised butter beans, escarole, and prosciutto or beef filet with roasted miataki mushrooms, broccoli rabe, and potato puree. While Trace may not demand destination-dining status, it's a great option if you're in the area and looking for a meal with style and substance.

Inside the W Hotel, 181 Third St. ℂ **415/817-7836.** www.trace-sf.com. Main courses $15–$40. AE, DC, DISC, MC, V. Mon–Thurs 6:30am–10:30am breakfast, 11:30am–2pm lunch, 6–10pm dinner; Fri 6:30am–10:30am breakfast, 11:30am–2pm lunch, 6–11pm dinner; Sat 10am–2pm brunch, 6–11pm dinner; Sun 10am–2pm brunch, 6–10pm dinner.

Waterbar ★★ SEAFOOD   Built in tandem with the EPIC Roasthouse (see above), Waterbar is the surf to EPIC's turf. As with EPIC, Waterbar was built just a few years ago from the ground up right on the Embarcadero waterfront. Whereas renowned restaurant designer Pat Kuleto went with a moderately conservative industrial look at the EPIC steakhouse, at Waterbar he unleashed his imagination and created the most visually playful decor since he opened Farallon in 1997. The focal point of the restaurant is a pair of radiant 19-foot floor-to-ceiling circular aquariums filled with fish and marine critters from the Pacific. The aquatic theme ebbs on with a beautiful glass "caviar" chandelier and a horse-shoe-shaped raw bar that has too few of the most coveted seats in town. Even the open kitchen is visually—and aromatically—pleasing. The menu offers a wide selection of market-driven, sustainable seafood such as oak-roasted Maine haddock with smoked butterball potatoes, ancho chili butter, and oyster broth; and local halibut poached in milk with grilled asparagus—but more fun can be had at the raw bar noshing on oysters and small plates. Either way, be sure to start off with the superb mahimahi ceviche with plantain *tostones*. If the weather is agreeable, ask the hostess for a table on the patio, which affords spectacular waterfront views. If the coastal chill has set in, opt for a table by the soaring windows inside instead to see San Francisco lit up in all her glory. ***Note:*** When bustling with the after-work crowd, Waterbar can get quite noisy; bear that in mind if you're seeking a quiet dining experience.

399 Embarcadero (at Harrison St.). ℂ **415/284-9922.** www.waterbarsf.com. Reservations recommended. Main courses $29–$36. AE, DC, DISC, MC, V. Daily 11:30am–2pm and 5:30–10pm. Valet parking $15 lunch, $10 dinner. Bus: 1, 12, 14, or 41. Streetcar: F. BART: Embarcadero.

Expensive

Anchor & Hope ★★ SEAFOOD   A stylish, convivial space, a location in SoMa, and a menu suitable for both noshing or more formal dining—Anchor & Hope bears all the markings of its owners, chefs Steven and Mitchell Rosenthal and Doug Washington, of Town Hall and Salt House (p. 124). They've gone fishing with their third restaurant, with a top-notch seafood menu now helmed by Chef Sarah Schafer. The restaurant is located down an alley in a lofty, warehouse-chic space with seafaring murals and paraphernalia throughout. As with the owners' other spaces, the genius of this interior is that it feels inviting for any party, from business clients to dates to families with kids to solo diners grabbing oysters and a beer at the bar (try one of 30+ brews). Whatever your occasion and attire, you'll be greeted with house-made kettle chips—the great equalizer. You might start off with the Angels on Horseback (clams wrapped in bacon with remoulade), and a decadent sea urchin with crab, tomato, and beurre blanc. Of the entrees we've tried, we enjoyed the wild king salmon with fava beans and shellfish butter, the bouillabaisse served with buttery garlic bread, and the satisfyingly meaty lobster roll. The bill occasionally surprises us here (maybe the potato chips throw us off)—which is why we're also fans of the Oyster & Stout Happy Hour (Wed 4:30–6pm).

83 Minna St. (at Second St.). ☎ **415/501-9100.** http://anchorandhopesf.com. Reservations recommended. Main courses $22–$30. AE, DC, DISC, MC, V. Mon–Fri 11:30am–2pm Mon–Thurs, and Sun 5:30 pm–10pm; Fri–Sat 5:30pm–11pm. Bus: 9, 10, 12, or 14. Streetcar: J, K, L, or M to Montgomery.

Chez Papa Resto ★★ FRENCH   When the folks behind Potrero Hill's popular Chez Papa announced they were going to open a new, swankier edition in the rehabbed Mint Plaza (a former homeless alley), more than a few skeptics took bets on their demise. Turns out, they needn't have worried. The stellar Provençal cuisine and impeccable wine service at Chez Papa Resto have enough star power to outshine any grittiness that might have lingered. Anyone finding himself or herself peckish in the vicinity of the Westfield Mall should definitely make a beeline here and settle into a bench table by the windows. Highlights on a recent lunch menu included, well, everything. But if I had to choose, I'd go for the smoked trout with potato salad and caper berries; the Alaskan black cod with oyster mushrooms, melted leeks, and black truffle emulsion; and the duck leg confit with lentils (get it with a glass of Châteauneuf du Pape, Domaine la Roquète). Afterward, stroll around the pedestrian plaza and into Blue Bottle Café, where coffee is elevated to an art form. (Order the Gibraltar—it's not on the menu. You can thank me later.)

4 Mint Plaza (at Fifth St.). ☎ **415/546-4134.** www.chezpaparesto.com. Dinner reservations recommended. Main courses $19–$33. AE, DISC, MC, V. Mon–Sat 11:30am–2:30pm; Mon–Thurs 5:30–10pm; Fri–Sat 5:30–10:30pm. Bus: 30 or 45. Streetcar: J, K, L, or M. See map p. 109.

MoMo's AMERICAN   With an abundance of patio seating, a huge swank-yet-casual dining room, and proximity to AT&T Park baseball stadium, festive MoMo's hits a home run if you're headed to a Giants game, but is not a destination in itself. Crowds of upscale sports fans make this a fun place to hang out on the patio and chow down on greasy-good thin sliced onion rings, refreshing seared ahi salad, thin-crust pizza, and awesome burgers. Come sundown, there are dozens of other restaurants where I'd prefer to spend my money, but singles appreciate the bar scene. Happy hour is hopping Monday through Friday in the baseball off season—especially when it's sunny. If you're headed here on a game day, make a reservation or arrive early, because party people form a line around the block to get in, and it's no fun trying to eat standing at the bar or wrestling for one of the coveted patio tables.

760 Second St. (at King St.). ☎ **415/227-8660.** www.sfmomos.com. Reservations recommended. Main courses $12–$39. AE, DC, DISC, MC, V. Sun–Wed 11:30am–9pm; Thurs–Sat 11:30am–10pm. Valet parking $8 lunch, $11 dinner, $20 game hours. Bus: 30, 45, or 80x. Streetcar: F, N, or T.

Twenty Five Lusk ★★ AMERICAN   This well-hidden new restaurant down the street from the ballpark hadn't even been open a month before it became difficult to snag a table without a reservation. And that's not for lack of space: There's a large mezzanine dining room overlooking a lounge area below full of places to lounge clustered around space age fireplaces—Twenty Five Lusk looks more like it would fit in the L.A. dining scene than San Francisco. Take a seat on the top level and get to ordering. Start with the asparagus risotto or the steamboat oysters with black radish, cucumber, caviar, micro celery, and lime mignonette. The roasted quail entree with wild arugula, nicoise olives, prosciutto, and rhubarb sauce is divine, as is the cod served with buckwheat noodles, grilled celery, pea leaves, cilantro, and ginger broth. Portion sizes are small, yet filling; like other establishments that focus on luxe cuisine, it's more about the flavors than the volume. For dessert, try something different like the chocolate ravioli with black-currant tea chocolate, glazed banana, and bergamot sauce. And don't neglect adding a cocktail (such as the Red Monkey—bourbon, bitter, sweet vermouth, and mint, angostura bitters) to your dining plan.

25 Lusk St. (at Harrison St.). ℂ **415/495-5875.** www.25lusk.com. Reservations recommended. Main courses $25–$29. AE, DC, DISC, MC, V. Mon–Thurs 5:30–10pm; Fri–Sun 5:30–11pm; brunch Sun 11am–2pm. Valet parking $10. Bus: 91. Streetcar: N.

Moderate

Gordon Biersch Brewery Restaurant ★ CALIFORNIAN   Popular with the young Republican crowd (loose ties and tight skirts predominate), this modern, two-tiered brewery and restaurant eschews traditional brewpub fare—no cheesy nachos on this menu—in an attempt to attract a more upscale clientele. And it works. Goat cheese ravioli is a bestseller, followed by the pecan-crusted half-chicken with garlic mashed potatoes. Start with the delicate and crunchy fried calamari appetizer or, if you're a garlic hound, the tangy Caesar salad. Most dishes can be paired with one of the brewery's lagers or ales. Couples bent on a quiet, romantic dinner can skip this place; when the lower-level bar fills up, you practically have to shout to be heard. Beer-lovers who want to pair their suds with decent grub, however, will be quite content.

2 Harrison St. (on the Embarcadero). ℂ **415/243-8246.** www.gordonbiersch.com. Reservations recommended. Main courses $18–$25. AE, DC, DISC, MC, V. Sun–Thurs 11:30am–midnight; Fri–Sat 11:30am–2am. Streetcar: N or T.

Salt House ★ AMERICAN   The self-proclaimed "jackasses" behind Town Hall—chefs Mitch and Steve Rosenthal, and front man Doug Washington—opened this modern urban tavern in 2006, figuring that SoMa and Financial District types would gravitate to a chic, neo-industrial spot that invites diners to eat

Twenty Five Lusk.

anywhere (dining room, bar, communal table, counter) anytime (they serve until midnight on weekends), and makes sure they do it with a drink in hand. They were mostly right, though at times the menu feels more bar bitey than full-fledged. Appetizers such as smoked trout with beets, broccoli di ciccio, and cauliflower in Meyer lemon–caper vinaigrette; and baked oysters with bacon and spinach certainly hit the spot. At lunch, the roasted pork Cubano sandwich is a don't miss.

545 Mission St. (btw. First and Second sts.). (✆ **415/543-8900**. www.salthousesf.com. Reservations recommended. Main courses $15–$24 lunch, $20–$27 dinner. AE, MC, V. Mon–Fri 11:30am–2pm and limited menu 2–5:30pm; Mon–Thurs 5:30–11pm; Fri–Sat 5:30pm–midnight; Sun 5–9:30pm. Bus: 10, 14, or 76. BART: Embarcadero or Montgomery.

Zuppa ★★ ITALIAN   If you're looking for a casual-chic dinner spot with good, affordable, rustic Italian food, lively ambience, and a somewhat hip crowd, Zuppa is it. Located among the warehouses of SoMa, this warm industrial room is awash with dark-wood tables and features a back-wall bar orchestrated by on-site owners Joseph and Mary (yes, really). Joe, whose career launched from Spago Hollywood more than 2 decades ago, oversees the menu while Mary works the front of the house. With a menu of items that don't top $20, this is the way San Francisco dining used to be—if you can't decide between the antipasti of grilled octopus, Yukon gold potatoes, arugula, and Cerignola olives, pizza with clams and garlic, or grilled pork chop, you can order all of them and not break the bank. Happy hour here (5–7pm Mon–Fri) is a downright bargain—50¢ oysters, half-price pizzas, $4 beers. A selection of cured meats and pizzas makes it easy to snack through a meal, but don't. The house-made pastas—particularly the pork ragout—are fantastic and shouldn't be missed, and the entrees are great as well—especially when paired with an Italian wine. *Take note:* Parking in local lots around here costs more on game days (the Giants ballpark is nearby)—expect to pay around $15. Otherwise, it's very affordable.

564 Fourth St. (btw. Brannan and Bryant sts.) (✆ **415/777-5900**. www.zuppa-sf.com. Reservations recommended. Main courses $16–$19. AE, DC, DISC, MC, V. Mon–Fri 11:30am–2:30pm; Mon–Thurs 5–10pm; Fri–Sat 5–11pm; Sun 5–9pm. Street parking or pay at nearby lots. Bus: 9X, 12, 30, 45, or 76.

Inexpensive

AsiaSF ★ ASIAN/CALIFORNIAN   Part restaurant, part gender-illusionist musical revue, AsiaSF manages to be both entertaining and satisfying. As you're entertained by mostly Asian men dressed as women (who lip-sync show tunes when they're not waiting on tables), you can nibble on superb grilled shrimp and herb salad; baby back pork ribs with honey tamarind glaze, pickled carrots, and sweet-potato crisps; or filet mignon with Korean dipping sauce, miso eggplant, and fried potato stars. The full bar, *Wine Spectator* award–winning wine list, and sake list add to the festivities. Fortunately, the food and the atmosphere are as colorful as the staff, which means a night here is more than a meal—it's a very happening event.

201 Ninth St. (at Howard St.). (✆ **415/255-2742**. www.asiasf.com. Reservations recommended. Main courses $9–$20. AE, DISC, MC, V (Mon–Wed $25 minimum). Sun 7–10pm; Wed–Thurs 7–10pm; Fri 7pm–2am; Sat 5pm–2am; cocktails and dancing until 2am on Fri–Sat. Bus: 9, 12, or 47. Streetcar: Civic Center on underground streetcar. BART: Civic Center. See map p. 153.

Dottie's True Blue Café ★ ☺ AMERICAN/BREAKFAST   This family-owned breakfast restaurant, one of our favorite downtown diners, moved to a new Mid-Market location but kept its legendary breakfast and brunch menu intact. This is the kind of place you'd expect to see off Route 66, where most customers are on a first-name basis with the staff and everyone is welcomed with a hearty hello and steaming mug of coffee. Dottie's serves far-above-average American morning fare (big portions of French toast, pancakes, bacon and eggs, omelets, and the like), delivered to tables laminated with old movie-star photos on rugged, diner-quality plates. Whatever you order arrives with delicious home-made bread, muffins, or scones, as well as house-made jelly. There are also daily specials and vegetarian dishes. See map p. 109.

28 Sixth St. (at Stevenson St.). *C* **415/885-2767.** Reservations not accepted. Breakfast $5–$11. DISC, MC, V. Wed–Mon 7:30am–3pm (lunch 11:30am–3pm). Bus: 14. Streetcar: Civic Center or Powell. BART: Civic Center or Powell.

Manora's ★ THAI   Manora's has been cranking out some of the best Thai food in town for 20 years and is well worth a jaunt to SoMa. But this is no relaxed affair: It's perpetually packed (unless you come early), and you'll be seated sar-dinelike at one of the cramped but well-appointed tables. During the dinner rush, the noise level can make conversation almost impossible, but the food is so darn good, you'll probably prefer to ignore people and stuff your face anyway. Start with a Thai iced tea or coffee and tangy soup or chicken satay, which comes with decadent peanut sauce. Follow these with any of the wonderful dinner dishes—which should be shared—and a side of rice. There are endless options, including a vast array of vegetarian plates. Every remarkably flavorful dish arrives seemingly seconds after you order it, which is great if you're hungry, a bummer if you were planning a long, leisurely dinner. *Tip:* Come before 7pm or after 9pm if you don't want a loud, rushed meal.

1600 Folsom St. (at 12th St.). *C* **415/861-6224.** www.manorathai.com. Reservations recommen-ded for 4 or more. Main courses $7–$15. MC, V. Mon–Thurs 11:30am–2:30pm; Mon–Sat 5:30–10:30pm; Sun 5–10pm. Bus: 9, 12, or 47. See map p. 153.

NOB HILL/RUSSIAN HILL

For a map of restaurants in this section, see the "San Francisco Restaurants" map on p. 106.

Very Expensive

La Folie ★★★ 🍴 FRENCH   I call this unintimidating, cozy, intimate French restaurant "the house of foie gras." Why? Because on my first visit, virtually every dish overflowed with the ultrarich delicacy. Subsequent visits proved that foie gras still reigns here, but more than that, it reconfirmed La Folie's long-standing reputation as one of the city's very best fine-dining experiences—and without any stuffiness to boot. Chef/owner Roland Passot, who unlike many celebrity chefs is actually in the kitchen each night, offers melt-in-your-mouth starters such as seared foie gras with caramelized pineapple and star anise vanilla Muscat broth. Generous main courses include rôti of quail and squab stuffed with wild mush-rooms and wrapped in crispy potato strings; butter-poached lobster with glazed blood oranges and *shiso,* scallion, carrot, and toasted almond salad; and roast venison with vegetables, quince, and huckleberry sauce. The staff is extremely approachable and knowledgeable, and the new surroundings (think deep wood paneling, mirrors, long, rust-colored curtains, and gold-hued Venetian plaster) are now as elegant as the food. Best of all, the environment is relaxed, comfort-able, and intimate. Finish with any of the delectable desserts. If you're not into the three-, four-, or five-course tasting menu, don't be deterred; the restaurant tells me they'll happily price out individual items.

2316 Polk St. (btw. Green and Union sts.). ✆ **415/776-5577.** www.lafolie.com. Reservations recommended. 3-course tasting menu $70; 4-course tasting menu $80; 5-course chef's tasting menu $90; vegetarian tasting menu $70. AE, DC, DISC, MC, V. Mon–Sat 5:30–10:30pm. Valet parking $15. Bus: 19, 41, 45, 47, 49, or 76.

Expensive

House of Prime Rib ★★ STEAKHOUSE Anyone who loves a huge slab of meat and old-school-style dining will feel right at home at this shrine to prime (rib)—catering to meat-loving San Franciscans since the 1940s. It's a fun and ever-packed affair within the men's club–like dining rooms (fireplaces included), where drinks are stiff, waiters are loose, and all the beef is offered English style—roasted in rock salt, sliced tableside, and served with creamed spinach, a baked or mashed potato, and a soufflé-like Yorkshire pudding. This is not the place to go if you're on a diet or you're looking for an adventure in dining: These guys do one thing, but they do it right, serving some 600 roast beef dinners every night, cut thin, thick, and in between (you can even get an extra slice "for dessert"). To placate the occasional non-meat eater, they also offer a fish-of-the-day special, but c'mon—if that's what you want, go to House of Prime Salmon.

1906 Van Ness Ave. (near Washington St.). ✆ **415/885-4605.** www.houseofprimerib.net. Reservations recommended. Complete dinners $28–$33. AE, MC, V. Mon–Thurs 5:30–10pm; Fri 5–10pm; Sat–Sun 4–10pm. Valet parking $7. Bus: 47 or 49.

Moderate

Nob Hill Cafe ★ 🍴 ITALIAN/PIZZA Considering the steep cost and formality of most Nob Hill restaurants, it's no wonder that residents don't mind waiting around for a table to open up at this cozy neighborhood bistro. This is the kind of place where you can come wearing jeans and sneakers, tuck into a large plate of linguine with clams and a glass of pinot, and leave fulfilled without blowing a wad of dough (pastas are in the humble $9–$15 range). The dining room is split into two small, simple rooms, with windows looking onto Taylor Street and bright local art on the walls. Service is friendly, and one of the owners is almost always on hand to make sure everyone's content. When the kitchen is "on," expect hearty Northern Italian comfort fare worth at least twice its price; even on off days, it's still a bargain. Start with a salad or the decadent polenta with pesto and Parmigiano, and then fill up on the veal piccata, any of the pastas or pizzas, or petrale sole. If you're into "celebrity" sightings, keep your eyes peeled for the original Doublemint twins, who dress alike and dine here frequently. *Tip:* Parking can be difficult in Nob Hill; fortunately, they offer valet parking a block away at the corner of Washington and Taylor streets.

1152 Taylor St. (btw. Sacramento and Clay sts.). ✆ **415/776-6500.** www.nobhillcafe.com. Reservations not accepted. Main courses $7–$17. DC, MC, V. Daily 11:30am–3pm and 5–10pm. Bus: 1.

Swan Oyster Depot ★★ 🍴 SEAFOOD Turning 100 years old in 2012, Swan Oyster Depot is a classic San Francisco dining experience you shouldn't miss. Opened in 1912, this tiny hole in the wall, run by the city's friendliest servers, is little more than a narrow fish market that decided to slap down some bar stools. There are only 20 or so stools here, jammed cheek-by-jowl along a long marble bar. Most patrons come for a quick cup of chowder or a plate of oysters on the half-shell with an Anchor Steam beer. The menu is limited to fresh Dungeness crab, shrimp, oyster, clam cocktails, a few types of smoked fish, Maine lobster, and Boston-style clam chowder, all of which are exceedingly fresh. *Note:* Don't let the lunchtime line dissuade you—it moves fast.

1517 Polk St. (btw. California and Sacramento sts.). ℂ **415/673-1101.** Reservations not accepted. Seafood cocktails $7–$15; clams and oysters on the half shell $7.95 per half-dozen. No credit cards. Mon–Sat 8am–5:30pm. Bus: 1, 19, 47, or 49.

CHINATOWN

For a map of restaurants in this section, see the "Chinatown & North Beach Restaurants" map on p. 129.

Inexpensive

Brandy Ho's Hunan Food ★ CHINESE   Fancy black-and-white granite tabletops and a large, open kitchen give you the first clue that the food at this casual restaurant is a cut above the usual Hunan fare. Take my advice and start immediately with fried dumplings (in sweet-and-sour sauce) or cold chicken salad, and then move on to fish-ball soup with spinach, bamboo shoots, noodles, and other goodies. The best main course is Three Delicacies, a combination of scallops, shrimp, and chicken with onion, bell pepper, and bamboo shoots, seasoned with ginger, garlic, and wine, and served with black-bean sauce. Most dishes are quite hot and spicy, but the kitchen will adjust the level to meet your specifications. A full bar includes Asian food–friendly libations like plum wine and sake from 11:30am to 11pm. There's a second location in the Castro at 4068 18th St. (at Castro St.; ℂ **415/252-8000**).

217 Columbus Ave. (at Pacific Ave.). ℂ **415/788-7527.** www.brandyhos.com. Reservations recommended. Main courses $8–$13. AE, DISC, MC, V. Sun–Thurs 11am–11pm; Fri–Sat 11am–midnight. Paid parking available at 170 Columbus Ave. Bus: 15 or 41.

Great Eastern ★ 🍴 CHINESE   If you like seafood and Chinese food and have an adventurous palate, you're going to love Great Eastern, which is well known among serious foodies for serving hard-to-find seafood pulled straight from the myriad tanks that line the walls. Rock cod, steelhead, sea conch, sea bass, shrimp, frogs, soft-shell turtle, abalone—if it's even remotely aquatic and edible, it's on the menu at this popular Hong Kong–style dinner house that's mostly frequented by Chinese locals (so you know it's good). The day's catch, sold by the pound, is listed on a board. Both upper- and lower-level dining rooms are stylish in a Chinatown sort of way, with shiny black and emerald furnishings. The dim sum is excellent here as well—some say it's even better than the venerable Yank Sing (p. 119)—so give it a try as well. *Tip:* Unless you can translate an authentic Hong Kong menu, order a set dinner (the crab version is fantastic) or point to another table and say, "I want that."

649 Jackson St. (btw. Kearny St. and Grant Ave.). ℂ **415/986-2500.** Most main courses $8–$13. AE, MC, V. Mon–Fri 10am–midnight; Sat–Sun 9am–midnight. Bus: 30, 41, or 45.

House of Nanking ★ CHINESE   This place would be strictly a tourist joint if it weren't for the die-hard fans who happily wait—sometimes up to an hour—for a coveted seat at this inconspicuous spot for Shanghai-style cuisine. Order the requisite pot stickers, green-onion-and-shrimp pancakes with peanut sauce, or any number of pork, rice, beef, seafood, chicken, or vegetable dishes from the menu, but I suggest you trust the waiter when he recommends a special (even if

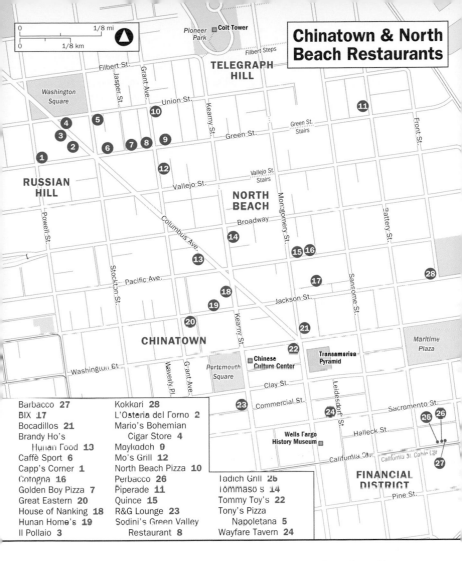

Chinatown & North Beach Restaurants

0 — 1/8 mi	
0 — 1/8 km	

Pioneer Park
Coit Tower
Filbert Steps

TELEGRAPH HILL

Filbert St.
Jasper St.
Grant Ave.
Union St.
Green St. Stairs
Green St.

Washington Square

Kearny St.

Front St.

RUSSIAN HILL

Powell St.

Columbus Ave.

Vallejo St.
Vallejo St. Stairs

NORTH BEACH

Broadway

Montgomery St.

Battery St.

Stockton St.
Pacific Ave.

Kearny St.

Jackson St.

Sansome St.

CHINATOWN

Waverly Pl.
Grant Ave.

Washington St.

Portsmouth Square

Chinese Culture Center

Transamerica Pyramid

Maritime Plaza

Clay St.

Leidesdorff St.

Commercial St.

Sacramento St.

Wells Fargo History Museum

Halleck St.

California St.

California St. Cable Car

FINANCIAL DISTRICT

Pine St.

Barbacco **27**	Kokkari **28**	Tadich Grill **26**
BIX **17**	L'Osteria del Forno **2**	Tommaso's **14**
Bocadillos **21**	Mario's Bohemian	Tommy Toy's **22**
Brandy Ho's	Cigar Store **4**	Tony's Pizza
Hunan Food **13**	Maykadeh **9**	Napoletana **5**
Caffè Sport **6**	Mo's Grill **12**	Wayfare Tavern **24**
Capp's Corner **1**	North Beach Pizza **10**	
Cotogna **16**	Perbacco **26**	
Golden Boy Pizza **7**	Piperade **11**	
Great Eastern **20**	Quince **15**	
House of Nanking **18**	R&G Lounge **23**	
Hunan Home's **19**	Sodini's Green Valley	
Il Pollaio **3**	Restaurant **8**	

you do specify your order, the waiter may tell you to get something else; roll with it, it's a longtime Chinatown tradition). Even with an expansion that doubled the available space, seating is tight, so prepare to be bumped around a bit and don't expect perky or attentive service—it's all part of the Nanking experience.

919 Kearny St. (at Columbus Ave.). ☎ **415/421-1429.** Reservations accepted for groups of 8 or more. Main courses $6–$12. MC, V. Mon–Fri 11am–10pm; Sat noon–10pm; Sun noon–9pm. Bus: 9, 12, or 30.

Hunan Home's ★★ CHINESE   One of Chinatown's best restaurants, Hunan Home's is a feast for the eyes—ubiquitous pink-and-white walls lined with big wall-to-wall mirrors that reflect armies of fish tanks and tacky chandeliers—as well as the palate. The rule of thumb here is not to put anything in your mouth until you're armed with a glass of water, because most every dish is *ooooweeeee* hot! Start with Home's excellent hot-and-sour soup (the acid test of every Chinese restaurant) or wonton soup (chock-full of shrimp, chicken, barbecued pork, squid, and vegetables), followed by the succulent bread appetizer, a platter of prawns with honeyed walnuts, and the scallops a la Hunan (sautéed along with snow peas, baby corn, celery, and mushrooms). Photographs of the more popular dishes are posted out front, though it's hard to tell which ones will singe your nose hairs.

622 Jackson St. (btw. Kearny St. and Grant Ave.). ✆ **415/982-2844.** Main courses $7.95–$12. AE, DC, DISC, MC, V. Sun–Thurs 11:30am–9:30pm; Fri–Sat 11:30am–10pm. Bus: 30, 41, or 45.

R&G Lounge ★ CHINESE It's tempting to take your chances and duck into any of the exotic restaurants in Chinatown, but if you want a sure thing, go directly to the three-story R&G Lounge. During lunch, all three floors are packed with hungry neighborhood workers who go straight for the $6 rice-plate specials. Even then, you can order from the dinner menu, which features legendary deep-fried salt-and-pepper crab (a little greasy for my taste), and wonderful chicken with black-bean sauce. A personal favorite is melt-in-your-mouth R&G Special Beef, which explodes with the tangy flavor of the accompanying sauce. I was less excited by the tired chicken salad, house specialty noodles, and bland spring rolls. But that was just fine since I saved room for generous and savory seafood in a clay pot and classic roast duck.

631 Kearny St. (at Clay St.). ✆ **415/982-7877.** www.rnglounge.com. Reservations recommended. Main courses $9.50–$30. AE, DC, DISC, MC, V. Daily 11am–9:30pm. Parking validated across the street at Portsmouth Square garage 24 hr. or Holiday Inn after 5pm. Bus: 1. Cable Car: California line.

NORTH BEACH/TELEGRAPH HILL

For a map of restaurants in this section, see the "Chinatown & North Beach Restaurants" map on p. 129.

Expensive

BIX ★★ 📷 AMERICAN/CALIFORNIAN The martini lifestyle may now be *en vogue,* but it was never out of style in this glamorous retro '30s-era supper club. BIX is utterly stylish, with curving mahogany paneling, giant silver pillars, and dramatic lighting, all of which sets the stage for live music and plenty of hobnobbing. Though the sleek setting has overshadowed the food in the past, the legions of diners entranced by the BIX experience don't seem to care—and it seems as of late BIX is "on" again. Chicken hash has been a menu favorite for the past 19 years, but newer luxury comfort-food dishes—such as caviar service, marrowbones with toast and shallot confit, steak tartare, and pan-roasted seasonal fish dishes—are developing their own fan clubs. ***Bargain tip:*** At lunch, the Bix-fixe menu goes for $20.

56 Gold St. (btw. Sansome and Montgomery sts.). ✆ **415/433-6300.** www.bixrestaurant.com. Reservations recommended. Main courses $16–$27 lunch, $20–$40 dinner. AE, DC, DISC, MC, V. Mon–Wed 4:30–10pm; Thurs 4:30–11pm; Fri 11:30am–11pm; Sat 5:30–11pm; Sun 5:30–10pm. Valet parking $10. Bus: 30, 41, or 45.

Moderate

Tony's Pizza Napoletana ★★ ITALIAN Tony Gemignani, the chef/owner of Tony's Pizza Napoletana, rocked Italy when he became the first American—and non-Neapolitan—to win Best Pizza Margherita at the World Pizza Cup in Naples

("Mio dio!"). He's now an 11-time World Pizza Champion and co-owner of the International School of Pizza in San Francisco. Believe the hype: Tony's Pizza Margherita is the best pizza I have ever tasted. But you have to get here early to try it, because he only bakes 73 Margheritas per day (ask your waiter why—it's an interesting story). But what's really unique about this North Beach pizza mecca is that the styles of pizzas served are determined by the temperature and types of Tony's seven different ovens. Styles include Neapolitan, Classic American and Italian, Sicilian, Pizza Romana, Gluten Free, and New York, Detroit, and St. Louis Style—all baked at different temperatures. *Note:* This place is always packed, and they don't take reservations, so be prepared to give your cellphone number to the hostess and walk around North Beach for an hour.

1570 Stockton St. (at Union St.). ✆ **415/835-9888.** www.tonyspizzanapoletana.com. No reservations. Main courses $13–$28. AE, DC, DISC, MC, V. Wed–Sun noon–11pm. Bus: 30, 39, 41, or 45. Cable car: Powell–Mason line.

Maykadeh PERSIAN/MIDDLE EASTERN   If you're looking to add a little exotic adventure to your North Beach dinner plans, this is the place to go. Surrounded by a sea of Italian bistros, Maykadeh is one of San Francisco's best and most elegant Persian restaurants. The Middle East may no longer be the culinary capital of the world, but at Maykadeh you can still sample the exotic flavors that characterize Persian cuisine. Of the dozen or so appetizers, some of the best are eggplant with mint garlic sauce; stuffed grape leaves; and lamb tongue with lime juice, sour cream, and saffron (c'mon, live a little). About eight mesquite-grilled items are on the menu, including filet of lamb marinated in lime, homemade yogurt, saffron, and onions. House specialties include half a dozen vegetarian dishes, among them eggplant braised with saffron, fresh tomato, and dried lime.

470 Green St. (btw. Kearny St. and Grant Ave.). ✆ **415/362-8286.** www.maykadehrestaurant. com. Reservations recommended. Main courses $15–$31. MC, V. Mon–Thurs 11:45am–10.30pm; Fri–Sat 11:45am–11pm; Sun 11:45am–10pm. Valet parking $7 lunch, $8 dinner. Bus: 30 or 41.

Piperade ★★ BASQUE   Chef Gerald Hirigoyen takes diners on a Basque adventure in this charming, small, and superbly authentic restaurant. Surrounded by a low wood-beamed ceiling, oak floors, and soft sconce lighting, it's a casual affair where diners indulge in small and large plates of Hirigoyen's flavorful Basque cuisine. Your edible odyssey starts with small plates—or plates to be shared—such as my personal favorites: piquillo peppers stuffed with goat cheese and a bright and simple salad of garbanzo beans with calamari, chorizo, and piquillo peppers. Share entrees, too. Indulge in New York steak with braised shallots and french fries, or sop up every drop of the sweet and savory red-pepper sauce with the braised seafood and shellfish stew. Save room for orange blossom beignets: Light and airy, with a delicate and moist web of dough within and a kiss of orange essence, the beignet is dessert at its finest. There's a communal table for drop-in diners and front patio seating during warmer weather.

1015 Battery St. (at Green St.). ✆ **415/391-2555.** www.piperade.com. Reservations recommended. Main courses $18–$30. AE, DC, DISC, MC, V. Mon–Fri 11:30am–3pm and 5:30–10:30pm; Sat 5:30–10:30pm. Closed Sun. Bus: 10, 12, 30, or 82x.

The Stinking Rose ITALIAN   Garlic is the "flower" from which this restaurant gets its name. From soup to ice cream, the supposedly healthful herb is a star ingredient in almost every dish. ("We season our garlic with food," exclaims the menu.) From a gourmet point of view, the Stinking Rose is unremarkable. Pizzas, pastas, and meats smothered in simple, overpowering sauces are tasty, but they're memorable only for their singular garlicky intensity. That said, this is a fun, albeit touristy place; the restaurant's lively atmosphere and odoriferous aroma combine for good entertainment. The best dishes include iron-skillet-roasted mussels, shrimp, and crab with garlic sauce; smoked mozzarella, garlic, and tomato pizza; salt-roasted tiger prawns with garlic parsley glaze; and 40-clove garlic chicken (served with garlic mashed potatoes, of course). They even serve garlic martinis and—what else?—garlic ice cream from garlic mecca Gilroy for dessert. *Note:* For those who are not garlic-inclined, they offer garlic-free "Vampire Fare."

325 Columbus Ave. (btw. Vallejo St. and Broadway). © **415/781-7673.** www.thestinkingrose. com. Reservations recommended. Main courses $19–$40. AE, DC, DISC, MC, V. Daily 11am–11pm. Bus: 30, 41, or 45.

Inexpensive

Caffè Sport ★ ITALIAN   People either love or hate this stodgy, garlic-smelling Sicilian eatery. Every square inch is cluttered with hanging hams, fishnets, decorative plates, dolls, mirrors, and over 2 decades' worth of dust; Caffè Sport was once a culinary landmark. Now it's better known for its surly staff and eclectic ambience than for its cream- and butter-heavy food. Still, the fare is served up with hearty portions of tongue-in-cheek attitude along with huge garlic-laden pasta dishes. Lunch is tame in comparison to dinner, when the Sport is mobbed and lively, and strangers might be packed together family style. Disregard the menu and just accept the waiter's "suggestions." Whatever arrives—whether calamari, mussels, or shrimp in tomato-garlic sauce, or pasta in pesto sauce—it's bound to be *bene*. Bring a huge appetite and plenty of cash (they don't take credit cards), but above all, don't be late if you have a reservation.

574 Green St. (btw. Grant and Columbus aves.). © **415/981-1251.** www.caffesport.ypguides. net. Reservations recommended. Main courses $15–$30. No credit cards. Tues–Sat noon–2pm and 5–10:30pm. Bus: 30, 41, or 45.

Capp's Corner ★ 🍴 ITALIAN   Capp's is a place of givens: It's a given that high-spirited regulars are hunched over the bar and that you'll be served huge portions of straightforward Italian fare at decent prices in a raucous atmosphere that prevails until closing. The waitresses are usually brusque and bossy, but always with a wink. Long tables are set up for family-style dining: bread, soup, salad, and a choice of around 20 classic main dishes (herb-roasted leg of lamb, spaghetti with meatballs, *osso buco* with polenta, fettuccine with prawns and white-wine sauce)—all for $18 or $20 or so per person, around $13 for kids. You might have to wait awhile for a table, but if you want fun and authentic old-school dining without pomp or huge prices, you'll find the wait worthwhile.

1600 Powell St. (at Green St.). © **415/989-2589.** www.cappscorner.com. Reservations accepted. Complete dinners $15–$17. AE, DC, MC, V. Daily 11:30am–2:30pm; Mon–Fri 4:30–10:30pm; Sat–Sun 4–11pm. Bus: 30 or 41.

Golden Boy Pizza ★ 🍴 ITALIAN/PIZZA   Pass by Golden Boy when the bars are hopping in North Beach and you'll find a crowd of inebriated sots savoring steamy slices of wondrously gooey pizza. But you don't have to be on a red-wine buzz to enjoy the big, doughy squares of Italian-style pizzas, each enticingly placed in the front windows (the aroma alone is deadly). Locals have flocked here for years to fill up on one of the cheapest and cheesiest meals in town. Expect to take your feast to go on busy nights, as there are only a few bar seats inside.

542 Green St. (btw. Stockton St. and Grant Ave.). ℂ **415/982-9738.** www.goldenboypizza.com. Pizza slice $2.75–$3.75. No credit cards. Sun–Thurs 11:30am–11:30pm; Fri–Sat 11:30am–2:30am. Bus: 30, 45, 39, or 41.

Il Pollaio ★ 🍴 ITALIAN/ARGENTINE   Simple, affordable, and consistently good is the winning combination at Il Pollaio. When I used to live in the neighborhood, I ate here at least once a week and I still can't make chicken this good. Seat yourself in the tiny, unfussy room, order, and wait expectantly for the fresh-from-the-grill lemon-infused chicken, which is so moist it practically falls off the bone. Each meal comes with a choice of salad or fries. If you're not in the mood for chicken, you can opt for rabbit, lamb, pork chop, or Italian sausage. On a sunny day, get your goods to go and picnic across the street at Washington Square.

555 Columbus Ave. (btw. Green and Union sts.). ℂ **415/362-7727.** Reservations not accepted. Main courses $8–$15. DISC, MC, V. Mon–Sat 11:30am–9pm. Bus: 30, 39, 41, or 45. Cable car: Powell–Mason line.

L'Osteria del Forno ★★ ITALIAN   L'Osteria del Forno might be only slightly larger than a walk-in closet, but it's one of the top three authentic Italian restaurants in North Beach. Peer in the window facing Columbus Avenue, and you'll probably see two Italian women with their hair up, sweating from the heat of the oven, which cranks out the best focaccia (and focaccia sandwiches) in the city. There's no pomp or circumstance here: Locals come strictly to eat. The menu features a variety of superb pizzas, salads, soups, and fresh pastas, plus a few daily specials and a roast of the day (pray for the roast pork braised in milk). Small baskets of warm focaccia keep you going until the arrival of the entrees, which should always be accompanied by a glass of Italian red (this tiny place actually has a full bar, with a nice selection of grappas). Good news for folks on the go: You can get pizza by the slice. Note that it's cash-only.

519 Columbus Ave. (btw. Green and Union sts.). ℂ **415/982-1124.** www.losteriadelforno.com. Reservations not accepted. Sandwiches $6–$7; pizzas $10–$18; main courses $6–$16. No credit cards. Sun–Mon and Wed 11:30am–10pm; Fri–Sat 11:30am–10:30pm. Bus: 30, 41, or 45.

Mario's Bohemian Cigar Store ★ 🍴 ITALIAN   Across the street from Washington Square is one of North Beach's most venerable neighborhood hang-outs. The century-old corner cafe—small, well worn, and perpetually busy—is one of the oldest and best original cappuccino cafes in the United States. I stop by at least once a month for a meatball or eggplant focaccia sandwich and a slice of Mario's house-made ricotta cheesecake, and then recharge with a cappuccino as I watch the world stroll by the picture windows. And no, they don't sell cigars.

566 Columbus Ave. (at Union St.). ℂ **415/362-0536.** Sandwiches $7.75–$11. MC, V. Daily 10am–10pm. Bus: 30, 41, or 45.

Mo's Grill ★★ ☺ AMERICAN   This simple diner offers a straightforward but winning combination: big, thick, grilled patties of fresh-ground, best-quality, center-cut chuck; fresh french fries; and a choice of cabbage slaw, sautéed garlic mushrooms, or chili. *Voilà!* You've got my burger of choice. (Zuni Café's is a contender, but is almost twice the price—p. 148.) The other food—spicy chicken sandwiches; steak with veggies, garlic bread, and potatoes; and token veggie dishes—is also up to snuff, but that messy, memorable burger is what keeps the carnivores captivated. (The sinisterly sweet shakes are fantastic, too.) Bargain-diners will appreciate the prices, with burgers ranging from $7 for a classic to $9 for an "Alpine" burger with Gruyère cheese and sautéed mushrooms. Entrees start at $10 for meatloaf with mashed potatoes, garlic bread, and a vegetable, and top out at $18 for New York steak. The classic breakfast menu is also a bargain. A second location at SoMa's Yerba Buena Gardens, 772 Folsom St., between Third and Fourth streets (℘ **415/957-3779**), is open Sunday and Monday from 11am to 5pm, Tuesday through Saturday from 11am to 8pm. It features breakfast and burgers.

1322 Grant Ave. (btw. Vallejo and Green sts.). ℘ **415/788-3779.** www.mosgrill.com. Main courses $7–$18. MC, V. Sun–Thurs 8:30am–10:30pm; Fri–Sat 8:30am–11:30pm. Bus: 9X, 30, 39, 41, or 45.

North Beach Pizza ★ ☺ ITALIAN/PIZZA   Whenever I order a North Beach pizza, I'm always disappointed by the measly amount of toppings that they give you. Then I eat the entire damn thing in one sitting. There's something about that uniquely gooey whole-milk mozzarella and hand-spun dough with thick, chewy edges that's so addictive it's been the most awarded and widely beloved pizza in the city for more than 2 decades. You *can* get a better pizza in the city—Pauline's (p. 154) and Little Star (p. 150) have them beat—but not in North Beach, not via free delivery throughout the city, and not at 2am on Saturday when you're drunk, stoned, and starving. Either create your own pizza from their list of 20 fresh ingredients (the sausage with black olives is the *bomb*), or choose from the house's 10 specialties such as the San Francisco Special—clams, garlic, cheese, and one brutal case of halitosis. There are numerous satellite NBPs throughout the city offering fast, free delivery until the wee hours.

1462 Grant St. (at Union St.). ℘ **415/433-2444.** www.northbeachpizza.com. Main courses $9–$21. AE, DC, DISC, MC, V. Mon–Thurs 5–11pm; Fri–Sat 10am–1am; delivery until 2am daily. Bus: 30, 41, or 45. Cable car: Powell–Mason line.

San Francisco Art Institute Café ▮ AMERICAN   Never in a million years would you stumble upon the Art Institute Café by accident. One of the best-kept secrets in San Francisco, this cafe offers fresh, affordable cafe standards for in-the-know residents and visitors as well as Art Institute students: a wide array of hearty breakfast dishes, fresh salads, sandwiches on homemade bread, daily ethnically inspired specials, and anything with caffeine in it—all priced at or under $7. The best reason to come here, though, is for the view, which extends from Alcatraz Island to Coit Tower and beyond—it's so phenomenal that the exterior served as the outside of Sigourney Weaver's chic apartment in the movie *Copycat*. To get to the upstairs cafe, walk through the contemplative courtyard, and pass by the art gallery housing *The Making of a Fresco* mural painted in 1931 by Diego Rivera, one of only four in the Bay Area.

800 Chestnut St. (btw. Jones and Leavenworth sts.). ℘ **415/749-4567.** Main courses $4–$6. No credit cards. Fall–spring Mon–Thurs 8am–5pm, Fri 8am–4pm; summer Mon–Fri 9am–2pm. Closed Sat–Sun. Hours dependent on school schedule; please call to confirm. Bus: 30 or 49. Cable car: Powell–Hyde or Powell–Mason line.

Sodini's Green Valley Restaurant ★ ITALIAN   Sodini's is everything you would expect from a classic Italian restaurant in North Beach—a family-owned-and-operated business run by a friendly, vivacious staff that serves hearty Italian classics on tables topped with wax-encrusted chianti bottle candles while the Chairman of the Board croons love songs in the background. There's usually a wait for a table; fortunately, the bar is a great place to hang out, shoot the breeze with the friendly bartender (most likely one of the owners), and get a little North

Beach history lesson. The clientele is a mix of locals and tourists, all getting hungrier by the minute as the aroma of garlic and fresh basil wafts from the kitchen. The large wood-fired pizzas are very good and worth moving that belt one more notch, but their best dish is the light and tender gnocchi. Regardless of what you order, you won't leave hungry or unhappy.

510 Green St. (at Grant St.). ☎ **415/291-0499.** Reservations not accepted. Main courses $10–$23. MC, V. Daily 5–10pm. Bus: 30, 41, or 45. Cable car: Powell–Mason line.

Tommaso's ★ ☺ ITALIAN   From the street, Tommaso's looks wholly unappealing—a drab, windowless brown facade sandwiched between sex shops. Then why are people always waiting in line to get in? Because everyone knows that Tommaso's, which opened in 1935, bakes one of San Francisco's best traditional-style pizzas. The center of attention in the downstairs dining room is the chef, who continuously tosses huge hunks of garlic and mozzarella onto pizzas before sliding them into the oak-burning brick oven. Nineteen different toppings make pizza the dish of choice, even though Italian classics such as veal Marsala, chicken cacciatore, superb lasagna, and wonderful calzones are also available. Tommaso's also offers half-bottles of house wines, homemade manicotti, and good Italian coffee. If you can overlook the seedy surroundings, this fun, boisterous restaurant is a great place to take the family.

1042 Kearny St. (at Broadway). ☎ **415/398-9696.** www.tommasos.com. Reservations not accepted. Pasta and pizza $14–$26; main courses $16–$22. AE, DC, DISC, MC, V. Tues–Sat 5–10:30pm, Sun 4–9:30pm. Closed Dec 19–Jan 11. Bus: 41.

FISHERMAN'S WHARF

For a map of restaurants in this section, see the "San Francisco Restaurants" map on p. 106.

Very Expensive

Forbes Island ★ 📷 FRENCH   Been there and done that in every San Francisco dining room? Then it's time for Forbes Island, a wonderfully ridiculous floating restaurant disguised as an island (complete with lighthouse and real 40-ft. palm trees) and unknown to even most locals. The idea's kitschy, but the execution's actually quite wonderful. Here's how it works: Arrive at the dock next to Pier 39, call the restaurant via the courtesy phone, climb aboard its pontoon boat that takes you on a 4-minute journey to the "island" located 75 feet from the city's famed sea lions, and descend into the island's bowels to find a surprisingly classy, Tudor-like wood-paneled dining room. Warmed by a fireplace and amused by fish swimming past the portholes (yes, the dining room is a wee bit underwater), guests dine on surprisingly well-prepared classic French food such as decadent wild mushroom risotto and goat cheese or roasted half-rack of lamb with herbed flageolet beans, minted edamame, and natural lamb reduction *jus*. The added "Sea Lion" room boasts the closest view you'll ever get of the creatures. *But be warned:* The menu is limited, the wine list features basic big-name producers without listing the vintage, and the "island" does gently rock. (Landlubbers need not apply or BYO Dramamine.) *One annoyance:* There is a mandatory $3 shuttle fee; the only other way to get there is to swim.

Water shuttle is just left of Pier 39. ☎ **415/951-4900.** www.forbesisland.com. Reservations recommended. Main courses $28–$39. AE, DC, MC, V. Wed–Sun arrive 5–10pm. Validated parking at Pier 39 garage, $8 for up to 6 hr.

Restaurant Gary Danko ★★★ FRENCH   James Beard Award–winning chef Gary Danko presides over my top pick for fine dining. Eschewing the white-glove formality of yesteryear's fine dining, Danko offers impeccable cuisine and perfectly orchestrated service in an unstuffy environment of wooden paneling and shutters and well-spaced tables (not to mention spa-style restrooms). The three- to five-course fixed-price seasonal menu is freestyle, so whether you want a sampling of appetizers or a flight of meat courses, you need only ask. Try his trademark buttery-smooth glazed oysters with lettuce cream, salsify, and Osetra caviar; the seared foie gras, which may be accompanied by peaches, caramelized onions, and *verjus* (a classic French sauce); and juniper-crusted venison with braised red cabbage, cranberries, cipollini onions, and chestnut gnocchi. Truthfully, I've never had a dish here that wasn't wonderful. And wine? The list is stellar, albeit expensive. If you pass on the glorious cheese cart or flambéed dessert of the day, a plate of petit fours reminds you that Gary Danko is one sweet and memorable meal. ***Tip:*** If you can't get a reservation, slip in and grab a seat at the bar, where you can also order a la carte.

800 North Point St. (at Hyde St.). ℂ **415/749-2060.** www.garydanko.com. Reservations required except at walk-in bar. 3-course fixed-price menu $69; 4-course menu $87; 5-course menu $102. AE, DC, DISC, MC, V. Daily 5:30–10pm. Bar daily 5–midnight. Valet parking $11. Bus: 10. Streetcar: F. Cable car: Hyde.

Scoma's ★ SEAFOOD   This is one of the few Fisherman's Wharf restaurants that still attracts the occasional local, along with the tourists. A throwback to the dining of yesteryear, Scoma's eschews trendier trout preparations and fancy digs for good old-fashioned seafood served in huge portions with lots of sauce and a windowed waterfront setting. If your idea of heaven is straightforward seafood classics—fried calamari, raw oysters, pesto pasta with rock shrimp, crab cioppino, lobster thermidor—served with a generous portion of old-time hospitality, then Scoma's is as good as it gets. Unfortunately, a taste of tradition will cost you big time. Prices are as steep as those at some of the finest restaurants in town. Personally, I'd rather splurge at nearby Gary Danko, but many of my out-of-town guests insist we meet at Scoma's—which is fine by me, since it's a change of pace from today's über-chic spots, and the parking's free.

Gary Danko won the prestigious James Beard Foundation's "Best New Restaurant" award in 2000—and still lives up to the acclaim.

Pier 47 and Al Scoma Way (btw. Jefferson and Jones sts.). ✆ **800/644-5852** or 415/771-4383. www.scomas.com. Reservations not accepted. Most main courses $16–$36. AE, DC, DISC, MC, V. Sun–Thurs 11:30am–10pm; Fri–Sat 11:30am–10:30pm. Bar opens 30 min. prior to lunch daily. Free valet parking. Bus: 10 or 47. Streetcar: F.

Expensive

Alioto's SEAFOOD   One of San Francisco's oldest restaurants, run by one of the city's most prominent families, the Aliotos, this Fisherman's Wharf landmark has a long-standing reputation for great cioppino (founder Nonna Rose is often credited with its invention). The curbside crab stand, Café 8, and the outdoor crab market are great for quick, inexpensive doses of San Francisco's finest. For more formal surroundings, continue up the stairs to the multilevel, harbor-view dining room. Don't mess around with the menu: If you're here, you're after Dungeness crab. Cracked, caked, stuffed, or stewed, it's impossible to get your fill, so bring plenty of money—particularly if you intend to order from Alioto's prodigious (and pricey) wine list. If you don't care for cracked crab, try the griddle-fried sand dabs or the rex sole served with tartar sauce.

8 Fisherman's Wharf (at Taylor St.). ✆ **415/673-0183.** www.aliotos.com. Reservations recommended. Main courses $15–$30 lunch; most main courses $15–$50 dinner. AE, DC, DISC, MC, V. Daily 11am–11pm. Bus: 10, 39, or 47. Streetcar: F. Cable car: Powell–Hyde line.

Ana Mandara ★ VIETNAMESE   Yes, Don Johnson is part owner. But more importantly, this Fisherman's Wharf favorite serves excellent, inventive Vietnamese food in an outstandingly beautiful setting. Chef Khai Duong is considered a pioneer of modern Vietnamese cuisine with stacks of awards to back up the claim. Amid a shuttered room with mood lighting, palm trees, and Vietnamese-inspired decor, diners (mostly tourists) splurge on crispy rolls, lobster ravioli with mango and coconut sauce, and wok-charred tournedos of beef tenderloin with sweet onions and peppercress. There is no more expensive Vietnamese dining room in town, but, along with the enjoyable fare, diners pay for the atmosphere, which, if they're in the neighborhood and want something more exotic than the standby seafood dinner, is worth the price.

891 Beach St. (at Polk St.) ✆ **415/771-6800.** www.anamandara.com. Reservations recommended. Main courses $22–$40. AE, DC, DISC, MC, V. Mon–Fri 11:30am–2pm; Sun–Thurs 5:30–9:30pm; Fri–Sat 5:30–10:30pm (bar until 1am). Valet parking Tues–Sun $9. Bus: 19, 30, or 45.

Moderate

Cafe Pescatore ★ ITALIAN   This cozy trattoria is one of the better bets in Fisherman's Wharf. Two walls of sliding glass doors offer pseudo-sidewalk seating when the weather's warm, although heavy vehicular traffic can detract from the alfresco experience. All the classics are well represented here: crisp Caesar salad, fried calamari, bruschetta, cioppino, pastas, chicken Marsala, and veal saltimbocca (sautéed veal scaloppini) with whipped baby potatoes, spinach, prosciutto, and lemon-caper butter sauce. The consensus is to order anything that's cooked in the open kitchen's wood-fired oven, such as pizza (Margherita), roasts (sea bass with pine-nut crust, or Atlantic salmon), or panini (lunch only; grilled chicken or grilled veggies). They serve a darn good breakfast, too.

2455 Mason St. (at North Point St., adjoining the Tuscan Inn). ✆ **415/561-1111.** www.cafe pescatore.com. Reservations recommended. Main courses $6.50–$12 breakfast, $9–$22 lunch and dinner. AE, DC, DISC, MC, V. Daily 7am–10pm. Bus: 39 or 42. Streetcar: F. Cable car: Powell–Mason line.

Fog City Diner ★ AMERICAN   When it opened, Fog City Diner was the "it" spot for locals in search of upscale California chow. These days, it gets a lot of mixed reviews for service and food, but I've always had a satisfying experience here. The restaurant looks like a genuine American metallic railroad diner—but only from the outside. Inside, dark polished woods, inspired lighting, and a well-stocked raw bar tell you this is no hash-slinger. Dressed-up diner dishes include juicy gourmet burgers with house-made pickles, huge salads, "warm breads," soups, sandwiches, cioppino, macaroni and Gouda cheese, and pork chops. Fancier fish and meat meals include grilled catches of the day and thick-cut steaks. Light eaters can make a meal out of the long list of small plates, which include crab cakes, quesadillas with asparagus and leeks, and their famous red-curry mussel stew. They've recently opened for weekend brunch as well. The food is fine, but if your heart is set on coming here, do so at lunch or for early evening cocktails and appetizers—you'll be better off elsewhere if you want a special dinner.

1300 Battery St. (at the Embarcadero). (*C* **415/982-2000.** www.fogcitydiner.com. Reservations recommended. Main courses $14–$24. DC, DISC, MC, V. Mon–Thurs 11:30am–10pm; Fri 11:30am–11pm; Sat 10:30am–11pm; Sun 10:30am–10pm. Streetcar: F.

Lou's Pier 47 STEAK/SEAFOOD/CAJUN   This popular restaurant and blues club is one of the few establishments on Fisherman's Wharf that locals will admit they've been to at least once. The bottom floor consists of a bar and bistro-style dining room, while the upstairs hosts blues bands every night of the week, with the occasional Motown, country, and R&B act thrown in for variety. Lunch and dinner items range from a variety of Cajun classics such as gumbo ya ya, jambalaya, and shrimp Creole to baby back ribs, steamed Dungeness crab, blackened swordfish, and New York steak. There's a lengthy starters menu if you just want to nosh on a Jamaica jerk salad, Louisiana crawfish bowl, or "peel 'em and eat" shrimp. **Budget tip:** The Saturday blues show from noon to 3pm is free; otherwise, the upstairs club cover is $3 to $10.

300 Jefferson St. (near Pier 47). (*C* **415/771-5687.** www.louspier47.com. Main courses $17–$23. AE, DC, MC, V. Daily 11am–11pm (club until 2am). Bus: 47. Streetcar: F. Cable car: Powell–Hyde line.

Inexpensive

Bistro Boudin at the Wharf DELI/AMERICAN   This industrial-chic Fisherman's Wharf shrine to the city's famous tangy French-style bread is impossible to miss. Even if you're not hungry, drop in to see bakers at work making 3,000 loaves daily, or take the tour and learn about the history of the city's sourdough bread (Boudin is the city's oldest continually operating business). Good, strong coffee is served at **Peet's Coffee** (another Bay Area great), and at **Bakers Hall** you'll find picnic possibilities such as handcrafted cheeses, fruit spreads, and chocolates, as well as a wall map highlighting the town's best places to spread a blanket and feast. There's also a casual **self-serve cafe** serving sandwiches, clam chowder bowls, salads, and pastries, and the more formal **Bistro Boudin** restaurant, which offers Alcatraz views with its Dungeness crab Louis, pizza, crab cakes, and burgers on sourdough buns.

160 Jefferson St., near Pier 43½. (*C* **415/928-1849.** www.boudinbakery.com. Reservations recommended at bistro. Main courses cafe $6–$10, bistro $11–$33. AE, DC, DISC, MC, V. Daily 11:45am–9pm. Bus: 47. Streetcar: F.

THE MARINA/PACIFIC HEIGHTS/ COW HOLLOW

For a map of restaurants in this section, see the "San Francisco Restaurants" map on p. 106.

Very Expensive

Harris' ★★ STEAKHOUSE   Every big city has a great steak restaurant, and in San Francisco it's Harris'—a comfortably elegant establishment where the seriously handsome and atmospheric wood-paneled dining room has high-backed booths, banquettes, high ceilings, hunting murals, stately waiters, a convivial bar scene with live jazz Thursday through Saturday, and even a meat counter for the carnivore on the go. Here, the point, of course, is steak, which can be seen hanging in a glass-windowed aging room off Pacific Avenue. The cuts are thick—New York style or T-bone—and are served with a baked potato and seasonal vegetables. You'll also find classic French onion soup, spinach and Caesar salads, and sides of delicious creamed spinach, sautéed shiitake mushrooms, or caramelized onions. Harris' also offers lamb chops, fresh fish, lobster, and occasionally venison, buffalo, and other seasonal game. Desserts, such as a sculptural beehivelike baked Alaska, are surprisingly good. If you're debating between this place and House of Prime Rib (p. 127), consider that aside from specializing in aged meats, this place is more "upscale" (the appetizer list includes an Eagle Rare Manhattan, and you can get 13 oz. of Kobe beef for $170), while HOPR features prime rib and a classic old school vibe.

2100 Van Ness Ave. (at Pacific Ave.). © **415/673-1888.** www.harrisrestaurant.com. Reservations recommended. Most main courses $25–$46. AE, DC, DISC, MC, V. Mon–Thurs 5:30–9pm; Fri 5:30–10pm; Sat 5–10pm; Sun 5–9pm. Valet parking $10. Bus: 12, 47, or 49.

Spruce ★ CONTEMPORARY AMERICAN   If you haven't heard of San Francisco's Pacific Heights neighborhood, it's where most of the city's old money lives, and now the ladies-who-lunch have a new place to hang their cloches: Spruce. In a beautifully restored 1930s era auto barn, Spruce consists of a restaurant, cafe, bar, and lounge under a single roof, making it both a destination restaurant and a neighborhood hangout. As you enter, there's a library nook on one side filled with newspapers, cookbooks, and so on, and a cafe on the other side offering gourmet take-away items. Farther inside is an elegant bar to the right and 70-seat restaurant to the left, both topped with a vast cathedral ceiling highlighted by a glass-and-steel skylight. With mohair couches, faux-ostrich chairs, and a black-and-chocolate decor, it's all quite visually appealing, but, alas, the cuisine isn't quite as impressive. The organic, locally sourced produce is wonderfully fresh, but many of the dishes I tried—spearmint and nettle ravioli, leek and fennel soup with salt cod dumplings, honey-lacquered duck breast—were lacking in flavor, and the service suffered from mysteriously long spells of absence. Spruce is still one of the exciting new restaurants in San Francisco, but it's best enjoyed from a seat at the bar while tucking into their fantastic all-natural burger and fries and pondering which wine to choose from their 70 by-the-glass selections.

3640 Sacramento St. (at Spruce St.). © **415/931-5100.** www.sprucesf.com. Reservations recommended. Main courses $26–$40. AE, DC, DISC, MC, V. Mon–Fri 11:30am–10pm; Sat–Sun 5–10pm. Valet parking $12 dinner only. Bus: 1 or 2.

Expensive

Baker & Banker ★★★ CONTEMPORARY AMERICAN   Baker & Banker is the most impressive restaurant to open in San Francisco in the past few years. When Quince occupied the same digs, it was far too stuffy for my liking—Baker & Banker moved in 2009, and co-owners and spouses Jeff Banker and Lori Baker have kept the cozy booths full thanks to their winning combination of superb cuisine and inviting atmosphere.

Jeff's signature dishes include the smoked trout, draped over a celery root latke and served with a horseradish crème fraîche with pickled beets and shaved fennel, and a black cod with foie gras–shiitake sticky rice accompanied by charred bok choy. But really you can't go wrong with anything you order, whether you opt for the crepes filled with butternut squash and *cavolo nero,* or the scallops with Dungeness crab, Sardinian couscous, Pernod-saffron sauce, and Satsuma mandarin salad. Just don't forget to save room for dessert, as that's one of Baker & Banker's specialties, thanks to Lori's penchant for the sweet. The hot spiced butterscotch with homemade vanilla marshmallows and olive oil–fleur de sel biscotti is particularly mouthwatering. The restaurant offers a very affordable chef's tasting menu for $55 a person, plus $35 for wine pairings. Baker & Banker also has a bakery component open during the day on the Bust Street side of the restaurant.

1701 Octavia St. (at Bush St.). *℃* **415/351-2500.** www.bakerandbanker.com. Reservations recommended. Main courses $20–$28. AE, MC, V. Tues–Sat 5:30–10pm; Sun 10am–2pm and 5–9pm. Valet parking $10 dinner. Bus: 1, 2, 3, 47, 49, 76, or 90.

Moderate

Ace Wasabi's Rock 'n' Roll Sushi ★ JAPANESE/SUSHI   What differentiates this Marina hot spot from the usual sushi spots around town are the unique combinations, the varied menu, and the young, hip atmosphere. The innovative rolls are a nice change for those bored with traditional styles, but don't worry if someone in your party isn't a raw fish fan: There are also plenty of non-seafood and cooked items on the menu. Don't miss the rainbow "Three Amigos" roll, or the "Flying Kamikaze" with spicy albacore tuna wrapped around asparagus and topped with ponzu and scallions. The service, like the surroundings, is jovial.

3339 Steiner St. (at Chestnut St.). *℃* **415/567-4903.** Some reservations; waitlist. Sushi $4–$14. AE, MC, V. Mon–Thurs 5:30–10pm; Fri–Sat 5:30–11pm; Sun 5–10pm. Bus: 30.

A16 ★★ ITALIAN   This sleek, casual, and wonderfully lively spot is one of San Francisco's best and busiest Italian restaurants, featuring thin-crust Neapolitan-style pizza and cuisine from the region of Campania. Named after the motorway that traverses the region, the divided space boasts a wine and beer bar up front, a larger dining area and open kitchen in the back, and a wall of wines in between. But its secret weapon is the creative menu of outstanding appetizers, pizza, and entrees—with ingredients sourced fresh from local farms. Even if you must hoard the insanely good roast Berkshire pork ribs and shoulder for yourself, start by sharing roasted Monterey sardines with citrus, fennel, and green olives, or artichoke and tuna *conserva* with dried favas, braised bitter greens, and housemade *croccantini.* If meatballs are on the menu, don't ask questions—get 'em. Co-owner and wine director Shelley Lindgren guides diners through one of the city's most exciting wine lists, featuring 40 wines by the half-glass, glass, and carafe.

The Marina/Pacific Heights/Cow Hollow

WHERE TO EAT

2355 Chestnut St. (btw. Divisadero and Scott sts.). ☎ **415/771-2216.** www.a16sf.com. Reservations recommended. Main courses $10–$16 lunch, $11–$25 dinner. AE, DC, MC, V. Wed–Fri 11:30am–2:30pm; Sun–Thurs 5–10pm; Fri–Sat 5–11pm. Bus: 22, 30, or 30X.

Betelnut ★ SOUTHEAST ASIAN Although San Francisco is teeming with Asian restaurants, few offer the posh, fashionable dining environment of this restaurant on upscale Union Street. As the menu explains, the restaurant is themed after Pejui Wu, a traditional Asian beer house offering local brews and savory dishes. But with the bamboo paneling, red Formica countertops, and low-hanging lamps, the place feels less like an authentic harbor restaurant and more like a set out of *Shanghai Surprise.* Still, the atmosphere is *en vogue,* with dimly lit booths, ringside seating overlooking the bustling stir-fry chefs, sidewalk tables (weather permitting), and body-to-body flirting at the cramped but festive bar. Lots of small plates make for a great night of grazing. Starters include sashimi and tasty salt-and-pepper whole gulf prawns; main courses to consider include wok-seared Mongolian beef and Singapore chili crab (seasonal). Whatever you do, order their heavenly signature dessert: a mouthwatering tapioca pudding with sweet red adzuki beans.

2030 Union St. (at Buchanan St.). ☎ **415/929-8855.** www.betelnutrestaurant.com. Reservations recommended. Main courses $9.50–$21. DC, DISC, MC, V. Sun–Thurs 11:30am–11pm; Fri–Sat 11:30am–midnight. Bus: 22, 41, or 45.

Dosa ★★ SOUTHERN INDIAN This favorite locals' spot has been dubbed the city's best Indian by the media for a reason. Dosa offers fresh, organic ingredients, reasonable prices, and a much more authentic cuisine than its Americanized competitors. This new outpost is more dressed up (read: swankier) than its casual Mission location (995 Valencia St.; ☎ **415/642-3672**) but serves the same winning dishes. The southern Indian menu has an entire section devoted to its namesake, *dosa* (a savory rice and lentil crepe with sambar and tomato and coconut chutney), as well as several *uttapam* dishes (a thicker pancakelike variation on the *dosa*). Order a couple of kinds to share, family style. For an entree, opt for the vegetable korma and *paratha* (cauliflower, green beans, peas, potatoes, poppy seeds, fennel, and coconut), or cilantro and chili fish with a side of basmati rice (aromatically flavored with either jasmine or lemon). Don't pass on dessert: The banana *uttapam* (layered with strawberries, chocolate, and white *shrikhand*) is divine. Drinks are creatively named and concocted. A signature four-course tasting menu is $39 and the best way to adequately sample the cuisine. Tack on $20 for wine pairings.

1700 Fillmore St. (at Post St.). ☎ **415/441-3672.** www.dosasf.com. Reservations recommended. Main courses $7–$28. AE, DISC, MC, V. Daily 11:30am–3pm and 5:30pm–midnight. Bus: 2, 3, 22, 38, or 38L.

E'Angelo Restaurant ★ ITALIAN Back when I was barely making enough to cover my rent, I would often treat myself to a night out at E'Angelo. All the house specialties, pastas, and pizzas cost less than $19; the atmosphere is casual and fun; tables are cozy-cramped; and the Italian staff is friendly. For me, the combination made not only for a hearty meal, but also for an opportunity to mingle with San Francisco: to live a little, eavesdrop on neighbors' conversations, and perhaps even run into local celebrities such as Robin Williams with his family. While years have passed, not much has changed at this traditional Italian hot spot: The place still won't take reservations or credit cards. It still serves decent portions of pastas, veal, lamb, chicken, and fish; a carafe of red or white wine for about 18 bucks (thrifty by-the-bottle prices, too); and one heck of a rich eggplant parmigiana. And unlike those at most of the neighboring restaurants, desserts are dirt-cheap.

2234 Chestnut St. (btw. Pierce and Scott sts.). ✆ **415/567-6164.** www.eangelo.com. Reservations not required. Main courses $13–$19. No credit cards. Tues–Sun 5–10:30pm; Sat–Sun 11am–3pm. Bus: 22, 30, or 30X.

Ella's ★★ AMERICAN/BREAKFAST   Well known throughout town as the undisputed queen of breakfasts, this restaurant's acclaim means you're likely to wait in line up to an hour on weekends. But midweek and in the wee hours of morning, it's possible to slide onto a counter or table seat in the colorful split dining room and lose yourself in outstanding and generous servings of chicken hash, crisped to perfection and served with eggs any way you like them, with a side of fluffy buttermilk biscuits. Pancakes, omelets, and the short list of other breakfast essentials are equally revered. Service can be woefully slow, but at least the busboys and -gals are quick to fill coffee cups. Come lunchtime, solid entrees like salads, chicken potpie, and grilled salmon with mashed potatoes remind you what's great about American cooking.

500 Presidio Ave. (at California St.). ✆ **415/441-5669.** www.ellassanfrancisco.com. Reservations accepted for lunch. Main courses $5.50–$11 breakfast, $9.75–$12 brunch, $9–$13 lunch. AE, DISC, MC, V. Mon–Fri 7am–3pm; Sat–Sun 8:30am–2pm. Bus: 1, 3, or 43.

Greens ★★ VEGETARIAN   In an old waterfront warehouse, with enormous windows overlooking the Golden Gate, boats, and the bay, Greens reigns over gourmet vegetarian—a pioneer in the city and one of the most renowned vegetarian restaurants in the country. Executive chef Annie Somerville (author of *Fields of Greens*) cooks with the seasons, using produce from local organic farms. Brunch is a boisterous affair, but on a weeknight, the dining room is quiet and romantic, especially when the fog is in. Dinner might feature such appetizers as grilled asparagus with Meyer lemon vinaigrette, shaved Andante cheese, and warm butter beans, or grilled portobello and endive salad. Entrees run the gamut from pizza with wilted escarole, red onions, lemon, and Parmesan to wild mushroom ravioli with chanterelle, hedgehog, and maitake mushrooms, savoy spinach, and spring onions. Those interested in the whole shebang should make reservations for the $49 four-course dinner served on Saturday only. Lunch and brunch are equally fresh, tasty—and crowded. The adjacent Greens To Go sells sandwiches, soups, salads, and so on.

Bldg. A, Fort Mason Center (enter Fort Mason opposite the Safeway at Buchanan and Marina sts.). ✆ **415/771-6222.** www.greensrestaurant.com. Reservations recommended. Main courses $11–$18 lunch, $15–$20 dinner; fixed-price dinner $48; Sun brunch $11–$17. AE, DISC, MC, V. Tues–Sat noon–2:30pm; Sun 10:30am–9pm; Mon–Sat 5:30–9pm. Greens To Go Mon–Thurs 8am–8pm; Fri–Sat 8am–5pm; Sun 10:30am–4pm. Parking in hourly lot $4 for up to 2½ hr. Bus: 28 or 30.

Isa ★★ FRENCH   Luke Sung, who trained with some of the best French chefs in the city, has captured many locals' hearts by creating the kind of menu we foodies dream of: a smattering of small dishes, served a la carte family style, that allow you to try numerous items in one sitting. It's a good thing that the menu, considered "French tapas," offers small portions at reasonable prices. After all, it's asking a lot to make a diner choose from mushroom ragout with veal sweetbreads, seared foie gras with caramelized apples, potato-wrapped sea bass in brown butter, and rack of lamb. Here a party of two can choose all of these plus one or two more and not be rolled out the door afterward. Adding to the allure is the warm boutique dining environment—70 seats scattered amid a small dining room in the front, and a large tented and heated patio out back that sets the mood with a warm yellow glow. Take a peek at the "kitchen," a shoebox of a cooking space, to appreciate Sung's accomplishments even more. Cocktailers, take note: You'll find only beer, wine, and *shoju* cocktails (a smooth alcohol made from sweet potato and used like vodka).

3324 Steiner St. (btw. Lombard and Chestnut sts.). 🕾 **415/567-9588.** www.isarestaurant.com. Reservations recommended. Main courses $9–$16. MC, V. Mon–Thurs 5:30–10pm; Fri–Sat 5:30–10:30pm; Sun 5:30–9:30pm. Bus: 22, 28, 30, 30X, 43, or 76.

Pane e Vino ★ ITALIAN While the rest of the city tries to modernize their manicotti, this ultracasual Italian spot focuses on huge helpings of classics that are fine for the traditional diner, but not fabulous for the gourmand. That said, prices are reasonable, and the mostly Italian-accented staff is always smooth and efficient under pressure (you'll see). The menu offers a wide selection of appetizers, including a fine carpaccio, *vitello tonnato* (sliced roasted veal and capers in lemony tuna sauce), and the hugely popular chilled artichoke stuffed with bread and tomatoes and served with vinaigrette. The broad selection of pastas includes flavorful *penne puttanesca* with tomatoes, capers, anchovies, garlic, and olives. Other specialties are grilled fish and meat dishes, including chicken breast marinated in lime juice and herbs. Top dessert picks are any of the Italian ice creams, panna cotta, and (but of course) creamy tiramisu.

1715 Union St. (at Gough St.). 🕾 **415/346-2111.** www.paneevinotrattoria.com. Reservations highly recommended. Main courses $14–$29. AE, MC, V. Sun–Thurs 5–10pm; Fri–Sat 5–10:30pm. No parking. Bus: 41 or 45.

Inexpensive

Barney's Gourmet Hamburgers ★ ☺ HAMBURGERS If you're on a perpetual quest for a good burger, a mandatory stop is Barney's Gourmet Hamburgers. Once you get past all the framed awards for the Bay Area's best burger, you're bombarded by a mind-boggling menu of beef, chicken, turkey, and vegetarian burgers to choose from, as well as sandwiches and salads. The ultimate combo is a humongous basket of fries (enough for a party of three), one-third-pound burger, and thick shake. Popular versions are the California Burger with jack cheese, bacon, Ortega chilies, and sour cream, or the Popeye Burger made with chicken, sautéed spinach, and feta cheese. Be sure to dine alfresco in the hidden courtyard in back. *Note:* There is another San Francisco location in Noe Valley at 4138 24th St., as well as eight other spots in the Bay Area.

3344 Steiner St. (btw. Chestnut and Lombard sts.). 🕾 **415/563-0307.** www.barneyshamburgers. com. Main courses $5–$8. No credit cards. Mon–Thurs 11am–9:30pm; Fri–Sat 11am–10pm; Sun 11am–9pm. Bus: 22, 28, 30, 30X, 43, 76, or 82X.

Eliza's ★ 🥢 CHINESE Despite the curiously colorful design of modern architecture, whimsy, and glass art, this perennially packed neighborhood haunt serves some of the freshest California-influenced Chinese food in town. Unlike comparable options, here the atmosphere (albeit unintentionally funky) and presentation parallel the food. The fantastically fresh soups, salads, seafood, pork, chicken, duck, and such specials as spicy eggplant are outstanding and are served on beautiful English and Japanese plates. (Get the sea bass with black-bean sauce and go straight to heaven!) I often come at midday and order the wonderful kung pao chicken lunch special (available weekdays only): a mixture of tender chicken, peanuts, chili peppers, subtly hot sauce, and perfectly crunchy vegetables. It's one of 32 main-course choices that come with rice and soup for around $6. The place is also jumping at night, so prepare to stand in line.

2877 California St. (at Broderick St.). ☎ **415/621-4819.** Reservations accepted for parties of 4 or more. Main courses $5–$7 lunch, $7–$15 dinner. MC, V. Mon–Fri 11am–3pm and 5–9:30pm; Sat–Sun 4:30–9:30pm. Bus: 1 or 24.

The Grove ★ CAFE   The Grove is the kind of place you go just to hang out and enjoy the fact that you're in San Francisco. That the heaping salads, lasagna, pasta, sandwiches, and daily specials are predictably good is an added bonus. I like coming here on weekday mornings for the easygoing vibe, strong coffee, and friendly, fast service. Inside you can sit at one of the dark-wood tables on the scuffed hardwood floor and people-watch through the large open windows, but on sunny days the most coveted seats are along the sidewalk. It's the perfect place to read the newspaper, sip an enormous mug of coffee, and be glad you're not at work right now. A second Pacific Heights location is at 2016 Fillmore St. between California and Pine streets (☎ 415/474-1419), and their third and newest location is in Hayes Valley at 301 Hayes St., at Franklin Street. (☎ 415/624-3953).

2250 Chestnut St. (btw. Scott and Pierce sts.). ☎ **415/474-4843.** Most main courses $6–$7. MC, V. Mon–Fri 7am–11pm; Sat–Sun 8am–11pm. Bus: 22, 28, 30, 30X, 43, 76, or 82X.

Home Plate ★ 🍴 BREAKFAST   Dollar for dollar, Home Plate just may be the best breakfast joint in San Francisco. Many Marina residents kick off their hectic weekends by carbo-loading here on big piles of buttermilk pancakes and waffles smothered with fresh fruit, or hefty omelets stuffed with everything from apple wood–smoked ham to spinach. You'll always start off with a coveted plate of freshly baked scones, best eaten with a bit of butter and a dab of jam. Be sure to look over the daily specials scrawled on the little green chalkboard before you order. And as every fan of this tiny cafe knows, it's best to call ahead and ask to have your name put on the waiting list before you slide into Home Plate.

2274 Lombard St. (at Pierce St.). ☎ **415/922-HOME** (4663). www.homeplatesf.com. Main courses $3.95–$7. DC, DISC, MC, V. Daily 7am–3pm. Bus: 28, 30, 43, or 76.

La Méditerranée ★ 🍴 MEDITERRANEAN   With an upscale-cafe ambience and quality Mediterranean/Middle Eastern food, La Méditerranée has long warranted its reputation as one of the most appealing inexpensive restaurants on upper Fillmore Street. Here you'll find freshly prepared traditional dishes that are worlds apart from the Euro-eclectic fare many restaurants now call "Mediterranean." Baba ghanouj, tabbouleh, dolmas, and hummus start out the menu. My favorite dish here is the chicken Cilicia, a phyllo-dough dish that's hand-rolled and baked with cinnamony spices, almonds, chickpeas, and raisins. Also recommended are the zesty chicken pomegranate drumsticks on a bed of rice. Both come with a green salad, potato salad, or soup for around $9.50. Ground lamb dishes, quiches, and combo plates round out the affordable menu, and wine comes by the glass and in half- or full liters. A second location is at 288 Noe St., at Market Street (☎ 415/431-7210).

2210 Fillmore St. (at Sacramento St.). ☎ **415/921-2956.** www.cafelamed.com. Main courses $8–$10 lunch, $10–$12 dinner. AE, MC, V. Sun–Thurs 11am–10pm; Fri–Sat 11am–10:30pm. Bus: 1, 3, or 22.

Mel's Drive-In ★ ☺ AMERICAN   Sure, it's contrived, touristy, and nowhere near healthy, but when you get that urge for a chocolate shake and banana cream pie at the stroke of midnight—or when you want to entertain the kids —no other place in the city comes through like Mel's Drive-In. Modeled after a classic 1950s diner, right down to the jukebox at each table, Mel's hearkens back to the halcyon days when cholesterol and fried foods didn't jab your guilty conscience with every greasy, wonderful bite. Too bad the prices don't reflect the '50s; a burger with fries and a Coke costs about $12.

Another Mel's, at 3355 Geary St. (© **415/387-2244**), is open from 6am to 1am Sunday through Thursday and 6am to 3am Friday and Saturday. Additional locations are 1050 Van Ness (© **415/292-6357**), open Sunday through Thursday 6am to 3am and Friday through Sunday 6am to 4am; and 801 Mission St. (© **415/227-4477**), open Sunday through Wednesday 6am to 1am, Thursday 6am to 2am, and Friday and Saturday 24 hours.

2165 Lombard St. (at Fillmore St.). © **415/921-2867.** www.melsdrive-in.com. Main courses $6.50–$12 breakfast, $7–$10 lunch, $8–$15 dinner. MC, V. Sun–Wed 6am–1am; Thurs 6am–2am; Fri–Sat 24 hr. Bus: 22, 30, or 43. Free parking.

Pluto's ★ 🍴 CALIFORNIAN   Catering to the Marina District's DINK (double income, no kids) crowd, Pluto's combines assembly-line efficiency with high quality. The result is cheap, fresh fare in the build-a-meal style: huge salads with a dozen choices of toppings, oven-roasted poultry and grilled meats (the tri-tip is great), sandwiches, and a wide array of sides such as crispy garlic potato rings, seasonal veggies, and barbecued chicken wings. Pluto's serves teas, sodas, bottled brews, and Napa wines as well as homemade desserts. The ordering system is bewildering to newcomers: Grab a checklist, and then hand it to the servers, who check off your order and relay it to the cashier. Seating is limited during the rush, but the turnover is fairly fast. A second Inner Sunset location is at 627 Irving St., at Eighth Avenue (© **415/753-8867**).

3258 Scott St. (at Chestnut St.). © **415/7-PLUTOS** (8867). www.plutosfreshfood.com. Reservations not accepted. Main courses $3.50–$5.75. MC, V. Mon–Fri 11am–10pm; Sat–Sun 10:30am–10pm. Bus: 28, 30, or 76.

JAPANTOWN

For a map of the restaurant in this section, see the "San Francisco Restaurants" map on p. 106.

Moderate

Takara ★ JAPANESE/SUSHI   When I'm in the mood for sushi, I often head to this unassuming restaurant tucked at the eastern end of Japantown. Not only is it large enough that you don't have to wait in a long line (unlike other local sushi spots), but the fish is also extremely fresh and affordable and the other offerings are fantastic. Along with standard nigiri, I always go for the seaweed with fabulously tangy vinegar and a floating quail egg. On the occasions that I can curb my sushi craving, I get more than my fill with their *yosenabe*. A meal for two that's under $20, it's a giant pot of soup brought to the table on a burner accompanied by a plate of fresh raw meat or seafood and vegetables. After you push the food into the liquid and briefly let it cook, you ladle it out and devour it. Even after serving two hungry people, there are always leftovers. Other favorites are anything with shrimp—pulled live from the tank—and sukiyaki, another tableside cooking experience. Bargain hunters should come for a lunch plate.

22 Peace Plaza, no. 202 (in Japan Center Miyako Mall). © **415/921-2000.** www.takararestaurant. com. Reservations recommended. Main courses $15–$23. MC, V. Daily 11:30am–2pm; Mon–Sat 5:30–9:30pm; Sun 5:30–9pm. Bus: 2 or 38.

CIVIC CENTER/HAYES VALLEY

For a map of restaurants in this section, see the "Mission District & Castro Area Restaurants" map on p. 153.

Very Expensive

Jardinière ★★ CALIFORNIAN/FRENCH   Jardinière is a pre- and post-symphony favorite, and it also happens to be the perfect setting for enjoying a cocktail with your significant other. A culinary dream team created the elegant dining room and sophisticated menu: owner-designer Pat Kuleto, who created the beautiful champagne-inspired decor, and owner-chef Traci Des Jardins, one of the city's most popular chefs. On most evenings the bi-level brick structure is abuzz with an older crowd (including ex-mayor Willie Brown, a regular) who sip cocktails at the centerpiece mahogany bar or watch the scene discreetly from the circular balcony. The restaurant's champagne theme extends to twinkling lights and clever ice buckets built into the balcony railing, making the atmosphere conducive to splurging in the best of style—especially when live jazz is playing (7:30pm nightly). The daily changing menu might include seared scallops with truffled potatoes and truffle reduction, sautéed petrale sole with Alsatian cabbage and Riesling sauce, or venison with celery root, red wine, braised cabbage, and juniper sauce. There's also an outstanding cheese selection and superb wine list—many by the glass, and over 500 bottles.

300 Grove St. (at Franklin St.). © **415/861-5555.** www.jardiniere.com. Reservations recommended. Main courses $26–$40; 7-course tasting menu $120. AE, DC, DISC, MC, V. Sun–Wed 5–10:30pm; Thurs–Sat 5–11:30pm. Valet parking $10. Bus: 19 or 21.

Expensive

NOPA ★★ MEDITERRANEAN   NOPA is an acronym for North of the Panhandle (the "pan" is Golden Gate Park)—but the only pan you need concern

sweet NOTHINGS

Hayes Valley will woo you with its cutesy boutiques, littering of sidewalk cafes, and specialty stores like **Flight 001,** a visually striking display of designer travel gear. But perhaps our favorite stop in the new "it" neighborhood is for a perfect macaroon at sweetshop **Miette** ★★, 449 Octavia St. (at Linden St.; © **415/626-6221**)—and maybe a bag of brightly colored, homemade candies to go, you know, since we've already come all this way—followed by a cup of joe across the way at **Blue Bottle Coffee** ★★, 315 Linden St., a well-hidden kiosk down a side alley that serves some of the city's best organic, gourmet, brewed-to-order coffee. Second locations for both can be found in the Ferry Building. You'll find two other Blue Bottle locations at 66 Mint St., at Jessie Street (© **415/495-3394**), which is home to a fancy $25,000 Japanese coffeemaker, and the new rooftop sculpture garden at SFMOMA. Also see the "I Scream For Artisanal Ice Cream" box on p. 156.

yourself with here is the one cooking your braised greens and the best damn pork chop in San Francisco. NOPA is big, tall, loud, crowded, and brimming with stylish 30-something singles who relish this kind of lively Big City dining scene. The kitchen specializes in Mediterranean-influenced cuisine made with seasonal ingredients sourced from local purveyors and served in straightforward presentations that always hit the mark. I start with the warm marinated olives, baked giant white beans with feta and oregano, the flatbread, and for the main course either the braised beef short ribs or the pork chop, but any meats emanating from their wood-fired oven will delight you. For a more casual affair, I highly recommend a seat at the bar, a half bottle of Storybook Mountain zin, and the wildly popular NOPA hamburger made from grass-fed beef. Be aware that reservations can be hard to secure on weekends, and the wait for a table can be long without one. Parking is even harder to score, but for $10 evening parking is available at the DMV lot on Broderick between Oak and Fell streets.

560 Divisadero St. (btw Fell & Hayes sts). € **415/864-8643.** www.nopasf.com. Reservations recommended. Main courses $12–$29. AE, DC, DISC, MC, V. Mon–Fri 6pm–1am; Sat–Sun 11am–1am. Bus: 1 or 24.

Moderate

Absinthe ★ FRENCH   This Hayes Valley hot spot is sexy, fun, reasonably priced, and frequented by everyone from the theatergoing crowd to the young and chic. Decor is all brasserie, with French rattan cafe chairs, copper-topped tables, a pressed-tin ceiling, soft lighting, period art, and a rich use of color and fabric, including leather and mohair banquettes. It's always a pleasure to unwind at the bar with a plate of Soft Garlic Pretzels and a Ginger Rogers—gin, mint, lemon juice, ginger ale, and a squeeze of lime. The lengthy lunch menu offers everything from oysters and caviar to Caesar salad and croque-monsieur, but I always end up getting their outstanding open-faced smoked-trout sandwich on grilled Italian bread. In the divided dining room, main courses are equally satisfying, from coq au vin and steak frites to roasted whole Dungeness crab with poached leeks in mustard vinaigrette, salt-roasted potatoes, and aioli. The best item on the weekend brunch menu is the creamy polenta, with mascarpone, maple syrup, bananas, and toasted walnuts.

398 Hayes St. (at Gough St.). € **415/551-1590.** www.absinthe.com. Reservations recommended. Brunch $8–$14; most main courses $12–$20 lunch, $14–$30 dinner. AE, DC, DISC, MC, V. Tues–Fri 11:30am–midnight (bar until 2am Fri); Sat 11am–midnight (bar until 2am); Sun 11am–10pm (bar until midnight). Valet parking (Tues–Sat after 5pm) $10. Bus: 21.

Hayes Street Grill ★ SEAFOOD   For 30 years, this small, no-nonsense seafood restaurant (owned and operated by revered food writer and chef Patricia Unterman) has maintained a solid reputation among San Francisco's picky epicureans for its impeccably fresh and straightforwardly prepared fish. The concise menu offers a dozen appetizers—most of which are fresh and lively salads—a half-dozen grilled fish selections cooked to perfection and matched with your sauce of choice (Szechuan peanut, tomatillo salsa, herb-shallot butter), and a side of signature fries. Fancier seafood specials, which change with the seasons and range from mahimahi (with Vietnamese dipping sauce, baby spinach, roasted peanuts, and basmati rice) to classic paella, are balanced by a few meat-driven dishes, which may include Niman Ranch (organic and wonderful) flatiron steak with mustard butter and balsamic onions. Finish your meal with the outstanding crème brûlée.

320 Hayes St. (near Franklin St.). ☏ **415/863-5545.** www.hayesstreetgrill.com. Reservations recommended. Main courses $20–$26 lunch, $20–$28 dinner. AE, DISC, MC, V. Mon–Fri 11:30am–2pm; Mon–Thurs 5–9pm; Fri–Sat 5–10:30pm; Sun 5–8:30pm. Bus: 19, 21, 31, or 38.

Sebo ★★★ JAPANESE/SUSHI *San Francisco* magazine created quite a fuss when they named this the "best sushi in the country." Neighborhood regulars could no longer get a table in the subdued 25-seat restaurant due to the lines out the door. Be sure to make a reservation or show up when they open their doors to get a taste of fish rarely seen inside the U.S. (most ingredients are flown in daily from Japan and the menu is dependent on what's available). Sit at the bar to watch owners/chefs Michael Black and Daniel Dunham prepare *sayori* (half beak), seared *kurodai* (daurade), or delicate *shiro ebi* (baby white shrimp). Everything changes on Sunday when they serve only *izakaya* (think pub food, Japanese style).

517 Hayes St. (btw. Laguna and Octavia sts.). ☏ **415/864-2122.** www.sebosf.com. Reservations recommended. Individual sushi $7–$18; *izakaya* items $5–$9. AE, DC, DISC, MC, V. Tues–Sun 6–10pm. Bus: 19, 21, 31, or 38.

Suppenküche ★★ GERMAN It's a challenge to create a German beer hall anywhere outside of Germany and not come off as a bit tawdry. But this Hayes Valley favorite proved all of my preconceived notions wrong. Diners sit at long wooden tables, often right next to other parties, and the food is as authentic as it comes, with Wiener schnitzel, spaetzle, potato pancakes, bratwurst and sauerkraut, and other familiar Bavarian fare served heartily. The drink menu is full of German, Austrian, and Belgian brews and wine, and those with a supreme thirst to quench should consider ordering Das Boot: 2 liters of your favorite beer served in a boot-shaped glass—if nothing else, it sure is fun to say. Drinks also come in 3-liter and 5-liter beer glasses, as well as the standard pint.

525 Laguna St. (at Hayes St.). ☏ **415/252-9289.** www.suppenkuche.com. Reservations recommended for parties of 6 or more. Main courses $14–$20. AE, DC, DISC, MC, V. Daily 5–10pm; Sun brunch 10am–2:30pm. Valet parking $7. Bus: 19, 21, 31, or 38.

Zuni Café ★★ 🏛 MEDITERRANEAN Zuni Café embodies the best of San Francisco dining: Its clientele spans young hipsters to hunky gay guys, the cuisine is consistently terrific, and the atmosphere is electric. Its expanse of windows overlooking Market Street gives the place a sense of space, despite the fact that it's always packed. For the full effect, stand at the bustling, copper-topped bar and order a glass of wine and a few oysters from the oyster menu (a dozen or so varieties are on hand at all times). Then, because *of course* you made advance reservations, take your seat in the stylish exposed-brick two-level maze of little dining rooms or on the patio. Then do what we all do: Splurge on chef Judy Rodgers's Mediterranean-influenced menu. Although the ever-changing menu always includes meat (such as hanger steak), fish (grilled or braised on the kitchen's wood grill), and pasta (tagliatelle with nettles, applewood-smoked bacon, butter, and Parmesan), it's almost sinful not to order her brick-oven-roasted chicken for two with Tuscan-style bread salad. I rarely pass up the polenta with mascarpone and a proper Caesar salad. But then again, if you're there for lunch or after 10pm, the hamburger on grilled rosemary focaccia bread is a strong contender for the city's best. Whatever you decide, be sure to order a stack of shoestring potatoes.

1658 Market St. (at Franklin St.). ☏ **415/552-2522.** www.zunicafe.com. Reservations recommended. Main courses $10–$19 lunch, $15–$29 dinner. AE, MC, V. Tues–Thurs 11:30am–11pm; Fri–Sat 11:30am–midnight; Sun 11am–11pm. Valet parking $10. Bus: 6 or 71. Streetcar: All Market St. streetcars.

Civic Center/Hayes Valley

WHERE TO EAT

Inexpensive

Frjtz Fries ★ BELGIAN   Although they serve great sandwiches and salads, Frjtz is best known for its addictively crisp french fries, piled high in a paper cone (how Euro) and served with a barrage of exotic dipping sauces such as chipotle rémoulade and balsamic mayo. Also try their crepes—try the grilled rosemary chicken and Swiss cheese—their big, leafy salad, or the chunky focaccia sandwich packed with roasted peppers, red onions, pesto mayo, grilled eggplant, and melted Gorgonzola. Wash it down with creamy Chimay Belgian ale. *Note:* There's a second Frjtz Fries at 590 Valencia St. (at 17th St.; *©* **415/863-8272**) in the Mission.

581 Hayes St. (at Laguna St.). *©* **415/864-7654.** www.frjtzfries.com. Reservations not accepted. Fries $3–$4.50; crepes $5–$8; sandwiches $7–$8.25. AE, DC, DISC, MC, V. Mon–Thurs 11:30am–10pm; Fri–Sat 11am–11pm; Sun 11am–9pm. Bus: 21.

Tacolicious ★★ MEXICAN   What started as a humble taco stand at Ferry Plaza Farmers Market has become the taco of the town (okay, bad pun). Realizing they were on to something, the owners opened up two sit-down restaurants in the Mission and Marina districts that specialize in *tacos de guisado*—tacos filled with braised meats such as beef short rib, shot-and-a-beer braised chicken, and fried rock cod, all sourced from local organic purveyors. And these little buggers are addictive—succulent, juicy, cheesy—so be sure to order twice as much as you planned because you don't want to get back in that line again. Non-taco dishes are also available, such as grilled squid Veracruz, skillet roasted mussels, and fried sweet plantains with heirloom beans (really, their entire menu will slay you). For *bebidas* try the house-made *agua frescas* or freshly squeezed margaritas. A second location is at 741 Valencia St. between 18th and 19th streets in the Mission district (*©* **415/626-1344**).

2031 Chestnut St. (at Fillmore St.) *©* **415/346-1966.** www.tacolicioussf.com. Reservations not accepted. Main courses $4–$12. AE, MC, V. Mon–Wed 11:30am–11 pm; Thurs–Sat 11:30am–midnight; Sun 11:30am–11pm. Bus: 22, 28, 30, 30X, 43, 76, or 82X.

Tommy's Joynt 🦴 ☺ AMERICAN   With its colorful mural exterior, it's hard to miss Tommy's Joynt, an over-60 (years and clientele) haven for cholesterol-be-damned holdouts from America's halcyon days and a late-night favorite for those in search of a cheap and hearty meal. The restaurant's exterior is tame in comparison to the interior, which looks like a Buffalo Bill museum that imploded: a wild collage of stuffed birds, a mounted buffalo head, an ancient piano, rusty firearms, fading prints, a beer-guzzling lion, and Santa Claus masks. The *hofbrau*-style buffet offers a cornucopia of rib-clinging a la carte dishes such as their signature buffalo stew (via a buffalo ranch in Wyoming), which resides under heat lamps among the stainless steel trays of whole turkeys and hams, sloppy joes, oxtails, corned beef, meatballs, mashed potatoes, and other classics. There's also a slew of seating on two levels, almost 100 varieties of beer, and a most interesting clientele of almost exclusively pre-cardiac-arrest males (some of whom have been coming to the "Joynt" for more than 40 years). It's all good stuff in a 'merican kind of way, the kind of place you take Grandpappy when he's in town just to show him that San Francisco's not entirely sissy.

1101 Geary Blvd. (at Van Ness Ave.). *©* **415/775-4216.** www.tommysjoynt.com. Reservations not accepted. Main courses $4–$7. No credit cards. Daily 10am–1:45am. Bus: 2, 3, or 38.

TASTY IN TIMBUKTU: RESTAURANTS OFF THE BEATEN PATH

They're on the way to nowhere, but because they're among the city's most unique, it would be a crime to leave out these destination restaurants. If you're not familiar with the streets of San Francisco, be sure to call first to get directions; otherwise, you'll spend more time driving than dining.

Thanh Long ★, 4101 Judah St. (at 46th Ave.; ✆ **415/665-1146;** www.an family.com; streetcar: N), is an out-of-the-way Sunset District Vietnamese standout that, long after my mom started taking me here as a tot for excellent roasted crab and addictive garlic noodles, has remained a San Francisco secret. Since the owners, the An family, have become rather famous for their aforementioned signature dishes now that they're served in sister restaurants Crustacean Beverly Hills and S.F.—suffice to say, the crab's out of the bag. But this location is still far enough on the outskirts of the city to keep it from becoming overcrowded. The restaurant is more visually pleasing than most Southeast Asian outposts (white tablecloths, tastefully exotic decor), but the extra glitz is reflected in the prices of luxury dishes (main courses run $14–$34) such as charbroiled tiger prawns with those famed garlic noodles and steamed sea bass with scallions and ginger sauce. On the plus side, unlike the cheaper options around town, there's a full bar here, too, serving fun cocktails such as the Pineapple and Litchi vodka infusion. Reservations are recommended. Thanh Long is open Sunday and Tuesday through Thursday from 5:30 to 9:30pm, Friday and Saturday from 5 to 10pm, and is closed on Mondays.

The **Ramp,** 855 Terry A. Francois St. (at the end of Mariposa St.; ✆ **415/621-2378;** www.ramprestaurant.com; bus 22 or 48), is an out-of-the-way mecca for seaside snacks, dancing, and drinking that's at its best when the sun is shining. If you're lucky enough to be in San Francisco on one of those rare hot days, head to this bayside hangout. The fare is of the basic pub grub variety—burgers, sandwiches, salads, and soups from $8 to $13—but the rustic boatyard environment and patio seating make this a relaxing place to dine in the sun. In summer, the place really rocks when live bands perform (4:30–8:30pm Fri–Sun Apr–Oct) and tanned, cocktailing singles prowl the area. It's open Monday through Friday from 11am to 10pm, and Saturday through Sunday from 9am to 10pm. The bar is open until 10pm on weekdays and later on weekends. From April to October, an outdoor barbecue is offered Saturday and Sunday from 4 to 7:30pm.

Little Star Pizza ★★, 846 Divisadero St. (at McAllister St.; ✆ **415/441-1118;** www.littlestarpizza.com; bus 5 or 24), may be on a dreary strip of busy Divisadero Street and feel like a bohemian speakeasy with its dark colored walls, low ceilings, and jukebox, but this joint is cranking out some of the best pizza in town. You're likely to have to wait for a seat at one of the well-spaced tables and you may have to strain to chat over the music and dining din, but there's little I wouldn't endure for one of Little Star's deep dish cornmeal-crust pizzas ($11–$22). Rather than inches of dough, these pies are thin and crisp with high sides that coddle fillings such as chicken, tomatoes, artichoke hearts, red bell peppers, sausage, and feta. These babies take about 25 minutes to bake, which is a great excuse to order chicken wings and a glass of wine for the wait. The place serves dinner Sunday and Tuesday through Thursday from 5 to 10pm, Friday and Saturday from 5 to 11pm, and is closed on Mondays. *Note:* There's a second location in the Mission District at 400 Valencia St., at 15th Street (✆ **415/551-7827**).

MISSION DISTRICT
Expensive

Bar Agricole ★ AMERICAN   Set back from the street in an otherwise industrial and warehouse-filled section of downtown, this hot new favorite among the
denizens of SoMa has become the talk of design publications across the nation.
A finalist in the prestigious James Beard Award for Outstanding Restaurant
Design, it's easy to see why the low-slung exterior, minimalist outdoor patio, and
sleek barnwood-paneled interior is so popular. This LEED-certified beauty
dishes up food whose central ingredients are locally harvested from organic and
biodynamic farms across the northern Bay Area. The distilled spirits and the concoctions that spring from them are from small-batch craftsmen and trend toward
the tart. The menu shifts weekly, is light-weight, packed with sensual delight and
such fascinating ingredients like cardoons (a thistlelike flowing plant), puntarelle
(a variety of chicory), cow tongue, or ciccioli (cured pig fat).

335 11th St. (at Harrison St.). ℭ **415/355-9400.** www.baragricole.com. Reservations recommended. Main courses $13–$28. AE, DC, DISC, MC, V. Sun–Wed 6–10pm; Thurs–Sat 6–11pm; Sun
brunch 11am–2pm. Bus: 6, 47, 49, 71, or 90. Streetcar: F, J, KT, L, M, N, or S.

Moderate

Bar Bambino ★★ ITALIAN   A welcome jewel in the gritty heart of the Mission, Bar Bambino shows a flair for well-made classic Italian fare, elegant yet
wholly accessible. Large parties can be accommodated at group tables on the
year-round outdoor patio. Couples on a date or friends meeting friends just for a
glass of wine from the expansive list will find comfortable seats at the bar or small
tables inside as well. Everyone will enjoy handmade pastas, braised meats, and a
wonderful, ever changing selection of salumis, cheeses, and bruschette. The
banana donuts with warm Nutella sauce are a perfect ending to a leisurely meal
at this unfussy spot. Daily lunch specials go for just $14.

2931 16th St. (btw. Capp St. and Van Ness Ave.). ℭ **415/701-8466.** www.barbambino.com.
Reservations recommended. Main courses $14–$28. AE, DC, DISC, MC, V. Mon–Thurs 5:30–
10pm; Fri–Sat 5pm–midnight. Bus: 33. BART: 16th St./Mission.

Bar Tartine ★★ AMERICAN   You've probably passed Bar Tartine a dozen
times and not even noticed it's there—it flies under the radar like that. But once
you discover it, you won't forget it anytime soon. Sister to the ever-popular Tartine Bakery down the street, which supplies the delicious homemade bread, Bar
Tartine opened in 2005 and quickly became a beloved Mission staple. Main
courses comprised of Fisherman's stew with white sea bass and Chicken papri-
kas with chard. Even if you're a dedicated chocoholic, you'd be wise to pass and
sample some of the other, more inventive desserts, such as pistachio ice cream,
cardamom coffee, chocolate krumkake, and white pumpkin and chestnut custard, pear, ginger bread. The wildly popular Tartine Bakery is located at 600
Guerrero St. (ℭ 415/487-2600; www.tartinebakery.com), and is open Monday
8am to 7pm, Tuesday and Wednesday 7:30am to 7pm, Thursday and Friday
7:30am to 8pm, Saturday 8am to 8pm, and Sunday 9am to 8pm.

561 Valencia St. (btw. 16th and 17th sts.). ℭ **415/487-1600.** www.bartartine.com. Reservations
recommended. Main courses $14–$38. AE, DISC, MC, V. Tues–Thurs and Sun 6–10pm; Fri–Sat
6–11pm; Sat–Sun 10:30am–2pm. Parking lot at 18th and Valencia sts., $8. Bus: 14, 22, 33, or 49.
Streetcar: J. BART: 16th St. station.

Beretta ★★ ITALIAN   Beretta is one of those restaurants that opened to so much buzz, it would be hard *not* to be let down. And yet, I wasn't. Its casual vibe and well-thought-out small bites have kept the place packed since its debut in early 2008. Pizzas are one-of-a-kind and what the place is known for: Choose one with *baccala,* potato, *panna,* onions, and capers, or the broccolini, pancetta, tomato, and mozzarella combo. If you're heading here after work for happy hour, nosh on antipasti plates like roasted beets with ricotta *salata,* meatballs in spicy tomato sauce, or eggplant *caponatina* with burrata. Need a heartier meal? Try one of the risotto dishes, like asparagus and *robiola* (Italian soft-ripened cheese) or saffron with *osso buco,* or a daily main course special like the herb-crusted halibut with fennel and olives. Don't feel guilty sampling an array of the unique cocktails, either: Beretta has numerous mixology titles—it would be a shame to let the drinks go untasted. *An added bonus:* If you forget to make a reservation in advance—and on most nights, this place is hopping—you can call 45 minutes prior to your arrival and have your name added to the list.

1199 Valencia St. (at 23rd St.). ℂ **415/695-1199.** www.berettasf.com. Reservations recommended. Pizzas $11–$15; main courses $12–$18. AE, DISC, MC, V. Mon–Fri 5:30pm–1am; Sat–Sun 11am–1am. Parking garage at 21st St. (btw. Mission and Valencia sts.). Bus: 14, 49, or 33. BART: 24th St. station.

Blowfish Sushi ★★ SUSHI   Located in a quiet neighborhood in the Mission District, Blowfish has everything I look for in a sushi restaurant: superb cuisine with beautiful presentations, a hip vibe with great energy and artwork, relaxed staff who know the menu well, a sophisticated cocktail and sake menu, and side-walk seating. Chef Tsuchida is a native of Tokyo and comes from a family that has been in the sushi business for several generations; the man knows his fish. I always start with the same dish: the Toro Tower—a swirling trio of expertly sliced sashimi that melts in your mouth. It's not on the regular menu so you have to ask for it. Other dishes you *will* find on the menu that I recommend are their signature Ritsu Roll, the Halibut Crudo (drizzled with white truffle oil, caviar, and mango salsa), and the Tokyo Queen roll. Consult your waiter—it's one of those "everything looks good" menus—and ask about the Russian Roulette shooters served in a revolver barrel.

2170 Bryant St. (btw. 19th and 20th sts.). ℂ **415/285-3848.** www.blowfishsushi.com. Reservations recommended. Main courses $7–$25. AE, DC, DISC, MC, V. Lunch Mon–Fri 11:30am–2:30pm; dinner Mon–Tues 5:30–10pm, Wed–Thurs 5:30–10:30pm, Fri–Sat 5:30–11pm; Sun 5:30–10pm. Bus: 27.

Delfina ★★ ITALIAN   Unpretentious warehouse-chic atmosphere, reasonable prices, and chef/co-owner Craig Stoll's superb seasonal Italian cuisine have made this family-owned restaurant one of the city's most cherished. Stoll, who was one of *Food & Wine*'s Best New Chefs in 2001 and a 2005 James Beard Award nominee, changes the menu daily, while his wife, Annie, works the front of the house (when she's not being a mom). Standards include Niman Ranch flatiron steak with french fries, and roasted chicken with Yukon Gold mashed potatoes and royal trumpet mushrooms. The winter menu might include slow-roasted pork shoulder or gnocchi with squash and chestnuts, while spring indulgences can include sand dabs with frisée, fingerling potatoes, and lemon-caper butter or lamb with polenta and sweet peas. Trust me—order the buttermilk *panna cotta* (custard) if it's available. *A plus:* A few tables and counter seating are reserved for walk-in diners. Delfina also has a heated and covered patio that's used mid-March through November—and don't miss **Pizzeria Delfina** next door (ℂ **415/437-6800;**

Mission District & Castro Area Restaurants

Absinthe **10**
AsiaSF **14**
Bar Agricole **15**
Bar Bambino **28**
Bar Tartino **27**
Beretta **37**
Bi-Rite Creamery and Bakeshop **29**
Blowfish Sushi **34**
Blue Bottle Coffee **9**
Café Flore **22**
Chow **18**
Commonwealth **32**
Delfina **30**
Flour + Water **35**
Foreign Cinema **36**
Frances **24**
Frjtz Fries **6**
Hayes Street Grill **12**
Humphry Slocombe **38**
Ike's Place **20**
Incanto **39**
Jake's on Market **19**
Jardiniere **11**
L'Ardoise **21**
Little Star Pizza **1**
Locanda **26**
Manora's **16**
Miette **8**

Mission Chinese Food **33**
Mitchell's Ice Cream **40**
NOPA **2**
Pauline's **17**
Sebo **7**
Starbelly **23**
Suppenküche **5**
Taqueria La Cumbre **25**
Tartine Bakery **31**
Thep Phanom **4**
Uva Enoteca **3**
Zuni Café **13**

www.pizzeriadelfina.com), where you can enjoy the same high-quality ingredients in a more casual, less expensive setting. *Note:* A second pizzeria is at 2406 California St. (at Fillmore St.; ☎ **415/440-1189**) in Pacific Heights.

3621 18th St. (btw. Dolores and Guerrero sts.). ☎ **415/552-4055.** www.delfinasf.com. Reservations recommended. Main courses $18–$26. MC, V. Mon–Thurs 5:30–10pm; Fri–Sat 5:30–11pm; Sun 5–10pm. Parking lot at 18th and Valencia sts., $8. Bus: 14, 33, or 49. Streetcar: J.

Flour + Water ★★ ITALIAN   As the name indicates, flour and water are the two main ingredients here. Don't let that fool you into thinking this is glorified prison food. The folks here are perfectionists—from carefully sourced ingredients and slavish preparations, to textures and flavors that are cultivated, coddled, and tinkered with until they meet exacting standards. Pastas are house-made daily; so is salumi—they butcher whole animals on-site and cook every part, snout to tail. Pizzas from the Italian wood-fired 900-degree oven take exactly 2 minutes to cook, and arrive achingly thin with perfectly blistered crusts. On a recent menu, the pappardelle with pork sausage and chanterelles just about melted in my mouth, and the *biancoverde* pizza with jersey ricotta, *fior di latte,* spinach, and garlic had to be one of the best things I've eaten in a long while. I still dream about it. Small, folksy, and unassuming (think menus on butcher paper), this place has been packed since the day it opened in 2009. They take limited reservations, so book as far in advance as you can, or chance it and try for one of the few walk-in spots.

2401 Harrison St. (at 20th St.). ☎ **415/826-7000.** www.flourandwater.com. Reservations recommended. Main courses $13–$24. AE, MC, V. Sun–Wed 5:30–11pm; Thurs–Sat 5:30pm–midnight. Bus: 12, 14, 14L, 27, or 49.

Foreign Cinema ★★ MEDITERRANEAN   This place is so chic and well hidden that it eludes me every time I drive past it on Mission Street. (*Hint:* Look for the valet stand.) The "cinema" here is a bit of a gimmick: It's an outdoor dining area (partially covered and heated, but still chilly) where mostly foreign films are projected onto the side of an adjoining building, with tableside minispeakers for audio. What's definitely not a gimmick, however, is the superb Mediterranean-inspired menu created by husband-and-wife team John Clark and Gayle Pirie. Snackers like me find solace at the oyster bar with a half-dozen locally harvested Miyagi oysters and a devilishly good *brandade* (fish purée) gratin. Heartier eaters can opt for grilled halibut with chanterelles and roasted figs in a fig vinaigrette, fried Madras curry–spiced chicken with gypsy peppers, or grilled natural rib-eye with Tuscan-style beans and rosemary-fried peppercorn sauce—all made from seasonal, sustainably farmed, organic ingredients when possible. Truth be told, even if the food weren't so good, I'd still come here—it's just that cool. If you have to wait for your table, consider stepping into their adjoining bar, Laszlo.

2534 Mission St. (btw. 21st and 22nd sts.). ☎ **415/648-7600.** www.foreigncinema.com. Reservations recommended. Main courses $18–$26. AE, MC, V. Mon–Thurs 6–10pm; Fri–Sat 5:30–11pm; Sun 5:30–10pm; brunch Sat–Sun 11am–3pm. Valet parking $10. Bus: 14, 14L, or 49.

Pauline's ★ PIZZA   Housed in a cheery yellow double-decker building that stands out like a beacon in a somewhat seedy neighborhood, Pauline's does only three things—pizzas, salads, and desserts—but it does them better than most restaurants in the city. Running the gauntlet of panhandlers for a slice of Louisiana andouille pizza topped with andouille sausage, bell peppers, and fontina cheese is completely worth it. Other gourmet toppings include house-made chicken sausage, French goat cheese, roasted eggplant, Danish fontina cheese,

Chef Chris Cosentino, of Incanto in Noe Valley and Boccalone in the Ferry Building.

and *tasso* (spiced pork shoulder). The salads are equally amazing: certified organic, handpicked by California growers, and topped with fresh and dried herbs (including edible flowers) from Pauline's own gardens in Berkeley. Don't forget to leave room for the house-made ice cream and sorbets or chocolate mousse and butterscotch pudding. The wine list offers a smart selection of low-priced wines, where Star Canyon Vineyards, yet another of the owners' pursuits, is showcased. Yes, prices are a bit steep (small pizzas start at $15), but what a paltry price to pay for perfection.

260 Valencia St. (btw. 14th St. and Duboce Ave.). ☎ **415/552-2050.** www.paulinespizza. com. Reservations accepted for parties of 8 or more. Pizzas $12–$25. MC, V. Tues–Sat 5–10pm. Bus: 14 or 49.

Inexpensive

Taqueria La Cumbre MEXICAN   If San Francisco commissioned a flag honoring its favorite food, we'd probably all be waving a banner of the Golden Gate Bridge bolstering a giant burrito—that's how much we love the mammoth tortilla-wrapped meals. Taqueria La Cumbre has been around forever and still retains its "Best Burrito" title, each deftly constructed using fresh pork, steak, chicken, or vegetables, plus cheese, beans, rice, salsa, and maybe a dash of guacamole or sour cream. The fact that it's served in a cafeteria-like brick-lined room with overly shellacked tables featuring a woman with overflowing cleavage makes it taste even better.

515 Valencia St. (btw. 16th and 17th sts.). ☎ **415/863-8205.** Reservations not accepted. Tacos and burritos $3.50–$6.50; dinner plates $5–$7. AE, MC, V. Daily 11am–2am. Bus: 14, 22, 33, or 49. BART: 16th St. Mission.

THE CASTRO & NOE VALLEY

For a map of restaurants in this section, see the "Mission District & Castro Area Restaurants" map on p. 153.

Expensive

Frances ★★★ CALIFORNIAN/MEDITERRANEAN   The much-accoladed Melissa Perello, who earned a Michelin star while helming Fifth Floor, has ventured out on her own with Frances. It's a cozy little spot tucked into the residential side of the Castro that merges a fine-dining sensibility with neighborhood casualness. The menu—inspired by what's available at local farmers' markets—is limited, and that's a good thing. Start with regular small-plate favorites, all priced at $6.50, including bacon beignets with crème fraîche and chives or the *panisse*

I SCREAM FOR ARTISANAL ice cream

You might not consider ice cream a standard treat in a city used to oft-cold and blustery summers, but on days when the fog burns off and temps rise above nippy, you'll have some delicious options, both old school and modern.

o **Swensen's** (1999 Hyde St., btw. Union St. and Warner Place; ℭ **415/775-6818;** www.swensensicecream.com) opened in 1948 and launched 300 outlets worldwide. It's old school through and through, with traditional flavors plus local favorites such as "Turkish coffee and sticky chewy chocolate" and "Swiss orange chip." A single scoop (4 oz.) is $3.35, a double $5.35.

o **Mitchell's Ice Cream** (688 San Jose Ave., btw. 29th and Valley sts.; ℭ **415/648-2300;** www.mitchellsicecream.com) in Noe Valley dates back to 1953. Each batch of ice cream and sorbet is made in-house daily, and flavors run from the norm to the more exotic like baby coconut, litchi, avocado, and purple yam. A single scoop (4–5 oz.) starts from $3.20, double $5.20.

o **Bi-Rite Creamery and Bakeshop** (3692 18th St., btw. Dolores and Oakwood sts.; ℭ **415/626-5600;** www.biritecreamery.com) racks up points for using local organic ingredients whenever possible and for originality of flavors: cardamom, crème fraîche, roasted banana, and salted caramel (it tastes just like roasted marshmallows)—they have popsicles, too! A single scoop is $3.50; a double $5. *Tip:* Bi-Rite's market across the street, at 3639 18th Street, sells ice cream by the pint. Skip the bakeshop's long lines, buy here, and bring your treat into nearby Dolores Park.

o **Humphry Slocombe** (2790 Harrison St., btw. 23rd and 24th sts.; ℭ **415/550-6971;** www.humphryslocombe. com; pictured) is the perfect end to a walking tour of murals along Balmy Alley and a visit to the Precita Eyes Mural Center (p. 199) in the Mission. The flavors are frankly crazy here—and out-of-this-world delicious: Try Tahitian vanilla, peanut butter curry, foie gras, or green tea with black sesame. Order a combo of the balsamic caramel and the McEvoy olive oil and get the added bonus of shouts of "Ice Cream Salad!" A single scoop is $3.25, a double $4.25.

o **The Ice Cream Bar** (815 Cole Street, btw Carl and Frederick sts; ℭ **415/742-4932;** www.theicecreambarsf.com) combines a classic ice cream parlor setting with modern mixology. Everything is made in-house (ice creams, cones, hot dog buns & more). Choose a single scoop for $2.75, a double for $3.75 or combine any of the available 75 tinctures (with flavors like bitter orange, bergamot, and dill weed) to build your own phosphate soda.

—David A. Lytle

frites (creamy-on-the-inside, crunchy-on-the-outside chickpea fritters with a "light and tart" Meyer lemon aioli), and then move on to perfectly seared scallops, a rich duck breast, or a vegetarian house-made pasta. Sides of seasonal vegetables are a la carte. Sommelier Paul Einbund has crafted a smart list of California and European wines, and desserts are a necessary end, especially those featuring locally produced Humphry Slocombe ice creams (see above).

3870 17th St. (at Pond St., btw. Noe and Sanchez sts.). ℂ **415/621-3870.** www.frances-sf.com. Reservations recommended. Main courses $16–$25. AE, DISC, MC, V. Tues–Thurs and Sun 5–10pm; Fri–Sat 5–10:30pm. Closed Mon. Bus: 24 or 33. Subway: F to 17th and Castro; K, L, or M to Castro.

Incanto ★★★ ITALIAN   The most difficult part of eating at this rustic Italian outpost in Noe Valley is simply deciding what to choose off of chef Chris Cosentino's wildly inventive menu: He highlights seasonal produce, handmade pastas, and a whole lot of meat. (Cosentino also operates **Boccalone,** a local salumeria in the Ferry Building, p. 174. Log onto www.boccalone.com.) Appetizers can be classic and simple, like cannellini bean spread with toast or a salad of marinated sardines with grapefruit and greens, or something truly new to most palates like calf brains or beef bone marrow. Cosentino is a champion of whole-animal cooking, and a recent remodel has also designed the restaurant for more head-to-tail and shared meal options. In addition to Whole Pig Dining and Leg of Beast Dining, there's also Ham in Hay—a whole ham, roasted in a crust of salt and fresh alfalfa hay, designed to be shared among 8 to 10 people. If you're more of a "safe" eater, try a little gem salad with Point Reyes blue cheese, or a simple pasta with pork ragout; the more adventurous can dive into sweetbreads, beef tendons, and pig trotters. Desserts are a big draw, with a perfect, slightly savory panna cotta topped with seasonal fruit, warm chocolate cake, or the daily sorbet. If you don't want a full meal, sit at the wine bar near the entrance and watch the chefs work in the open kitchen while you enjoy a wine flight creatively assembled by wine director Edward Ruiz.

1550 Church St. (at Duncan St., btw. 27th and 28th sts.). ℂ **415/641-4500.** www.incanto.biz Reservations recommended. Main courses $18–$25. AE, DC, DISC, MC, V. Wed–Sat 5:30–10pm; Sun–Mon 5:30–9:30pm. Closed Tues. Subway: J to 24th St.

Moderate

Jake's on Market ★★ AMERICAN   Jake's Executive Chef Erik Hopfinger has unleashed his secret family recipe for fried chicken upon delighted locals, who have been clucking about Jake's since it replaced the venerable 2223 Restaurant in early 2012. You'll like Jake's the second you walk in—it exudes that relaxed aura of a lively upscale diner with warm colors, bright lighting, and a hearty welcome from the staff. Chances are good that you'll be greeted tableside by one of the two owners—Tim Travelstead and Brad Becker—long-time Castro residents who named the restaurant after their son. Chef Erik offers a seasonally changing menu of small and large plates, all made with locally sourced and organic ingredients wherever possible. Must-try dishes include "East Coast vs. West Coast" crab cakes featuring Maryland blue crab vs. local Dungeness, the apple cider-brined double cut pork chop, and of course Erik's Southern fried chicken—the best I've ever had—served with a house-made buttermilk cheddar chive biscuit, mashed potatoes, homestyle gravy, and honey poppy slaw. If you're nostalgic for a holiday dinner, Chef Erik serves an organic free-range turkey

TOP CHEF'S YIGIT PURA PICKS
YOUR NEXT dessert

The winner of Top Chef Just Desserts Season 1, Yigit Pura (pronounced "Yeet") started cooking in his hometown of Ankara, Turkey, worked with Daniel Boulud in New York and Las Vegas, and now lives here in San Francisco, where he works as Executive Pastry Chef for Taste Catering (www.tastecatering.com). We posed a question slightly less taxing than a Quickfire Challenge: "Which local bakeries and desserts excite you?"

Acme Bread: Their breads are by far some of the best I've had in the United States, especially their rustic country loaves—great crunchy crust with the perfect tender chewy texture inside!

Bi-Rite Creamery, p. 156: The Lavender Honey Ice Cream here is so satisfying. It's creamy, without having too much of an egg flavor, and instead, the bright flavors of the European honey shines in a very masculine manner. I love it with their berry compote and gingersnap croutons.

Boulette's Larder: I love everything in this space. It is all made with such precision and love. I especially love their fresh house-made English muffins, which they have on Saturdays at 10am. If you get up early enough to go to the Ferry Plaza Farmers' Market (p. 175), treat yourself to one.

Kika's Treats (various retailers; http://kikastreats.com): Kika (Cristina Besher) is only sweeter than her desserts. She

makes wholesale baked goods here in SF, and you can find her products in most retail stores. I am addicted to her caramelized graham crackers enrobed in milk chocolate. I'm certain she puts sea salt in the base, which makes it so addictive!

Tartine Bakery: Every once in a blue moon they will make "Bostoc," which in essence is a slice of thick brioche soaked in light orange flower syrup, baked with almond cream and sliced almonds. Tartine takes this and adds kumquat jam, and they bake it super dark. It's heaven. Sweet, bitter, chewy goodness!

—Yigit Pura

Yigit Pura
Pastry Chef

dinner with all the trimmings: corn bread stuffing, whipped potatoes, green beans, cranberry orange compote, and homestyle gravy—all for only $15.50.

2223 Market St. (btw Sanchez & 16th sts.). (C) **415/431-0692.** www.jakesonmarket.com. Reservations recommended. Main courses $12–$29. AE, DC, DISC, MC, V. Brunch Sat–Sun 10am–3pm; dinner Mon–Thu 5pm–midnight; Fri–Sat 5pm–1am; Sun 5pm–midnight. Bus: 8, 22, 24, or 37. Streetcar: F, K, L, or M.

5

The Castro & Noe Valley

WHERE TO EAT

L'Ardoise ★★ FRENCH   This charming little Duboce Triangle neighbor-hood restaurant's name (*ardoise* means "chalk" in French) is a reference to the daily menus displayed on chalkboards outside Parisian bistros—and chef and owner Thierry Clement certainly knows his way around classic French bistro fare. You'll find standard appetizers like escargot, butter lettuce with delicate and sweet anchovies, and charcuterie platters. Main courses include steak frites, a rich duck leg confit, and creamy mushroom risotto. Specials change daily dependent upon what's locally available (and the chef's whim) and have included veal with sweetbreads (a personal favorite), roasted salmon, and other seafood. The selec-tive wine list is outstanding, highlighting the best affordable French (white Bor-deaux and offbeat Languedoc), Californian (smart pinot noirs and not-too-buttery chardonnays), and sparkling wines from around the globe. To really feel French for an evening, sit at the zinc bar. Desserts are merely passable.

151 Noe St. (at Henry St.). ✆ **415/437-2600.** www.lardoisesf.com. Reservations recommended. Main courses $14–$20. AE, DC, DISC, MC, V. Tues–Thurs 5:30–10pm; Fri–Sat 5–11pm. Subway: F to Noe/Market; N to Duboce Park.

Starbelly ★★ CALIFORNIAN   A huge communal dining counter runs down the middle of this large, high-ceilinged cafe in the Castro, a brother to the Mis-sion-based Beretta (p. 152). Look for thin, crispy pizzas (pear, blue cheese, and arugula), savory sandwiches (especially the *porchetta*), and heartier entrees (lamb chops, grilled fish, handmade pasta, or a simple and juicy burger) for lunch and dinner throughout the week. The weekend brunches really shine, particularly if you can score a table in the outdoor patio. Opt for traditional fare such as thick bacon, eggs, pillowy sourdough pancakes, or granola with yogurt and fruit, or go a little further out with the pulled chicken sandwich with jalapeño slaw or the squash-and-sage pizza. Wash it all down with a recommended microbrewed beer or a *calimocho*—a mix of Italian cola and red wine. Share any of a rotating selection of Dynamo donuts (candied orange blossom, chocolate star anise, *banana de leche*—yum!) for a sweet ending. *Tip:* You can call in 45 minutes before your estimated arrival time to get your name on the waiting list.

3583 16th St. (at Noe and Market sts.). ✆ **415/ 252-7500.** www.starbellysf.com. Reservations recommended. Main courses $11–$22. AE, DC, DISC, MC, V. Mon–Thurs 11:30am–11pm; Fri 11:30am–midnight; Sat 10:30am–midnight; Sun 10:30am–11pm. Bus: 24. Subway: F to Noe/Market; K, L, M to Castro Station.

Inexpensive

Café Flore 🐟 CALIFORNIAN   Because of its large and lively patio over-looking a busy section of Market Street, Café Flore is the top sunny-day meet-me-for-coffee spot within the Castro community. And boy is the people-watching good here—leather-wrapped

The *calimocho* at Starbelly combines red wine and cola.

bears, drag queens, trannies (Dad, is that you?), gym bunnies, and other anti-establishment types saunter down Market Street in full glory. As for dining at the cafe, here's how it works: You order drinks and desserts inside at the bar, then find a seat indoors or outside on the patio or sidewalk, and claim a spot. Next, go to the kitchen counter (there are no waiters), place your meal order and get a number, and the food will be delivered to your table. Many of the menu items are composed of mostly organic ingredients and include a succulent version of roasted chicken over rice, Niman Ranch hamburgers, soups, salads, and pastas. Breeders are always welcome as long as they behave, and breakfast is served until 3pm.

2298 Market St. (at Noe St.). ℂ **415/621-8579.** www.cafeflore.com. Reservations not accepted. American breakfast $5.95; main courses $4.50–$10. MC, V. Sun–Thurs 7am–1am; Fri–Sat 7am–2am (kitchen closes at 10pm). Metro: F.

Chow ★ 🍴 AMERICAN   Chow claims to serve American cuisine, but the management must be thinking of today's America, because the menu is not exactly meatloaf and apple pie. And that's just fine for eclectic and cost-conscious diners. After all, what's not to like about starting with a Cobb salad before moving on to Thai-style noodles with steak, chicken, peanuts, and spicy lime-chili garlic broth, or cioppino? Better yet, everything except the fish of the day costs under $15, especially the budget-wise daily sandwich specials, which range from meatball with mozzarella (Sun) to grilled tuna with Asian-style slaw, pickled ginger, and a wasabi mayonnaise (Mon); both come with salad, soup, or fries. Although the food and prices alone would be a good argument for coming here, beer on tap, a great inexpensive wine selection, and the fun, tavernlike environment clinch the deal. A second location, **Park Chow,** is at 1240 Ninth Ave. (ℂ **415/665-9912**). You can't make reservations unless you have a party of eight or more, but if you're headed their way, you can call ahead to place your name on the waiting list (recommended).

215 Church St. (near Market St.). ℂ **415/552-2469.** www.chowfoodbar.com. Reservations not accepted except for parties of 8 or more. Main courses $7–$15. DISC, MC, V. Sun–Thurs 8am–11pm; Fri–Sat 8am–midnight. Bus: 8, 22, or 37. Streetcar: F, J, K, L, or M.

Ike's Place ★ 🍴 CAFE/VEGETARIAN   From an inconspicuous doorway in the Castro emerges drippy, warm, and deee-licious sandwiches filled with hand-shredded ingredients that you have to taste to believe. The line often snakes around the block for this little shop started up by native San Franciscan Ike Shehadeh, but the wait is worth it (sometimes up to 2 hr., due to its online following). All sandwiches come with Dirty Sauce, Ike's house garlic- and herb-laden aioli, which is spread over your choice of unbaked roll once you place your order, the roll is baked and then respread with sauce. Well over 200 different sandwiches are offered on the menu with meats taking up the goodly portion. Turkey and chicken are hand-shredded, meatball sandwiches are hot and messy, and even vegan selections sound tasty. Personal favorites so far are Name of the Girl I'm Dating and the Montana to Rice. Ike's is also popular with vegetarians and vegans for options like the Meatless Mike and the Vegan Backstabber.

   Tip: Look online before you go—the wall menu doesn't have room for nearly all the options. Or, better yet, call your order in to get a pickup time so you don't have to wait in that line (ideally call at 10am, when they open, for a noon pickup). Insiders go for secret unlisted sandwiches; try www.hiddenmenu.com for a few.

3489 16th St. (at Sanchez St.). ℂ **415/553-6888.** www.ilikeikesplace.com. Sandwiches $7–$10. MC, V. Mon–Sat 10am–7pm. Metro: F to Sanchez and Market.

HAIGHT-ASHBURY

For a map of restaurants in this section, see the "San Francisco Restaurants" map on p. 106. **Note:** The Upper Haight and Lower Haight are two distinct neighborhoods separated by a giant hill 10 blocks apart from one another, so plan accordingly.

Upper Haight
INEXPENSIVE

Cha Cha Cha ★★ 🍴 CARIBBEAN This is one of my all-time favorite places to get festive, but it's not for everybody. Dining at Cha Cha Cha is not about a meal; it's about an experience. Put your name on the waiting list, crowd into the minuscule bar, and sip sangria while you wait. When you do get seated (it can take up to two pitchers of sangria, but by then you really don't care), you'll dine in a loud—and I mean *loud*—dining room with Santería altars, banana trees, and plastic tropical-themed tablecloths. The best thing to do is order from the tapas menu and share the dishes family style. Fried calamari, fried new potatoes, Cajun shrimp, and mussels in saffron broth are all bursting with flavor and accompanied by luscious sauces—whatever you choose, you can't go wrong. This is the kind of place where you take friends in a partying mood and make an evening of it. If you want the flavor without the festivities, come during lunch. Their second, larger location, in the Mission District, at 2327 Mission St., between 19th and 20th streets (📞 **415/824-1502**), is open for dinner only and has a full bar specializing in mojitos.

1801 Haight St. (at Shrader St.). 📞 **415/386-7670.** www.cha3.com. Reservations not accepted. Tapas $4–$9; main courses $12–$15. AE, DISC, MC, V. Daily 11:30am–4pm; Sun–Thurs 5–11pm; Fri–Sat 5–11:30pm. Bus: 6, or 71. Streetcar: N.

Citrus Club ★ NOODLES When you're a starving writer you quickly discover that the cheapest, healthiest, and most satisfying things to eat in San Francisco are burritos and noodles. Citrus Club does noodles. Large, heaping bowls of thick Asian noodles, served hot in bone-warming broth or cool, minty, and refreshing. In typical Upper Haight fashion, the Club has sort of a cheap Polynesian-chic feel—love those Vietnamese straw hat lamps—a young, hip staff and clientele, and the omnipresent world-beat rhythms. Most items on the menu are unlike anything you've seen before, so take my advice and walk around the two dining rooms to see what looks good before ordering. A refreshing starter is the citrus salad made with mixed greens, mint, fried noodles, and a tangy citrus vinaigrette. Popular cold noodle selections are the spicy lime and coconut, and the orange-mint. For hot noodles, try the marmalade shrimp or sweet chili-glazed tofu and greens. If you're in a party mood, order a sake margarita; otherwise, a big pot of ginger tea goes well with any of the noodle dishes.

1790 Haight St. (at Shrader St.). 📞 **415/387-6366.** www.citrusclubsf.com. Main courses $6–$10. MC, V. Sun–Thurs 11:30am–10pm; Fri–Sat 11:30am–11pm. Bus: 6, 66, or 71. Muni Metro: N.

Kan Zaman ★ 🎁 MIDDLE EASTERN An evening dining at Kan Zaman is one of those quintessential Haight-Ashbury experiences that you can't wait to tell your friends about back in Ohio. As you pass through glass-beaded curtains, you're led by the hostess to knee-high tables under a billowed canopy tent. Shoes removed, you sit cross-legged with your friends in cushioned comfort. The most adventurous of your group requests an *argeeleh,* a large hookah pipe filled with fruity honey or apricot tobacco. Reluctantly at first, everyone simultaneously sips the sweet smoke from the cobralike tendrils emanating from the hookah; then dinner arrives—inexpensive platters offering a variety of classic Middle Eastern cuisine: smoky baba ghanouj, *kibbe* (cracked wheat with spiced lamb) meat pies, Casablanca beef couscous, spicy hummus with pita bread, succulent lamb and chicken kabobs. The spiced wine starts to take effect, just in time for the beautiful, sensuous belly dancers who glide across the dining room, mesmerizing the rapt audience with their seemingly impossible gyrations. The evening ends, the bill arrives: $17 each. Perfect. **Note:** Belly dancing starts at 9pm Thursday through Saturday only.

1793 Haight St. (at Shrader St.). ℂ **415/751-9656.** www.kanzamansf.com. Main courses $5–$14. MC, V. Mon–Thurs 5pm–midnight; Fri 5pm–2am; Sat noon–2am; Sun noon–midnight. Bus: 6, 66, or 71. Metro: N.

Lower Haight

INEXPENSIVE

Thep Phanom ★ THAI   It's the combination of fresh ingredients, attractive decor, and friendly service, and that heavenly balance of salty, sweet, hot, and sour flavors, that have made Thep Phanom one of the city's most beloved Thai restaurants. Those who like to play it safe will be more than happy with standards such as pad Thai, coconut-lemon-grass soup, and prawns in red curry sauce, but consider diverting from the usual suspects for such house specialties as Thaitanic Beef (stir-fried beef and string beans in a spicy sauce), prawns with eggplant and crisped basil, and *ped sawan*—duck with a delicate honey sauce served over spinach. There's good people-watching here as well—the restaurant's reputation attracts a truly diverse San Francisco crowd. Be sure to make reservations or prepare for a long wait on weekend nights, and don't leave anything even remotely valuable in your car. See map p. 153.

400 Waller St. (at Fillmore St.). ℂ **415/431-2526.** www.thepphanom.com. Reservations recommended. Main courses $9–$13. AE, DC, DISC, MC, V. Daily 5:30–10:30pm. Bus: 6, 22, 66, or 71.

Uva Enoteca ★★ ITALIAN   The Haight has seen a recent resurgence in its dining scene, which can largely be attributed to the arrival of gems like Uva Enoteca. The narrow wine bar with its exposed brick and intimate setting could easily be found in New York's West Village and is a breath of fresh air among Haight Street's other shoddy offerings. Start with a speck and apple purée bruschetta and meat-and-cheese assortment; if you're unsure of which of the local varieties to order, ask Boris, and he'll bring you out a delectable pairing. If you still have stomach space to spare, follow that with a panino or *piadina* (flatbread sandwich), like my favorite, the pine-nut butter, raisins, bitter greens, and balsamic selection, and pasta or pizza. The wine selection changes weekly, with 80 or so types—all Italian, all the time—always on tap, which you can order by the bottle, 20 ounces, 6 ounces, or 8 ounces. The gelato, made special for the restaurant by a local company, is a can't-miss, with flavors like avocado, honey granola, bergamot, and kiwi (alongside more normal types like chocolate and vanilla). One thing's for sure: You'll want to make repeat visits to Uva Enoteca to be able to taste everything on the menu and feel as if you've done it justice. See map p. 153.

568 Haight St. (btw. Fillmore and Steiner sts.). ℂ **415/829-2024.** www.uvaenoteca.com. Reservations recommended. Panini $8; pasta $14; pizza $13. DISC, MC, V. Mon–Thurs 5–11pm; Fri–Sat 5–11:30pm; Sun 5–10pm; brunch Sat–Sun 11am–2pm. Bus: 6, 22, or 71.

RICHMOND/SUNSET DISTRICTS

Yes, it's a long haul from downtown to "the Avenues," but these restaurants wouldn't be in the guidebook if they weren't worth the trip. For a map of restaurants in this section, see the "Richmond & Sunset Districts Restaurants" map on p. 165.

Moderate

Aziza ★★ MOROCCAN   If you're looking for something really different—or a festive spot for a large party—head deep into the Avenues for an exotic taste of Morocco. Chef-owner Mourad Lahlou creates an excellent dining experience through colorful and distinctly Moroccan surroundings combined with a modern yet authentic take on the cuisine of his homeland. In any of the three opulently adorned dining rooms (the front room features private booths, the middle room is more formal, and the back has lower seating and a Moroccan lounge feel), you can indulge in the seasonal five-course tasting menu ($75) or individual treats such as kumquat-enriched lamb shank; saffron guinea hen with preserved lemon and olives; or Paine Farm squab with wild mushrooms, bitter greens, and a *ras el hanout* reduction (a traditional Moroccan blend of 40 or so spices). Consider finishing off with my favorite dessert (if it's in season): rhubarb galette with rose-and geranium-scented crème fraîche, vanilla aspic, and rhubarb consommé.

5800 Geary Blvd. (at 22nd Ave.) ☎ **415/752-2222**. www.aziza-sf.com. Reservations recommended. Main courses $15–$28. AE, MC, V. Wed–Mon 5:30–10pm. Valet parking $8 weekdays, $10 weekends. Bus: 29 or 38.

Beach Chalet Brewery & Restaurant ★ AMERICAN   While Cliff House (see below) has more historical character and better ocean views, the Beach Chalet is where the locals go. The Chalet occupies the upper floor of a restored historic public lounge adorned with WPA frescoes that originally opened in 1900. Dinner is pricey, and the ocean view disappears with the sun, so come for lunch or an early dinner, when you can eat your hamburger, buttermilk-fried calamari, or grilled Atlantic salmon with one of the best vistas around. In the evening, it's a more local crowd, especially on Tuesday through Sunday evenings, when live bands accompany the cocktails and house-brewed ales. Breakfast is served here as well. In early 2004, owners Lara and Greg Truppelli added the adjoining **Park Chalet** restaurant to the Beach Chalet. The 3,000-square-foot glass-enclosed extension behind the original landmark building offers more casual fare—with entrees ranging from $11 to $23—including rib-eye steak, fish and chips, roasted chicken, and pizza. **Note:** Be careful getting into the parking lot (accessible only from the northbound side of the highway)—it's a quick, sandy turn.

1000 Great Hwy. (at west end of Golden Gate Park, near Fulton St.) ☎ **415/386-8439**. www. beachchalet.com. Main courses $8–$17 breakfast, $11–$27 lunch/dinner. AE, MC, V. Beach Chalet: Sun–Thurs 9am–10pm; Fri–Sat 9am–11pm; brunch Sat–Sun 9am–2pm. Park Chalet: Mon–Thurs 9am–10pm; Fri 9am–11pm; Sat 8am–11pm; Sun 8am–10pm; brunch Sat–Sun 11am–2pm. Bus: 5, 18, 31, or 38. Streetcar: N.

Cliff House ★ CALIFORNIAN/SEAFOOD   In the old days (we're talking way back), Cliff House was *the* place to go for a romantic night on the town. Nowadays, the revamped San Francisco landmark caters mostly to tourists who arrive to take a gander at the Sutro Baths remains next door or dine at the two remodeled restaurants. The more formal (and pricey) **Sutro's** has contemporary decor, spectacular panoramic views, and a fancy seafood-influenced American menu that showcases local ingredients. The food, while nothing revolutionary, is well prepared and features the likes of roasted organic beet salad; lobster and crab cakes with shaved fennel, romesco sauce, and caramelized Meyer lemon; and a mighty fine grilled lamb sirloin sandwich (at lunch). The same spectacular views in less dramatic but still beautiful surroundings can be found at the **Bistro,** which offers big salads, sandwiches, burgers, and other soul-satisfiers. For the most superb ocean views, come for sunset, so long as it looks like the fog will let up. Alternatively, overindulge to the tune of live harp music at the Sunday champagne buffet in the **Terrace Room.** (Reserve well in advance; it's a popular event.)

1090 Point Lobos (at Merrie Way). ✆ **415/386-3330.** www.cliffhouse.com. Reservations accepted for Sutro's only. Bistro main courses $9–$26 breakfast/lunch, $13–$26 dinner. Sutro main courses $19–$32 lunch, $29–$39 dinner; 3-course prix-fixe $25 lunch and $35 dinner (Mon–Fri only). AE, DC, DISC, MC, V. Bistro: Mon–Sat 9am–9:30pm; Sun 8:30am–9:30pm. Sutro: Daily 11:30am–3:30pm and 5–9:30pm; brunch Sun 10am–3:30pm. Bus: 18 or 38.

Khan Toke Thai House ★★ ⚜ THAI   Khan Toke Thai is so traditional you're asked to remove your shoes before being seated. Popular for special occasions, this Richmond District fixture is easily the prettiest Thai restaurant in the city; lavishly carved teak interiors evoke the ambience of a Thai temple. To start, I suggest ordering the *tom yam gong* soup of lemon grass, shrimp, mushroom, tomato, and cilantro. Follow with such well-flavored dishes as ground pork with fresh ginger, green onion, peanuts, and lemon juice; prawns with hot chilies, mint leaves, lime juice, lemon grass, and onions; or chicken with cashews, crispy chilies, and onions. For a real treat, have the deep-fried pompano topped with sautéed ginger, onions, peppers, pickled garlic, and yellow-bean sauce or deep-fried red snapper with "three-flavors" sauce and basil leaves. A complete dinner, including appetizer, soup, salad, two main courses, dessert, and coffee, is a great value.

5937 Geary Blvd. (btw. 23rd and 24th aves.). ✆ **415/668-6654.** Reservations recommended Fri–Sat for parties of 3 or more. Main courses $6–$13; fixed-price dinner $20. AE, MC, V. Daily 5–10pm. Bus: 38.

Outerlands ★★ CALIFORNIAN   It's perhaps only a tad of an exaggeration to say that Outerlands could be the place that makes the Outer Sunset District (once a culinary wasteland) a destination dining neighborhood. Located deep in the fog belt, the tiny wooden outpost instantly hooks you with the smell of fresh baking bread and simmering soups. The decor—salvaged graying fence and barn wood that's been converted into arty sculptures, tables, walls, and chairs—feels at once homey and retro stylish. The menu, composed almost entirely of local, organic, and sustainable ingredients, is a marvel of home-cooked simplicity, with such comforting offerings as galette of fried egg, cipollini onions, gypsy peppers, pancetta, and manchego cheese, and cauliflower soup with truffle oil toast. Dinner is lovely, but brunch is sublime: Dutch pancakes, Moroccan French toast, and "eggs in jail" served with a side of Zoe's bacon and house-made levain toast.

4001 Judah St. (at 45th Ave.). ✆ **415/661-6140.** www.outerlandssf.com. No reservations. Main courses $8–$14. MC, V. Tues–Sat 11am–3pm and 6–10pm; Sun 10am–2:30pm. Streetcar: N Judah.

Inexpensive

Burma Superstar ★★ ⚜ BURMESE   Despite its gratuitous name, this basic dining room garners two-star status by offering exceptional Burmese food

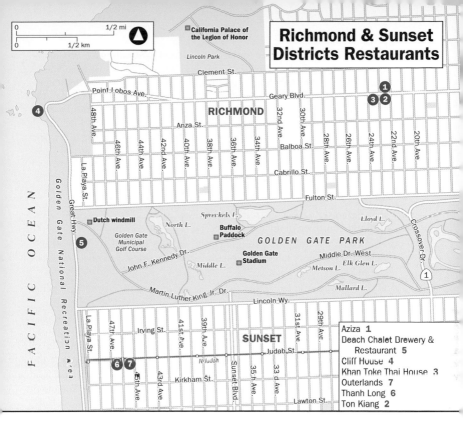

California Palace of
the Legion of Honor

Lincoln Park

Clement St.

Point Lobos Ave.

Geary Blvd.

RICHMOND

Anza St.

Balboa St.

Cabrillo St.

Fulton St.

PACIFIC OCEAN

Golden Gate National Recreation Area

Dutch windmill

Spreckels L.

North L.

**Buffalo
Paddock**

Lloyd L.

Crossover Dr.

Golden Gate
Municipal
Golf Course

GOLDEN GATE PARK

John F. Kennedy Dr.

Golden Gate
Stadium

Middle Dr. West

Elk Glen L.

Middle L.

Metson L.

Mallard L.

Martin Luther King Jr. Dr.

Lincoln Wy.

Irving St.

SUNSET

Judah St.

N Judah

Kirkham St.

Sunset Blvd.

Lawton St.

Aziza	**1**
Beach Chalet Brewery & Restaurant	**5**
Cliff House	**4**
Khan Toke Thai House	**3**
Outerlands	**7**
Thanh Long	**6**
Ton Kiang	**2**

at rock-bottom prices. Unfortunately, the allure of the tea-leaf salad, Burmese-style curry with potato, and sweet tangy sesame beef is one of the city's worst-kept secrets. Add to that a no-reservations policy, and you can count on waiting in line for up to an hour. (FYI, parties of two are seated more quickly than larger groups, and it's less crowded at lunch.) On the bright side, you can pencil your cellphone number onto the waiting list and browse the Clement Street shops until you receive a call—or else, head 2 blocks east to the sister restaurant, **B Star Bar** (127 Clement St.; ☏ **415/933-9900**), which essentially serves the same dishes for the same prices, but in a prettier, more polished setting without nearly the wait.

309 Clement St. (at Fourth Ave.). ☏ **415/387-2147.** www.burmasuperstar.com. Reservations not accepted. Main courses $8–$16. MC, V. Daily 11:30am–3:30pm; Mon–Thurs 5–10pm; Fri–Sat 5–10:30pm. Bus: 2, 38, or 44.

Ton Kiang ★★ CHINESE/DIM SUM   Ton Kiang is probably the number-one place in the city to have dim sum (served daily), only partially due to the fact that they make all their sauces, pickles, and other delicacies in-house. The experience goes like this: Wait in line (which is out the door 11am–1:30pm on week-ends), get a table on the first or second floor, and get ready to say yes to dozens of delicacies, which are rolled past the table for your approval. From stuffed crab claws, roast Beijing duck, and a gazillion dumpling selections (including scallop and vegetable, shrimp, and beef), to the delicious and hard-to-find *doa miu* (snow pea sprouts flash-sautéed with garlic and peanut oil) and a mesmerizing mango pudding, every tray of morsels coming from the kitchen is an absolute delight. Though it's hard to get past the dim sum, which is served all day every day, the full menu of Hakka cuisine is worth investigation as well—fresh and flavorful soups; an array of seafood, beef, and chicken; and clay-pot specialties.

5821 Geary Blvd. (btw. 22nd and 23rd aves.). $\textcircled{C}$ **415/387-8273.** www.tonkiang.net. Reservations accepted for parties of 8 or more. Dim sum $2–$6.50; main courses $9–$25. AE, DC, DISC, MC, V. Mon–Thurs 10am–9pm; Fri 10am–9:30pm; Sat 9:30am–9:30pm; Sun 9am–9pm. Bus: 38.

PRACTICAL INFORMATION

Although dining in San Francisco is almost always a hassle-free experience, here are a few things to keep in mind:

- If you want a table at the restaurants with the best reputations, you probably need to book 6 to 8 weeks in advance for weekends, and a couple of weeks ahead for weekdays.

- If there's a long wait for a table, ask if you can order at the bar, which is often faster and more fun.

- Don't leave *anything* valuable in your car while dining, particularly in or near high-crime areas such as the Mission, downtown, or—believe it or not—Fisherman's Wharf. (Thieves know tourists with nice cameras and a trunk full of mementos are headed there.) Also, it's best to give the parking valet only the key to your car, *not* your hotel room or house key.

- No smoking. It is against the law to smoke in any restaurant in San Francisco, even if it has a separate bar or lounge area. You're welcome to smoke outside, however—at least for the time being.

- This ain't New York: Plan on dining early. Most restaurants close their kitchens around 10pm.

- If you're driving to a restaurant, add extra time to your itinerary for parking, which can be an especially infuriating exercise in areas like the Mission, downtown, the Marina, and, well, pretty much everywhere. Expect to pay at least $10 to $13 for valet service, *if* the restaurant offers it.

6

EXPLORING SAN FRANCISCO

S an Francisco's parks, museums, tours, and landmarks are favorites for travelers the world over and offer an array of activities to suit every visitor. But no particular activity or place makes the city one of the most popular destinations in the world. It's San Francisco itself—its charm, its atmosphere, its perfect blend of big metropolis with small-town hospitality. No matter what you do while you're here—whether you spend all your time in central areas like Union Square or North Beach, or explore the outer neighborhoods—you're bound to discover the reason millions of visitors keep leaving their hearts in San Francisco.

FAMOUS SAN FRANCISCO SIGHTS

Alcatraz Island ★★★ ☺   Visible from Fisherman's Wharf, Alcatraz Island (also known as the Rock) has seen a checkered history. In 1775, Juan Manuel Ayala was the first European to discover it. He named it after the many alcatraces, or pelicans that nested on the island. From the 1850s to 1933, it served as a military fortress, protecting the bay's shoreline, as well as a military prison. In 1934, the government converted the buildings of the military outpost into a maximum-security civilian penitentiary. Given the sheer cliffs, treacherous tides and currents, and frigid water temperatures, it was believed to be totally escape-proof. Among the famous gangsters who occupied cellblocks A through D were Al Capone; Robert Stroud, the so-called Birdman of Alcatraz (an expert in ornithological diseases); Machine Gun Kelly; and Alvin "Creepy" Karpis, a member of Ma Barker's gang. It cost a fortune to keep them imprisoned here because all supplies, including water, had to be shipped in. In 1963, after an apparent escape in which no bodies were recovered, the government closed the prison. It moldered abandoned until 1969, when a group of Native Americans chartered a boat to the island and symbolically reclaimed the island for the Indian people. They occupied the island until 1971—the longest occupation of a federal facility by Native Americans to this day—but eventually were forcibly removed by the U.S. government. (See www.nps.gov/archive/alcatraz/indian.html for more information on the Native American occupation of Alcatraz.) The next year the island was given over to the National Park Service, natural habitats were restored, and the wildlife that was driven away during the prison years began to return. Today, you can see black-crested night herons and other seabirds here on a trail along the island's perimeter. Tours of the former prison, including an audio tour narrated by former guards and inmates, are offered daily.

Allow about 2½ hours for the round-trip boat ride and the tour. Wear comfortable shoes (the National Park Service notes that there are a lot of hills to

PREVIOUS PAGE: **Enjoy a grand view of downtown from Coit Tower.**

climb) and take a heavy sweater or windbreaker, because even when the sun's out, it's cold and windy on Alcatraz. You should also bring snacks and drinks with you if you think you'll want them. Although there is a beverage-and-snack bar on the ferry, the options are limited and expensive, and only water is available on the island. The excursion to Alcatraz is very popular and space is limited, so purchase tickets as far in advance as possible (up to 90 days) via the Alcatraz Cruises website at www.alcatraz cruises.com. You can also purchase tickets in person by visiting the Hornblower Alcatraz Landing ticket office at Pier 33. The first departure, called the "Early Bird," leaves at 9am, and ferries depart about every half-hour afterward

> ### 📎 Finding Your Way
>
> When asking for directions in San Francisco, be careful not to confuse numerical avenues with numerical streets. Numerical avenues (Third Ave. and so on) are in the Richmond and Sunset districts in the western part of the city. Numerical streets (Third St. and so on) are south of Market Street in the eastern and southern parts of the city. Get this wrong and you'll be an hour late for dinner.

until 4pm. Two night tours (highly recommended) are also available, offering a more intimate and wonderfully spooky experience.

For those who want to get a closer look at Alcatraz without going ashore, two boat-tour operators offer short circumnavigations of the island. (See "Self-Guided & Organized Tours" on p. 212 for complete information.)

Pier 33, near Fisherman's Wharf. © **415/981-7625.** www.alcatrazcruises.com or www.nps.gov/alcatraz. Admission (includes ferry trip and audio tour) $26 adults, $25 seniors 62 and older, $16 children 5–11. Night tours $33 adults, $31 seniors 62 and older, $20 children 5–11. Arrive at least 20 min. before departure time.

AT&T Park ★★ 📷   If you're a baseball fan, you'll definitely want to schedule a visit to the magnificent AT&T Park, home of the San Francisco Giants and hailed by the media as one of the finest ballparks in America. From April through October, an often sellout crowd of 40,800 fans packs the $319-million ballpark—which has a smaller, more intimate feel than Candlestick Park (where the

AT&T Park.

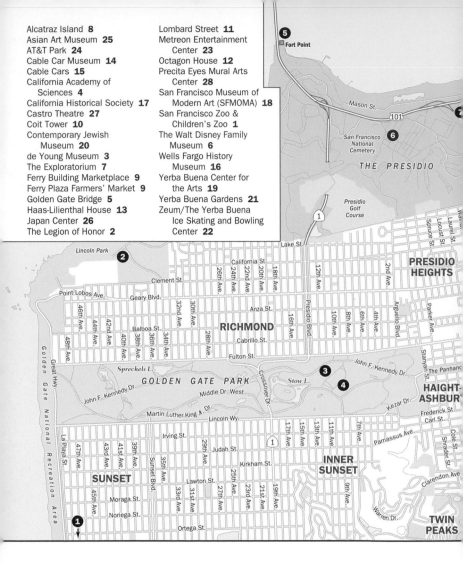

49ers play) as well as prime views of San Francisco Bay—and roots for the National League's Giants.

During the season, tickets to the game can be hard to come by (and expensive when you find them), but you can try to join the Bleacher Bums by purchasing one of the 500 bleacher-seat tickets sold every day before the game. They make you work for it: You have to show up at the ballpark 4 hours early, and then come back 2 hours before the game to get your tickets (maximum four per person). The upside is that the tickets are only $9 to $10.

If you can't even get bleacher seats, you can always join the "knothole gang" at the Portwalk (located behind right field) to catch a free glimpse of the game through cutout portholes into the ballpark. In the spirit of sharing, Portwalk peekers are encouraged to take in only an inning or two before giving way to fellow fans.

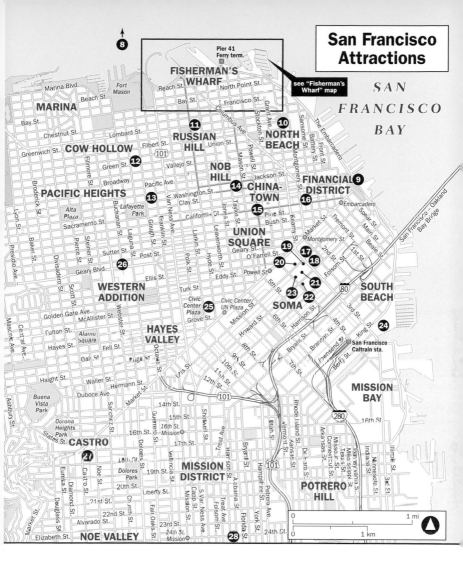

One guaranteed way to get into the ballpark is to take a guided tour of AT&T Park and go behind the scenes where you'll see the press box, the dugout, the visitor's clubhouse, a luxury suite, and more. All tours run daily at 10:30am and 12:30pm. Ticket prices are $13 for adults, $11 for seniors 56 and over, and $7.50 for kids 12 and under. There are no tours on game days, and limited tours on the day of night games. To buy tickets online log onto www.sfgiants.com, and then click on "AT&T Park" and "Ballpark Tours" from the drop-down list. You can also buy tour tickets at any Giants Dugout Store or Tickets.com outlet. For more tour information, call ✆ **415/972-2400.**

At the southeast corner of SoMa at the south end of the Embarcadero (bounded by King, Second, and Third sts.). ✆ **415/972-2000.** www.sfgiants.com. Bus: 10, 30, 45, or 47. Metro: N line.

Boudin at the Wharf ★ After more than 30 years of being an inconspicuous bread shop in the heart of Fisherman's Wharf, the Boudin Bakery was super-sized a few years ago. The new, ultramodern, 26,000-square-foot flagship baking emporium is now nearly half a block long, housing not only their demonstration bakery but also a museum, gourmet marketplace, cafe, espresso bar, and restaurant. The Boudin (pronounced Bo-deen) family has been baking sourdough French bread in San Francisco since the gold rush, using the same simple recipe and original "mother dough" for more than 150 years. About 3,000 loaves a day are baked within the glass-walled bakery; visitors can watch the entire process from a 30-foot observation window along Jefferson Street or from a catwalk suspended directly over the bakery (it's quite entertaining). You'll smell it before you see it: The heavenly aroma emanating from the bread ovens is purposely blasted out onto the sidewalk.

The best time to arrive is in the morning when the demo bakery is in full swing. Catch the action along Jefferson Street; then, when your appetite is stoked, head to the cafe for an inexpensive breakfast of sourdough French toast or their Bread Bowl Scrambler filled with eggs, bacon, cheddar, onions, and bell peppers. After breakfast, spend some time browsing the museum and marketplace. On the upper level is Bistro Boudin, a full-service restaurant serving lunch, dinner, and weekend brunch. Tours of the bakery are available as well. ***Tip:*** If the line at the cafe is too long, walk across the parking lot to the octagon-shaped building, which serves the same items—Boudin chowder bowls, salads, pizzas—in a serve-yourself setting.

160 Jefferson St. (btw. Taylor and Mason sts.). ✆ **415/928-1849.** www.boudinbakery.com. Bakery/cafe/marketplace daily 10am–7pm.

Cable Cars ★★★ 📷 ☺ Although they may not be San Francisco's most practical means of transportation, cable cars are certainly the best loved and are a must-experience when visiting the city. Designated official moving historic landmarks by the National Park Service in 1964, they clank up and down the city's steep hills like mobile museum pieces, tirelessly hauling thousands of tourists each day to Fisherman's Wharf at the brisk pace of 9 miles per hour.

The city's cable car system was the first of its kind in the world when it debuted in 1873.

As the story goes, London-born engineer Andrew Hallidie was inspired to invent the cable cars after witnessing a heavily laden carriage pulled by a team of overworked horses, slip and roll backwards down a steep San Francisco slope, dragging the horses behind it. Hallidie resolved to build a mechanical contraption to replace horses, and in 1873, the first cable car made its maiden voyage from the top of Clay Street. Promptly ridiculed as "Hallidie's Folly," the cars were slow to gain acceptance. One early onlooker voiced the general opinion by exclaiming, "I don't believe it—the damned thing works!"

Even today, many visitors have difficulty believing that these vehicles, which have no engines, actually work. The cars, each weighing about 6 tons, run along a steel cable, enclosed under the street on a center rail. You can't see the cable

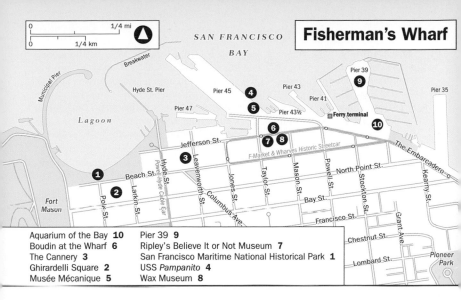

Aquarium of the Bay **10**	Pier 39 **9**
Boudin at the Wharf **6**	Ripley's Believe It or Not Museum **7**
The Cannery **3**	San Francisco Maritime National Historical Park **1**
Ghirardelli Square **2**	USS *Pampanito* **4**
Musée Mécanique **5**	Wax Museum **8**

unless you peer straight down into the crack, but you'll hear its characteristic clickity-clacking sound whenever you're nearby. The cars move when the gripper (they don't call themselves drivers) pulls back a lever that closes a pincerlike "grip" on the cable. The speed of the car, therefore, is determined by the speed of the cable, which is a constant 9½ mph—never more, never less.

The two types of cable cars in use hold a maximum of 90 and 100 passengers, and limits are rigidly enforced. The best view (and the most fun) is from a perch on the outer running boards—but hold on tightly, especially around corners.

Hallidie's cable cars were imitated and used throughout the world, but all have been replaced by more efficient means of transportation. San Francisco planned to do so, too, but met with so much opposition that the cable cars' perpetuation was actually written into the city charter in 1955. The mandate cannot be revoked without the approval of a majority of the city's voters—a distant and doubtful prospect.

San Francisco's three existing cable car lines form the world's only surviving system, which you can experience for yourself should you choose to wait in the often long lines (up to a 2-hr. wait in summer). For more information on riding them, see "Getting Around" in chapter 12.

Powell–Hyde and Powell–Mason lines begin at the base of Powell and Market sts.; California St. line begins at the foot of Market St. at the Embarcadero. $5 per ride.

The Secret to Catching Cable Cars

Here's the secret to catching a ride on a cable car: Don't wait in line with all the tourists at the turnaround stops at the beginning and end of the lines. Walk a few blocks up the line (follow the tracks) and do as the locals do: Hop on when the car stops, hang on to a pole, and have your $5 ready to hand to the brakeman (hoping, of course, that he'll never ask). On a really busy weekend, however, the cable cars often don't stop to pick up passengers en route because they're full, so you might have to stand in line at the turnarounds.

The Cannery   The Cannery was built by Del Monte in 1907 as the world's largest fruit-canning plant. It was converted into a mall in the 1960s and now contains 30-plus shops and several restaurants, including Jack's Cannery Bar and Oyster Pier (*C* **415/931-6400).** Vendors' stalls and sidewalk cafes occupy the courtyard amid a grove of century-old olive trees, and weather permitting, street performers are usually out in force, entertaining tourists (but very few locals). Shops are open Monday to Saturday at 10am and Sunday at 11am, while the restaurants generally open at 11:30am.

2801 Leavenworth St. (btw. Beach and Jefferson sts.). *C* **415/771-3112.** www.thecannery.com. Bus: 30 or 47. Streetcar: F to Hyde St.

Coit Tower ★★   In a city known for its great views and vantage points, Coit Tower is one of the best. Located atop Telegraph Hill, just east of North Beach, the round stone tower offers panoramic views of the city and the bay.

Completed in 1933, the tower is the legacy of Lillie Hitchcock Coit, a wealthy eccentric who left San Francisco a $125,000 bequest "for the purpose of adding beauty to the city I have always loved." Though many believe the tower is a fire hose–shaped homage to San Francisco firefighters (Coit had been saved from a fire as a child and became a lifelong fan and mascot for Knickerbocker Engine Co. #5), the tower is merely an expression of Coit's esteem; a memorial to firefighters lies down below in Washington Square Park.

Inside the base of the tower are impressive and slightly controversial (by 1930s standards) murals entitled *Life in California* and *1934,* which were completed under the Depression-era Public Works Art Project. Depicting California agriculture, industry, and even its leftist leanings (check out the socialist references in the library and on the newsstands), the murals are the collaborative effort of more than 25 artists, many of whom had studied under Mexican muralist Diego Rivera.

The only bummer: The narrow street leading to the tower is often clogged with tourist traffic. If you can, find a parking spot in North Beach and hoof it. The Filbert and Greenwich steps leading up to Telegraph Hill are one of the most beautiful walks in the city (p. 219).

Telegraph Hill. *C* **415/362-0808.** Admission is free to enter; elevator ride to the top is $5 adults, $3.50 seniors and youth 13–17, $1.50 children 6–12. Daily 10am–5pm. Bus: 39 (Coit).

Ferry Building Marketplace ★★★ 🎁   There's no better way to enjoy a San Francisco morning than strolling this gourmet marketplace in the Ferry

San Francisco Segway Tours

Segways are those weird-looking upright scooters you've probably seen on TV. The two-wheeled "human transporter" is an ingenious electric-powered transportation device that uses gyroscopes to emulate human balance. After the free 40-minute lesson, riding a Segway becomes intuitive: lean forward, go forward; lean back, go back; stand upright, stop. Simple. The **San Francisco Electric Tour Company** offers Segway-powered

narrated 2-hour tours of the San Francisco waterfront daily, starting from Fisherman's Wharf and heading out all the way to the Marina Green. For $70 it's not a bad deal, and it's the closest you'll come to being a celebrity (everyone checks you out). **Note:** You have to be at least 12 years old to join the tour. For more information, log onto www.sfelectrictour.com or call *C* **415/474-3130.**

LEFT: **Local favorites Cap'n Mike and Sally sell their smoked salmon at the Ferry Plaza Farmers' Market.** RIGHT: **Cowgirl Creamery sells fine cheeses at the Ferry Building.**

Building and snacking your way through breakfast or lunch. San Franciscans—writers and editors of this guide included—can't get enough of this place; we're still amazed at what a fantastic job they did renovating the interior. The Marketplace is open daily and includes much of Northern California's best gourmet bounty: Cowgirl Creamery's Artisan Cheese Shop, Recchiuti Confections (amazing chocolate), Acme Breads, Hog Island Oysters, gourmet fast food from Gott's Roadside out of Napa, famed Vietnamese restaurant the Slanted Door, one of our favorite lunch spots Il Cane Rosso, and myriad other restaurants, delis, gourmet coffee shops, specialty foods, and wine bars. Check out the Imperial Tea Court, where you'll be taught the traditional Chinese way to steep and sip your tea; buy fancy cooking items at the Sur La Table shop; grab a bite and savor the bayfront views from in- and outdoor tables; or browse the Farmers' Market when it's up and running: Tuesdays and Thursdays 10am to 2pm (usually with food trucks) and Saturdays from 8am to 2pm (this is the big market that draws the big vendors and crowds, including local chefs). Trust us, you'll love this place.

The Embarcadero, at Market St. (© **415/693-0996.** www.ferrybuildingmarketplace.com. Most stores daily 10am–6pm; restaurant hours vary. Bus: 2, 12, 14, 21, 66, or 71. Streetcar: F. BART: Embarcadero.

Ferry Plaza Farmers' Market ★★★

If you're heading to the Ferry Building Marketplace or just happen to be in the area at the right time (especially a sunny Sat), make a point of visiting the Farmers' Market, which is held in the outdoor areas in front of and behind the marketplace. This is where San Francisco foodies and many of the best local chefs—including the famed Alice Waters of Chez Panisse—gather, hang out, and peruse stalls hawking the finest Northern California fruits, vegetables, breads, meats, dairy, flowers, ready-made snacks, and to-go meals by local restaurants. You'll be amazed at the variety and quality, and the crowded scene itself is something to behold. Drop by on Saturday from 9am to noon for a serious social fest, including tours of the market and culinary demos by city chefs.

The Embarcadero, at Market St. (© **415/291-3276.** www.cuesa.org. Year-round Tues 10am–2pm; Sat 8am–2pm. Bus: 2, 12, 14, 21, 66, or 71. Streetcar: F. BART: Embarcadero.

Fisherman's Wharf ☺   Few cities in America are as adept at wholesaling their historical sites as San Francisco, which has converted Fisherman's Wharf into one of the most popular tourist attractions in the world. Unless you come early in the morning to watch the few remaining fishing boats depart, you won't find many traces of the traditional waterfront life that once existed here—the only trolling going on at Fisherman's Wharf these days is for tourist dollars. Nonetheless, everyone always seems to be enjoying himself or herself while strolling down Pier 39 on a sunny day, especially the kids.

Originally called Meiggs' Wharf, this bustling strip of waterfront got its present moniker from generations of fishermen who used to dock their boats here. A small fleet of fewer than 30 fishing boats still set out from here, but mostly it's one long shopping and entertainment mall that stretches from Ghirardelli Square at the west end to Pier 39 at the east.

Accommodating a total of 300 boats, two marinas flank Pier 39 and house the sightseeing ferry fleets, including departures to Alcatraz Island. Twenty years ago, hundreds of California sea lions took up residence on the floating docks, attracted by herring (and free lodging). They can be seen most days sunbathing, barking, and belching in the marina—some nights you can hear them all the way from Washington Square. Weather permitting, the Marine Mammal Center (*©* **415/289-SEAL** [7325]) offers an educational talk at Pier 39 daily from 10am to 5pm that teaches visitors about the range, habitat, and adaptability of the California sea lion. *Note:* After their population ballooned to more than 1,700 in the fall of 2009 the sea lions abruptly abandoned the docks, disappointing some onlookers. They returned in 2010, though in weaker numbers.

Some people love Fisherman's Wharf; others can't get far enough away from it. Most agree that, for better or for worse, it has to be seen at least once in your lifetime. There are still some traces of old-school San Francisco character here that I will always enjoy, particularly the convivial seafood street vendors who dish out piles of fresh Dungeness crab and clam chowder from their steaming stainless steel carts. Also worth a look-see is the wonderful Musée Mécanique at Pier 45, an antique arcade featuring dozens of old-fashioned coin operated amusements, including fortunetellers, an enormous mechanical carnival, and "Laffing Sal," the guffawing bust that

Coit Tower.

Seafood shopping at Fisherman's Wharf.

FUNKY FAVORITES AT fisherman's wharf

The following attractions clustered on or near Fisherman's Wharf are great fun for kids, adults, and kitsch-lovers of all ages. My favorite is the ominous-looking World War II submarine **USS *Pampanito*,** Pier 45, Fisherman's Wharf (ⓒ 415/775-1943; www.mari time.org), which saw plenty of action in the Pacific. It has been completely restored, and visitors are free to crawl around inside and play Das Boot. Admission is $10 for ages 13 and older, $6 for seniors 62 and older, $4 for children 6 to 12, and free for children 5 and under; the family pass (two adults, up to four kids) costs $20. The *Pampanito* is open daily at 9am.

Ripley's Believe It or Not! Museum, 175 Jefferson St. (ⓒ 415/771-6188; www.ripleysf.com), has drawn curious spectators through its doors for over 30 years. Inside, you'll experience a world of improbabilities: a ⅓-scale matchstick cable car, a shrunken human torso once owned by Ernest Hemingway, a dinosaur made from car bumpers, a walk through a kaleidoscope tunnel, and video displays and illusions. Robert LeRoy Ripley's infamous arsenal may lead you to ponder whether truth is, in fact, stranger than fiction. What it won't do is blow your mind or feel truly worth the money. That said, with the right attitude, it's easy to enjoy an hour here playing amid the goofy and interactive displays with lots of laughs included in the admission price, which is $20 for adults, $10 for children 5 to 12, and free for children 4 and under. Hours are Sunday through Thursday 9am to 11pm, and 9am until midnight on Friday and Saturday (open 10am in winter months).

Conceived and executed in the **Madame Tussaud mold,** San Francisco's Wax Museum, 145 Jefferson St. (ⓒ 800/ 439-4305 or 415/202-0402; www.wax museum.com), has long been a kitschy-fun tourist trap. The museum has more than 270 lifelike figures, including Oprah Winfrey, Johnny Depp, Marilyn Monroe, John Wayne, former president George W. Bush, former Giants baseball star Barry Bonds, rap artist Eminem, and "Feared Leaders" such as Fidel Castro. The Chamber of Horrors features Dracula, Frankenstein, and a werewolf, along with bloody victims hanging from meat hooks. Other galleries include King Tut's Tomb, the Palace of Living Art, and for all you geeks out there, Nobel Prize–Winning Scientists. Admission is $14 for adults, $10 for juniors 12 to 17 and seniors 55 and older, $7 for children 6 to 11, and free for children 5 and under. The complex is open from 10am to 9pm every day of the year.

once terrified children outside Playland at the Beach. A walk-through aquarium, a real World War II submarine, a blues bar, and the Rainforest Cafe offer enough entertainment to amuse everyone here, even us snobby locals.

At Taylor St. and the Embarcadero. ⓒ 415/674-7503. www.fishermanswharf.org. Bus: 30, 39, 47, or 82X. Streetcar: F. Cable car: Powell–Mason line to the last stop and walk to the wharf. If you're arriving by car, park on adjacent streets or on the wharf btw. Taylor and Jones sts. for $16 per day, $8 with validation from participating restaurants.

Ghirardelli Square This National Historic Landmark property dates from 1864, when it served as a factory making Civil War uniforms, but it's best known

Watching a dessert in the works at Ghirardelli Square.

as the former chocolate and spice factory of Domingo Ghirardelli (pronounced Gear-ar-dell-y), who purchased it in 1893. The factory has since been converted into an unimpressive three-level mall containing 30-plus stores and five dining establishments. Street performers entertain regularly in the West Plaza and fountain area. Incidentally, the Ghirardelli Chocolate Company still makes chocolate, but its factory is in a lower-rent district in the East Bay. Still, if you have a sweet tooth, you won't be disappointed at the mall's fantastic (and expensive) old-fashioned soda fountain, which is open until midnight. Their "world famous" hot fudge sundae is good, too. (Then again, have you ever had a bad hot fudge sundae?) As if you need another excuse to laze the day away in this sweet spot, the square now boasts free wireless Internet.

900 North Point St. (btw. Polk and Larkin sts.). ℂ **415/775-5500.** www.ghirardellisq.com. Stores generally daily 10am–9pm in summer; Sun–Fri 10am–6pm, Sat 10am–9pm rest of year. Parking $2.25 per 20 min. (1–1½ hr. free with purchase and validation, maximum $30).

Golden Gate Bridge ★★★ ☺ The year 2007 marked the 70th birthday of possibly the most beautiful, and certainly the most photographed, bridge in the world. Often half-veiled by the city's trademark rolling fog, San Francisco's Golden Gate Bridge, named for the strait leading from the Pacific Ocean to the San Francisco Bay, spans tidal currents, ocean waves, and battering winds to connect the City by the Bay with the Redwood Empire to the north.

With its gracefully suspended single span, spidery bracing cables, and zooming twin towers, the bridge looks more like a work of abstract art than one of the 20th century's greatest practical engineering feats. Construction was completed in May 1937 at the then-colossal cost of $35 million (plus another $39 million in interest being financed entirely by bridge tolls).

The 1¾-mile bridge (including the approach), which reaches a height of 746 feet above the water, is awesome to cross. Although kept to a maximum of 45 miles an hour, traffic usually moves quickly, so crossing by car won't give you too much time to see the sights. If you drive from the city, take the last San Francisco exit, right before the toll plaza, park in the southeast parking lot, and make the crossing by foot. Back in your car, continue to Marin's Vista Point, at the bridge's northern end. Look back, and you'll be rewarded with one of the finest views of San Francisco.

Millions of people visit the bridge each year, gazing up at the tall orange towers, out at the vistas of San Francisco and Marin County, and down into the stacks of oceangoing liners. You can walk out onto the span from either end, but be prepared—it's usually windy and cold, and the traffic is noisy. Still, walking even a short distance is one of the best ways to experience the immense scale of the structure and the perfect place to sing "San Francisco . . . open your Golden Gate."

Hwy. 101 N. www.goldengatebridge.org. $6 cash toll collected when driving south. Bridge-bound Golden Gate Transit buses (©️ 511) depart hourly during the day for Marin County, starting from Mission and First sts. (across the street from the Transbay Terminal and stopping at Market and Seventh sts., at the Civic Center, along Van Ness Ave., at Lombard and Fillmore sts., and at Francisco and Richardson sts.).

Lombard Street ★ Known (erroneously) as the "crookedest street in the world," this whimsically winding block of Lombard Street draws thousands of visitors each year (much to the chagrin of neighborhood residents, most of whom would prefer to block off the street to tourists). The angle of the street is so steep that the road has to snake back and forth to make a descent possible. The brick-lined street zigzags around the residences' bright flower gardens, which explode with

Golden Gate Bridge by the Numbers

Span: 6,450 feet
Total length: 8,981 feet
Completion date: May 28, 1937
Cost: $35 million
Date paid in full: July 1971
Engineer: Joseph B. Strauss
Road height: 260 feet
Tower height: 746 feet
Swing span: 27 feet
Deepest foundation: 110 feet under water
Cable thickness: 37 inches
Cable length: 7,650 feet
Steel used: 83,000 pounds
Concrete used: 389,000 cubic yards
Miles of wire cable: 80,000
Gallons of paint annually: 10,000
Color: international orange
Rise, in cold weather: 5 feet
Drop, in hot weather: 10 feet
Traffic: 3 million vehicles per month
Toll: $6 (southbound only)

Joseph B. Strauss's creation.

GoCar Tours of San Francisco

If the thought of walking up and down San Francisco's brutally steep streets has you sweating already, considering renting a talking GoCar instead. The tiny yellow three-wheeled convertible cars are easy and fun to drive—every time I see one of these things, the people riding in them are grinning from ear to ear—and they're cleverly guided by a talking GPS (Global Positioning System), which means that the car always knows where you are, even if you don't. The most popular computer-guided tour is a 2-hour loop around the Fisherman's Wharf area, out to the Marina District, through Golden Gate Park, and down Lombard Street, the "crookedest street in the world." As you drive, the talking car tells you when to turn and what landmarks you're passing. Even if you stop to check something out, as soon as you turn your GoCar back on, the tour picks up where it left off. Or you can just cruise around wherever you want (but not across the Golden Gate Bridge). There's a lockable trunk for your things, and the small size makes parking a breeze. Keep in mind, this isn't a Ferrari—two adults on a long, steep hill may involve one of you walking (or pushing).

You can rent a GoCar from 1 hour (about $49) to a full day. You'll have to wear a helmet, and you must be a licensed driver of at least 18 years of age. The GoCar rental shop is at 2715 Hyde St., between Beach and North Point streets at Fisherman's Wharf. For more information call ℂ **800/91-GOCAR** (46227) or 415/441-5695, or log onto their website at www.gocartours.com.

color during warmer months. This short stretch of Lombard Street is one-way, downhill, and fun to drive. Take the curves slowly and in low gear, and expect a wait during the weekend. Save your film for the bottom where, if you're lucky, you can find a parking space and take a few snapshots of the silly spectacle. You can also take staircases (without curves) up or down on either side of the street. In truth, most locals don't understand what the fuss is all about. I'm guessing the draw is the combination of seeing such a famous landmark, the challenge of negotiating so many steep curves, and a classic photo op. **FYI:** Vermont Street, between 20th and 22nd streets in Potrero Hill, is even more crooked, but not nearly as picturesque.

Btw. Hyde and Leavenworth sts.

Pier 39 👍 Pier 39 is a multilevel waterfront complex a few blocks east of Fisherman's Wharf. Constructed on an abandoned cargo pier, it is, ostensibly, a re-creation of a turn-of-the-20th-century street scene, but don't expect a slice of old-time maritime life here: Today, Pier 39 is a busy mall welcoming millions of visitors per year. It has more than 110 stores, 13 bay-view restaurants, a two-tiered Venetian carousel, a Hard Rock Cafe, Players Sports Grill and Arcade, and the Aquarium of the Bay (see below) for the kids. And everything here is slanted toward helping you part with your travel dollars. This is the place that locals love to hate, but kids adore it. That said, it does have a few perks: absolutely beautiful natural surroundings and bay views, entertaining street performers, and sunbathing sea lions lounging along its neighboring docks.

On the waterfront at the Embarcadero and Beach St. © **415/705-5500.** www.pier39.com. Shops daily 10am–8pm, with extended hours during summer and on weekends.

MUSEUMS

For information on museums in Golden Gate Park, see the "Golden Gate Park" section, beginning on p. 204.

Aquarium of the Bay ☺ This $38-million, 1-million-gallon marine attraction at Pier 39 is filled with sharks, stingrays, and other sea creatures that visitors can get up close and personal with via touch tanks and clear acrylic tunnels that you pass through on a people-mover. (Being here during an earthquake would be really interesting.) Although the tunnel is an engineering marvel, the overall experience pales in comparison to the Monterey Bay Aquarium, but the kids sure seem to get a kick out of all the fish swimming above and around them.

The Embarcadero at Beach St. © **888/SEA-DIVE** (732 3483) or 415/623-5333. www.aquariumof thebay.com. Aquarium admission $17 adults, $10 seniors and children 3–11, free for children 2 and under; family (2 adults, 2 children) package $38. Behind-the scenes tour $22 per person, $14 seniors and children 5–11, including admission to the aquarium. Summer daily 9am–8pm; rest of year Mon–Thurs 10am–6pm, Fri–Sun 10am–7pm. Closed Dec 25.

Asian Art Museum ★ Previously in Golden Gate Park and reopened in a stunning space that was once the Beaux Arts–style main library, San Francisco's Asian Art Museum is one of the Western world's largest museums devoted to Asian art. Its collection boasts more than 15,000 art objects, including world-class sculptures, paintings, bronzes, ceramics, and jade items, spanning 6,000 years of history and regions of south Asia, west Asia, Southeast Asia, the Himalayas, China, Korea, and Japan. Inside you'll find 40,000 square feet of gallery space showcasing 2,500 objects at any given time. Add temporary exhibitions, live demonstrations, learning activities, the very good Cafe Asia, and a store, and you've got one very good reason to head to the Civic Center.

200 Larkin St. (btw. Fulton and McAllister sts.). © **415/581-3500.** www.asianart.org. Admission $17 adults, $13 seniors 65 and over, $7 youths 13–17, $12 college students with ID, free for children 12 and under. $10 flat rate for all (except children 12 and under who are free) after 5pm Thurs. $5 1st Sun of the month. Tues–Wed and Fri–Sun 10am–5pm; Thurs 10am–9pm. Bus: All Market St. buses. Streetcar: Civic Center.

Cable Car Museum ★ ⚓ ☺ If you've ever wondered how cable cars work, this nifty museum explains (and demonstrates) it all. The Cable Car Museum is no stuffed shirt; it's the living powerhouse, repair shop, and storage place of the cable car system and is in full operation. Built for the Ferries and Cliff House Railway in 1887, the building underwent an $18-million reconstruction to restore its original gaslight-era look, install an amazing spectators' gallery, and add a museum of San Francisco transit history.

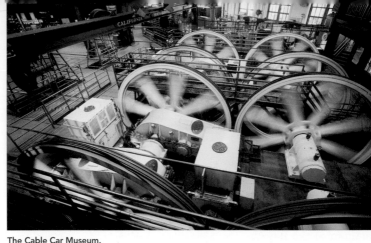

The Cable Car Museum.

The exposed machinery, which pulls the cables under San Francisco's streets, looks like a Rube Goldberg invention. Stand in the mezzanine gallery and become mesmerized by the massive groaning and vibrating winches as they thread the cable that hauls the cars through a huge figure-eight and back into the system using slack-absorbing tension wheels. For a better view, move to the lower-level viewing room, where you can see the massive pulleys and gears operating underground.

Also on display here is one of the first grip cars developed by Andrew S. Hallidie, operated for the first time on Clay Street on August 2, 1873. Other displays include an antique grip car and trailer that operated on Pacific Avenue until 1929, and dozens of exact-scale models of cars used on the various city lines. There's also a shop where you can buy a variety of cable car gifts. You can see the whole museum in about 45 minutes, and the best part—it's free.

1201 Mason St. (at Washington St.). ✆ **415/474-1887.** www.cablecarmuseum.org. Free admission. Apr–Sept daily 10am–6pm; Oct–Mar daily 10am–5pm. Closed Thanksgiving, Christmas, and New Year's Day. Cable car: Both Powell St. lines.

California Academy of Sciences ★★★ ☺ San Francisco's California Academy of Sciences has been entertaining locals and tourists for more than 150 years, and with the grand opening of the all-new Academy in 2008, it's now going stronger than ever. Four years and $500 million in the making, the new Academy is the "greenest" museum in the world, and the only institution in the world to combine an aquarium, planetarium, natural history museum, and scientific research program under one roof. The spectacular new complex has literally reinvented the role of science museums in the 21st century, a place where visitors interact with animals, educators, and biologists at hands-on exhibits such as a four-story living rainforest dome complete with flitting butterflies and birds, and the world's deepest living coral reef display. Even the Academy's 2½-acre undulating living garden roof is an exhibit, planted with 1.7 million native California plants, including thousands of flowers.

More than 38,000 live animals fill the new Academy's aquarium and natural history exhibits. Highlights include the Morrison Planetarium, the world's largest all-digital planetarium, which takes you on a guided tour of the solar system and beyond using current data from NASA to produce the most accurate and interactive digital universe ever created; the Philippine Coral Reef, the world's deepest living coral reef tank where 4,000 sharks, rays, sea turtles, giant clams, and other aquatic creatures live in a Technicolor forest of coral; and the Rainforests of the World, a living rainforest filled with mahogany and palm trees, croaking frogs, chirping birds, leaf cutter ants, bat caves, chameleons, and hundreds of tropical butterflies. You can climb into the treetops of Costa Rica, descend in a glass elevator into the Amazonian flooded forest, and walk along an acrylic tunnel beneath the Amazonian river fish that swim overhead.

Even the dining options here are first-rate, as both the Academy Café and Moss Room restaurant are run by two of the city's top chefs, Charles Phan and Loretta Keller, and feature local, organic, sustainable foods. The only thing you won't enjoy here is the entrance fee—a whopping $30 per adult—but it includes access to all the Academy exhibits and the planetarium shows, and if you arrive by public transportation, they'll knock $3 off the fee (how very green). *Tip:* The boozy "Nightlife" Thursdays from 6 to 10pm are just $12, draw big (but not too packed) crowds, and let you see much of the museum. No kids.

55 Concourse Dr., Golden Gate Park. ✆ **415/379-8000.** www.calacademy.org. Admission $30 adults, $25 seniors 65 and over, $25 youths 12–17, $20 children 7–11, free for children 6 and under. Free to all 3rd Wed of each month. Mon–Sat 9:30am–5pm; Thurs "Nightlife" 6pm; Sun 11am–5pm. Closed Thanksgiving and Christmas. Bus: 5, 21, 44, or 71.

California Historical Society   As part of the plan to develop the area around Yerba Buena Gardens as the city's cultural hub, the California Historical Society opened to house a research library and an ever-changing roster of exhibits that pertain to California's rich past. A 2-hour walking tour of the Bay Area is offered by local eccentric Gary L. Holloway, and there's an outlet of the very fine William Stout Architectural Books in the lobby. Call or check the website for current exhibit and walking tour information.

678 Mission St. (btw. Third and New Montgomery sts.). ✆ **415/357-1848.** www.californiahistorical society.org. $3 adults, $1 seniors/students. North Baker Research Library Wed–Fri noon–5pm. Galleries Wed–Sat noon–4:30pm. Bus: 5, 9, 14, 30, or 45. Streetcar F line or Metro to Montgomery St.

The aquarium at the California Academy of Sciences.

The de Young Museum.

Contemporary Jewish Museum ★

Maybe the best reason to visit this new addition to the Yerba Buena Gardens area is the building. Carved out of a 1907 power substation designed by Willis Polk, New York architect Daniel Libeskind married the old Beaux Arts brick facade to a shiny, modern blue-steel cube that looks a bit like an alien spaceship crashed into the roof. Libeskind actually based the design on the Hebrew letters of the word chai (life). Inside, the look is geometry-meets-modern-industrial, with soaring skylights and enormous windows that illuminate exhibits on Jewish culture, history, art, and ideas. The cafe offers sandwiches, salads, and traditional Jewish fare such as matzo ball soup, latkes, and bagels with lox.

Frederick William MacMonnies' Diana, at the de Young Museum.

736 Mission St. (btw. Third and Fourth sts.). ℂ **415/655-7800.** www.thecjm.org. Admission $12 adults, $10 seniors/students. $5 Thurs after 5pm. Fri–Tues 11am–5pm; Thurs 1–8pm. Closed Passover, July 4, Rosh Hashanah, Yom Kippur, Thanksgiving, and New Year's Day. Bus: 5, 9, 14, 15, 30, or 45. Streetcar: F line or Metro to Montgomery St.

de Young Museum ★★★   After closing for several years, San Francisco's oldest museum (founded in 1895) reopened in late 2005 in its state-of-the-art Golden Gate Park facility. Its vast holdings include one of the finest collections of American paintings in the United States from Colonial times through the 20th century, as well as decorative arts and crafts; Western and non-Western textiles; and arts from Africa, Oceania, and the Americas. Along with superb revolving exhibitions, the de Young has long been beloved for its educational programs for both children and adults, and now it's equally enjoyed for its stunning architecture and sculpture-graced garden. The striking facade consists of 950,000 pounds of textured and perforated copper that's intended to patinate with age, while the northeast corner of the building features a 144-foot tower that slowly spirals from the ground floor and culminates with an observation floor offering panoramic views of the entire city (from a distance, it has the surreal look of a rusty aircraft carrier cruising through the park). Surrounding sculpture gardens and lush, grassy expanses are perfect for picnicking. Adding to the allure is surprisingly good and healthy organic fare at the grab-and-go or order-and-wait cafe/restaurant. *Note:* Underground parking is accessed at 10th Avenue and Fulton Street. Also, admission tickets to the de Young may be used on the same day for free entrance to the Legion of Honor (see below).

50 Hagiwara Tea Garden Dr. (inside Golden Gate Park, 2 blocks from the park entrance at Eighth Ave. and Fulton). (*C*) **415/750-3600** or 863-3330. www.famsf.org. Admission adults $11, seniors $8, youths 13–17 and college students with ID $7, children 12 and under free. Free 1st Tues of the month. $2 discount for Muni riders with Fast Pass or transfer receipt. Tues–Sun 9:30am–5:15pm (Fri until 8:45pm [except Dec]). Closed New Year's Day, Thanksgiving, and Christmas. Bus: 5, 21, 44, or 71.

The Exploratorium ★★★ ☺ *Scientific American* magazine rated the Exploratorium "the best science museum in the world"—and I couldn't agree more. Inside you'll find hundreds of exhibits that give you hands-on access to everything from giant-bubble blowing to Einstein's theory of relativity. It's like a mad scientist's penny arcade, an educational fun house, and an experimental laboratory all rolled into one. Touch a tornado, shape a glowing electrical current, or take a sensory journey in total darkness in the Tactile Dome ($3 extra, and call (*C*) **415/561-0362** to make advance reservations)—even if you spent all day here you couldn't experience everything. Every exhibit at the Exploratorium is designed to be interactive, educational, safe, and, most importantly, fun. And don't think it's just for kids; parents inevitably end up being the most reluctant to leave. I went here recently and spent 3 hours in just one small section of the museum, marveling at all the mind-blowing hands-on exhibits related to light and eyesight. On the way out, be sure to stop in the wonderful gift store, which is chock-full of affordable brain candy.

The museum is in the Marina District at the beautiful **Palace of Fine Arts ★★**, the only building left standing from the Panama Pacific Exposition of 1915. The adjoining park with lagoon—the perfect place for an afternoon picnic—is home to ducks, swans, sea gulls, and grouchy geese, so bring bread.

3601 Lyon St., in the Palace of Fine Arts (at Marina Blvd.). (*C*) **415/EXPLORE** (397-5673) or 561-0360 (recorded information). www.exploratorium.edu. Admission $15 adults; $12 seniors, youth 13–17, visitors with disabilities, and college students with ID; $10 children 4–12; free for children 3 and under. Free for all 1st Wed of month. Tues–Sun 10am–5pm. Closed Mon except MLK, Jr., Day, Presidents' Day, Memorial Day, and Labor Day. Free parking. Bus: 28, 30, or Golden Gate Transit.

Haas-Lilienthal House Of the city's many gingerbread Victorians, this handsome Queen Anne house is one of the most flamboyant. The 1886 structure features all the architectural frills of the period, including dormer windows, flying cupolas, ornate trim, and a winsome turret. The elaborately styled house is now the only Victorian house museum in the city that has its rooms fully furnished with period

The Haas-Lilienthal House.

Italian-Style Saturday Singalong

If you haven't completely fallen in love with San Francisco yet, then show up at **Caffe Trieste** in North Beach on most Saturdays between 1 and 5pm. That's when the stringed instruments are tuned up, the chairs are scooted against the walls, and the locals entertain the crowd with their lively version of classic Italian operas and heartwarming folk songs. Everybody's so high on caffeine that it quickly becomes one big happy party and the highlight of everyone's vacation. (Even jaded locals—myself included—still get a kick out of it.) This family-owned corner institution is one of San Francisco's most beloved cafes—a Beat Generation hangout that's been around since 1956 serving locally roasted Italian coffee and playing the muse to numerous artists, including Francis Ford Coppola, who supposedly penned The Godfather here. You'll find it at 601 Vallejo St. at Grant Avenue (✆ **415/392-6739**; www.caffetrieste. com). Call to confirm that the show's on.

pieces and is open to the public. The San Francisco Architectural Heritage maintains the house and offers docent-led 1-hour tours (the only way to see the house), which start every 20 to 30 minutes on Wednesdays, Saturdays, and Sundays.

2007 Franklin St. (at Washington St.). ✆ **415/441-3000.** www.sfheritage.org. 1-hr. guided tour $8 adults, $5 seniors and children 12 and under. Wed and Sat noon–3pm; Sun 11am–4pm. (**Note:** Some Sat the house is closed for private functions, so call to confirm.) Bus: 1, 12, 19, 27, 47, or 49. Cable car: California St. line.

The Legion of Honor ★★   Designed as a memorial to California's World War I casualties, this neoclassical structure is an exact replica of the Legion of Honor Palace in Paris, right down to the inscription HONNEUR ET PATRIE above the portal. The exterior's grassy expanses, cliff-side paths, and incredible view of the Golden Gate and downtown make this an absolute must-visit attraction before you even get in the door. The inside is equally impressive: The museum's permanent collection covers 4,000 years of art and includes paintings, sculpture, and decorative arts from Europe, as well as international tapestries, prints, and drawings. The chronological display of 4,000 years of ancient and European art includes one of the world's finest collections of Rodin sculptures. The sunlit Legion Cafe offers indoor and outdoor seating at moderate prices. Plan to spend 2 or 3 hours here.

In Lincoln Park (34th Ave. and Clement St.). ✆ **415/750-3600** or 863-3330 (recorded information). www.famsf.org. Admission $11 adults, $8 seniors 65 and over, $7 youths 13–17 and college students with ID, free for children 12 and under. Fees may be higher for special exhibitions. Free 1st Tues of each month. Free admission with same-day tickets from the de Young Museum. Tues–Sun 9:30am–5:15pm. Bus: 18.

Metreon Entertainment Center ☺   This 350,000-square-foot high-tech mall on the corner of 4th and Mission was never really embraced by locals, but with a new $30-million makeover that includes a lighter, brighter redesign, and 470-seat dining terrace facing Yerba Buena Gardens with free Wi-Fi and iPad hookups, and the only Target in the city, everyone is hoping the "reimagined" mall will be the new darling of SoMa. Within its gleaming walls are an AMC movie theater, an IMAX theater, and a bevy of new retail outlets and restaurants such as SoGreen Yogurt, San Francisco Soup Co., Cako Creamery, and La Boulange Bakery. The whole place is wired with free Wi-Fi, which now makes it an ideal place to spend an alfresco lunch while fiddling with your tablet.

101 Fourth St. (at the corner of Mission St.). ☎ **415/369-6000.** www.metreon.com. Building 10am–10pm daily; individual businesses may have different hours. Bus: 5, 9, 14, 30, or 45. Streetcar: Powell or Montgomery.

Octagon House   This unusual, eight-sided, cupola-topped house dates from 1861 and is maintained by the National Society of Colonial Dames of America. Its design was based on a past theory that people living in a space of this shape would live longer, healthier lives. Inside is a small museum where you'll find Early American furniture, portraits, silver, pewter, looking glasses, and English and Chinese ceramics. There are also some historic documents, including signatures of 54 of the 56 signers of the Declaration of Independence. Even if you're not able to visit the inside, this atypical structure is worth a look from the outside.

2645 Gough St. (at Union St.). ☎ **415/441-7512.** Free admission; donation suggested. Feb–Dec 2 Sun noon–3pm; 2nd and 4th Thurs of each month noon–3pm. Tours by appointment are the only way to see the house. Closed holidays. Bus: 41 or 45.

San Francisco Maritime National Historical Park ★ ☺   This park includes several marine-themed sites within a few blocks of each other. The park's signature Maritime Museum—on Beach Street at Polk Street, shaped like an Art Deco ship, and filled with sea-faring memorabilia—reopened in 2010 after major renovations. Be sure to pop in to check out the murals. Head 2 blocks east to the corner of Hyde and Jefferson streets and you'll find SFMNHP's state-of-the-art Visitor's Center, which offers a fun, interactive look at the city's maritime heritage. Housed in the historic Haslett Warehouse building, the Center tells the stories of voyage, discovery, and cultural diversity. Across the street, at the park's Hyde Street Pier, are several historic ships, which are moored and open to the public.

The *Balclutha,* one of the last surviving square-riggers and the handsomest vessel in San Francisco Bay, was built in Glasgow, Scotland, in 1886 and carried grain from California at a near-record speed of 300 miles a day. The ship is now completely restored.

The 1890 *Eureka* still carries a cargo of nostalgia for San Franciscans. It was the last of 50 paddle-wheel ferries that regularly plied the bay; it made its final trip in 1957. Restored to its original splendor at the height of the ferryboat era, the side-wheeler is loaded with deck cargo, including antique cars and trucks.

The black-hulled, three-masted *C. A. Thayer,* built in 1895 and recently restored, was crafted for the lumber trade and carried logs felled in the Pacific Northwest to the carpentry shops of California.

Other historic ships docked here include the tiny two-masted *Alma,* one of the last scow schooners to bring hay to the horses of San Francisco; the *Hercules,* a huge 1907 oceangoing steam tug; and the *Eppleton Hall,* a side-wheel tugboat built in England in 1914 to operate on London's River Thames.

At the pier's small-boat shop, visitors can follow the restoration progress of historic boats from the museum's collection. It's behind the maritime bookstore on your right as you approach the ships.

Visitor's Center: Hyde and Jefferson sts. (near Fisherman's Wharf). ☎ **415/447-5000.** www.nps.gov/safr. No fee for Visitor's Center. Tickets to board ships $5, free for children 16 and under. Visitor's Center: Memorial Day–Sept 30 daily 9:30am–5:30pm; Oct 1–Memorial Day daily 9:30am–5pm. Ships on Hyde St. Pier: Memorial Day–Sept 30 daily 9:30am–5:30pm; Oct 1–Memorial Day daily 9am–5pm. Bus: 19, 30, or 47. Cable car: Powell–Hyde St. line to the last stop.

San Francisco Museum of Modern Art (SFMOMA) ★   Swiss architect Mario Botta, in association with Hellmuth, Obata, and Kassabaum, designed this $65-million museum, which has made the area south of Market Street, or SoMa, one of the more popular areas to visit for tourists and residents alike. The museum's permanent collection houses the West Coast's most comprehensive collection of 20th-century art, including painting, sculpture, photography, architecture, design, and media arts. The collection, including a new infusion of some 1,100 pieces from late Gap founder Don Fisher, features master works by Ansel Adams, Bruce Conner, Joseph Cornell, Salvador Dalí, Richard Diebenkorn, Eva Hesse, Frida Kahlo, Ellsworth Kelly, Yves Klein, Sherrie Levine, Henri Matisse, Piet Mondrian, Pablo Picasso, Robert Rauschenberg, Diego Rivera, Cindy Sherman, Alfred Stieglitz, Clyfford Still, and Edward Weston, among many others, as well as an ever-changing program of special exhibits. Unfortunately, few works are on display at one time, and for the money the experience can be disappointing—especially compared to museums in New York. However, this is about as good as it gets in our boutique city, so take it or leave it. Docent-led tours take place daily. Times are posted at the admission desk. Phone or check SFMOMA's website for current details of upcoming special events and exhibitions.

The Caffè Museo, to the right of the museum entrance, offers very good quality fresh soups, sandwiches, and salads. Be sure to visit the MuseumStore, which carries a wonderful array of modern and contemporary art books, innovative design objects and furniture, jewelry and apparel, educational children's books and toys, posters, and stationery: It's one of the best gift shops in town.

151 Third St. (2 blocks south of Market St., across from Yerba Buena Gardens). ℂ 4**15/357-4000.** www.sfmoma.org. Admission $18 adults, $12 seniors, $11 students 13 and over with ID, free for children 12 and under. Half-price for all Thurs 6–9pm. Free to all 1st Tues of each month. Thurs 11am–8:45pm; Fri–Tues 11am–5:45pm. Closed Wed and major holidays. Bus: 30 or 45. Streetcar: J, K, L, or M to Montgomery.

San Francisco Museum of Modern Art (SFMOMA).

SAN FRANCISCO'S OLD-FASHIONED
arcade museum

"Fun for all ages" isn't a trite expression when describing **San Francisco's Musée Méca-nique,** a truly unique penny arcade museum containing one of the largest privately owned collections of antique coin-operated mechanical musical instruments in the world—160 machines dating back from the 1880s through the present (and they still work!). You can pay Grand-Ma Fortune Teller a quarter to see what she has to say about your future, or watch little kids cower in fear as Laughing "Fat Lady" Sal gives her infa-mous cackle of a greeting. Other yesteryear seaside resort games include antique movie

machines, 19th-century music boxes, old-school strength testers, and mechanical cranes. The museum is located at Pier 45 at the end of Taylor Street at Fisherman's Wharf. It's open Monday through Friday from 10am to 7pm and Saturday and Sunday from 10am to 8pm. Admission is free (✆ **415/346-2000;** www. museemechanique.org).

San Francisco Zoo (& Children's Zoo) ☺   Located between the Pacific Ocean and Lake Merced in the southwest corner of the city, the San Francisco Zoo, which once had a reputation for being a bit shoddy and out-of-date, has come a long way in recent years (that is, until the notorious tiger-attack incident in 2007, when a Siberian tiger escaped and attacked three visitors, killing one). Though grown-ups who are into wildlife will enjoy the visit, it's really aimed at kids, who get a kick out of attractions like the hands-on Children's Zoo, the flock of shockingly pink flamin-gos, Grizzly Gulch, the giant anaconda, and the ageless Little Puffer train.

Founded at its present site near the ocean in 1929, the zoo is spread over 100 acres and houses more than 930 animals, including some 245 species of mammals, birds, reptiles, amphibians, and invertebrates. Exhibit highlights include the Lip-man Family Lemur Forest, a forest setting for five endangered species of lemurs from Madagascar; Jones Family Gorilla World, a tranquil setting for a family group of western lowland gorillas; Koala Crossing, which connects to the Australian Walk-about exhibit with its kangaroos, wallaroos, and emu; Penguin Island, home to a large breeding colony of Magellanic Penguins (join them for lunch at 2:30pm daily); and the Primate Discovery Center, home to rare and endangered monkeys. Puente al Sur (Bridge to the South) has a pair of giant anteaters and some capybaras. The Lion House is home to rare Sumatran and Siberian tigers and African lions. You can watch the big cats get fed every day at 2pm (except Mon). African Savanna is a 3-acre mixed-species habitat with giraffes, zebras, antelopes, and birds.

The 6-acre Children's Zoo offers kids and their families opportunities for close-up encounters with rare domestic breeds of goats, sheep, ponies, and horses in the Family Farm. Touch and feel small mammals, reptiles, and amphibians along the Nature Trail and gaze at eagles and hawks stationed on Hawk Hill. Don't miss a visit to the fascinating Insect Zoo or the Meerkat and Prairie Dog exhibit, where kids can crawl through tunnels and play in sand, just like these amazing burrowing species.

There's a coffee cart by the entrance as well as two decent cafes inside, definitely good enough for a bite with the kids (though the lines can be long and slightly confusing if you're handling food and kid duty at the same time).

Great Highway btw. Sloat Blvd. and Skyline Blvd. (✆ **415/753-7080.** www.sfzoo.org. Admission $15 adults, $12 for seniors 65 and over and youth 12–17, $9 for children 3–11, free for children 2 and under. San Francisco residents receive a discount. Free to all 1st Wed of each month, except $2 fee for Children's Zoo. Carousel $2. Daily 10am–5pm. Bus: 23 or 18. Streetcar: L from downtown Market St. to the end of the line.

The Walt Disney Family Museum ★ ☺ Dedicated to the life, career, and art of Walt Disney, this new museum offers a fascinating look at the man behind the mouse. Opened in 2009 by the Walt Disney Family Foundation (headed up by Walt's oldest daughter, Diane, who lives in Northern California), the museum occupies an inconspicuous spot on the main post of the Presidio. The architecture alone is reason to visit the wonderful world of Disney. Repurposed out of an old army barracks and gymnasium, the deceptively large space blends seamlessly into its historic surroundings. In fact, it's easy to pass right by the tidy brick facade, until you notice the uniformed usher with the über-friendly smile beckoning you toward the door. Once inside, you'll find a museum that is as appealing to adults as to children (okay, maybe a tad more to adults, but don't tell that to our kids). The galleries are set up chronologically, beginning with Walt's early cartoons for his high school yearbook and ending with his death in 1966. Highlights include an interactive gallery documenting Disney's innovations in sound synchronization where kids can add sound effects to a Steamboat Willie cartoon; absorbing audio narratives about Disney's run-ins and ultimate triumphs over swindlers who tried to cash in on early successes; an original multiplane camera that shows you how Disney developed dimensional animation; and the nail-biting tale of how the Disney brothers financed *Snow White and the Seven Dwarfs.* Along the way, there are plenty of old-fashioned cartoons to watch—which we suspect kids and grown-ups will enjoy for different reasons. It's part of what makes this new museum such a winner.

In the Presidio, Main Post, 104 Montgomery St. (at Sheridan Ave.). (✆ **415/345-6800.** www. waltdisney.org. Admission $20 adults, $15 for students with valid IDs and seniors 65 and over, $12 for children 6–17. Wed–Mon 10am–6pm. Bus: 28 or 43.

Wells Fargo History Museum Wells Fargo, one of California's largest banks, got its start in the Wild West. Its history museum, at the bank's head office, houses hundreds of genuine relics from the company's whip-and-six-shooter days, including pistols, photographs, early banking articles, posters, a stagecoach, and mining equipment.

420 Montgomery St. (at California St.). (✆ **415/396-2619.** www.wellsfargohistory.com. Free admission. Mon–Fri 9am–5pm. Closed bank holidays. Bus: Any to Market St. Cable car: California St. line. BART: Montgomery St.

Yerba Buena Center for the Arts ★ 🎁 ☺ The YBCA, which opened in 1993, is part of the large outdoor complex that takes up a few city blocks across the street from SFMOMA, and sits atop the underground Moscone Convention

Outside the Yerba Buena Center for the Arts.

Penguins at the zoo are fed at 2:30pm daily.

Center. It's the city's cultural facility, similar to New York's Lincoln Center but far more fun on the outside. The Center's two buildings offer music, theater, dance, and visual arts programs and shows. James Stewart Polshek designed the 755-seat theater, and Fumihiko Maki designed the Galleries and Arts Forum, which features three galleries and a space designed especially for dance. Cutting-edge computer art, multimedia shows, contemporary exhibitions, and performances occupy the center's high-tech galleries.

701 Mission St. ℐ **415/978-ARTS** (2787) (box office). www.ybca.org. Admission for gallery $7 adults; $5 seniors, teachers, and students. Free to all 1st Tues of each month. Free for seniors and students with ID every Thurs. Tues–Wed and Sun noon–5pm; Thurs–Sat noon–8pm. Closed Mon. Contact YBCA for times and admission to theater. Bus: 5, 9, 14, 15, 30, or 45. Streetcar: Powell or Montgomery.

Yerba Buena Gardens ★ Unless you're at Yerba Buena to catch a perfor-mance, you're more likely to visit the 5-acre gardens, a great place to relax in the grass on a sunny day and check out architecture, artworks, and a revolving sea of humanity. The most dramatic outdoor piece is an emotional mixed-media memo-rial to Martin Luther King, Jr. Created by sculptor Houston Conwill, poet Estella Majozo, and architect Joseph De Pace, it features 12 panels, each inscribed with quotations from King, sheltered behind a 50-foot-high waterfall. There are also several actual garden areas here, including a Butterfly Garden, the Sister Cities Garden (highlighting flowers from the city's 13 sister cities), and the East Gar-den, blending Eastern and Western styles. Don't miss the view from the upper terrace, where old and new San Francisco come together in a clash of styles that's fascinating. May through October, Yerba Buena Arts & Events puts on a series of free outdoor festivals featuring dance, music, poetry, and more by the San Fran-cisco Ballet, Opera, Symphony, and others.

Located on 2 square city blocks bounded by Mission, Folsom, Third, and Fourth sts. www.yerba buenagardens.com. Free admission. Daily 6am–10pm. Contact Yerba Buena Arts & Events: ℐ **415/543-1718** or www.ybgf.org for details about the free outdoor festivals. Bus: 5, 9, 14, 30, or 45. Streetcar: Powell or Montgomery.

free CULTURE

To beef up attendance and give indigent folk like us travel writers a break, almost all of San Francisco's art galleries and museums are open free to the public 1 day of the week or month (or both), and several never charge admission. Use the following list to plan your week around the museums' free-day schedules; see the individual attraction listings in this chapter for more information on each museum.

FIRST TUESDAY
- **Center for the Arts at Yerba Buena Gardens** (p. 190)
- **de Young Museum** (p. 184)
- **The Legion of Honor** (p. 186)
- **San Francisco Museum of Modern Art** (p. 188)

FIRST WEDNESDAY
- **The Exploratorium** (p. 185)
- **San Francisco Zoo** (p. 189)

THIRD WEDNESDAY
- **California Academy of Sciences** (p. 182)

ALWAYS FREE
- **Cable Car Museum** (p. 181)
- **Glide Memorial United Methodist Church** (p. 206)
- **Musée Mécanique** (p. 189)
- **San Francisco Maritime National Historical Park and Museum** (there's a fee to board ships; p. 187)
- **Wells Fargo History Museum** (p. 190)

Zeum/The Yerba Buena Ice Skating and Bowling Center ★ ☺ Also in Yerba Buena Gardens you'll find Zeum, an innovative, hands-on multimedia, arts, and technology museum for kids of all ages. Next to Zeum is the fabulous 1906 carousel that once graced the city's bygone oceanside amusement park, Playland-at-the-Beach, and there's a Children's Garden, a cafe, and a fun store. Right behind Zeum, you'll find the Yerba Buena Ice Skating and Bowling Center, a great stopover if you're looking for fun indoor activities, including a 12-lane bowling alley and an ice-skating rink with public sessions daily.

Zeum: 221 Fourth St. (at Howard St.). ℂ **415/820-3320.** www.zeum.org. Admission $10 adults; $8 seniors, students, and youth 3–18; free for children 2 and under. Summer Tues–Sun 11am–5pm; during the school year Wed–Fri 1–5pm, Sat–Sun 11am–5pm. Carousel $3 per person, each ticket good for 2 rides. Daily 11am–6pm. Yerba Buena Ice Skating and Bowling Center: 750 Folsom St. ℂ **415/820-3521.** Bowling alley: $34–$40 per lane/per hour. Sun–Thurs 10am–10pm; Fri–Sat 10am–midnight. Skating rink: Call for hours and admission. Bus: 5, 9, 14, 30, or 45. Streetcar: Powell or Montgomery.

NEIGHBORHOODS WORTH A VISIT

To really get to know San Francisco, break out of the downtown and Fisherman's Wharf areas to explore the ethnically and culturally diverse neighborhoods. Walk the streets, browse the shops, grab a bite at a local restaurant; you'll find that San

Francisco's beauty and charm are around every corner, not just at the popular tourist destinations.

Note: For information on Fisherman's Wharf, see its entry under "Famous San Francisco Sights," on p. 176. For information on San Francisco neighborhoods and districts that aren't discussed here, see "Neighborhoods in Brief," in chapter 3, beginning on p. 41.

Nob Hill

When the cable car started operating in 1873, this hill became the city's exclusive residential area. Newly wealthy residents who had struck it rich in the gold rush and the railroad boom (and were known by names such as the "Big Four" and the "Bonanza kings") built their mansions here, but they were almost all destroyed by the 1906 earthquake and fire. The only two surviving buildings are the Flood Mansion, which serves today as the Pacific Union Club, and the Fairmont Hotel, which was under construction when the earthquake struck and was damaged but not destroyed. Today, the sites of former mansions hold the city's luxury hotels—the InterContinental Mark Hopkins, the Stanford Court, the Huntington Hotel, and spectacular Grace Cathedral, which stands on the Crocker mansion site. Nob Hill is worth a visit if only to stroll around delightful Huntington Park with its cherubic fountain (a copy of the Tartarughe fountain in Rome), attend a Sunday service at the cathedral, or ooh and aah your way around the Fairmont's spectacular lobby.

South of Market (SoMa)

From Market Street to Townsend Street and the Embarcadero to Division Street, SoMa has become the city's cultural and multimedia center. The process started when alternative clubs began opening in the old warehouses in the area nearly 2 decades ago. A wave of entrepreneurs followed, seeking to start new businesses in what was once an extremely low-rent area compared to the neighboring Financial District. Once the dot.commers moved in, it was gentrification and high rents all the way. The building boom started with the construction of the Moscone

Huntington Park.

fortune cookie **FACTORY**

At 56 Ross Alley is the **Golden Gate Fortune Cookie Factory** (© **415/781-3956**), a tiny Chinatown storefront where, since 1962, three women sit at a conveyor belt, folding messages into thousands of fortune cookies as the manager invariably calls out to tourists, beckoning them to stroll in, watch the cookies being made, and buy a bag of 40 for about $3. Sure, there are other fortune cookie bakeries in the city, but this is the only one left where the cookies are still made by hand the old-fashioned way. You can purchase regular fortunes, unfolded flat cookies without fortunes, or, if you bring your own fortunes, they can create custom cookies (great for dinner parties) at around $6 for 50 cookies—a very cheap way to impress your friends. The factory is open daily 8am to 8pm. Admission is free.

Convention Center and continued with the Yerba Buena Center for the Arts, Yerba Buena Gardens, and the San Francisco Museum of Modern Art in the early '90s. During the dot.com years, the Four Seasons Hotel, W Hotel, St. Regis Hotel, and scads of chic live-work lofts appeared on the scene. The last few years, SoMa has been ground zero for a new wave of mega high-rises, including Millennium Tower and One Rincon Hill. Much of the city's nightlife takes place in former warehouse spaces throughout the district.

North Beach

In the late 1800s, an enormous influx of Italian immigrants to North Beach firmly established this aromatic area as San Francisco's "Little Italy." Dozens of Italian restaurants and coffeehouses continue to flourish in what is still the center of the city's Italian community. Walk down Columbus Avenue on any given morning and you're bound to be bombarded by the wonderful aromas of roasting coffee and savory pasta sauces. Although there are some interesting shops and bookstores in the area, it's the dozens of eclectic little cafes, delis, bakeries, and coffee shops that give North Beach its Italian-bohemian character.

For more perspective on this neighborhood, follow the detailed walking tour in chapter 7 (beginning on p. 233) or sign up for a guided Javawalk with coffee nut Elaine Sosa.

Chinatown

The first Chinese immigrants came to San Francisco in the early 1800s to work as laborers. By 1851, 25,000 Chinese people were working in California, and most had settled in San Francisco's Chinatown. Fleeing famine and the Opium Wars, they had come seeking the good fortune promised by the "Gold Mountain" of California and hoped to return with wealth to their families in China. For the majority, the reality of life in California did not live up to the promise. First employed as workers in the gold mines during the gold rush, they later built the railroads, working as little more than slaves and facing constant prejudice. Yet the community, segregated in the Chinatown ghetto, thrived. Growing prejudice led to the Chinese Exclusion Act of 1882, which halted all Chinese immigration for 10 years and severely limited it thereafter. (The Chinese Exclusion Act was not repealed until 1943.) Chinese people were also denied the opportunity to buy homes outside the Chinatown ghetto until the 1950s.

Today, San Francisco has one of the largest communities of Chinese people in the United States. More than 80,000 people live in Chinatown, but the majority of Chinese people have moved out into newer areas like the Richmond and Sunset districts. Although frequented by tourists, the area continues to cater to Chinese shoppers, who crowd the vegetable and herb markets, restaurants, and shops. Tradition runs deep here, and if you're lucky, through an open window you might hear women mixing mah-jongg tiles as they play the centuries-old game. (**Be warned:** You're likely to hear and see lots of spitting around here, too—it's part of local tradition.)

The gateway at Grant Avenue and Bush Street marks the entry to Chinatown. The heart of the neighborhood is Portsmouth Square, where you'll find locals playing board games or just sitting quietly.

On the newly beautified and renovated Waverly Place, a street where the Chinese celebratory colors of red, yellow, and green are much in evidence, you'll find three Chinese temples: Jeng Sen (Buddhist and Taoist) at no. 146, Tien Hou (Buddhist) at no. 125, and Norras (Buddhist) at no. 109. If you enter, do so quietly so that you do not disturb those in prayer.

A block west of Grant Avenue, Stockton Street, from 1000 to 1200, is the community's main shopping street, lined with grocers, fishmongers, tea sellers, herbalists, noodle parlors, and restaurants. Here, too, is the Buddhist Kong Chow Temple, at no. 855, above the Chinatown post office. Explore at your

---

🎁 This City's for the Birds!

If you're walking around San Francisco—especially Telegraph Hill or Russian Hill—and you suddenly hear lots of loud squawking and screeching overhead, look up. You're most likely witnessing a fly-by of the city's famous green flock of wild parrots. These are the scions of a colony that started out as a few wayward house pets—mostly cherry-headed conures, which are indigenous to South America—who found each other, and bred. Years later they've become hundreds strong, traveling in chatty packs through the city (with a few parakeets along for the ride), and stopping to rest on tree branches and delight residents who have come to

consider them part of the family. To learn just how special these birds are to the city, check out the book **The Wild Parrots of Telegraph Hill**, or see the heartwarming movie of the same name.

leisure. A Chinatown walking tour is outlined in chapter 7, beginning on p. 225. Visit www.sanfranciscochinatown.com for more info.

Japantown

More than 12,000 citizens of Japanese descent (1.5% of the city's population) live in San Francisco, or Soko, as the Japanese who first emigrated here often called it. Initially, they settled in Chinatown and SoMa, along Stevenson and Jessie streets from Fourth to Seventh streets. After the earthquake in 1906, SoMa became a light industrial and warehouse area, and the largest Japanese concentration took root in the Western Addition between Van Ness Avenue and Fillmore Street, the site of today's Japantown, now over 100 years old. By 1940, it covered 30 blocks.

In 1913, the Alien Land Law was passed, depriving Japanese Americans of the right to buy land. From 1924 to 1952, the United States banned Japanese immigration. During World War II, the U.S. government froze Japanese bank accounts, interned community leaders, and removed 112,000 Japanese Americans—two-thirds of them citizens—to camps in California, Utah, and Idaho. Japantown was emptied of Japanese people, and war workers took their place. Upon their release in 1945, the Japanese found their old neighborhood occupied. Most of them resettled in the Richmond and Sunset districts; some returned to Japantown, but it had shrunk to a mere 6 or so blocks. Today, the community's notable sights include the Buddhist Church of San Francisco, 1881 Pine St. (at Octavia St.), www.bcsfweb.org; the Konko Church of San Francisco, 1909 Bush St. (at Laguna St.); the Sokoji–Soto Zen Buddhist Temple, 1691 Laguna St. (at Sutter St.); Nihonmachi Mall, 1700 block of Buchanan Street between Sutter and Post streets, which contains two steel fountains by Ruth Asawa;

and the Japan Center, a Japanese-oriented shopping mall occupying 3 square blocks bounded by Post, Geary, Laguna, and Fillmore streets. At its center stands the five-tiered Peace Pagoda, designed by world-famous Japanese architect Yoshiro Taniguchi "to convey the friendship and goodwill of the Japanese to the people of the United States." Surrounding the pagoda, through a network of arcades, squares, and bridges, you can explore dozens of shops featuring everything from TVs and tansu chests to pearls, bonsai, and kimonos. Kabuki Springs & Spa (see the "Urban Renewal" box below) is the center's most famous tenant. But locals also head here for its numerous authentic restaurants, teahouses, shops, and the Sundance multiplex movie theater.

There is often live entertainment on summer weekends and during spring's cherry blossom festival, including Japanese music and dance

The Sokoji–Soto Zen Buddhist Temple.

○ **Kabuki Springs & Spa,** 1750 Geary Blvd. (🕾 **415/922-6000;** www.kabuki springs.com), the Japan Center's most famous tenant, was once an authentic, traditional Japanese bathhouse. The Joie de Vivre hotel group bought and renovated it, however, and it's now more of a Pan-Asian spa with a focus on wellness. The deep ceramic communal tubs—at a very affordable $22 to $25 per person—private baths, and shiatsu massages remain. The spa is open from 10am to 9:45pm daily; joining the baths is an array of massages and ayurvedic treatments, body scrubs, wraps, and facials, which cost from $60 to $150.

○ **Spa Radiance,** 3011 Fillmore St. (🕾 **415/346-6281;** www.sparadiance. com), is an utterly San Francisco spa experience due to its unassuming Victorian surroundings and its wonderfully luxurious treatments such as facials, body treatments, massages, manicures, pedicures, Brazilian waxing, spray-tanning, and makeup application by in-house artists.

○ A more posh and modern experience is yours at **International Orange,** 2044 Fillmore St., second floor (🕾 **888/894-8811;** www.internationalorange.com). The self-described spa yoga lounge offers just what it says in a chic white-on-white space on the boutique-shopping stretch of Fillmore Street. They've also got a great selection of clothing and face and body products, including one of my personal favorites, locally made In Fiore body balms.

○ In the **St. Regis Hotel,** Remède Spa, 125 Third St. (🕾 **415/284-4060;** www. remede.com), has two whole floors dedicated to melting away all your cares, worries, kinks, and knots—not to mention primping. Expect wonderful massage, facials, manis and pedis, waxes, and more. A few doors down in the W Hotel is the city's outpost of New York's Bliss Spa, 181 Third St., fourth floor (🕾 **415/281-0990;** www. blissworld.com). The hip version to St. Regis's chic, it offers a similar spa menu, including wedding specialties.

○ Opened in 2003, **Tru,** 750 Kearny St. (🕾 **415/399-9700;** www.truspa.com), is a sleek, modern-day spa with options that go way beyond your average hot stone massage. Signature treatments include oxygen facials and the world's only tropical rainforest water treatment room—a full immersion experience involving steam, tropical rainstorms, and a 100-gallon-a-minute waterfall. It's located inside the Hilton Hotel, between Union Square and the Financial District.

Kabuki Springs.

performances, tea ceremonies, flower-arranging demonstrations, martial-arts presentations, and other cultural events. **The Japan Center** (🕾 415/922-7765) is open daily from 10am to midnight, although most shops close much earlier. To get there, take bus no. 2 or 3 (exit at Buchanan and Sutter sts.) or no. 22 or 38 (exit at the northeast corner of Geary Blvd. and Fillmore St.).

Haight-Ashbury

Few of San Francisco's neighborhoods are as varied—or as famous—as Haight-Ashbury. Walk along Haight Street, and you'll encounter everything from drug-dazed drifters begging for change to an armada of the city's funky-trendy shops, clubs, and cafes. Turn anywhere off Haight, and instantly you're among the clean-cut, young urban professionals who can afford the steep rents in this hip 'hood. The result is an interesting mix of well-to-do and well-screw-you aging flower children, former Dead-heads, homeless people, and throngs of tourists who try not to stare as they wander through this most human of zoos. Some find it depressing, others find it fascinating, but everyone agrees that it ain't what it was in the free-lovin' psychedelic Summer of Love. Is it still worth a visit? Not if you are here for a day or two, but it's certainly worth an excursion on longer trips, if only to enjoy a cone of Cherry Garcia at the now-famous Ben & Jerry's Ice Cream Store on the corner of Haight and Ashbury streets, and then to wander and gawk at the area's intentional freaks.

The Castro

Castro Street, between Market and 18th streets, is the center of the city's gay community as well as a lovely neighborhood teeming with shops, restaurants, bars, and other institutions that cater to the area's colorful residents. Among the landmarks are Harvey Milk Plaza and the Castro Theatre (www.castrotheatre. com), a 1930s movie palace with a Wurlitzer organ. The gay community began to move here in the late 1960s and early 1970s from a neighborhood called Polk Gulch, which still has a number of gay-oriented bars and stores. Castro is one of the liveliest streets in the city and the perfect place to shop for gifts and revel in free-spiritedness. Check www.castroonline.com for more info.

The Mission District

Once inhabited almost entirely by Irish immigrants, the Mission District is now the center of the city's Latino community as well as a mecca for young, hip

A Precita Eyes tour of Balmy Alley.

residents. It's an oblong area stretching roughly from 14th to 30th streets between Potrero Avenue on the east and Dolores Avenue on the west. In the outer areas, many of the city's finest Victorians still stand, although they seem strangely out of place in the mostly lower-income neighborhoods. The heart of the community lies along 24th Street between Van Ness and Potrero avenues, where dozens of excellent ethnic restaurants, bakeries, bars, and specialty stores attract people from all over the city. The area surrounding 16th Street and Valencia Street is a hotbed for impressive—and often impressively

A detail from *Enrique's Journey* by Josue Rojas in Balmy Alley.

cheap—vintage stores, artisanal coffee shops, restaurants, and bars catering to the city's hipsters. The Mission District at night doesn't feel like the safest place (although in terms of creepiness, the Tenderloin, a few blocks off Union Square, beats the Mission by far), and walking around the area should be done with caution, but it's usually quite safe during the day and is highly recommended.

For an even better insight into the community, go to the **Precita Eyes Mural Arts Center** ★★, 2981 24th St., between Harrison and Alabama streets (© **415/285-2287;** www.precitaeyes.org), and take one of the 1½- to 2-hour tours conducted on Saturdays and Sundays at 11am and 1:30pm, where you'll see 60 murals in an 8-block walk. Group tours are available during the week by appointment. The 11am tour costs $12 for adults, $8 for students with ID, $5 for seniors, and $2 for children 17 and under; the 1:30pm tour, which is half an hour longer and includes a slide show, costs $15 for adults, $8 for students with ID, and $5 for seniors and children 17 and under. All but the Saturday morning tour (which leaves from 3325 24th St. at the Café Venice) leave from the center's 24th Street location.

Other signs of cultural life in the neighborhood are progressive theaters such as **Theatre Rhinoceros** (www.therhino.org) and **Theater Artaud** (www.artaud.org). At 16th Street and Dolores Avenue is the Mission San Francisco de Asís, better known as **Mission Dolores** (p. 208). It's the city's oldest surviving building and the district's namesake.

THE PRESIDIO & GOLDEN GATE NATIONAL RECREATION AREA

The Presidio

In October 1994, the Presidio passed from the U.S. Army to the National Park Service and became one of a handful of urban national parks that combines historical, architectural, and natural elements in one giant arboreal expanse. (It also contains a previously private golf course and a home for George Lucas's production company.) The 1,491-acre area incorporates a variety of terrain—coastal scrub, dunes, and prairie grasslands—that shelter many rare plants and more than 200 species of birds, some of which nest here.

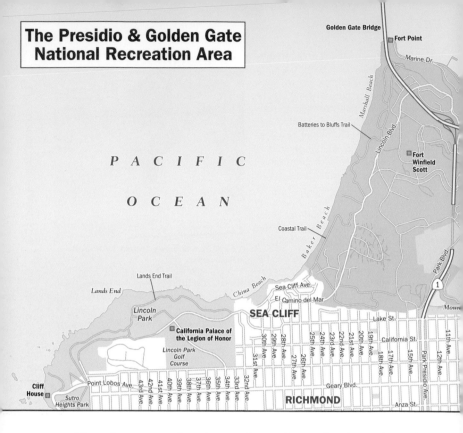

The Presidio & Golden Gate National Recreation Area

PACIFIC

OCEAN

Golden Gate Bridge

Fort Point

Marine Dr.

Marshall Beach

Batteries to Bluffs Trail

Lincoln Blvd.

Fort Winfield Scott

Coastal Trail

Baker Beach

Lands End Trail

Lands End

China Beach

Sea Cliff Ave.

El Camino del Mar

SEA CLIFF

Lincoln Park

California Palace of the Legion of Honor

Lincoln Park Golf Course

Point Lobos Ave.

Cliff House

Sutro Heights Park

Lake St.

California St.

Park Presidio Ave.

Geary Blvd.

RICHMOND

Anza St.

This military outpost has a 220-year history, from its founding in September 1776 by the Spanish under José Joaquin Moraga to its closure in 1994. From 1822 to 1846, the property was in Mexican hands.

During the war with Mexico, U.S. forces occupied the fort, and in 1848, when California became part of the Union, it was formally transferred to the United States. When San Francisco suddenly became an important urban area during the gold rush, the U.S. government installed battalions of soldiers and built Fort Point to protect the entry to the harbor. It expanded the post during the Civil War and during the Indian Wars of the 1870s and 1880s. By the 1890s, the Presidio was no longer a frontier post but a major base for U.S. expansion into the Pacific. During the war with Spain in 1898, thousands of troops camped here in tent cities awaiting shipment to the Philippines, and the Army General Hospital treated the sick and wounded. By 1905, 12 coastal defense batteries were built along the headlands. In 1914, troops under the command of Gen. John Pershing left here to pursue Pancho Villa and his men. The Presidio expanded during the 1920s, when Crissy Army Airfield (the first airfield on the West Coast) was established, but the major action was seen during World War II, after the attack on Pearl Harbor. Soldiers dug foxholes along nearby beaches, and the Presidio became the headquarters for the Western Defense Command. Some 1.75 million men were shipped out from nearby Fort Mason to fight in the Pacific; many returned to the Presidio's hospital, whose capacity peaked one year at 72,000

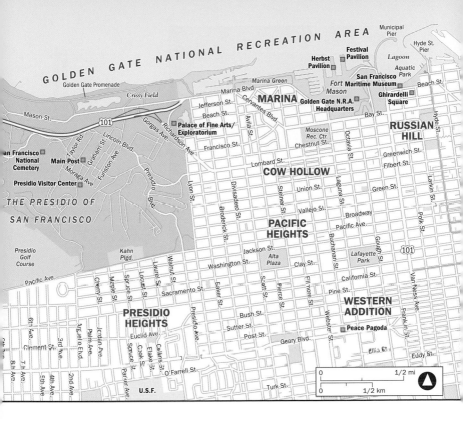

patients. In the 1950s, the Presidio served as the headquarters for the Sixth U.S. Army and a missile defense post, but its role slowly shrank. In 1972, it was included in new legislation establishing the Golden Gate National Recreation Area; in 1989, the Pentagon decided to close the post and transfer it to the National Park Service.

Today, the area encompasses more than 470 historic buildings, a scenic golf course, a national cemetery, the Walt Disney Family Museum (see listing earlier), several good restaurants, 22 hiking trails (to be doubled over the next decade), and a variety of terrain and natural habitats. The National Park Service offers walking and biking tours around the Presidio (reservations are suggested) as well as a free shuttle called "PresidioGo." For more information, call the **Presidio Visitors Center** at 𝄐 **415/561-4323.** Take bus no. 28, 45, 76, or 82X to get there.

Golden Gate National Recreation Area

The largest urban park in the world, GGNRA makes New York's Central Park look like a putting green, covering three counties along 28 miles of stunning, condo-free shoreline. Run by the National Park Service, the Recreation Area wraps around the northern and western edges of the city, and just about all of it is open to the public with no access fees. The Muni bus system provides transportation to the more popular sites, including **Aquatic Park, Cliff House, Fort Mason,** and **Ocean Beach.** For more information, contact the **National Park**

TOP: **The Walt Disney Family Museum.**
RIGHT: **You'll find joggers, picnickers, and kite-fliers along the Golden Gate Promenade.**

Service (© 415/561-4700; www.nps.gov/goga). For more detailed information on particular sites, see the "Getting Outside" section, later in this chapter.

Here is a brief rundown of the salient features of the park's peninsula section, starting at the northern section and moving westward around the coastline:

Aquatic Park, adjacent to the Hyde Street Pier, has a small swimming beach, although it's not that appealing (and darned cold). Far more entertaining is a visit to the **San Francisco Maritime National Historical Park's Visitor Center** a few blocks away (p. 187 for more information).

Fort Mason Center, from Bay Street to the shoreline, consists of several buildings and piers used during World War II. Today they hold a variety of museums, theaters, shops, and organizations, and **Greens** vegetarian restaurant (p. 142), which affords views of the Golden Gate Bridge. For information about Fort Mason events, call © 415/345-7500 or visit www.fortmason.org. The park headquarters is also at Fort Mason.

Farther west along the bay at the northern end of Laguna Street is **Marina Green,** a favorite local spot for kite-flying, jogging, and walking along the Promenade. The **St. Francis Yacht Club** is also here.

Next comes the 3.5-mile paved **Golden Gate Promenade ★**, San Francisco's best and most scenic biking, jogging, and walking path. It runs along the shore past **Crissy Field** (www.crissyfield.org) and ends at Fort Point under the Golden Gate Bridge. (Be sure to stop and watch the gonzo windsurfers and kite surfers, who catch major wind here, and admire the newly restored marshlands.) **The Crissy Field Café and Bookstore** is open from 9am to 5pm Wednesday through Sunday and offers yummy, organic soups, salads, sandwiches, coffee drinks, and a decent selection of outdoor-themed books and cards.

Fort Point ★ (© 415/556-1693; www.nps.gov/fopo) was built between 1853 and 1861 to protect the narrow entrance to the harbor. It was designed to house 500 soldiers manning 126 muzzle-loading cannons. By 1900, the fort's soldiers and obsolete guns had been removed, but the formidable brick edifice remains. Fort Point is open Friday through Sunday only from 10am to 5pm, and guided tours and cannon demonstrations are given at the site once or twice a day on open days, depending on the time of year.

Lincoln Boulevard sweeps around the western edge of the bay to **Baker Beach,** where the waves roll ashore—a fine spot for (often nude) sunbathing, walking, or fishing. Hikers can follow the **Coastal Trail** (www.coastwalk.org) from Fort Point along this part of the coastline all the way to Lands End.

A short distance from Baker Beach, China Beach is a small cove where swimming is permitted. Changing rooms, showers, a sun deck, and restrooms are available.

A little farther around the coast is **Land's End ★**, looking out to Pyramid Rock. A lower and an upper trail offer hiking amid wind-swept cypresses and pines on the cliffs above the Pacific.

Still farther along the coast lie **Point Lobos,** the ruins of **Sutro Baths** (www.sutrobaths.com), and the **Cliff House ★**. The Cliff House (www.cliff house.com), which recently underwent major renovations, has been serving refreshments to visitors since 1863. It's famed for its views of Seal Rocks (a colony of sea lions and many marine birds) and the Pacific Ocean. Immediately northeast of Cliff House you'll find traces of the once-grand Sutro Baths, a swimming facility that was a major summer attraction accommodating up to 24,000 people until it burned down in 1966.

A little farther inland at the western end of California Street is **Lincoln Park,** which contains a golf course and the spectacular **Legion of Honor Museum** (p. 186)

At the southern end of Ocean Beach, 4 miles down the coast, is **Fort Funston** (© 415/561-4323), where there's an easy loop trail across the cliffs. Here you can watch hang gliders take advantage of the high cliffs and strong winds. It's also one of the city's most popular dog parks.

Farther south along Route 280, Sweeney Ridge affords sweeping views of the coastline from the many trails that crisscross its 1,000 acres. From here the

The Lawn Bowling Club gathers at the courts at 150 Bowling Green Dr., in Golden Gate Park.

expedition led by Don Gaspar de Portolá first saw San Francisco Bay in 1769. It's in Pacifica; take Sneath Lane off Route 35 (Skyline Blvd.) in San Bruno.

The GGNRA extends into Marin County, where it encompasses the **Marin Headlands, Muir Woods National Monument,** and **Olema Valley** behind the **Point Reyes National Seashore.** See chapter 10 for information on Muir Woods.

GOLDEN GATE PARK ★★★

Everybody loves Golden Gate Park—people, dogs, birds, frogs, turtles, bison, trees, bushes, and flowers. Literally, everything feels unified here in San Francisco's enormous arboreal front yard. Conceived in the 1860s and 1870s, this great 1,017-acre landmark, which stretches inland from the Pacific coast, took shape in the 1880s and 1890s thanks to the skill and effort of John McLaren, a Scot who arrived in 1887 and began landscaping the park.

When he embarked on the project, sand dunes and wind presented enormous challenges. But McLaren had developed a new strain of grass called "sea bent," which he planted to hold the sandy soil along the Firth of Forth back home, and he used it to anchor the soil here, too. Every year the ocean eroded the western fringe of the park, and ultimately he solved this problem, too, though it took him 40 years to build a natural wall, putting out bundles of sticks that the tides covered with sand. He also built the two windmills that stand on the western edge of the park to pump water for irrigation. Under his brilliant eye, the park took shape.

Today the park consists of hundreds of gardens and attractions connected by wooded paths and paved roads. While many worthy sites are clearly visible, there are infinite treasures that are harder to find, so pick up information at **McLaren Lodge and Park Headquarters** (at Stanyan and Fell sts.; ℂ 415/831-2700) if you want to find the more hidden spots. It's open daily and offers park maps for $3. Of the dozens of special gardens in the park, most recognized are **McLaren Memorial Rhododendron Dell,** the **Rose Garden, Botanical Gardens,** and, at the western edge of the park, a springtime array of thousands of tulips and daffodils around the **Dutch windmill.**

In addition to the highlights described in this section, the park contains lots of recreational facilities: tennis courts; baseball, soccer, and polo fields; a golf course; riding stables; and fly-casting pools. **The Strawberry Hill boathouse** handles boat rentals. The park is also the home of the **de Young Museum,** 50 Hagiwara Tea Garden Dr. (ℂ **415/750-3600** or 863-3330). For more information, see p. 184.

For further information, call the **San Francisco Visitor Information Center** at ℂ **415/283-0177.** Enter the park at Kezar Drive, an extension of Fell Street; bus riders can take no. 5, 6, 66, or 71.

Park Highlights

Conservatory of Flowers ★★   Opened to the public in 1879, this glorious Victorian glass structure is the oldest existing public conservatory in the Western Hemisphere. After a bad storm in 1995, delayed renovations kept the museum closed and visitors were only able to imagine what wondrous displays existed within the striking glass assemblage. Thankfully, a $25-million renovation, including a $4-million exhibit upgrade, was completed a few years ago, and now the Conservatory is a cutting-edge horticultural destination with over 1,700 species of plants. Here you can check out the rare tropical flora of the Congo,

The Conservatory of Flowers in Golden Gate Park.

Philippines, and beyond within the stunning structure. As one of only four public institutions in the U.S. to house a highland tropics exhibit, its five galleries also include the lowland tropics, aquatic plants, the largest Dracula orchid collection in the world, and special exhibits. It doesn't take long to visit, but make a point of staying awhile; outside there are good sunny spots for people-watching as well as paths leading to impressive gardens begging to be explored. If you're around during summer and fall, don't miss the Dahlia Garden to the right of the entrance in the center of what was once a carriage roundabout—it's an explosion of colorful Dr. Seuss–like blooms. The conservatory is open Tuesday through Sunday from 9am to 5pm, closed Mondays. Admission is $7 for adults; $5 for youth 12 to 17 years of age, seniors, and students with ID; $2 for children 5 to 11; and free for children 4 and under and for all visitors the first Tuesday of the month. For more information, visit www.conservatory offlowers.org or call ⓒ **415/831-2090.**

Japanese Tea Garden ☺ John McLaren, the man who began landscaping Golden Gate Park, hired Makoto Hagiwara, a wealthy Japanese landscape designer, to further develop this garden originally created for the 1894 Midwinter Exposition. It's a quiet place with cherry trees, shrubs, and bonsai crisscrossed by winding paths and high-arched bridges over pools of water. Focal points and places for contemplation include the massive bronze Buddha (cast in Japan in 1790 and donated by the Gump family), the Buddhist wooden pagoda, and the Drum Bridge, which, reflected in the water,

Japanese Tea Garden in Golden Gate Park.

205

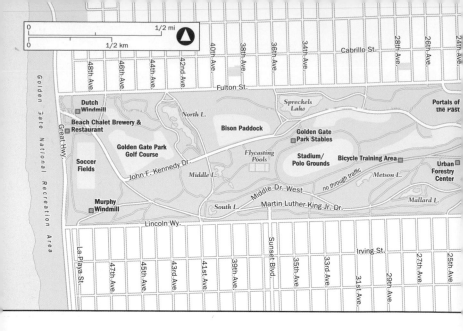

looks as though it completes a circle. The garden is open daily November through February from 8:30am to 5pm (teahouse 10am–4:30pm), March through October from 8:30am to 6pm (teahouse 10am–5:30pm). For information on admission, call ✆ **415/752-4227.** For the teahouse, call ✆ **415/752-1171.**

San Francisco Botanical Gardens at Strybing Arboretum More than 7,000 plant species grow here, among them some ancient plants in a special "primitive garden," rare species, and a grove of California redwoods. Docent tours begin at 1:30pm daily, with an additional 10:20am tour on weekends. Strybing is open Monday through Friday from 8am to 4:30pm, and Saturday, Sunday, and holidays from 10am to 5pm. Admission is free. For more information, call ✆ **415/661-1316** or visit www.strybing.org.

Strawberry Hill/Stow Lake Rent a paddle boat or rowboat and cruise around the circular Stow Lake as painters create still lifes, joggers pass along the grassy shoreline, ducks waddle around waiting to be fed, and turtles sunbathe on rocks and logs. Strawberry Hill, the 430-foot-high artificial island and highest point in the park that lies at the center of Stow Lake, is a perfect picnic spot; it boasts a bird's-eye view of San Francisco and the bay. It also has a waterfall and peace pagoda. For the boathouse, call ✆ **415/386-2531.** Boat rentals are available Wednesday through Sunday from 10am to 4pm, weather permitting; four-passenger rowboats go for $19 per hour, and four-person paddle boats run $24 per hour; fees are cash-only.

RELIGIOUS BUILDINGS WORTH CHECKING OUT

Glide Memorial United Methodist Church ★★ 📷 The best way to spend a Sunday morning in San Francisco is to visit this Tenderloin-area church to witness the exhilarating and lively sermons accompanied by an amazing gospel

Golden Gate Park

choir. Reverend Cecil Williams's enthusiastic and uplifting preaching and singing with the homeless and poor of the neighborhood has attracted nationwide fame over the past 40-plus years. In 1994, during the pastor's 30th-anniversary celebration, singers Angela Bofill and Bobby McFerrin joined comedian Robin Williams, author Maya Angelou, and talk-show queen Oprah Winfrey to honor him publicly. Even former president Clinton has joined the crowd. Cecil Williams now shares pastor duties with Douglas Fitch and alternates presiding over the roof-raising Sunday services in front of a diverse audience that crosses all socioeconomic boundaries. Go for an uplifting experience and some hand-clapping, shoulder-swaying gospel choir music—it's an experience you'll never forget. ***Tip:*** Arrive about 20 minutes early to make sure you get a seat; otherwise it's standing room only.

330 Ellis St. (west of Union Square). ✆ **415/674-6000.** www.glide.org. Services Sun at 9 and 11am. Bus: 27. Streetcar: Powell. BART: Powell.

Grace Cathedral Although this Nob Hill cathedral, designed by architect Lewis P. Hobart, appears to be made of stone, it is in fact constructed of reinforced concrete beaten to achieve a stonelike effect. Construction began on the site of the Crocker mansion in 1928 but was not completed until 1964. Among the more interesting features of the building are its stained-glass windows, particularly those by the French Loire studios and Charles Connick, depicting such modern figures as Thurgood Marshall, Robert Frost, and Albert Einstein; the replicas of Ghiberti's bronze Doors of Paradise at the east end; the series of religious murals completed in the 1940s by Polish artist John De Rosen; and the 44-bell carillon. Along with its magical ambience, Grace lifts spirits with services, musical performances (including organ recitals and evensong, or evening prayer, on many Sun), and its weekly Forum (Sun 9:30–10:30am except during summer and major holidays), where guests lead discussions about spirituality in modern times and have community dialogues on social issues.

1100 California St. (btw. Taylor and Jones sts.). ✆ **415/749-6300.** www.gracecathedral.org.

Mission Dolores   San Francisco's oldest standing structure, the Mission San Francisco de Asís (also known as Mission Dolores), has withstood the test of time, as well as two major earthquakes, relatively intact. In 1776, at the behest of Franciscan missionary Junípero Serra, Father Francisco Palou came to the Bay Area to found the sixth in a series of 21 missions along El Camino Real (the King's Hwy.). From these humble beginnings grew what was to become the city of San Francisco. The mission's small, simple chapel, built solidly by Native Americans who were converted to Christianity, is a curious mixture of native construction methods and Spanish-colonial style. A statue of Father Serra stands in

The Mission Dolores.

the mission garden, although the portrait looks somewhat more contemplative, and less energetic, than he must have been in real life. The cemetery garden out back houses the remains of many notable First Californians, including some 5,000 Native Americans who succumbed to Western diseases. A 45-minute self-guided tour costs $5; otherwise, admission is $3 for adults and $2 for children.

16th St. (at Dolores St.). ✆ **415/621-8203.** www.missiondolores.org. Admission $5 adults, $2 children. Summer daily 9am–5pm; winter daily 9am–4pm; spring daily 9am–4:30pm; Good Friday 9am–noon. Closed Thanksgiving, Easter, and Dec 25. Bus: 14 or 33 to Church and 16th sts. Streetcar: J.

ARCHITECTURAL HIGHLIGHTS
Must-Sees for Architecture Buffs

ALAMO SQUARE HISTORIC DISTRICT   San Francisco's collection of Victorian houses, known as **Painted Ladies,** is one of the city's most famous assets.

The Painted Ladies of Alamo Square.

City Hall.

Most of the 14,000 extant structures date from the second half of the 19th century and are private residences. Spread throughout the city, many have been beautifully restored and ornately painted. The small area bordered by Divisadero Street on the west, Golden Gate Avenue on the north, Webster Street on the east, and Fell Street on the south—about 10 blocks west of the Civic Center—has one of the city's greatest concentrations of Painted Ladies. One of the most famous views of San Francisco—seen on post-cards and posters all around the city (and p. 1 of this guide)—depicts sharp-edged Financial District skyscrapers behind a row of Victorians. This fantastic juxtaposition can be seen from Alamo Square, in the center of the historic district, at Fulton and Steiner streets.

CITY HALL & CIVIC CENTER   Built between 1913 and 1915, City Hall, located in the Civic Center District, is part of this "City Beautiful" complex done in the Beaux Arts style. The dome rises to a height of 306 feet on the exterior and is ornamented with oculi and topped by a lantern. The interior rotunda soars 112 feet and is finished in oak, marble, and limestone, with a monumental marble staircase leading to the second floor. With a major renovation completed in the late 1990s, the building was returned to its former splendor. No doubt you saw it on TV during early 2004, when much of the hoopla surrounding the gay marriage proceedings was depicted on the front steps. (Remember Rosie O'Donnell emerging from this very building after getting married to her girlfriend?) Public tours are given Monday through Friday at 10am, noon, and 2pm. Call ✆ **415/554-4933** for details.

Other Architectural Highlights

San Francisco is a center of many architecturally striking sights. This section concentrates on a few highlights.

The Union Square and Financial District areas have a number of buildings worth checking out. One is the former **Circle Gallery,** 140 Maiden Lane. Now a gallery housing Folk Art International, Xanadu Tribal Arts, and Boretti Amber & Design, it's the only building in the city designed by Frank Lloyd Wright (in 1948). The gallery was the prototype for the Guggenheim's seashell-shaped circular gallery space, even though it was meant to serve as a retail space for V. C. Morris, a purveyor of glass and crystal. Note the arresting exterior, a solid wall with a circular entryway to the left. Maiden Lane is just off Union Square between Geary and Post streets.

The Hallidie Building, 130–150 Sutter St., designed by Willis Polk in 1917, is an ideal example of a glass-curtain building. The vast glass facade is miraculously suspended between the two cast-iron cornices. The fire escapes that course down each side of the building complete the proscenium-like theatrical effect.

Two prominent pieces of San Francisco's skyline are in the Financial District. **The Transamerica Pyramid,** 600 Montgomery St., between Clay and Washington streets, is one of the tallest structures in San Francisco. This corporate headquarters was completed in 1972, stands 48 stories tall, and is capped by a 212-foot spire. The former

The Hallidie Building's iconic fire escape.

Bank of America World Headquarters, 555 California St., was designed by Wurster, Bernardi, and Emmons with Skidmore, Owings, and Merrill. This carnelian-marble-covered building dates from 1969 and is 52 stories tall. The focal point of the building's formal plaza is an abstract black granite sculpture, known locally as the "Banker's Heart," designed by Japanese architect Masayuki Nagare.

The Medical Dental Building, 450 Sutter St., is a steel-frame structure beautifully clad in terra cotta. It was designed by Miller and Pflueger in 1929. The entrance and the window frames are elaborately ornamented with Mayan relief work; the lobby ceiling is similarly decorated with gilding. Note the ornate elevators.

At the foot of Market Street you will find the **Ferry Building.** Built between 1895 and 1903, it served as the city's major transportation hub before the Golden Gate and Bay bridges were built; some 170 ferries docked here daily unloading Bay Area commuters until the 1930s. The tower that soars above the building was inspired by the Campanile of Venice and the Cathedral Tower in Seville. In 2003, a 4-year renovation was completed and the building is now a spectacular mixed-use landmark building featuring a 660-foot-long, skylit nave, which had been partially filled in and destroyed in the 1950s. If you stop by the Ferry Building, you might also want to go to **Rincon Center,** 99 Mission St., to see the WPA (Works Progress Administration) murals painted by the Russian artist Refregier in the post office.

Several important buildings are on or near Nob Hill. **The Flood Mansion,** 2222 Broadway St., at Webster Street, was built between 1885 and 1886 for James Clair Flood. Thanks to the Comstock Lode, Flood rose from being a bartender to one of the city's wealthiest men. He established the Nevada bank that later merged with Wells Fargo. The house cost $1.5 million to build at the time; the fence alone cost $30,000. It was designed by Augustus Laver and modified by Willis Polk after the 1906 earthquake to accommodate the Pacific Union Club. Unfortunately, you can't go inside: The building is now a private school.

Built by George Applegarth in 1913 for sugar magnate Adolph Spreckels, the **Spreckels Mansion,** 2080 Washington St., is currently home to romance novelist Danielle Steel (don't even try to get in to see her!). The extraordinary building has rounded-arch French doors on the first and second floors and curved balconies on the second floor. Inside, the original house featured an indoor pool in the basement, Adamesque fireplaces, and a circular Pompeian room with a fountain.

Finally, one of San Francisco's most ingenious architectural accomplishments is the **San Francisco–Oakland Bay Bridge.** Although it's visually less appealing than the nearby Golden Gate Bridge (except at night when it's lit up), the Bay Bridge is in many ways more spectacular. The silvery giant that links San Francisco with Oakland is one of the world's longest steel bridges (8¼ miles). It opened in 1936, 6 months before the Golden Gate. Each of its two decks contains five automobile lanes. The Bay Bridge is not a single bridge at all, but a superbly dovetailed series of spans joined midbay, at Yerba Buena Island, by one of the world's largest (in diameter) tunnels. To the west of Yerba Buena, the bridge is actually two separate suspension bridges, joined at a central anchorage. East of the island is a 1,400-foot cantilever span, followed by a succession of truss bridges. This east span of the bridge is finally being replaced after being damaged in the 1989 Loma Prieta earthquake and a years-long fight between city residents, planners, and designers. And it looks even more complex than it

ESPECIALLY FOR kids

The following San Francisco attractions appeal to kids of all ages:

- Alcatraz Island (p. 168)
- Cable Car Museum (p. 181)
- Cable Cars (p. 172)
- California Academy of Sciences (p. 182)
- The Exploratorium (p. 185)
- Golden Gate Bridge (p. 178)
- Golden Gate Park, including the Children's Playground, Bison Paddock, and Japanese Tea Garden (p. 204)
- Maritime Museum (San Francisco Maritime National Historical Park) and the historic ships anchored at Hyde Pier (p. 187)
- Metreon Entertainment Center (p. 186)
- San Francisco Zoo (p. 189)

In addition to the sights listed above, a number of playgrounds are of particular interest to kids. One of the most enormous tricked-out playgrounds for kids is in **Golden Gate Park,** where you'll find a fantastic kids' playland just west of the Stanyan Street entrance. Other playful park areas include Stow Lake's boats and the bison paddock. Apartment buildings surround the **Cow Hollow Playground,** Baker Street between Greenwich and Filbert streets, on three of four sides. The landscaped playground features a bi-level play area fitted with well-conceived, colorful play structures, including a tunnel, slides, swings, and a miniature cable car. **Huntington Park,** Taylor Street between Sacramento and California streets, sits atop Nob Hill. This tiny play area contains several small structures particularly well suited to children 4 and under. **Julius Kahn Playground,** West Pacific Avenue at Spruce Street, is a popular playground inside San Francisco's great Presidio Park. Larger play structures, a trickling canal, and forested surroundings make this area attractive to children and adults alike. Go to www.parks.sfgov.org.

sounds. You can drive across the bridge (the toll is $4, paid westbound), or you can catch a bus at the Transbay Terminal (Mission St. at First St.) and ride to downtown Oakland.

SELF-GUIDED & ORGANIZED TOURS

The 49-Mile Scenic Drive ★★

The self-guided, 49-mile drive is an easy way to orient yourself and to grasp the beauty of San Francisco and its extraordinary location. It's also a flat-out stunning and very worthy excursion. Beginning in the city, it follows a rough circle around the bay and passes virtually all the best-known sights, from **Chinatown** to the **Golden Gate Bridge, Ocean Beach, Seal Rocks, Golden Gate Park,** and **Twin Peaks.** Originally designed for the benefit of visitors to San Francisco's 1939 and 1940 Golden Gate International Exposition, the route is marked by blue-and-white sea gull signs. Although it makes an excellent half-day tour, this mini-excursion can easily take longer if you decide, for example, to stop to walk across the Golden Gate Bridge or to have tea in Golden Gate Park's **Japanese Tea Garden.**

The **San Francisco Visitor Information Center,** at Powell and Market streets (p. 404), distributes free route maps, which are handy since a few of the Scenic Drive marker signs are missing. Try to avoid the downtown area during the weekday rush hours from 7 to 9am and 4 to 6pm.

A BART Tour

One of the world's best commuter systems, **Bay Area Rapid Transit (BART)** runs along 104 miles of rail, linking 43 stations between San Francisco, Millbrae, and the East Bay. Under the bay, BART runs through one of the longest underwater transit tubes in the world. This link opened in September 1972, 2 years

BART arrives.

The 49-mile drive's inspiring views may spark some romance.

behind schedule and 6 months after the general manager resigned under fire. The train cars are 70 feet long and were designed to represent the latest word in public transport luxury. Four decades later, they no longer seem futuristic, but they're still attractively modern, with carpeted floors, tinted picture windows, air-conditioning, and recessed lighting. The trains can hit a top speed of 80 mph; a computerized control system monitors and adjusts their speed.

The people who run BART think so highly of their trains and stations that they sell a $5.20 "Excursion Ticket," which allows you, in effect, to "sightsee" the BART system, or basically ride it. "Tour" the entire system as much as you like for up to 3 hours; you must exit at the station where you entered. (If you get out anywhere else along the line, the gate instantly computes the normal fare.) For more information, call ℂ **415/989-BART** (2278) or visit www.bart.gov, where you can also download trip plans directly to your iPod, PDA, or wireless.

Boat Tours

One of the best ways to look at San Francisco is from a boat bobbing on the bay. There are several cruises to choose from, and many of them start from Fisherman's Wharf.

Blue & Gold Fleet, Pier 39, Fisherman's Wharf (ℂ **415/705-8200;** www.blueandgoldfleet.com), tours the bay year-round in a sleek, 350-passenger sightseeing boat, complete with food and beverage facilities. The fully narrated, 1-hour cruise passes beneath the Golden Gate Bridge and comes within yards of Alcatraz Island. Don a jacket, bring the camera, and make sure it's a clear day for the best bay cruise. Frequent daily departures from Pier 39's West Marina begin at 10:45am daily during winter and 10am daily during summer. Tickets cost $29 for adults, $26 for seniors 63 and over and juniors 12 to 18, and $21 for children 5 to 11; children 4 and under are admitted free. There's a $2.25 charge for ordering tickets by phone; discounts are available on their website.

The **Red & White Fleet,** Pier 43½ (ℂ **415/673-2900;** www.redandwhite.com), offers daily Bay Cruises tours that leave from Pier 43½. The tour boats cruise along the city waterfront, beneath the Golden Gate Bridge, past Angel Island, and around Alcatraz and are narrated in eight languages. Prices are $24 for adults, $16 for seniors and children 5 to 17. Discounts are available through online purchase.

Bus Tours

Gray Line (ℂ **888/428-6937** or 415/434-8687; www.sanfranciscosightseeing.com) is San Francisco's largest bus-tour operator. It offers numerous itineraries daily (far too many to list here). Free pickup and return are available between centrally located hotels and departure locations. Advance reservations are required for all tours except motorized cable car and trolley tours. Day and evening tours depart from Pier 43½ at Fisherman's Wharf; motorized cable car tours depart from Pier 39 and Pier 41.

Air Tours

For those of you seeking a little thrill and adventure during your vacation, consider booking a flight with San Francisco Seaplane Tours, the Bay Area's only seaplane tour company. For more than 60 years, this locally owned outfit has provided its customers a bird's-eye view of the city, flying directly over San

Francisco at an altitude of about 1,500 feet. Sights you'll see during the narrated excursions include the Golden Gate and Bay Bridges, Alcatraz, Tiburon, and Sausalito. Half the fun, however, is taking off and landing on the water (which is surprisingly smooth). Trips depart from Sausalito, and they offer complimentary shuttle pickup at Pier 39. Prices range from $149 per person for the 20-minute Golden Gate Tour to $195 for the 30-minute Champagne Sunset Flight, which includes a bottle of bubbly and a cozy backseat for two. Children's rates are also available, and cameras are welcome. (On calm days, the pilot will even roll the window down.) For more information or reservations, log onto www.seaplane. com or call © **415/332-4843.**

Equally thrilling (and perhaps more so if you've never been in a helicopter) is a tour of San Francisco and the bay via San Francisco Helicopters. The $160 Vista package includes free shuttle pickup from your hotel or Pier 39, and a 20-minute tour that takes you under—yes, under—the Golden Gate Bridge, over the city, and past the Bay Bridge and Alcatraz Island. After takeoff, the pilot gives a narrated tour and answers questions while the background music adds a bit of Disney-ride quality to the experience. (***Tip:*** The view from the front seat is the best.) Picnic lunch and sunset dinner packages are available as well. For more information or reservations, log onto www.sfhelicopters.com or call © **800/400-2404** or 650/635-4500.

But the bird's-eye experience that trumps all other air tours in (and of) the Bay Area is a trip with **Airship Ventures,** which rolled out its operation starting in November 2008. Airship Ventures' massive white zeppelin floats low and slow enough for passengers to truly absorb Northern California's natural beauty, like the intricate system of veinlike channels and mud flats that fringe the Bay. In fact, prior to your ride, you'll likely see it from the ground as you comb the city streets; the airship hovers so low it appears to just graze the tops of the skyscrapers. The 246-foot zeppelin is the world's largest airship and stretches 15 feet longer than a 747. It holds 12 passengers and offers tours from its base at Moffett Field, near

A bird's-eye view.

Mountain View, as well as from Oakland. Tour options range from 45-minute experiences to a full 2-hour loop around the Bay. On this grand adventure, expect to see **Coit Tower, Golden Gate Park,** the **Transamerica Pyramid, Alcatraz,** the **Pacific Coastline,** the **Richmond–San Rafael Bridge, Mount Diablo,** the **Marin Headlands,** and, of course, the **Golden Gate Bridge.** South Bay routes showcasing Silicon Valley are also offered. Tickets start at $375 for a 45-minute flight. One-hour tours are $495 per person and 2-hour flights run $950 per person. In addition to individual tours, custom charters, daylong airship cruises along the California coastline, and a 2-day pilot experience are also available. For more information or for tour times and reservations, log onto www.airshipventures.com or call ✆ 650/969-8100 weekdays from 9am to 5pm or weekends from 9am to 3pm.

Walking Tours

Cruisin' the Castro (✆ 415/255-1821; www.cruisinthecastro.com) is an informative historical tour of San Francisco's most famous gay quarter, which will give you new insight into the contribution of the gay community to the city's political maturity, growth, and beauty. This fun and easy walking tour is for all ages, highlighting gay and lesbian history from 1849 to present. Stops include **America's only Pink Triangle Park and Memorial,** the original site of the AIDS Quilt Name Project, **Harvey Milk's residence** and photo shop (now the **Human Rights Campaign and Action Center**), and the **Castro Theatre.** Tours run Monday through Saturday (except Wed) from 10am to 12:30pm and meet at the Rainbow Flag at the Harvey Milk Plaza on the corner of Castro and Market streets above the Castro Muni station. Reservations are required. The tour costs $35 per adult, $25 for children 5 to 12. A **Harvey Milk Tour** is offered Wednesday, and costs $45 per adult, $35 for children 5 to 12.

On the **Haight-Ashbury Flower Power Walking Tour** (✆ 415/863-1621), you explore hippie haunts with Pam and Bruce Brennan (the "Hippy Gourmet"). You'll revisit the Grateful Dead's crash pad, Janis Joplin's house, and other reminders of the Summer of Love in 2½ short hours. Tours begin at 9:30am on Tuesdays and Saturdays, and Fridays at 11am. The cost is $20 per person (cash only). Reservations are required. You can purchase tickets online at www.hippyg ourmet.com. (Click on the "Walking Tour" link at the bottom left of the website.)

San Francisco's Chinatown is always fascinating, but for many visitors with limited time it's hard to know where to search out the "nontouristy" shops, restaurants, and historical spots in this microcosm of Chinese culture. **Wok Wiz Chinatown Walking Tours & Cooking Center,** 250 King St., Ste. 268 (✆ 650/355-9657; www.wokwiz.com), founded over 2 decades ago by the late beloved author and cooking instructor Shirley Fong-Torres, is the answer. The Wok Wiz tours take you into Chinatown's nooks and crannies. Guides are Chinatown natives, speak fluent Cantonese, and are intimately acquainted with the neighborhood's alleys and small enterprises, as well as Chinatown's history, folklore, culture, and food. Tours are conducted daily from 10am to 1pm and include a seven-course dim sum lunch (a Chinese meal made up of many small plates of food). There's also a less expensive tour that does not include lunch. The walk is easy, as well as fun and fascinating. Groups are generally held to a maximum of 15, and reservations are essential. Prices (including lunch) are $50 for adults and $35 for children 10 and under; without lunch, prices are $35 and $25, respectively. Tickets can be purchased online at www.wokwiz.com, or by calling ✆ 212/209-3370. Wok Wiz also operates an **I Can't Believe I Ate My Way Through Chinatown**

Michael Meadows of City Tours explains the seasonal detailing of these four Victorian row-houses in Upper Haight neighborhood. They represent winter, spring, summer, and fall.

tour. It starts with breakfast, moves to a wok shop, and stops for nibbles at a vegetarian restaurant, dim sum place, and a marketplace, before taking a break for a sumptuous authentic Cantonese luncheon. It's offered on most Saturdays and costs $90 per person, food included.

Jay Gifford, founder of the **Victorian Homes Historical Walking Tour** (✆ **415/252-9485;** www.victorianwalk.com) and a San Francisco resident for more than 2 decades, communicates his enthusiasm and love for San Francisco throughout this highly entertaining walking tour. The 2½-hour tour, set at a leisurely pace, starts at the corner of Powell and Post streets at Union Square and incorporates a wealth of knowledge about San Francisco's Victorian architecture and the city's history—particularly the periods just before and after the great earthquake and fire of 1906. You'll stroll through Japantown, Pacific Heights, and Cow Hollow. In the process, you'll see more than 200 meticulously restored Victorians, including the sites where *Mrs. Doubtfire* and *Party of Five* were filmed. Jay's guests often find that they are the only ones on the quiet neighborhood streets, where tour buses are forbidden. The tour ends in Cow Hollow, where you can have lunch on your own, or return via bus to Union Square, passing through North Beach and Chinatown. Tours run daily and start at 11am rain or shine; cost is $25 per person (cash only).

The best bargains in town, however, are the 30 or so walking tours conducted by **San Francisco City Guides** (✆ **415/557-4266;** www.sfcityguides.org), a group of 200 trained volunteers who lead free history and architectural walking tours all over San Francisco. Sponsored by the public library, tours range from City Scapes & Public Places to Ghosts, Sinners, & Secret Places, and last 1½ to 2 hours.

GETTING OUTSIDE

Half the fun in San Francisco takes place outdoors. If you're not in the mood to trek it, there are other things to do that allow you to enjoy the surroundings.

BALLOONING   Although you must drive an hour to get to the tour site, hot-air ballooning over the Wine Country is an ethereal experience. **Adventures**

Aloft, P.O. Box 2500, Vintage 1870, Yountville, CA 94599 (☎ **800/627-2759** or 707/944-4400; www.nvaloft.com), is Napa Valley's oldest hot-air balloon company, staffed with full-time professional pilots. Groups are small, and each flight lasts about an hour. The cost of $230 per person (children $190) includes a post-adventure champagne brunch and a framed "first-flight" certificate. Flights launch daily at sunrise (weather permitting).

BEACHES Most days it's too chilly to hang out at the beach, but when the fog evaporates and the wind dies down, one of the best ways to spend the day is ocean-side in the city. On any truly hot day, thousands flock to the beach to worship the sun, build sand castles, and throw a ball around. Without a wet suit, swimming is a fiercely cold endeavor and is not recommended. In any case, dip at your own risk—there are no lifeguards on duty and San Francisco's waters are cold and have strong undertows. On the South Bay, **Baker Beach** is ideal for picnicking, nude sunning, walking, or fishing against the backdrop of the Golden Gate (though pollution makes your catch not necessarily worthy of eating).

Ocean Beach, at the end of Golden Gate Park, on the westernmost side of the city, is San Francisco's largest beach—4 miles long. Just offshore, at the northern end of the beach, in front of Cliff House, are the jagged **Seal Rocks,** inhabited by various shorebirds and a large colony of barking sea lions (bring binoculars for a close-up view). To the left, **Kelly's Cove** is one of the more challenging surf spots in town. Ocean Beach is ideal for strolling or sunning, but don't swim here—tides are tricky, and each year bathers drown in the rough surf.

Stop by Ocean Beach bus terminal at the corner of Cabrillo and La Playa streets to learn about San Francisco's history in local artist Ray Beldner's whimsically historical sculpture garden. Then hike up the hill to explore Cliff House and the ruins of the **Sutro Baths.** These baths, once able to accommodate 24,000 bathers, were lost to fire in 1966.

A whale **OF A TALE**

Not many people outside of California know about the **Farallon Islands,** nor do many people get to visit up close. The entire Gulf of Farallones National Marine Sanctuary is off-limits to civilians, so visitors must gaze from the deck of a fishing or whale-watching boat if they want a peek firsthand.

This veteran eco-tourism company offers trips out to the desolate outcropping of rock off the coast of San Francisco that is home to birds, sea lions, seals, dolphins, and the ever-present great white shark. Typically on the search for migrating gray, humpback, or blue whales, expeditions leave from Gas House Cove Marina at Fort Mason and pass underneath the majestic Golden Gate Bridge on the 27-mile trip out to the islands. Captain Jim Robertson has a crew of trained naturalists who accompany each voyage and will stop the Outer Limits catamaran at the first sign of water spouts on the 6- to 8-hour weekend trips.

For more information, call ☎ **415/331-6267** or visit **www.sfbaywhale watching.com.**

Get Your Blood Pumping

When Eric Kipp, a certified yogi, conceptualized his wildly popular concept of **Hiking Yoga,** he aimed to bring tourists and locals alike out and about for some fresh air, intense cardio, and fantastic city views. Kipp's 90-minute urban treks, which take place several times a day, most days of the week, depart from the clock tower at the Ferry Building and wind their way up to Coit Tower and around Telegraph Hill. Routes vary, but the formula is always the same:

Participants enjoy intense and fast-paced hill hiking—this is no leisurely walk in the park—while stopping at four stations throughout the city for a series of yoga poses. The program, which originated in San Francisco in 2007, was such a hit, Kipp has now taken it to more than a dozen cities. For information or a schedule of hikes, visit **www.hikingyoga.com** or call ✆ **415/261-3641.** Reservations are required, and each session costs $20. Package deals are available.

BIKING   The San Francisco Parks and Recreation Department maintains two city-designated bike routes. One winds 7½ miles through Golden Gate Park to Lake Merced; the other traverses the city, starting in the south, and continues over the Golden Gate Bridge. These routes are not dedicated to bicyclists, who must exercise caution to avoid crashing into pedestrians. Helmets are recommended for adults and required by law for kids 17 and under. A bike map is available from the **San Francisco Visitor Information Center,** at Powell and Mason streets, for $3 (p. 404), and from bicycle shops all around town.

Ocean Beach has a public walk- and bikeway that stretches along 5 waterfront blocks of the Great Highway between Noriega and Santiago streets. It's an easy ride from Cliff House or Golden Gate Park.

Avenue Cyclery, 756 Stanyan St., at Waller Street, in the Haight (✆ **415/387-3155**), rents bikes for $8 per hour or $30 per day. It's open daily, April through September from 10am to 7pm and October through March from 10am to 6pm. For cruising Fisherman's Wharf and the Golden Gate Bridge, your best bet is **Blazing Saddles** (✆ **415/202-8888;** www.blazing saddles.com), which has five locations around Fisherman's Wharf. Bike rentals start at $32 per day, and include maps, locks, and helmets; tandem bikes are available as well.

BOATING   At the **Golden Gate Park Boat House** (© 415/368-2531) on Stow Lake, the park's largest body of water, you can rent a rowboat or pedal boat by the hour and steer over to Strawberry Hill, a large, round island in the middle of the lake, for lunch. There's usually a line on weekends. The boathouse is open daily from 10am to 4pm, weather permitting.

Cass'Marina, 1702 Bridgeway, Sausalito (© 800/472-4595 or 415/332-6789; www.cassmarina.com), is a certified sailing school that rents sailboats measuring 22 to 38 feet. Sail to the Golden Gate Bridge on your own or with a licensed skipper. In addition, large sailing yachts leave from Sausalito on a regularly scheduled basis. Call or check the website for schedules, prices, and availability of sailboats. The marina is open Wednesday through Monday from 9am to sunset.

CITY STAIR CLIMBING ★★   Many health clubs have stair-climbing machines and step classes, but in San Francisco, you need only go outside. The following city stair climbs will give you not only a good workout, but seriously stunning neighborhood, city, and bay views as well. Check **www.sisterbetty. org/stairways** for more ideas.

Filbert Street Steps, between Sansome Street and Telegraph Hill, are a particular challenge. Scaling the sheer eastern face of Telegraph Hill, this 377-step climb winds through verdant flower gardens and charming 19th-century cottages. Napier Lane, a narrow, wooden plank walkway, leads to Montgomery Street. Turn right and follow the path to the end of the cul-de-sac, where another stairway continues to Telegraph's panoramic summit and Coit Tower.

The **Lyon Street Steps,** between Green Street and Broadway, were built in 1916. This historic stairway street contains four steep sets of stairs

The Filbert Street Steps.

totaling 288 steps. Begin at Green Street and climb all the way up, past manicured hedges and flower gardens, to an iron gate that opens into the Presidio. A block east, on Baker Street, another set of 369 steps descends to Green Street.

FISHING   **Berkeley Marina Sports Center,** 225 University Ave., Berkeley (✆ **510/237-3474;** www.berkeleysportfishing.com), offers daily trips for ling cod, rock fish, and many other types of game fish year-round; trips for salmon run April through October. Fishing equipment is available; the cost, including boat ride and bait, is about $95 per person. Reservations are required, as are licenses for adults. One-day licenses can be purchased for $12 before departure. Find out the latest on the season by contacting their hot line at ✆ **510/486-8300** (press 3). Excursions run daily from 6am to 3:30pm. Fish are cleaned, filleted, and bagged on the return trip for a small fee (free for salmon fishing).

GOLF   San Francisco has a few beautiful golf courses. One of the most lavish is the **Presidio Golf Course** (✆ **415/561-4661;** www.presidiogolf.com). Greens fees are $125 for nonresidents Monday to Thursday, $145 Friday to Sunday. Twilight rates drop to $85 and $93, respectively, and then to $49 after 3pm for everyone. Carts are included.

There are also two decent municipal courses in town. The 18-hole **Harding Park,** Skyline Boulevard at Harding Road (✆ **415/664-4690;** www.harding-park.com), charges greens fees of $150 per person Monday through Thursday, $170 Friday through Sunday. Opened in 1925, it was completely overhauled in 2002, and the new Harding has been getting rave reviews ever since. In 2004, it was named by *Golf* magazine as the number-two best municipal golf course in America; in 2009 it hosted the President's Cup. The course, which skirts the shores of Lake Merced, is a 6,743-yard, par-72. You can also play the easier Fleming executive 9. The 18-hole **Lincoln Park Golf Course,** 34th Avenue and Clement Street (✆ **415/221-9911;** www.lincolnparkgc.com), charges greens fees of $34 per person Monday through Thursday, $38 Friday through Sunday, with rates decreasing after 4pm in summer, 2pm in winter. It's San Francisco's prettiest municipal course, with terrific views and fairways lined with Monterey cypress and pine trees. The 5,181-yard layout plays to par 68, and the 17th hole has a glistening ocean view. This is the oldest course in the city and one of the oldest in the West. It's open daily at daybreak.

HANDBALL   The city's best handball courts are in **Golden Gate Park,** opposite Seventh Avenue, south of Middle Drive East. Courts are available free, on a first-come, first-served basis.

PARKS   In addition to **Golden Gate Park** and the **Golden Gate National Recreation Area** (p. 204 and 201, respectively), San Francisco boasts more than 2,000 acres of parkland, most of which is perfect for picnicking or throwing around a Frisbee.

Smaller city parks include **Buena Vista Park** (Haight St. btw. Baker and Central sts.), which affords fine views of the Golden Gate Bridge and the area around it and is also a favored lounging ground for gay trysts; **Ina Coolbrith Park** (Taylor St. btw. Vallejo and Green sts.), offering views of the Bay Bridge and Alcatraz; and **Sigmund Stern Grove** (19th Ave. and Sloat Blvd.) in the Sunset District, which is the site of a famous free summer music festival.

One of my personal favorites is **Lincoln Park,** a 270-acre green space on the northwestern side of the city at Clement Street and 34th Avenue. **The Legion of Honor** is here (p. 186), as is a scenic 18-hole municipal golf course (see "Golf," above). But the best things about this park are the 200-foot cliffs that overlook the Golden Gate Bridge and San Francisco Bay. To get to the park, take bus no. 38 from Union Square to 33rd and Geary streets, and then walk a few blocks.

RUNNING   The **Bay to Breakers Foot Race** ★ (𝄮 415/359-2800; www.zazzle baytobreakers.com) is an annual 7.5-mile run from downtown to Ocean Beach. About 80,000 entrants take part in it, one of San Francisco's trademark events. Costumed participants and hordes of spectators add to the fun. The event is held on the third Sunday of May.

The **San Francisco Marathon** takes place annually at the end of July or first weekend in August. For more information, visit www.thesfmarathon.com (𝄮 888/958-6668).

Great jogging paths include the entire expanse of Golden Gate Park, the shoreline along the Marina, and the Embarcadero.

TENNIS   The **San Francisco Parks and Recreation Department** (𝄮 415/753-7001) maintains more than 132 courts throughout the city. Almost all are available free, on a first-come, first-served basis. An additional 21 courts are available in Golden Gate Park, which cost $5 for 90 minutes during weekdays and $10 on weekends. Check the website for details on rules for reserving courts (www.parks.sfgov.org)

WALKING & HIKING   The **Golden Gate National Recreation Area** offers plenty of opportunities. One incredible walk (or bike ride) is along the Golden Gate Promenade, from Aquatic Park to the Golden Gate Bridge. The 3.5-mile paved trail heads along the northern edge of the Presidio out to Fort Point, passing the marina, Crissy Field's restored wetlands, a small

Bay to Breakers Foot Race, now sponsored by Zazzle.

beach, and plenty of athletic locals. You can also hike the **Coastal Trail** all the way from the Fort Point area to Cliff House. The park service maintains several other trails in the city. For more information or to pick up a map of the Golden Gate National Recreation Area, stop by the park service head-quarters at Fort Mason; enter on Franklin Street (© **415/561-4700**).

Although most people drive to this spectacular vantage point, a more rejuvenating way to experience **Twin Peaks** is to walk up from the back roads of U.C. Medical Center (off Parnassus Ave.) or from either of the two roads that lead to the top (off Woodside or Clarendon aves.). The best time to trek is early morning, when the city is quiet, the air is crisp, and sightseers haven't crowded the parking lot. Keep an eye out for cars, however, because there's no real hiking trail, and be sure to walk beyond the lot and up to the highest vantage point.

SPECTATOR SPORTS

The Bay Area's sports scene includes several major professional franchises. Check the local newspapers' sports sections for daily listings of local events.

Major League Baseball

The 2010 World Series Champion **San Francisco Giants** ★ play at AT&T Park, Third and King streets (© **415/972-2000;** www.sfgiants.com), in the China Basin section of SoMa. From April to October, 41,503 fans fill the seats here to root for the National League Giants. Tickets are hard to come by, but you can usually obtain some through Tickets.com (© **800/225-2277;** www.tickets.com). Go Giants!

The American League's **Oakland Athletics** play across the bay at the Coliseum, Hegenberger Road exit from I-880, Oakland (© **510/430-8020;** www.athletics.mlb.com). The stadium holds over 50,000 spectators and is accessible through BART's Coliseum station. Tickets are available from the **Coliseum Box Office** or by phone through Tickets.com (© **800/225-2277;** www.tickets.com).

The Giants' Brian Wilson gets the wheatpaste treatment, courtesy of artist Get Up (www.twitter.com/getupart).

Pro Basketball

The **Golden State Warriors** of the NBA play at the **ORACLE Arena,** a 19,200-seat facility at 7000 Coliseum Way in Oakland (© **510/986-2200;** www.nba.com/warriors). The season runs November through April, and most games start at 7:30pm. Tickets are available at the arena, online, and by phone through **Tickets.com** (© **800/225-2277;** www.tickets.com).

Pro Football

The **San Francisco 49ers** (www.sf49ers.com) play at **Candlestick Park,** Giants Drive and Gilman Avenue, on Sundays August through December; kick-off is usually at 1pm. Tickets sell out early in the season but are available at higher prices through ticket agents beforehand and from "scalpers" (illegal ticket-sellers who are usually at the gates). Ask your hotel concierge for the best way to track down tickets.

The 49ers' archenemies, the **Oakland Raiders** (www.raiders.com), play at the **Oakland-Alameda Coliseum,** off the I-880 freeway (Nimitz). Call ✆ **800/ RAIDERS** (724-3377) for ticket information.

7

CITY STROLLS

Hills schmills. Don't let a few steep slopes deter you from one of San Francisco's greatest pleasures—walking around the neighborhoods and exploring the city for yourself. Here are a couple of introductory walks that hit the highlights of our favorite neighborhoods for touring on foot.

WALKING TOUR 1: **CHINATOWN: HISTORY, CULTURE, DIM SUM & THEN SOME**

START: **Corner of Grant Avenue and Bush Street.**
PUBLIC TRANSPORTATION: **Bus no. 2, 3, 9X, 30, 38, 45, or 76.**
FINISH: **Commercial Street between Montgomery and Kearny streets.**
TIME: **2 hours, not including museum or shopping stops.**
BEST TIMES: **Daylight hours, when the streets are most active.**
WORST TIMES: **Early or late in the day, because shops are closed and no one is milling around.**
HILLS THAT COULD KILL: **None.**

This tiny section of San Francisco, bounded loosely by Broadway and by Stockton, Kearny, and Bush streets, is said to harbor one of the largest Chinese populations outside Asia. Daily proof is the crowds of Chinese residents who flock to the herbal stores, vegetable markets, restaurants, and businesses. Chinatown, specifically Portsmouth Square, also marks the original spot of the city center. On this walk, you'll learn why Chinatown remains intriguing to all who wind through its narrow, crowded streets, and how its origins are responsible for the city as we know it.

To begin the tour, make your way to the corner of Bush Street and Grant Avenue, 4 blocks from Union Square and all the downtown buses, where you can't miss the:

1 Chinatown Gateway Arch

Traditional Chinese villages have ceremonial gates like this one. A lot less formal than those in China, this gate was built more for the benefit of the tourist industry than anything else.

Once you cross the threshold, you'll be at the beginning of Chinatown's portion of:

2 Grant Avenue

This is a mecca for tourists who wander in and out of gift shops that offer a variety of unnecessary junk interspersed with quality imports. You'll also find decent restaurants and grocery stores frequented by Chinese residents, ranging from children to the oldest living people you've ever seen.

PREVIOUS PAGE: **A streetlamp in Chinatown.**

Tear yourself away from the shops and turn right at the corner of Pine Street. Cross to the other side of Pine and on your left you'll come to:

3 St. Mary's Square

Here you'll find a huge metal-and-granite **statue of Dr. Sun Yat-sen**, the founder of the Republic of China. A native of Guangdong (Canton) Province, Sun Yat-sen led the rebellion that ended the reign of the Qing Dynasty.

Note also the second monument in the square, which honors Chinese-American victims of World War I and World War II.

Walk to the other end of the square, toward California Street, turn left, cross California Street at Grant Street, and you'll be standing in front of:

4 Old St. Mary's Cathedral

The first Catholic cathedral in San Francisco and the site of the Chinese community's first English-language school, St. Mary's was built primarily by Chinese laborers and dedicated on Christmas Day 1854.

Step inside to find a written history of the church and turn-of-the-20th-century photos of San Francisco.

Upon leaving the church, take a right, walk to the corner of Grant Avenue and California Street, and go right on Grant. Here you'll find a shop called:

5 Canton Bazaar

Of the knickknack and import shops lining Grant Avenue, this is one of the most popular; it's located at 616 Grant Ave.

Continue in the same direction on Grant Avenue and cross Sacramento Street to the northwest corner of Sacramento and Grant. You'll be at the doorstep of the:

6 Bank of America

This bank is an example of traditional Chinese architectural style. Notice the dragons subtly portrayed on many parts of the building.

Chinese New Year parade.

Chinatown at dusk.

Walking Tour: Chinatown

Head in the same direction (north) on Grant Avenue, and a few doors down is the:

7 Chinatown Kite Shop

This store, located at 717 Grant Ave., has an assortment of flying objects, including attractive fish kites, nylon or cotton windsock kites, hand-painted Chinese paper kites, wood-and-paper biplanes, and pentagonal kites.

Cross Grant Avenue and you'll arrive at:

8 The Wok Shop

Here's where you can purchase just about any cleaver, wok, cookbook, or vessel you might need for Chinese-style cooking in your own kitchen. It's located at 718 Grant Ave.

When you come out of the Wok Shop, go right. Walk past Commercial Street and you'll arrive at the corner of Grant Avenue and Clay Street; cross Clay and you'll be standing on the:

9 Original Street of "American" California

Here an English seaman named William Richardson set up the first tent in 1835, making it the first place that an Anglo set up base in California.

Continue north on Grant Avenue to Washington Street. Turn right and at 743 Washington St. you will be standing in front of the former Bank of Canton, now known as the:

10 United Commercial Bank

This building boasts the oldest (from 1909) Asian-style edifice in Chinatown. The three-tiered temple-style building once housed the China Telephone Exchange, known as "China-5" until 1945.

You're probably thirsty by now, so follow Washington Street a few doors down (east); on your right-hand side, at 733 Washington St., you will come upon:

11 Washington Bakery & Restaurant ☕

No need to have a full meal here—the service can be abrupt. Do stop in, however, for a little potable adventure: snow red beans with ice cream. The sugary-sweet drink mixed with whole beans and ice cream is not something you're likely to have tried elsewhere, and it happens to be quite tasty.

Head back to Grant Avenue, cross Washington Street, cross Grant, and follow the west side of Grant 1 block to:

12 Ten Ren Tea Co., Ltd.

In this amazing shop at 949 Grant Ave., you can sample a freshly brewed tea variety and check out the dozens of drawers and canisters labeled with more than 40 kinds of tea. Like Washington Bakery, Ten Ren offers unusual

drinks worth trying: delightful hot or iced milk teas containing giant blobs of jelly or tapioca. Try black tea or green tea and enjoy the outstanding flavors and the giant balls of tapioca slipping around in your mouth.

Leave Ten Ren, make a left, and when you reach Jackson Street, make another left. Follow Jackson Street until you reach Ross Alley and turn left into the alley.

13 Ross Alley

As you walk along this narrow street, just one of the many alleyways that crisscrossed Chinatown to accommodate the many immigrants who jammed into the neighborhood, it's not difficult to believe that this block once was rife with gambling dens.

As you follow the alley south, on the left side of the street you'll encounter the:

Dazzling a crowd at the corner of Grant and Commercial streets. That's a preserved Banksy mural in the background (only partially visible here—see it for yourself).

14 Golden Gate Fortune Cookie Company

Located at 56 Ross Alley, this store is little more than a tiny place where three women sit at a conveyer belt, folding messages into warm cookies as the manager invariably calls out to tourists, beckoning them to buy a big bag of the fortune-telling treats.

You can purchase regular fortunes, unfolded flat cookies without fortunes, or, if you bring your own fortunes, make custom cookies (I often do this when I'm having dinner parties) at around $6 for 50 cookies—a very cheap way to impress your friends! Or, of course, you can just take a peek and move on.

As you exit the alley, cross Washington Street, take a right heading west on Washington, and you're in front of the:

15 Great China Herb Co.

For centuries, the Chinese have come to shops like this one, at 857 Washington St., which are full of exotic herbs, roots, and other natural substances. They buy what they believe will cure all types of ailments and ensure good health and a long life. Thankfully, unlike owners in many similar area shops, Mr. and Mrs. Ho speak English, so you will not be met with a blank stare when you inquire what exactly is in each box, bag, or jar arranged along dozens of shelves. It is important to note that you should not use Chinese herbs without the guidance of a knowledgeable source such as an herb doctor. They may be natural, but they also can be quite powerful and are potentially harmful if misused.

Take a left upon leaving the store and walk to:

16 Stockton Street

The section of Stockton Street between Broadway and Sacramento streets is where most of the residents of Chinatown do their daily shopping.

One noteworthy part of this area's history is **Cameron House** (actually up the hill at 920 Sacramento St., near Stockton St.), which was named after Donaldina Cameron (1869–1968). Called Lo Mo, or "the Mother," by the Chinese, she spent her life trying to free Chinese women who came to America in hopes of marrying well but who found themselves forced into prostitution and slavery. Today, the house still helps women free themselves from domestic violence.

Wander up Stockton Street to absorb the atmosphere and street life of this less-tourist-oriented Chinese community before doubling back to Washington Street. At 1068 Stockton St. you'll find **AA Bakery & Café,** an extremely colorful bakery with Golden Gate Bridge–shaped cakes, bright green and pink snacks, moon cakes, and a flow of Chinese diners catching up over pastries. Another fun place at which to peek is **Gourmet Delight B.B.Q.,** at 1045 Stockton St., where barbecued duck and pork are supplemented by steamed pigs' feet and chicken feet. Everything's to go here, so if you grab a snack, don't forget napkins. Head farther north along the street and you'll see live fish and fowl awaiting their fate as the day's dinner.

Meander south on Stockton Street to Clay Street and turn west (right) onto Clay. Continue to 965 Clay St. (Make sure you come Tues–Fri noon–5pm or Sat or Sun noon–4pm.) You've arrived at the:

17 Chinese Historical Society of America Museum

Founded in 1963, this museum (© **415/391-1188**) has a small but fascinating collection that illuminates the role of Chinese immigrants in American history, particularly in San Francisco and the rest of California.

The interesting artifacts on display include a shrimp-cleaning machine, 19th-century clothing and slippers of the Chinese pioneers, Chinese herbs and scales, historic hand-carved and painted shop signs, and a series of photographs that document the development of Chinese culture in America.

The goal of this organization is not only to "study, record, acquire, and preserve all suitable artifacts and such cultural items as manuscripts, books, and works of art . . . which have a bearing on the history of the Chinese living in the United States of America," but also to "promote the contributions that Chinese Americans living in this country have made to the United States of America." It's an admirable and much-needed effort, considering what little recognition and appreciation the Chinese have received throughout American history.

The museum is open Tuesday through Friday from noon to 5pm and Saturday and Sunday from noon to 4pm. Admission is $3 for adults, $2 for college students with ID and seniors, and $1 for kids 6 to 17.

Retrace your steps, heading east on Clay Street back toward Grant Avenue. Turn left onto:

18 Waverly Place

Also known as "the Street of Painted Balconies," Waverly Place is probably Chinatown's most popular side street or alleyway because of its painted balconies and colorful architectural details—a sort of Chinese-style New Orleans street. And though you can admire the architecture only from the ground, because most of the buildings are private family associations or temples, with a recent beautification and renovation by the city, it's definitely worth checking out.

One temple you can visit (but make sure it's open before you climb the long, narrow stairway) is the **Tin How Temple,** at 125 Waverly Place. Accessible via the stairway three floors up, this incense-laden sanctuary, decorated in traditional black, red, and gold lacquered wood, is a house of worship for Chinese Buddhists, who come here to pray, meditate, and send offerings to their ancestors and to Tin How, the Queen of the Heavens and Goddess of the Seven Seas. There are no scheduled services, but you are welcome to visit. Just remember to quietly respect those who are here to pray and be as unobtrusive as possible. It is customary to give a donation (put it in one of those little red envelopes) or buy a bundle of incense during your visit.

Once you've finished exploring Waverly Place, walk east on Clay Street, past Grant Avenue, and continue until you come upon the block-wide urban playground that is also the most important site in San Francisco's history.

19 Portsmouth Square

This very spot was the center of the region's first township, which was called Yerba Buena before it was renamed San Francisco in 1847. Around 1846, before any semblance of a city had taken shape, this plaza lay at the foot of the bay's eastern shoreline. There were fewer than 50 non–Native American residents in the settlement, there were no substantial buildings to speak of, and the few boats that pulled into the cove did so less than a block from where you're standing.

In 1846, when California was claimed as a U.S. territory, the marines who landed here named the square after their ship, the USS *Portsmouth*. (Today a bronze plaque marks the spot where they raised the U.S. flag.)

Yerba Buena remained a modest township until the gold rush of 1849 when, over the next 2 years, the population grew from under 1,000 to over 19,000, as gold seekers from around the world made their way here.

When the square became too crowded, long wharves were constructed to support new buildings above the bay. Eventually, the entire area became landfill. That was almost 150 years ago, but today the square still serves as an important meeting place for neighborhood Chinese—a sort of communal outdoor living room.

Throughout the day, the square is heavily trafficked by children and—in large part—by elderly men, who gamble over Chinese cards and play chess. If you arrive early in the morning, you might come across people practicing tai chi.

It is said that Robert Louis Stevenson used to love to sit on a bench here and watch life go by. (At the northeast corner of the square, you'll find a monument to his memory, consisting of a model of the *Hispaniola*, the ship in Stevenson's novel *Treasure Island*, and an excerpt from his "Christmas Sermon.")

A game of mah-jongg in Portsmouth Square.

Once you've had your fill of the square, exit to the east at Kearny Street. Directly across the street, at 750 Kearny St., is the Holiday Inn. Cross the street, enter the hotel, and take the elevator to the third floor, where you'll find the:

20 Chinese Culture Center

This center is oriented toward both the community and tourists, offering interesting display cases of Chinese art and a gallery with rotating exhibits of Asian art and writings. The center is open Tuesday through Saturday from 10am to 4pm.

When you leave the Holiday Inn, take a left on Kearny Street and go 3 short blocks to Commercial Street. Take a left onto Commercial and note that you are standing on the street once known as the site of:

21 Joshua A. Norton's Home

Norton, the self-proclaimed "Emperor of the United States and Protector of Mexico," used to walk around the streets in an old brass-buttoned military uniform, sporting a hat with a "dusty plume." He lived in a fantasy world, and San Franciscans humored him at every turn.

Norton was born around 1815 in the British Isles and sailed as a young man to South Africa, where he served as a colonial rifleman. He came to San Francisco in 1849 with $40,000 and proceeded to double and triple his fortune in real estate. Unfortunately for him, he next chose to go into the rice business. While Norton was busy cornering the market and forcing prices up, several ships loaded with rice arrived unexpectedly in San Francisco's harbor. The rice market was suddenly flooded, and Norton was forced into bankruptcy.

A spicy crab dish at the R&G Lounge.

He left San Francisco for about 3 years and must have experienced a breakdown (or revelation) of some sort, for upon his return, Norton thought he was an emperor.

Instead of ostracizing him, however, San Franciscans embraced him as their own homegrown lunatic and gave him free meals.

When Emperor Norton died in 1880 (while sleeping at the corner of California St. and Grant Ave.), approximately 10,000 people passed by his coffin, which was bought with money raised at the Pacific Union Club, and more than 30,000 people participated in the funeral procession. Today you won't see a trace of his character, but it's fun to imagine him cruising the street.

From here, if you've still got an appetite, you should go directly to 631 Kearny St. (at Clay St.), home of the R&G Lounge.

22 R&G Lounge 🍴

The R&G Lounge is a sure thing for tasty $5 rice-plate specials, chicken with black-bean sauce, and gorgeously tender and tangy R&G Special Beef.

Otherwise, you might want to backtrack on Commercial Street to Grant Avenue, take a left, and follow Grant back to Bush Street, the entrance to Chinatown. You'll be at the beginning of the Union Square area, where you can catch any number of buses (especially on Market St.) or cable cars, or do a little shopping. Or you might backtrack to Grant, take a right (north), and follow Grant to the end. You'll be at Broadway and Columbus, the beginning of North Beach, where you can venture onward for our North Beach tour (see below).

WALKING TOUR 2: **GETTING TO KNOW NORTH BEACH**

START:	**Intersection of Montgomery Street, Columbus Avenue, and Washington Street.**
PUBLIC TRANSPORTATION:	**Bus no. 10, 12, 15, 30X, or 41.**
FINISH:	**Washington Square.**
TIME:	**3 hours, including a stop for lunch.**
BEST TIMES:	**Monday through Saturday between 11am and 4pm.**
WORST TIMES:	**Sunday, when shops are closed.**
HILLS THAT COULD KILL:	**The Montgomery Street hill from Broadway to Vallejo streets; otherwise, this is an easy walk.**

Along with Chinatown, North Beach is one of the city's oldest neighborhoods. Originally the Latin Quarter, it became the city's Italian district when Italian immigrants moved "uphill" in the early 1870s, crossing Broadway from the Jackson Square area and settling in. They quickly established restaurants, cafes, bakeries, and other businesses familiar to them from their homeland. The "Beat Generation" helped put North Beach on the map, with the likes of Jack Kerouac and Allen Ginsberg holding court in the area's cafes during the 1950s. Although most of the original Beat poets are gone, their spirit lives on in North Beach, which is still a haven for bohemian artists and writers. The neighborhood, thankfully, retains its Italian village feel; it's a place where residents from all walks of life enjoy taking time for conversation over pastries and frothy cappuccinos.

If there's one landmark you can't miss, it's the familiar building on the corner of Montgomery Street and Columbus Avenue, the Transamerica Pyramid (take bus no. 15, 30X, or 41 to get there).

1 Transamerica Pyramid

Noted for its spire (which rises 212 ft. above the top floor) and its "wings" (which begin at the 29th floor and stop at the spire), this pyramid is San Francisco's tallest building and a hallmark of the skyline. You might want to take a peek at one of the rotating art exhibits in the lobby or go around to the right and into ½-acre Redwood Park, which is part of the Transamerica Center.

The Transamerica Pyramid occupies part of the 600 block of Montgomery Street, which once held a historic building called:

The Transamerica Pyramid.

2 The Montgomery Block

Originally four stories high, the Montgomery Block was the tallest building in the West when it was built in 1853. San Franciscans called it "Halleck's Folly" because it was built on a raft of redwood logs that had been bolted together and floated at the edge of the ocean (which was right at Montgomery St. at that time). The building was demolished in 1959 but is fondly remembered for its historical importance as the power center of the city. Its tenants included artists and writers of all kinds, among them Jack London, George Sterling, Ambrose Bierce, Bret Harte, and Mark Twain. This is a picturesque area, but there's no particular spot to direct you to. It's worth looking around, however, if only for the block's historical importance.

From the southeast corner of Montgomery and Washington streets, look across Washington to the corner of Columbus Avenue and you'll see the original Transamerica Building, located at 4 Columbus Ave.

3 Original Transamerica Building

The original Transamerica Building is a Beaux Arts flatiron-shaped building covered in terra cotta; it was also the home of Sanwa Bank and Fugazi Bank. Built for the Banco Populare Italiano Operaia Fugazi in 1909, it was originally a two-story building and gained a third floor in 1916. In 1928, Fugazi merged his bank with the Bank of America, which was started by A. P. Giannini, who also created the Transamerica Corporation. The building now houses a Church of Scientology.

Cross Washington Street and continue north on Montgomery Street to no. 730:

4 Golden Era Building

Erected around 1852, this San Francisco historic landmark building is named after the literary magazine *The Golden Era*, which was published here. Some of the young writers who worked on the magazine were known as "the Bohemians"; they included Samuel Clemens (also known as Mark Twain) and Bret Harte (who began as a typesetter here). Backtrack a few dozen feet and stop for a minute to admire the exterior of the annex, at no. 722, which, after years of neglect and lawsuits, has finally been stabilized and is going to be developed. The Belli Annex, as it is currently known, is registered as a historic landmark.

Continue north on Washington Street and take the first right onto Jackson Street. Continue until you hit the:

5 400 Block of Jackson Square

Here's where you'll find some of the only commercial buildings to survive the 1906 earthquake and fire. The building at 415 Jackson St. (ca. 1853) served as headquarters for the Ghirardelli chocolate company from 1855 to 1894. The Hotaling Building (no. 451) was built in 1866 and features pediments and quoins of cast iron applied over the brick walls. At no. 441 is another of the buildings that survived the disaster of 1906. Constructed between 1850 and 1852 with ship masts for interior supporting columns, it served as the French Consulate from 1865 to 1876.

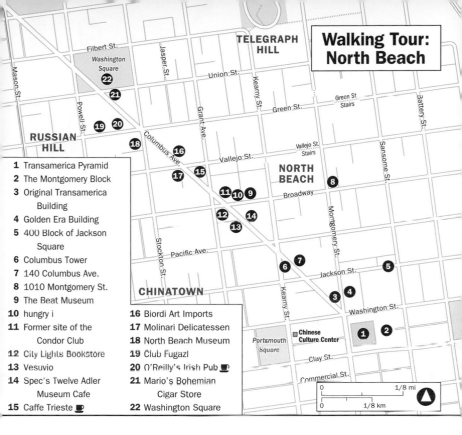

Walking Tour: North Beach

TELEGRAPH HILL

Filbert St.

Washington Square **22**

21

Union St.

19 **20**

RUSSIAN HILL

18

16

17 **15**

Vallejo St.

NORTH BEACH

8

11 **10** **9**

Broadway

12

14

13

Pacific Ave.

CHINATOWN

6 **7**

Jackson St.

5

3 **4**

Washington St.

Portsmouth Square

Chinese Culture Center

Clay St.

1 **2**

Commercial St.

0 — 1/8 mi
0 — 1/8 km

Mason St. · Powell St. · Columbus Ave. · Stockton St. · Kearny St. · Jasper St. · Grant Ave. · Kearny St. · Green St. · Green St. Stairs · Vallejo St. Stairs · Montgomery St. · Sansome St. · Battery St.

1 Transamerica Pyramid
2 The Montgomery Block
3 Original Transamerica Building
4 Golden Era Building
5 400 Block of Jackson Square
6 Columbus Tower
7 140 Columbus Ave.
8 1010 Montgomery St.
9 The Beat Museum
10 hungry i
11 Former site of the Condor Club
12 City Lights Bookstore
13 Vesuvio
14 Spec's Twelve Adler Museum Cafe
15 Caffe Trieste

16 Biordi Art Imports
17 Molinari Delicatessen
18 North Beach Museum
19 Club Fugazi
20 O'Reilly's Irish Pub
21 Mario's Bohemian Cigar Store
22 Washington Square

Cross the street and backtrack on Jackson Street. Continue toward the intersection of Columbus Avenue and Jackson Street. Turn right on Columbus and look across the street for the small triangular building at the junction of Kearny Street and Columbus Avenue, Columbus Tower (also known as the Sentinel Building).

6 Columbus Tower

If you walk a little farther, turn around, and look back down Columbus Avenue, you'll be able to get a better look at Columbus Tower (officially the Sentinel Bldg.). The flatiron beauty, a building shaped to a triangular site, went up between 1905 and 1907. Movie director and producer Francis Ford Coppola bought and restored it in the mid-1970s; it is now home to his film production company, American Zoetrope Studios. The building's cafe offers panini, pasta, pizzas, and antipasti; the store showcases all things Coppola, including his wines, olive oil, and Parmesan cheese. It's a great place for a glass of wine, an espresso, or a snack.

Across the street from Columbus Tower on Columbus Avenue is:

7 140 Columbus Ave.

Although it was closed for a few years, the Purple Onion (© 415/956-1653), famous for its many renowned headliners who often played here before they became famous, is again host to an eclectic mix of music and comedy. Let's hope the next Phyllis Diller—who was still struggling when she played a 2-week engagement here in the late 1950s—will catch her big break here, too.

Continue north on Columbus Avenue and then turn right on Pacific Avenue. After you cross Montgomery Street, you'll find brick-lined Osgood Place on the left. A registered historic landmark, it is one of the few quiet—and car-free—little alleyways left in the city. Stroll up Osgood and go left on Broadway to 1010 Montgomery St. (at Broadway).

Outside the Beat Museum: Neal Cassady and Jack Kerouac.

8 1010 Montgomery St.

This is where Allen Ginsberg lived when he wrote his legendary poem, *Howl,* first performed on October 13, 1955, in a converted auto-repair shop at the corner of Fillmore and Union streets. By the time Ginsberg finished reading, he was crying and the audience was going wild. Jack Kerouac proclaimed, "Ginsberg, this poem will make you famous in San Francisco."

Continue along Broadway toward Columbus Avenue. This stretch of Broadway is San Francisco's answer to New York's Times Square, complete with strip clubs and peep shows that are being pushed aside by restaurants, clubs, and endless crowds.

9 The Beat Museum

You can purchase *Howl* and other Beat works and memorabilia at this museum, which has among its collection a $450 first edition of *On the Road* and a replica of Kerouac's '49 Hudson. The car was featured in Walter Salles *On the Road* film adaptation (2012) and is on permanent loan from the director. Tickets to the museum within the store are $5.

Continue along Broadway to:

10 hungry i

Now a seedy strip club (at 546 Broadway), the original hungry i (at 599 Jackson St., which is under construction for senior housing) was owned and operated by the vociferous "Big Daddy" Nordstrom. If you had been here while Enrico Banducci was in charge, you would have found only a plain room with an exposed brick wall and director's chairs around small tables. A who's who of nightclub entertainers fortified their careers at the original hungry i, including Lenny Bruce, Billie Holiday (who sang "Strange Fruit" there), Bill Cosby, Richard Pryor, Woody Allen, and Barbra Streisand.

At the corner of Broadway and Columbus Avenue, you will see the:

11 Former Site of the Condor Club

The Condor Club was located at 300 Columbus Ave.; this is where Carol Doda scandalously bared her breasts and danced topless for the first time in 1964. Note the bronze plaque claiming the Condor Club as BIRTHPLACE OF THE WORLD'S FIRST TOPLESS & BOTTOMLESS ENTERTAINMENT. Go inside what is now the Condor Sports Bar and have a look at the framed newspaper clippings that hang around the dining room. From the elevated back room, you can see Doda's old dressing room and, on the floor below, an outline of the piano that would descend from the second floor with her atop it.

City Lights Bookstore, still operated by founder Lawrence Ferlinghetti, is a historic landmark.

When you leave the Condor Sports Bar, cross to the south side of Broadway. Note the mural of jazz musicians painted on the entire side of the building directly across Columbus Avenue. Diagonally across the intersection from the Condor Sports Bar is:

12 City Lights Booksellers & Publishers

Founded in 1953 and owned by one of the first Beat poets to arrive in San Francisco, Lawrence Ferlinghetti, City Lights is now a city landmark and literary mecca. Located at 261 Columbus Ave., it's one of the last of the Beat-era hangouts in operation. An active participant in the Beat movement, Ferlinghetti

The mural on the wall outside Vesuvio's, once a favored Beat hangout.

established his shop as a meeting place where writers and bibliophiles could (and still do) attend poetry readings and other events. A vibrant part of the literary scene, the well-stocked bookshop prides itself on its collection of art, poetry, and political paperbacks.

Upon exiting City Lights bookstore, turn right, cross aptly named Jack Kerouac Street, and stop by Vesuvio, the bar on your right.

13 Vesuvio

Because of its proximity to City Lights bookstore, Vesuvio became a favorite hangout of the Beats. Dylan Thomas used to drink here, as did Jack Kerouac, Ferlinghetti, and Ginsberg. Even today, Vesuvio, which opened in 1949, maintains its original bohemian atmosphere. The bar is located at 255 Columbus Ave. (at Jack Kerouac St.); the building dates from 1913. It is an excellent example of pressed-tin architecture.

Facing Vesuvio across Columbus Avenue is another favorite spot of the Beat Generation:

14 Spec's Twelve Adler Museum Cafe

Located at 12 Saroyan Place, this is one of the city's funkiest bars, a small, dimly lit watering hole with ceiling-hung maritime flags and exposed brick walls crammed with memorabilia. Within the bar is a minimuseum that consists of a few glass cases filled with mementos brought by seamen who frequented the pub from the '40s and onward.

From here, walk back up Columbus Avenue across Broadway to Grant Avenue. Turn right on Grant and continue until you come to Vallejo Street. At 601 Vallejo St. (at Grant Ave.) is:

Caffe Trieste.

15 Caffe Trieste

Yet another favorite spot of the Beats and founded by Gianni Giotta in 1956, Caffe Trieste is still run by family members. The quintessential San Francisco coffeehouse, Trieste features opera on the jukebox, and the real thing, performed by the Giottas, on Saturday afternoons. Any day of the week is a good one to stop in for a cappuccino or espresso—the beans are roasted right next door.

Go left out of Caffe Trieste onto Vallejo Street, turn right on Columbus Avenue, and bump into the loveliest shop in all of North Beach, Biordi Art Imports, located at 412 Columbus Ave.

16 Biordi Art Imports

This store has carried imported hand-painted majolica pottery from the hill towns of central Italy for more than 50 years. Some of the colorful patterns date from the 14th century. Biordi handpicks its artisans, and its catalog includes biographies of those who are currently represented.

Across Columbus Avenue, at the corner of Vallejo Street, is the:

17 Molinari Delicatessen

This deli, located at 373 Columbus Ave., has been selling its pungent, air-dried salamis since 1896. Ravioli and tortellini are made in the back of the shop, but it's the sandwiches and the mouthwatering selection of cold salads, cheeses, and marinades up front that captures the attention of most folks. One Italian sub is big enough for two hearty appetites.

Walk north to the lively intersection of Columbus, Green, and Stockton streets, and look for the U.S. Bank at 1435 Stockton St. On the second floor of the bank, you'll find the:

18 North Beach Museum

The North Beach Museum displays historical artifacts that tell the story of North Beach, Chinatown, and Fisherman's Wharf. Just before you enter the museum, you'll find a framed, handwritten poem by Lawrence Ferlinghetti that captures his impressions of this primarily Italian neighborhood. After passing through the glass doors, visitors see many photographs of some of the first Chinese and Italian immigrants, as well as pictures of San Francisco after the 1906 earthquake. You can visit the museum any time the bank is open (unfortunately, it's closed on weekends), and admission is free.

Now backtrack toward Columbus Avenue and go left on Green Street to Club Fugazi, at 678 Green St.

19 Club Fugazi

It doesn't look like much from the outside, but Fugazi Hall was donated to the city (and more important, the North Beach area) by John Fugazi, the founder of the Italian bank that was taken over by A. P. Giannini and turned into the original Transamerica Corporation. For many years, Fugazi Hall has been staging the zany and whimsical musical revue Beach Blanket Babylon. The show evolved from Steve Silver's Rent-a-Freak service, which consisted of a group of partygoers who would attend parties dressed as any number of characters in outrageous costumes. The fun caught on and soon became Beach Blanket Babylon, now the longest-running musical revue in the nation.

If you love comedy and enormous hats, you'll love this show. We don't want to spoil it for you by telling you what it's about, but if you get tickets and they're in an unreserved-seat section, you should arrive fairly early because you'll be seated around small cocktail tables on a first-come, first-served basis. (Two sections have reserved seating, four don't, and all of them frequently sell out weeks in advance; however, sometimes it is possible to get tickets at the last minute on weekdays.) You'll want to be as close to the stage as possible. This supercharged show (p. 270 for more information) is definitely worth the price of admission.

20 O'Reilly's Irish Pub ☕

Head back the way you came on Green Street. Before you get to Columbus Avenue, you'll see this pub, at 622 Green St., a homey watering hole that dishes out good, hearty Irish food and a fine selection of beers (including Guinness, of course) that are best enjoyed at one of the sidewalk tables. Always a conversation piece is the mural of Irish authors peering from the back wall. How many can you name?

As you exit O'Reilly's, turn left, cross Columbus Avenue, and then take a left onto Columbus. Proceed 1 block northwest to:

21 Mario's Bohemian Cigar Store

Located at 566 Columbus Ave., across the street from Washington Square, this is one of North Beach's most popular neighborhood hangouts. No, it does not sell cigars, but the cramped and casual space overlooking Washington Square does sell killer focaccia sandwiches, coffee drinks, beer, and wine.

Our next stop, directly across Union Street, is:

22 Washington Square

This is one of the oldest parks in the city. The land was designated a public park in 1847 and has undergone many changes since then. Its current landscaping dates from 1955. You'll notice **Saints Peter and Paul Church** (the religious center for the neighborhood's Italian community) on the northwest end. Take a few moments to go inside and check out the traditional Italian interior. Note that this is the church in which baseball great Joe DiMaggio married his first wife, Dorothy Arnold. He wasn't allowed to marry Marilyn Monroe here because he had been divorced. He married Monroe at City Hall and came here for publicity photos.

Today the park is a pleasant place in which to soak up the sun, read a book, or chat with a retired Italian octogenarian who has seen the city grow and change.

From here, you can see the famous **Coit Tower** at the top of Telegraph Hill to the northwest. If you'd like to get back to your starting point at Columbus and Montgomery, walk south (away from the water) on Columbus.

SHOPPING

L ike its population, San Francisco's shopping scene is incredibly diverse. Every style, era, fetish, and financial status is represented here—not in huge, sprawling shopping malls, but in hundreds of boutiques and secondhand stores scattered throughout the city. Whether it's a pair of Jimmy Choo shoes, a Chanel knockoff, or Chinese herbal medicine you're looking for, San Francisco's got it. Just pick a shopping neighborhood, wear some sensible shoes, and you're sure to end up with at least a few take-home treasures.

THE SHOPPING SCENE
Major Shopping Areas

San Francisco has many shopping areas, but the following places are where you'll find most of the action.

UNION SQUARE & ENVIRONS   San Francisco's most congested and popular shopping mecca is centered on Union Square and bordered by Bush, Taylor, Market, and Montgomery streets. Most of the big department stores and many high-end specialty shops are here. Be sure to venture to Grant Avenue, Post and Sutter streets, and Maiden Lane. This area is a hub for public transportation; all Market Street and several other buses run here, as do the Powell–Hyde and Powell–Mason cable car lines. You can also take the Muni streetcar to the Powell Street station.

CHINATOWN   When you pass through the gate to Chinatown on Grant Avenue, say goodbye to the world of fashion and hello to a swarm of cheap tourist shops selling everything from linen and jade to plastic toys and $2 slippers. But that's not all Chinatown has to offer. The real gems are tucked away on side streets or are small, one-person shops selling Chinese herbs, original art, and jewelry. Grant Avenue is the area's main thoroughfare, and the side streets between Bush Street and Columbus Avenue are full of restaurants, markets, and eclectic shops. Stockton Street is best for grocery shopping (including live fowl and fish). Walking is the way to get around, because traffic through this area is slow and parking is next to impossible. Most stores in Chinatown are open daily from 10am to 10pm. Take bus no. 1, 9X, 30, 41, or 45.

UNION STREET   Union Street, from Fillmore Street to Van Ness Avenue, caters to the upper-middle-class crowd. It's a great place to stroll, window-shop the plethora of boutiques, try the cafes and restaurants, and watch the beautiful people parade by. Take bus no. 22, 41, 45, 47, 49, or 76.

CHESTNUT STREET   Parallel and a few blocks north, Chestnut Street is a younger version of Union Street. It holds endless shopping and dining

PREVIOUS PAGE: **Card prints of taco trucks, from Eric Rewitzer of www.3fishstudios.com.**

The shops along Fillmore Street.

choices, and an ever-tanned, superfit population of postgraduate singles who hang around cafes and scope each other out. Take bus no. 22, 28, 30, 43, or 76.

FILLMORE STREET   Some of the best shopping in town is packed into 5 blocks of Fillmore Street in Pacific Heights. From Jackson to Sutter streets, Fillmore is the perfect place to grab a bite and peruse the high-priced boutiques, crafts shops, and incredible housewares stores. (Don't miss Zinc Details; p. 258.) Take bus no. 1, 2, 3, 12, 22, or 24

HAIGHT STREET   Green hair, spiked hair, no hair, or mohair—even the hippies look conservative next to Haight Street's dramatic fashion freaks. The shopping in the 6 blocks of upper Haight Street between Central Avenue and Stanyan Street reflects its clientele. It offers everything from incense and European and American street styles to furniture and antique clothing. Bus nos. 6, 66, and 71 run the length of Haight Street, and nos. 33 and 43 run through upper Haight Street. The Muni streetcar N line stops at Waller Street and Cole Street.

SOMA   Although this area isn't suitable for strolling, you'll find almost all the discount shopping in warehouse spaces south of Market. You can pick up a discount-shopping guide at most major hotels. Many bus lines pass through this area.

HAYES VALLEY   It's not the prettiest area in town, with some of the shadier housing projects a few blocks away. But while most neighborhoods cater to more conservative or trendy shoppers, lower Hayes Street, between Octavia and Gough streets, celebrates anything vintage, chic, artistic, or downright funky. With new shops opening frequently, it's definitely the most interesting new shopping area in town, with furniture and glass stores, thrift shops, trendy shoe stores, and men's and women's clothiers. You can find lots of great antiques shops south on Octavia Street and on nearby Market Street. Take bus no. 21.

FISHERMAN'S WHARF & ENVIRONS   The tourist-oriented malls along Jefferson Street include hundreds of shops, restaurants, and attractions. Among them are Ghirardelli Square, Pier 39, the Cannery, and the Anchorage. See "Shopping Centers & Complexes" on p. 260.

Just the Facts: Hours, Taxes & Shipping

Store hours are generally Monday through Saturday from 10am to 6pm and Sunday from noon to 5pm. Most department stores stay open later, as do shops around Fisherman's Wharf, the most heavily visited area (by tourists).

Sales tax in San Francisco is 9.5%, which is added on at the register for all goods and services purchased. If you live out of state and buy an expensive item,

you might want to have the store ship it home for you. You'll have to pay for shipping, but you'll escape paying the sales tax.

Most of the city's shops can wrap your purchase and ship it anywhere in the world. If they can't, you can send it yourself, through UPS (✆ **800/742-5877**), FedEx (✆ **800/463-3339**), or the U.S. Postal Service.

SHOPPING A TO Z

Antiques

Jackson Square, a historic district just north of the Financial District's Embarcadero Center, is the place to go for the top names in fine furniture and fine art. More than a dozen dealers on the 2 blocks between Columbus and Sansome streets specialize in European furnishings from the 17th to the 19th centuries. Most shops here are open Monday through Friday from 9am to 5pm and Saturday from 11am to 4pm.

Bonhams & Butterfields   This renowned auction house holds preview weekends for upcoming auctions of furnishings, silver, antiques, art, and jewelry. Call for auction schedules. 220 San Bruno Ave. (at 16th St.). ✆ **800/223-2854** or 415/861-7500. www.bonhams.com/us.

Therien & Co.   For the best in Scandinavian, French, and eastern European antiques, head beyond SoMa's design center to this boutique, where you can find the real thing or antique replicas, as well as made-to-order furniture from their neighboring custom furniture shop. 411 Vermont St. (at 17th St.). ✆ **415/956-8850.** www. therien.com.

Art

The *San Francisco Bay Area Gallery Guide,* a comprehensive, bimonthly publication listing the city's current shows, is available free by mail. Send a self-addressed, stamped envelope to San Francisco Bay Area Gallery Guide, 1369 Fulton St., San Francisco, CA 94117 (✆ **415/921-1600**); or pick one up at the San Francisco Visitor Information Center at 900 Market St. Most of the city's major art galleries are clustered downtown in the Union Square area.

Catharine Clark Gallery ✦   Catharine Clark is a different kind of gallery experience. Although many galleries focus on established artists and out-of-this-world prices, Catharine's exhibits works by up-and-coming contemporary as well as established artists (mainly from California). It nurtures beginning collectors by offering a purchasing plan that's almost unheard of in the art business. You can buy a piece on layaway and take up to a year to pay for it—interest free! Prices here make art a realistic purchase for almost everyone for a change, but serious collectors also frequent the shows because Clark has such a keen eye for talent. Shows change every 6 weeks. Open Tuesday through Friday 10:30am to 5:30pm and Saturday 11am to 5:30pm. Closed Sunday and Monday. 150 Minna St., ground floor (btw. Third and New Montgomery sts.). ℰ **415/399-1439.** www.cclarkgallery.com.

Fraenkel Gallery   This photography gallery features works by contemporary American and European artists. Excellent shows change every 2 months. Open Tuesday through Friday 10:30am to 5:30pm and Saturday 11am to 5pm. Closed Sunday and Monday. 49 Geary St. (btw. Grant Ave. and Kearny St.), 4th floor. ℰ **415/981-2661.** www.fraenkelgallery.com.

Hang 🖌   Check out this amazingly affordable gallery for attractive pieces by yet-to-be-discovered Bay Area artists. The staff is friendly and helpful, and the gallery is designed to cater to new and seasoned collectors who appreciate original art at down-to-earth prices. 567 Sutter St. ℰ **415/434-4264.** www.hangart.com.

Images of the North   The highlight here is one of the most extensive collections of Canadian and Alaskan Inuit art in the United States. There's also a small collection of Native American masks and jewelry. Open Tuesday through Saturday 11am to 5:30pm and by appointment. 2036 Union St. (at Buchanan St.). ℰ **415/673-1273.** www.imagesnorth.com.

Meyerovich Gallery   Paintings, sculptures, and works on paper here are by modern and contemporary masters, including Chagall, Matisse, Miró, and Picasso. Meyerovich's new Contemporary Gallery, across the hall, features works by Lichtenstein, Stella, Motherwell, Dine, and Hockney. Open Monday through Friday 10:30am to 6:30pm and Saturday 10:30am to 5:30pm. Closed Sunday. 251 Post St. (at Stockton St.), 4th floor. ℰ **415/421-7171.** www.meyerovich.com.

Body Products

Showroom by In Fiore 🎁   I'm totally addicted to In Fiore—a high end line of body balms, oils, perfumes, and facial serums—so I was especially thrilled when San Francisco–based founder Julie Elliott opened her by-appointment-only shop in what she calls the "Tender Nob" (on the border of Nob Hill and the Tenderloin near Union Sq). Come here to check out her whole line, as well as limited-edition balms, and see why celebrities like Julia Roberts and Meg Ryan are fans. Open Tuesday through Saturday and by appointment only. 868 Post St. (btw. Leavenworth and Hyde sts.). ℰ **415/928-5661.** www.infiore.net.

Books

Book Passage   If you're moseying through the Ferry Building Marketplace, drop into this cozy independent that emphasizes (for tourists and locals alike) local travel, boating on the bay, food, cooking, sustainable agriculture and ecology, fiction, culinary and regional history and literature, and photo and gift books about the Bay Area. The store also hosts lots of author events: Check their website for details. Ferry Bldg. Marketplace (at the Embarcadero and Market St.). ℰ **415/835-1020.** www.bookpassage.com.

The Booksmith   Haight Street's best selection of new books is in this large, well-maintained shop. It carries all the top titles, along with works from smaller presses, and more than 1,000 different magazines. 1644 Haight St. (btw. Clayton and Cole sts.). ℰ **800/493-7323** or 415/863-8688. www.booksmith.com.

City Lights Booksellers & Publishers 🎁   Brooding literary types browse this famous bookstore owned by Lawrence Ferlinghetti, the renowned Beat Generation poet. The three-level bookshop prides itself on a comprehensive

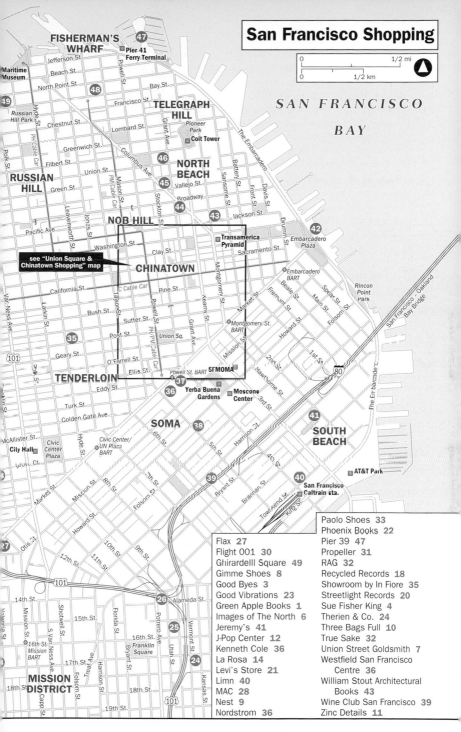

San Francisco Shopping

FISHERMAN'S WHARF
47 Pier 41 Ferry Terminal
Jefferson St.
Beach St.
Maritime Museum
North Point St.
49
48
Russian Hill Park
Chestnut St.
Francisco St.
Bay St.
TELEGRAPH HILL
Pioneer Park
Coit Tower
Lombard St.
Greenwich St.
46 NORTH BEACH
45 Vallejo St.
RUSSIAN HILL
Green St.
Broadway
44
43 Jackson St.
NOB HILL
Washington St.
Transamerica Pyramid
42 Embarcadero Plaza
Clay St.
Sacramento St.
see "Union Square & Chinatown Shopping" map
CHINATOWN
Embarcadero BART
California St.
Pine St.
Rincon Point Park
Bush St.
Sutter St.
Post St.
Union Sq.
Montgomery St. BART
35
Geary St.
O'Farrell St.
80
TENDERLOIN
Ellis St.
Powell St. BART
SFMOMA
37
36 Yerba Buena Gardens
Moscone Center
Eddy St.
Turk St.
Golden Gate Ave.
SOMA
38
41 SOUTH BEACH
McAllister St.
Civic Center Plaza
City Hall
Civic Center/ UN Plaza BART
39
40 San Francisco Caltrain sta.
AT&T Park
MISSION DISTRICT

SAN FRANCISCO BAY

Flax 27
Flight 001 30
Ghirardelll Square 49
Gimme Shoes 8
Good Byes 3
Good Vibrations 23
Green Apple Books 1
Images of The North 6
Jeremy's 41
J-Pop Center 12
Kenneth Cole 36
La Rosa 14
Levi's Store 21
Limn 40
MAC 28
Nest 9
Nordstrom 36

Paolo Shoes 33
Phoenix Books 22
Pier 39 47
Propeller 31
RAG 32
Recycled Records 18
Showroom by In Fiore 35
Streetlight Records 20
Sue Fisher King 4
Therien & Co. 24
Three Bags Full 10
True Sake 32
Union Street Goldsmith 7
Westfield San Francisco Centre 36
William Stout Architectural Books 43
Wine Club San Francisco 39
Zinc Details 11

247

collection of art, poetry, and political paperbacks, as well as more mainstream books. Open daily until midnight. 261 Columbus Ave. (at Broadway). ℭ **415/362-8193.** www.citylights.com.

Green Apple Books  The local favorite for used books, Green Apple is crammed with titles—more than 60,000 new and 100,000 used books and DVDs. Its extended sections in psychology, cooking, art, and history; collection of modern first editions; and rare graphic comics are superseded only by the staff's superlative service. *Note:* There's a separate music, fiction, and DVD annex next door. 506 Clement St. (at Sixth Ave.). ℭ **415/387-2272.** www.greenapplebooks.com.

Phoenix Books  One of the city's most beloved independent bookstores, Phoenix recently moved to a bigger space in Noe Valley, giving loyal customers, many of whom are toddlers, a little more breathing room. New and used books share equal billing on the well-stocked shelves, so check the inside covers for discounted prices before you pay full retail. The large sales tables offer real bargains—even on bestsellers—and if you're not sure what you want, the fabulously well-informed staff will guide you to their current favorites. 3957 24th St. (btw. Church and Sanchez sts.). ℭ **415/821-3477.** www.dogearedbooks.com.

William Stout Architectural Books  Step inside this shrine to all things architectural, and even if you think you're not interested in exquisite bathrooms, Southern California's modern homes, or great gardens, you can't help but bury yourself in the thousands of design books. An expansion to a second level means that if they don't have what you're looking for, it probably doesn't exist. *Tip:* There's also a new, small outpost inside the California Historical Society, located at Mission and Third streets. 804 Montgomery St. (at Jackson St.). ℭ **415/391-6757.** www.stoutbooks.com.

China, Silver & Glass

Gump's  Founded over a century ago, this San Francisco retail institution offers gifts and treasures ranging from Asian antiquities to contemporary art glass and exquisite jade and pearl jewelry. Many items are made specifically for the store. Gump's also has one of the city's most revered holiday window displays and is hugely popular for wedding registries (and don't they know it). 135 Post St. (btw. Kearny St. and Grant Ave.). ℭ **800/766-7628** or 415/982-1616. www.gumps.com.

Crafts

The Canton Bazaar Amid a wide variety of handicrafts, here you'll find an excellent selection of rosewood and carved furniture, cloisonné enamelware, porcelain, carved jade, embroideries, jewelry, and antiques from mainland China. Open daily until 10pm. 616 Grant Ave. (btw. Sacramento and California sts.). ℭ **415/362-5750.** www. cantonbazaar.com.

Try Gump's department store near Union Square for designer home goods.

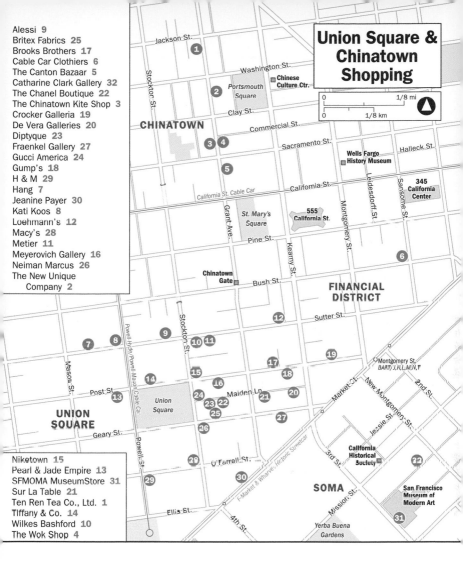

Alessi **9**
Britex Fabrics **25**
Brooks Brothers **17**
Cable Car Clothiers **6**
The Canton Bazaar **5**
Catharine Clark Gallery **32**
The Chanel Boutique **22**
The Chinatown Kite Shop **3**
Crocker Galleria **19**
De Vera Galleries **20**
Diptyque **23**
Fraenkel Gallery **27**
Gucci America **24**
Gump's **18**
H & M **29**
Hang **7**
Jeanine Payer **30**
Kati Koos **8**
Loehmann's **12**
Macy's **28**
Metier **11**
Meyerovich Gallery **16**
Neiman Marcus **26**
The New Unique
   Company **2**

Niketown **15**
Pearl & Jade Empire **13**
SFMOMA MuseumStore **31**
Sur La Table **21**
Ten Ren Tea Co., Ltd. **1**
Tiffany & Co. **14**
Wilkes Bashford **10**
The Wok Shop **4**

The New Unique Company   Primarily a calligraphy- and watercolor-sup-
plies store, this shop also has a good assortment of books on these topics. In addition, there's a wide selection of carved stones for use as seals on letters and
documents. Should you want a special design or group of initials, the store will
carve seals to order. 838 Grant Ave. (btw. Clay and Washington sts.). ℂ **415/981-2036.**
www.newunique.com.

Department Stores (Downtown)

Bloomingdale's   This massive 338,550-square-foot department store is the
anchor of the Westfield San Francisco Centre at Fifth and Market streets. See
"Shopping Centers & Complexes" on p. 260. It's the largest Bloomies outside of
New York's flagship 59th Street store, and even sports the same black-and-white

polished checkerboard marble. It's owned by the same company that runs Macy's, but fashions—for both men and women—tend to be more high-end and forward. Highlights include '60s-inspired fashions by Biba, knitwear by Sonia Rykiel, handbags by Louis Vuitton, and absurdly expensive shoes by Jimmy Choo. 845 Market St. (at Fifth St.). ℰ **415/856-5300.** www.bloomingdales.com.

Macy's   The seven-story Macy's West features contemporary fashions for women, juniors, and children, plus jewelry, fragrances, cosmetics, and accessories. The sixth floor offers a "hospitality suite" where visitors can leave their coats and packages, grab a cup of coffee, or find out more about the city from the concierge. The top floors contain home furnishings, and the Cellar sells kitchenware and gourmet foods. You'll even find a Boudin Cafe (though the food is not as good compared to their food at other locations) and a Wolfgang Puck Cafe on the premises. Across the street, Macy's East has five floors of men's fashions. Stockton and O'Farrell sts., Union Sq. ℰ **415/397-3333.**

Neiman Marcus   Some call this Texas-based chain "Needless Mark-ups." But those who can afford the best of everything can't deny that the men's and women's clothes, precious gems, and conservative formalwear are some of the most glamorous in town. The Rotunda Restaurant, located on the fourth floor, is a beautiful place for lunch and afternoon tea that was recently renovated along with the rest of the store. 150 Stockton St. (btw. Geary and O'Farrell sts.), Union Sq. ℰ **415/362-3900.**

Nordstrom   Located in the newly renovated San Francisco Shopping Centre, Nordstrom is renowned for its personalized service. Equally devoted to women's and men's fashions, the store has one of the best shoe selections in the city and thousands of suits in stock. The Bistro, on the fourth floor, has a panoramic view and is ideal for an inexpensive lunch or light snack. Spa Nordstrom, on the fifth floor, is the perfect place to relax after a hectic day of bargain hunting. 865 Market St. (at Fifth St.). ℰ **415/243-8500.**

Discount Shopping

Burlington Coat Factory   As its name hints, you'll find hundreds of coats here—from cheapies to designer—as well as men's and women's clothing, shoes, and accessories. These items will particularly come in handy for those visitors who don't heed our advice and pack a parka for July travel (one of the unexpectedly chilliest months in the Bay Area). But the best deal is the home section, where designer bedding, bath accessories, and housewares go for a fraction of their normal retail prices. 899 Howard St. (at Fifth St.). ℰ **415/495-7234.** www.coat.com.

Jeremys ✦   This boutique is a serious mecca for fashion hounds thanks to the wide array of top designer fashions, from shoes to suits, at rock-bottom prices. There are no cheap knockoffs here, just good men's and women's clothes and accessories that the owner scoops up from major retailers—last season's items and overruns to sale samples and returns. 2 S. Park (btw. Bryant and Brannan sts. at Second St.). ℰ **415/882-4929.** www.jeremys.com.

Loehmann's   San Francisco's branch of Loehmann's—the nation's only upscale off-price specialty retailer—caters to a sophisticated white-collar crowd, offering professional clothing, shoes, and accessories at bargain prices. Be sure to check out the Back Room, where designer clothes are sold for 30% to 65% less than the Union Square department stores. ***Note:*** There's a separate men's store

at 211 Sutter St. 222 Sutter St. (btw. Kearny St. and Grant Ave.). ℂ **415/982-3215.** www.
loehmanns.com.

Fabrics

Britex Fabrics   A San Francisco institution since 1952 and newly renovated,
Britex offers an absurd quantity and variety of fabrics, lace, ribbons, and trims—
four floors in all. The top floor is for bargains and remnants; the third floor houses
more than 40,000 buttons. Closed Sundays. 146 Geary St. (btw. Stockton and Grant
sts.). ℂ **415/392-2910.** www.britexfabrics.com.

Fashion

See also "Vintage Clothing," later in this section.

MEN'S FASHIONS

Brooks Brothers   In San Francisco, this bulwark of tradition is 1 block east
of Union Square. Brooks Brothers introduced the button-down collar and single-
handedly changed the standard of the well-dressed businessman. The multilevel
shop also sells traditional casual wear, including sportswear, sweaters, and shirts.
150 Post St. (at Grant Ave.). ℂ **415/397-4500.** www.brooksbrothers.com.

Cable Car Clothiers   Dapper men head to this fashion institution for traditional attire, such as three-button suits with natural shoulders, Aquascutum
coats, McGeorge sweaters, and Atkinson ties. Closed Sundays. 200 Bush St. (at
Sansome St.). ℂ **415/397-4740.** www.cablecarclothiers.com.

The Levi's Store   Levi's Castro shop is geared for the boys, with a tasteful
array of jeans, jean jackets, boots, and everything in between—plus some witty
touches like the handlebar moustaches on the mannequins and a poster that
gives an eyeful of beefcake bottom en route to the changing rooms. 525 Castro St.
(btw. 18th and 19th sts.). ℂ **415/255-6726.**

UNISEX

A-B Fits   This North Beach boutique is the place to pop in for jeans to
fit all shapes, styles, and sizes, as well
as smart and sassy contemporary wear
for gals and guys on the go. The snugly
fitting stock with over 100 styles of
jeans and pants ranges from Chip &
Pepper, Earnest Sewn, Edwin, Notify,
and Rogan, to chic wear from the likes
of Twelfth Street by Cynthia Vincent,
Ya-Ya, and Twinkle by Wenlan. 1519
Grant Ave. (at Union and Filbert sts.).
ℂ **415/982-5726.** www.abfits.com.

Gucci America   Donning Gucci's
golden Gs is not a cheap endeavor. But
if you've got the cash, you'll find all the
latest lines of shoes, leather goods,
scarves, and pricey accessories here,

A mannequin at the Levi's Store in the Castro.

such as a $9,000 handmade crocodile bag. 240 Stockton St. (btw. Geary and Post sts.).
© **415/392-2808.** www.gucci.com.

H & M   This ever-trendy and cheap Swedish clothing chain opened in Union Square at the end of 2004 and had lines out the door all through the holiday season—and not just for their collection by Stella McCartney. Drop in anytime for trendy cuts and styles sure to satisfy the hip him and her along on the trip. 150 Powell St. (btw. Ellis and O'Farrell sts.). © **415/986-4215.** www.hm.com/us.

MAC 🎁   No, we're not talking cosmetics. The more-modern-than-corporate stock at this hip and hidden shop (Modern Appealing Clothing) just combined its men's and women's fashion meccas in a new space in oh-so-trendy Hayes Valley. Drop in for men's imported tailored suits and women's separates in new and intriguing fabrics as well as gorgeous ties, vibrant sweaters, and a few choice home accouterments. Lines include Belgium's Dries Van Noten and Martin Margiela, New York's John Bartlett, and local sweater sweetheart Laurie B. The best part? Prices are more reasonable than at many of the trendy clothing stores in the area. 387 Grove St. (at Gough St.). © **415/863-3011.**

Niketown   Here it's not "I can," but "I can spend." At least that's what the kings of sportswear were banking on when they opened this megastore in 1997. As you'd expect, inside the doors shoppers find themselves in a Nike world offering everything the merchandising team could create. 278 Post St. (at Stockton St.). © **415/392-6453.** http://store.nike.com.

Three Bags Full   Snuggling up in a cozy sweater can be a fashionable event if you do your shopping at this pricey boutique, which carries the gamut in handmade, playful, and extravagant knitwear. 3314 Sacramento St. (at Presidio Ave.). © **415/923-1454.** www.threebagsfull.com.

Wilkes Bashford 🎁   Wilkes Bashford, who recently staved off closure by merging with an East Coast retail chain, is one of the most expensive and best-known clothing stores in the city. In its 4-plus decades in business, the boutique has garnered a reputation for stocking only the finest clothes in the world (which can often be seen on former and current mayors, and the city's social elite). Most fashions come from Italy and France; they include women's designer sportswear and couture and men's Kiton and Brioni suits (at $2,500 and up, they're considered the most expensive suits in the world). Closed Sundays. 375 Sutter St. (at Stockton St.). © **415/986-4380.** www.wilkesbashford.com.

WOMEN'S FASHIONS

Ambiance   This chain of Bay Area boutiques is laden with designer wear, often found at heavily discounted prices. On my last visit, I left with a knockout BCBG dress and a Diane von Furstenberg shift marked down to just $100, an absolute steal. Other labels commonly found on the racks include Tibi, Milly, and Nanette Lepore. There are also inexpensive jewelry bins by the counter that are worth a glance. *Just be wary:* The shop girls are extremely good at their jobs, and you'll often walk out with far more than you intended to buy. 1458 Haight St. © **415/552-5095.** Additional locations are at 3985–3989 24th St. (© **415/647-7144**) and 1858–1864 Union St. (© **415/923-9797**). www.ambiancesf.com.

The Chanel Boutique   Ever fashionable and expensive, Chanel is appropriately located on Maiden Lane, the quaint downtown side street where the most exclusive stores and spas cluster. You'll find here what you'd expect from Chanel:

clothing, accessories, scents, cosmetics, and jewelry. 155 Maiden Lane (btw. Stockton St. and Grant Ave.). ✆ **510/478-7622.** www.chanel.com.

emily lee   More mature fashionistas head to the quaint shopping area of Laurel Village, a block-long strip mall of shops that includes emily lee, for everything from artsy-designer garb to sportswear—all stylish, sensible, and loose fitting. Designers include the likes of Blanque, Eileen Fisher, Flax, Ivan Grundahl, and Three Dots. 3509 California St. (at Locust St.). ✆ **415/751-3443.**

Métier 🎁   Discerning and well-funded shoppers consider this the best women's clothing shop in town. Within its walls you'll find classic, sophisticated, and expensive creations, which include European ready-to-wear lines and designers: fashions by Italian designers Anna Molinari, Hache, and Blumarine, and by French designer Martine Sitbon. You will also find a distinguished collection of antique-style, high-end jewelry from L.A.'s Cathy Waterman, as well as ultra-popular custom-designed poetry jewelry by Jeanine Payer. Closed Sunday. 355 Sutter St. (btw. Stockton and Grant sts.). ✆ **415/989-5395.** www.metiersf.com.

RAG 🎁   If you want to add some truly unique San Francisco designs to your closet, head to RAG, or Residents Apparel Gallery, a co-op shop where around 55 local emerging designers showcase their latest creations. Prices are great; fashions are forward, young, and hip; and if you grab a few pieces, no one at home's going to be able to copy your look. 541 Octavia St. (btw. Hayes and Grove sts.). ✆ **415/621-7718.** www.ragsf.com.

Food

Boulangerie 🎁   A bit of Paris on Pine Street, this true blue bakery sells authentically French creations, from delicious and slightly sour French country wheat bread to rustic-style desserts, including the locally famous cannelés de Bordeaux, custard baked in a copper mold. And if you're looking for a place to eat Boulangerie bread and pastries, visit their cafes—Boulange de Polk, at 2300 Polk St. near Green Street (✆ 415/345-1107); Boulange de Cole, at 1000 Cole St. at Parnassus Street (✆ 415/242-2442); or Boulange de Noe, 3898 24th St. (✆ 415/821-1050). 2325 Pine St. (at Fillmore St.). ✆ **415/440-0356,** ext. 204. www.laboulangebakery.com.

Cowgirl Creamery Cheese Shop 🎁   San Francisco is fanatical about cheese, and much of the local enthusiasm can be attributed to the two women who created the small-production Cowgirl Creamery up in Point Reyes. Their city outpost is located in the Ferry Building Marketplace and offers all their signature cheeses—robust Red Hawk to smooth, creamy Mt. Tam. Here's how you do it: Sample a few, buy a hefty slice of your favorite cheese, and then enjoy it on the waterfront with some crusty Acme Bread and a piece of fruit from Capay Farms (all within the same building). Ferry Bldg. Marketplace, no. 17. ✆ **415/362-9354.** www.cowgirlcreamery.com.

Ferry Building Marketplace 🎁   A one-stop shop for some of the city's finest edibles, the renovated historic Ferry Building is home to the revered Acme Bread Company, Scharffen Berger Chocolate, the Imperial Tea Court, Peet's Coffee, Cowgirl Creamery Cheese Shop (see above), Recchiuti Confections, and more. There's no better place to load up on the Bay Area's outstanding bounty. Ferry Bldg. Plaza (at the foot of Market St. at the Embarcadero). ✆ **415/983-8030.** www.ferrybuildingmarketplace.com.

amazing **GRAZING**

There's no better way to spend a sunny Saturday morning in San Francisco than to stroll the **Ferry Building Marketplace** and **Farmers' Market,** snacking your way through some of America's finest organic produce—it's one of the most highly acclaimed farmers' markets in the United States. While foraging among the dozens of stalls crammed with Northern California fruit, vegetables, bread, shellfish, and dairy items, you're bound to bump elbows with the dozens of Bay Area chefs who do their shopping here. The enthusiastic vendors are always willing to educate visitors about the pleasures of organic produce and often provide free samples. It's a unique opportunity for city dwellers to buy freshly picked organic produce directly from small family-operated farms.

On Saturday mornings the market is in its full glory. Nearly the entire building is enrobed with local meat ranchers, artisan cheese makers, bread bakers, specialty food purveyors, and farmers. On Saturdays, make sure you arrive by 10:30am to watch Meet the Farmer, a half-hour interview with one of the farmers, food artisans, or other purveyors who give the audience in-depth information about how and where their food is produced. Then, at 11am, Bay Area chefs give cooking demonstrations using ingredients purchased that morning from the market. (You get to taste their creations, then leave with the recipe in hand.) Several local restaurants also have food stalls selling their cuisine—including breakfast items—so don't eat before you arrive. You can also pick up locally made vinegars, preserves, herbs, and oils, which make wonderful gifts.

If you decide you want a local foodie to lead you on a culinary excursion of the Marketplace and Farmers' Market, my friend Lisa Rogovin, an "Epicurean Concierge" and founder of **In the Kitchen with Lisa,** offers guided culinary excursions. Some of Lisa's top noshing tips include:

Ten Ren Tea Co., Ltd. 🎁 At the Ten Ren Tea Co. shop, you will be offered a steaming cup of tea when you walk in the door. In addition to a selection of almost 50 traditional and herbal teas, the company stocks a collection of cold tea drinks, tea-related paraphernalia such as pots, cups, and infusers, and pearl, tapioca, and bubble tea. If you can't make up your mind, take home a mail-order form. The shop is open daily from 9am to 9pm. 949 Grant Ave. (btw. Washington and Jackson sts.). ✆ **415/362-0656.** www.tenren.com.

Gifts

Art of China Amid a wide variety of collectibles, this shop features exquisite, hand-carved Chinese figurines. You'll also find a lovely assortment of ivory beads, bracelets, necklaces, and earrings. Pink-quartz dogs, jade figurines, porcelain vases, cache pots, and blue-and-white barrels suitable for use as table bases are just some of the many items stocked here. 839–843 Grant Ave. (btw. Clay and Washington sts.). ✆ **415/981-1602.** www.artsofchinasf.com.

Cost Plus World Market At the Fisherman's Wharf cable car turntable, Cost Plus is a vast warehouse crammed to the rafters with Chinese baskets, Indian camel bells, Malaysian batik scarves, and innumerable other items from

- Mortgage Lifter heirloom tomatoes dipped in special Rosemary Salt from **Eatwell Farm**

- Creamy and sweet Barhi dates from **Flying Disk Ranch,** spread on an épi baguette from **Acme Bread Company** with a touch of fresh Panir cheese from **Cowgirl Creamery**

- Whatever's in season at **Hamada Farms,** such as their Tahitian pomelos and Oro Blanco grapefruits

- Fleur de Sel chocolates at **Recchiuti Confections**

- **Scharffen Berger**'s Bittersweet Mocha chocolate bars made with ground Sumatra coffee beans from Peet's Coffee & Tea

- Warm liquid Valrhona chocolate at **Boulette's Larder** (nirvana, she says)

For more information about Lisa's guided culinary tours, log on to her website at www.inthekitchenwithlisa. com, or call her at ℰ **415/806-5970.**

The Ferry Building Marketplace is open Monday through Friday from 10am to 6pm, Saturday from 9am to 6pm, and Sunday from 11am to 5pm. The Farmers' Market takes place year-round, rain or shine, every Tuesday 10am to 2pm and Saturday 8am to 2pm. The Ferry Building is located on the Embarcadero at the foot of Market Street (about a 15-min. walk from Fisherman's Wharf). Call ℰ **415/693-0996** for more information or log onto www. ferryplazafarmersmarket.com or www. ferrybuildingmarketplace.com.

Algeria to Zanzibar. More than 20,000 items from 50 nations, imported directly from their countries of origin, pack this warehouse. There's also a mammoth gourmet imports selection and a decent wine shop. It's open Monday through Saturday from 10am to 9pm and Sunday from 10am to 7pm. 2552 Taylor St. (btw. North Point and Bay sts.). ℰ **415/928-6200.** www.worldmarket.com.

Dandelion 🎁 Tucked in an out-of-the-way location in SoMa is the most wonderful collection of gifts, collectibles, and furnishings. There's something for every taste and budget here, from an excellent collection of teapots, decorative dishes, and gourmet foods to silver, books, cards, and picture frames. Don't miss the Zen-like second floor, with its peaceful furnishings in Indian, Japanese, and Western styles. The store is closed Sunday and Monday except during November and December, when it's open daily. Hours are 10am to 6pm. 55 Potrero Ave. (at Alameda St.). ℰ **415/436-9500.** www.dandelionsf.com.

Flax If you're the kind of person who goes into an art store for a special pencil and comes out $300 less later, don't go near this shop. Flax has everything you can think of in art and design supplies, an amazing collection of blank bound books, children's art supplies, frames, calendars—you name it. There's a gift for

Ceramic cattle heads from A&G Merch.

every type of person here, especially you. 1699 Market St. (at Valencia and Gough sts.). © **415/552-2355.** www.flaxart.com.

Good Vibrations A laypersons' sex-toy, book, and video emporium, Good Vibrations is a women-owned, worker-owned cooperative. Unlike most sex shops, it's not a back-alley business, but a straightforward shop with healthy, open attitudes about human sexuality. It also has a vibrator museum. 603 Valencia St. (at 17th St.). © **415/522-5460** or 800/BUY-VIBE (289-8423) for mail order. A 2nd location is at 1620 Polk St., at Sacramento St. (© **415/345-0400**), and a 3rd is at 899 Mission St., at 5th St. (© **415/513-1635**). www.goodvibes.com.

J-Pop Center Fans of manga, anime, and all things Japanese culture have a new mecca in the $15-million J-Pop Center (aka New People World), which offers five levels of J-awesomeness. The basement offers a THX-certified theater to showcase Japanese cinema; the first floor includes Blue Bottle coffee and Bentos snack shop; the main floor offers a New People shop that offers "all that is kawaii, fun, fabulous and bizarre"; second-floor shops include Baby the Stars Shine Bright and Black Peace Now; and the third level features Japanese artists at the Superfrog Gallery. 1746 Post St. (btw. Buchanan and Webster sts.). www.newpeople world.com.

Kati Koos Need a little humor in your life? Previously called Smile, this store specializes in whimsical art, furniture, one-of-a-kind clothing, jewelry, and American crafts guaranteed to make you grin. Closed Sunday. 500 Sutter St. (btw. Powell and Mason sts.). © **415/362-3437.** www.katikoos.com.

SFMOMA MuseumStore 🎁 With an array of artistic cards, books, jewelry, housewares, furniture, knickknacks, and creative tokens of San Francisco, it's virtually impossible not to find something here you'll consider a must-have. (Check out the FogDome!) Aside from being one of the locals' favorite shops, it offers far more tasteful mementos than most Fisherman's Wharf options. Open late (until 9:30pm) on Thursday nights. 151 Third St. (2 blocks south of Market St., across from Yerba Buena Gardens). © **415/357-4035.** www.sfmoma.org.

Housewares/Furnishings

A&G Merch Lion butt magnets, ceramic cattle heads, and bird pillows—oh my! This Brooklyn import, an offshoot brand of the pricier The Future Perfect, opened on Market in 2011 and mixes antique and modern sensibilities in a way that feels very San Francisco. We like their Altered Antique Plates, which feature images of *The Exorcist,* Mr. T, and Pee Wee Herman, among others. 2279 Market (btw. Sanchez and 16th sts.). ✆ 415/503-1173. www.aandgmerch.com.

Alessi   Italian designer Alberto Alessi, who's known for his whimsical and colorful kitchen-utensil designs, such as his ever-popular spiderlike lemon squeezer, opened a flagship store here. Drop by for everything from gorgeous stainless-steel double boilers to corkscrews shaped like maidens. 424 Sutter St. (at Stockton St.). ✆ 415/434-0403. www.alessi.com.

Biordi Art Imports 🎁   Whether you want to decorate your dinner table, color your kitchen, or liven up the living room, Biordi's Italian majolica pottery is the most exquisite and unusual way to do it. The owner has been importing these hand-painted collectibles for 60 years, and every piece is a showstopper. Call for a catalog. They'll ship anywhere. Closed Sundays. 412 Columbus Ave. (at Vallejo St.). ✆ 415/392-8096. www.biordi.com.

Diptyque   If the idea of spending $40 on a candle makes you laugh, this isn't the place for you. But if you're the type willing to throw down good money to "scentualize" your living space, don't skip this French shop offering dozens of spectacular flaming fragrances. I'm such a fan that every time I went to Paris I'd weigh down my luggage with these 50-hour burners (before the horrible exchange rate, that is). But now I can scoop them up in my own backyard. They also make great gifts. 171 Maiden Lane (near Stockton St.). ✆ 415/402-0600.

Limn   For the latest in Europe's trendsetting and ultramodern furniture and lighting, go straight to SoMa celebrity Limn, which also showcases artworks in its adjoining gallery. 290 Townsend St. (at Fourth St.). ✆ 415/543-5466. www.limn.com.

Nest 🎁   Don't come into Fillmore Street's cutest French interiors store without your credit cards. Nest carries adorable throws, handmade quilts, must-have slippers and sleepwear, and a number of other things you never knew you needed until now. 2300 Fillmore St. (at Clay St.). ✆ 415/292-6199. www.nestsf.com.

Propeller 🎁   This airy skylight lit shop is a must stop for lovers of the latest in über-modern furniture and home accessories. Owner/designer Lorn Dittfeld hand-picks pieces done by emerging designers from as far away as Sweden, Italy, and Canada as well as a plethora of national newbies. Drop in to lounge on the hippest sofas, grab pretty and practical gifts such as ultracool magnetic spice racks, or adorn your home with Bev Hisey's throws and graphic pillows, diamond-cut wood tables by William Earle, or hand-tufted graphic rugs by Angela Adams. 555 Hayes St. (btw. Laguna and Octavia sts.). ✆ 415/701-7767. www.propellermodern.com.

Propeller modern lighting.

Sue Fisher King 🎁   For sumptuous tablecloths, silk pillows, bed linens, and beyond, head to this exclusive neighborhood boutique known by the society set as the only home store to shop. It's filled with items like exquisite cashmere blankets, Turkish towels, china, silver flatware, Italian chandeliers, and more. Closed Sunday. 3067 Sacramento St. (at Baker St.). ℂ **415/922-7276.** www.suefisherking.com.

Sur La Table   Cooks should beeline it to this shop that specializes in all things culinary. Its floors are packed to the rafters with pricey but stylish high-quality pots and pans, utensils, tabletop items, books, and more coupled with an extremely helpful and knowledgeable staff. Ferry Bldg. Marketplace, stall #37. ℂ **415/262-9970.** A 2nd location is at 845 Market St., at the Cable Car Turnaround (ℂ **415/ 814-4691**). www.surlatable.com.

The Wok Shop   This shop has every conceivable implement for Chinese cooking, including woks, brushes, cleavers, circular chopping blocks, dishes, oyster knives, bamboo steamers, and strainers. It also sells a wide range of kitchen utensils, baskets, handmade linens from China, and aprons. 718 Grant Ave. (at Clay St.). ℂ **415/989-3797.** www.wokshop.com.

Zinc Details 🏮   This contemporary furniture and knickknack shop has received accolades everywhere from *Elle Decor Japan* to *Metropolitan Home* to *InStyle* for its amazing collection of locally crafted modern furniture, glass vases, pendant lights, rugs, wall coverings, and ceramics from all over the world. A portion of these true works of art is made specifically for the store. 1905 Fillmore St. (btw. Bush and Pine sts.). ℂ **415/776-2100.** www.zincdetails.com.

Jewelry

Dianne's Old & New Estates   Many local girls get engagement rings from this fantastic little shop featuring top-of-the-line antique jewelry—pendants, diamond rings, necklaces, bracelets, and pearls. For a special gift, check out the collection of platinum wedding and engagement rings and vintage watches. Don't worry if you can't afford it now—the shop offers 1-year interest-free layaway. And, if you buy a ring, they'll send you off with a thank-you bottle of celebration bubbly. 2181A Union St. (at Fillmore St.). ℂ **888/346-7525** or 415/346-7525. www. diannesestatejewelry.com.

Jeanine Payer   If you want to buy a trinket that is truly San Franciscan, stop by this boutique hidden on the street level of the beautifully ornate Phelan Building where designer Jeanine Payer showcases gorgeous, handmade contemporary jewelry that she crafts in sterling silver and 18-karat gold five stories above in her studio. All of her pieces, including fabulous baby gifts, feature her engraved poetry, which can even be customized. Celebrities such as Sheryl Crow, Debra Messing, and Ellen DeGeneres are fans. 762 Market St. (at O'Farrell St.). ℂ **866/359-3579.** www.jeaninepayer.com.

Tiffany & Co.   Even if you don't have lots of cash with which to buy an exquisite bauble that comes in Tiffany's famous light-blue box, you can enjoy this renowned store by window shopping—a la Audrey Hepburn in *Breakfast at Tiffany's*. The designer collection features Paloma Picasso, Jean Schlumberger, and Elsa Peretti in both silver and 18-karat gold, and there's an extensive gift collection in sterling, china, and crystal. 350 Post St. (at Powell St.). ℂ **415/781-7000.** www.tiffany.com.

Union Street Goldsmith   A showcase for Bay Area goldsmiths, this exquisite shop sells a contemporary collection of fine custom-designed jewelry in platinum and all karats of gold. Many pieces emphasize colored stones. 1909 Union St. (at Laguna St.). ℂ **415/776-8048.** www.unionstreetgoldsmith.com.

Amoeba Music.

Music

Amoeba Music   Don't be scared off by the tattooed, pierced, and fierce-looking employees (and other shoppers!) in this beloved new and used record store highlighting indie labels. They're actually more than happy to recommend some great music to you. If you're looking for the latest from Britney, this might not be the store for you (though they do have everything), but if you're into interesting music that's not necessarily on every station all the time, check this place out. You can buy, sell, and trade in this cavernous, loud Haight Street hot spot. Haight St. (btw. Shrader and Stanyan sts.). ℓ **415/831-1200.** A 2nd location is at 2455 Telegraph Ave. in Berkeley, at Haste St. (ℓ **510/549-1125**). www.amoeba.com.

Recycled Records 🎀   Easily one of the best used-record stores in the city, this loud shop in the Haight has cases of used "classic" rock LPs, sheet music, and tour programs. It's open from 10am to 8pm daily. 1377 Haight St. (btw. Central and Masonic sts.). ℓ **415/626-4075.** www.recycled-records.com.

Streetlight Records   Overstuffed with used music in all three formats, this place is best known for its records and excellent CD collection. It also carries new and used DVDs and computer games. Rock music is cheap (especially in the bargain bins—"Get the Knack" anyone?), and the money-back guarantee guards against defects. 2350 Market St. (btw. Castro and Noe sts.). ℓ **415/282-8000.** www.streetlightrecords.com.

Shoes

Bulo   If you have a fetish for foot fashions, you must check out Bulo, which carries nothing but imported Italian shoes. The selection is small but styles run the gamut, from casual to dressy, reserved to wildly funky. New shipments come in every 3 to 4 weeks, so the selection is ever-changing, eternally hip, and, unfortunately, ever-expensive, with many pairs going for close to $200. 418 Hayes St. ℓ **415/255-4939.** www.buloshoes.com.

Gimme Shoes   The staff is funky-fashion snobby, the prices are steep, and the European shoes and accessories are utterly chic. 2358 Fillmore St. (at Washington St.). ℓ **415/441-3040.** Additional location at 416 Hayes St. (ℓ **415/864-0691**). www.gimmeshoes.com.

Kenneth Cole   This trendy shop carries high-fashion footwear for men and women. There is also an innovative collection of handbags and small leather goods and accessories. 865 Market St. (in the San Francisco Shopping Centre). ℓ **415/227-4536.** www.kennethcole.com.

Paolo Shoes This Italian import store is run by owner Paolo Iantorno, who actually designs the shoes for his hipster shops. If gorgeous, handcrafted, colorful shoes are what you're looking for, this is the shop for you. You can get your low-heeled slip-ons here—this store features men's and women's footwear and bags—but they might be in silver python. Check out the men's perforated orange slip-ons—not for the faint of heart or fashion-modest. You might not even mind that many shoes are upwards of 200 bucks when you realize that Paolo's women's shoes are so sexy and comfortable, you won't want to take them off. 524 Hayes St. (℗**415/552-4580.** A 2nd location is at 2000 Fillmore St. ((℗ **415/771-1944**). www.paoloshoes.com.

Shopping Centers & Complexes

Crocker Galleria Modeled after Milan's Galleria Vittorio Emanuele, this glass-domed, three-level pavilion, about 3 blocks east of Union Square, features around 40 high-end shops with expensive and classic designer creations. Fashions include Aricie lingerie, Gianni Versace, and Polo/Ralph Lauren. Closed Sunday. 50 Post St. (at Kearny St.). (℗ **415/393-1505.** www.thecrockergalleria.com.

Ghirardelli Square This former chocolate factory is one of the city's quaintest shopping malls and most popular landmarks. It dates from 1864, when it served as a factory making Civil War uniforms, but it's best known as the former chocolate and spice factory of Domingo Ghirardelli (say "Gear-ar-dell-y"). A clock tower, an exact replica of the one at France's Château de Blois, crowns the complex. Inside the tower, on the mall's plaza level, is the fun Ghirardelli soda fountain. It still makes and sells small amounts of chocolate, but the big draw is the old-fashioned ice-cream parlor. Stores range from a children's club to a perfumery, cards and stationery to a doggie boutique. The main plaza shop and restaurant hours are 10am to 6pm Sunday through Thursday and 10am to 9pm Friday and Saturday, with extended hours during the summer. The square has recently undergone a major face-lift, which not only jazzed up its appearance a bit, but brought free Wi-Fi to the area. Along with elegant Vietnamese restaurant Ana Mandara (p. 137), there's now an English tea experience (Crown & Crumpet), wine bar (Cellar360), cupcake bakery, and more. 900 North Point St. (at Polk St.). (℗ **415/775-5500.** www.ghirardellisq.com.

Pier 39 ✋ This bayside tourist trap also happens to have stunning views. To residents, that pretty much wraps up Pier 39—an expensive spot where out-of-towners go to waste money on worthless souvenirs and greasy fast food. For vacationers, though, Pier 39 does have some redeeming qualities—fresh crab (in season), playful sea lions, phenomenal views, and plenty of fun for the kids. If you want to get to know the real San Francisco, skip the cheesy T-shirt shops and limit your time here to one afternoon, if at all. Located at Beach St. and the Embarcadero.

Westfield San Francisco Centre Opened in 1988 and given a $460-million expansion in 2006, this ritzy 1.5-million-square-foot urban shopping center is one of the few vertical malls (multilevel rather than sprawling) in the United States. Its most attractive feature is a spectacular atrium with a century-old dome that's 102 feet wide and three stories high. Along with Nordstrom (p. 250) and **Bloomingdale's** (p. 249) department stores and a Century Theatres multiplex, there are more than 170 specialty stores, including Abercrombie & Fitch, Herve Leger, bebe, Juicy Couture, and J. Crew. The bottom level is sprinkled with probably the best food-court fare you've ever had, along with a gourmet market and deli, and a fast-service (but not fast food) outlet for Charles Phan's Slanted Door, called Out the Door. 865 Market St. (at Fifth St.). (℗ **415/512-6776.** www.westfield.com/sanfrancisco.

Toys

The Chinatown Kite Shop   This shop's playful assortment of flying objects includes attractive fish kites, windsocks, hand-painted Chinese paper kites, wood-and-paper biplanes, pentagonal kites, and do-it-yourself kite kits, all of which make great souvenirs or decorations. Computer-designed stunt kites have two or four control lines to manipulate loops and dives. Open daily from 10am to 8pm. 717 Grant Ave. (btw. Clay and Sacramento sts.). ☏ **415/989-5182.** www.chinatownkite.com.

Travel Goods

Flight 001   Jet-setters zoom into this space-shuttle-like showroom for hip travel accessories. Check out the sleek luggage, "security friendly" manicure sets, and other mid-air must-haves. 525 Hayes St. (btw. Laguna and Octavia sts.). ☏ **415/487-1001.** A 2nd location is out in Berkeley at 1774 4th St. (☏ **510/526-1001**). www.flight001.com.

Vintage Clothing

Buffalo Exchange   This large and newly expanded storefront on upper Haight Street is crammed with racks of antique and new fashions from the 1960s, 1970s, and 1980s. It stocks everything from suits and dresses to neckties, hats, handbags, and jewelry. Buffalo Exchange anticipates some of the hottest new street fashions. 1555 Haight St. (btw. Clayton and Ashbury sts.). ☏ **415/431-7733.** A 2nd shop is at 1210 Valencia St., at 24th St. (☏ **415/647-8332**). www.buffaloexchange.com.

Good Byes 🎁   One of the best new- and used-clothes stores in San Francisco, Good Byes carries only high-quality clothing and accessories, including an exceptional selection of men's fashions at unbelievably low prices (for example, $350 pre-owned shoes for $35). Women's wear is in a separate boutique across the street. 3464 Sacramento St. and 3483 Sacramento St. (btw. Laurel and Walnut sts.). ☏ **415/346-6388** (men's) and **415/674-0151** (women's). www.goodbyessf.com.

Flight 001 specializes in stylish, travel-size items.

La Rosa   On a street packed with vintage-clothing shops, this is one of the more upscale options. Since 1978, it has featured a selection of high-quality, dry-cleaned secondhand goods. Formal suits and dresses are its specialty, but you'll also find sport coats, slacks, and shoes. The more moderately priced sister store, Held Over, is located at 1543 Haight St., near Ashbury (© **415/864-0818**), and their discount store, Clothes Contact, is located at 473 Valencia St., at 16th St. (© **415/621-3212**). 1711 Haight St. (at Cole St.). © **415/668-3744.**

Wine & Sake

True Sake   Amid woven sea grass flooring, colorful backlit displays, and a so-hip Hayes Valley location are more than 140 varieties of Japanese-produced sake ranging from an $8,300ml bottle of Ohyama to a $180,720ml bottle of Kotsu-zumi Rojohanaari—which, incidentally, owner Beau Timken (who is on hand to describe each wine) says is available at no other retail store in the U.S. 560 Hayes St. (btw. Laguna and Octavia sts.). © **415/355-9555.** www.truesake.com.

Wine Club San Francisco ✦   The Wine Club is a discount warehouse that offers bargains on more than 1,200 domestic and foreign wines. Bottles cost between $4 and $1,100. 953 Harrison St. (btw. Fifth and Sixth sts.). © **415/512-9086.** www.thewineclub.com.

SAN
FRANCISCO
AFTER DARK

9

F or a city with fewer than a million full-time inhabitants, San Francisco boasts an impressive after-dark scene. Dozens of piano bars and top-notch lounges augment a lively dance-club culture, and skyscraper lounges offer dazzling city views. The city's arts scene is also extraordinary: The opera is justifiably world renowned, the ballet is on its toes, and theaters are high in both quantity and quality. In short, there's always something going on in the city, and unlike in Los Angeles or New York, you don't have to pay outrageous cover charges or wait to be "picked" to be a part of the scene.

For up-to-date nightlife information, turn to the *San Francisco Weekly* (www. sfweekly.com) and the *San Francisco Bay Guardian* (www.sfbg.com), both of which run comprehensive listings. They are available for free at bars and restaurants and from street-corner boxes all around the city. *Where* (www.wheresf. com), a free tourist-oriented monthly, also lists programs and performance times; it's available in most of the city's finer hotels. The Sunday edition of the *San Francisco Chronicle* features a "Datebook" section, printed on pink paper, with information on and listings of the week's events. If you have Internet access, it's a good idea to check out www.citysearch.com or www.sfstation.com for the latest in bars, clubs, and events. And if you want to secure seats at a hot-ticket event, either buy well in advance or contact the concierge of your hotel and see if they can swing something for you.

Tix Bay Area (also known as **TIX;** ✆ **415/430-1140;** www.tixbayarea.org) sells half-price tickets on the day of performances and full-price tickets in advance to select Bay Area cultural and sporting events. TIX is also a Ticketmaster outlet and sells Gray Line tours and transportation passes. Tickets are primarily sold in person with some half-price tickets available on their website. To find out which shows have half-price tickets, call the TIX info line or check out their website. A service charge, ranging from $1.75 to $6, is levied on each ticket depending on its full price. You can pay with cash, traveler's checks, Visa, MasterCard, American Express, or Discover with photo ID. TIX, located on Powell Street between Geary and Post streets, is open Tuesday through Friday from 11am to 6pm, Saturday from 10am to 6pm, and Sunday from 10am to 3pm. *Note:* Half-price tickets go on sale at 11am.

You can also get tickets to most theater and dance events through **City Box Office,** 180 Redwood St., Ste. 100, between Golden Gate and McAllister streets off Van Ness Avenue (✆ **415/392-4400;** www.cityboxoffice.com). MasterCard and Visa are accepted.

Tickets.com (✆ **800/225-2277;** www.tickets.com) sells computer-generated tickets (with a hefty service charge of $3–$19 per ticket!) to concerts, sporting events, plays, and special events. **Ticketmaster** (✆ **415/421-TIXS** [8497];

PREVIOUS PAGE: **Alembic owner Daniel Hyatt pours you a cocktail.**

www.ticketmaster.com) also offers advance ticket purchases (also with a service charge).

For information on local theater, check out www.theatrebayarea.org. For information on major league baseball, pro basketball, pro and college football, and horse racing, see "Spectator Sports" in chapter 6, p. 222.

And don't forget that this isn't New York: Bars close at 2am, so get an early start if you want a full night on the town in San Francisco.

THE PERFORMING ARTS

Special concerts and performances take place in San Francisco year-round. **San Francisco Performances,** 500 Sutter St., Ste. 710 (𝒸 **415/398-6449;** www.performances.org), has brought acclaimed artists to the Bay Area for more than 30 years. Shows run the gamut from chamber music to dance to jazz. Performances are in several venues, including the Herbst Theater and the Yerba Buena Center for the Arts. The season runs from late September to June. Tickets cost from $12 to $50 and are available through **City Box Office** (𝒸 **415/392-4400)** or through the San Francisco Performances website.

Classical Music

Philharmonia Baroque Orchestra This orchestra of baroque, classical, and "early Romantic" music performs in San Francisco and all around the Bay Area. The season lasts September through April. Performances are in Herbst Theater, 401 Van Ness Ave. Tickets are sold through City Box Office, 𝒸 **415/392-4400** (box office), or call 252-1288 (administrative offices). www.philharmonia.org. Tickets $30–$75.

San Francisco Symphony Founded in 1911, the internationally acclaimed San Francisco Symphony has long been an important part of the city's cultural life under such legendary conductors as Pierre Monteux and Seiji Ozawa. In 1995, Michael Tilson Thomas took over from Herbert Blomstedt; he has led the orchestra to new heights and crafted an exciting repertoire of classical and modern music. The season runs September through June. Summer symphony activities include a Summer Festival and a Summer in the City series. Tickets are very hard to come by, but if you're desperate, you can usually pick up a few outside the hall the night of the concert. Also, the box office occasionally has a few last-minute tickets. Performing at Davies Symphony Hall, 201 Van Ness Ave. (at Grove St.). 𝒸 **415/864-6000** (box office). www.sfsymphony.org. Tickets $25–$114.

Opera

In addition to San Francisco's major opera company, you might check out the amusing **Pocket Opera,** 469 Bryant St. (𝒸 **415/972-8930;** www.pocketopera.org). From early March to mid-July, the comic company stages farcical performances of well-known operas in English. The staging is intimate and informal, without lavish costumes and sets. The cast ranges from 3 to 16 players, supported by a chamber orchestra. The rich repertoire includes such works as *Don Giovanni, The Barber of Seville,* and over 80 other operas. Performances are Friday at 7:30pm, throughout the day on Saturday, and Sunday at 2pm. Call the box office for complete information, location (which varies), and showtimes. Tickets cost from $20 (students) to $37.

San Francisco Opera The San Francisco Opera was the second municipal opera in the United States and is one of the city's cultural icons. Brilliantly

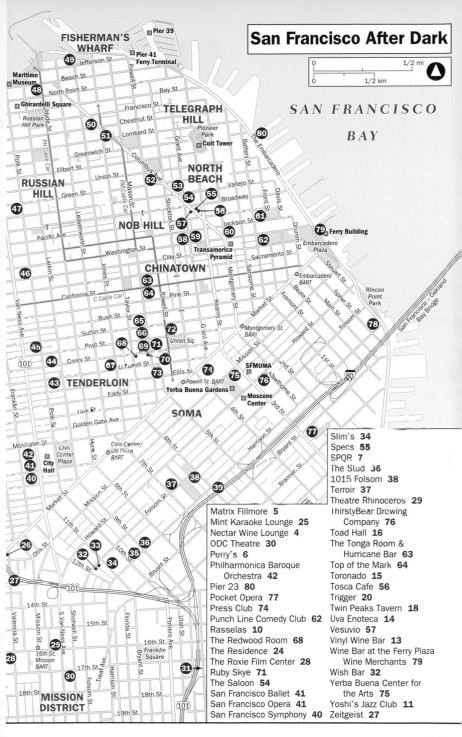

San Francisco After Dark

FISHERMAN'S WHARF

Pier 39
Pier 41 Ferry Terminal

Maritimo Museum **48**

Ghirardelli Square

Russian Hill Park

49 Jefferson St.
Beach St.
North Point St.
Bay St.
Francisco St.
Chestnut St.
Lombard St.

50
51

Greenwich St.
Union St.
Filbert St.
Green St.

TELEGRAPH HILL

Pioneer Park
Coit Tower

NORTH BEACH

52
53
54 **55** Broadway
56

80

SAN FRANCISCO

BAY

RUSSIAN HILL
47

NOB HILL

57
58 **59** **60**
Transamerica Pyramid

61
62

79 Ferry Building
Embarcadero Plaza

Pacific Ave.
Washington St.
Clay St.
Sacramento St.

CHINATOWN

46

California St.
C Cable Car
Pine St.
Bush St.
Sutter St.
Post St.
Geary St.

63
64

Embarcadero BART

Beale St.
Fremont St.
Main St.
Spear St.
Steuart St.

Rincon Point Park

San Francisco–Oakland Bay Bridge

45
44

65
66 **72**
68 **69** **71**
70

Montgomery St. BART
Union Sq.

Montgomery St. BARI

Howard St.
Folsom St.

78

TENDERLOIN
43

67 O'Farrell St.
Ellis St.
73

74 **75** SFMOMA
Moscone Center

Powell St. BART
Yerba Buena Gardens

Eddy St.
Turk St.
Golden Gate Ave.

SOMA

42
41 City Hall
40

Civic Center/ UN Plaza BART

Market St.
Mission St.
Folsom St.

Harrison St.
Bryant St.
Brannan St.

77

26
27

33
32 **34** **35** **36**

Otis St.

101

29
28
30

16th St. Mission BART
Franklin Square

31

MISSION DISTRICT

balanced casts may feature celebrated stars like Frederica Von Stade and Plácido Domingo along with promising newcomers and regular members in productions that range from traditional to avant-garde. All productions have English supertitles. The season starts in September, lasts 14 weeks, takes a break for a few months, and then picks up again in June and July. During the interim winter period, future opera stars are featured in showcases and recitals. Performances are held most evenings, except Monday, with matinees on Sunday. Tickets go on sale as early as June for subscribers and August for the general public, and the best seats sell out quickly. Some less coveted seats are usually available until curtain time. War Memorial Opera House,

The San Francisco Opera House.

301 Van Ness Ave. (at Grove St.). *C* **415/864-3330** (box office). www.sfopera.com. Tickets $15–$250; standing room $10 cash only; student rush $15 cash only.

Theater

American Conservatory Theater (A.C.T.) 🎁 The Tony Award–winning American Conservatory Theater made its debut in 1967 and quickly established itself as the city's premier resident theater group and one of the nation's best. Numerous big-name actors have tread the boards here, including Annette Bening and Nicolas Cage. The A.C.T. season runs September through July and features both classic and experimental works. Its home is the fabulous Geary Theater, a national historic landmark that is regarded as one of America's finest performance spaces. Performing at the Geary Theater, 415 Geary St. (at Mason St.). *C* **415/749-2ACT** (2228). www.act-sf.org. Tickets $14–$82.

Eureka Theatre Company Eureka houses contemporary performances throughout the year, usually Wednesday through Sunday. Check their website or call the theater for information on upcoming shows and how to purchase tickets (but be aware: Since they don't produce the shows themselves, they won't take reservations for any shows at the theater or sell them online). 215 Jackson St. (btw. Battery and Front sts.). For information, *C* **415/788-7469**, for tickets 255-8207. www.theeureka theatre.org. Ticket prices vary by company but are generally $22–$38.

Lorraine Hansberry Theatre San Francisco's top African-American theater group performs in a 300-seat state-of-the-art theater. It mounts special adaptations

---

Free Opera

Every year, the San Francisco Opera stages a number of free performances, beginning with Opera in the Park every September to kick off the season. They follow it with occasional free performances throughout the city as part of the Brown Bag Opera program. Schedule details can be found on the company's website at www.sfopera.com.

from literature along with contemporary dramas, classics, and music. Performing at 620 Sutter St. (at Mason St.). ✆ **415/345-3980**. www.lhtsf.org. Tickets $25–$32.

The Magic Theatre   The highly acclaimed Magic Theatre, which celebrated its 40th season in 2006, is a major West Coast company dedicated to presenting new plays; over the years, it has nurtured the talents of such luminaries as Sam Shepard and David Mamet. Shepard's Pulitzer prize–winning play *Buried Child* had its premiere here, as did Mamet's *Dr. Faustus*. The season usually runs from October through June; performances are held Tuesday through Sunday. A perk for anyone who's been in previous years: In 2005 and 2006, they redecorated the lobby and added new seats in one of the theaters. Performing at Bldg. D, Fort Mason Center, Marina Blvd. (at Buchanan St.). ✆ **415/441-8822**. www.magictheatre.org. Tickets $20–$60; discounts for students, educators, and seniors.

Theatre Rhinoceros   Founded in 1977, this was America's first (and remains its foremost) theater ensemble devoted solely to works addressing gay, lesbian, bisexual, and transgender issues. The company presents main-stage shows and studio productions of new and classic works each year. The theater is 1 block east of the 16th Street/Mission BART station. 2926 16th St. ✆ **800/838-3006**. www.therhino.org. Tickets $15–$25.

Dance

In addition to the highly regarded local dance companies such as **ODC, Alonzo King's Lines Ballet,** and **Smuin Ballet,** top traveling troupes like the **Joffrey Ballet** and **American Ballet Theatre** make regular appearances in San Francisco. Primary modern dance spaces include **Yerba Buena Center for the Arts,** 701 Mission St. (✆ **415/978-2787**; www.ybca.org); the **Cowell Theater,** at Fort Mason Center, Marina Boulevard at Buchanan Street (✆ **415/345-7575**; www.fortmason.org); and the **ODC Theatre,** 3153 17th St., at Shotwell Street in the Mission District (✆ **415/863-9834**; www.odcdance.org). Tickets cost $15 to $25. Check the local papers for schedules or contact the theater box offices for more information.

San Francisco Ballet   Founded in 1933, the San Francisco Ballet is the oldest professional ballet company in the United States and is regarded as one of the country's finest. It performs an eclectic repertoire of full-length neoclassical and contemporary ballets. The Repertory Season generally runs February through May; the company performs *The Nutcracker* in December. The San Francisco

Ten lads-a-leaping at the San Francisco Ballet.

Ballet Orchestra accompanies most performances. War Memorial Opera House, 301 Van Ness Ave. (at Grove St.). ℂ **415/865-2000** for tickets and information. www.sfballet.org. Tickets $20–$205.

COMEDY & CABARET

BATS Improv ★ 💼 Combining improvisation with competition, BATS performs hilarious improvisational tournaments in which teams of actors compete against each other in scenes, songs, and games, based on suggestions from the audience. There are also long-form shows throughout the year with improvisations of movies, musicals, and even Shakespeare; audience members supply suggestions for titles and plot points, and characters and dialogue are then made up and performed immediately onstage. Main Company shows are Fridays and Saturdays at 8pm; student performance ensemble shows are Sundays at 7pm. Reservations and discount tickets available through their website. Remaining tickets are sold at the box office the night of the show. Performing at Bayfront Theatre at the Fort Mason Center, Bldg. B, no. 350, 3rd floor. ℂ **415/474-8935.** www.improv.org. Tickets $5–$15.

Beach Blanket Babylon ★★ 📷 A San Francisco tradition, Beach Blanket Babylon evolved from Steve Silver's Rent-a-Freak service—a group of "party guests" extraordinaire who hired themselves out as a "cast of characters" complete with fabulous costumes and sets, props, and gags. After their act caught on, it moved into the Savoy-Tivoli, a North Beach bar. By 1974, the audience had grown too large for the facility, and Beach Blanket has been at the 400-seat Club Fugazi ever since. The show is a comedic musical send-up that is best known for outrageous costumes and oversize headdresses. It's been playing for over 30 years, and almost every performance sells out. The show is updated often enough that locals still attend. Those 20 and under are welcome at both Sunday matinees (2 and 5pm), when no alcohol is served; photo ID is required for evening performances. Write for weekend tickets at least 3 weeks in advance, or get them through their website or by calling their box office. **Note:** Only a handful of tickets per show are assigned seating; all other tickets are within specific sections depending on price, but seating is first-come, first-seated within that section. Performances are Wednesday and Thursday at 8pm, Friday and Saturday at 6:30 and 9:30pm, and Sunday at 2 and 5pm. At Club Fugazi, Beach Blanket Babylon Blvd.,

678 Green St. (btw. Powell St. and Columbus Ave.). © **415/421-4222.** www.beachblanket babylon.com. Tickets start at $25.

Cobb's Comedy Club Cobb's features such national headliners as Joe Rogan, Brian Regan, Tracy Morgan, Roseanne Barr, and Jake Johannsen. Comedy reigns Wednesday through Sunday, including a 15-comedian All-Pro Wednesday showcase (a 3-hr. marathon). Cobb's is open to those 18 and over, and occasionally to kids 16 and 17 when accompanied by a parent or legal guardian (call ahead). Shows are held Wednesday, Thursday, and Sunday at 8pm, Friday and Saturday at 8 and 10:15pm. 915 Columbus Ave. (at Lombard St.). © **415/928-4320.** www.cobbscomedy. com. Cover $10–$35. 2-beverage minimum.

Punch Line Comedy Club Adjacent to the Embarcadero One office

Al Gore gets the Beach Blanket Babylon treatment.

building, this is the largest comedy nightclub in the city. Three-person shows with top national and local talent are featured here Tuesday through Saturday. Showcase night is Sunday, when 15 comics take the mic. There's an all-star showcase or a special event on Monday. Doors always open at 7pm and shows are Sunday through Thursday at 8pm, Friday and Saturday at 8 and 10pm (18 and over; two-drink minimum). They serve a full menu—think wings, chicken sandwiches, ravioli, pizzas, appetizers, and salads. 444 Battery St. (btw. Washington and Clay sts.), plaza level. © **415/397-4337** or 397-7573 for recorded information. www. punchlinecomedyclub.com. Cover Mon $7.50, Tues–Thurs $13–$15; Fri–Sat $18 $20; Sun $12. Prices are subject to change for more popular comics, maxing out at a price of $45. 2-beverage minimum.

THE CLUB & MUSIC SCENE

The greatest legacy from the 1960s is the city's continued tradition of live entertainment and music, which explains the great variety of clubs and music enjoyed by San Francisco. The hippest dance places are south of Market Street (SoMa), in former warehouses; the artsy bohemian scene centers are in the Mission; and the most popular cafe culture is still in North Beach.

Note: The club and music scene is always changing, often outdating recommendations before the ink can dry on a page. Most of the venues below are promoted as different clubs on various nights of the week, each with its own look, sound, and style. Discount passes and club announcements are often available at clothing stores and other shops along upper Haight Street.

Drinks at most bars, clubs, and cafes follow most big-city prices, ranging from about $5 to $10, unless otherwise noted.

Rock & Blues Clubs

In addition to the following listings, see "Dance Clubs," below, for (usually) live, danceable rock.

Club-Hopping Tour

If you prefer to let someone else take the lead (and the driver's seat) for a night out, contact **3 Babes and a Bus** (© **800/414-0158; www.threebabes.com**). The nightclub tour company will take you and a gaggle of 20- to 40-something partyers (mostly single women) out on the town, skipping lines and cover charges, for $39 per person.

Bimbo's 365 Club ★★   Originally located on Market Street when it opened in 1931, this North Beach destination is a swank Ricky Ricardo–style spot to catch outstanding live rock, jazz, and smaller, eclectic acts like Flight of the Conchords. Amid glamorous leather banquettes, audiences dance and sip grown-up cocktails. Grab tickets in advance at the box office, which is open Monday through Friday, 10am to 4pm. 1025 Columbus Ave. (at Chestnut St.). © **415/474-0365.** www.bimbos365club.com.

Biscuits and Blues   With a crisp, blow-your-eardrums-out sound system, New Orleans–speak-easy (albeit commercial) appeal, and a nightly lineup of live, national acts, there's no better place to muse the blues than this basement-cum-nightclub. From 7pm on, they serve drink specials, along with their signature fried chicken; namesake moist, flaky biscuits; some new small-plate entrees dubbed "Southern tapas"; and a newly expanded wine list. Menu items range from $8 to $17. 401 Mason (at Geary St.). © **415/292-2583.** www.biscuitsandblues.com. Cover (during performances) $15–$22.

The Boom Boom Room 🍸   The late John Lee Hooker and his partner Alex Andreas bought this Western Addition club years back and used Hooker's star power to pull in some of the best blues bands in the country (even the Stones showed up for an unannounced jam session). Though it changed focus and is now a roots music–oriented club, it's still a fun, dark, small, cramped, and steamy joint where you can hear good live tunes—ranging from New Orleans funk, soul, and new wave, to trance jazz, live drum 'n' bass, electronica, house, and more—Tuesday through Sunday until 2am. If you're going to the Fillmore (see below) to see a band, stop by here first for a drink and come back after your show for more great music. The neighborhood's a bit rough, so be sure to park in the underground lot across the street. 1601 Fillmore St. (at Geary Blvd.). © **415/673-8000.** www.boomboomblues.com. Cover varies from free to $15.

Bottom of the Hill 🍸   Voted one of the best places to hear live rock in the city by the *San Francisco Bay Guardian,* this popular neighborhood club attracts a diverse crowd ranging from rockers to real-estate salespeople; it also offers tons of all-ages shows. The main attraction is an eclectic range of live music almost

Scope-a-Scene

The local newspapers won't direct you to the city's underground club scene, nor will they advise you which of the dozens of clubs are truly hot. To get dialed in, check out reviews from the ravers themselves at www.sfstation.com. The far more commercial **Club Line** (© **415/339-8686; www.sfclubs.com**) offers up-to-date schedules for the city's larger dance venues.

every night (focusing on indie punk with the occasional country band thrown in), but the club also offers pretty good burgers, a bar menu, and outdoor seating on the back patio Wednesday through Friday from 4pm to 2am, Saturday through Tuesday 8:30pm to 2am. Happy hour runs Wednesday to Friday from 4 to 7pm. 1233 17th St. (at Missouri St.). © **415/621-4455.** www.bottomofthehill.com. Cover $8–$16.

The Boom Boom Room.

Cafe du Nord  If you like your clubs dim, sexy, and with a heavy dose of old-school ambience, you will definitely dig Cafe du Nord. This subterranean supper club has rightfully proclaimed itself as the place for a "slightly lurid indie pop scene set in a beautiful old 1907 speakeasy." It's also where an eclectic crowd gathers to linger at the front room's 40-foot mahogany bar, or dine on the likes of panko-crusted prawns and blackened mahimahi. The small stage hosts an eclectic mix of local and visiting artists ranging from Shelby Lynne (country) to the Dickdusters (punk) and local favorite Ledisi (R&B). The popular storytelling series Porchlight often calls the cafe home. 2174 Market St. (at Sanchez St.). ℂ **415/861-5016.** www.cafedunord.com. Cover $8–$20. Food $5–$15.

The Fillmore Made famous by promoter Bill Graham in the 1960s, the Fillmore showcases big rock names in a moderately sized standing-room-only space. Check listings in papers, call the theater, or visit their website for information on upcoming events. And if you make it to a show, check out the fabulous collection of vintage concert posters chronicling the hall's history. 1805 Geary Blvd. (at Fillmore St.). ℂ **415/346-6000.** www.thefillmore.com. Tickets $17–$45.

Grant & Green Saloon The atmosphere at this historic North Beach dive bar is not that special, but Mondays feature jazz, Tuesdays are DJ and karaoke, and the local bands on Thursday through Saturday are decent. All in all, the space is an all-around great place to let your hair down. Not to mention, most shows are free, and you really can't beat that. 1371 Grant Ave. (at Green St.). ℂ **415/693-9565.**

Great American Music Hall ★★ Built in 1907 as a restaurant/bordello, the Great American Music Hall is likely one of the most gorgeous rock venues you'll encounter. With ornately carved balconies, frescoed ceilings, marble columns, and huge hanging light fixtures, you won't know whether to marvel at the structure or watch the acts, which have ranged from Duke Ellington and Sarah Vaughan to Arctic Monkeys, the Radiators, and She Wants Revenge. All shows are all ages (6 and up) so you can bring your family, too. You can buy a ticket for

DRINKING & SMOKING laws

The drinking age is 21 in California, and bartenders can ask for a valid photo ID, no matter how old you look. Some clubs demand identification at the door, so it's a good idea to carry it at all times. Once you get through the door, however, forget about cigarettes—smoking is banned in all California bars. The law is generally enforced and though San Francisco's police department has not made bar raids a priority, people caught smoking in bars can be—and occasionally are—ticketed and fined. Music clubs strictly enforce the law and will ask you to leave if you light up. If you must smoke, do it outside. Also, the dreaded last call for alcohol usually rings out at around 1:30am, since state laws prohibit the sale of alcohol from 2 to 6am every morning. *A very important word of warning:* Driving under the influence of alcohol is a serious crime in California, with jail time for the first offense. You are likely to be legally intoxicated (.08% blood alcohol) if you have had as little as one alcoholic drink an hour. When in doubt, take a taxi.

just the show and order bar snacks (such as nachos, black bean and cheese flautas, burgers, and sandwiches), or buy a ticket that includes a complete dinner (an extra $25), which changes nightly but always includes a salad and a choice of a meat, fish, or veggie entree. You can purchase tickets over the phone (✆ **888/233-0449**) for a $2-to-$7 service fee or download a form from the website and fax it to 415/885-5075 with your Visa or MasterCard info; there is a service charge of $2 per ticket. You can also stop by the box office to purchase tickets directly the night of the performance for no charge (assuming the show isn't sold out), or buy them online at www.gamhtickets.com or Tickets.com (✆ **800/225-2277**). Valet parking is available for select shows; check the website for additional parking information. 859 O'Farrell St. (btw. Polk and Larkin sts.). ✆ **415/885-0750.** www.music hallsf.com. Ticket prices and starting times vary; call or check website for individual show information.

Lou's Pier 47 Club   You won't find many locals in the place, but Lou's happens to be good, old-fashioned fun. It's a casual spot where you can relax with Cajun seafood (downstairs) and live blues bands (upstairs) nightly. A vacation attitude makes the place one of the more, um, jovial spots near the wharf. 300 Jefferson St. (at Jones St.). ✆ **415/771-5687.** www.louspier47.com. $3–$10 cover during prime hours.

Pier 23   If there's one good-time destination that's an anchor for San Francisco's party people, it's the Embarcadero's Pier 23. Part ramshackle patio spot and part dance floor with a heavy dash of dive bar, here it's all about fun for a startlingly diverse clientele (including a one-time visit by Bill Clinton!). The well-worn box of a restaurant with tented patio is a prime sunny-day social spot for white collars, but on weekends, it's a straight-up people zoo where every age and persuasion coexists more peacefully than the cast in a McDonald's commercial. Expect to boogie down shoulder-to-shoulder to 1980s hits and leave with a contagious feel-good vibe. Pier 23, at the Embarcadero (at Battery St.). ✆ **415/362-5125.** www. pier23cafe.com. Cover $5–$12 during performances.

The Saloon   An authentic gold rush survivor, this North Beach dive is the oldest bar in the city. Popular with both bikers and daytime pinstripers, it schedules live blues nightly and afternoons Friday through Sunday. 1232 Grant Ave. (at Columbus St.). ✆ **415/989-7666.** Cover $5–$15 Fri–Sat.

Slim's Co-owned by musician Boz Scaggs, this glitzy restaurant and bar serves California cuisine and seats 200, but it's usually standing room only during almost nightly shows by performers of homegrown rock, jazz, blues, and alternative music. An added bonus for the musically inclined family: All ages are always welcome. Call or check their website for a schedule; hot bands sell out in advance. 333 11th St. (at Folsom St.). ✆ **415/255-0333.** www.slims-sf.com. Cover free–$30.

Bars with DJ Grooves

The Bliss Bar Surprisingly trendy for sleepy, family-oriented Noe Valley, this small, stylish, and friendly bar is a great place to stop for a varied mix of locals, colorful cocktail concoctions, and a DJ spinning at the front window from 9pm to 2am every night except Sunday and Monday. If it's open, take your cocktail into the too-cool back Blue Room. And if you're on a budget, stop by from 4 to 7pm when martinis, lemon drops, and cosmos are only $4. 4026 24th St. (btw. Noe and Castro sts.). ✆ **415/826-6200.** www.blissbarsf.com.

Wish Bar Swathed in burgundy and black with exposed cinder-block walls, cement floors, and red-shaded sconces aglow with candlelight, even you will look cool at this mellow SoMa bar in the popular night-crawler area around 11th and Folsom streets. With a bar in the front, a DJ spinning upbeat lounge music in the back, and seating—including cushy leather couches—in between, it's often packed with a surprisingly diverse (albeit youthful) crowd. Closed Sundays. 1539 Folsom St. (btw. 11th and 12th sts.) ✆ **415/431-1661.** www.wishsf.com.

Dance Clubs

The Endup This legendary party space with a huge, heated outdoor deck (complete with waterfall and fountain, no less), indoor fireplace, and eclectic clientele has always thrown some of the most intense all-nighters in town. In

underground **ENTERTAINMENT**

If you'd rather slit your wrists than visit hokey tourist attractions like Pier 39, log on to www. laughingsquid.com and see what the locals are up to during your vacation. Since 1995, the Laughing Squid has been the Bay Area's sine qua non online resource for art, culture, and technology. Along with links to local art and culture events, the Laughing Squid also hosts the **"Squid List,"** a daily event announcements list. There's some really freaky fringe stuff on this website, with plenty of garbage-level entertainment among several gems, including the **Great Pillow Fight** that usually happens around Valentine's Day (so you can take out your aggression on your partner before giving him or her chocolates?). Either way, this site offers entertaining surfing.

San Francisco's Great Pillow Fight.

fact, it's practically a second home to the city's DJs. There's a different theme every night: Friday Ghettodisco, Super Soul Sundayz, and so on. The Endup is ever-popular with the sleepless dance-all-day crowd that comes here after the other clubs close, hence the name. It's open Saturday morning from 6am to noon and then nonstop from Saturday night around 10pm until Sunday night/Monday morning at 4am. The Sunday morning t-dance, a long-held tradition, begins at 6am. Call or check the website to confirm nights—offerings change from time to time. 401 Sixth St. (at Harrison St.). ☎ **415/646-0999.** www.theendup.com. Cover free–$15.

Harry Denton's Starlight Room 📷 If that new cocktail dress is burning a hole in your suitcase, get yourself dolled up tonight and say hello to Harry, our city's de facto party host. His celestial crimson-infused cocktail lounge and night-club, perched on the top floor of the Sir Francis Drake Hotel, is a throwback to 1930s San Francisco, when red-velvet banquettes, chandeliers, and fashionable duds were de rigueur. The 360-degree view of the city is worth the cover charge alone, but what draws tourists and locals of all ages is a night of Harry Denton–style fun, which usually includes plenty of drinking, live music, and unrestrained dancing, regardless of age. The bar stocks a pricey collection of single-malt Scotches and champagnes, and you can snack from the "Lite" menu. If you make a reservation to guarantee a table, you will also have a place to rest between songs. Early evening is more relaxed, but come the weekend this place gets loose. *Tip:* Come dressed for success (no casual jeans, open-toed shoes for men, or sneakers), or you'll be turned away at the door. Atop the Sir Francis Drake Hotel, 450 Powell St., 21st floor. ☎ **415/395-8595.** www.harrydenton.com. Cover $10 Wed–Fri after 8:30pm; $15 Sat after 8:30pm.

Holy Cow Its motto, "Never a cover, always a party," has been the case since 1987 when this industrial SoMa nightclub opened. The local clubbers rarely come here anymore, but it's still a reliable place for tourists and geezers like me who want to break a sweat on the dance floor to DJs spinning club classics and Top 40. Nightly drink specials make it difficult to leave sober, so plan your transportation accordingly. *Note:* The bar's only open Thursday through Saturday from 9pm to 2am. 1535 Folsom St. (btw. 11th and 12th sts.). ☎ **415/621-6087.** www.theholycow.com.

Ruby Skye Downtown's most glamorous and colossal nightspot led a previous life as an 1890s Victorian playhouse, and many of the beautiful Art Nouveau trimmings are still in place. Mission District clubbers won't go near the place—way too disco and full of the "bridge and tunnel" crowd—but for tourists it's a safe bet for a dance-filled night in the city. The light and sound system here is amazing, and on weekend nights the huge ballroom floor is packed with sweaty bodies dancing to thumping DJ beats or live music. When it's time to cool off, you can chill on the mezzanine or fire up in the smoking room. Be sure to call or check the website to make sure there isn't a private event taking place. 420 Mason St. (btw. Geary and Post sts.). ☎ **415/693-0777.** www.rubyskye.com. Cover $10–$25.

1015 Folsom The ginormous party warehouse—total capacity is 2,000 persons—has three levels of dance floors that make for an extensive variety of dancing venues. DJs pound out house, disco, funk, acid-jazz, and more, with lots of groovy lasers and LED lights to stimulate the eye. Each night is a different club that attracts its own crowd, ranging from yuppie to hip-hop. Open Thursday through Saturday 10pm to 2am. 1015 Folsom St. (at Sixth St.). ☎ **415/431-1200.** www.1015.com. Cover varies.

Harry Denton's Starlight Room.

Yoshi's Jazz Club.

Jazz & Latin Clubs

Rasselas Large, casual, and comfortable with couches and small tables, Rasselas is a popular locals spot for jazz, blues, soul, and R&B combos 7 days a week. The adjacent restaurant serves good Ethiopian cuisine nightly from 5 to 10pm, which, combined with the live music, makes for quite the cultural evening. 1534 Fillmore St. (at Geary Blvd.) ✆ 415/346-8696. www.rasselasjazzclub.com. Cover $10 Fri–Sat. 2-drink minimum.

Yoshi's Jazz Club ★★ What started out in 1977 as a modest sushi and jazz club in Oakland has become one of the most respected jazz venues in the world. For more than 3 decades, San Franciscans had to cross the Bay Bridge to listen to Stanton Moore, Branford Marsalis, and Diana Krall in such an intimate setting. With the grand opening of Yoshi's in San Francisco's Fillmore District, now locals can take a taxi. The two-story, 28,000-square-foot, state-of-the-art jazz venue features the finest local, national, and international jazz artists, as well as first-rate Japanese cuisine at the adjoining restaurant. The elegant club is awash in gleaming dark and blond woods, big sculptural Japanese lanterns, and sensuously curved walls that envelop the intimate stage. Don't worry about the seating chart; there's not a bad seat in the house. It's the perfect place for a romantic date that starts with hamachi and ends with Harry Connick, Jr., so be sure to check Yoshi's website to see who's playing while you're in town and make reservations ASAP—you'll be glad you did. 1330 Fillmore St. (at Eddy St.). ✆ 415/655-5600. www.yoshis.com.

THE BAR SCENE

Finding your kind of bar in San Francisco has a lot to do with which district it's in. The following is a very general description of what types of bars you're likely to find throughout the city:

- Marina/Cow Hollow bars attract a yuppie post-collegiate crowd.
- The opposite of the Marina/Cow Hollow crowd: Hipsters frequent the Mission District haunts.
- Haight-Ashbury caters to eclectic neighborhood cocktailers and beer-lovers.
- The Tenderloin, though still dangerous at night (take a taxi), is now a new hot spot for serious cocktails.
- Tourists mix with conventioneers at downtown pubs.

- North Beach serves all types, mostly tourists.
- Russian Hill's Polk Street has become the new Marina/Cow Hollow scene.
- The Castro caters to gay locals and tourists.
- SoMa offers an eclectic mix from sports bars to DJ lounges.

The following is a list of a few of San Francisco's more interesting bars. Unless otherwise noted, these bars do not have cover charges.

Alembic   In the heart of the Haight is one of the city's premier cocktail bars—with fine-tuned classics, some unusual originals from bartender Daniel Hyatt, such as the Southern Exposure (gin, mint, lime, sugar, and celery juice), a menu of greasy and sophisticated snacks from lamb sliders to bone barrow, and barbacks eager to whip up custom drinks such as funky Manhattan variations (our beverage of choice). On the last Sunday of the month, they'll hand you a copy of the classic *Savoy Cocktail Book* and offer to make anything in its nearly 300 pages. 1725 Haight St. (btw. Cole and Shrader sts.). ✆ **415/666-0822.** www.alembic bar.com.

Blackbird 🛉   Blackbird provides some much needed balance to the plenitude of dark, cruisy gay bars in the Castro. This is exactly what a neighborhood hangout should be. There's plenty of room (when it's not crowded on the weekends) for groups of friends to meet after work and actually be able to sit (not stand) together and catch up. Chatty bartenders mix classic and house-invented cocktails and pour beers from an impressive list of little-known craft brewers. The relaxed vibe is echoed in the pickled wood dropped ceiling, spacious orange benches, and a mix tape soundtrack played at just the right volume—you can enjoy the music and still hear yourself think. Rotating art contrasts nicely with the oak bar and walls papered with front page stories of historic disasters. *Note:* This bar is cash only. 2124 Market St. (btw. Church and Sanchez sts.). ✆ **415/503-0630.** www.blackbirdbar.com.

Bourbon & Branch 🛉   An unmarked door on the corner of Jones and O'Farrell streets opens to unveil the dimly lit interior of Bourbon & Branch, where you're only admitted upon presenting the correct password. Anyone can make a reservation (online or by phone) to receive the code for entry, but it's often necessary to do so weeks in advance, and you're only allotted a space for 2 hours—but not a second more. Although fairly well known and wildly popular among the locals, this is one of those secrets we tend to like to keep to ourselves

Bourbon & Branch.

out of fear that we'll no longer be able to get a table. In fact, if you don't plan a few days—sometimes even a week—in advance, it's already difficult to get seating. Although if you don't have a reservation, it's not a problem if you don't mind sitting at the bar. After ringing the buzzer, give the hostess the password "books," and you'll be allowed into the hidden room accessed by way of a moving bookcase. Just don't fail to meticulously study the speak-easy's house rules before you go: They mean business. The drinks menu is as extensive as they come, with favorites such as the Old Fashioned or Sidecar mingling with more nouveau creations such as a cucumber gimlet or an elderflower-and-champagne concoction. 501 Jones St. (at O'Farrell St.). ℂ **415/346-1735.** www.bourbonandbranch.com. No cover.

Buddha Lounge 🏮 If you like colorful dive bars, you'll love the Buddha Lounge. This heart of-Chinatown bar is a great glimpse into Chinatown's neighborhood culture. Of course, most tourists shy away from what appears to be yet another dark, seedy watering hole, but it's really just a cheery neighborhood bar. Be brave. Step inside, order a drink, and pretend you're in a Charlie Chan movie. The best part is when the Chinese woman behind the bar answers the phone: "HELLO BUDDHA!" 901 Grant Ave. (at Washington St.). ℂ **415/362-1792.** No cover.

Buena Vista Café 📷 "Did you have an Irish coffee at the Buena Vista?" The popular myth is that the Irish coffee was invented at the Buena Vista, but the real story is that this wharf-side cafe was the first bar in the country to serve Irish coffee after a local journalist came back from a trip to Dublin and described the drink to the bartender. Since then, the bar has poured more of these addictive pick-me-up drinks than any other bar in the world, and ordering one has become a San Francisco must-do. Heck, it's entertaining just to watch the venerable tenders pour up to 10 whiskey-laden coffees at a time (a rather messy event). The cafe is in a prime tourist spot along the wharf, so plan on waiting for a stool or table to free up on weekends. And if you need a snack to soak up the booze, they serve food here as well. 2765 Hyde St. (at Beach St.). ℂ **415/474-5044.** www.thebuenavista.com.

Edinburgh Castle Since 1958 this legendary Scottish pub has been known for having rare British ales on tap and one of the best selections of single-malt Scotches in the city. The homey pub is festively decorated with a mishmash of across the-pond mementos, including an authentic Ballantine caber (a long wooden pole) used in the annual Scottish games. Fish and chips (served in newspaper, of course) and other traditional British foods are available until 11pm. The Edinburgh also features author readings and performances and has hosted such noteworthy writers as Po Bronson, Beth Lisick, and Anthony Swofford. Open 5pm to 2am daily. 950 Geary St. (btw. Polk and Larkin sts.). ℂ **415/885-4074.** www.castlenews.com.

Hemlock Tavern This former gay dance club is now one of the most popular bars on Polk Street and always packed on weekends. There's lots of dark wood, warm colors, a line for the bathroom, and an enclosed back room that's dedicated just to smokers. The crowd is a bit younger than the Edinburgh Castle crew, but there's a similar mix of locals, hipsters, musicians, and visitors who would never think of themselves as tourists. The jukebox is sweet, and you can chow down on warm peanuts (toss the shells on the floor) and wash 'em down with a good selection of beers on tap. 1131 Polk St. (at Sutter St.). ℂ **415/923-0923.** www.hemlock tavern.com. No cover.

Li Po Cocktail Lounge 🏮 A dim, divey, and slightly spooky Chinese bar that was once an opium den, Li Po's alluring character stems from its mishmash clutter of dusty Asian furnishings and mementos, including an unbelievably huge ancient rice-paper lantern hanging from the ceiling and a glittery golden shrine to Buddha behind the bar. The bartenders, who pour a mean Li Po Special Mai Tai, love to creep out patrons with tales of opium junkies haunting the joint. Bands and DJs occasionally whip up a sweaty dance scene in the basement, but it's a hit-or-miss schedule. 916 Grant Ave. (btw. Washington and Jackson sts.). ✆ **415/982-0072.**

Martuni's 🍸   San Francisco has plenty of bars with pianos in them, but for the real singalong piano bar experience you'll want to head to Martuni's. After a couple of stiff martinis you'll loosen up enough to join the eclectic crowd in rousing renditions of everything from Cole Porter to Elton John. If you're not up for singing, you can cuddle with your date in the dark alcoves and watch the fun; otherwise, saddle up to the piano and let 'er rip. 4 Valencia St. (at Market St.). ✆ **415/241-0205.**

Matrix Fillmore   The Matrix represents the best and worst of the Marina/Cow Hollow young-'n-yuppie scene: It attracts some of the city's top eye candy, but also has L.A.-style attitude in abundance. (I was once asked to give up my fireplace love seat to someone more important.) Dress in black, order a mojito, say "like" a lot, and you'll do just fine. The slick lounge atmosphere is further enhanced by dyed concrete floors, flatscreen TVs, and free-standing centerpiece fireplace with its "Zen minimalist" mantel. One plus: The bar offers 10 wines by the glass and a large by-the-bottle selection, including cult classics like Dalla Valle. Valet parking is available at the nearby Balboa Café (Fillmore and Greenwich sts.). 3138 Fillmore St. (btw. Greenwich and Filbert sts.). ✆ **415/563-4180.** www.matrixfillmore.com.

Perry's   If you read *Tales of the City,* you may remember that this bar and restaurant has a colorful history as a pickup place for Pacific Heights and Marina singles. Although the times are not as wild today, locals still come to check out the happenings at the dark mahogany bar. A separate dining room offers breakfast, lunch, dinner, and weekend brunch. It's a good place for hamburgers, simple fish dishes, and pasta. Menu items range from $6 to $22. 1944 Union St. (at Laguna St.). ✆ **415/922-9022.** www.perryssf.com.

The Redwood Room   Best known for its gorgeous redwood paneling made from a single 2,000-year-old tree, the Clift Hotel's Redwood Room bar and lounge has a plush, modern feel that's illuminated by beautiful original Deco sconces. If you know who Ian Schrager and Philippe Starck are, then you know their scene: Amex Platinum posers and randy businessmen who mix, mingle, and never balk at the high drink prices ($9–$25). But even if that's not your scene, it's worth poking your head in to admire the classy decor. In the Clift Hotel, 495 Geary St. ✆ **415/929-2372.** www.clifthotel.com.

The Residence   The bar-formerly-known-as Amber closed on New Year's Day 2010 and reemerged a few weeks later as a completely new place altogether. Gone are the secondhand couches, graffitied and peeling walls, and years of smoke damage. It's gone decidedly retro—way retro. Now you'll find a quiet space lined with wood paneling and flocked wallpaper, 19th-century divans, fainting couches, and ottomans. It's opium den meets Mary Poppins. It's still owned and operated by the same people, who also took the opportunity to rethink what and how they serve. Enjoy the free chocolates served on silver trays at the bar while you scan the thoughtful drinks list. Look for both classic and modern drinks from inky, smooth Black Manhattans to sparkling sake cocktails. 718 14th St. (btw. Belcher and Church sts.). ✆ **415/797-8866.**

Specs' 🍸   The location of Specs'—look for a tiny nook on the east side of Columbus Avenue just south of Broadway—makes it a bit tough to find but well worth the search. Specs' historically eclectic decor—maritime flags hang from the ceiling while dusty posters, photos, and oddities like dried whale penises line the walls—offers plenty of visual entertainment while you toss back a cold Bud (sans glass, of course). A "museum" displayed under glass contains memorabilia and items brought back by long-dead seamen who dropped in between voyages. There are plenty of salty and slightly pickled regulars to match the motif, so you may not want to order a cosmo while doing your nails at the bar. 12 Saroyan Place (at 250 Columbus Ave.). ℂ **415/421-4112.**

The Tonga Room & Hurricane Bar 🍴 This was the original rainforest cafe long before there was ever an enterprise of the same name. It's kitschy as all get-out, but there's no denying the goofy Polynesian pleasures of the Fairmont Hotel's tropical oasis. Drop in and join the crowds for an umbrella drink—mai tais are the house specialty—a simulated thunderstorm and downpour, and a heavy dose of whimsy that escapes most San Francisco establishments. If you're on a budget, you'll definitely want to stop by for the weekday happy hour from 5 to 7pm, when you can stuff your face at the all-you-can-eat bar-grub buffet (baby back ribs, chow mein, pot stickers) for $9.50 and the cost of one drink. Settle in and you'll catch live Top-40 music after 8pm Wednesday through Sunday, when there's a $5 cover. In the Fairmont Hotel, 950 Mason St. (at California St.). ℂ **415/772-5278.** www.tongaroom.com.

Toronado Gritty Lower Haight isn't exactly a charming street, but there's plenty of nightlife here, catering to an artistic/grungy/skateboarding 20-something crowd. While Toronado definitely draws in the young'uns, its 50-plus microbrews on tap and 100 bottled beers also entice a more eclectic clientele in search of beer heaven. The brooding atmosphere matches the surroundings: an aluminum bar, a few tall tables, minimal lighting, and a back room packed with tables and chairs. Happy hour runs 11:30am to 6pm every day for $1 off pints. 547 Haight St. (at Fillmore St.). ℂ **415/863-2276.** www.toronado.com.

Tosca Cafe 🍴 Open Tuesday through Saturday from 5pm to 2am, and Sunday 7pm to 2am, Tosca is a low-key and large popular watering hole for local politicos, writers, media types, incognito celebrities such as Johnny Depp or

The Ear Scene

Head to the Tonga Room for kitsch, fruity drinks, and a stuff-your-face pupu platter.

Nicolas Cage, and similar cognoscenti of unassuming classic characters. Equipped with dim lights, red leather booths, and high ceilings, it's everything you'd expect an old North Beach legend to be. No credit cards. 242 Columbus Ave. (btw. Broadway and Pacific Ave.). ℭ 415/986-9651. www.toscacafesf.com.

Vesuvio   Situated along Jack Kerouac Alley, across from the famed City Lights bookstore, this renowned literary beatnik hangout is packed to the second-floor rafters with neighborhood writers, artists, songsters, wannabes, and everyone else ranging from longshoremen and cabdrivers to businesspeople, all of whom come for the laid-back atmosphere. The convivial space consists of two stories of cocktail tables, complemented by changing exhibitions of local art. In addition to drinks, Vesuvio features an espresso machine. 255 Columbus Ave. (at Broadway). ℭ 415/362-3370. www.vesuvio.com.

Zeitgeist   The front door is black, the back door is adorned with a skeleton Playboy bunny, and inside is packed to the rafters with tattooed, pierced, and hard-core-looking partyers. But forge on. Zeitgeist is such a friendly and fun punk-rock-cum-biker-bar beer garden that even the occasional yuppie can be spotted mingling around the slammin' jukebox that features tons of local bands or in the huge back patio filled with picnic tables. (There tend to be cute girls here, too.) Along with fantastic dive-bar environs, you'll find 30 beers on draft, a pool table, and pinball machines. The regular crowd, mostly locals and bike messengers, come here to kick back with a pitcher, and welcome anyone else interested in the same pursuit. And if your night turns out, um, better than expected, there's a hotel upstairs. Cash only. 199 Valencia St. (at Duboce Ave.). ℭ 415/255-7505.

Brewpubs

Gordon Biersch Brewery Restaurant   Gordon Biersch Brewery is San Francisco's largest brew restaurant, serving decent food and tasty beer to an attractive crowd of mingling professionals. There are always several house-made beers to choose from, ranging from light to dark. Menu items run $5.50 to $28 (see p. 124 for more information). 2 Harrison St. (on the Embarcadero). ℭ 415/243-8246. www.gordonbiersch.com.

ThirstyBear Brewing Company   Nine superb, handcrafted varieties of brew are always on tap at this stylish high-ceilinged brick edifice. Good Spanish food is served here, too. Pool tables and dartboards are upstairs, and live flamenco can be heard on Sunday nights. 661 Howard St. (1 block east of the Moscone Center). ℭ 415/974-0905. www.thirstybear.com.

Cocktails with a View

See "Dance Clubs," earlier, for a full review of Harry Denton's Starlight Room. Unless otherwise noted, these establishments have no cover charge.

Leatherneck Steakhouse & Lounge   This sky-view restaurant and bar at the top of the Marines Memorial Club may just be the best-kept secret in town. Open since 1946, the club is a living memorial to U.S. Marines who served in the Pacific during World War II, as well as a hotel. The small rooftop lounge next to the restaurant—not much more than a handful of stools and a bar—is the kind of place where elderly gents in suit coats belly up and reminisce about the war years over a strong cocktail. The dress code may be "resort casual," but the views are big-city spectacular. No cover, and the drinks are very reasonable (especially during 4–6pm happy hour). It's open Sunday and Monday 11am to 9pm, Tuesday to

Thursday 11am to 10pm, and Friday and Saturday 11am to 11pm. In the Marines Memorial Club & Hotel, 609 Sutter St. (at Mason St.). ☏ **415/673-6672.** www.marineclub.com.

Top of the Mark 📷   This is one of the most famous cocktail lounges in the world, and for good reason—the spectacular glass-walled room features an unparalleled 19th-floor view. During World War II, Pacific-bound servicemen toasted their goodbyes to the States here. While less dramatic today than they were back then, evenings spent here are still sentimental, thanks to the romantic atmosphere. Live bands play throughout the week; a jazz pianist on Tuesdays starts at 7pm; salsa on Wednesdays begins with dance lessons at 8pm and the band starts up at 9pm; on Thursdays Stompy Jones brings a swing vibe from 7:30pm; and a dance band playing everything from '50s hits through contemporary music keeps the joint hopping Fridays and Saturdays starting at 9pm. Drinks range from $9 to $12. A $59 three-course fixed-price sunset dinner is served Friday and Saturday at 7:30pm. Sunday brunch, served from 10am to 2pm, costs $59 for adults and includes a glass of champagne; for children 4 to 12, the brunch is $30. In the Mark Hopkins InterContinental, 1 Nob Hill Place (btw. California and Mason sts.). ☏ **415/616-6916.** www.topofthemark.com. Cover $5–$10.

Sports Bar

Greens Sports Bar   If you think San Francisco sports fans aren't as enthusiastic as those on the East Coast, well, you're right. These days it's pretty easy to find an empty seat at Greens during a '49ers or Giants game. The city's de facto sports bar is a classic, cozy hangout with lots of dark wood, polished brass, windows that open onto the street, and an array of elevated TVs showing various sporting events via satellite. Highlights include 18 beers on tap, a pool table, and a boisterous happy-hour scene every Monday through Friday from 4 to 7pm. Food isn't served, but you can place an order from the various restaurants along Polk Street and eat at the bar. (They even provide a selection of menus.) 2239 Polk St. (at Green St.). ☏ **415/775-4287.**

Top of the Mark offers an incredible view of the city.

EUGENIO PICKS YOUR NEXT wine bar

Eugenio Jardim is the gregarious sommelier at the restaurant Jardinière (p. 146), where patrons in jeans enjoy Chef Traci des Jardins's food alongside a theater crowd in tuxedos and gowns. He was named Sommelier of the Year by *Sunset Magazine* in 2010. We asked him: "What are your favorite local wine bars?"

When it comes to grabbing a good glass of wine in the Bay Area, I think restaurants are still a step ahead of wine bars on what's new and exciting. In general, Bay Area wine lovers want some food with their wine (hallelujah to that). Wine bars are back in full force, but I find them a bit gimmicky these days. I do understand the need to offer something unique that will set one apart but, let's be frank, what should really matter is the quality of the wine you offer, right? Having said that, I still think it is really great that we San Franciscans now have so many more options of places to enjoy wines.

Among the most creative concepts of late is the Pop-Up spot, which with a turn of a key or the ring of the clock turns a coffee shop into a happening wine bar. From the relentlessly creative mind of wine kid Mark Bright, **Vinyl Wine Bar,** 359 Divisadero St. (✆ **415/621-4132;** www.facebook.com/vinylwinebar), is born. No one knows exactly what comes next, but he and his partners managed to cram into a single room a movie projector, a communal table

made up from the old Embarcadero Freeway Broadway Exit sign, a bar, and a kitchen. Oh, did I forget the hordes of youngsters who flock there for the Pizza night, or for the Pasta night, or even for the night when a food truck stops by to feed the patrons?

When it comes to quality of wine and service, associated with some of the most fun people-watching spots, the **Wine Bar at the Ferry Plaza Wine Merchants** (✆ **415/391-9400;** www.fpwm.com), in

Wine & Champagne Bars

The Bubble Lounge   This two-level champagne bar—looking ever so chic with its red velvet sofas, brick walls, and floor-to-ceiling draperies—chills more than 300 champagnes and sparkling wines, including about 30 by the glass. As one would expect at a Financial District bubbly bar, there's a soupçon of pretentiousness emanating from the BMW-driving clientele and perpetually unshaven bartenders. If you're the type that prefers beer and free pretzels you'll hate it here, particularly if you have to wait in line for a $20 flute of something you can't even pronounce, but the pickup scene really perks up as the bubbly flows into the Ferry Building (p. 174), is second to none! Silas and Jason are usually in command from behind the bar, stirring the crowds to try the latest discoveries by "Wine Mama" Debbie Zachareas. They serve delicious wines in every pour size imaginable, and if you find something in the adjacent wine shop, just grab it and they will serve it to you for a mere $6 corkage fee. Their food selections include some of the city's best treats: Salumi from Boccalone, cheeses from Cowgirl Creamery, bread from ACME, and chocolates from Michael Recchiuti, all housed in the Ferry Building as well. Every Wednesday night they host a local or visiting winemaker, for what's become the best opportunity to have a one-on-one with the people behind the wine.

Uva Enoteca, 568 Haight St. (*©* **415/829-2024;** www.uvaenoteca. com), is unashamedly "all about Italy" and the "double 'B' team" of Ben and Boris create an amazing environment for the enjoyment of casual Italian-inspired foods and wines. The wine list covers the entire "boot" with great local wines from every region. Their mouthwatering menu is, without a doubt, the greatest bargain in town! Located in the heart of the very festive (and young) Lower Haight area of the city, this rustic Italian jewel makes you feel like you are just hanging out with friends in your own kitchen, and life feels just right!

When Shelley Lindgren set out to open her second restaurant in the city, we all held our breath. Now, a couple of years later, **SPQR,** a Roman Trattoria at 1911 Fillmore St. (*©* **415/771-7779;** www.spqrsf.com), still has a new and exciting feel about it. The food is inspired and wholesome, and the wines—oh my, the wines! Shelley is not only the nicest person in the business, but also possesses one of the finest palates out there. With A-16, her first restaurant, she not only taught San Francisco about the delicious foods and wines of Campania and the South of Italy, but she also created a great center for the passionate and eager wine novices to learn about Italian wines. Emily, one of Shelley's brightest apprentices, is probably the third generation of these young Somms, but she absolutely knows her stuff, and when I go to this bustling trattoria I rarely book a reservation because I love to sit with her at the bar. I normally pick the food and let my fabulous young Somm decide what I will be drinking with it. I am often delighted and surprised but never disappointed.

—Eugenio Jardim

the night. 714 Montgomery St. (btw. Washington and Jackson sts.). *©* **415/434-4204.** www. bubblelounge.com.

First Crush   If you're staying downtown and in the mood for a glass of fine wine, take a stroll to this popular restaurant and wine lounge. Amid a stylish and dimly lit interior, an eclectic mix of visitors and locals nosh on reasonably priced "progressive American cuisine" that's paired, if desired, with a large selection of all-California wines served by the glass. But plenty of folks also drop by just to sample flights of wine and talk shop with the wine-savvy staff. This also is a good late-night-bite spot, as it's open until midnight Thursday through Saturday. 101

Cyril Magnin St. (also known as Fifth St., just north of Market St., at Ellis St.). ℂ **415/982-7874.** www.firstcrush.com.

Nectar Wine Lounge   Catering to the Marina's young and beautiful, this hip place to sip pours about 50 globally diverse wines by the glass (plus 800 choices by the bottle) along with creative small plates; pairings are optional. Soothing shades of browns lend a relaxing ambience to the lounge's industrial-slick decor that includes lots of polished woods and hexagonal highlights. 3330 Steiner St. (at Chestnut St.). ℂ **415/345-1377.** www.nectarwinelounge.com.

Press Club   This "urban wine tasting bar" near the Four Seasons Hotel is a mix of Northern California–sourced wine cellar and slick, modern lounge—it's that rare wine bar that might please both Alice Waters and Hugh Hefner. Sample from the space's eight separate bars, and chat up reps from the six Northern California wineries featured (the list of wineries rotates). If you like what you taste, they'll sell you a case and even ship it home for you. Swipe the Press Club card you're given at the door to register each purchase, and then as you leave pay off your card—that's where the VIP Press treatment ends. Small bites for nibbling include Cowgirl Creamery cheeses, popcorn with truffle butter, meatloaf sliders, and mini-cupcakes. 20 Yerba Buena Lane. ℂ **415/744-5000.** www.pressclubsf.com.

Terroir 🎁   The full name—Terroir Natural Wine Merchant—only tells you a little about what you'll find inside this SoMa area wine-shop-slash-bar. The shop sells a handpicked selection of natural wines (dry farmed, organic, chemical free, and wild-yeast fermented), which you can taste at a tiny zinc bar in the back. Owners Luc Ertoran, Guilhaume Gerard, and Dagan Ministero pour by the glass, half-bottle, or bottle and will guide you through your selections, telling you as much or as little as you want to know. Seats at this bar are prime real estate for getting a backdoor education on the art and science of biodynamic winemaking. Or, take your glass and perhaps a simple charcuterie plate up to the library loft space and kick back. *Tip:* If you want some filling and authentic French fare, Chez Spencer's mobile kitchen (known as Spencer to Go) pulls up across the street on Thursday nights. 1116 Folsom St. (btw. Seventh and Langton sts.). ℂ **415/558-9946.** www.terroirsf.com.

The Press Club.

San Francisco Drag Shows

If you're out on a Friday night and looking for something to do that's definitely off the straight-laced path, head to the Cinch (see below) for its weekly **Charlie Horse** drag show, hosted by the sassy Miss Trannyshack 2005, Anna Conda. Every week is a different theme, such as "Valley of the Dolls Night" based on the scandalous Jacqueline Susann novel, or "What Is Your Take on Old School," where the "ladies" of the evening masquerade as their favorite divas such as Dolly Parton or Joni Mitchell. There's no cover charge, no drink minimum, and the performance is free. An added bonus: The show comes with complimentary popcorn.

If you prefer your drag queens with a slice of quiche, **Harry Denton's Starlight Room** (p. 276) hosts a weekly **Sunday's a Drag** brunch performance, where divas perform female impersonation acts and lip-sync Broadway tunes. The "brunch with an attitude" has two seatings every Sunday, at noon and 2:30pm. The price of brunch is $45 per person, which includes entertainment, brunch, coffee, tea, and fresh juices. For reservations, call (✆ **415/395-8595** or e-mail reservations@harrydenton.com.

GAY & LESBIAN BARS & CLUBS

Check the free weeklies such as the *San Francisco Bay Guardian* and *San Francisco Weekly* for listings of events and happenings around town. The *Bay Area Reporter* is a gay paper with comprehensive listings, including a weekly community calendar. All these papers are free and distributed weekly on Wednesday or Thursday, and can be found stacked at the corners of 18th and Castro streets and Ninth and Harrison streets, as well as in bars, bookshops, and other stores around town. See "LGBT Travelers," in chapter 12, beginning on p. 396, for further details on gay-themed guidebooks. Also check out the rather homely but very informative site titled "Queer Things to Do in the San Francisco Bay Area" at www.sfqueer.com, or www.gaywired.com for more gay happenings.

The Café 🏳️‍🌈 When this place first opened, it was the only predominantly lesbian dance club on Saturday nights in the city. Once the guys found out how much fun the girls were having, they joined the party. Today, after completing a multimillion-dollar remodel in July 2009, it's a hugely popular mixed gay and lesbian scene with three bars; two pool tables; a steamy, free-spirited dance floor; and a small, heated patio and balcony with a retractable glass skylight where smoking and schmoozing are allowed. *An added perk:* They open at 5pm weekdays and 3pm weekends (2pm on Sun). 2369 Market St. (at Castro St.). (✆ **415/834-5840.** www.cafesf.com.

The Cinch Part cruisy neighborhood bar, part modern-day penny arcade, the Cinch features free Wi-Fi, two pool tables, five TVs, video games, an Internet

Find leather daddies at the Folsom Street Fair every September. See p. 37.

jukebox, pinball, and an outdoor smoking patio. They even have their own softball team, the Renegades. With happy hour Monday through Friday 4 to 8pm (all night on Mon), progressive music by DJs on Thursday and Friday nights, and a host of other fun theme nights, the bar attracts a mixed crowd of gays, lesbians, and gay-friendly straights. 1723 Polk St. (near Washington St.). ℂ **415/776-4162.**

The Endup Open 24 hours, this club is where you're likely to "end up" after a night on the town, likely at 6am and not sober. It's a different nightclub every night of the week, but regardless of who's throwing the party, the place is always throbbing with DJ beats and sweaty bodies. There are two pool tables, a fireplace, an outdoor patio, and, on the dance floor, a mob of gyrating souls—particularly on Friday nights. Some nights are straight or mixed, so call ahead if you care. (See p. 275 for more information.) 401 Sixth St. (at Harrison St.). ℂ **415/646-0999.** www.theendup.com. Cover $20.

Lone Star Saloon Expect lesbians and a heavier, furrier motorcycle crowd (both men and women) here most every night. The Thursday night "beer bust" and Saturday and Sunday afternoon "beverage benefits" on the patio are especially popular and cost $9 per person. 1354 Harrison St. (btw. Ninth and 10th sts.). ℂ **415/863-9999.** www.lonestarsf.com.

The Lookout This bar provides the neighborhood with DJs spinning and the best view of the Castro District from its large, second-floor, wraparound balcony. People of all ages come here for the friendliness of the bartenders, the flow of drag queens, and the highly charged, cruisy atmosphere. There's a pizza joint next door in case you get hungry—it's all you can eat on Tuesdays from 6 to 9:30pm for just $9.95. 3600 16th St. (at Market and Noe sts.). ℂ **415/431-0306.** www.lookoutsf.com.

The Mint Karaoke Lounge This is a gay and lesbian karaoke bar—sprinkled with a heavy dash of straight folks on weekends—where you can get up and sing your heart out every night. Along with song, you'll encounter a mixed 20- to 40-something crowd that combines cocktails with do-it-yourself cabaret. Want to eat and listen at the same time? Feel free to bring in the Japanese food from the attached restaurant. Sashimi goes for about $7, main entrees $8, and sushi combo plates about $11. 1942 Market St. (at Laguna St.). ℂ **415/626-4726.** www.themint.net. 2-drink minimum.

The Stud The Stud, which has been around for almost 40 years, is one of the most successful gay establishments in town. The interior has an antiques-shop look. Music is a balanced mix of old and new, and nights vary from cabaret to oldies to disco-punk. Check their website in advance for the evening's offerings.

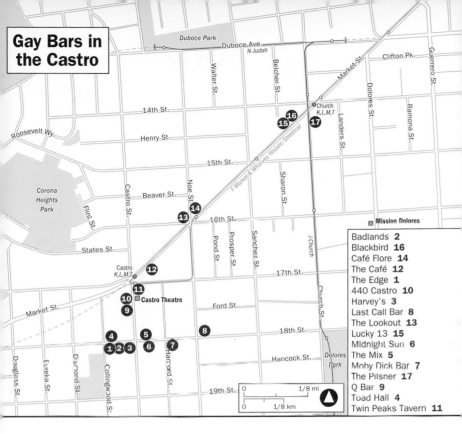

Gay Bars in the Castro

Mission Dolores

Badlands	**2**
Blackbird	**16**
Café Flore	**14**
The Café	**12**
The Edge	**1**
440 Castro	**10**
Harvey's	**3**
Last Call Bar	**8**
The Lookout	**13**
Lucky 13	**15**
Midnight Sun	**6**
The Mix	**5**
Moby Dick Bar	**7**
The Pilsner	**17**
Q Bar	**9**
Toad Hall	**4**
Twin Peaks Tavern	**11**

Drink prices range from $3 to $8. Happy hour runs Monday through Saturday 5 to 9pm with $1 off well drinks. 399 Ninth St. (at Harrison St.) ☎ **415/863-6623** or 252-STUD (7883) for event info. www.studsf.com. Cover $6–$10.

Toad Hall   Named after a former Castro watering hole that was featured prominently in scenes in the film *Milk,* this new addition to the gayborhood provides a bit of respite from the seedier Badlands and the Edge just across 18th Street. It's a bit cruisy and a bit boozy—the bar runs the length of the room. A small elevated stage is dedicated to showing your moves to the DJ's selection of the latest (Lady Gaga, Beyoncé, or BritBrit) and greatest (Donna Summer, Weather Girls) dance tracks. When you start to feel claustrophobic, head out to the smoking-friendly back patio, where you can indulge your craving for just one more drink at the outdoor bar. 4146 18th St. (btw. Castro and Collingwood sts.). ☎ **415/621-2811.** www.toadhallbar.com.

Trigger   In the mood for buff, barely dressed bartenders and thumping house music in a glam industrial setting? Head to Trigger. Once you're past the doormen and velvet ropes, you'll be greeted by an energetic crowd of revelers ready to dance and maybe check each other out. Bartenders—male and female—double as the entertainment, whether it's dancing in a gilded cage or performing acrobatics on the trapeze overhead as the lights swirl. If you're feeling special, opt for bottle service in the VIP balcony. 2344 Market St. (btw. 16th and Noe sts.). ☎ **415/551-2582.** www.clubtrigger.com.

Roughly 25 of the city's 40+ gay bars are in the Castro. We asked legendary drag queen Heklina to give quick takes on all of them for you. For the full list of Heklina's reviews of bars outside the Castro, search Frommers.com. For more on Heklina, visit www.trannyshack.com. *Note:* As we go to print, Lime, at 2247 Market Street, is closing and will reopen as a gay sports bar, Hi Tops. Trigger, at 2344 Market Street, is closing, with no immediate plans to reopen.

Twin Peaks: This legendary Castro bar, long derided as "God's waiting room" because of its older clientele, is actually the best bar on Castro Street for people-watching. Great martinis.

Midnight Sun: Longest running video bar in the Castro. The two-for-one happy hour is responsible for many, many hangovers.

Moby Dick: Castro institution, famous for its 250-gallon saltwater fish tank above the bar. Daily drink specials.

Blackbird: Extremely trendy (as in, recently opened), great ambience, great drinks. Perfect for before-dinner drinks.

The Pilsner: A slightly off-the-beaten-path neighborhood bar. Pool table, patio.

440 Castro: "Booze, Music, Fun" is the slogan for this Castro bar, and they live up to it with their infamous five, four, three, two, one drink specials.

Harvey's: Location, location! On the gayest corner on earth, 18th and Castro. Stop here for a bite to eat before seeing a film at the Castro Theater or heading off to a more interesting bar.

The Mix: Very laid-back, unpretentious. Pool table, jukebox. Spacious outdoor patio site of numerous fund-raisers and drag shows. Quintessential Castro bar.

Last Call: Formerly known as Men's Room, perfectly located 2 blocks away from Castro Street. Close, but not too close if you want to get away from the insanity. Cozy is the word; it even has a fireplace.

Toad Hall: I confess I have not given this one much of a chance, but if you think this is something more than yet another faceless, soulless new bar to pop up in the Castro, please convince me otherwise.

Twin Peaks Right at the intersection of Castro, 17th, and Market streets is one of the Castro's most famous (at 35 years old) gay hangouts. It caters to an older crowd but often has a mixture of patrons and claims to be the first gay bar in America. Because of its relatively small size and desirable location, the place becomes fairly crowded and convivial by 8pm, earlier than many neighboring bars. 401 Castro St. (at 17th and Market sts.). © **415/864-9470.**

FILM

The **San Francisco International Film Festival** (© **415/561-5000;** www. sffs.org), which celebrated its 50th birthday in 2006, is held at the end of April and reigns as one of America's longest-running film festivals. Entries include new films by new and established directors. Call or surf ahead for a schedule or information, and check out their website for more information on purchasing tickets, which are relatively inexpensive.

9

Film

SAN FRANCISCO AFTER DARK

Badlands: I much preferred the old, seedy Badlands of lore (hay on the floor, pinball machines, country vibe). The sterile "New Improved" version (now going on 10 years old) could be Anywhere, USA. Still, it's very popular, especially if you're into twinks.

The Edge: Popular neighborhood bar. Numerous charity events are produced here, sometimes featuring performances on a comically tiny stage.

Q Bar: Castro Street bar with a younger crowd. Mondays (Wanted) and Wednesdays (Booty Call) are the most popular nights. Can be twink heaven.

Café Flore: Beloved cafe in the heart of the Castro neighborhood. Outdoor seating available for people-watching. Popular Sunday brunch location.

The Lookout: Centrally located with a wraparound balcony perfect for people-watching. Great food, especially the pizza. Don't miss "JOCK" Sundays, from 3 to 9pm every week.

The Café: Another in a long line of formerly great bars that underwent a remodel and had whatever character and personality it possessed stripped away . . . but hey, that's just my opinion.

Lucky 13: Not a gay bar, but in the Castro, so if you wander in by mistake enjoy the free popcorn, smoking patio, and great jukebox.

If you're not here in time for the festival, don't despair. The classic, independent, and mainstream cinemas in San Francisco are every bit as good as the city's other cultural offerings.

Repertory Cinemas

Castro Theatre Built in 1922 by renowned Bay Area architect Timothy Pflueger and listed as a City of San Francisco registered landmark, the beautiful Castro Theatre is known for its screenings of classics and for its Wurlitzer organ, which is played before each evening show. A different film is featured almost nightly, and more often than not it's a double feature. They also play host to a number of festivals throughout the year and the occasional movie premiere, such as the 2008 Oscar contender *Milk*. Bargain matinees are usually offered on Wednesday, Saturday, Sunday, and holidays. Phone or visit their website for schedules, prices, and showtimes. 429 Castro St. (near Market St.). ✆ **415/621-6120.** www.castrotheatre.com.

The Roxie Film Center Founded in 1909, the Roxie is the oldest continu-ally running theater in San Francisco, and so when it almost went under in 2005, a private donor saved it with a huge donation and a great idea: The theater merged with the New College of California and is now a nonprofit film center serving both students and the general public. Management has promised that the programming will stay the same and that they will continue to screen the best new alternative films anywhere, as well as host filmmakers such as Werner Her-zog. The low-budget contemporary features are largely devoid of Hollywood candy coating; many are West Coast premieres. If you're here in February, catch a flick at SF Indie Fest, which calls the Roxie home. Phone for schedules, prices, and showtimes. Admission is $5 to $9.75 adults, $5 seniors 65 plus and children 11 and under; $5 matinee is the first show on weekends. 3117 16th St. (at Valencia St.). ℂ **415/863-1087.** www.roxie.com.

SIDE TRIPS FROM SAN FRANCISCO

10

The City by the Bay is, without question, captivating, but don't let it ensnare you to the point of ignoring its environs. The surrounding region offers beautiful natural areas such as Mount Tamalpais and Muir Woods, scenic bayside communities such as Tiburon and Sausalito, and vibrant neighboring cities such as Oakland and Berkeley.

From San Francisco, you can reach any of these points in an hour or less by car. Public transportation options are also listed throughout the chapter. Another option is to hitch a ride with **San Francisco Sightseeing** (✆ **888/428-6937** or 415/434-8687; www.sanfranciscosightseeing.com), which runs regularly scheduled bus tours to neighboring towns and the countryside. Half-day trips to Muir Woods and Sausalito, and full-day trips to Napa and Sonoma are available, as are excursions to Yosemite and the Monterey Peninsula. Phone for prices and schedules.

BERKELEY

10 miles NE of San Francisco

Berkeley is best known as the home of the University of California at Berkeley, which is world renowned for its academic standards, 18 Nobel prize winners (seven are active staff), and protests that led to the most famous student riots in U.S. history. Today, there's still hippie idealism in the air, but the radicals have aged; the 1960s are present only in tie-dye and paraphernalia shops. The biggest change the town is facing is yuppification; as San Francisco's rent and property prices soar out of the range of the average person's budget, everyone with less than a small fortune is seeking shelter elsewhere, and Berkeley is one of the top picks (although Oakland is quickly becoming a favorite, too). Berkeley is a lively city teeming with all types of people, a beautiful campus, vast parks, great shopping, and some incredible restaurants.

Essentials

The **Berkeley Bay Area Rapid Transit (BART)** station is 2 blocks from the university. The fare from San Francisco is less than $4 one-way. Call ✆ **511** or visit www.bart.gov for trip info, or fares, or to download trip planners to your iPod, mobile phone, or PDA.

If you are coming **by car** from San Francisco, take the Bay Bridge (go during the evening commute, and you'll think Los Angeles traffic is a breeze). Follow I-80 east to the University Avenue exit, and follow University Avenue until you hit the campus. Parking is tight, so either leave your car at the Sather Gate parking lot at Telegraph Avenue and Durant Street, or expect to fight for a spot.

PREVIOUS PAGE: **Muir Woods tends to dwarf—and exhilarate—visitors.**

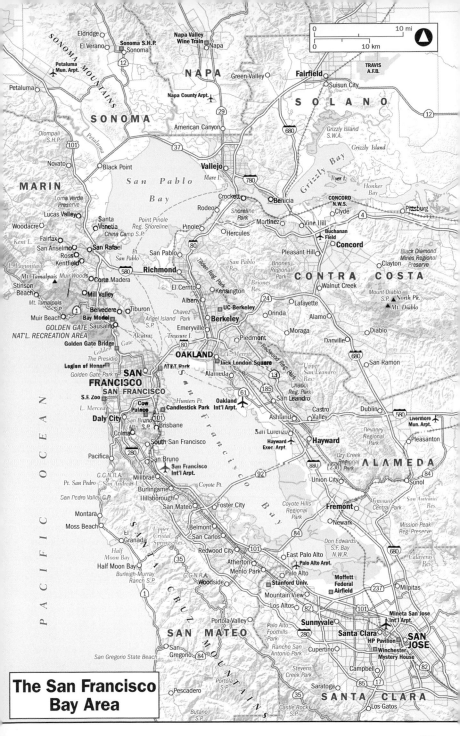

The San Francisco Bay Area

What to See & Do

Hanging out is the preferred Berkeley pastime, and the best place to do it is **Telegraph Avenue,** the street that leads to the campus's southern entrance. Most of the action lies between Bancroft Way and Dwight Way, where coffeehouses, restaurants, shops, great book and record stores, and crafts booths (with vendors selling everything from T-shirts and jewelry to I Ching and tarot-card readings) swarm with life. Pretend you're a local: Plant yourself at a cafe, sip a latte, and ponder something intellectual, or survey the town's unique residents.

If used and antiquarian books are your thing, stop by **Moe's Books,** 2476 Telegraph Ave. (© **510/849-2087;** www.moesbooks.com). After exploring four floors of new, used, and out-of-print books, you're unlikely to leave empty-handed.

You can also catch a performance at the Tony Award–winning **Berkeley Repertory Theatre,** 2025 Addison St. (© **510/647-2949;** www.berkeleyrep. org). Tickets range from $27 (cheap seats for shows still in previews) to $71 (premium Sat-night seats).

UC BERKELEY CAMPUS

The University of California at Berkeley (www.berkeley.edu) is worth a stroll. It's a beautiful campus with plenty of woodsy paths, architecturally noteworthy buildings, and, of course, 33,000 students. Among the architectural highlights of the campus are a number of buildings by Bernard Maybeck, Bakewell and Brown, and John Galen Howard.

Contact the **Visitor Information Center,** 101 University Hall, 2200 University Ave., at Oxford Street (© **510/642-5215;** www.berkeley.edu/visitors), to join a free 90-minute campus tour. Reservations are required; see the website for details. Tours are available year-round Monday through Saturday at 10am and Sunday at 1pm. Weekday tours depart from the visitor center and weekend tours start from Sather Bell Tower in the middle of campus. Electric cart tours are available year-round for travelers with disabilities for $50, 2 weeks' advance reservations required; no tours are given the week between Christmas and New Year's Day. Or stop by the office and pick up a self-guided walking-tour brochure or a free Berkeley map. *Note:* The information center is closed on weekends, but you can find the latest information on their website.

The university's southern, main entrance is at the northern end of Telegraph Avenue, at Bancroft Way. Walk through the entrance into Sproul Plaza, and when school is in session, you'll encounter the gamut of Berkeley's inhabitants: colorful street people, rambling political zealots, and ambitious students. You might be lucky enough to stumble upon some impromptu musicians or a heated debate. There's always something going on here, so stretch out on the grass for a few

10

SIDE TRIPS | Berkeley

Berkeley

RESTAURANTS

Bear's Lair Brew Pub **10**
Bette's Ocean View Diner **3**
Cafe Fanny **4**
Cafe Rouge **2**
Chez Panisse **6**
Golden Bear Cafe **10**
Meritage **14**
O Chamé **1**
Rivoli **5**
Terrace **9**

ATTRACTIONS

Lawrence Hall of Science **7**
UC Berkeley Art Museum **11**
University of California
 Botanical Garden **8**

HOTELS

Claremont Resort & Spa **14**
Hotel Durant **12**
Rose Garden Inn **13**

297

minutes and take in the Berkeley vibe. You'll also find the student union, complete with a bookstore, cafes, and an information desk on the second floor where you can pick up the student newspaper (also found in dispensers throughout campus).

For viewing more traditional art forms, there are some noteworthy museums, too. **The Lawrence Hall of Science ★**, east of campus on Centennial Drive, just above the **Botanical Gardens** (*©* **510/642-5132; www.lawrence hallofscience.org**), offers hands-on science exploration for kids of all ages. It's open daily from 10am to 5pm and is a wonderful place to watch the sunset. Included in the admission price is an outdoor science park called Forces That Shape the Bay, which lets visitors explore ongoing geologic forces. The site includes activity stations such as earthquake simulators, a geologic uplift bench, a water feature, telescopes, BayLab programs and demonstrations, an audio tour, and picnic sites. Admission is $12 for adults; $9 for seniors 62 and over, students, and children 7 to 18; $6 for children 3 to 6; and free for kids 2 and under. **The UC Berkeley Art Museum ★**, 2626 Bancroft Way, between College and Telegraph avenues (*©* **510/642-0808;** www.bampfa.berkeley.edu), is open Wednesday through Sunday from 11am to 5pm. Admission is $8 for adults; $5 for seniors, non-UCB students, visitors with disabilities, and children 17 and under; and $4 for UCB students. This museum contains a substantial collection of Hans Hofmann paintings, a sculpture garden, and the marvelous Pacific Film Archive, where they screen art-house films, rarities, and documentaries.

PARKS

Unbeknownst to many travelers, Berkeley has some of the most extensive and beautiful parks around. If you want to wear the kids out or enjoy hiking, swimming, sniffing roses, or just getting a breath of California air, jump in your car and make your way to **Tilden Park ★**. On the way, stop at the colorful terraced

The campus at UC Berkeley.

The Botanical Gardens at UC Berkeley.

WPA-era **Rose Garden** ★ in north Berkeley on Euclid Avenue between Bay View Place and Eunice Street. Then head high into the Berkeley hills to Tilden Park, where you'll find plenty of flora and fauna, hiking trails, an old steam train and merry-go-round, a farm and nature area for kids, and a chilly tree-encircled lake. The East Bay's public transit system, AC Transit (© **511;** www.actransit. org), runs the air-conditioned no. 67 bus line around the edge of the park on weekdays and all the way to the Tilden Visitors Center on Saturdays and Sundays. Call © **888/327-2757** or see www.ebparks.org for further information.

Another worthy nature excursion is the **University of California Botanical Garden** (© **510/643-2755;** www.botanicalgarden.berkeley.edu), which features a vast collection of native California herbage ranging from cacti to redwoods. It's on campus in Strawberry Canyon on Centennial Drive. Unfortunately no public bus can take you directly there, so driving is the way to go. Call for directions. Open daily from 9am to 5pm; closed the first Tuesday of every month; docent-led tours on Thursdays, Saturdays, and Sundays at 1:30pm. Admission is $7 adults, $5 seniors 65 and over and youth 13 to 17, $2 for youth 5 to 12, and free for children 2 and under and UC students.

SHOPPING

If you're itching to exercise your credit cards, head to one of two places. College Avenue from Dwight Way to the Oakland border overflows with eclectic boutiques, antiques shops, and restaurants. The other, more upscale option is Fourth Street, in west Berkeley, 2 blocks north of the University Avenue exit. This shopping strip is the perfect place to go on a sunny morning. Grab a cup of java and outstanding pancakes and scones at **Bette's Ocean View Diner,** 1807 Fourth St. (© **510/644-3932**). Read the paper at a patio table, and then hit the **Crate & Barrel Outlet,** 1785 Fourth St., between Hearst and Virginia streets (© **510/528-5500**). Prices are 30% to 70% off retail. It's open daily from 10am to 6pm. This area also boasts small, wonderful stores crammed with imported and locally made housewares. Nearby is **REI,** the Bay Area's favorite outdoors outfitter, 1338 San Pablo Ave., near Gilman Street (© **510/527-4140**). It's open Monday through Friday from 10am to 9pm, Saturday from 10am to 8pm, and Sunday from 11am to 6pm.

The Claremont Resort & Spa.

Where to Stay

Unfortunately, Berkeley is not even close to being a good hotel town. Most accommodations are extremely basic motels and funky B&Bs. The one exception (though it's overpriced) is the **Claremont Resort & Spa,** 41 Tunnel Rd., Berkeley (**www.claremontresort. com;** © **800/551-7266** or 510/843-3000), a grand Victorian hotel, also on the border of Oakland, with a fancy spa and gym, three restaurants, a hip bar, and grandiose surroundings. Rates are nearly half of what they were prerecession, ranging from $209 to $309. Or you can contact the **Berkeley & Oakland Bed and Breakfast Network** (www.bbonline.com/ca/berkeley-oakland; ☎ 510/848-1431), which books visitors into private homes and apartments.

MODERATE

Hotel Durant ★   It only takes walking into the lobby of Hotel Durant to get the feeling you're living out a game of Clue—or else pursuing a degree of higher learning. The lobby mimics an old-fashioned library (with contemporary furnishings like a bright blue leather couch), and the rooms give the feeling that you might be enrolling in the neighboring University of California at Berkeley any day now. (The location is within spitting distance of the campus itself and 1 block off of bustling Telegraph Ave.) Shower curtains are emblazoned with dictionary entries, posters from classics like *The Graduate* adorn the walls, even the key cards are made to look like student IDs. It's very whimsical, while being quite cool at the same time. Best of all, like other Joie de Vivre properties, Hotel Durant is pet friendly, so you can bring your furry friend along; rooms are equipped with dog beds and food bowls, and pets are given organic treats and toy footballs.

2600 Durant Ave. (at College St.), Berkeley, CA 94704. www.hoteldurant.com. ☎ **800/238-7268** or 510/845-8981. Fax 510/486-8336. 143 units. $105–$290 double. AE, DC, DISC, MC, V. Uncovered parking $16; valet parking $26. **Amenities:** Restaurant; bar. *In room:* TV, DVD, hair dryer, minibar, MP3 docking station, free Wi-Fi.

Rose Garden Inn   Like a Merchant Ivory movie, the accommodations within this 40-room/five-building inn range from English Country to Victorian, making it a favorite for visiting grandparents and vacationing retirees. Despite your age or design sense, the stunning and expansive garden exploding with rosebushes, hydrangeas, and an abundance of flora and fauna is sure to delight, as well as erase all memories that you're on a characterless stretch of Telegraph Avenue a few blocks south of the student action. Rooms, many of which have fireplaces, cable TVs, and all the basic amenities, show some wear and tend to be a little dark, but they are spacious, updated, and very clean, despite the obvious age of some bathroom nooks and crannies.

2740 Telegraph Ave. (at Stuart St.), Berkeley, CA 94705. www.rosegardeninn.com. ☎ **800/992-9005** or 510/549-2145. Fax 510/549-1085. 40 units. $139–$235 double. Rates include breakfast, coffee, and afternoon cookies. AE, DC, DISC, MC, V. Free parking on a space-available basis. *In room:* TV, hair dryer, free Wi-Fi.

Where to Eat

East Bay dining is a relaxed alternative to San Francisco's gourmet scene. There are plenty of ambitious Berkeley restaurants and, unlike in San Francisco, plenty of parking, provided you're not near the campus.

If you want to dine student style, eat on campus Monday through Friday. Buy something at a sidewalk stand or in the building directly behind the Student Union. There's also the Bear's Lair Brew Pub and Coffee House, and the Terrace. All the university eateries have both indoor and outdoor seating.

Telegraph Avenue has an array of small ethnic restaurants, cafes, and sandwich shops. Follow the students: If the place is crowded, it's good, supercheap, or both.

EXPENSIVE

Chez Panisse ★★★ CALIFOR-
NIAN   California cuisine is so
much a product of Alice Waters's
genius that all other restaurants following in her wake should be dated A.A.W.
(After Alice Waters). Most of the produce and meat comes from local farms
and is organically produced, and after
all these years, Alice still tends her restaurant with great integrity and innovation. In the upstairs cafe are displays of
pastries and fruit and an oak bar
adorned with large bouquets of fresh
flowers. At lunch or dinner, the menu
might feature delicately smoked grav-
lax or roasted eggplant soup with pesto,
followed by lamb ragout garnished

Alice Waters.

with apricots, onions, and spices and served with couscous.

The cozy downstairs restaurant, strewn with blossoming floral bouquets, is
an appropriately warm environment in which to indulge in the fixed-price four-
course gourmet dinner, which is served Tuesday through Thursday. Monday is
bargain night, with a three-course dinner for $60. Every Saturday, the restaurant
posts the following week's menu, which changes daily. The wine list is also excellent, with bottles ranging from $23 to $560.

1517 Shattuck Ave. (btw. Cedar and Vine). © **510/548-5525** for main restaurant reservations,
548-5049 for cafe reservations. Fax 510/548-0140. www.chezpanisse.com. Reservations required
for the dining room and taken 1 month prior to calendar date requested. Reservations are
recommended for the cafe, but walk-ins are welcome. Restaurant fixed-price menu $75–$95;
cafe main courses $15–$28. AE, DC, DISC, MC, V. Restaurant seatings Mon–Sat 6–8:30pm and
8:30–9:15pm most times of the year (in slower months, like Jan–Mar, times vary; please call to
confirm). Cafe Mon–Thurs 11:30am–3pm and 5–10:30pm; Fri–Sat 11:30am–3:30pm and
5–11:30pm. BART: Downtown Berkeley. From I-80 N., take the University Ave. exit and turn left
onto Shattuck Ave.

Meritage ★★★ CALIFORNIAN/FRENCH   In the trendy Claremont Spa
& Resort, which recently underwent a very pricey remodel, this restaurant (formerly Jordan's) reopened at the close of 2009 to much acclaim and attention.
With good reason—Chez Panisse aside, it's one of the only spots east of the Bay
Bridge where you'll find such bold fare. Boasting contemporary Californian cui-
sine in a classy French setting (minus the pretention), Meritage has many fine
attributes, but its *pièce de résistance* is the world-class wine list. Crafted around
the chef's menu—which largely relies on the crops and stocks of local farmers
and purveyors—each wine is paired to perfection with a suggested dish. While
Meritage carries 190 selections from around the world, the focal point is on
Northern California wines, and 18 types are offered by the 3- or 6-ounce glass.
Executive chef Josh Thomsen, who has been in the kitchen of some of the state's
best dining establishments, including Yountville's French Laundry, L.A.'s Hotel
Bel Air, and the Lodge at Pebble Beach, helms the restaurant. ***Best of all:*** All

courses are served in either half- or full-size portions, so you can sample several, and divided into categories by wine, such as "spicy and earthy reds" or "full-bodied whites." Do yourself a favor and check into one of the Claremont's upgraded rooms for the night so you can enjoy yourself to the fullest and not worry about stumbling home at evening's end.

41 Tunnel Rd. (inside the Claremont). (©) **800/551-7266.** www.meritageclaremont.com. Reservations recommended. Main courses $13–$37. AE, DC, DISC, MC, V. Restaurant Mon–Sat 6:30–11am; Tues–Sat 6–11pm. Lounge Mon–Sat 5–11pm; Sat 11am–2:30pm; Sun 6:30am–1:30pm.

MODERATE

Cafe Rouge ★ MEDITERRANEAN After cooking at San Francisco's renowned Zuni Cafe for 10 years, chef-owner Marsha McBride launched her own restaurant, a sort of Zuni East. She brought former staff members with her, and now her sparse, loftlike dining room serves salads, rotisserie chicken with oil and thyme, grilled lamb chops, steaks, and homemade sausages. East Bay carnivores are especially happy with the burger; like Zuni's, it's top-notch. Tuesday, Wednesday, and Thursday are $1 oyster nights from 5:30 to 9:30pm. During warm days, outdoor dining overlooking the shopping square is ideal.

1782 Fourth St. (btw. Delaware and Hearst). (©) **510/525-1440.** www.caferouge.net. Reservations recommended. Main courses $12–$36. MC, V. Mon–Fri 11:30am–3pm; Tues–Thurs 5:30–9:30pm; Fri–Sat 5:30–10pm; Sun 5–9:30pm; brunch Sun 10am–2:30pm.

Rivoli ★★ CALIFORNIAN One of the favored dinner destinations in the East Bay, Rivoli offers top-notch food at amazingly reasonable prices. Aside from a few house favorites, the menu changes entirely every 3 weeks to feature whatever's freshest and in season; the wine list follows suit, with around 10 by-the-glass options handpicked to match the food. While many love the portobello-mushroom fritter, a gourmet variation of the fried zucchini stick, we weren't wowed. However, plenty of dishes shine, including chicken cooked with prosciutto di Parma, wild mushroom chard and ricotta cannelloni, Marsala jus, snap peas, and baby carrots; and braised lamb shank with green garlic risotto, sautéed spinach, and oven-dried tomatoes. Finish the evening with an assortment of cheeses or a warm chocolate truffle torte with hazelnut ice cream, orange crème anglaise, and chocolate sauce.

1539 Solano Ave. (©) **866/496-2489** or 510/526-2542. www.rivolirestaurant.com. Reservations recommended. Main courses $18–$25. AE, DC, DISC, MC, V. Mon–Thurs 5:30–9:30pm; Fri 5:30–10pm; Sat 5–10pm; Sun 5–9pm.

INEXPENSIVE

Cafe Fanny ★★ FRENCH/ITALIAN Alice Waters's (of Chez Panisse fame) cafe is one of those local must-do East Bay breakfast traditions. Don your Birkenstocks and earth-tone apparel, grab the morning paper, and head here to wait in line for a simple yet masterfully prepared French breakfast. The menu offers such items as soft-boiled farm-fresh eggs on Levain toast, buckwheat crepes with house-made preserves, cinnamon toast, and an assortment of superb pastries. Lunch is more of an Italian experience featuring seasonal selections. Sandwiches—such as Alice's baked ham and watercress on focaccia or grilled chicken breast wrapped in prosciutto, sage, and aioli on Acme bread—might convince you that maybe Berkeley isn't such a crazy place to live after all. There's also a selection of pizzettas, salads, and soup. Eat inside at the stand-up food bar (one bench) or outside at one of the cafe tables.

1603 San Pablo Ave. (at Cedar St.). © **510/524-5447.** www.cafefanny.com. Breakfast items $3–$9.45; lunch $7.45–$9.45. MC, V. Mon–Fri 7am–3pm; Sat 8am–4pm; Sun 8am–3pm. Breakfast until 11am; Sun all day. Closed major holidays.

O Chamé ★★ JAPANESE   Spare and plain in its decor, this spot has a meditative air to complement the traditional, experimental, and extremely fresh Japanese-inspired cuisine. The menu, which changes daily, offers meal-in-a-bowl dishes ($13–$16) that allow a choice of soba or udon noodles in a clear soup with a variety of toppings—from shrimp and wakame seaweed to beef with burdock root and carrot. Appetizers include a flavorful melding of grilled shiitake mushrooms, as well as portobello mushrooms and green-onion pancakes. Their main entree selection always includes delicious roasted salmon, but you can also easily fill up on a bowl of soba or udon noodles with fresh, wholesome fixings (think roasted oysters, sea bass, and tofu skins).

1830 Fourth St. (near Hearst). © **510/841-8783.** www.ochame.com. Reservations recommended Fri–Sat dinner. Main courses $9–$19 lunch, $18–$24 dinner. AE, MC, V. Mon–Sat 11:30am–3pm; Mon–Thurs 5:30–9pm; Fri–Sat 5:30–9:30pm.

OAKLAND

10 miles E of San Francisco

Although it's less than a dozen miles from San Francisco, Oakland is worlds apart from its sister city across the bay. Originally little more than a cluster of ranches and farms, Oakland exploded in size and stature practically overnight, when the last mile of transcontinental railroad track was laid down. Major shipping ports soon followed and, to this day, Oakland remains one of the busiest industrial ports on the West Coast.

The price for economic success, however, is Oakland's lowbrow reputation as a predominantly working-class city; it is forever in the shadow of chic San Francisco. However, as the City by the Bay has become crowded and expensive in the past few years, Oakland has experienced a rush of new residents, businesses, and quality restaurants. As a result, "Oaktown" is in the midst of a renaissance, and its future continues to look brighter. A 2012 *New York Times* ranking of Oakland as the fifth most desirable destination to visit in the world, just above Tokyo, raised some eyebrows in San Francisco—but the city's profile is undoubtedly on the rise.

Rent a sailboat on Lake Merritt, stroll along the waterfront, see a show at the Paramount Theatre, explore the fantastic Oakland Museum—they're all great reasons to hop the bay and spend a fog-free day exploring one of California's largest and most ethnically diverse cities.

Essentials

BART connects San Francisco and Oakland through one of the longest underwater transit tunnels in the world. Fares range from $3 to $4 one-way, depending on your station of origin; children 4 and under ride free. BART trains operate Monday through Friday from 4am to midnight, Saturday from 6am to midnight, and Sunday from 8am to midnight. Exit at the 12th Street station for downtown Oakland. Call ☎ **511** or visit www.bart.gov for more info.

By car from San Francisco, take I-80 across the San Francisco–Oakland Bay Bridge and follow signs to downtown Oakland. Exit at Grand Avenue South for the Lake Merritt area. *Note:* Make sure you have a map of Oakland or GPS device—you do not want to get lost in Oakland and end up in a bad neighborhood.

For a calendar of events in Oakland, contact the **Oakland Convention and Visitors Bureau,** 463 11th St., Oakland, CA 94607 (☎ **510/839-9000; www.oaklandcvb.com**). The city also sponsors eight free guided tours, including African-American Heritage and downtown tours held Wednesdays and Saturdays May through October; call ☎ **510/238-3234** or visit **www.oaklandnet. com/walkingtours** for details.

Downtown Oakland lies between Grand Avenue on the north, I-980 on the west, Inner Harbor on the south, and Lake Merritt on the east. Between these landmarks are three BART stations (12th St., 19th St., and Lake Merritt), City Hall, the Oakland Museum, Jack London Square, and several other sights.

What to See & Do

Lake Merritt is one of Oakland's prime tourist attractions, along with Jack London Square (see below). Three and a half miles in circumference, the tidal lagoon was bridged and dammed in the 1860s and is now a wildlife refuge that is home to flocks of migrating ducks, herons, and geese. The 122-acre Lakeside Park, a popular place to picnic, feed the ducks, and escape the fog, surrounds the lake on three sides. Visit www.oaklandnet.com/parks for more info. At the **Municipal Boathouse ★** (☎ **510/238-2196**), in Lakeside Park along the north shore, you can rent sailboats, rowboats, pedal boats, canoes, or kayaks for $10 to $25 per hour (cash only). Or you can take an hour-long gondola ride with **Gondola Servizio** (☎ **888/737-8494;** www.gondolaservizio.com). Experienced gondoliers will serenade you, June through October, as you glide across the lake; the cost ranges from $45 to $225 for two, depending on the time and gondola style.

Another site worth visiting is Oakland's **Paramount Theatre ★**, 2025 Broadway (☎ **510/893-2300;** www.paramounttheatre.com), an outstanding National Historic Landmark and example of Art Deco architecture and decor. Built in 1931 and authentically restored in 1973, it's the city's main performing-arts center, hosting big-name performers like Smokey Robinson and Alicia Keys. Guided tours of the 3,000-seat theater are given the first and third Saturday morning of each month, excluding holidays. No reservations are necessary; just show up at 10am at the box office entrance on 21st Street at Broadway. The tour lasts 2 hours, cameras are allowed, and admission is $5.

If you take pleasure in strolling sailboat-filled wharves or are a die-hard fan of Jack London, you might enjoy a visit to **Jack London Square ★** (☎ **866/295-9853;** www.jacklondonsquare.com). A relatively low-key version of San Francisco's Fisherman's Wharf, Oakland's only patently tourist area shamelessly plays up the fact that Jack London spent most of his youth along the waterfront. The square fronts the harbor, housing a mostly tourist-tacky complex of boutiques and eateries, as well as a more locals-friendly farmers' market year-round on Sundays from 10am to 2pm. Recently, a couple of top-quality restaurants—Cocina Poblana and Miss Pearl's Jam House—have been added to the mix, and a new

ATTRACTIONS
Heinold's First and Last Chance
   Saloon **13**
Oakland Museum of California **8**
Paramount Theatre **6**
Potomac Visitor Center **10**

HOTELS
Oakland Marriott City Center **7**
Waterfront Hotel **11**

RESTAURANTS
A Côté **2**
BayWolf **3**
Bocanova **12**
Commis **4**
Oliveto Cafe & Restaurant **1**
Plum **5**
Yoshi's Jazz Club & Japanese
   Restaurant **9**

Oakland

THE USS POTOMAC: FDR'S floating white house

It took the Potomac Association's hundreds of volunteers more than 12 years—at a cost of $5 million—to restore the 165-foot presidential yacht *Potomac*, President Franklin D. Roosevelt's beloved "Floating White House." Now a proud and permanent memorial berthed at the Port of Oakland's FDR Pier at Jack London Square, the revitalized *Potomac* is open to the public for dockside tours, as well as 2-hour History Cruises along the San Francisco waterfront and around Treasure and Alcatraz islands. Prior to departure, a 15-minute video, shown at the nearby Potomac Visitor Center, provides background on FDR's presidency and FDR's legacy concerning the Bay Area.

The dockside tours are available year-round on Wednesdays and Fridays from 10am to 2:30pm, and on Sundays from noon to 3pm. Admission is $10 for ages 13 to 59, $8 for seniors age 60 and over, and free for children age 12 and under. The History Cruise runs on Thursdays and Saturdays from early May to mid-November; the departure time is 11am. History Cruise fares are $45 for ages 13 to 59, $40 for seniors 60 and older, $25 for children 6 to 12, and free for kids 5 and under. Due to the popularity of the cruises, advance purchase is strongly recommended.

Hours and cruise schedules are subject to change, so be sure to call the Potomac Visitor Center before arriving. Tickets for the Dockside Tour can be purchased at the Visitor Center upon arrival; tickets for the History Cruise can be purchased in advance via **Ticketweb** (© **866/468-3399**; www.ticketweb.com) or by calling the **Potomac Visitor Center** (© **510/627-1215**; www.usspotomac.org). The Visitor Center is located at 540 Water St., at the corner of Clay and Water streets adjacent to the FDR Pier at the north end of Jack London Square.

marketplace showcasing local epicure is under construction, offering new hope for the area. Most shops are open daily from 11am to 6pm (some restaurants stay open later). One of the best reasons to come here is the live jazz at **Yoshi's Jazz Club & Japanese Restaurant ★**, 510 Embarcadero W. (© **510/238-9200;** www.yoshis.com), which attracts top international performers and serves some fine sushi in its adjoining restaurant. In the center of the square is a small model of the Yukon cabin in which Jack London lived while prospecting in the Klondike during the gold rush of 1897.

In the middle of Jack London Square is a more authentic memorial, **Heinold's First and Last Chance Saloon** (© **510/839-6761; www.heinoldsfirstand lastchance.com**), a funky, friendly little bar and historic landmark. This is where London did some of his writing and most of his drinking.

Jack London Square is at Broadway and Embarcadero. Take I-880 to Broadway, turn south, and drive to the end. Or you can ride BART to the 12th Street station and then walk south along Broadway (about half a mile). Or take bus no. 72R or 72M to the foot of Broadway.

Oakland Museum of California ★   Two blocks south of Lake Merritt, the Oakland Museum of California incorporates just about everything you'd want to know about the state and its people, history, culture, geology, art, environment, and ecology. Inside a low, modern building set among sweeping gardens and terraces, it's actually three museums in one: exhibitions of works by California artists from Bierstadt to Diebenkorn; collections of historic artifacts, from Pomo Indian basketry to Country Joe McDonald's guitar; and re-creations of California habitats from the coast to the Sierra Mountains. The museum holds major shows of California artists as well as exhibitions dedicated to California's rich nature and history. Two new exhibit halls—the Gallery of California Art and the Gallery of California History—opened in spring of 2010, showcasing thousands of artworks and artifacts.

Forty-five-minute guided tours leave from the gallery information desks on request or by appointment. There's a fine cafe, a **Collector's Gallery** (© **510/834-2296**) that sells works by California artists, and a museum shop. The cafe is open Wednesday through Saturday from 10:30am to 4pm, Sunday from 1:30 to 4pm.

1000 Oak St. (at 10th St.). © **510/238-2200.** www.museumca.org. Admission $12 adults, $9 students and seniors, $6 youth (ages 9–17), and free for children 8 and under. 2nd Sun of the month is free (special exhibitions excepted). Wed–Sat 10am–5pm (until 9pm 1st Fri of the month); Sun noon 5pm. Closed Jan 1, July 4, Thanksgiving, and Dec 25. BART: Lake Merritt station; follow the signs posted in the station. From I-880 N., take the Oak St. exit; the museum is 5 blocks east. Or take I-580 to I-980 and exit at the Jackson St. ramp.

Where to Stay

Two fine midrange hotel options in Oakland are the **Waterfront Hotel,** 10 Washington St., Jack London Square (www.jdvhotels.com/hotels/waterfront; © **888/842-5333** or 510/836-3800), and the **Oakland Marriott City Center,** 1001 Broadway (www.marriott.com; © **800/228-9290** or 510/451-4000; fax 510/835-3466). Most major motel chains also have locations (and budget prices) around town and near the airport. The **Claremont Resort & Spa** (listed on p. 299), which borders both Berkeley and Oakland, is also an option; it's not downtown, but it's just a quick drive to all the action, and it's near the fabulous shopping and dining neighborhood of Oakland's Rockridge.

Where to Eat

Note that **Meritage ★★★** in the Claremont Hotel, on the border between Berkeley and Oakland, is listed earlier in the Berkeley section.

EXPENSIVE

Bocanova ★★ LATIN AMERICAN   Bocanova bills itself as a "Pan-America Grill." Well, I don't know about you, but I've never tasted food this good south of the border. The new Jack London Square restaurant, with stellar waterfront views, can be best described as a roller coaster for your taste buds, as you'll twist and turn, dip and ride over a plethora of flavors—many of which you might never have heard of before. When you see ingredients you don't recognize on the menu—and you will—don't hesitate to ask the knowledgeable servers for tips.

The menu is divided up by preparation: the Pantry, the Raw Bar, the Garden, the Freidora, the Stove, the Ovens, La Plancha, the Grill. Starters like Dungeness crab deviled eggs in chipotle aioli; walu crudo with mango, papaya, and rocoto pepper; and halibut ceviche are all staples. Main courses run the gamut of pork tenderloin with pineapple and chili sauce, Peruvian marinated chicken, and Kobe-style bavette steak with chipotle sauce. The sweet potato and chipotle gratin and the Parmesan cauliflower au gratin are must-order sides to pair with the rest of the perfect cooked-to-order meal. Don't forget to wash it all down with one of the Latin American–style cocktails, such as a Pisco sour. The roasted banana cake with cream cheese ice cream and cashew brittle at the end of the meal is the cherry on top.

55 Webster St. (on Jack London Sq.). ℭ **510/444-1233.** www.bocanova.com. Reservations recommended. Main courses $12–$36. MC, V. Mon–Fri 11:30am–3pm; Sat 11am–3pm; Mon–Thurs 5–10pm; Fri–Sat 5–11pm; Sun 5–9:30pm; brunch Sun 11am–3:30pm.

Oliveto Cafe & Restaurant ★★★ ITALIAN   Opened 25 years ago by Bob and Maggie Klein, and now under the helm of executive chef Jonah Rhodehamel, Oliveto is one of the top Italian restaurants in the Bay Area (and certainly the best in Oakland). Local workers pile in at lunchtime for wood-fired pizzas, simple salads, and sandwiches served in the lower-level cafe. The upstairs restaurant—with suave neo-Florentine decor and a partially open kitchen—is more elegant

and packed nightly with fans of the mind-blowing house-made pastas, sausages, and prosciutto. Oliveto has a wood-burning oven, flame-broiled rotisserie, and a full bar that sports a high-end liquor cabinet. An assortment of pricey grills, braises, and roasts anchors the daily changing menu, but the heavenly pastas, pizzettas, and awesome salads offer the most bang for your buck. Still, the Arista (classic Italian pork with garlic and rosemary and pork jus) is insanely good, and no one does fried calamari, onion rings, and lemon slices better than Oliveto. *Tip:* Free parking is available in the lot at the rear of the Market Hall building.

Oliveto.

Rockridge Market Hall, 5655 College Ave. (off the northeast end of Broadway at Shafter/ Keith St., across from the Rockridge BART station). ℭ **510/547-5356.** www.oliveto.com. Reservations recommended for restaurant. Main courses cafe $2.50–$12 breakfast, $4–$8 lunch, $12–$15 dinner; restaurant $13–$16 lunch, $13–$29 dinner. AE, DC, MC, V. Cafe Mon–Fri 7am–9pm; Sat–Sun 11:30am–10pm. Restaurant Mon–Fri 11:30am–2pm; Mon–Thurs 5:30–9pm; Fri–Sat 5:30–10pm; Sun 5–9pm.

Plum CALIFORNIAN   When Plum opened in 2010, it arrived to much fanfare. By the time it was 6 months old, it had already been named one of the best restaurants in the Bay Area by the *San Francisco Chronicle* and covered by every national travel magazine to pass through town. And not without cause. Its design, while aesthetically pleasing, is quite simple—communal-style wood banquettes, high loftlike ceilings, various picture collages of plums on the wall—as is the menu, at least in length. But simple doesn't have to translate to boring. The brainchild of Daniel Patterson, Plum's menu is broken up into four categories: Snacks, To Start, Vegetables and Grains, and Animal. Within each category, there are only four dishes, many of which are vegetable heavy. While the menu changes regularly, expect to see similar offerings to artichoke terrine, beet boudin noir, and turnip apple soup as smaller starters. The beef cheek and oxtail burger; slow-cooked farm egg with fried farro, chicken, and sprouts; and Manila clams are popular orders for the main event. Desserts, served in mason jars, are not only artfully presented but even more delicious than they look. For example, panna cotta was never my favorite—until I discovered Plum, which serves it at the perfect consistency with a glaze of quince compote and thyme on top.

2214 Broadway (at Grand Ave.). *(𝄞* **510/444-7586.** www.plumoakland.com. Reservations recommended. Small plates $4–$13; main courses $12 $18. AE, DC, MC, V. Sun–Thurs 5–10pm; Fri–Sat 5–11pm.

MODERATE

A Côté ★★ FRENCH TAPAS   Jack and Daphne Knowles look to chef Matthew Colgan to serve up superb rustic Mediterranean-inspired small plates at this loud, festive, and warmly lit joint. A "limited reservations" policy means there's usually a long wait during prime dining hours, but once seated, you can join locals in a nosh fest featuring the likes of croque-monsieur, *pommes frites* with aioli, wood-oven cooked mussels in Pernod, grilled pork tenderloin with creamy polenta and pancetta, and cheese plates—and wash it down with Belgian ales, perky cocktails, or excellent by-the-glass or -bottle selections from the great wine list. **Note:** The heated and covered outdoor seating area tends to be quieter.

5478 College Ave. (at laft Ave.). *(𝄞* **510/655-6469.** www.acoterestaurant.com. Limited reservations accepted. Small plates $8–$16. MC, V. Sun Tues 5:30–10pm; Wed–Thurs 5:30–11pm; Fri–Sat 5:30pm–midnight.

BayWolf ★ CALIFORNIAN   The life span of most Bay Area restaurants is about a year; BayWolf, one of Oakland's most revered restaurants, has, fittingly, been going strong for over 3 decades. The converted brown Victorian is a comfortably familiar sight for most East Bay diners, who have come here for years to let executive chef and owner Michael Wild do the cooking. BayWolf enjoys a reputation for simple yet sagacious preparations using only fresh ingredients. Main courses include Liberty Ranch duck three ways (grilled breast, braised leg, and crépinette) with turnips, curly endive, apples, and Calvados; flavorful seafood stew seasoned with saffron; and tender braised osso buco with creamy polenta and gremolata. Informal service means you can leave the tie at home. The front deck has heat lamps and a radiant heat floor, allowing for open-air evening dining year-round—a treat that San Franciscans rarely experience.

3853 Piedmont Ave. (off Broadway btw. 40th St. and MacArthur Blvd.). *(𝄞* **510/655-6004.** www. baywolf.com. Reservations recommended. Main courses $8–$18 lunch, $10–$26 dinner. AE, MC, V. Mon–Fri 11:30am–2pm; Tues–Sun 5:30–9:30pm. Paid parking at Piedmont Ave. and Yosemite St.

ANGEL ISLAND & TIBURON

8 miles N of San Francisco

A California State Park, **Angel Island** is the largest of San Francisco Bay's three islets (the others are Alcatraz and Yerba Buena). The island has been, at various times, a prison, a quarantine station for immigrants, a missile base, and even a favorite site for duels. Nowadays, most visitors are content with picnicking on the large green lawn that fronts the docking area; loaded with the appropriate recreational supplies, they claim a barbecue pit, plop their fannies down on the lush, green grass, and while away an afternoon free of phones, televisions, and traffic. Hiking, mountain biking, and guided tram tours are other popular activities here.

Tiburon, situated on a peninsula of the same name, looks like a cross between a fishing village and a Hollywood Western set—imagine San Francisco reduced to toy dimensions. The seacoast town rambles over a series of green hills and ends up at a spindly, multicolored pier on the waterfront, like a Fisherman's Wharf in miniature. In reality, it's an extremely plush patch of yacht-club suburbia, as you'll see by the marine craft and the homes of their owners. Ramshackle, color-splashed old frame houses line Main Street, sheltering chic boutiques, souvenir stores, antiques shops, art galleries, and dockside restaurants. Other roads are narrow, winding, and hilly and lead up to dramatically situated homes. The view from here of San Francisco's skyline and the islands in the bay is a good enough reason to pay the precious price to live here.

Although there is a hotel in Tiburon, I wouldn't recommend staying there: It's a 1-block town, and the hotel is very expensive. There are no hotels on Angel Island. Both destinations are better as day trips.

Essentials

Ferries of the **Blue & Gold Fleet** (© **415/705-5555;** www.blueandgoldfleet. com) from Pier 41 (Fisherman's Wharf) travel to both Angel Island and Tiburon.

Angel Island and Tiburon.

Boats run on a seasonal schedule; phone or look online for departure information. The round-trip fare is $15 to Angel Island, $8.50 for kids 6 to 12, and free for kids 5 and under. The fare includes state park fees. Tickets to Tiburon are $11 each way for adults, $6.75 for kids 5 to 11, and free for kids 4 and under. Tickets are available at Pier 41, online, or over the phone.

By car from San Francisco, take U.S. 101 to the Tiburon/Hwy. 131 exit and then follow Tiburon Boulevard all the way downtown, a 40-minute drive from San Francisco. Catch the **Tiburon–Angel Island Ferry** (✆ **415/435-2131;** www.angelislandferry.com) to Angel Island from the dock at Tiburon Boulevard and Main Street. The 15-minute round-trip costs $14 for adults, $12 for children 5 to 11, and $1 for bikes. One child 2 or under is admitted free of charge with each paying adult (after that it's $3.50 each). Boats run on a seasonal schedule, but usually depart hourly from 10am to 5pm on weekends, with a more limited schedule on weekdays. Call ahead or look online for departure information. Tickets can only be purchased when boarding and include state park fees. No credit cards.

What to See & Do on Angel Island

Passengers disembark from the ferry at **Ayala Cove,** a small marina abutting a huge lawn area equipped with tables, benches, barbecue pits, and restrooms. During the summer season, there's also a small store, a gift shop, the Cove Cafe (with surprisingly good grub), and an overpriced mountain-bike rental shop at Ayala Cove.

Angel Island's 12 miles of hiking and bike trails include the **Perimeter Road,** a paved path that circles the island. It winds past disused troop barracks, former gun emplacements, and other military buildings; several turnoffs lead to the top of Mount Livermore, 776 feet above the bay. Sometimes referred to as the "Ellis Island of the West," Angel Island was used as a holding area for detained Chinese immigrants awaiting admission papers from 1910 to 1940. You can still see faded Chinese characters on some of the walls of the barracks where the immigrants were held.

The 1-hour audio-enhanced open-air **Tram Tour** of the island costs $14 for adults, $13 for seniors, $9.50 for children 6 to 12, and is free for children 5 and under; schedules vary depending on the time of year. Tours generally run at 10:30am, 12:15, and 1:45pm on weekdays, with an additional run at 3pm on weekends and holidays. But check in at the Cove Cafe upon arrival on the island for the current day's tram schedule.

Guided **Segway tours** of the island are available as well, March through November. The 2½-hour interpretive tour circles the island's paved Perimeter Trail and costs $65, plus a $3 processing fee. Tours leave at 10:30am and 12:30pm daily. All riders must be 16 years or older. To make tour reservations, call ✆ **415/435-3392** or visit www.angelisland.com.

During the warmer months you can camp at a limited number of reserved sites; call **Reserve America** at ✆ **800/444-7275** or visit www.reserveamerica. com to find out about environmental campgrounds at Angel Island. Reservations are taken 2 days to 7 months in advance.

Guided **sea-kayak tours** ★ are also available. The 2½-hour trips combine the thrill of paddling stable, two- or three-person kayaks with an informative, naturalist-led tour around the island (conditions permitting). All equipment is provided (including a much-needed wet suit), kids are welcome, and no experience is necessary. Rates run $65 to $75 per person. For more information, contact the Sausalito-based **Sea Trek** at ℂ **415/488-1000** or www.seatrekkayak.com. *Note:* Tours depart from Sausalito, not Angel Island.

For more information about activities on Angel Island, call ℂ **415/897-0715** or log onto www.angelisland.com.

What to See & Do in Tiburon

The main thing to do in tiny Tiburon is stroll along the waterfront, pop into the stores, and spend an easy $50 on drinks and appetizers before heading back to the city. For a taste of the Wine Country, stop at **Windsor Vineyards,** 72 Main St. (ℂ **800/289-9463;** www.windsorvineyards.com)—its Victorian tasting room dates from 1888. Twenty or more choices are available for a free tasting. Wine accessories and gifts—glasses, cork pullers, carry packs (which hold six bottles), gourmet sauces, posters, and maps—are also available. Ask about personalized labels for your selections. The shop is open Sunday through Thursday from 10am to 6pm, Friday and Saturday from 10am to 7pm.

Where to Eat in Tiburon

Guaymas MEXICAN   Guaymas offers authentic Mexican regional cuisine and a spectacular panoramic view of San Francisco and the bay. In good weather, the two heated outdoor patios are almost always packed with diners soaking in the sun and scene. Inside the large dining room, colorful Mexican artwork and tons of colored paper cutouts strewn overhead on string brighten the beige walls. Should you feel chilled, to the rear of the dining room is a beehive-shaped adobe fireplace.

Guaymas is named after a fishing village on Mexico's Sea of Cortez, and both the town and the restaurant are famous for their camarones (giant shrimp). The restaurant also features ceviche, handmade tamales, and chargrilled beef, seafood, and fowl. It's not fancy, nor is it gourmet, but it is a good place to come with large parties or family. In addition to a small selection of California and Central American wines, the restaurant offers an exceptional variety of tequilas and Mexican beers.

5 Main St. ℂ **415/435-6300.** www.guaymas restaurant.com. Reservations recommended. Main courses $13–$23. AE, DC, DISC, MC, V. Mon–Thurs 11am–10pm; Fri–Sat 11am–11pm; Sun 10am–10pm. Ferry: Walk about 10 paces from the landing. From U.S. 101, exit at Tiburon/Hwy. 131; follow Tiburon Blvd. 5 miles and turn right onto Main St. Restaurant is behind the bakery.

The Windsor tasting room.

Sam's Anchor Café ★ 🎁 SEAFOOD   Summer Sundays are liveliest in Tiburon, when weekend boaters tie up at the docks of waterside restaurants like this one, and good-time cyclists pedal from the city to kick back here. Sam's is the kind of place where you and your cronies can take off your shoes and have a fun, relaxing time eating burgers and drinking margaritas outside on the pier. The fare is typical—sandwiches, salads, and such—but the quality and selection are inconsequential: Beer, burgers, and a designated driver are all you really need.

27 Main St. ⓒ **415/435-4527.** www.samscafe.com. Main courses $12–$18 brunch, $13–$25 lunch, $21–$27 dinner. AE, DC, DISC, MC, V. Mon–Thurs 11am–9:30pm; Fri 11am–10pm; Sat 9:30am–10pm; Sun 9:30am–9:30pm. Ferry: Walk from the landing. From U.S. 101, exit at Tiburon/Hwy. 131; follow Tiburon Blvd. 4 miles and turn right onto Main St.

SAUSALITO

5 miles N of San Francisco

Just off the northeastern end of the Golden Gate Bridge is the picturesque little town of Sausalito, a slightly bohemian adjunct to San Francisco. With fewer than 8,000 residents, Sausalito feels rather like St. Tropez on the French Riviera (minus the beach). Next to the pricey bayside restaurants, antiques shops, and galleries, you'll see hamburger joints, ice-cream shops, and secondhand bookstores. Sausalito's main strip is Bridgeway, which runs along the water; on a clear day the views of San Francisco far across the bay are spectacular. After admiring the view, those in the know make a quick detour to Caledonia Street, 1 block inland; not only is it less congested, but it also has a better selection of cafes and shops. Since the town is all along the waterfront and only stretches a few blocks, it's best explored on foot and easy to find your way around.

Essentials

The **Golden Gate Ferry Service** fleet, Ferry Building (ⓒ **415/923-2000**; www.goldengate.org), operates between the San Francisco Ferry Building, at the foot of Market Street, and downtown Sausalito. Service is frequent, running at reasonable intervals every day of the year except January 1, Thanksgiving, and December 25. Phone for an exact schedule The ride takes a half-hour, and one-way fares are $7.45 for adults; $3.70 for youth 6 to 18, seniors 65 plus, and passengers with disabilities (50% off full fare); children 5 and under ride free (limit two children per full-fare adult). Family rates are available on weekends.

Ferries of the **Blue & Gold Fleet** (ⓒ **415/705-5555**; www.blueandgold fleet.com) leave from Pier 41 (Fisherman's Wharf); the one-way cost is $11 for adults, $6.75 for kids 5 to 11. Boats run on a seasonal schedule; phone or log onto their website for departure information.

By car from San Francisco, take U.S. 101 N. and then take the first right after the Golden Gate Bridge (Alexander exit). Alexander becomes Bridgeway in Sausalito.

What to See & Do

Above all else, Sausalito has scenery and sunshine, for once you cross the Golden Gate Bridge, you're out of the San Francisco fog patch and under blue California sky (we hope). Houses cover the town's steep hills, overlooking a forest of masts on the waters below. Most of the tourist action, which is almost singularly limited to window-shopping and eating, takes place at sea level on Bridgeway.

Sausalito is a mecca for shoppers seeking handmade, original, and offbeat clothes and footwear, as well as arts and crafts. Many of the town's shops are in the alleys, malls, and second-floor boutiques reached by steep, narrow staircases on and off Bridgeway. Caledonia Street, which runs parallel to Bridgeway 1 block inland, is home to more shops.

Bay Area Discovery Museum ☺ If you just can't stand the thought of one more trip to Pier 39 or Fisherman's Wharf and are looking for something else to do with your kids (infants to 8 years old), check out this museum. Located on 7½ acres in the Golden Gate National Recreation Area at Fort Baker, the museum offers spectacular (jaw-dropping even!) views of the city and Golden Gate Bridge (you're literally at the northern base of the bridge) and is also the ultimate indoor-outdoor interactive kids' adventure. Tot Spot is tops for crawlers and toddlers (up to 42 in.); Lookout Cove is a 2½-acre outdoor area with a scaled-down model of the bridge that kids can add rivets to, a shipwreck to explore, tidal pools, and lovely site-specific art; Art Studios splits kids into age groups 5 and under and 6 and older; and the Wave Workshop re-creates the habitat under the bridge. There's even a small cafe that serves yummy, organic food far better than typical family-friendly fare. Chef Chad Newton serves up local, sustainable sandwiches, salads, soups, and burgers for kids and adults to nosh on after a long day of exploring. *One thing to note:* If you're here alone with two kids of different ages, it can be difficult to navigate, as they do keep the little ones separate from the older ones in the Tot Spot. If you explain your situation, they'll give your older ones (12 and up) a "Tot Spot Helper" sticker and let them in, but they won't be allowed to play and will have to stick by you. But if it's a nice day, you can spend the whole time in Lookout Cove with both kids, have lunch outside, and still feel like you got your money's worth.

E. Fort Baker, 557 McReynolds Rd. ✆ **415/ 339-3900.** www.baykidsmuseum.org. Admission $10 adults, $8 children, free for children under 1 and members. Discounts available to AAA members and members of reciprocal museum organizations (see website). Tues–Fri 9am–4pm; Sat–Sun 10am–5pm. Closed Mon and all major holidays. By car: Cross the Golden Gate Bridge and take the Alexander Ave. exit. Follow signs to E. Fort Baker and the Bay Area Discovery Museum.

Bay Model Visitors Center ☺ The U.S. Army Corps of Engineers once used this high-tech, 1½-acre model of San Francisco's bay and delta to resolve problems and observe the impact of changes in water flow. Today the model is strictly for educational purposes and reproduces (in scale) the rise and fall of tides and the flows and currents of water. There's a 10-minute

The Golden Gate Bridge gets its own Mini Me at the Bay Model Visitors Center.

film, self-guided and audio tours ($3 donation requested), and a 1-hour tour (free; book a reservation), but the most interesting time to visit is when the model is in operation, so call ahead.

2100 Bridgeway. ℭ **415/332-3871.** www.spn.usace.army.mil/bmvc. Free admission. Tues–Sat 9am–4pm.

Where to Stay

Sausalito is such a desirable enclave that it offers little in the way of affordable lodging. On the bright side, it's so close to San Francisco that it takes only about 15 minutes to get here, traffic permitting. Although the hotels listed below are great destinations in themselves, Sausalito itself is more day trip than destination.

VERY EXPENSIVE
The Inn Above Tide ★★

Perched directly over the bay atop well-grounded pilings, this former luxury-apartment complex underwent a $4-million transformation in 2004 into one of Sausalito's—if not the Bay Area's—finest accommodations. The view clinches it: Every room affords an unparalleled panorama of the San Francisco Bay, including a postcard-quality vista of the city glimmering in the distance. Should you manage to tear yourself away from your private deck, you'll find that 23 of the sumptuously appointed rooms sport romantic little fireplaces. Soothing warm earth tones highlight the decor, which blends in well with the bayscape outside. Be sure to request that your breakfast and newspaper be delivered to your deck and then cancel your early appointments—on sunny mornings, nobody checks out early.

Sausalito

ATTRACTIONS
Bay Area Discovery Museum **9**
Bay Model Visitors Center **1**

HOTELS
Casa Madrona Hotel & Spa **3**
Cavallo Point **8**
The Inn Above Tide **6**

RESTAURANTS
Hamburgers **5**
Horizons **7**
Poggio **4**
Sushi Ran **2**

30 El Portal St. (next to the Sausalito Ferry Landing), Sausalito, CA 94965. www.innabovetide. com. ℰ **800/893-8433** or 415/332-9535. Fax 415/332-6714. 29 units. $305–$1,025 double. Rates include continental breakfast and evening wine and cheese. AE, DC, MC, V. Valet parking $18. **Amenities:** Concierge. *In room:* A/C, TV/DVD, CD player, fridge, hair dryer, minibar, free Wi-Fi.

EXPENSIVE

Casa Madrona Hotel & Spa ★★   Sooner or later, most visitors to Sausalito look up and wonder at the ornate mansion on the hill. It's part of Casa Madrona, a hideaway by the bay built in 1885 by a wealthy lumber baron. The epitome of luxury in its day, the mansion had slipped into decay when John Gallagher purchased it in 1910 and converted it into a hotel. By 1976, it was damaged and facing the threat of demolition when John Mays acquired the property and revitalized the hotel. Successive renovations and extensions added a rambling, New England–style building to the hillside below the main house. Now listed on the National Register of Historic Places, the hotel offers whimsically decorated rooms, suites, and cottages, which are accessed by steep, gorgeously landscaped pathways. The 16 free-standing units, the seven cottages, and the rooms in the mansion have individual themes such as Lilac and Lace, Renoir, and the Artist's Loft. Some have claw-foot tubs and others have fireplaces. Rooms in the newer adjoining building have a chic contemporary decor, four-poster beds, marble bathrooms, and great marina views from some rooms. The classy Italian Poggio restaurant (see below) has been a Sausalito favorite since opening, and the hotel's full-service spa offers a wide assortment of treatments and getaway packages.

801 Bridgeway, Sausalito, CA 94965. www.casamadrona.com. ℰ **415/332-0502.** Fax 415/332-2537. 63 units. $169–$389 double. AE, DC, DISC, MC, V. Valet parking $24. Ferry: Walk across the street from the landing. From U.S. 101 N., take the 1st right after the Golden Gate Bridge (Alexander exit); Alexander becomes Bridgeway. **Amenities**: Restaurant, Poggio (see review, below); babysitting upon request; concierge; room service; spa. *In room:* TV, VCR upon availability, hair dryer, minibar.

Cavallo Point ★★   This new über-eco lodge, which occupies Golden Gate National Park's century-old former army quarters in Fort Baker, opened its doors in 2008 after nearly a decade in the making. The 17 red-roofed, colonial-style buildings form a horseshoe overlooking the San Francisco skyline at the bay's edge, with Adirondack chairs throughout the knee-high grassy knolls for lounging.

You have your pick of rooms: Roughly half are repurposed old officers' quarters in the historic lodging, which give off a rustic, nostalgic feel—prices start a bit lower for these than the more dressed-up rooms—while the newer buildings have a more contemporary flair. At least, that's what the hotel employees will tell you—there aren't too many discernible differences between the two models. The majority of rooms have unobstructed views of the Golden Gate Bridge, which practically towers over Cavallo's entities. For dinner, you needn't even head into downtown Sausalito, which is just a mile up the road; the on-site restaurant, Murray Circle, combining French, Mediterranean, and California influences in its fare, is about the finest around.

One of the four properties comprising the high-rolling Passport Resorts, Cavallo Point also offers an interesting mix of classes and activities, spanning a cooking school to sunrise yoga sessions, in its 11,000-square-foot Healing Arts

Centers. Check the blackboard in the main lobby daily to see what's on tap for the coming week.

601 Murray Circle, Sausalito, CA 94965. www.cavallopoint.com. ℂ **888/651-2003** or 415/339-4700. Fax 415/339-4792. 142 units. $240–$750 double; $300–$800 suite. AE, DC, DISC, MC, V. Valet parking $20. Pets are allowed for $75 (some rooms). **Amenities:** Restaurant; concierge; room service; spa. *In room:* TV, hair dryer, minifridge, MP3 docking station, free Wi-Fi.

Where to Eat

EXPENSIVE

Horizons ★ SEAFOOD/AMERICAN   Eventually, every San Franciscan ends up at Horizons to meet a friend for Sunday bloody marys. It's not much to look at from the outside, but it gets better as you head past the 1960s-era dark-wood interior toward the waterside terrace. On warm days, it's worth the wait for alfresco seating if only to watch dreamy sailboats glide past San Francisco's distant skyline. The food here can't touch the view, but it's well portioned and satisfying enough. Seafood dishes are the main items, including steamed clams and mussels, freshly shucked oysters, and a variety of seafood pastas. In fine Marin tradition, Horizons has an "herb tea and espresso" bar.

558 Bridgeway. ℂ **415/331-3232.** www.horizonssausalito.com. Reservations accepted weekdays only. Main courses $9–$27; salads and sandwiches $6–$11. AE, MC, V. Mon–Thurs 11:30am–9pm; Fri 11am–10:30pm; Sat 10:30am–10pm; Sun 10:30am–9pm. Valet parking $4.

Poggio ★★ ITALIAN   Sausalito has long been low on upscale dining options, but all that changed with the late-2003 opening of elegant Poggio; the name is a loose Italian translation for "special hillside place." Adjoining the Casa Madrona Hotel & Spa and across the street from the marina, everything is special here, from the floor-to-ceiling doors opening to the sidewalk, to its interior with arches and earthen colors, mahogany accents, well-directed light, and centerpiece

A picnic lunch, SAUSALITO-STYLE

If the crowds are too much or the prices too steep at Sausalito's bayside restaurants, grab a bite to go for an impromptu picnic in the park fronting the marina. It's one of the best and most romantic ways to spend a warm, sunny day in Sausalito. The best source for a la carte eats is the Mediterranean-style **Venice Gourmet Delicatessen** at 625 Bridgeway, located right on the waterfront just south of the ferry landing. Since 1964, this venerable deli has offered all the makings for a superb picnic: wines, cheeses, fruits, stuffed vine leaves, salami, lox, prosciutto, salads, quiche, made-to-order sandwiches, and fresh-baked pastries. It's open daily from 9am to 6pm (ℂ **415/332-3544;** www.venicegourmet.com).

wood-burning oven manned by a cadre of chefs; to the wine cellar, terra-cotta-tiled floors, comfy mohair banquettes, and white linen-draped tables. The daily changing menu features items like a superb salad of endive, Gorgonzola, walnuts, figs, and honey; pizzas; addictively excellent pastas (try the spinach ricotta gnocchi with beef ragout); and entrees such as whole local petrale sole deboned and served tableside, or grilled lamb chops with roasted fennel and gremolata. Special seasonal meals are offered throughout the year, including the highly anticipated white truffle dinner in November. With a full bar, well-priced wine list, and great desserts, this is Sausalito's premier dining destination—excluding the more casual Sushi Ran (see below).

777 Bridgeway (at Bay St.). ✆ **415/332-7771.** www.poggiotrattoria.com. Italian-style breakfast a la carte $2.50–$5.50; main courses lunch $8–$18, dinner $13–$25. AE, DC, DISC, MC, V. Daily 6:30 11am; Sun–Thurs 11:30am–10pm; Fri–Sat 11:30am–11pm. Free valet parking at Casa Madrona Hotel & Spa.

Sushi Ran ★★ SUSHI/JAPANESE   San Francisco isn't exactly stellar in its Japanese-food selection, but right across from the Golden Gate Bridge is a compact, but fashionable, destination for seriously delicious sushi and cooked dishes. All walks of sushi-loving life cram into the sushi bar, window seats, and more roomy back dining area for Nori Kusakabe's nigiri sushi and standard and specialty rolls. You'll also find a slew of creative dishes by executive chef Scott Whitman, such as generously sized and unbelievably moist and buttery miso-glazed black cod (a must-have), oysters on the half shell with ponzu sauce and tobiko (fish eggs), and a Hawaiian-style ahi poke (Hawaiian-style minced raw fish) salad with seaweed dressing that's authentic enough to make you want to hula.

107 Caledonia St. ✆ 4**15/332-3620.** www.sushiran.com. Reservations recommended. Sushi $5–$14; main courses $8.50–$16. AE, MC, V. Mon–Fri 11:45am–2:30pm; Mon–Sat 5:30–11pm; Sun 5–10:30pm. From U.S. 101 N., take the 1st right after the Golden Gate Bridge (Alexander exit); Alexander becomes Bridgeway in Sausalito. At Johnson St. turn left, and then right onto Caledonia.

INEXPENSIVE

Hamburgers CAFE   Like the name says, the specialty at this tiny, narrow cafe is juicy flame-broiled hamburgers, arguably Marin County's best. Look for the rotating grill in the window off Bridgeway, and then stand in line and salivate with everyone else. Chicken burgers are a slightly healthier option. Order a side of fries, grab a bunch of napkins, and head to the park across the street.

737 Bridgeway. ✆ **415/332-9471.** Sandwiches $5.50–$6.50. No credit cards. Daily 11am–5pm. From U.S. 101 N., take the 1st right after the Golden Gate Bridge (Alexander exit); Alexander becomes Bridgeway in Sausalito.

MARIN, MUIR WOODS & MOUNT TAMALPAIS

N of the Golden Gate Bridge

Muir Woods

While the rest of Marin County's redwood forests were being devoured to feed San Francisco's turn-of-the-20th-century building spree, Muir Woods, in a

Muir Woods.

remote ravine on the flanks of Mount Tamalpais, escaped destruction in favor of easier pickings.

Although the magnificent California redwoods have been successfully transplanted to five continents, their homeland is a 500-mile strip along the mountainous coast of southwestern Oregon and Northern California. The coast redwood, or Sequoia sempervirens, is one of the tallest living things known to man (!); the largest known specimen in the Redwood National Forest towers 368 feet. It has an even larger relative, the Sequoiadendron giganteum of the California Sierra Nevada, but the coastal variety is stunning enough. Soaring toward the sky like a wooden cathedral, Muir Woods is unlike any other forest in the world and an experience you won't soon forget.

Granted, Muir Woods is tiny compared to the Redwood National Forest farther north, but you can still get a pretty good idea of what it must have been like when these giants dominated the entire coastal region. What is truly amazing is that they exist a mere 6 miles (as the crow flies) from San Francisco—close enough, unfortunately, that tour buses arrive in droves on the weekends. You can avoid the masses by hiking up the **Ocean View Trail,** turning left on **Lost Trail,** and returning on the **Fern Creek Trail.** The moderately challenging hike shows off the woods' best sides and leaves the lazy-butts behind.

To reach Muir Woods from San Francisco, cross the Golden Gate Bridge heading north on Hwy. 101, take the Stinson Beach/Hwy. 1 exit heading west, and follow the signs (and the traffic). The park is open daily from 8am to sunset, and the admission fee is $5 per person 17 and over. There's also a small gift shop, educational displays, and ranger talks. For more information, call the **National Parks Service at Muir Woods** (✆ **415/388-2596**) or visit www.nps.gov/muwo.

If you don't have a car, you can book a bus trip with **San Francisco Sightseeing** (✆ **888/428-6937** or 415/434-8687; www.sanfranciscosightseeing. com), which takes you straight to Muir Woods and makes a short stop in Sausalito on the way back. The 3½-hour tour runs twice daily at 9:15am and 2:15pm and costs $41 for adults, $39 for seniors, $20 for children 5 through 11, and free for kids 4 and under. Pickup and return are offered from select San Francisco hotels. Call for information and departure times.

Mount Tamalpais

The birthplace of mountain biking, Mount Tam—as the locals call it—is the Bay Area's favorite outdoor playground and the most dominant mountain in the region. Most every local has his or her secret trail and scenic overlook, as well as an opinion on the raging debate between mountain bikers and hikers (a touchy subject). The main trails—mostly fire roads—see a lot of foot and bicycle traffic on weekends, particularly on clear, sunny days when you can see a hundred miles in all directions, from the foothills of the Sierra to the western horizon. It's a great place to escape from the city for a leisurely hike and to soak in breathtaking views of the bay.

To get to Mount Tamalpais **by car,** cross the Golden Gate Bridge heading north on Hwy. 101, and take the Stinson Beach/Hwy. 1 exit. Follow the signs up the shoreline highway for about 2½ miles, turn onto Pantoll Road, and continue for about a mile to Ridgecrest Boulevard. Ridgecrest winds to a parking lot below East Peak. From there, it's a 15-minute hike up to the top. You'll find a visitor center with a small museum, video, diorama, and store, as well as informative "Mount Tam Hosts" who are more than happy

Hiking Mount Tamalpais.

to help you plan a hike, identify plants, and generally share their love of the mountain. Visitor center admission is free; it's open Saturday and Sunday from 11am to 4pm (standard time), and Saturday and Sunday 10am to 5:30pm (daylight saving time). Park hours are 7am to 6pm daily in winter, 7am to 9pm for about 1 month during the height of summer. Two-hour, 2-mile moonlight hikes, among many others, are offered (✆ **415/388-2070;** www.mttam.net).

Where to Stay

Pelican Inn ★★   Perhaps one of the most charming facets of the Pelican Inn is that it's beloved by locals but relatively unknown in the travel industry. The 16th-century-style English inn (which, ironically, was built in 1979) has seven rooms accessed by a tight-fitting stairwell in the back "Snug Room" (open only to inn guests and a great place for lounging at the end of a long day). Some quarters have four-poster beds and tapestry rugs; all have that quintessential old-world charm. Even if you're just rushing through, stop by the pub for a bite; it serves up some classic English fare like shepherd's pie and bangers and mash with a contemporary California spin. On sunny days, the lawn is filled with bikers and hikers—a popular coastal trail cuts in right beside the inn—and those just visiting nearby Muir Beach. The inn prides itself on being "organic," meaning service is minimal and not too attentive; also, rooms are free of outside distractions like phones, TVs, and VCRs.

10 Pacific Way (Hwy. 1), Muir Beach, CA 94965. www.pelicaninn.com. ✆ **415/383-6000.** 7 units. $190–$280 double. Rates include a full English breakfast. MC, V. **Amenities:** Restaurant.

Where to Eat

The Tavern at Lark Creek ★★ AMERICAN   It used to be the pricey Lark Creek Inn; now it's a neighborhood pub where you can grab a bite—and a damn tasty one, at that—for under $15. Housed in a stately Victorian, the interior is warm and inviting, with soaring sky-lit ceilings and ample dining space—much cozier, more convivial, and less snobby than its former state. The menu has a nice mixture of comfort fare like shrimp and grits or mac and cheese croquettes (tempura-battered), as well as heartier gastro-pub eats like short ribs and wood-oven-baked, lamb-sausage moussaka. The restaurant even offers ongoing vegan options, such as quinoa-and-red-potato cakes or pumpkin risotto, and a build-your-own prix-fixe menu for $30.

234 Magnolia Ave., Larkspur. © **415/924-7766.** www.tavernatlarkcreek.com. Reservations recommended. Main courses $8.95–$19. AE, DC, DISC, MC, V. Mon–Thurs 5:30–9:30pm; Fri–Sat 5–10pm; Sun 10am–2pm and 5–9:30pm. Free valet parking.

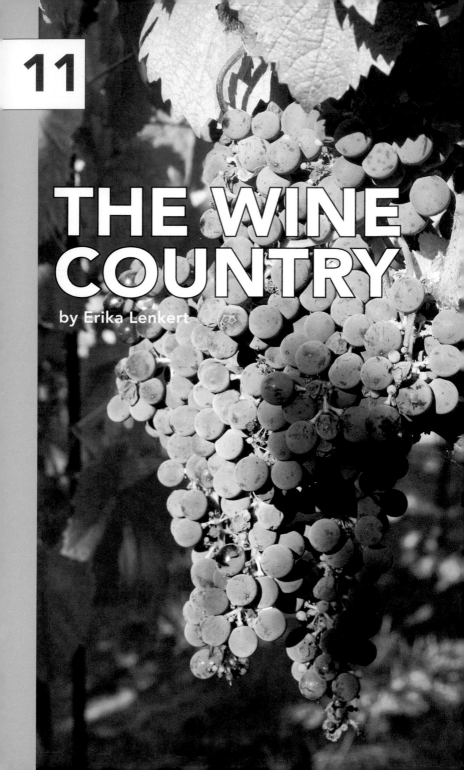

THE WINE COUNTRY

by Erika Lenkert

Anyone with a penchant for the good life and a day or more to spare on his or her San Francisco itinerary should beeline directly to the Wine Country, an hour or so north by car. Amid mountains dipping into grapevine-trellised valleys, you'll experience an entirely different Northern California: fresh country air, mustard-flower-draped hillsides in spring, gloriously hot weather during summer and fall, romantically chilly and wet days during winter, and nothing to do but indulge all year round—be it in the tasting rooms of some of the world's finest wineries, around the tables at the region's legendary restaurants, or within the resorts and spas tucked within the valleys and mountains. Even the rotten economy can't spoil the fun to be found in this Disneyland for grown-ups. If anything, the economic downturn has made a table at previously inaccessible restaurants easier to come by and proprietors that much more eager to make your experience truly memorable.

To help you decide which of the Wine Country's two distinct valleys (Napa and Sonoma) you prefer to visit, consider their differences: The most obvious is size—Napa Valley dwarfs Sonoma Valley in population, number of wineries, and sheer volume of tourism (and traffic). Napa is definitely the more commercial of the two, with many more wineries and spas to choose from (including more formal tours and seminars for those who want to learn about the world of winemaking), and a superior selection of restaurants, hotels, and quintessential Wine Country activities, like hot-air ballooning, wine tasting, and shopping. Meanwhile, Sonoma Valley is paradise for those who are in the less-is-more camp. Napa Valley's neighbor has fewer wineries (about 45), fewer big hotels and restaurants, and a less commercial feel. As a result, there are fewer crowds on the low-key country roads; more down-home charm in the country communities, B&Bs, and little family-run restaurants; and, in general, more opportunities for intimate pastoral experiences. For more on Sonoma Valley's offerings (as spectacular as Napa Valley's but more low-key), see the "Sonoma Valley" section, later in this chapter.

If you're planning a more extensive trip to the area, consult *Frommer's Napa & Sonoma Day by Day* (Wiley).

NAPA VALLEY

Just 55 miles north of San Francisco, the city of Napa and its neighboring towns have an overall tourist-centric feel. You'll see plenty of rolling hills, flora and

PREVIOUS PAGE: **Pinot noir grapes from Carneros vineyards.**

fauna, and vast stretches of vine-yards, but they come hand-in-hand with upscale restaurants (which are shockingly increasing by the day despite the down economy), designer discount outlets, rows of hotels, and, in summer, traffic clustered more tightly than grapes on the vines. Even with hordes of visitors during the high season (think Mar–Oct), Napa is still pretty sleepy, focusing on day-time attractions (wine, outdoor activities, and spas) and, of course, food. Nightlife is very limited, but after indulging all day, most visitors are ready to turn in early anyway.

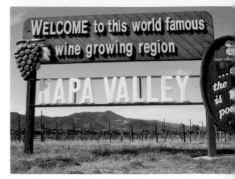

Napa welcomes more than five million visitors a year.

Although the name "Napa Valley" is larger than life, the actual area is relatively condensed and a mere 35 miles long. When the traffic cooperates, you can venture from the town of Napa all the way to Calistoga in a half-hour.

Essentials

GETTING THERE From San Francisco, cross the Golden Gate Bridge and continue north on U.S. 101. Turn east on California Hwy. 37; turn left onto the Hwy. 12/121 turnoff and follow it through the Carneros District to Hwy. 29, the main road through the Wine Country. Head north on Hwy. 29. Downtown Napa is a few minutes ahead, while Yountville, Oakville, Rutherford, St. Helena, and Calistoga are farther along.

Hwy. 29 (the St. Helena Hwy.) runs the length of Napa Valley. You really can't get lost—there's just one north-south road, on which most of the

A slice of Tuscany in California.

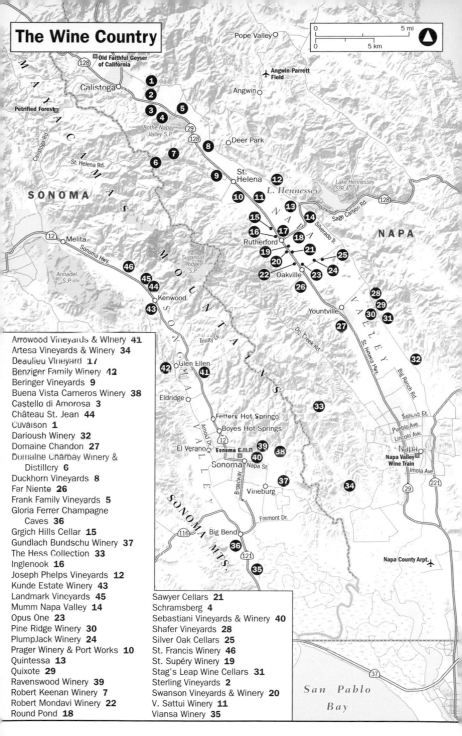

The Wine Country

Old Faithful Geyser of California

Pope Valley

Angwin-Parrett Field

Angwin

Calistoga

Petrified Forest

Bothe-Napa Valley S.P.

Deer Park

St. Helena

L. Hennessey

Lake Hennessey S.R.A.

SONOMA

MAYACAMAS

Melita

Annadel S.P.

Sonoma Hwy.

Sugarloaf Ridge S.P.

Kenwood

Rutherford

Oakville

NAPA

Yountville

MOUNTAINS

Trinity Dr.

Dry Creek Rd.

St. Helena Hwy.

Big Ranch Rd.

Glen Ellen

Eldridge

Fetters Hot Springs

Boyes Hot Springs

El Verano

Sonoma C.H.H.

Sonoma

Napa St.

Vineburg

Fremont Dr.

Pueblo Ave.

Lincoln Ave.

Napa

Napa Valley Wine Train

Imola Ave.

SONOMA MTS.

Big Bend

Napa County Arpt.

San Pablo Bay

wineries, hotels, shops, and restaurants are located. The other main thoroughfare, which parallels Hwy. 29, is the Silverado Trail. You'll find lots of great wineries here, too.

VISITOR INFORMATION   Once you're in Napa Valley, you can stop at the **Napa Valley Welcome Center,** 600 Main St., Napa, CA 94559 (*©* **707/251-5895;** www.legendarynapavalley.com), open Tuesday through Thursday 9am to 5pm and 9am to 6pm on Friday. You can call or write in for the *Napa Valley Guidebook,* which includes information on lodging, restaurants, wineries, and other things to do, along with a winery map; the guidebook is free of charge to U.S. residents.

Another good source is WineCountry.com, where you'll find tons of information on all of California's wine-producing regions as well as articles written by moi.

Touring the Napa Valley & Wineries

Napa Valley claims more than 45,000 acres of vineyards, making it the most densely planted winegrowing region in the United States. The venture from one end to the other is easy; you can drive it in around a half-hour (but expect it to take closer to 50 min. during high season, Apr–Nov). With more than 300 wineries tucked into the nooks and crannies surrounding Hwy. 29 and the Silverado Trail—most of which offer tastings and sales—it's worthwhile to research which wineries you'd like to visit before you hit the wine trails. If you'd like a map detailing the region's wineries, you can grab one from the visitor center—or see *Frommer's Portable California Wine Country.*

Reservations at Wineries

Plenty of wineries' doors are open to everyone, without reservations, between 10am and 4:30pm. Most wineries that require reservations for visits do so because of local permit laws—not because they're snobby—while some do so to create a more intimate tasting experience (usually with lofty prices to match). It's always best to call ahead if you have your heart set on visiting a certain winery.

Conveniently, most of the large wineries—as well as most of the hotels, shops, and restaurants—are along a single road, Hwy. 29. It starts at the mouth of the Napa River, near the north end of San Francisco Bay, and continues north to Calistoga and the northern limits of the grape-growing region. When planning your tour, keep in mind that most wineries are closed on major holidays.

Each of the Napa Valley establishments in this chapter—every town, winery, hotel, and restaurant—is organized below from south to north, beginning in the city of Napa, and can be reached from the main thoroughfare of Hwy. 29.

NAPA ★

55 miles N of San Francisco

The city of Napa serves as the commercial center of the Wine Country and the gateway to Napa Valley—hence the high-speed freeway that whips you right past it and on to the "tourist" towns of St. Helena and Calistoga. However, if you veer off the highway, you'll be surprised to discover a small but burgeoning community

Napa Valley Traffic

Travel the Silverado Trail as often as possible to avoid California Hwy. 29's traffic. The Trail runs parallel to and about 2 miles east of Hwy. 29. You get there from the city of Napa or by taking any of the "crossroads" from Hwy. 29. Crossroads are not well signposted, but they're clearly defined on most maps. If you take the Trail, keep us locals happy by driving at least the speed limit. Slow rubberneckers are no fun to follow when you're trying to get from one end of the valley to the other. Also, avoid passing through Main Street in St. Helena (on Hwy. 29) during high season. While a wintertime ride from Napa to Calistoga can take 30 minutes, in summer you can expect the trek to take closer to 50 minutes.

of around 75,000 residents with the most "cosmopolitan" atmosphere in the county (though I use that term loosely)—and some of the most affordable accommodations in the valley (Calistoga also has good deals). Still in the process of gentrification for the past decade, and deeply affected by the economic downturn, it continues to house surprisingly fancy hotels, condos, and restaurants, while the city center's small storefront spaces remain glaringly abandoned. Heading north on either Hwy. 29 or the Silverado Trail leads you to Napa's wineries and the more quintessential Wine Country atmosphere of vineyards and wide-open country views.

Artesa Vineyards & Winery ★★ 📷 Views, modern architecture, seclusion, and region-specific pinot noir flights are the reasons this is one of my favorite stops. Arrive on a day when the wind is blowing less than 10 mph, and the fountains are captivating, they automatically shut off with higher winds. Step into the winery, and there's plenty to do. You can wander through the very tasteful gift shop, browse a room that outlines history and details of the Carneros region, or head to the long bar for $10 to $15 flights of everything from chardonnays and pinot noirs to cabernet sauvignon and merlot. Sorry, but Artesa's permits don't allow for picnicking.

A sculpture at Artesa.

1345 Henry Rd., Napa. ✆ **707/224-1668.** www.artesawinery.com. Daily 10am–5pm; tours daily at 11am and 2pm. From Hwy. 12/121, turn north on old Sonoma Rd., turn left on Dealy Lane, which becomes Henry Rd.

Darioush Winery ★ With architecture based on Persepolis, the capital city of ancient Persia, this 22,000-square-foot winery features the dazzling 16 monumental 18-foot-tall free-standing columns at the entrance, a state-of-the-art visitor center, and opulent landscaping—all in honor of Persian-American owner Darioush Khaledi's homeland. (He immigrated during the Islamic Revolution and found his fortune in a grocery chain.) It's free to stroll the property, but expensive tastings ($35) include their well-regarded merlot, cabernet sauvignon, viognier, and chardonnay, as well as addictive Persian pistachios. Opt for the appointment-only $50 private tasting with cheese pairing and you'll get to savor local Sonoma artisan cheeses with your wine and tour the facilities. Throw down $150 and you're privy to an elaborate wine and food pairing featuring limited release wines.

4240 Silverado Trail (south of Oak Knoll Ave.), Napa. ℂ **707/257-2345.** www.darioush.com. Daily 10:30am–5pm. Private tasting with cheese pairing daily at 2pm and by appointment. Tours available by appointment.

The Hess Collection ★★ 🎁 Tucked into the hillside of rural Mount Veeder, this winery brings art and wine together like no other destination in the valley. Swiss art collector Donald Hess is behind the 1978 transformation of the Christian Brothers' 1903 property into a winery–art gallery exhibiting huge, colorful works by the likes of Frank Stella, Francis Bacon, and Andy Goldsworthy. A free self-guided tour leads through the collection and offers glimpses through tiny windows into the winemaking facilities. Guided tours and food and wine pairings, which include four wines and seasonal noshes, are available by appointment only Thursday through Saturday for $35 to $50 per person. But you can drop by the tasting room anytime, pay $10, and sample the current cabernet and chardonnay and three other featured wines; $15 to $30 gets you a reserve tasting. Current-release bottles go from $18 to $120. They've got a decent gift shop and very picturesque courtyard, too.

4411 Redwood Rd., Napa. ℂ **707/255-1144.** www.hesscollection.com. Daily 10am–5:30pm, except some holidays. From Hwy. 29 north, exit at Redwood Rd. west, and follow Redwood Rd. for 6½ miles.

Pine Ridge Winery More for the serious wine taster, intimate Pine Ridge welcomes guests with a pretty hillside location, less tourist traffic than most, and coveted cabernet sauvignon. Outside, vineyards surround the well-landscaped property. Across the parking lot is a demonstration vineyard, which is somewhat educational if you know something about grape growing and even more helpful if you take their $40 tour (by appointment), which also covers the cellar and barrel tastings. Otherwise, tastings, which are held inside a modest room, range from $20 to $40 for current releases. White-wine lovers should definitely sample their chenin-blanc viogner blend; it's divine.

5901 Silverado Trail, Napa. ℂ **800/575-9777** or 707/253-7500. www.pineridgewinery.com. Daily 10:30am–4:30pm. Tours by appointment at 10am, noon, and 2pm.

📎 Paying to Taste

It used to be unusual to have to pay for wine tasting, and when the tides first started to change, I wasn't really for it. But over the past decade, sipping through the region has become such a pastime that in the more popular—and cheap or free—tasting spots you'll often find yourself competing for room at the bar, never mind a refill or a little wine chatter with your host. As a result, I've changed my view on paying a premium to taste. With the flash of a 10- or 20-spot per person, you not only avoid crowding in with the hundreds of tipsy souls who come merely for the fun and the buzz, but you also usually get a more intimate experience, complete with attention from staff and usually far more exclusive (and sometimes even seated) surroundings.

The architectural whimsy of Quixote winery.

Quixote ★★ 🎁 Due to zoning laws, this spectacular and truly one-of-a-kind Stags' Leap District winery welcomes up to eight guests per day, all of whom are likely to find themselves as awestruck by the architecture as they are by the powerful petite syrahs and cabernet sauvignons. The hidden, hillside property owned by longtime industry power player Carl Doumani is the only U.S. structure designed by late great European artist Friedensreich Hundertwasser. Whimsical and captivating even to those who know nothing about design, it's a structural fantasy world with undulating lines, a gilded onion dome, and a fearless use of color. During the $25-per-person reservation-only sit-down tasting and tour, visitors can fill their agape mouths with tastes of the winery's current releases.

6126 Silverado Trail, Napa. ✆ **707/944-2659.** www.quixotewinery.com. Tastings by appointment only Tues–Sun.

Shafer Vineyards ★★ 🎁 For an intimate, off-the-beaten-track wine experience, make an appointment to tour and taste at this spectacularly low-key destination producing legendary wine. Unlike many Napa wineries, this one is family owned—by John and Doug Shafer—who, along with winemaker Elias Fernandez, use sustainable farming and solar energy to make truly outstanding wines, including chardonnay, merlot, cabernet sauvignon, and syrah. Though they produce only 32,000 cases per year, they have still managed to make their Hillside Select famous. But more importantly, they share it and their winemaking philosophy with you during a truly enjoyable and relaxed $45-per-person 1½-hour tour and tasting. Most wines go for $48 to $70, but their Hillside Select cabernet will cost you $225 (and, should you get your hands on some, is immediately worth more). **FYI:** Book your tasting tour 4 to 6 weeks in advance online or by phone; the tours are intimate and popular.

6154 Silverado Trail, Napa. ✆ **707/944-2877.** www.shafervineyards.com. By appointment only Mon–Fri 9am and 4pm; closed weekends and holidays.

Stag's Leap Wine Cellars Founded in 1972, Stag's Leap shocked the oenological world in 1976 when its 1973 cabernet won first place over French wines in a Parisian blind tasting. Visit the charmingly landscaped, unfussy winery and its very cramped "tasting room" where, for $15 per person, you can try a selection of four current release wines. Be prepared to pay $25 for estate wines, which, incidentally are very tasty. A 1-hour tour and tasting runs through everything from the vineyard and production facilities to the ultraswank $5-million wine caves.

5766 Silverado Trail, Napa. ✆ **707/944-2020.** www.cask23.com. Daily 10am–4:30pm. Tours by appointment only. From Hwy. 29, go east on Trancas St. or Oak Knoll Ave., and then north to the cellars.

YOUNTVILLE ★★

68 miles N of San Francisco

As tiny a town as it is, Yountville (pop. around 3,000) is a serious power player in the world of food and wine. Why? Two words: Thomas Keller. One of the nation's most revered chefs, he has not one, but four dining destinations here. But there's more to munch on than fabulous French-inspired food. TV Chef Michael Chiarello (who became famous decades ago as Tra Vigne's chef) has an Italian restaurant here, too, right alongside his NapaStyle home style and gift shop. You'll also find several other well-established culinary legends who have long given visitors reason to veer off Hwy. 29 to overindulge. Fortunately, the town also has lots of places to sleep off food comas. Most are midlevel luxury resorts, which are subtly sprinkled along the thoroughfare, including **Hotel Luca ★★** (6774 Washington St.; www.hotellucanapa.com; ✆ **707/944-8080**), a charming 20-room destination in downtown Yountville that conjures Tuscan decadence, complete with giant, opulently appointed rooms, a centerpiece courtyard with outdoor fireplace, outdoor pool, a polished restaurant, and basement spa that also delivers. Highfalutin travelers flock to **Bardessono** (6526 Yount St., ✆ **707/204-6000;** www.bardessono.com; $400–$800 double), a "sustainable luxury" resort that boasts some of the sexiest and best-appointed rooms around, supermodern style, and easy access to the town's top restaurants.

Domaine Chandon ★★ 🎁 Founded in 1973 by French champagne house Moët et Chandon, the valley's most renowned sparkling winemaker rises to the grand occasion with elegant grounds, a party vibe, and trendy decor. Manicured gardens showcase locally made sculpture, and guests linger—glasses fizzing with bubbly and tables covered with fancy snacks—in the festive tasting Salon or under its patio's umbrella shade. In the restaurant, diners indulge in a formal Michelin-star-awarded French-inspired meal (a more casual menu is available at lunchtime). If you can pull yourself away from the Salon's bubbly or still wine (sold in tastes for $18–$25), the comprehensive tours and tastings, which range in scope and price, are interesting, very informative, and friendly. *Note:* The reservations-required restaurant is closed on Tuesday and Wednesday and has even more restricted winter hours.

1 California Dr. (at Hwy. 29), Yountville. ✆ **707/944-2280.** www.chandon.com. Daily 10am–5pm; hours vary by season, so call to confirm. Call or check website for free tour schedules and seasonal hours.

OAKVILLE

70 miles N of San Francisco

Driving farther north on Hwy. 29 brings you to Oakville, most easily recognized by Oakville Cross Road.

Far Niente ★ This storybook stone winery is a serious treat for wine, garden, and classic car lovers, even if it can feel a little intimidating and formal. Founded in 1885, it was abandoned for 60 years around Prohibition, purchased in 1979 by Gil Nickel (of nearby Nickel & Nickel winery, where tours and tastings are $50), and opened to the public for the first time in spring 2004. The $50 by-appointment tour here includes a walk around the beautiful historic stone property, caves, private car collection (truly stunning!), and a huge azalea garden. It finishes with a sampling of five wines (including a delicious chardonnay, cabernet

Domaine Chandon offers a unique sculpture garden in addition to the bubbly.

sauvignon, and Dolce—their spectacular semillon and sauvignon blanc dessert blend that's sure to make converts of even sweet wine naysayers). Wine prices range from $56 for chardonnay to $125 for the estate cabernet sauvignon.

1350 Acacia Dr., Oakville. (𝄇 **800/363-6523** or 707/944-2861. www.farniente.com. (See also www.nickelandnickel.com and www.dolcewine.com.) Tours and tastings by appointment only daily 10am–4pm.

Silver Oak Cellars   Long known for producing the go-to cabernet for label-conscious big spenders, Silver Oak has more to it than a notable name. Its focus on the big red varietal means its 30,000 annual case production is dedicated to fine Napa Valley cabernet sauvignon. (An additional 70,000 cases are produced annually at their Alexander Valley winery in Geyserville.) Tastings in their Mediterranean-style tasting room, which include a keepsake bordeaux glass, are $10. No picnic facilities are available.

915 Oakville Cross Rd. (at Money Rd.), Oakville. (𝄇 **800/273-8809** or 707/944-8808. www.silver oak.com. Tasting room Mon–Sat 9am–5pm; Sun 11am–5pm.

PlumpJack Winery   If most wineries are like a Brooks Brothers suit, modest PlumpJack stands out as the Todd Oldham of wine tasting: chic, colorful, a little wild, and popular with a young, hip crowd as well as aficionados. Like the franchise's PlumpJack San Francisco restaurants and wine shop, and its Lake Tahoe resort, this playfully medieval-themed winery is a welcome diversion from the same old same old. With Getty bucks behind what was once Villa Mt. Eden winery, the budget covers far more than just atmosphere: There's some serious winemaking going on here, too. For $15 you can stand at the bar and sample sauvignon blanc, merlot, syrah, and chardonnay. Alas, there are no tours or picnic spots.

620 Oakville Cross Rd. (just west of the Silverado Trail), Oakville. (𝄇 **707/945-1220.** www. plumpjack.com. Daily 10am–4pm. Reservations required for groups of 8 or more.

Robert Mondavi Winery ★ 🎁

Mission-style Mondavi is home to the most comprehensive tours in the valley. Basic jaunts, which cost $25 and last about an hour and 15 minutes, take you through the vineyards and through their winemaking facilities. After the tour, you taste the results of all this attention to detail in selected current wines. If you're really into learning more about wine, ask about their myriad in-depth tours, such as their $100 "Harvest of Joy" tour, which includes a tour of the winery and a three course luncheon with wine pairing. In summer, the winery features exceptional outdoor concerts where locals (and visitors) bring their own picnic and dance in the grass to the likes of Chris

Holding your glass up to the sky—or any pale or white background—is a good way to check the wine's color.

Isaak, Colbie Caillet, or k.d. Lang. If you can swing it, don't pass up the opportunity to attend a show; it's one the most magical experiences available in these parts. Call about upcoming events.

7801 St. Helena Hwy. (Hwy. 29), Oakville. ⓒ **888/766-6328,** ext. 2000, or 707/226-1395. www. robertmondaviwinery.com. Daily 10am–5pm. Reservations recommended for guided tour; book 1 week ahead, especially for weekend tours. Closed Easter, Thanksgiving, Christmas Day, and New Year's Day.

Opus One   A serious and stately affair, the Opus One experience includes a formal (read: stiff) but educational winery tour and a steeply priced but satisfying swig of the famed (and pricey) red wine developed in a partnership between wine legends Robert Mondavi and Baron Philippe de Rothschild. Architecture buffs in particular will appreciate the tour, which takes in both the impressive Greco-Roman-meets-20th-century building and the no-holds-barred ultra-high-tech production and aging facilities. Wine lovers will appreciate the attention to detail: The entire facility caters to one ultrapremium wine, which is offered here for a whopping $35 per 4-ounce taste (and a painful $210 per bottle). Grab your glass and head to the redwood rooftop deck to enjoy the view.

7900 St. Helena Hwy. (Hwy. 29), Oakville. ⓒ **707/944-9442.** www.opusonewinery.com. Daily 10am–4pm. Tours daily by appointment only; in high season, book a month in advance.

RUTHERFORD

3 miles N of Oakville

If you so much as blink after Oakville, you're likely to overlook Rutherford, the next small town that borders on St. Helena. Each town in Napa Valley has its share of spectacular wineries, but you won't see most of them while driving along Hwy. 29.

Swanson Vineyards & Winery ★★ 🎁   The valley's most untraditionally chic and playful wine tasting is part and parcel of the experience at Swanson, which was founded and continues to be owned and operated by the family behind the famed frozen dinner brand of the same name. Make a reservation, pay $65, and you and up to seven other guests sit at a centerpiece round table in a vibrant coral New Orleans–inspired parlor and take in the refined yet whimsical atmosphere. The table's set more for a dinner party than for a tasting, with fancy stemware, caviar on potato crisps, slivers of a fine cheese or two, crackers, and one chocolate-and-red-wine-ganache-filled bonbon, which are also available for purchase in an adorable black and pink hatbox. Over the course of the hour-or-more snack-and-sip event, a winery host will pour four to seven wines, perhaps a bright pinot grigio, merlot, and hearty Alexis, their signature cab-syrah blend, and let you carry on fun conversation along with lighthearted but informative wine banter. Definitely a must-do for those who don't mind spending the money. Want the fun without the advance commitment or expense? Check out the adjacent Sip Shoppe (www.sipshoppe.com; appointment recommended), for a less formal, more fun tasting experience.

1271 Manley Lane, Rutherford. ✆ **707/967-3500.** www.swansonvineyards.com. Tasting appointments available Thurs–Mon 11am–4pm.

Sawyer's winemaker Brad Warner.

Sawyer Cellars 🎁 The most attractive thing about Sawyer, aside from its clean and tasty wines, is its dedication to extremely high quality while it maintains a humble, accommodating attitude. Step into the simple restored 1920s barn to see what I mean. Whatever you ask, the tasting-room host will answer. Whatever your request, they do their best to accommodate it. Here you can tour the property on a little tram or learn more about winemaker Brad Warner, who spent 30 years at Mondavi before embarking on this exclusive endeavor. Plunk down $15 to taste delicious estate-made wines: sauvignon blanc, merlot, cabernet sauvignon, and Meritage with prices ranging from $22 to $49 (for current releases). With a total production of only 4,200 cases and a friendly attitude, this winery is a rare treat.

8350 St. Helena Hwy. (Hwy. 29), Rutherford. ✆ **707/963-1980.** www.sawyercellars.com. Tasting by appointment. Tours by appointment. Daily 10am–5pm.

St. Supéry Winery 😊 The outside looks like a modern corporate office building, but inside you'll find a functional, welcoming winery that encourages first-time tasters to learn more about oenology. On the self-guided tour, you can wander through the demonstration vineyard, where you'll learn about growing techniques. Inside, kids gravitate toward coloring books and "SmellaVision," an interactive display that teaches one how to identify different wine ingredients. For $25, you can sample four wines, which hopefully include their excellent and very well priced sauvignon blanc. Even the prices make visitors feel at home: Bottles start at $20 and the tag on their high-end cabernet sauvignon is $85.

8440 St. Helena Hwy. (Hwy. 29), Rutherford. ℂ **800/942-0809** or 707/963-4507. www.stsupery.com. Daily 10am–5pm.

A tasting at Inglenook, formerly Rubicon.

Inglenook ★★ Since being purchased by Francis Ford Coppola in 1995, this spectacular 1880s ivy-draped historic stone winery and grounds has had more reincarnations than Madonna! Originally known as Inglenook Vineyards, then Niebaum-Coppola, and later Rubicon Estate, it's now back to Inglenook. Regardless, it's still where Coppola's Hollywood meets Napa winemaking history. You'll have to fork over $25 to visit the estate, but that includes valet parking, a tasting of five wines (they make a gazillion different kinds), a tour of the impeccably renovated grounds, and access to the giant wine bar and retail center and room showcasing Coppola film memorabilia, from Academy Awards to trinkets from *The Godfather* and *Bram Stoker's Dracula*. Wine, food, and gift items dominate the cavernous tasting area, where wines such as an estate-grown blend, cabernet franc, merlot, and zinfandel made from organically grown grapes are sampled. Bottles range from around $19 to more than $100. Along with the basic tour, you can pay extra for more exclusive, specialized tours as well.

1991 St. Helena Hwy. (Hwy. 29), Rutherford. ℂ **800/782-4266** or 707/968-1100. www.inglenook.com. Daily 10am–5pm. Tours daily.

Beaulieu Vineyard Bordeaux native Georges de Latour founded the third-oldest continuously operating winery in Napa Valley in 1900. With the help of legendary oenologist André Tchelistcheff, de Latour produced world-class, award-winning wines that have been served at the White House since Franklin D. Roosevelt was at the helm. The brick-and-redwood tasting room isn't much to look at, but with Beaulieu's (Bowl-you) reputation, it has no need to visually impress. Tastings range in price from $15 to $35 and a number of bottles sell for under $20. The Reserve Tasting Room offers a taste of five reserve wines for $35 and bottles that cost upwards of $100.

1960 St. Helena Hwy. (Hwy. 29), Rutherford. ℂ **707/967-5233.** www.bvwines.com. Daily 10am–5pm.

Grgich Hills Cellar Croatian émigré and winemaking Hall of Famer Miljenko (Mike) Grgich (Grr-gitch) made his presence known to the world when his 1973 Chateau Montelena chardonnay bested the top French white burgundies at the famous 1976 Paris tasting. Since then, the master vintner teamed up with Austin Hills (of the Hills Bros. coffee fortune) and started this extremely successful and respected winery featuring estate-grown wines from organically and biodynamically farmed vineyards.

The ivy-covered stucco building and its tasting room are more modest than many, but people don't come here for the scenery: As you might expect, Grgich's chardonnays are legendary—and priced accordingly. The smart buys are the outstanding zinfandel and cabernet sauvignon, which cost around $35 and $60, respectively. The winery also produces a fantastic fumé blanc for around $30 a bottle. Before you leave, be sure to poke your head into the barrel-aging room and inhale the divine aroma. Tastings cost $15 (which includes the glass), and during harvest, there's often an affordable ($10; reservations required) grape stomp! No picnic facilities are available.

1829 St. Helena Hwy. (Hwy. 29), north of Rutherford Cross Rd., Rutherford. ℭ 707/963-2784. www.grgich.com. Daily 9:30am–4:30pm. $35 and up tours by appointment only.

Mumm Napa Valley   Housed in a big redwood barn, Mumm is a fun place to stop for a glass (or bottle) of bubbly and a stroll past its exceptional photography exhibits. Just beyond the extensive gift shop (filled with all sorts of namesake mementos) is the tasting room, where you can purchase sparkling wine by the glass ($7–$16), three-wine flights ($10–$25), or the bottle ($20–$85). You can also take a 45-minute free educational tour and stroll through the impressive fine-art photography gallery, which features a permanent Ansel Adams collection and ever-changing photography exhibits. Sorry, there's no food or picnicking here.

8445 Silverado Trail (just south of Rutherford Cross Rd.), Rutherford. ℭ 800/686-6272 or 707/967-7730. www.mummnapa.com. Daily 10am–5pm. Complimentary tours offered daily at 10am. $20 tour and tasting 11am–3pm.

Round Pond ★★   Surrounded by imported blue agave, palm, and olive trees, ultrachic Round Pond's sleek and minimalist digs are a stunning stage for the annual production of a minuscule 3,000 cases of cabernet sauvignon and about 100 cases of Nebbiolo. (Here only the best grapes make the cut, and bottle prices, ranging $24–$95, reflect as much.) The estate also grows Spanish and Italian olives, which has resulted in award-winning oils, and red-wine vinegars. Book an appointment for one of the three tastings, which range from the $30 estate tasting to the very sexy (and pricey) $250 twilight tasting and dinner.

875 Rutherford Rd., btw. the Silverado Trail and Hwy. 29, Rutherford. ℭ 888/302-2575. www.roundpond.com. Winery daily 11am–3:30pm. Tours and tastings by appointment only. Olive Mill 7 days a week by appointment.

Quintessa ★   Beyond the stunning winery design by San Francisco–based Walker Warner Architects the draw here is simple: It's the place to taste from the winery's annual 8,000 cases of one very good and well-known cabernet sauvignon, merlot, and cabernet franc blend. Along the way you'll learn a little background in biodynamic farming, a sustainable farming technique that works around the moon's cycles and creating a naturally symbiotic growing environment (hence the property's cows and chickens, which are believed to "calm the vines"). If you're lucky, you'll also experience Ugo, Quintessa's oldest employee, who warbles to the wine in the underground barrel caves. It may seem a bit hippie-dippy, but the $65 private tour and tasting with food pairings may just turn you into a believer. If you want to take a potable memento for the road, a bottle of wine is a commitment at $145.

1601 Silverado Trail, Rutherford. ℭ 707/967-1601. www.quintessa.com. Daily 10am–4pm by appointment only.

ST. HELENA

73 miles N of San Francisco

Located 17 miles north of Napa on Hwy. 29, this former Seventh-day Adventist village maintains a pseudo–Old West feel while catering to upscale shoppers with deep pockets. St. Helena is a quiet, attractive little town, where you'll find a slew of beautiful old homes and first-rate restaurants, boutiques, and accommodations.

V. Sattui Winery ★ ☺ 🎁   Touristy and crowded, this winery is also a fun, family-friendly picnic-party stop thanks to a huge gourmet deli and grassy expanse. The gourmet store stocks more than 200 cheeses, sandwich meats, pâtés, breads, exotic salads, and desserts such as white-chocolate cheesecake. (It would be an easier place to graze were it not for the continuous mob scene at the counter.) Meanwhile, the extensive wine offerings—all of which are only available here, so buy something if you love it—flow at the long wine bar in the back. (A case purchase will get you membership into their private cellar and its less crowded, private tasting room.) Wine prices start at around $13, with many in the $18 neighborhood; reserves top out at around $125. *Note:* To use the usually packed picnic area, you must buy food and wine here. On summer weekends, check out the barbecues for $7 to $10.

1111 White Lane (at Hwy. 29), St. Helena. ☏ **707/963-7774.** www.vsattui.com. Daily 9am–6pm; winter daily 9am–5pm.

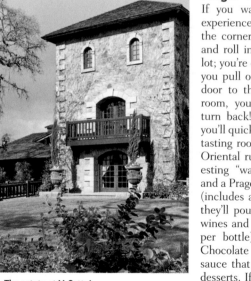

The estate at V. Sattui.

Prager Winery & Port Works 🎁   If you want an off-the-beaten-track experience, Prager's can't be beat. Turn the corner from Sutter Home winery and roll into the small gravel parking lot; you're on the right track, but when you pull open the creaky old wooden door to this shack of a wine-tasting room, you'll begin to wonder. Don't turn back! Pass the oak barrels, and you'll quickly come upon the clapboard tasting room, made homey with a big Oriental rug, some of the most interesting "wallpaper" you've ever seen, and a Prager family host. Fork over $15 (includes a complimentary glass), and they'll pour you five samples of their wines and ports (which cost $32–$80 per bottle). Also available is Prager Chocolate Drizzle, a chocolate liqueur sauce that tops ice creams and other desserts. If you're looking for a special gift, consider their bottles, which can be custom etched in the design of your choice for around $85, plus the cost of the wine.

1281 Lewelling Lane (just west of Hwy. 29, behind Sutter Home), St. Helena. ☏ **800/969-7678** or 707/963-7678. www.pragerport.com. Mon–Sat 10:30am–4:30pm; Sun 11am–4:30pm. Appointment required.

Joseph Phelps Vineyards ★   Visitors interested in intimate, comprehensive tours and a knockout tasting should schedule a tour at this winery founded in 1973 by major wine world player Joseph Phelps. A favorite stop for serious wine lovers, primarily due to their ever-popular and expensive Insignia wine, this modern, state-of-the-art winery and big-city vibe are proof that Phelps's annual 80,000 cases prove fruitful in more ways than one. While at first meeting it seems seriousness hangs heavier than harvest grapes, the mood lightens during the hour-plus $25 informal tasting or any of the $40 "seminars" (think blending or wine appreciation), which include tastings of five or six wines. The three excellently located picnic tables, on the terrace overlooking the valley, are available on a first-come, first-served basis, with preference given to Phelps wine club members (join and get wine shipped a certain number of times per year) who are also able to make a reservation.

200 Taplin Rd. (off the Silverado Trail), St. Helena. ℂ **800/707-5789** or 707/963-2745. www.josephphelps.com. Mon–Fri 10am–5pm; Sat–Sun 10am–4pm. $40–$60 seminars and tastings by appointment only weekends at 11am and 2pm, weekdays at 11am and 2:30pm. $15 per person for 1-oz. pour of Insignia.

Robert Keenan Winery 🛏 It's a winding, uphill drive to reach secluded Robert Keenan, but this far off the tourist track you're guaranteed more elbowroom at the tasting bar and a quieter, less commercial experience.

Behind the 10,000-case annual production of primarily full-bodied reds is native San Franciscan Robert Keenan, who ran his own insurance agency for 20 years before purchasing his "retirement property" and launching a second career. But the 176-acre estate (48 acres of which are now planted with grapes), dates back to 1890 when it was founded as the Conradi Winery.

Drop by to sip mountain cab, merlot, chardonnay, cabernet franc, and zin, which range from $29 to $57 per bottle. Older vintages, which you won't find elsewhere, are for sale here as well. Take the tour to learn about the vineyards, production facilities, and winemaking in general. Those looking for a pastoral picnic spot should consider spreading their blankets out here. The three tables, situated right outside the winery and surrounded by vineyards, offer stunning views.

3660 Spring Mountain Rd. (off Hwy. 29), St. Helena. ℂ **707/963-9177.** www.keenanwinery.com. Daily; by appointment only.

Domaine Charbay Winery & Distillery After you finally reach this mountaintop hideaway, affectionately called "the Still on the Hill," you immediately get the sense that something special is going on here. Owner Miles Karakasevic considers himself more of a perfume maker than a 12th-generation master distiller, and it's easy to see why. The tiny distillery is crammed with bottles of his latest fragrant potions, such as brandy, whole-fruit-flavor-infused vodkas, grappa, and pastis. He's also become known for other elixirs: black walnut liqueur, apple brandy, a line of ports, several cabernet sauvignons, and the charter product—Charbay (pronounced Shar-bay)—a brandy liqueur blended with chardonnay.

The low-key tour—which costs $20 per person, is private and exclusive, and includes tastes of premade cocktails—centers on a small, 25-gallon copper alembic still and the distilling process.

4001 Spring Mountain Rd. (5 miles west of Hwy. 29), St. Helena. ℂ **800/634-7845** or 707/963-9327. www.charbay.com. Daily (except holidays).

Beringer Vineyards ★ 🛏 You won't find a personal experience at this tourist-heavy stop. But you will get a taste of history within the regal 1876 estate founded by brothers Jacob and Frederick Beringer and hand-dug tunnels in the hillside. The oldest continuously operating winery in Napa Valley, Beringer managed to stay open even during Prohibition by cleverly making sacramental wines. White zinfandel is the winery's most popular seller, but plenty of other varietals are available to enjoy. Tastings of current vintages, which range from $15 to $25, are conducted in newer facilities. Reserve wines are available for tasting in the remarkable Rhine House for $25 (applied toward purchase), and tours range from the $20 standard to the $30 "Taste of Beringer Tour."

Beringer ages its wine in "custom-toasted" French Nevers oak barrels.

2000 Main St. (Hwy. 29), St. Helena. ✆ **707/963-7115.** www.beringer.com. Oct–May 10am–5pm (last tour 4pm, last tasting 4:45pm); June–Sept 10am–6pm (last tour 5:15pm, last tasting 5:30pm).

CALISTOGA

81 miles N of San Francisco

Calistoga, the last tourist town in Napa Valley, got its name from Sam Brannan, entrepreneur extraordinaire and California's first millionaire. After making a bundle supplying miners during the gold rush, he went on to take advantage of the natural geothermal springs at the north end of the valley by building a hotel and spa here in 1859. Flubbing up a speech, in which he compared this natural California wonder to New York State's Saratoga Springs resort town, he serendipitously coined the name "Calistoga," and it stuck. Today, this small, simple resort town, with fewer than 6,000 residents and an old-time main street (no building along the 6-block stretch is more than two stories high), is popular with city folk who come here to unwind. Calistoga is a great place to relax and indulge in mineral waters, mud baths, Jacuzzis, massages, and, of course, wine. The vibe is more casual—and a little groovier—than you find in neighboring towns to the south.

Frank Family Vineyards ★ 🎁 "Wine dudes" Dennis, Tim, Jeff, Rick, and Pat will do practically anything to maintain their rightfully self-proclaimed reputation as the "friendliest winery in the valley." Here it's all about down-home, friendly fun. No muss, no fuss, no intimidation factor. At Frank Family, you're part of their family—no joke. They'll greet you like a long-lost relative and serve you all the bubbly you want (three to four varieties: blanc de blanc, blanc de noir, reserve, and rouge, at $32–$135 a bottle). Still-wine lovers can slip into the equally casual back room to sample chardonnay and a very well-received cabernet sauvignon. Behind the tasting room is a choice picnic area, situated under the oaks and overlooking the vineyards.

1091 Larkmead Lane (just off the Silverado Trail), Calistoga. ✆ **707/942-0859.** www.frankfamily vineyards.com. Daily 10am–5pm. No tours offered.

Castello di Amorosa ★ 🎁 The rumors are true: There is a medieval-style stone castle in Calistoga. Though it's only a few years old, the eight-level

THE INS & OUTS OF shipping wine HOME

Perhaps the only things more complex than that $800 case of cabernet you just purchased are the rules and regulations about shipping it home. Because of absurd and forever fluctuating laws—which supposedly protect the business of the country's wine distributors—wine shipping is limited by regulations that vary in each of the 50 states. Shipping rules also vary from winery to winery.

Every single time I write this book, the rules change. This go-round the government is said to be phasing out reciprocity laws and requiring that each state be approved to ship or receive wine. Individual wineries must buy permits for each state they want to ship to, making it difficult for smaller wineries to ship to many states (so most will probably opt only for the states that brandish the most visitors or mail-order demands). Technically, only wineries with permits are allowed to ship wine; shipping stores are not supposed to ship any wine or liquor. That said, they do it anyway, so don't fret if you want to send wine.

If you do get stuck shipping illegally (not that I'm recommending you do that, but believe me, it's done all the time and most shipping companies are well aware of it), you might want to package your wine in an unassuming box and head to a post office, UPS, or other shipping company outside the Wine Country area. It's less obvious that you're shipping wine from Vallejo or San Francisco than from Napa Valley.

However, you can try these companies. They are likely to help you out.

NAPA VALLEY SHIPPING COMMUNITIES

The **UPS Store**, at 1436 Second St., in Napa (© 707/265-6011), claims to pack and ship anything anywhere. Rates for a case of wine were quoted at approximately $40 for ground shipping to Los Angeles and $65 to New York.

St. Helena Mailing Center, 1241 Adams St., at Hwy. 29, St. Helena (© 707/963-2686), says it will pack and ship to certain states within the U.S. Rates for prewrapped shipments are around $34 per case for ground delivery to Los Angeles.

SONOMA VALLEY SHIPPING COMMUNITIES

The **UPS Store**, 19201 Sonoma Hwy., in Maxwell Village, Sonoma (© 707/935-3438), has a lot of experience with shipping wine. It claims it will ship your wine to any state. Prices vary from $38 to Los Angeles to as much as $79 to the East Coast and $198 to Hawaii and Alaska.

---

structure, complete with 90 feet of caves, a dungeon, and torture chamber, is surprisingly authentic (as evidenced by how tired and achy my legs and feet were after tromping on cobblestones). Drop by to get a glimpse of old-world grandiosity and pay $18 to sample a variety of wines, including chardonnay, merlot, cabernet, and dessert wines. (Prices aren't too bad at $20–$100 per bottle.) Or make a reservation for the nearly 2-hour tour, which costs $33 ($22 for children 5 or older; 4 and under are not permitted). Though the castle is a far cry from quintessential wine country (some liken it to Disneyland), it is fun to browse this stunning architectural accomplishment.

4045 N. St. Helena Hwy., Calistoga. © **707/942-8200** or 967-7084 (for events). www.castello diamorosa.com. Tasting Apr–Nov daily 9:30am–6pm, Oct–Mar daily 9:30am–5pm. Tours by reservation only: on the hour Mon–Fri 9:30am–4:30pm, and on the half-hour Sat–Sun and holi-days 9:30am–5pm.

Schramsberg ★★★ 🎁 A landmark once frequented by Robert Louis Ste-venson and the second-oldest property in Napa Valley, this 217-acre sparkling wine estate is one of the valley's all-time best places to explore. Schramsberg is the label that presidents serve when toasting dignitaries from around the globe, and there's plenty of historical memorabilia in the winery's front room to prove it. But the real mystique begins when you enter the sparkling wine caves, which wind 2 miles (reputedly the longest in North America) and were partly hand-carved by Chinese laborers in the 1800s. The caves have an authentic Tom Sawyer ambi-ence, complete with dangling cobwebs and seemingly endless passageways; you can't help but feel you're on an adventure. The comprehensive, unintimidating tour ends in a charming, cozy tasting room, where you'll sample four surprisingly varied selections of their high-end bubbly. At $45 per person, tasting isn't cheap, but it's money well spent. Note that tastings are offered only to those who take the free tour, and you must make reservations in advance.

1400 Schramsberg Rd. (off Hwy. 29), Calistoga. (℡ **707/942-2414.** www.schramsberg.com. Daily 10am–4pm. Tours and tastings by appointment only. At 10 and 11:30am, 12:30, 1:30, and 2:30pm.

Sterling Vineyards 😊 🎁 One of the more commercial wine-tasting experi-ences in the area, Sterling has one thing going for it that no other winery can boast: an aerial tram offering stunning valley views while en route to its white Mediterranean-style winery perched 300 feet up on a rocky knoll. The ride, which costs $25 ($10 for kids) and includes wine tasting, leads to a self-guided tour of the winemaking process and a panoramic tasting room offering samples of five varietals. However, more sophisticated sips—limited releases or reserve flights—cost from $5 to $25, respectively. Expect to pay from $14 to $100+ for a souvenir bottle.

1111 Dunaweal Lane (off Hwy. 29, just south of downtown Calistoga), Calistoga. (℡ **707/942-3344.** www.sterlingvineyards.com. Daily 10:30am–4:30pm.

Duckhorn Vineyards ★ With quintessential pastoral surroundings (think meadow views), Victorian farmhouse surroundings (hello verandas!), and a selec-tion of extremely good wines on hand, Duckhorn Vineyards has much to offer for visitors interested in spending time to relax and taste. The tasting room, complete with cafe tables and a centerpiece bar, is an unexpectedly modern place where you'll pay $20 for a flight of four current-release wines, or $30 for a semiprivate estate-wine tasting, the latter of which you can book in advance. The fee may be a bit higher than elsewhere, but this is not your run-of-the-mill drink and dash. You'll get plenty of attention and information on their current releases of sauvi-gnon blanc, merlot, and cabernet sauvignon.

1000 Lodi Lane (at the Silverado Trail), St. Helena. (℡ **707/963-7108.** www.duckhorn.com. Daily 10am–4pm. Reservations recommended.

Cuvaison Chardonnay lovers, take note: Cuvaison, pronounced Koo-vay-sawn (a French term for wine fermentation using skins), was founded in 1969 by Silicon Valley engineers Thomas Cottrell and Thomas Parkhill and is known for its production of the lush, round, and very food-friendly white grape. Still, its 400 acres and a 63,000-case annual production aren't exclusively reserved to its most

🎁 ENJOYING art & nature

Anyone with an appreciation for art absolutely must visit di **Rosa Preserve** (5200 Carneros Hwy. [Hwy. 12/121], look for the gate; 💲 707/226-5991; www.dirosaart.org). Rene and Veronica di Rosa collected contemporary American art for more than 40 years and then converted their 215 acres of prime property into a monument to Northern California's regional art, including Seated Woman with Vase, pictured, by Viola Frey. Veronica and Rene have passed on, but their legacy remains through their world-renowned collection featuring nearly 2,300 works in all mediums, by more than 900 Greater Bay Area artists.

Today the day-to-day operations are run by a nonprofit staff, but you will be privy to Rene's treasures, which are on display practically everywhere—along the shores of the property's 35-acre lake and in each nook and cranny of their 125-year-old winery-turned-residence, adjoining building, two newer galleries, and gardens. With hundreds of surrounding acres of rolling hills (protected under the Napa County Land Trust), this place is a must-see for both art and nature lovers. Tours (Wed–Fri) range from a $10 1-hour overview at 11am and noon to the $15 2-hour extended home tour at 10am and 1pm. On Saturdays, you may take a guided 2½-hour tour for $15. Reservations recommended. Drop-ins are welcome at the Gatehouse Gallery Tuesday through Friday from 9:30am to 3pm; Saturday is by appointment. Suggested donation is $3. Check the website for times. Reservations recommended.

famous varietal. Winemaker Steven Rogstad also produces a limited amount of merlot, pinot noir, cabernet sauvignon, and zinfandel within the handsome Spanish mission–style structure.

Tastings are an affordable $15, which includes a glass and four tastings. Wine prices range from $22 for a chardonnay to as much as $85 for a cabernet sauvignon. Beautiful picnic grounds are situated amid 350-year-old moss-covered oak trees.

4550 Silverado Trail (just south of Dunaweal Lane), Calistoga. 💲 **707/942-6266.** www.cuvaison. com. Daily 10am–5pm.

Beyond the Wineries: What to See & Do in Napa Valley

NAPA/ST. HELENA

If you have plenty of time and a penchant for Victorian architecture, seek out the **Napa Valley Welcome Center,** 600 Main St. (💲 **707/251-5895;** www.legendary napavalley.com), which offers a free map for self-guided walking tours of the town's historic buildings.

📎 **Sip Tip**

You can cheaply sip your way through downtown Napa without ever getting behind the wheel with the "Taste Napa Downtown" wine card. For a mere $20, you get 10¢ tasting privileges at 10 local wine-centric watering holes and tasting rooms, all of which are within walking distance of each other. Plus you'll get 10% discounts at tasting rooms. Available at the **Napa Valley Welcome Center** (600 Main St.; 📞 **707/251-5895**). Learn more at **www.napadowntown.com**.

A MARKETPLACE ★★ **The Oxbow Market,** 610 and 644 First St. (📞 **707/ 226-6529;** www.oxbowpublicmarket.com), is a bustling gourmet co-op featuring a cornucopia of tasty tenants, including a number of sources for quick, delicious, affordable meals (think rotisserie chicken—try the potatoes too!; gourmet tacos; cheeses galore; a fresh oyster outpost; a wine bar and shop; an outstanding organic ice-cream vendor; and more). There's also a food-related antiques shop, spectacular herbs and spices source, and many other reasons to loosen your belt and your grip on your wallet. Adjoining the main shopping hall is yet another outpost of **Gott's Roadside Tray Gourmet** (a gourmet burger joint, p. 362). In other words, definitely drop by hungry! Open daily. Check the website for hours of operation for specific vendors.

BIKING The quieter northern end of the valley is an ideal place to rent a bicycle and ride the **Silverado Trail. St. Helena Cyclery,** 1156 Main St. (📞 **707/963-7736;** www.sthelenacyclery.com), rents bikes for $11 per hour or $37 a day, including rear rack, helmet, lock, and bag in which you can pack a picnic.

SHOPPING Shopaholics should make a beeline to the **Napa Premium Outlets** (📞 **707/226-9876;** www.premiumoutlets.com), where Barneys New York can inspire even a jaded local to take the First Street exit off Hwy. 29 and brave the crowds. Unfortunately, Barneys usually carries only cheap outlet-store stuff. But you'll find multiple places to part with your money, including TSE (killer cashmere at bargain prices), Banana Republic, Calvin Klein, Nine West, Benetton, Jones New York, BCBG, more fashion shops, a few kitchenware and gift shops, a food court, and a decent (but expensive) sushi restaurant. Shops are open Monday through Thursday from 10am to 8pm, Friday and Saturday from 10am to 9pm, and Sunday from 10am to 6pm. Call for seasonal hours.

    St. Helena's Main Street ★ is the best place to go if you're suffering from serious retail withdrawal. Here you'll find trendy fashions at Pearl, 1219 Main St. (📞 **707/963-3236**), Jimmy Choo shoes at **Footcandy,** 1239 Main St. (📞 **707/963-2040**), chic pet gifts at **Fideaux,** 1312 Main St. (📞 **707/967-9935**), custom-embroidered French linens at Jan de Luz, 1219 A Main St. (📞 **707/963-1550**), and estate jewelry at **Patina,** 1342 Main St. (📞 **707/963-5445**), along with locally frequented restaurants.

    Most stores are open 10am to 5pm daily; the mall is on Main Street, between Pope and Pine streets, St. Helena.

    One last favorite stop: **Napa Valley Olive Oil Manufacturing Company,** 835 Charter Oak Ave., at the end of the road behind Tra Vigne restaurant (📞 **707/963-4173**). The tiny market presses and bottles its own oils and sells them at a fraction of the price you'll pay elsewhere. In addition, it has an extensive selection of Italian cooking ingredients, imported snacks, great deals on dried mushrooms, and a picnic table in the parking lot. You'll love the age-old method for totaling the bill, which you simply must find out for yourself. Drop by any day between 9am and 5:30pm.

SPA-ING IT If the Wine Country's slow pace and tranquil vistas aren't soothing enough for you, the region's diverse selection of spas can massage, bathe, wrap, and steam you into an overly pampered pulp. Should you choose to indulge, do so toward the end of your stay—when you've wined and dined to the point where you have only enough energy left to make it to and from the spa. Good choices include **Dr. Wilkinson's Hot Springs,** 1507 Lincoln Ave., Calistoga (© **707/942-4102;** www.drwilkinson.com), and **Meadowood,** 900 Meadowood Lane, St. Helena (© **707/963-3646; www.meadowood.com**).

LIVE ENTERTAINMENT Despite the lack of a true nightlife scene (though the bar at Napa's Morimoto can seriously jump), Napa has two venues that regularly feature surprisingly big acts. The first is the stunning, renovated **Art Deco Uptown Theatre,** 350 Third St., Napa (© **707/259-0123;** www.uptowntheatrenapa.com), which recently hosted the likes of comedienne Lisa Lampanelli, Montrose, Ani DiFranco, and Lucinda Williams. The other is the **Napa Valley Opera House,** 1030 Main St., Napa (© **707/226-7372;** www.nvoh.org), which features dance and comedy performances as well as concerts by talents such as singer Natalie Cole and saxophonist Branford Marsalis.

CALISTOGA

BIKING Cycling enthusiasts can rent bikes from **Getaway Adventures/Wine Country Adventures** (© **800/499-2453** or 707/568-3040; www.getawayadventures.com). Full-day group tours cost $149 per person, including lunch and a visit to four or five wineries, $195 per person for private groups of six or more. Bike rental without a tour costs $30 per day. You can also inquire about the company's kayaking and hiking tours.

MUD BATHS The one thing you should do while you're in Calistoga is what people have been doing here for the past 150 years: Take a mud bath. The natural baths contain local volcanic ash, imported peat, and naturally boiling mineral hot-springs water, mulled together to produce a thick mud that simmers at a temperature of about 104°F (40°C). Sinking into a

On most bicycling tours of Napa, you bike 3 to 6 miles between each winery.

cement tub filled with hot, dense peat and mud is creepy-fun—and very memorable.

Indulge yourself at any of these Calistoga spas: **Golden Haven Hot Springs Spa,** 1713 Lake St. (✆ **707/942-6793;** www.goldenhaven.com); **Calistoga Spa Hot Springs,** 1006 Washington St. (✆ **707/942-6269;** www.calistogaspa.com;); **Calistoga Village Inn & Spa,** 1880 Lincoln Ave. (✆ **707/942-0991;** www.greatspa.com); **Indian Springs Resort,** 1712 Lincoln Ave. (✆ **707/942-4913;** www.indianspringscalistoga.com); or **Roman Spa Motel,** 1300 Washington St. (✆ **707/942-4441;** www.romanspahotsprings.com).

NATURAL WONDERS Old Faithful Geyser of California, 1299 Tubbs Lane (✆ **707/942-6463;** www.oldfaithfulgeyser.com), is one of only three "old faithful" geysers in the world. It's been blowing off steam at regular intervals for as long as anyone can remember. On average, the 350°F (176°C) water spews at a height of about 40 to 60 feet every 40 minutes, day and night, and the performance lasts about 3 minutes. (*Note:* Height and length of time are weather-dependent.) You can bring a picnic lunch to munch on between spews. An exhibit hall, gift shop, and snack bar are open every day. Admission is $10 for adults, $7 for seniors, $3 for children 6 to 12, and free for children 5 and under. Check the website for discount coupons. The geyser is open daily from 9am to 6pm (to 5pm in winter). To get there, follow the signs from downtown Calistoga; it's between Hwy. 29 and Calif. 128.

You won't see thousands of trees turned into stone, but you'll still find many interesting petrified specimens at the **Petrified Forest,** 4100 Petrified Forest Rd. (✆ **707/942-6667;** www.petrifiedforest.org). Volcanic ash blanketed this area after an eruption near Mount St. Helena 3 million years ago. You'll find redwoods that have turned to rock through the slow infiltration of silicas and other minerals, a .25-mile walking trail, a museum, a discovery shop, and picnic grounds. Admission is $10 for adults, $9 for seniors 60 and over and juniors 12 to 17, $5 for children 6 to 11, and free for children 5 and under; look on the website for discount coupons. The forest is open daily from 9am to 7pm (to 5pm in winter). Heading north from Calistoga on Calif. 128, turn left onto Petrified Forest Road, just past Lincoln Street.

Where to Stay in Napa Valley

Accommodations in Napa Valley run the gamut—from standard motels and floral-and-lace Victorian-style B&Bs to world-class luxury retreats—and all are easily accessible from the main highway that stretches across the valley and leads to its attractions. Most of the romantically pastoral options (think hidden hillside spots with vineyard views or quaint small-town charmers) are found on the outskirts of historic St. Helena, which has the best walking/shopping street, and the equally storied but more laid-back and affordable hot-springs-heavy Calistoga, which also boasts some of the region's most affordable options. The few commercial blocks of rural Yountville have become a destination in itself thanks to a number of famous restaurants (including world-renowned French Laundry) as well as a handful of high-end hotels and middle-end B&Bs. The most "reasonably priced" (a relative term in this high-priced area) choices are the B&Bs, small hotels, and national chain options in downtown Napa, the closest thing you'll find to a city in these parts. Fortunately, the workaday town continues to add more reasons to visit, including impressive restaurants (Hello, Morimoto—home

PRICE CATEGORIES

Very Expensive	$300 and up
Expensive	$200–$299
Moderate	$150–$199
Inexpensive	Under $150

to Iron Chef Morimoto's high-end Japanese cuisine, p. 354). No matter where you stay, you're just a few minutes—or less—away from world-class wineries.

NAPA

While there are a few rural resorts in Napa, most accommodations are in the walkable downtown area, including **Embassy Suites,** 1075 California Blvd., Napa, CA 94559 (www.napavalley.embassysuites.com; ✆ **800/362-2779** or 707/253-9540), which offers 205 two-room suites that include a galley kitchen complete with coffeemaker, fridge, microwave, a wet bar, two TVs, and access to indoor and outdoor pools and a restaurant. Rates range from $189 to $390 and include cooked-to-order breakfast, 2-hour beverage reception from 5:30 to 6:30pm, complimentary access to a health club, and free parking. The 272-room **Napa Valley Marriott,** 3425 Solano Ave., Napa, CA 94558 (www.marriott. com; ✆ **800/228-9290** or 707/253-8600), gives lots of bang for the buck, with a large resort feel, an exercise room, a heated outdoor pool and spa, and a restaurant; rates range from $99 to $398 for rooms, $350 to $500 for suites.

Best For: Travelers in search of reasonable prices and easy access to the town's numerous restaurants, the wonderful co-op foodie shopping hall Oxbow Market, and farmers' market.

Drawbacks: The few "rural" options tucked into surrounding hillsides aside, it doesn't have the romantic pastoral scenery associated with the region.

Expensive

Cedar Gables Inn ★★ 🏠 This grand, romantic Shakespearean/Renaissance style B&B in Old Town Napa was built in 1892 and boasts rooms that reflect that era with rich tapestries and stunning gilded antiques. Four rooms have fireplaces, five have whirlpool tubs, and all feature queen-size (and one king-size) brass, wood, or iron beds. Guests meet each evening in front of the roaring fireplace in the lower "English tavern" for wine and cheese. At other times, the family room is a perfect place to cuddle up and watch the large-screen TV. Bonuses include a three-course gourmet breakfast each morning, port in every room, and VIP treatment at many local wineries. Cooking classes, led by hot local chefs and fetching $150 per person for wine-paired dinners, are offered once or twice a month at the inn's kitchen. The inn is nonsmoking.

486 Coombs St. (at Oak St.), Napa, CA 94559. www.cedargablesinn.com. ✆ **800/309-7969** or 707/224-7969. Fax 707/224-4838. 9 units. $199–$359 double. Rates include full breakfast, evening wine and cheese, and port. AE, DISC, MC, V. From Hwy. 29 N., exit onto First St., and follow signs to downtown; turn right onto Jefferson St., and left on Oak St.; house is on the corner. In room: A/C, hair dryer, free Wi-Fi.

Napa River Inn ★★ If you want chic-boutique hotel charm, reasonable prices, and the very best downtown Napa location, you can't get much better

WHAT YOU'LL REALLY PAY

The prices associated with a stay in Wine Country can be jaw-dropping. Here, luxury abodes can set you back close to $1,000 per night. But more startling, even a standard motel room can go for upward of $250 per night over the weekend during high season. Why? Because there tend to be more people who want to visit than there are hotels to accommodate them. In other words, it's a seller's market. So, if budget travel is essential to your itinerary, definitely avoid visiting during high season—March to November—when most hotels charge peak rates, sell out completely on weekends, and often have a 2-night minimum. That said, there are still deals to be had, so when you browse the rates listed here, which are "rack rates" or the maximum possible charge per night, keep in mind that you may be able to book a room for substantially cheaper; it's always worth asking. You can also find deals through flash sale sites like LivingSocial and Groupon, though restrictions may apply. If you need help organizing your Wine Country vacation, contact an agency. **Bed & Breakfast Inns of Napa Valley** (✆ **707/944-4444**; www.bbinv.com), an association of B&Bs, provides descriptions and lets you know who has rooms available. **Napa Valley Reservations Unlimited** (✆ **800/251-6272** or 707/252-1985; www.napavalleyreservations.com) is also a source for booking everything from hot-air balloon rides to wine-tasting tours by limousine.

than this three-building hotel located in the renovated 1884 historic Napa Mill and Hatt Market. Each of the well-appointed rooms in the main building romances with burgundy-colored walls, original brick, wood furnishings, plush fabrics, a gas fireplace, and a claw-foot tub. The more modern themed addition overlooking the river and ground floor marketplace's dining patio boasts urban loft appeal. Yet another riverfront building houses the more masculine (and in my opinion less pretty) nautically themed mustard-and-brown rooms, which also have less daylight. Perks include instant access to the best downtown dining (Angèle, one of my faves, is right out the front door), complimentary vouchers to breakfast at adorable Sweetie Pie's bakery, and wine at the nearby swank wine bar, the Bounty Hunter.

500 Main St., Napa, CA 94559. www.napariverinn.com. ✆ **877/251-8500** or 707/251-8500. Fax 707/251-8504. 66 units. $249–$399 double; $299–$499 suite. Rates include vouchers to a full breakfast at Sweety Pies and first wine tasting at the nearby Bounty Hunter. AE, DISC, MC, V. Pets $25 per night. **Amenities:** 2 restaurants; concierge. *In room:* A/C, TV, CD clock radio/MP3 docking station, fridge, hair dryer, free Wi-Fi.

Inexpensive

Best Western Elm House Inn ★★ Unlike most Napa Valley hotels, this sweet family-owned and -run downtown Napa option provides true value at surprisingly reasonable prices. While rooms may be just a step up from motel flair, their sizes are generous and are accompanied by lots of perks and thoughtful human touches—including friendly personal service, an above-par breakfast with thick made-to-order waffles, and freshly baked afternoon cookies. With a well-appointed lobby with a large fireplace and garden with meticulous landscaping, this special find has all the personality and charm of a B&B with all the privacy of a hotel. It's also within walking distance of Napa's downtown center and close to Hwy. 29, the region's thoroughfare.

800 California Blvd., Napa, CA 94559. www.bestwestern.com. 📞 **888/849-1997** or 707/255-1831. Fax 707/255-8609. 22 units. $119–$299 double. Rates include full breakfast and evening cookies. AE, DISC, MC, V. From Hwy. 29 north, take the First St. exit, take a right onto California Blvd., and the hotel is on the corner of Second St. and California Blvd. **Amenities:** Access to washer/dryer. *In room:* A/C, hair dryer, free Wi-Fi.

Chablis Inn ★   There's no way around it: If you want to sleep cheaply in a town where the average room rate tops $200 per night in high season, you're destined for a motel. Look on the bright side: Because your room is likely to be little more than a crash pad after a day of eating and drinking, a clean bed and a remote control are all you really need anyway. And Chablis offers much more than that. All the motel-style rooms are super clean, and some even boast kitchenettes or whirlpool tubs. Guests have access to a heated outdoor pool and hot tub. *Note:* Second-floor rooms are quieter, though require you to hoof it upstairs. 3360 Solano Ave., Napa, CA 94558. www.chablisinn.com. 📞 **800/443-3490** or 707/257-1944. Fax 707/226-6862. 34 units. May to mid Nov $99–$179 double; mid Nov to Apr $89–$159 double. AE, DISC, MC, V. **Amenities:** Jacuzzi; heated outdoor pool. *In room:* A/C, satellite TV, fridge, hair dryer, Wi-Fi.

YOUNTVILLE

Far less "developed" in look and feel than neighboring Napa, this tiny town has about 4 long blocks of hotels and restaurants—with a little shopping thrown in for good measure.

Best For: Travelers who enjoy resorts and their amenities and instant access to destination restaurants.

Drawbacks: A stay here doesn't come cheaply, even if you end up in a relatively plain B&B.

Very Expensive
Napa Valley Lodge ★ 👜   Boasting the four-diamond award from AAA and thumbs up from me, this relaxed yet polished retreat, located just off Hwy. 29, beyond a wall that does a good job of blocking the road, adds a personal touch to its well-appointed offerings. The large, clean guest rooms are better appointed than many in the area and have spacious bathrooms with dual shower heads. (Many also have vaulted ceilings, and 39 have fireplaces.) Rooms come with a king-size or two queen-size beds, wicker furnishings, robes, and a private balcony or a patio. Ground-level units are smaller and get less sunlight than those on the second floor. Suites boast king-size beds and Jacuzzi tubs. Extras include a concierge, afternoon tea and cookies in the lobby, Friday evening wine tasting in the library, and a continental breakfast. Ask about winery tour packages and winter discounts, the latter of which can be as high as 30%. 2230 Madison St., Yountville, CA 94599. www.napavalleylodge.com. 📞 **800/368-2468** or 707/944-2468. Fax 707/944-9362. 55 units. $295–$595 double. Rates include champagne breakfast buffet, afternoon tea and cookies, and Fri evening wine tasting. AE, DISC, MC, V. **Amenities:** Concierge; small exercise room; Jacuzzi; heated outdoor pool; spa. *In room:* A/C, ceiling fan, TV w/pay movies, hair dryer, minibar, free Wi-Fi.

Villagio Inn & Spa ★★   Set next to a small vineyard in the center of walkable Yountville, this, the largest luxury resort in the small town, with immaculately maintained grounds, is a choice spot for bachelorette parties, girlfriend getaways, and a younger, hipper set (as well as an older clientele). Everyone loves the opportunities to lounge by a pool while pop music plays, indulge in spa treatments at the swank spa, and linger over complimentary champagne breakfast (served each morning). Perks include a complimentary bottle of chardonnay upon arrival, a four-poster queen-size bed, flatscreen TVs, a balcony or porch, a Jacuzzi for two in the bathroom, and a fireplace in most rooms.

6481 Washington St., Yountville 94599. www.villagio.com. ✆ **800/351-1133** or 707/944-8877. Fax 707/944-8855. 112 units. $250–$720 double. Rates include champagne breakfast buffet and complimentary wine upon arrival. AE, DISC, MC, V. **Amenities:** Concierge; Jacuzzi; pool; spa; tennis court. In room: A/C, TV/VCR w/on-demand movies, fridge, free Wi-Fi.

Inexpensive

Maison Fleurie ★★   One of the prettiest garden-set B&Bs in the Wine Country, this property, run by the ever-classy Four Sisters Inn company, comprises a trio of beautiful 1873 brick-and-fieldstone buildings overlaid with ivy. The main house—a charming Provençal replica with thick brick walls, terra-

cotta tile, and paned windows—holds seven rooms; the rest are in the old bakery building and the carriage house. Some feature private balconies, patios, sitting areas, Jacuzzi tubs, and fireplaces. An above-par breakfast is served in the quaint little dining room; afterward, you're welcome to wander the landscaped grounds or hit the wine-tasting trail, returning in time for afternoon hors d'oeuvres and wine.

6529 Yount St. (btw. Washington St. and Yountville Cross Rd.), Yountville, CA 94559. www.maisonfleurienapa.com. ✆ **800/788-0369** or 707/944-2056. Fax 707/944-9342. 13 units. $145–$295 double. Rates include full breakfast and afternoon hors d'oeuvres. AE, DISC, MC, V. **Amenities:** Free use of bikes; Jacuzzi; heated outdoor pool. In room: A/C, TV, hair dryer, free Wi-Fi.

Maison Fleurie.

OAKVILLE & RUTHERFORD

Mere blips on the map, these rural towns don't have much in the way of commercial spaces, but they do have very revered wineries.

Best For: Luxury lovers who want to experience the divine digs of Auberge du Soleil, or anyone looking to sleep surrounded by vineyards.

Drawbacks: You won't find much in the way of reasonably priced rooms here.

Very Expensive

Auberge du Soleil ★★★ 📷   This spectacular Relais & Châteaux member is one of the most exclusive luxury retreats in all of California. Set high above Napa Valley in a 33-acre olive grove, contemporary California bungalow-like rooms are large enough to get lost in—and you might want to, once you discover

Room with a view at the Auberge du Soleil.

all the amenities. Rooms, which are frequented by celebrities and other worldly VIPs, beckon with cushy furniture, a fireplace, CD selection, two flatscreen TVs, (***Downsides:*** poor TV channel selection and screen quality), and a grand bathroom with aggressive double shower heads and tubs for two with romance-friendly accouterments like candles and bath oils. Fresh flowers, original art, wood floors, and a minibar loaded with free drinks and snacks are the best of luxury home-away-from-home. Each sun-washed private deck has spectacular views of the valley. All guests have access to a celestial swimming pool, exercise room, and a fabulous spa. Although only guests can use the spa, you can savor Auberge's romantic grandeur without staying overnight if you dine in their destination restaurant overlooking the valley (p. 359 for more info). ***Parents take note:*** This is not a kid-friendly place.

180 Rutherford Hill Rd., Rutherford, CA 94573. www.aubergedusoleil.com. (2) **800/348-5406** or 707/963-1211. Fax 707/963-8764. 50 units. $600–$1,275 double; $1,350–$2,875 suite. Rates include breakfast and daily newspaper. AE, DISC, MC, V. From Hwy. 29 in Rutherford, turn right on Calif. 128 and go 3 miles to the Silverado Trail; turn left and head north about 600 ft. to Rutherford Hill Rd.; turn right. **Amenities:** Restaurant, Auberge du Soleil (review, p. 359); bikes; concierge; health club and full-service spa; outdoor Jacuzzi; 3 outdoor pools ranging from hot to cold; room service; sauna; tennis court. *In room:* A/C, TV/DVD w/HBO, hair dryer, kitchenette, minibar, MP3 docking station, free Wi-Fi.

Moderate

Rancho Caymus Inn ★ This cozy Spanish-style hacienda, with two floors opening onto wisteria-covered balconies and a centerpiece courtyard with an enormous outdoor fireplace, overflows with personality. Hardly the cookie-cutter style of newer hotels, this one was the passionate creation of sculptor Mary Tilden Morton (whose dad was a forestry baron; Berkeley's Tilden Park is named for him). Morton wanted each room in the hacienda to be a work of art, so she employed the most skilled craftspeople she could find. As a result, you'll find Morton-designed adobe fireplaces in 22 of 26 rooms, and artifacts she gathered in Mexico and South America.

The mix-and-match decor is eclectic, with imported carved wood furnishings and unique handmade accessories as well as wet bars, sitting areas with sofa beds, and small private patios. Most of the suites have fireplaces, one has a kitchenette, and five have whirlpool tubs. Breakfast, which includes fresh fruit, granola, orange juice, and pastries, is served in the inn's dining room.

1140 Rutherford Rd. (P.O. Box 78), Rutherford, CA 94573. www.ranchocaymus.com. (2) **800/845-1777** or 707/963-5387. Fax 707/963-5387. 26 suites. $175–$435 double; $215–$410 master suite; $275–$450 2-bedroom suite. Rates include continental breakfast. AE, MC, V. From Hwy. 29 N., turn right onto Rutherford Rd./Calif. 128 east; the hotel is on your left. *In room:* A/C, TV/DVD, fridge, hair dryer, kitchenette in 1 room, minibar, free Wi-Fi.

ST. HELENA

Perfectly situated between the winery-heavy towns of Yountville, Oakville, and Rutherford to the south and Calistoga to the north and rife with famed wine brands of its own, this charming historic town provides easy access to a wide variety of the region's offerings.

Best For: Deep-pocketed travelers who appreciate small-town charm and boutique shopping, or those looking for exceptional resort living, which can be found at Meadowood.

Drawbacks: It's a half-hour drive—or more, during traffic—to downtown Napa.

Very Expensive

Harvest Inn ★★   One of the valley's few sprawling resorts, this 74-unit property has wonderfully spacious accommodations, all of which are uniquely decorated with warm, homey furnishings and nestled into 8 acres of flora; most have fireplaces. Extensive grounds (which include two swimming pools and hot tubs, a spa, and a wine bar) and well-appointed suites make the place popular with wedding parties and families. Although you can't reserve specific rooms in advance, request an abode away from the highway upon arrival. Also, if you're not into climbing stairs, ask for a ground-level room, as some accommodations are on a second story and don't have elevator access. The inn offers free wine tastings Friday and Saturday evenings.

1 Main St., St. Helena, CA 94574. www.harvestinn.com. ✆ **800/950-8466** or 707/963-9463. Fax 707/963-4426. 74 units. $259–$560 double; $499–$950 suite. Rates include breakfast. AE, MC, DISC, V. Free parking. From Hwy. 29 N., turn left into the driveway at the large HARVEST INN sign. **Amenities:** Wine bar; 2 hot tubs; 2 heated outdoor pools. *In room:* A/C, TV/DVD, fridge, hair dryer, free Wi-Fi.

Meadowood Napa Valley ★★ 🎁   If Auberge du Soleil is the luxury spot for hiding out, this first-class country resort surrounded by 250 secluded acres of pristine mountainside is a place to be out and about, enjoying the property's shared offerings. Here, free-standing luxury accommodations (featuring beamed ceilings, private patios, stone fireplaces, forest views, and American country classic furnishings) are private, available in various sizes and floor plans, and scattered throughout the vast hillside property. Most are individual suite-lodges so far removed from the common areas that you must drive to get to them—and hoof it a bit to get to the restaurant or spa. Lazier folks can beckon a complimentary ride or opt for more centrally located rooms.

Reasons to explore include golf on a challenging 9-hole course, tennis on seven championship courts, croquet (yes, croquet) on two international regulation lawns, and a posh pool scene in summertime. There are private hiking trails, a health spa, yoga, two heated pools, and two whirlpools. An added bonus for lazy travelers: Their formal Restaurant at Meadowood has Michelin-star-award-winning talent cranking out delicious multicourse meals that focus on the seasons and local ingredients.

900 Meadowood Lane, St. Helena, CA 94574. www.meadowood.com. ✆ **800/458-8080** or 707/963-3646. Fax 707/963-3532. 85 units. $475–$825 double; $775–$1,250 1-bedroom suite; $1,400–$3,400 2-bedroom suite; $1,875–$4,775 3-bedroom suite; $2,350–$6,150 4-bedroom suite. Ask about promotional offers and off-season rates. 2-night minimum stay. AE, DISC, MC, V. **Amenities:** 2 restaurants; concierge; golf course; health club and full-service spa; Jacuzzi; 2 large heated outdoor pools (adult and family pools); room service; sauna; 7 tennis courts. *In room:* A/C, TV, hair dryer, kitchenette in some rooms, minibar, free Wi-Fi.

Expensive

Wine Country Inn ★★   Just off the highway behind Freemark Abbey vineyard is one of the Wine Country's most personable choices. The attractive wood-and-stone property, complete with a French-style mansard roof and turret, overlooks a pastoral landscape of vineyards. The individually decorated rooms contain antique furnishings and handmade quilts; most have fireplaces and private terraces overlooking the valley, and others have private hot tubs. The five luxury cottages include king-size beds, sitting areas, fireplaces, private patios, and three-headed walk-in showers. Suites come with two-person jetted tubs, stereos, plenty of space, and lots of privacy. The family that runs this place puts personal touches everywhere and makes every guest feel welcome. They serve wine and plenty of appetizers nightly, along with a big dash of hotel-staff hospitality in the inviting living room. A full buffet breakfast is served there, too. *Note:* TV junkies book elsewhere. There are no tubes in rooms here.

1152 Lodi Lane, St. Helena, CA 94574. www.winecountryinn.com. (℃ **888/465-4608** or 707/963-7077. Fax 707/963-9018. 29 units, 12 with shower only. $235–$680 double; $535–$660 for cottages. Rates include breakfast and appetizers. DISC, MC, V. **Amenities:** Concierge; Jacuzzi; heated outdoor pool; spa services; free Wi-Fi. *In room:* A/C, hair dryer.

Inexpensive

El Bonita Motel ★ ☺ ✒   This 1940s Art Deco motel is a bit too close to Hwy. 29 for comfort, but the awesome price and 2½ acres of beautifully landscaped gardens behind the building (away from the road) help even the score. The rooms, while small and nothing fancy (think motel basic), are spotlessly clean and decorated with newer furnishings and kitchenettes; some have whirlpool bathtubs. It ain't heaven, but it is cheap for St. Helena.

195 Main St. (at El Bonita Ave.), St. Helena, CA 94574. www.elbonita.com. (℃ **800/541-3284** or 707/963-3216. Fax 707/963-8838. 41 units. $80–$280 double. Rates include continental breakfast. AE, DISC, MC, V. **Amenities:** Jacuzzi; heated outdoor pool; sauna. *In room:* A/C, TV, fridge, hair dryer, free Wi-Fi.

CALISTOGA

Four blocks of shops and restaurants, about a dozen low-key spas—most of which offer access to natural hot springs—and a profusion of reasonably priced hotels make Calistoga a popular choice.

Best For: Visitors interested in mud baths, hot springs, relaxed surroundings, and budget-friendly rooms.

Drawbacks: At the opposite end of the valley, a trip to Napa is a 40-minute drive. This area is also the hottest during summer, with temperatures regularly cresting 100°F (38°C).

Very Expensive

Calistoga Ranch ★★★   Tucked into the eastern mountainside on 157 pristine hidden-canyon acres, the 46 rural-chic free-standing luxury cottages may cost more than a month's rent, but if you've got the cash, it's one of the most spectacular temporary homes in the state. Auberge's sister property boasts stunning grounds and rooms packed with every conceivable amenity (including fireplaces, and private patios, often with outdoor hot tubs) along a wooded area, and cushy outdoor furnishings. Reasons not to leave include a giant swimming pool, a good gym, an incredibly designed indoor-outdoor spa with a natural thermal pool, massages and other spectacular treatments (ask for a massage from Doug!), individual pavilions with private-garden soaking tubs, and a restaurant with stunning views of the property's Lake Lommel (and unfortunately just okay food). Need more enticement? They offer free activities like yoga, biking, and hiking. Add architecture that intentionally tries to blend with the natural surroundings, and you've got a romantically rustic slice of Wine Country heaven.

580 Lommel Rd., Calistoga, CA 94515. www.calistogaranch.com. (℃ **707/254-2800.** Fax 707/254-2888. 46 cottages. $675–$4,200 double. AE, DISC, MC, V. **Amenities:** Restaurant; concierge; gym; Jacuzzi; large heated outdoor pool; room service; spa; free Wi-Fi throughout. *In room:* A/C, TV/ DVD w/DVDs, fax upon request, fridge, hair dryer, full kitchen in 4 lodges, minibar.

Expensive

Cottage Grove Inn ★   Standing in two parallel rows at the end of the main strip in Calistoga are adorable cottages that, though on a residential street (with a paved road running btw. two rows of accommodations), seem removed from the action once you've stepped across the threshold. Each compact guesthouse has a wood-burning fireplace, homey furnishings, a king-size bed with down comforter, and an enormous bathroom with a skylight and a deep, two-person Jacuzzi tub. Guests enjoy such niceties as gourmet coffee, a flatscreen TV, a stereo with CD player, a DVD (the inn has a complimentary DVD library), and a wet bar. Several local spas are within walking distance. This is a top pick if you want to do the Calistoga spa scene in comfort and style. Bicycles are provided for cruises around town, and guests can recoup a few bucks by using the complimentary tasting passes to more than a dozen nearby wineries.

1711 Lincoln Ave., Calistoga, CA 94515. www.cottagegrove.com. (℃ **800/799-2284** or 707/942-8400. Fax 707/942-2653. 16 cottages. $260–$450 double. Rates include breakfast and evening wine and cheese. AE, DISC, MC, V. *In room:* A/C, TV/DVD, fridge, hair dryer, free Wi-Fi.

Solage ★★   The more affordable, chic sister of Calistoga Ranch, this valley floor destination is a spacious yet petite resort complete with free-standing accommodations, family and adult swimming pools and Jacuzzis, a Michelin-ranked restaurant (SolBar; p. 362), and a wonderfully relaxed vibe. Rooms are smartly appointed and include patios or balconies, plus access to cruising bikes for roaming the property and beyond.

755 Silverado Trail, Calistoga, CA 94515. www.solagecalistoga.com. (℃ **866/942-7442** or 707/226-0800. Fax 707/226-0809. 89 units. $325–$725 double; $580–$995 suite. Rates include in-room coffee and tea and use of bicycles. AE, DISC, MC, V. **Amenities:** Restaurant; concierge; gym; Jacuzzi; 2 large heated outdoor pools; room service; spa; free Wi-Fi throughout; free bicycle use. *In room:* A/C, TV/DVD/CD player, MP3 docking station, fridge, hair dryer, minibar.

Moderate

Chanric Inn ★★   Channing McBride and Ric Pielstick, life partners and co-owners of Chanric Inn (get it? Chan-ric?), take B&B hospitality to the next level at their Calistoga gem. Splendid decor, little touches like gourmet biscotti and Aveda bath products in the rooms, and Ric's unforgettable cuisine are merely starting perks. Adding to the allure is a downstairs wet bar that's open 24/7, outdoor pool and hot tub with a view, and daily three-course breakfast (think trademark muffins, red Anjou pear with sabayon mousseline, and a soufflé of wild mushrooms and Gruyère cheese). Cooking classes are often offered on the premises, and the resident golden retriever, Dinnegan, is always around to further ensure that you're enjoying yourself accordingly.

1805 Foothill Blvd., Calistoga, CA 94515. www.thechanric.com. ✆ **877/281-3671** or 707/942-4535. 6 units. $209–$349 double. Rates include breakfast. AE, MC, V. *In room:* Hair dryer, free Wi-Fi.

Euro Spa & Inn ★★   In a quiet residential section of Calistoga, this small inn and spa provides a level of solitude and privacy that few other spas can match. The horseshoe-shaped inn consists of 13 boutique hotel rooms, a spa center, and an outdoor patio, where an expanded continental breakfast and snacks are served. The rooms, although small, are pleasantly decorated and come equipped with whirlpool tubs, decks, gas woodstoves, and kitchenettes. Spa treatments range from foot reflexology to minifacials.

1202 Pine St. (at Myrtle St.), Calistoga, CA 94515. www.eurospa.com. ✆ **707/942-6829.** Fax 707/942-1138. 13 units. $98–$275 double. Rates include expanded continental breakfast. 7 packages available. AE, DISC, MC, V. **Amenities:** Jacuzzi; outdoor heated pool; spa. *In room:* A/C, TV, hair dryer, kitchenette, free Wi-Fi.

Inexpensive
Calistoga Spa Hot Springs ★ ☺ 🔥   Very few hotels in the Wine Country cater specifically to families with children, which is why I recommend Calistoga Spa Hot Springs if you're bringing the little ones: They classify themselves as a family resort and are accommodating to visitors of all ages. In any case, it's a great bargain, offering unpretentious yet comfortable rooms, as well as a plethora of spa facilities. All of Calistoga's best shops and restaurants are within easy walking distance, and you can even whip up your own grub at the barbecue grills near the large pool and patio area.

1006 Washington St. (at Gerard St.), Calistoga, CA 94515. www.calistogaspa.com. ✆ **866/822-5772** or 707/942-6269. 57 units. $120–$247 double. Discounted rates available weekdays Oct–Mar, excluding holidays. MC, V. **Amenities:** Exercise room; 4 heated outdoor pools and kids' wading pool; spa. *In room:* A/C, TV, hair dryer, kitchenette, free Wi-Fi.

Dr. Wilkinson's Hot Springs Resort ★   This spa/"resort," in the heart of Calistoga, is one of the best deals in Napa Valley—and also offers all the spa treatments the town is famous for. The rooms range from attractive Victorian-style accommodations to cozy guest rooms in the main 1960s-style motel. All rooms, some of which have flatscreen TVs and iPod players, are spiffier than most of the area's other hotels, with tasteful textiles and basic motel-style accouterments. The bungalows have refrigerators and/or kitchens. Facilities include three mineral-water pools (two outdoor and one indoor), a Jacuzzi, a steam room, and mud baths. All kinds of body treatments are available in the spa, including famed mud baths, steams, and massage—all of which I highly recommend. Be sure to inquire about their excellent packages and their sister property, Hideaway Cottages, which offers fully equipped multiroom cottages at amazingly good prices.

1507 Lincoln Ave. (Calif. 29, btw. Fairway and Stevenson aves.), Calistoga, CA 94515. www.drwilkinson.com. ✆ **707/942-4102.** 42 units. $149–$299 double; $164–$600 for the Hideaway cottages. Weekly discounts and packages available. AE, MC, V. **Amenities:** Jacuzzi; 2 pools; spa; free Wi-Fi in lobby. *In room:* A/C, TV, hair dryer.

Roman Spa Hot Springs Resort ★   Reasonable prices, a central location just a block off Calistoga's main drag, trusty accommodations, a garden setting, and mineral pools make this low-key destination a sure thing for luxury lovers on a budget. Like most old-school "resorts" (a term used loosely in these parts) in the area, the focus is on the spa, which includes three mineral pools—one indoor pool, one outdoor pool, and one outdoor whirlpool—dry "Finnish" saunas, and mud bath and massage facilities. Accommodations are clean, comfortable, and, depending on what you get, somewhat outdated, and upgrades include a whirl-pool tub, full kitchen, or two-room "family" suite.

1300 Washington St., Calistoga, CA 94515. www.romanspahotsprings.com. (✆ **800/914-8957** or 707/942-4441. 60 units. $140–$250 double; $230–$450 suite. AE, DISC, MC, V. **Amenities:** 3 mineral pools; sauna; spa. *In room:* AC, TV, fridge, hair dryer.

Where to Eat in Napa Valley

Napa Valley's restaurants draw as much attention to the valley as its award-winning wineries. Nowhere else in the state are kitchens as deft at mixing fresh seasonal, local, organic produce into edible magic, which means that menus change constantly to reflect the best available ingredients. Add that to a great bottle of wine and stunning views, and you have one heck of an eating experience. If foodie destinations are your trip's focus, your reservations are likely to focus around Yountville and Napa, though there are a few worthy dining rooms in St. Helena, which means you are likely to cover a lot of ground. Regardless, to best enjoy Napa's restaurant scene, keep one thing in mind: Reserve in advance—especially for a seat in a famous room.

NAPA
Expensive
Morimoto Napa ★★ JAPANESE/SUSHI   Here the menu created by Iron Chef Masaharu Morimoto is the initial draw, but there's more to the spot's celebrity, including a hopping bar scene and sprawling industrial-chic interior, with spacious dining areas accented with glass, rich wood, and gnarled grapevines. You might skip the sushi, which is expensive and, during my visit, perched atop too-cold rice. Entrees such as whole-roasted lobster with Indian spices and lemon crème fraîche are decadent but trumped by appetizers such as Toro Tartare (with a presentation you must see for yourself), the buttery goodness that is Wagyu beef carpaccio, and foie gras chawan mushi (a savory custard with duck breast): pure edible glamour. Add a couple of Morimotinis and you've got a night well spent.

610 Main St., Napa. (✆ **707/252-1600.** www.morimotonapa.com. Reservations recommended. Main courses $26–$80. AE, DC, MC, V. Daily 11:30am–2:30pm; Sun–Thurs 5pm–midnight, Fri–Sat 5pm–1am.

Moderate
Angèle ★★ COUNTRY FRENCH   I, along with other locals, love this riverside spot for three reasons: The food is consistently great, it's reasonably priced (comparatively), and the surroundings are some of the best in the valley. Its cozy combo of raw wood beams, taupe-tinted concrete-slab floors, bright yellow leather bar stools, candlelight, and a heated, shaded patio (weather permitting) has always been great for intimate dining. The menu is regularly peppered with seasonal specialties, but it also holds on to local favorites like crispy roast chicken, which, depending on the time of year, may be ornamented with summer corn, chanterelles, lardons, baby potatoes, and jus or something more wintery. Also expected: outstanding burgers and tasty seafood such as roasted Columbia river

sturgeon with sunchokes, black trumpet mushrooms, and sauce daube. During winter eves, opt for the rustic-chic indoors; for summer, settle into one of the outdoor seats.

540 Main St. (in the Hatt Bldg.). ✆ **707/252-8115.** www.angelerestaurant.com. Reservations recommended. Main courses $18–$32. AE, MC, V. Sun–Thurs 11:30am–9pm; Fri–Sat 11:30am–10pm.

BarBersQ ★ BARBECUE   Located in a Napa strip mall, this crowded eatery has garnered three stars from San Francisco's most persnickety critic and a fiercely loyal following for its "American Heritage cuisine" (think Memphis-style barbecue, classic comfort foods, and meat, meat, and more meat). The menu covers all the grease and gristle faves, from legendary fried chicken (served only on Sun) to ribs, brisket, whole roast chicken for two, beans and ham, and mac and cheese. Add chocolate bourbon pecan pie, Key lime pie, or a hot fudge sundae, and you'll be hard-pressed to get out the door with your pants buttoned. Like most Napa Valley restaurants, this one does decadence with a "healthy" twist, employing fresh, local, organic ingredients when possible. While this effort doesn't cut calories, it may mitigate any potential guilt attached to unabashed indulgence. Also, FYI, service is uneven—also a Napa norm—and takeout is a popular option.

3900 D Bel Aire Plaza. ✆ **707/224-6600.** www.barbersq.com. Reservations recommended. Main courses $17–$36. AE, MC, V. Sun–Thurs 11:30am–8:30pm; Fri–Sat 11:30am–9pm.

Bistro Don Giovanni ★★ REGIONAL ITALIAN   Donna and Giovanni Scala own this bright, large, bustling, and cheery Italian restaurant (hence the name), which also happens to be one of my favorite restaurants in Napa Valley. Fare prepared by longtime chef/partner Scott Warner highlights quality ingredients and California flair and never disappoints, especially when it comes to the thin-crusted pizzas and house-made pastas. I almost always order beets and haricots verts, the pasta with duck Bolognese, or seared salmon filet perched atop a tower of buttermilk mashed potatoes. On the rare occasion that I stray, I am equally smitten with outstanding classic pizza Margherita fresh from the wood-burning oven and steak frites. Yet, not all is perfect. Service often leaves a little to be desired (unless you sit at the bar—always a social adventure!), and appetizer prices are a bit steep for the size. But don't let these drawbacks deter you. Alfresco dining overlooking the vineyards is available—and highly recommended on a warm, sunny day. Desserts seriously rock, so take my advice and order unabashedly—even if your stomach protests.

4110 Howard Lane (at St. Helena Hwy.). ✆ **707/224-3300.** www.bistrodongiovanni.com. Reservations recommended. Main courses $21–$38. AE, DC, DISC, MC, V. Sun–Thurs 11:30am–10pm; Fri–Sat 11:30am–11pm.

Ubuntu ★ VEGETARIAN   This Michelin-starred spot in downtown Napa offers decadent vegetarian cuisine made from sustainably, locally grown ingredients (often plucked from owner Sandy Lawrence's biodynamic garden). The edible action takes place in an eco-friendly room characterized by high stone walls, a large centerpiece community table, and a partitioned upstairs that acts as a yoga studio. While the space has a subdued palette, the food is colorful and vibrant. A recent fall visit included warm focaccia with bronze fennel-spiced eggplant, tomato, and ricotta, and a warm yam pudding with cranberry granita, cinnamon fluff, and poached quince. Because dishes are based on what's fresh and seasonally available, the menu changes regularly. You don't need to be crunchy to dine here—everything about this place is grown-up and elegant.

1140 Main St., near Pearl, Napa. ☎ **707/251-5656.** www.ubuntunapa.com. Reservations recommended. AE, DC, DISC, MC, V. Lunch Sat–Sun 11:30am–2:15pm; dinner Thurs–Mon 5:30–9pm.

Inexpensive

Alexis Baking Company ★ BAKERY/CAFE   Alexis (also known as ABC) is a quaint, casual hangout for residents and in-the-know tourists who don't mind the limited menu in exchange for quality food and relaxed, bright coffeehouse-style surroundings. On weekend mornings—especially Sunday, which is when you might find me devouring their out-of-this-world huevos rancheros and classic eggs Benedict—the line stretches out the door. Order from the counter during the week and at the table on Sunday, find a seat, and relax—there's really nothing else to do. Start your day with spectacular pastries, coffee drinks, and breakfast goodies like pumpkin pancakes with sautéed pears. Lunch also bustles with locals who come for simple, fresh fare like grilled hamburgers with Gorgonzola, grilled-chicken Caesar salad, roast lamb sandwich with minted mayo and roasted shallots on rosemary bread, and lentil bulgur orzo salad. (Sorry, fries lovers; you won't find any here.) Desserts run the gamut; during the holidays, they include a moist and magical steamed persimmon pudding. Oh, and the pastry counter's cookies and cakes beg you to take something for the road.

1517 Third St. (btw. Main and Jefferson sts.). ☎ **707/258-1827.** www.alexisbakingcompany.com. Main courses $6–$17 breakfast, $7–$13 lunch. MC, V. Mon–Fri 7am–3pm; Sat 7:30am–3pm; Sun 8am–2pm.

Norman Rose Tavern ★ AMERICAN   Despite its unsavory name, Napa's favorite stop for good American grub is a welcome departure from the region's pervasive French and Italian menus. Here, within a handsome yet relaxed dining room, it's all about dressed-up classic American comfort foods. All the standbys are present and accounted for—from a build-your-own burger with optional fix-in's like an organic fried egg, thyme-roasted mushrooms, or smoked bacon to four types of fries (including chili 'n' cheese!) to grilled flatiron steak. Equally uncommon for the area are the moderate prices, which is why locals have been instant loyalists since the doors opened in late 2009. FYI, this joint is owned and operated by the folks behind Pizza Azzurro (see below).

1401 First St. (at Franklin St.), Napa. ☎ **707/258-1516.** www.normanrosenapa.com. Main courses $17–$23 lunch and dinner. AE, MC, V. Mon–Thurs 11:30am–9:30pm; Fri 11:30am–1pm; Sat 10am–10pm; Sun 10am–9pm.

Pizza Azzurro ★ ITALIAN   This casual, cheery, family-friendly restaurant serves the best fancy thin-crust pies in downtown Napa. Unlike many Valley dining rooms, the place has an authentic neighborhood feel thanks to a very low-key atmosphere, and the continual presence of chef/owner Michael Gyetvan, who spent 10 years in the kitchens of Tra Vigne, One Market, and Lark Creek Inn. While killer thin-crust pizzas—such as the incredible salsiccia (tangy tomato sauce, rustic Sonoma-made fennel pork sausage, crunchy red onion, and mozzarella)—star here, they've got great salads, too. Pastas (such as rigatoni in red sauce with hot Italian sausage and mushrooms) play it safe, while manciatas—soft, lightly cooked pizza dough meant to be folded and eaten like a soft taco—are very satisfying. (Try the B.B.L.T. version.) Although Bistro Don Giovanni (see above) is king of fancy pasta and pizza fixes, Azzurro is cheaper and far better if you've got the kids in tow or want to have a low-key or fast dinner.

1260 Main St. (at Clinton St.). (707/255-5552. www.azzurropizzeria.com. No reservations except for 8 or more. Main courses $13–$16. AE, MC, V. Mon–Wed 11:30am–9:30pm; Thurs–Sat 11:30am–10pm; Sun 11:30am–9:30pm.

ZuZu ★★ TAPAS   A local place to the core, ZuZu lures neighborhood regulars with a no-reservation policy, a friendly, cramped wine-and-beer bar, and affordable Mediterranean/Latin American small plates, which are meant to be shared. The comfortable, warm, and not remotely corporate atmosphere extends from the environment to the food, which includes sizzling mini-skillets of tangy and fantastic paella, addictive prawns with chipotle and paprika, light and delicate sea scallop ceviche salad, and Tunisian brik pastry stuffed with Dungeness crab. Desserts aren't as fab, but with a bottle of wine and tastier plates than you can possibly devour, who cares?

829 Main St. (707/224-8555. www.zuzunapa.com. Reservations not accepted. Tapas $4–$15. AE, MC, V. Mon–Thurs 11:30am–10pm; Fri 11:30am–11pm; Sat 4–11pm; Sun 4–9:30pm.

YOUNTVILLE
Very Expensive
The French Laundry ★★★ CLASSIC AMERICAN/FRENCH   The world-famous French Laundry is unlike any other dining experience. Part of its appeal has to do with intricate, mouthwatering preparations, often finished tableside and always presented with uncommon artistry and detail, from the food itself to the surface it's delivered on. Other strengths are the service (superfluous, formal, and attentive) and the sheer length of time it takes to ride chef Thomas Keller's culinary magic carpet. The atmosphere is as serious as the diners who quietly swoon over the parade of bite-size delights. Seating ranges from downstairs to upstairs to seasonal garden tables. Technically, the prix-fixe menu offers a choice

of nine courses (including a vegetarian menu), but after several presentations from the kitchen, everyone starts to lose count. Signature dishes include Keller's "foie gras en terrine" (Moulard duck with spiced raisins, celery branch, and candied peanuts) and "Fricassée" (sweet butter-poached Maine lobster with pomegranate, caramelized shallots, watercress, and garnet yam mousse). The experience defies description, so if you absolutely love food, you'll simply have to try it for yourself. Portions are small, but only because Keller wants his guests to taste as many things as possible. Trust me, nobody leaves hungry.

The staff is well acquainted with the wide selection of regional wines; there's a $50 corkage fee if you bring your own bottle, which is only

A sous chef perfects a dish at the French Laundry.

welcome if it's not on the list. **Hint:** If you can't get a reservation, try walking in—no-shows are rare but possible, especially during lunch on rainy days. Reservations are accepted 2 months in advance of the date, starting at 10am. Anticipate hitting redial many times. Also, insiders tell me that fewer people call on weekends, so you have a better chance at getting beyond the busy signal. You can also try www.opentable.com, though online reservations are still taken 2 months in advance.

6640 Washington St. (at Creek St.). ℭ **707/944-2380.** www.frenchlaundry.com. Reservations required. Dress code: no jeans, shorts, or tennis shoes; men should wear jackets; ties optional. 9-course tasting menu (including vegetarian option) $270. AE, MC, V. Fri–Sun 11am–1pm; daily 5:30–9:15pm.

Expensive

Redd ★★ CONTEMPORARY AMERICAN   Chef Richard Reddington may have put his name on the culinary map at nearby resort Auberge du Soleil, but he secured a spot among the valley's very best chefs when he opened his own restaurant at the end of 2005. Though the modern and stark dining room is a wee too stark and white-on-white for my taste, the menu is definitely full-flavored. Expect exceptional appetizers such as a delicate sashimi hamachi with edamame, cucumber, ginger, and sticky rice, as well as a cold foie gras trio with pistachios and brioche. For entrees, the Alaskan halibut with salsify barigoule and herb butter is a dream dish that simultaneously manages to be rich and light. If your budget allows, definitely let the sommelier wine-pair the meal for you. He's bound to turn you on to some new favorites. Also, if you're looking for a lush brunch spot, this is it!

6480 Washington St. ℭ **707/944-2222.** www.reddnapavalley.com. Reservations recommended. Main courses brunch $15–$27, lunch $15–$27, dinner $15–$31; 5-course tasting menu $80, $125 with wine pairing. AE, DISC, MC, V. Mon–Sat 11:30am–2:30pm; Sun 11am–2:30pm; daily 5:30–9:30pm. Bar menu served daily 2:30–11pm.

Moderate

Bistro Jeanty ★ FRENCH BISTRO   This famous casual, warm bistro, with muted buttercup walls, two dining rooms divided by the bar, and patio seats, is where chef Philippe Jeanty creates seriously rich French comfort food for legions of fans. The all-day menu includes legendary tomato soup in puff pastry, foie gras pâté, steak tartare, and home-smoked trout with potato slices. No meal should start without a paper cone filled with fried smelt (it's often on the list of specials), and none should end without the crème brûlée, made with a thin layer of chocolate cream between classic vanilla custard and a caramelized sugar top. In between, it's a rib-gripping free-for-all including coq au vin, cassoulet, and juicy, slow-roasted pork shoulder with butternut squash gratin and Brussels sprouts. Alas, quality has suffered since Jeanty has branched out to three restaurants, but when the kitchen is on it's still a fine place to sup.

6510 Washington St. ℭ **707/944-0103.** www.bistrojeanty.com. Reservations recommended. Appetizers $8.75–$16; most main courses $17–$38. AE, MC, V. Daily 11:30am–10:30pm.

Bottega Ristorante ★ ITALIAN   Decorated in the Italian equivalent of the steakhouse—dark leather, pin lights, and brick walls—this sexy Italian hot spot is owned and operated by Food Network star Michael Chiarello, which at least partially explains its popularity. But Chiarello has more going for him than a smile that's made for TV. The guy is a good cook, and evidence can be found in dishes such as grilled loin of lamb with saffron braised potatoes, pistachio pesto, and rosemary scented lamb jus; and pumpkin and fontina risotto with meat Bolognese. Not everything wows, but no matter. With (relatively) reasonable prices, an awesome scene, and the famed chef himself regularly schmoozing the tables, even on the occasion you do get a just-okay dish, there's much to enjoy here.

6525 Washington St., behind the NapaStyle store. ℂ **707/945-1050.** www.botteganapavalley. com. Reservations recommended. Main courses lunch and dinner $15–$28. AE, DC, DISC, MC, V. Tues–Sun 11:30am–2:30pm; Mon–Thurs 5–9:30pm; Fri–Sat 5–10pm; Sun 5–9:30pm.

Bouchon ★ FRENCH BISTRO   Famed chef Thomas Keller (of French Laundry, p. 357) is behind this sexy French brasserie. Along with posh environs, expect a raw bar, textbook renditions of steak frites, mussels meunière, grilled-cheese sandwiches, and other French classics (try the expensive and rich foie gras pâté, which is made at the French Laundry). The Bibb lettuce salad is a must try (seriously, trust me on this) and french fries are perhaps the best in the valley. A bonus, especially for restless residents and off-duty restaurant staff, is the late hours, although they offer a more limited menu when the crowds dwindle.

6534 Washington St. (at Humboldt St.). ℂ **707/944-8037.** www.bouchonbistro.com. Reservations recommended during the week, required on weekends. Main courses $18–$35. AE, MC, V. Daily 11:30am–midnight.

Mustards Grill ★ CALIFORNIAN   Here the promise is simple: Hyperflavored (and undeniably tasty) comfort classics with exotic spins in heaping portions. As a popular valley standard for more than 20 years, you should also expect to wait for a table within the convivial, barn-style space—even, annoyingly, if you have a reservation. But once you're settled in with a selection from the 300 New World wine list and raise fork to mouth, all is easily forgiven. Do start with seared ahi tuna or moist and meaty crab cakes and broaden your culinary horizons (not to mention your waistline) with favorites such as Mongolian-style pork chop with hot mustard sauce or sautéed lemon-garlic half-chicken with mashed potatoes and fresh herbs. And definitely end with their famed lemon-lime tart, which is easily identified by its Bart Simpson–hairdo-like meringue topping.

7399 St. Helena Hwy. (Hwy. 29). ℂ **707/944-2424.** www.mustardsgrill.com. Reservations recommended. Main courses $15–$27. AE, DC, DISC, MC, V. Mon–Thurs 11:30am–9pm; Fri 11:30am–10pm; Sat 11am–10pm; Sun 11am–9pm.

RUTHERFORD
Expensive
Auberge du Soleil ★★ 📖 WINE COUNTRY CUISINE   With the absolute best valley view on the terrace by day, outstanding formal cuisine by Chef Robert Curry anytime, and polished, warm service, Auberge is an excellent choice for a special-occasion or food lover's meal. The seasonally inspired, local-ingredient-focused menu changes frequently, but hopefully it includes the stunning Hiramasa crudo with slow-cooked hen egg, soba, yuzu, and "Hong Kong" vinaigrette; seared tuna with glazed pork belly, tempura, and seasoned dashi; and venison tournedos with pancetta, raddichio, sweet potato Napoleon, and huckleberry.

WHERE TO STOCK UP FOR A
gourmet picnic

You can easily plan your whole trip around restaurant reservations, but gather one of the world's best gourmet picnics, and the valley's your oyster.

One of the finest gourmet-food stores in the Wine Country, if not all of California, is the **Oakville Grocery Co.**, 7856 St. Helena Hwy., at Oakville Cross Road, Oakville (© 707/944-8802; www.oakvillegrocery.com). You can put together the provisions for a memorable picnic or, with at least 24 hours' notice, the staff can prepare a picnic basket for you. The store, with its small-town vibe and claustrophobia-inducing crowds, can be quite an experience. You'll find shelves crammed with the best breads and choicest cheeses in the northern Bay Area, as well as pâtés, cold cuts, crackers, top-quality olive oils, fresh foie gras (domestic and French, seasonal), smoked Norwegian salmon, and, of course, an exceptional selection of California wines. The store is open daily from 9am to 5pm. There's also an espresso bar tucked in the corner (Mon–Thurs 7am–5pm, Fri–Sat 7am–6pm, Sun 8am–5pm), offering lunch items, a complete deli, and house-baked pastries.

Another of my favorite places to fill a picnic basket is New York's version of a swank European marketplace, **Dean & DeLuca**, 607 S. St. Helena Hwy. (Hwy. 29), north of Zinfandel Lane and south of Sulphur Springs Road, St. Helena (© 707/967-9980; www.deandeluca.com). The ultimate in gourmet grocery stores is more like a world's fair of foods, where everything is beautifully displayed and often painfully pricey. As you pace the barn-wood plank floors, you'll stumble upon more high-end edibles than you've probably ever seen under one roof. They include local organic produce (delivered daily); 300 domestic and imported cheeses (with an on-site aging room to ensure proper ripeness); shelves and shelves of tapenades, pastas, oils, hand-packed dried herbs and spices, chocolates, sauces, cookware, and housewares; an espresso bar; one hell of a bakery section; and more. Along the back wall, you can watch the professional chefs prepare gourmet takeout, including salads, rotisserie meats, and sautéed vegetables. You can also snag a pricey bottle from the wine section's 1,400-label collection. The store is open Sunday to Thursday 7am to 7pm, Friday and Saturday 7am to 8pm. (The espresso bar is open daily at 7am.)

Wash it down with a bottle from the impressive (and pricey) wine list, with over 30 available by the glass, and you're living like the rich and famous who regularly stay here. For those who want to experience VIP living without paying full price, dine at the bar (which also has patio seats), where you can have a more casual feast of ahi tuna tartare, grilled chicken panini, a good ol' burger, and oysters on the half shell, along with 25 wines by the glass. And breakfast is destination-worthy, too.

180 Rutherford Hill Rd. © **707/967-3111.** www.aubergedusoleil.com. Reservations required. Main courses $28–$42 lunch; 4-course fixed-price dinner $115; 6-course $140, $222 with wine pairings per person; vegetarian tasting menu $98; bar menu $7–$34. AE, DISC, MC, V. Daily 7–11am, 11:30am–2:30pm, and 5:30–9:30pm. Bar daily 11am–11pm.

ST. HELENA

Expensive

Terra/Bar Terra ★★ CONTEMPORARY AMERICAN   In 2011, Terra doubled its destination-worthy fun, offering two entirely different experiences—one a casual bar area with relaxed dining and one a refined fine dining room that pays tribute to the cooking that made Terra one of the valley's most renowned restau-

Fish dish at Terra. Save room for dessert.

rants. Conceptualized by Lissa Doumani and her husband, Hiro Sone, a Japanese master chef (who are also behind San Francisco's famed Ame restaurant), the new bar menu offers seasonal cocktails made from fruits and herbs grown by the owners (plus a full bar) and a menu featuring a broad range of small dishes and prices that allows diners to mix and match a meal to suit their appetites and pocketbooks. (Don't even think of missing the legendary fried rock shrimp; tuna belly with daikon salad and wasabi sauce,

grilled edamame; or kimchi.) The fine-dining menu continues to reflect Sone's full use of the region's bounty and his formal training in classic European and Japanese cuisine. But now the affair is a four- or five-course extravaganza, with options ranging from understated and refined (two must-tries: forest mushrooms salad, and broiled sake-marinated cod with shrimp dumplings and shiso broth) to rock-your-world flavorful. I cannot express the importance of saving room for dessert (or forcing it even if you don't). Doumani's recipes, which include to-die-for tiramisu, are heavenly.

1345 Railroad Ave. (btw. Adams and Hunt sts.). ℭ **707/963-8931.** www.terrarestaurant.com. Reservations recommended. Bar: Plates $6–$26. Dining room: 4 course $67; 5 course $82; 6-course $94; chef's menu changes nightly. AE, DC, MC, V. Mon, Wed, Thurs–Fri 6–9pm; Sat–Sun 6–9:30pm. Closed 2 weeks in early Jan.

Moderate

Tra Vigne Restaurant ★ ITALIAN   Tra Vigne's got the best outdoor dining scene around, period. Sit in the astoundingly romantic and lush Tuscan-style courtyard and share a chilled bottle of white wine, and you'll bask in the glory of superb alfresco dining regardless of whether the kitchen is on the money or missing the mark (both of which happen). Inside, the bustling, cavernous dining room and happening bar are fine for chilly days and eves, but they're not nearly as magical. You can also count on wonderful bread (served with house-cured olives); a menu of robust California dishes, cooked Italian style; a daily oven-roasted pizza special; lots of pastas; and tried-and-true standbys like short ribs and fritto misto.

1050 Charter Oak Ave. ℭ **707/963-4444.** www.travignerestaurant.com. Reservations recommended. Main courses $16–$30. DC, DISC, MC, V. Summer daily 11:30am–10pm; winter Mon–Thurs 11:30am–9pm, Fri–Sat 11:30am–10pm, Sun 11am–9:30pm.

Inexpensive

Gillwoods Café AMERICAN   In a town like this—where if you order mushrooms on your burger, the waiter's likely to ask, "What kind?"—this plain old American restaurant is a godsend. At this homey haunt, with its wooden benches and original artwork, it's all about the basics. You'll find a breakfast of bakery goods, fruit, pancakes, omelets (with pronounceable ingredients), and a decent eggs Benedict, and a lunch menu of burgers, sandwiches, lots of salads, and chicken-fried steak. Lunch is available starting at 10:30am, but late risers can order breakfast all day. A second location is in downtown Napa at 1320 Napa Town Center (✆ **707/253-0409**).

1313 Main St. (Hwy. 29, at Spring St.). ✆ **707/963-1788.** www.gillwoodscafe.com. Breakfast $9–$12; lunch $9–$13. AE, MC, V. Daily 7:30am–2:30pm. Napa location daily 7am–3pm.

Gott's Roadside Tray Gourmet DINER   This gourmet roadside burger shack built in 1949 and previously known as Taylor's Refresher draws huge lines of tourists who love the notion of ordering at the counter and feasting alfresco. But truth be told, its burgers, onion rings, and fries are overrated, especially considering the inflated prices. However, it's still the only outdoor burger joint in St. Helena (it also offers ahi tuna burgers and various sandwiches, tacos, soups, and salads), and its ever-bustling status proves everyone knows it. A second location in Napa at 644 First St. (near Soscol Ave.) is open daily 10:30am to 9pm.

933 Main St. ✆ **707/963-3486.** www.gottsroadside.com. Main courses $7–$14. AE, MC, V. Daily 10:30am–9pm (until 10pm during summer).

CALISTOGA

Expensive

SolBar ★★ CALIFORNIAN   This Michelin-rated resort dining room in the chic Solage resort is hands down the sexiest dinner spot in the valley. It's not merely the mood-lit modern barn environs with mountain views. Or that half the restaurant is bar and leather couch seating where a guitarist might be helping set the sultry tone. (Never mind the patio seating with a sculptural outdoor fireplace, which is awesome for lunch and warm-weather dinners.) It's that the restaurant manages to feel refined, cozy, and happening all at the same time. Pair the winning ambience with Nantucket Bay scallops with salt-roasted fennel, smoked potatoes, sunchokes, Meyer lemon, and pequillo peppers or wagyu brisket with Yukon Gold potato gnocchi, Swiss chard, and beer-battered onion rings, and you're destined for a culinary love affair. Incidentally, they are a contender for Best Breakfast, too. Order the "Sol-Pe," or crispy masa cake with chorizo, black beans, jack cheese, scrambled eggs, chile verde, and sour cream, and you're sure to agree.

755 Silverado Trail. ✆ **866/942-7442.** www.solagecalistoga.com/dining. Reservations recommended. Main courses dinner $21–$36, lunch $15–$19, breakfast $11–$17. AE, DC, DISC, MC, V. Daily 7am–10pm. Bar until midnight.

SONOMA VALLEY

A pastoral contrast to Napa, Sonoma manages to maintain a backcountry ambience, thanks to its far lower density of wineries, restaurants, and hotels. Small, family-owned wineries are Sonoma's mainstay; tastings are low-key and come with plenty of friendly banter with the winemakers. Basically, this is the valley to target if your ideal vacation includes visiting a handful of wineries along quiet woodsy roads, avoiding shopping outlets and Napa's high-end glitz, and simply enjoying the laid-back country atmosphere.

The valley is some 17 miles long and 7 miles wide, and it's bordered by two mountain ranges: the Mayacamas to the east and the Sonomas to the west. Unlike in Napa Valley, you won't find much in the way of palatial wineries with million-dollar art collections or aerial trams. Rather, the Sonoma Valley offers a refreshing dose of family-owned winery reality, where modestly sized wineries are integrated into the community. If Napa Valley feels like a fantasyland, where everything exists to service the almighty grape and the visitors it attracts, then the Sonoma Valley is its antithesis, an unpretentious gaggle of ordinary towns, ranches, and wineries that welcome tourists but don't necessarily rely on them. The result is a chance to experience what Napa Valley must have been like long before the Seagrams and Moët et Chandons of the world turned the Wine Country into a major tourist destination.

As in Napa, you can pick up *Wine Country Review* throughout Sonoma. It gives you the most up-to-date information on wineries and related area events.

Essentials

GETTING THERE   From San Francisco, cross the Golden Gate Bridge and stay on U.S. 101 N. Exit at Hwy. 37; after 10 miles, turn north onto Hwy. 121. After another 10 miles, turn north onto Hwy. 12 (Broadway), which takes you directly into the town of Sonoma.

VISITOR INFORMATION   While you're in Sonoma, stop by the **Sonoma Valley Visitors Bureau,** 453 First St. E. (© **866/996-1090** or 707/996-1090; www.sonomavalley.com). It's open Monday through Saturday from 9am to 5pm (6pm in summer Fri–Sat) and Sunday 10am to 5pm. An additional Visitors Bureau is a few miles south of the square at Cornerstone Festival of Gardens at 23570 Arnold Dr. (Hwy. 121; © **866/996-1090**); it's open daily from 9am to 4pm, 5pm during summer.

If you prefer advance information from the bureau, you can contact the Sonoma Valley Visitors Bureau to order the free *Sonoma Valley Visitors Guide,* which lists almost every lodge, winery, and restaurant in the valley.

Touring the Sonoma Valley & Wineries

Sonoma Valley is currently home to about 45 wineries (including California's first winery, Buena Vista, founded in 1857) and 13,000 acres of vineyards. It produces roughly 76 types of wines, totaling more than five million cases a year. Unlike the rigidly structured tours at many of Napa Valley's corporate-owned wineries, on the Sonoma side of the Mayacamas Mountains, tastings are usually low-key and tours free.

The towns and wineries covered below are organized geographically from south to north, starting at the intersection of Hwy. 37 and Hwy. 121 in the Carneros District and ending in Kenwood. The wineries tend to be a little more spread out here than they are in Napa Valley, but they're easy to find. Still, it's best to decide which wineries you're most interested in and devise a touring strategy before you set out, so you don't do too much backtracking.

I review some of my favorite Sonoma Valley wineries here—more than enough to keep you busy tasting wine for a long weekend. If you'd like a complete list of local wineries, be sure to pick up one of the free guides available at the Sonoma Valley Visitors Bureau (see "Visitor Information," above).

For a map of the wineries below, please see "The Wine Country" map on p. 325.

THE CARNEROS DISTRICT

As you approach the Wine Country from the south, you must first pass through the Carneros District, a cool, wind-swept region that borders San Pablo Bay and marks the entrance to both the Napa and Sonoma valleys. Until the latter part of the 20th century, this mixture of marsh, sloughs, and rolling hills was mainly used as sheep pasture (carneros means "sheep" in Spanish). However, after experimental plantings yielded slow-growing, high-quality grapes—particularly chardonnay and pinot noir—several Napa and Sonoma wineries expanded their plantings here. They eventually established the Carneros District as an American Viticultural Appellation, a legally defined wine-grape growing area. Although about a dozen wineries are spread throughout the region, there are no major towns or attractions—just plenty of gorgeous scenery as you cruise along Hwy. 121, the major route between Napa and Sonoma.

It's not just the grapes: Steve Sangiacomo discusses how competing winemakers use the same grapes to produce very different wines.

Viansa Winery and Italian Marketplace ★ 🎁   A sprawling, and extremely romantic, Tuscan-style villa sitting atop a knoll overlooking the entire lower valley, Viansa was founded by descendants of the Sebastianis (one of the nation's earliest Italian winemaking families). Here you'll find everything old-world wine dynasties cherish, including wine, food, and gorgeous views along with a large room crammed with a cornucopia of artisan snacks and gifts.

The winery, which does extensive mail-order business through the Tuscan Club, features Italian varietals. Tastings cost $5 per person for four villa wines and $10 for four reserve wines and are offered at the east and west ends of the marketplace. The self-guided tour includes a trip through the underground barrel-aging cellar, adorned with colorful hand-painted murals. Viansa is also one of the few wineries in Sonoma Valley that sells deli items—the focaccia sandwiches are delicious.

25200 Arnold Dr. (Calif. 121), Sonoma. 𝒞 **800/995-4740** or 707/935-4700. www.viansa.com. Daily 10am–5pm. Daily self-guided tours.

Gloria Ferrer Champagne Caves ★ 🎁   Gloria Ferrer, the grande dame of Sonoma Valley's sparkling-wine producers, is named after José Ferrer's wife, whose family has made sparkling wine for 5 centuries. The family business, Freixenet, is the world's largest producer of sparkling wine. That legacy amounts

A Garden Detour

Garden lovers should pull over for a gander at **Cornerstone Festival of Gardens**, 23570 Arnold Dr., Sonoma (© 707/933-3010; www.cornerstone gardens.com). Modeled in part after the International Garden festival at Chaumont-sur-Loire in France's Loire Valley and the Grand-Métis in Quebec, Canada, the 9-acre property is the first gallery-style garden exhibit in the United States and includes a series of 22 ever-changing gardens designed by famed landscape architects and designers. There are

several interesting shops here, too, including a personal favorite and L.A. transplant: **Zipper ★★**, which is packed with incredible home finds and gifts at very reasonable prices. Open 10am to 5pm daily (gardens close at 4pm), year-round (cafe opens at 9am). Admission to the gardens is free. You can take a self-guided tour anytime; installations are marked with descriptive plaques. Docent tours are available for groups of 10 or more by appointment.

to big bucks, and certainly a good chunk of change went into building this palatial estate. It glimmers like Oz, high atop a gently sloping hill, overlooking the verdant Carneros District. On a sunny day, enjoying a glass of dry brut while soaking in the magnificent views is a must.

If you're unfamiliar with the term méthode champenoise, take the $10 tasting and 30-minute tour of the fermenting tanks, bottling line, and caves brimming with racks of yeast-laden bottles. Afterward, retire to the elegant tasting room, order a glass of one of seven sparkling wines ($5–$10 a glass) or tastes of their eight still wines ($2–$3 per taste), find an empty chair on the veranda, and say, "Ahhh. This is the life." There are picnic tables, but it's usually too windy for comfort. You must buy a bottle (from around $20–$50) or glass of sparkling wine to reserve a table.

23555 Carneros Hwy. (Calif. 121), Sonoma. © **707/996-7256,** www.gloriaferrer.com, Daily 10am–5pm. Tours daily 11am, 1, and 3pm, $10.

SONOMA

At the northern boundary of the Carneros District along Hwy. 12 is the centerpiece of Sonoma Valley. The midsize town of Sonoma owes much of its appeal to Mexican general Mariano Guadalupe Vallejo, who fashioned this pleasant, slow-paced community after a typical Mexican village—right down to its central plaza, Sonoma's geographical and commercial center. The plaza sits at the top of a "T" formed by Broadway (Hwy. 12) and Napa Street. Most of the surrounding streets form a grid pattern around this axis, making Sonoma easy to negotiate. The plaza's Bear Flag Monument marks the spot where the crude Bear Flag was raised in 1846, signaling the end of Mexican rule; the symbol was later adopted by the state

The grand view from Gloria Ferrer's patio.

of California and placed on its flag. The 8-acre park at the center of the plaza, complete with two ponds populated by ducks, is perfect for an afternoon siesta in the cool shade.

Gundlach Bundschu Winery ★★   If it looks like the people working here are actually enjoying themselves, that's because they are. Gundlach Bundschu (pronounced Gun-lock Bun-shoe) is the quintessential Sonoma winery—nonchalant in appearance but obsessed with wine: The GB clan are a nefarious lot, infamous for wild stunts such as holding up Napa's Wine Train on horseback and—egad!—serving Sonoma wines to their captives; the small tasting room looks not unlike a bomb shelter, the Talking Heads is their version of Muzak, and the "art" consists of a dozen witty black-and-white posters promoting GB wines.

This is the oldest continually family-owned and -operated winery in California, going into its sixth generation since Jacob Gundlach harvested his first crop in 1858. Drop in to sample chardonnay, pinot noir, merlot, cabernet, and more. Prices for the 14 distinct wines range from $24 per bottle for the Mountain Cuvee to $80 for the Vintage reserve cabernet sauvignon. Tastings are $10, and tours, which include a trip into the 430-foot cave, start at $20 and are by appointment only.

Gundlach Bundschu has the best picnic grounds in the valley, though you have to walk to the top of Towles' Hill to earn the sensational view. They also have great activities (Midsummer Mozart Festival, film fests), so call or check the website if you want to join the fun.

2000 Denmark St. (off Eighth St. E.), Sonoma. ℗ **707/938-5277.** www.gunbun.com. Daily 11am–4:30pm. Tours last 1 hr. and are by appointment only. Groups of 8 or more should make an appointment.

A tasting room at Gundlach Bundschu.

Buena Vista Carneros Winery   Count Agoston Haraszthy, the Hungarian émigré who is universally regarded as the father of California's wine industry, founded this historic winery in 1857. A close friend of Mexico's General Vallejo, Haraszthy returned from Europe in 1861 with 100,000 of the finest vine cuttings, which he made available to all growers. Although Buena Vista's winemaking now takes place at an ultramodern facility in the Carneros District, the winery maintains a tasting room inside the restored 1862 Press House. The beautiful stone-crafted room brims with wines, wine-related gifts, and accessories.

Tastings are $10 for a flight of seven wines. You can take the self-guided tour any time during operating hours; their $20 "Carneros Experience" requires a

TOURING THE SONOMA VALLEY by bike

Sonoma and its neighboring towns are so small, close together, and relatively flat that it's not difficult to get around on two wheels. In fact, if you're in no great hurry, there's no better way to tour the Sonoma Valley than by bicycle, even though there are no great bike routes (it's all along the road for the most part). You can rent a bike from the **Goodtime Bicycle Company** ★ ((*C* 888/525-0453 or 707/938-0453; www.good timetouring.com). The staff will happily point you toward easy bike trails, or you can take an organized excursion to Kenwood-area wineries, south Sonoma wineries, or even northern Sonoma's Russian River and Dry Creek areas. Goodtime also provides a gourmet lunch featuring local Sonoma products. If you purchase wine along the way, Goodtime will carry it for you and help with shipping arrangements. Lunch rides start at 10:30am and end around 3:30pm. The cost, including food and equipment, is $135 per person (that's a darn good deal). Rentals cost $25 a day and include helmets, locks, everything else you'll need, and delivery and pickup to and from local hotels.

Mountain bikes, helmets, and locks are also available for rent from **Sonoma Valley Cyclery**, 20093 Broadway, Sonoma ((*C* 707/935-3377), for $25 to $65 a day. Hybrid bikes (better for casual wine-tasting cruisers) are $25 per day, helmet and lock included.

reservation and pairs five wines with a small plate of food, including cheeses. After tasting, grab your favorite bottle, a selection of cheeses from the Sonoma Cheese Factory, salami, bread, and spreads (all available in the tasting room), and plant yourself at one of the many picnic tables in the lush, verdant setting.

18000 Old Winery Rd. (off E. Napa St., slightly northeast of downtown), Sonoma. (*C* **800/926-1266** or 707/265-1472. www.buenavistacarneros.com. Daily 10am–5pm.

Sebastiani Vineyards & Winery The name Sebastiani is practically synonymous with Sonoma. What started in 1904, when Samuele Sebastiani began producing his first wines, has in three generations grown into a small empire, producing some 350,000 cases a year. The original 1904 property is open to the public with a free educational tour, an 80-foot S-shaped tasting bar, and lots of gift shopping opportunities. In the contemporary tasting room's minimuseum area, you can see the winery's original turn-of-the-20th-century crusher and press, as well as the world's largest collection of oak-barrel carvings, crafted by bygone local artist Earle Brown. If it's merely wine that interests you, you can sample a flight of seven Sonoma County wines for $10. Bottle prices are reasonable, ranging from $13 to $90. A picnic area adjoins the cellars; a far more scenic spot is across the parking lot in Sebastiani's Cherryblock Vineyards.

389 Fourth St. E., Sonoma. (*C* **800/888-5532** or 707/933-3200. www.sebastiani.com. Daily 11am–5pm. Tours daily at 11am, 1, and 3pm.

Ravenswood Winery ★ The first winery in the United States to focus primarily on zinfandel—the versatile red grape known here for being big, ripe, juicy, and powerful—Ravenswood underscores its zest for zin with their motto, "No Wimpy Wines." While zins make up about three-quarters of their astonishing one-million-case production, they also produce merlot, cabernet sauvignon, Rhone varietals, and a small amount of chardonnay.

The winery is smartly designed—recessed into the hillside to protect its treasures from the simmering summers. Tours ($15 per person) follow the wine-making process from grape to glass and include a visit to the aromatic oak-barrel aging rooms. You're welcome to bring your own picnic basket to any of the tables, and don't forget to check their website or call to find out if they're having one of their famous ongoing barbecues or winter celebrations. Regardless, tastings are $10 for five Sonoma County wines to $15 for the Vineyard Designate series. Bottles average around $35.

18701 Gehricke Rd. (off Lovall Valley Rd.), Sonoma. ℭ **888/669-4679** or 707/933-2332. www. ravenswoodwinery.com. Daily 10am–4:30pm. Tours at 10:30am; reservations recommended for groups of 8 or more.

GLEN ELLEN

About 7 miles north of Sonoma on Hwy. 12 is the town of Glen Ellen. Although just a fraction of the size of Sonoma, Glen Ellen is home to several of the valley's finest wineries, restaurants, and inns. Aside from the addition of a few new restaurants, this charming town hasn't changed much since the days when Jack London settled on his Beauty Ranch, about a mile west. Other than the wineries, you'll find few real signs of commercialism; the shops and restaurants, along one main winding lane, cater to a small, local clientele—that is, until the summer tourist season begins and traffic nearly triples on the weekends. If you haven't decided where you want to set up camp during your visit to the Wine Country, I highly recommend this lovable little rural region.

Arrowood Vineyards & Winery   Richard Arrowood had already established a reputation as a master winemaker at Château St. Jean when he and his wife, Alis Demers Arrowood, set out on their own in 1986. Their picturesque winery stands on a gently rising hillside lined with perfectly manicured vineyards. Tastings take place in the Hospitality House, the newer of Arrowood's two stately gray-and-white buildings. They're fashioned after New England farmhouses, complete with wraparound porches. Richard's focus is on making world-class wine with minimal intervention, and his results are impressive: More than one of his recent releases scored over 90 points in *Wine Spectator, Wine Advocate*, or *Wine Enthusiast.* Mind you, excellence isn't free: A taste here is $5 for five Sonoma County wines or $10 for five limited-production wines, while a winery, vineyard, and cellar tour is $20, but if you're curious about what near-perfection tastes like, it's well worth it. *Note:* No picnic facilities are available here.

14347 Sonoma Hwy. (Calif. 12), Glen Ellen. ℭ **707/935-2600.** www.arrowoodvineyards. com. Daily 10am–4:30pm. Tours by appointment only.

Benziger Family Winery ★★ 📠

A visit here confirms that this is indeed a family winery. At any given time, two generations of Benzigers (Ben-zigger) may be running around tending to chores, and they instantly make you feel as if you're part of the clan. The pastoral, user-friendly property features

Benziger Winery.

an exceptional self-guided tour of the certified biodynamic winery ("The most comprehensive tour in the wine industry," according to *Wine Spectator*), gardens, and a spacious tasting room staffed by amiable folks. Definitely pay the $20 for adults and $5 for kids 20 and under for the 45-minute tram tour, pulled by a beefy tractor. Both informative and fun, it winds through the estate vineyards and to caves, and ends with a tasting. *Tip:* Tram tickets—a hot item in the summer— are available on a first-come, first-served basis, so either arrive early or stop by in the morning to pick up afternoon tickets.

Tastings of the standard-release wines are $10. Tastes including several limited-production wines or estate wines cost $20. The winery also offers several scenic picnic spots

1883 London Ranch Rd. (off Arnold Dr., on the way to Jack London State Historic Park), Glen Ellen. **(C) 888/490-2739** or 707/935-3000. www.benziger.com. Tasting room daily 10am–5pm. Tram tours daily (weather permitting) $20 adults, $5 children, every half-hour, 11am–3:30pm (except noon).

KENWOOD

A few miles north of Glen Ellen along Hwy. 12 is the tiny town of Kenwood, the valley's northernmost outpost. Although Kenwood Vineyards' wines are well known throughout the United States, the town itself consists of little more than a few restaurants, wineries, and modest homes on the wooded hillsides. The nearest lodging, the luxurious Kenwood Inn & Spa (p. 376), is about a mile south of the vineyards. Kenwood makes for a pleasant half-day trip from Glen Ellen or downtown Sonoma. Take an afternoon tour of Château St. Jean (see below) and have dinner at Kenwood Restaurant (p. 382).

Kunde Estate Winery Expect a friendly, unintimidating welcome at this scenic winery, run by five generations of the Kundes since 1904. One of the largest grape suppliers in the area, the Kunde family (pronounced Kun-dee) has devoted 700 acres of its 2,000-acre ranch to growing ultrapremium-quality grapes. This abundance allows them to make nothing but estate wines. (Wines made from grapes grown on the property, as opposed to also using grapes purchased from other growers.)

The giant tasting room and gift shop, located in a 17,000-square-foot winemaking facility, offers samples of six estate releases for $10 and reserve tastings for $20; bottle prices range from $15 for a Magnolia Lane sauvignon blanc to $40 for a Drummond Vineyards cabernet sauvignon; most labels are priced in the high teens. The tour of the property's extensive wine caves includes a history of the winery. Private tours are available by appointment, but most folks are happy to just stop by to sip and sun at one of the many patio tables around a man-made pond. Animal lovers will appreciate Kunde's preservation efforts: The property has a duck estuary with more than 50 species (which can be seen by appointment only).

9825 Sonoma Hwy., Kenwood. **(C) 707/833-5501.** www.kunde.com. Tastings daily 10:30am–5pm. Complimentary cave tours daily on the hour 11am–3pm.

Château St. Jean ★ 🍴 Château St. Jean is notable for its exceptionally beautiful buildings, expansive landscaped grounds, gourmet market–like tasting room, and tasty wines. Among California wineries, it's a pioneer in vineyard designation—the procedure of making wine from, and naming it for, a single vineyard. A private drive takes you to what was once a 250-acre country retreat built in 1920; a well-manicured lawn overlooking the meticulously maintained vineyards is now a picnic area, complete with a fountain and picnic tables.

In the huge tasting room—with a charcuterie shop and housewares for sale—you can sample Château St. Jean's bounty, from chardonnays and cabernet sauvignon to fumé blanc, merlot, Johannesburg Riesling, and Gewürztraminer. Tastings are $10 per person, $20 per person for reserve wines.

8555 Sonoma Hwy. (Calif. 12), Kenwood. ℂ **800/543-7572** or 707/833-4134. www.chateau stjean.com. Tasting daily 10am–5pm. At the foot of Sugarloaf Ridge, just north of Kenwood and east of Hwy. 12.

St. Francis Winery Although St. Francis Winery makes commendable chardonnay, zinfandel, and cabernet sauvignon, they're best known for their highly coveted merlot.

Tastings at the chic tasting room are $10 per person for a choice of five wines from a selection of nationally known brands and wines only available at the winery. For $35, you can try their wine and food pairing, which includes a flight of four wines paired with seasonal hors d'oeuvres. Now that St. Francis is planning more special activities, it's worthwhile to call or check the website for its calendar of events.

100 Pythian Rd. (Calif. 12/Sonoma Hwy.), Santa Rosa (at the Kenwood border). ℂ **800/543-7713,** ext. 242, or 707/833-4666. www.stfrancis winery.com. Daily 10am–5pm.

St. Francis.

Landmark Vineyards One of California's oldest exclusively chardonnay estates was first founded in 1972 in the Windsor area of Northern Sonoma County. When new housing development started encroaching on the winery's territory, proprietor Damaris Deere W. Ethridge (great-great-granddaughter of John Deere, the tractor baron) moved her operation to Northern Sonoma Valley in 1990. The winery, which produces 27,000 cases annually, is housed in a modest, mission-style building set on 11 acres of vineyards. The tasting room offers $15 samples of current releases and pours reserve tastings. (Notice the wall-to-wall mural behind the tasting counter painted by noted Sonoma County artist Claudia Wagar.) Wine prices range from $28 for the Overlook chardonnay to $65 for a reserve pinot noir.

The winery has a pond-side picnic area, as well as what is probably the only professional bocce court in the valley (yes, you can play, and yes, they provide instructions). Also available from Memorial Day to Labor Day are free Belgian horse–drawn wagon tours through the vineyards, offered every Saturday from 1 to 4pm.

101 Adobe Canyon Rd. (just east of Hwy. 12), Kenwood. ℂ **800/452-6365** or 707/833-1144. www.landmarkwine.com. Daily 10am–4:30pm. Tours available by appointment.

Where to Stay in Sonoma Valley

The biggest choice you need to make when considering where to shack up is whether to stay in downtown Sonoma, which allows for easy access to its walkable shopping and dining square, or anywhere else in the valley, which promises more rural small-town surroundings and guaranteed time in the car to get to any activities. Regardless, you're destined to spend time behind the wheel, as the wineries and attractions are scattered. Keep in mind that during the peak season and on weekends, most B&Bs and hotels require a minimum 2-night stay. Of course, that's assuming you can find a vacancy; make reservations as far in advance as possible. If you are having trouble finding a room, call the **Sonoma Valley Visitors Bureau** (② **866/996-1090** or 707/996-1090; www.sonoma valley.com). The staff will try to refer you to a lodging that has a room to spare but won't make reservations for you. Another option is the **Bed and Breakfast Association of Sonoma Valley** (② **800/969-4667**), which can refer you to a B&B that belongs to the association. You can also find updated information on their website, www.sonomabb.com.

SONOMA

The southernmost town in Sonoma Valley is also the most "townlike," with an extremely charming town square encircled by hotels, restaurants, boutiques, and a historic California mission. It's also a short drive from many of the wineries.

Best For: Visitors who want instant access to shopping, restaurants, and bars.

Drawbacks: It's far more bustling than other areas and requires longer time in the car when exploring wineries to the north.

Very Expensive

Fairmont Sonoma Mission Inn & Spa ★★ Set on 12 meticulously groomed acres, the Fairmount Sonoma Mission Inn is the only choice for visitors looking for a world class resort. Known for its old-world glamorous looks (think massive three story replica of a California mission built in 1927 and painted pink, and an array of satellite wings housing numerous superluxury suites), it's even more famous for its unparalleled spa facilities, which showcase, among more modern conveniences, the property's original draw: naturally heated artesian mineral pools and whirlpools. It's got all the other outdoor bells and whistles, too, including golf, tennis, and enough picture-perfect wedding spots to keep the brides and grooms coming. Rooms range from understated country elegance, and sometimes a wood-burning fireplace, in the original hotel to fancier, more modern rooms with plantation-style shutters, ceiling fans, down comforters, oversize bath towels, and fireplaces. For the ultimate in luxury, the opulently appointed Mission Suites are the way to go. Golfers will be glad to know the resort is also home to the nearby Sonoma Golf Club, host of the PGA championship every October.

101 Boyes Blvd., corner of Boyes Blvd. and Calif. 12, P.O. Box 1447, Sonoma, CA 95476. www. fairmont.com/sonoma. ② **800/441-1414** or 707/938-9000. Fax 707/938-4250. 226 units. $149–$1,259 double. Rates include free wine tasting (4:30–5:30pm) and free bottle of wine upon arrival. AE, DC, MC, V. Valet parking is free for day use (spagoers) and $25 for overnight guests. From central Sonoma, drive 3 miles north on Hwy. 12 and turn left on Boyes Blvd. **Amenities:** 2 restaurants; babysitting; bike rental; concierge; golf course; health club and spa; Jacuzzi; 3 large, heated outdoor pools; room service; sauna. In room: A/C, TV, hair dryer, high-speed Internet access ($14 per day), minibar.

MacArthur Place ★★   A lower-key alternative to the Fairmont Sonoma Mission Inn & Spa (see above) is this much smaller and more intimate luxury property and spa located 4 blocks south of Sonoma's plaza. The 5½-acre "country estate" is replete with landscaped gardens and tree-lined pathways, free-standing accommodations, a spa, and a heated swimming pool and whirlpool. Most of the individually decorated guest rooms are Victorian-modern attached cottages scattered throughout the resort; all are exceedingly well stocked. Some suites come with fireplaces, porches, wet bars, six-speaker surround sound, and whirlpool tubs that often have shutters opening to the bedroom. Everyone has access to complimentary wine and cheese in the evening and the DVD library anytime. The full-service spa offers a fitness center, body treatments, skin care, and massages. Within the resort's restored century-old barn is Saddles, Sonoma's only steakhouse specializing in grass-fed beef, organic and sustainably farmed produce, and whimsically classy Western decor. An array of other excellent restaurants—as well as shops, wineries, and bars—is within biking distance. *Note:* All rooms are nonsmoking.

29 E. MacArthur St., Sonoma, CA 95476. www.macarthurplace.com. ℂ **800/722-1866** or 707/938-2929. 64 units. Sun–Thurs $239–$650 double; Fri–Sat $349–$699 double. Rates include continental breakfast and evening wine and cheese. AE, DISC, MC, V. Free parking. **Amenities:** Restaurant and bar specializing in martinis; rental bikes; concierge; exercise room; outdoor Jacuzzi; outdoor heated pool; room service; full-service spa; free Wi-Fi throughout. *In room:* A/C, TV/DVD, hair dryer, minibar.

Expensive
The Renaissance Lodge at Sonoma ★★   Downtown Sonoma's only large-scale property is one of my favorite places to stay in the area because it's well equipped, well located, and chic in its country decor, and it has a killer spa. At the center of this resort is a U-shaped building with a classic big-hotel lobby and a large courtyard swimming pool with plenty of lounge chairs. The modern and spacious accommodations in the main building are decorated in earth tones and come complete with prints by local artists, artistic lighting fixtures, balconies or patios, and some fireplaces and tubs with shutters that open from the bathroom to the bedroom. The two-story cottages along the property are especially appealing because they're surrounded by trees, flowers, and shrubs, and offer a sense of seclusion. The Raindance Spa, where I've consistently had exceptional massages, makes excellent use of its outdoor public space, with a number of small pools surrounded by lush plants. And as a bonus after your treatment, you get to hang around the pool all day if you want to. *Another perk:* The on-property restaurant cranks out surprisingly good food—and is extremely accommodating to youthful palates.

1325 Broadway, Sonoma, CA 95476. www.thelodgeatsonoma.com. ℂ **888/710-8008** or 707/935-6600. Fax 707/935-6829. 182 units. $249–$449 double. AE, MC, V. **Amenities:** Restaurant; concierge; health club and spa; Jacuzzi; large heated outdoor pool; limited room service; wine tasting. *In room:* A/C, TV w/pay movies, hair dryer, MP3 docking station, free Wi-Fi.

Moderate
Best Western Sonoma Valley Inn ☺   Perfect for the traveling family, this simple inn with updated rooms offers plenty for kids along for the ride. There's room to run around, plus a large, heated outdoor saltwater pool, gazebo-covered

spa, and sauna to play in. The rooms come with a few nice perks, such as conti-nental breakfast delivered to your room each morning, and satellite TV with HBO (they also offer a host of paid movies). Recently all rooms were newly fur-nished with love seats, new window treatments, and brand-new designer bed-ding. Most rooms have either a balcony or a deck overlooking the inner courtyard. *An added bonus:* If you need someone to help you get the kinks out, you can reserve one of the two new spa rooms and have the staff book an outside com-pany to come in and give you an on-site massage. The inn is also in a convenient location, just a block from Sonoma's plaza.

550 Second St. W. (1 block from the plaza), Sonoma, CA 95476. www.sonomavalleyinn.com. © **800/334-5784** or 707/938-9200. Fax 707/938-0935. 80 units. $99–$399 double. Rates include continental breakfast. AE, DISC, MC, V. **Amenities:** Exercise room; Jacuzzi; heated outdoor pool. *In room:* A/C, TV, fridge, hair dryer, free Wi-Fi.

El Dorado Hotel ★   This 1843 mission revival building may look like a 19th-century Wild West relic from the outside, but inside it's all 21st-century deluxe. Each modern, handsomely appointed guest room has French windows and tiny balconies. Some rooms offer lovely views of the plaza; others overlook the private courtyard and heated lap pool. Most rooms are on the second floor, and there's no elevator. However, if you're against hoofing it, you can request one of the four so-called bungalows on the ground floor, which were upgraded in 2006 and have partially enclosed patios. The only major drawback is noise; it's enough that man-agement offers guests ear plugs, so if you're a light sleeper, think twice. A "mar-ket," opened late 2007, serves light breakfast and lunch fare, coffee, and ice cream. Though prices reflect its prime location on Sonoma Square, this is still one of the more charming options within its price range—especially when you factor in instant access to the ground-floor El Dorado Kitchen, which is one of the valley's best restaurants.

405 First St. W., Sonoma, CA 95476. www.eldoradosonoma.com. © **800/289-3031** or 707/996-3030. Fax 707/996-3148. 27 units. $165–$225 double. 2-night minimum weekends and holidays. AE, DISC, MC, V. **Amenities:** Restaurant, El Dorado Kitchen (review, p. 377); heated outdoor pool. *In room:* A/C, flatscreen TV, DVD/CD player, fridge, hair dryer, free Wi-Fi.

Victorian Garden Inn   A small picket fence, a wall of trees, and an acre of gardens enclose an adorable Victorian garden brimming with violets, roses, camellias, and peonies, all shaded under flowering fruit trees. It's truly a marvel-ous sight in the springtime. The guest units—three in the century-old water tower and one in the main building (an 1870s Greek Revival farmhouse), as well as a cottage—continue the Victorian theme, with white wicker furniture, floral prints, padded armchairs, and claw-foot tubs. The most popular units are the Top o' the Tower and the Woodcutter's Cottage. Each has its own entrance and a gar-den view; the cottage boasts a sofa and armchairs set in front of the fireplace. After a hard day of wine tasting, spend the afternoon cooling off in the pool or on the shaded wraparound porch, enjoying a mellow merlot while soaking in the sweet garden smells. New parents, take note: The property recommends you leave young tots behind.

316 E. Napa St., Sonoma, CA 95476. www.victoriangardeninn.com. © **800/543-5339** or 707/996-5339. 4 units, 1 cottage. $159–$359 double. Rates include breakfast. AE, MC, V. **Amenities:** Concierge; hot tub; free Internet access; outdoor pool. *In room:* A/C.

Inexpensive

El Pueblo Inn ★   Located on Sonoma's main east-west street, 8 blocks from the center of town, this isn't Sonoma's fanciest hotel, but it is well cared for and offers some of the best-priced accommodations around. The rooms here are pleasant enough, with individual entrances, post-and-beam construction, exposed brick walls, light-wood furniture, down comforters, recliners, and geometric prints. A new addition in 2002 resulted in 20 new larger rooms, with high ceilings, DVDs, and fireplaces in some rooms. Each room also now opens to a courtyard with a fountain. The new reception area doubles as a breakfast room for its continental breakfast and leads to a small meeting room. Reservations should be made at least a month in advance for the spring and summer months.

896 W. Napa St., Sonoma, CA 95476. www.elpuebloinn.com. ✆ **800/900-8844** or 707/996-3651. Fax 707/935-5988. 53 units. Apr–Nov $194–$309 double; Dec–Mar $119–$179 double. Rates include continental breakfast. Corporate, AAA, and senior discounts available. AE, DISC, MC, V. **Amenities:** Fitness room; Jacuzzi; seasonal heated outdoor pool. *In room:* A/C, TV, DVD (newer rooms only), fridge, hair dryer, free high-speed Internet access.

Sonoma Hotel ★   This cute little historic hotel on Sonoma's tree-lined town plaza emphasizes 19th-century elegance and comfort. Built in 1880 by Swiss immigrant Henry Weyl, it has attractive guest rooms decorated in early California style, with French country furnishings, wood and iron beds, and pine armoires. In a bow to modern luxuries, recent additions include private bathrooms, cable TV, and (this is crucial) air-conditioning. Perks include fresh coffee and pastries in the morning and wine in the evening. Its lovely restaurant, the girl & the fig (p. 377), serves California-French cuisine. *Tip:* For a quieter stay, request a room that doesn't front the street.

110 W. Spain St., Sonoma, CA 95476. www.sonomahotel.com. ✆ **800/468-6016** or 707/996-2996. Fax 707/996-7014. 16 units. Summer $110–$248 double; winter $99–$220 double. 2-night minimum required for summer weekends. Rates include continental breakfast and evening wine. AE, DC, MC, V. **Amenities:** Restaurant, the girl & the fig (p. 377). *In room:* A/C, TV.

GLEN ELLEN

A 10- to 20-minute drive (traffic permitting) from downtown Sonoma provides a far more rural experience, with little more than a 1-block town, lush overgrown surroundings, and accommodations ranging from intimate to grand and budget to wallet-busting.

Best For: People seeking a heavy dose of country charm.

Drawbacks: You'll have to get in the car to do pretty much anything other than dine at the few local restaurants.

Very Expensive

Gaige House Inn ★★ 🎁   Set on a 3-acre oasis with perfectly manicured lawns and gardens, the Wine Country's finest B&B combines intimate surroundings with luxury appointments within its 1890 Queen Anne–Italianate building and Garden Annex. Spacious rooms offer everything you could want—firm mattresses, silky-soft Sferra linens, and stylish plantation-style decor with Asian and Indonesian influences. For aquatic enjoyment, four rooms have Jacuzzi tubs, one has a Japanese soaking tub, and the 13 spa garden suites have, among other delights, granite soaking tubs. There's also an outdoor 40-foot heated pool for all to use. For chilly country nights, fireplaces (in 17 rooms) definitely come in handy. Bathrooms are equally luxe, range in size, and are stocked with Aveda products and slippers.

Evenings are best spent in the reading parlor, sipping premium wines. Appetizers at the wine hour might include freshly shucked oysters or a sautéed scallop served ready-to-slurp on a Chinese soupspoon. Breakfast is a momentous event, accented with herbs from the inn's garden. On sunny days, the meal can be served at individual tables on the large terrace.

13540 Arnold Dr., Glen Ellen, CA 95442. www.gaige.com. *C* **800/935-0237** or 707/935-0237. Fax 707/935-6411. 23 units. Summer $365–$395 double, $595–$695 suite; winter $239–$269 double, $369–$419 suite. Rates include breakfast, complimentary bottle of wine and welcome reception. AE, DISC, MC, V. **Amenities:** Large heated pool. *In room:* A/C, TV/DVD, fridge, hair dryer, free Wi-Fi.

Inexpensive

Beltane Ranch ★★ 🏠 The word ranch conjures up a big ol' two-story house in the middle of hundreds of rolling acres, the kind of place where you laze away the day in a hammock watching the grass grow or in the garden pitching horseshoes. You can have all that and more at the well-located Beltane Ranch, a century-old buttercup-yellow manor that's been everything from a bunkhouse to a brothel to a turkey farm. You simply can't help but feel your tensions ease away as you prop your feet up on the shady wraparound porch overlooking the quiet vineyards, sipping a cool, fruity chardonnay. Each room is uniquely decorated with American and European antiques; all have sitting areas and separate entrances. A big country breakfast is served in the garden or on the porch overlooking the vineyards. For

Beltane Ranch.

exercise, you can play tennis on the private court or hike the trails meandering through the 105-acre estate. The staff here is knowledgeable and helpful. *Tip:* Request one of the upstairs rooms for the best views.

11775 Sonoma Hwy./Hwy. 12, P.O. Box 395, Glen Ellen, CA 95442. www.beltaneranch.com. *C* **707/996-6501.** 5 units, 1 cottage. $150–$240 double. Rates include full breakfast. DISC, MC, V. **Amenities:** Outdoor, unlit tennis court. *In room:* No phone, free Wi-Fi.

KENWOOD

The northernmost town is also the least developed, with stretches of vineyards, a handful of wineries and restaurants, and the renowned luxury retreat listed below; it's also the gateway to Northern Sonoma, a Wine Country destination in itself.

Best For: Anyone who wants to truly "get away from it all" or venture up to Northern Sonoma while staying in the valley.

Drawbacks: You'll have to do more driving to get to the rest of the area's attractions.

Very Expensive

Kenwood Inn & Spa ★★   Inspired by the villas of Tuscany, the Kenwood Inn's honey-colored Italian-style buildings, flower-filled flagstone courtyard, and pastoral views of vineyard-covered hills provide one of the region's most romantic backdrops. Add spacious rooms lavishly and exquisitely decorated with imported tapestries, velvets, and antiques, plus a fireplace, balcony (except on the ground floor), private bathroom (many with spa tubs), feather bed, CD player, and down comforter, and you've got amore in the making. With no TVs, relaxation is inevitable—especially if you book treatments at their Caudalie Vinotherapie Spa. A minor caveat is road noise, which you're unlikely to hear from your room but can be slightly audible over the tranquil pumped-in music around the courtyard and decent-size pool.

An impressive three-course gourmet breakfast is served in the courtyard or in the Mediterranean-style dining room. *A note for traveling families:* Kenwood Inn doesn't welcome kids 17 or under.

10400 Sonoma Hwy., Kenwood, CA 95452. www.kenwoodinn.com. ✆ **800/353-6966** or 707/833-1293. Fax 707/833-1247. 29 units. May–Oct from $425 double; Nov–Apr from $325 double. Rates include gourmet breakfast. 2-night minimum on weekends. AE, MC, V. No pets allowed. Children 17 and under not recommended. **Amenities:** Concierge; 2 outdoor hot tubs; heated outdoor pool; indoor soaking tub; full-service spa. *In room:* A/C, CD player, hair dryer, free high-speed Internet access.

Where to Eat in Sonoma Valley

While the majority of restaurants are clustered around downtown Sonoma's square, there are some winners sprinkled farther out in the tiny towns to the north. However, unlike Napa, Sonoma Valley doesn't have the kind of world-class restaurants that would inspire you to drive great distances in 100°F (38°C) weather in heavy traffic, which means you can pretty much eat anywhere near where you are and do just fine.

SONOMA

Moderate

Cafe La Haye ★★ ECLECTIC   Everything about this cafelike restaurant is charming. The atmosphere within the small split-level dining room is smart and intimate. The vibe is small business—a welcome departure from Napa Valley's big-business restaurants. The straightforward, seasonally inspired cuisine, which chefs bring forth from the tiny open kitchen, is delicious and wonderfully well-priced. Although the menu is small, it offers just enough options. Expect a risotto special; pasta such as rigatoni with sweet Italian sausage and fresh mozzarella; and pan-roasted chicken breast, perhaps with tomato-leek broth, ricotta gnocchi, grilled squash and pesto. Meat eaters are sure to be pleased with filet of beef seared with black pepper and lavender and served with Gorgonzola-potato gratin.

140 E. Napa St. ✆ **707/935-5994.** www.cafelahaye.com. Reservations recommended. Main courses $19–$33. AE, MC, V. Tues–Sat 5:30–9pm.

El Dorado Kitchen ★ CALIFORNIAN   Downtown Sonoma's most hip and contemporary restaurant, which has sexy seating indoors and out, entices with a seasonal menu ("Mediterranean-inspired bistro cuisine") of familiar items with unfamiliar twists—such as griddled prosciutto and Vermont cheddar with San Marzano tomato soup, curry fritto misto (lightly battered and fried apples, cauliflower, and fall squash served with curry salt and aioli), and a Caesar salad that pays homage to Southern France with the addition of niçoise olives. Entrees might include sautéed Scottish salmon with French green lentils, root vegetables, bacon lardons, and mushroom sauce, or lamb loin with rosemary polenta, piquillo peppers, Swiss chard, and niçoise olive sauce. Don't hesitate to order the white truffle and Parmesan french fries and one of their house drinks. In an area where dinner prices can run upwards of the cost of some people's monthly house payments, El Dorado Kitchen's prices are surprisingly reasonable and portions are generous.

405 First St. W. ℭ **707/996-3030.** www.eldoradosonoma.com. Reservations recommended. Lunch $14–$26; dinner $24–$32; brunch $12–$24. AE, MC, V. Mon–Sat 11:30am–2:30pm and 5:30–9pm; Sun 11am–2:30pm and 5:30–9pm.

the girl & the fig ★ COUNTRY FRENCH   Well established in its downtown Sonoma digs (it used to be in Glen Ellen), this modern, attractive, and cozy eatery, with lovely patio seating, is the home for Sondra Bernstein's (the girl) beloved restaurant. Here the cuisine is nouveau country with French nuances, garden-fresh produce, and local meats, poultry, and fish whenever possible. And yes, figs are sure to be on the menu in one form or another. The wonderful fig and arugula salad contains pancetta, pecans, dried figs, Laura Chenel goat cheese, and fig-and-port vinaigrette. Other favorites include grilled pork chops or duck confit. For dessert, try the lavender crème brûlée, a glass of Botrytis Late Harvest Roussanne, and a sliver of one of their delicious offerings from the cheese list. The wine list features Rhone varietals

the girl & the fig.

(yum!), and staff will happily help you choose the best accompaniment for your meal. Looking for brunch? Head here on Sunday, when it's served until 3pm.

110 W. Spain St. ℭ **707/938-3634.** www.thegirlandthefig.com. Reservations recommended. Main courses $18–$25. AE, DISC, MC, V. Daily 11:30am–10pm; Sun brunch 10am. Late-night brasserie menu until 11pm Fri–Sat.

Harvest Moon ★★ REGIONAL SEASONAL AMERICAN   Napa may have better restaurants in general, but the feasts to the east have nothing on this new downtown Sonoma restaurant. Chef/owner Nick Demarest's experience at

Berkeley's world-famous Chez Panisse is evidenced by his use of outstanding ingredients combined into dishes of clean, pure, and glorious flavors. His chicory salad with mustard vinaigrette, house-cured bacon, and Gruyère is a case-in-point appetizer that's easily backed up by entrees such as pan-fried local rock cod with Swiss chard, fingerling potatoes, and beurre rouge. Sweetening the already delicious deal, his wife Jen is a pedigreed pastry chef with experience at Napa's fancy La Toque. The space itself is quirky, which means you can expect great seats at the wine bar and a scattering of tables tucked within a cramped and warm historic adobe room. Inside, you'll see the chef hard at work within the shoebox open kitchen. Outside, weather permitting, is a spacious garden dining area. Regardless, if it's a good meal you're after, you will not find a better one this side of the Mayacamas.

487 First St. W. ✆ **707/933-8160.** www.harvestmooncafesonoma.com. Reservations recommended. Main courses $17–$27. AE, DISC, MC, V. Sun–Thurs 5:30–9pm; Fri–Sat 5:30–9:30pm; Sun brunch 10am–2pm.

Meritage ★ SOUTHERN FRENCH/NORTHERN ITALIAN   Chef-owner Carlo Cavallo, formerly executive chef for Giorgio Armani, combines the best of southern French and northern Italian cuisines (hence "Meritage," after a blend made with traditional bordeaux varieties), giving Sonomans yet another reason to eat out. The menu, which changes twice daily, is a good read: chicken ravioli sautéed in a tomato and baby artichoke chardonnay sauce; seafood stew with tiger prawns, Manila clams, mussels, and mixed fresh fish in a spicy tomato saffron broth; and wild boar baby back ribs braised in a Porcini cabernet shallot sauce. Shellfish fans can't help but love the oyster raw bar with options of fresh crab and lobster, and cocktailers revel in the new martini bar. A lovely garden patio is prime positioning for sunny brunches and lunches and summer dinners. Such edible enticement—combined with reasonable prices, excellent service, a stellar wine list, and Carlo's practiced charm—make Meritage a trustworthy option.

165 W. Napa St. ✆ **707/938-9430.** www.sonomameritage.com. Reservations recommended. Main courses $18–$40; chef tasting menu $60; vegetarian tasting menu $50. AE, MC, V. Mon–Thurs 5–9pm; Fri–Sat 5–9:30pm; brunch Sat–Sun 10:30am–3pm.

Swiss Hotel ★ CONTINENTAL/NORTHERN ITALIAN   With its slanting floors and beamed ceilings, the historic Swiss Hotel, located right in the town center, is very much the local favorite for fine food served at reasonable prices. The turn-of-the-20th-century oak bar at the left of the entrance is adorned with black-and-white photos of pioneering Sonomans. Conversely, the white dining room and sidewalk patio seats are brighter spots to enjoy lunch specials such as penne with chicken, mushrooms, and tomato cream; hot sandwiches; and California-style pizzas fired in a wood-burning oven. But the secret spot is the atmospheric back garden patio, a secluded oasis shaded by a wisteria-covered trellis and adorned with plants, a fountain, gingham tablecloths, and a fireplace. Dinner main courses run the gamut. I like the linguine and prawns with garlic, hot pepper, and tomatoes; the blue cheese–encrusted filet mignon; and roasted rosemary chicken. The food may not knock your socks off, but it's all simply satisfying.

18 W. Spain St. (at First St. W.). ✆ **707/938-2884.** www.swisshotelsonoma.com. Reservations recommended. Main courses lunch $8–$17, dinner $14–$29. AE, MC, V. Daily 11:30am–2:30pm; Sun–Thurs 5–9pm; Fri–Sat 5–10pm. Bar daily 11:30am–2am.

Inexpensive
Basque Boulangerie Café BAKERY/DELI   If you prefer a lighter morning meal and strong coffee, stand in line with the locals at the Basque Boulangerie Café, the most popular gathering spot in Sonoma Valley. Most everything—sourdough Basque breads, pastries, quiches, soups, salads, desserts, sandwiches, cookies—is made in-house and made well. Daily lunch specials, such as a grilled-veggie sandwich ($6.25), are listed on the chalkboard out front. Seating is scarce, and if you can score a sidewalk table on a sunny day, consider yourself one lucky person. A popular option is ordering to go and eating in the shady plaza across the street. The cafe also sells wine by the glass, as well as a wonderful cinnamon bread by the loaf that's ideal for making French toast.

460 First St. E. (✆) **707/935-7687.** www.basqueboulangerie.com. Menu items $3–$12. AE, DISC, MC, V. Daily 7am–6pm.

Black Bear Diner ☺ DINER   When you're craving a classic American breakfast with all the cholesterol and the fixin's (perhaps to counterbalance that wine hangover), make a beeline for this old-fashioned diner. First, it's fun, with its over-the-top bear paraphernalia, gazette-style menu listing local news from 1961 and every possible diner favorite, and absurdly friendly waitstaff. Second, it's darned cheap. Third, helpings are huge. What more could you want? Kids get a kick out of coloring books, old-timers reminisce over Sinatra playing on the jukebox, and everyone leaves stuffed on omelets, scrambles, and pancakes. Lunch and dinner feature steak sandwiches, salads, and comfort food faves like barbecued pork ribs, Cobb salad, fish and chips, and burgers—they grind their own beef. But unless you like old-school run-of-the-mill diner fare, your best bet is to dine elsewhere.

201 W. Napa St. (at Second St.). (✆) **707/935-6800.** www.blackbeardiner.com. Main courses breakfast $5–$8.50, lunch and dinner $5.50–$17. AE, DISC, MC, V. Daily 6am–9:30pm (closing varies on weekends, depending on business).

Della Santina's ★★ TUSCAN   For those who just can't swallow another chichi California meal, follow the locals to this friendly, traditional Italian restaurant. How traditional? Ask father-and-son team Dan and Robert, who proudly point out Signora Santina's hand-embroidered linen doilies and discuss her Tuscan recipes. Their pride is merited: Dishes are authentic and well flavored, without overbearing sauces or one hint of California pretentiousness. Start with traditional antipasti, particularly sliced mozzarella and tomatoes, move on to one of the nine authentic pasta dishes, or opt for spit-roasted chicken, pork, turkey, rabbit, or duck—or a selection of three. **Perk:** You can guiltlessly order a bottle of wine since many choices here go for under $40. Portions are huge, but save room for dessert, like the creamy panna cotta. Though the inside's small, a huge back

The gnocci at Della Santina's.

patio covered in blooming trellises is full practically every night in the summer (the wait's never too bad), and they've recently tented part of it, so you can eat back there in winter, too, weather permitting.

133 E. Napa St. (just east of the square). ℭ **707/935-0576.** www.dellasantinas.com. Reservations recommended. Main courses $12–$19. AE, DISC, MC, V. Daily 11:30am–3pm and 5–9:30pm.

Freemont Diner ★★ SOUTHERN A diner in the truest sense, this sweet roadside shack en route to Napa lures food fanatics from miles around with its simple combination of honest rib-gripping food with local sensibility and absurd amounts of homespun charm. Nowhere else in these parts can you find griddle and smoker goodness in the form of burgers, grilled cheese, brisket, and Ruben sandwiches alongside gumbo, chicken and waffles, mac and cheese, "Figs in blankets" (wine soaked figs wrapped in ham!), pies, and fancy sodas, shakes, floats, beer, and wine. (Plus an awesome breakfast with plenty of biscuits.) Equally savory are the surrounds, which include indoor dining nooks within the shack and picnic tables outside, antiques galore, and mismatched tables, chairs, and pretty much everything else. Every visual detail is authentic and intentional, from the printed menu to the patinaed decorative cash register outside. Like the rest of the dining experience, service is warm and relaxed.

2660 Fremont Dr., Sonoma. ℭ **707/938-7370.** www.thefremontdiner.com. Reservations recommended. Main courses breakfast $9–$14, lunch $7.50–$12. MC, V. Mon–Fri 8am–3pm; Sat–Sun 8am–4pm.

Juanita Juanita MEXICAN Everyone loves this roadside shack hawking fresh Mexican specialties and hearty sides of who-gives-a-heck attitude. Lines out the door during weekends prove the point. But if you've gotta have a killer quesadilla, nachos, enchiladas, tacos, and their fabulous "plate" specials (think grilled chicken with chipotle cream sauce on a bed of spinach and avocado with rice, beans, and tortillas), it's worth the wait. Besides, the place is fun. Here the decor and vibe are about as casual as you can get. Plop down at the counter, pull up a chair at one of the mix-and-match tables, or grab a table on the patio, kick up your heels, dig into the plastic bucket of tortilla chips and side o' salsa, sip on an ice-cold beer, and revel in the oh-so-Sonoma-casual vibe as you fill up on the huge portions. Kids dig the place, too, and have their own specialties offered at pint-size prices of $4.75.

19114 Arnold Dr. (just north of W. Napa St.). ℭ **707/935-3981.** www.juanitajuanita.com. No reservations. Main courses $7.50–$15. No credit cards. Mon–Sun 11am–8pm; closed Tues.

Taste of the Himalayas ★ NEPALESE/INDIAN If you're looking for something other than the usual pizzas, pastas, and burritos, this is your spot. Just what does a Nepalese meal entail? Start with crisp samosas (a mild blend of potatoes and peas served with mint sauce) or momos (small steamed dumplings stuffed with either lamb or veggies). Move on to entrees such as curry or Tandoori dishes, which wash down nicely with Indian Taj Mahal beer. All entrees come with a delicious bowl of mild daal bhat, the traditional Indian lentil soup, your choice of basmati rice or naan, and casual but attentive service.

464 First St. E. ℭ **707/996-1161.** Reservations recommended, but walk-ins welcome. Main courses $10–$18. AE, MC, V. Daily 11am–2:30pm and 5–10pm.

BOYES HOT SPRINGS
Expensive

Santé ★★ CALIFORNIA/FRENCH   If fine dining is part of your Sonoma dream vacation, this award-winning spot is the restaurant to book. Located inside luxurious Sonoma Mission Inn resort, the white-tablecloth dining room is relaxed enough that you can wear jeans, but special enough that you'll want to dress for dinner—if only to match the elegance of the food. The three- or four-course fixed-price seasonal menu features local bounty whipped into stellar renditions of the likes of "grown-up" macaroni and cheese with lobster and black truffles; butter-poached lobster with decadent lobster bisque emulsion, sunchokes, cipollini onions, and Yorkshire pudding; and double-cut American "Kobe"-style steak with glazed baby veggies, to-die-for mashed potatoes, and béarnaise and bordelaise sauces. A cheese cart, beautiful desserts (try the coconut panna cotta!), and an impressive wine program (let the sommelier do the pairing!) round out the menu, which provides a la carte options as well.

Inside Sonoma Mission Inn, 100 Boyes Blvd., Sonoma. ℂ **707/938-9000.** www.fairmont.com/sonoma. Reservations recommended. 3 courses $75; 4 courses $85. AE, DC, MC, V. Daily 6–9pm.

GLEN ELLEN
Moderate

the fig café & wine bar ★★ NEW AMERICAN   The girl & the fig's (p. 377) sister restaurant is more casual than its downtown Sonoma sibling. But don't let the bucolic neighborhood vibe, airy environs, and soothing sage-and-mustard color scheme fool you. From his open kitchen, general manager and chef de cuisine Bryan Jones brings you the kind of rustic sophistication more commonly associated with urban restaurants. Consider starting with a thin-crust pizza, fried calamari with spicy lemon aioli, a cheese plate, or the signature fig and arugula salad; move on to braised pot roast with mashed potatoes or mussels in a garlic, leek, and tarragon sauce with fries; and finish with a fantastic chocolate brownie with vanilla ice cream. *A perk:* The "Rhone Alone" wine selections are available by the flight, glass, or bottle, free corkage.

13690 Arnold Dr. (at Madrone Rd.). ℂ **707/938-2130.** www.thefigcafe.com. Reservations not accepted. Main courses $13–$20. AE, DISC, MC, V. Sun–Thurs 5:30–9pm; Fri–Sat 5:30–9:30pm; brunch Sat–Sun 10am–3pm.

Glen Ellen Inn Oyster Grill & Martini Bar ★ CALIFORNIAN   Christian and Karen Bertrand have made this place so quaint and cozy that you feel as if you're dining in their home, and that's exactly the place's charm. Garden seating is the favored choice on sunny days, but the covered, heated patio is also always welcoming. Courses from Christian's open kitchen are exotic—think ginger tempura calamari with wasabi or brie fondue with sourdough toast points for starters. Entrees, which change with the seasons, range from pumpkin ravioli with roasted butternut squash sauce to grilled salmon with tomatillo sauce and corn cake. And let's not forget the eponymous oyster grill and martini bar, which includes half-size martinis (genius!) and oysters any way you want 'em. If that doesn't do it for you, the 550-plus wine selection list offers numerous bottles from Sonoma, as well as more than a dozen wines by the glass. *Tip:* There's a small parking lot behind the restaurant.

13670 Arnold Dr. (at O'Donnell Lane). ℂ **707/996-6409.** www.glenelleninn.com. Reservations recommended. Main courses $16–$26. AE, DISC, MC, V. Mon–Sun 11:30am–9pm (dinner from 5pm); Wed 5–9pm. Closed 1 week in Jan.

Hot Box Grill NEW AMERICAN A wholesome, satisfying dining experience, Hot Box Grill elevates familiar dishes through stellar and—often local artisan—ingredients and love from a talented kitchen staff. That means duck-fat fries are sprinkled with smoked prosciutto, truffle oil, and Grana Padano cheese; pasta is handmade and slathered with slow-cooked rabbit, escarole, walnut cream, and breadcrumbs; and grilled "cowboy steak" for two comes with horseradish crème fraîche, Brussels sprouts with pancetta and garlic, twice baked potato, crisp shoestring onions, and gravy. A low-key exterior and relaxed environment echoes the neighborhood and clientele, many of whom are local devotees.

18350 Sonoma Hwy., Sonoma. ℂ 707/939-8383. www.hotboxgrill.com. Reservations recommended. Main courses $16–$26. AE, MC, V. Tues–Thurs and Sun 5:30–10pm; Fri–Sat 5:30–11pm.

Wolf House ★ ECLECTIC The most polished dining room in Glen Ellen is elegant yet relaxed, whether you're seated in the dining room—smartly adorned with maple floors, gold walls, dark-wood wainscoting, and a corner fireplace—or outside on the multilevel terrace under a canopy of trees with serene views of adjacent Sonoma Creek. The menu adds fancy finishes to old favorites. At lunch, that equates to a fresh grilled ahi tuna niçoise sandwich or a juicy half-pound burger with Point Reyes Original Blue cheese. During dinner, seared roasted Liberty Farms duck breast pecan with dried cherry strudel, sautéed cider cabbage, and braised kumquat demi, or pan-roasted salmon with sweet asparagus, baby arugula salad, and sunchoke mash do the trick. The reasonably priced wine list offers many by-the-glass options as well as a fine selection of Sonoma wines. At brunch, locals love the nepalas rancheros (chorizo, pinto beans, roasted chilies, and fried eggs), Dungeness crab-cake Benedict, omelets, and almond-crusted French toast.

13740 Arnold Dr. (at London Ranch Rd.). ℂ 707/996-4401. www.jacklondonlodge.com/wolf_house.htm. Reservations recommended. Main courses brunch and lunch $11–$16, dinner $15–$27. AE, MC, V. Mon–Fri 11:30am–3pm; daily 5:30–9pm; brunch Sat–Sun 11am–3pm.

KENWOOD
Moderate
Kenwood Restaurant & Bar ★★ CALIFORNIAN/CONTINENTAL This is what Wine Country dining should be. From the terrace of the Kenwood Restaurant, diners enjoy a view of the vineyards set against Sugarloaf Ridge as they imbibe Sonoma's finest at umbrella-covered tables. On nippy days, you can retreat inside to the Sonoma-style roadhouse, with its vibrant artwork and cushioned rattan chairs at white cloth–covered tables. Regardless, the cuisine is perfectly balanced between tradition and innovation, complemented by a reasonably priced wine list. Great starters are Dungeness crab cake with herb mayonnaise; super-fresh sashimi with ginger, soy, and wasabi; and a wonderful Caesar salad. The main dish might be poached salmon in salsa beurre blanc, or prawns with saffron Pernod sauce. But the Kenwood doesn't take itself too seriously: Great sandwiches and burgers are also available.

9900 Sonoma Hwy. (just north of Dunbar Rd.). ℂ 707/833-6326. www.kenwoodrestaurant.com. Reservations recommended. Main courses $16–$34. MC, V. Wed–Sat 12:30–8:30pm; Sun noon–8pm.

Inexpensive

Café Citti NORTHERN ITALIAN   If a casual, tasty meal is on your itinerary, head to Café Citti (pronounced Cheat-ee), a roadside do-it-yourself Italian trattoria that is both good and cheap. You order from the huge menu board displayed above the open kitchen. Afterward, you grab a table (the ones on the patio, shaded by umbrellas, are the best on warm afternoons), and a server will bring your meal. It's all hearty, home-cooked Italian. Standout dishes are the green-bean salad, tangy Caesar salad, focaccia sandwiches, and roasted rotisserie chicken stuffed with rosemary and garlic. Wine is available by the bottle, and the espresso is plenty strong. Everything on the menu board is available to go, which makes Café Citti an excellent resource for picnic supplies.

9049 Sonoma Hwy. (C) **707/833-2690.** www.cafecitti.com. Main courses $12–$16. MC, V. Daily 11am–3:30pm; Sun–Thurs 5–8:30pm; Fri–Sat 5–9pm.

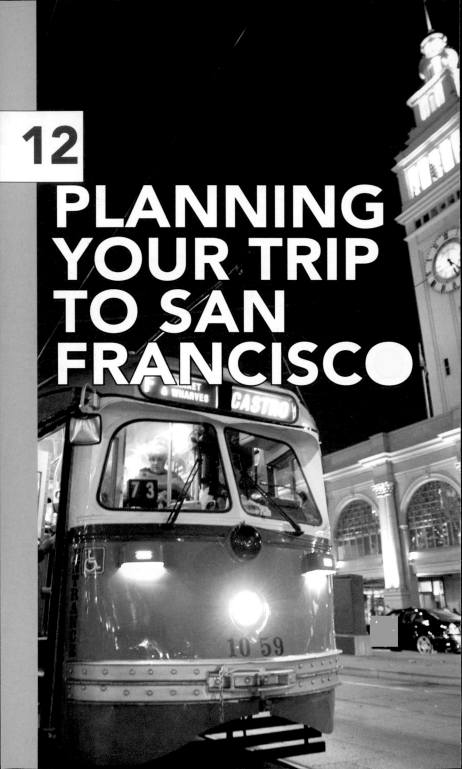

12

PLANNING YOUR TRIP TO SAN FRANCISCO

GETTING THERE
By Plane

The northern Bay Area has two major airports: San Francisco International and Oakland International.

SAN FRANCISCO INTERNATIONAL AIRPORT Almost four dozen major scheduled carriers serve **San Francisco International Airport** (SFO; ℂ 650/821-8211; www.flysfo.com), 14 miles directly south of downtown on U.S. 101. Drive time to downtown during commuter rush hour is about 40 minutes; at other times, it's about 20 to 25 minutes. You can also ride BART from the airport to downtown and the East Bay.

You can also call ℂ 511 or visit www.511.org for up-to-the-minute information about public transportation and traffic.

OAKLAND INTERNATIONAL AIRPORT About 5 miles south of downtown Oakland, at the Hegenberger Road exit of Calif. 17 (U.S. 880; if coming from south, take 98th Ave.), **Oakland International Airport** (ℂ 800/247-6255 or 510/563-3300; www.oaklandairport.com) primarily serves passengers with East Bay destinations. Some San Franciscans prefer this less-crowded, more accessible airport, although it takes about a half-hour to get there from downtown San Francisco (traffic permitting). The airport is also accessible by BART via a shuttle bus.

ARRIVING AT THE AIRPORT

IMMIGRATION & CUSTOMS CLEARANCE International visitors arriving by air, no matter what the port of entry, should cultivate patience and resignation before setting foot on U.S. soil. U.S. airports have considerably beefed up security clearances in the years since the terrorist attacks of September 11, 2001, and clearing Customs and Immigration can take as long as 2 hours.

GETTING INTO TOWN FROM THE AIRPORT

The fastest and cheapest way to get from SFO to the city is to take BART (Bay Area Rapid Transit; ℂ 415/989-2278; www.bart.gov), which offers numerous stops within downtown San Francisco. This route, which takes about 35 minutes, avoids traffic on the way and costs a heck of a lot less than taxis or shuttles. (A BART ticket is about $7 each way, depending on exactly where you're going.) Just jump on the airport's free shuttle bus to the International terminal, enter the BART station there, and you're on your way to San Francisco. Trains leave approximately every 15 minutes.

A cab from the airport to downtown costs $40 to $50, plus tip, and takes about 30 minutes, traffic permitting.

SuperShuttle (ℂ 800/BLUE-VAN [2583-826], or 415/558-8500; www.supershuttle.com) is a private shuttle company that offers door-to-door airport service, in which you share a van with a few other passengers. They will take you anywhere in the city, charging $17 per person to a residence or business. On the return trip, add $10 to $17 for each additional person depending on whether you're traveling from a hotel or a residence. The shuttle stops at least every 20 minutes, sometimes sooner, and picks up passengers from the marked areas outside the terminals' upper levels. Reservations are required for the return trip to

PREVIOUS PAGE: **The F-Market & Wharves train makes an evening stop at the Ferry Building.**

the airport only and should be made 1 day before departure. These shuttles often demand they pick you up 2 hours before your domestic flight and 3 hours before international flights and during holidays. Keep in mind that you could be the first one on and the last one off, so this trip could take awhile; you might want to ask before getting in. For $75, you can either charter the entire van for up to seven people or an **Execucar** private sedan for up to four people. For more info on the Execucar, call ℂ **800/410-4444.**

The **San Mateo County Transit system, SamTrans** (ℂ **800/660-4287** in Northern California, or 650/508-6200; www.samtrans.com), runs two buses between SFO and the Transbay Terminal at First and Mission streets. Bus no. 292 costs $2 and makes the trip in about 55 minutes. The KX bus costs $4 and takes just 35 minutes but permits only one carry-on bag. Both buses run daily. The no. 292 starts at 5:25am Monday through Friday and 5:30am on weekends; both run until 1am and run every half-hour until 7:30pm, when they run hourly. The KX starts at 5:53am and ends at 10:37pm Monday through Friday. On weekends, service runs from 7:19am to 9:30pm, runs every half-hour until 6:30pm, and then changes to an hourly schedule.

GETTING INTO TOWN FROM OAKLAND INTERNATIONAL AIRPORT

Taxis from the Oakland Airport to downtown San Francisco are expensive—approximately $60, plus tip. The cheapest way to reach downtown San Francisco is to take the shuttle bus from the Oakland Airport to **BART** (Bay Area Rapid Transit; ℂ **510/464-6000;** www.bart.gov). The **AirBART shuttle bus** runs about every 15 minutes Monday through Saturday from 5am to 12:05am and Sunday from 8am to 12:05am. It makes pickups in front of terminals 1 and 2 near the ground transportation signs. Tickets must be purchased at the Oakland Airport's vending machines prior to boarding. The cost is $2 for the 10-minute ride to BART's Coliseum station in Oakland. BART fares vary, depending on your destination; the trip to downtown San Francisco costs about $4 and takes 15 minutes once you're on board. The entire excursion should take around 45 minutes.

By Car

San Francisco is easily accessible by major highways: I-5, from the north, and U.S. 101, which cuts south-north through the peninsula from San Jose and across the Golden Gate Bridge to points north. If you drive from Los Angeles, you can take the longer coastal route (437 miles and 11 hr.) or the inland route (389 miles and 8 hr.). From Mendocino, it's 156 miles and 4 hours; from Sacramento, 88 miles and 1½ hours; from Yosemite, 210 miles and 4 hours.

If you are driving and aren't already a member, it's worth joining the **American Automobile Association** (AAA; ℂ **800/922-8228;** www.csaa.com). It charges $49 to $79 per year (with an additional one-time joining fee), depending on where you join, and provides roadside and other services to motorists. **Amoco Motor Club** (ℂ **800/334-3300;** www.bpmotorclub.com) is another recommended choice.

International visitors should note that insurance and taxes are almost never included in quoted rental car rates in the U.S. Be sure to ask your rental agency about additional fees for these. They can add a significant cost to your rental car.

By Train

Traveling by train takes a long time and usually costs as much as, or more than, flying. Still, if you want to take a leisurely ride across America, rail may be a good option.

San Francisco–bound **Amtrak** (© **800/872-7245** or 800/USA-RAIL [872-7245]; www.amtrak.com) trains leave from New York and cross the country via Chicago. The journey takes about 3½ days, and seats sell quickly. At this writing, the lowest round-trip fare costs about $300 from New York and $270 from Chicago. Round-trip tickets from Los Angeles range from $120 to as much as $200. Trains arrive in Emeryville, just north of Oakland, and connect with regularly scheduled buses to San Francisco's Ferry Building and the Caltrain station in downtown San Francisco.

Caltrain (© **800/660-4287** or 415/546-4461; www.caltrain.com) operates train service between San Francisco and the towns of the peninsula. The city depot is at 700 Fourth St., at Townsend Street.

GETTING AROUND

For a map of San Francisco's public transportation options, see the inside back cover of this guide. You can also call © **511** for current transportation and traffic information or check www.511.org.

By Public Transportation

The **San Francisco Municipal Transportation Agency,** 1 S. Van Ness Ave.,, better known as "Muni" (© **415/673-6864;** www.sfmuni.com), operates the city's cable cars, buses, and streetcars. Together, these three services crisscross the entire city. Fares for buses and streetcars are $2 for adults, 75¢ for seniors 65 and over, children 5 to 17, and riders with disabilities. Cable cars, which run from 6:30am to 12:50am, cost a whopping $6 for all people 6 and over ($3 for seniors and riders with disabilities before 7am or after 9pm). Needless to say, they're packed primarily with tourists. Exact change is required on all vehicles except cable cars (unless you have Clipper, CityPASS, or Passport; see the box in this section). Fares are subject to change. If you're standing waiting for Muni and have wireless Web access (or from any computer), check www.nextmuni.com to get up-to-the-minute information about when the next bus or streetcar is coming. Muni's NextBus uses satellite technology and advanced computer modeling to track vehicles on their routes.

CABLE CAR San Francisco's cable cars might not be the most practical means of transport, but the rolling historic landmarks are a fun ride. The three lines are concentrated in the downtown area. The most scenic, and exciting, is the Powell–Hyde line, which follows a zigzag route from the corner of Powell and Market streets, over both Nob Hill and Russian Hill, to a turntable at gas-lit Victorian Square in front of Aquatic Park. The Powell–Mason line starts at the same intersection and climbs Nob Hill before descending to Bay Street, just 3 blocks from Fisherman's Wharf. The least scenic is the California Street line, which begins at the foot of Market Street and runs a straight course through Chinatown and over Nob Hill to Van Ness Avenue. All riders must exit at the last stop and wait in line for the return trip. The cable car system operates from approximately 6:30am to 12:50am, and each ride costs $5.

CLIPPER, CITYPASS, OR PASSPORT: WHICH IS RIGHT FOR YOU?

You will need one of several available cards or passes to ride Muni or BART.

For long-term stays or short visits with light sightseeing: Locals use **Clipper cards**, available at Muni metro stations or at pharmacies, including Walgreens. Load them with money for use on all forms of transportation (see individual fare prices in this section). Monthly passes are $64 (Muni-only) or $74 (Muni and BART), or just $22 for seniors 65 and over, students ages 5 to 17, and travelers with disabilities. See www.clippercard.com.

For short visits with heavy sightseeing and transportation-hopping: **CityPASS** entitles you to unlimited Muni rides (including cable car rides, normally $6) for 7 days, plus admission to these specific attractions (regular adult prices listed in parentheses so you can calculate your savings): **California Academy of Sciences** ($30), either **Blue & Gold Fleet Bay Cruise Adventure** ($25) or **Alcatraz Island Tour** ($26), **SFMOMA** ($18), **Aquarium of the Bay** ($17), and either the **Exploratorium** ($15) or the **de**

Young Museum ($10). CityPASS is $69 for adults or $39 for children ages 5 to 12, so your savings obviously increase the more you use the pass. Buy at www.citypass.com or at any CityPASS attractions, and be sure to click on "Alcatraz Option" if that's your preference.

If you won't visit your money's worth of CityPASS sites: **Passports** focus solely on transportation and entitle you to unlimited rides on all Muni vehicles, including buses, trains, and cable cars. A Passport costs $14 for 1 day, $21 for 3 days, and $27 for 7 consecutive days. Passports are sold daily from 8am to midnight at the information booths in the baggage claim areas at San Francisco International Airport. You can also buy a Passport or CityPASS at the San Francisco Visitor Information Center, Powell–Market cable car booth, Holiday Inn Civic Center, and TIX Bay Area booth at Union Square, among other outlets. See www.sfmta.com/cms/mfares/passports.htm.

BUS Buses reach almost every corner of San Francisco and beyond—they even travel over the bridges to Marin County and Oakland. Overhead electric cables power some buses; others use conventional gas engines. All are numbered and display their destinations on the front. Signs, curb markings, and yellow bands on adjacent utility poles designate stops, and most bus shelters exhibit Muni's transportation map and schedule. Many buses travel along Market Street or pass near Union Square and run from about 6am to midnight. After midnight, there is infrequent all-night "Owl" service. For safety, avoid taking buses late at night.

Popular tourist routes include bus nos. 5, 7, and 71, all of which run to Golden Gate Park; 41 and 45, which travel along Union Street; and 30, which runs between Union Square and Ghirardelli Square. A bus ride costs $2 for adults and 75¢ for seniors 66 and over, children 5 to 17, and riders with disabilities.

STREETCAR Six of Muni's seven streetcar lines, designated J, K, L, M, N, and T, run underground downtown and on the streets in the outer neighborhoods. The sleek rail cars make the same stops as BART (see below) along Market Street, including Embarcadero Station (in the Financial District), Montgomery and

Powell streets (both near Union Square), and the Civic Center (near City Hall). Past the Civic Center, the routes branch off: The J line takes you to Mission Dolores; the K, L, and M lines run to Castro Street; and the N line parallels Golden Gate Park and extends all the way to the Embarcadero and AT&T Park. The newest one (called T-Third Street, opened in 2007) runs to AT&T Park and the San Francisco Caltrain station and then continues south along Third Street, ending near Monster (Candlestick) Park.

Streetcars run about every 15 minutes, more frequently during rush hours. They operate Monday through Friday from 5am to 12:15am, Saturday from 6am to approximately 12:15am, and Sunday from approximately 8am to 12:20am. The L and N lines operate 24 hours a day, 7 days a week, but late at night, regular buses trace the L and N routes, which are normally underground, from atop the city streets. Because the operation is part of Muni, the fares are the same as for buses, and passes are accepted.

The most recent line to this system is not a newcomer at all, but is, in fact, an encore performance of rejuvenated 1930s streetcars from all over the world. The beautiful, retro multicolored F-Market & Wharves streetcar runs from 17th and Castro streets to the Embarcadero; every other streetcar continues to Jones and Beach streets in Fisherman's Wharf. This is a quick, charming, and tourist-friendly way to get up- and downtown without any hassle.

BART **BART,** an acronym for Bay Area Rapid Transit (© **415/989-2278;** www.bart.gov), is a futuristic-looking, high-speed rail network that connects San Francisco (starting just south of the airport) with the East Bay—Oakland, Richmond, Concord, Pittsburg, and Fremont. Four stations are on Market Street (see "Streetcar," above). One-way fares range from $1.75 to $11, depending on how far you go. Machines in the stations dispense tickets that are magnetically encoded with a dollar amount. Computerized exits automatically deduct the correct fare. Children 4 and under ride free. Trains run every 15 to 20 minutes, Monday through Friday from 4am to midnight, Saturday from 6am to midnight, and Sunday from 8am to midnight. In keeping with its futuristic look, BART now offers online trip planners that you can download to your smartphone or tablet.

The 33-mile BART extension, which extends all the way to San Francisco International Airport, opened in June 2003. See above for information on getting into town from the airport.

By Taxi

This isn't New York, so don't expect a taxi to appear whenever you need one—if at all. If you're downtown during rush hour or leaving a major hotel, it won't be hard to hail

---

Taxi Apps Are Uber Handy

Considering the weak (sometimes horrible) state of taxis in San Francisco, you'll want to plug into these taxi apps: Set up a profile with **Uber** (www.uber.com), **Cabulous** (www.cabulous.com), or **Taxi Magic** (www.taximagic.com); hail a nearby taxi with a simple text or a few taps on your phone; then track the cab on your phone as it approaches you. Rates tend to be slightly higher than traditionally hailing cabs, but your fare will be charged automatically to your credit card. Uber offers hybrid cars or pricier black town cars and gets our vote for reliability.

a cab; just look for the lighted sign on the roof that indicates the vehicle is free. Otherwise, it's a good idea to call one of the following companies to arrange a ride; even then, there's been more than one time when the cab never came for us. The companies are **Veteran's Cab** (© **415/552-1300**), **Luxor Cabs** (© **415/282-4141**), **De Soto Cab** (© **415/970-1300**), and **Yellow Cab** (© **415/626-2345**). Rates are approximately $3.50 for the first ⅕ mile and 55¢ each fifth of a mile thereafter.

By Car

You don't need a car to explore downtown San Francisco. In fact, with the city becoming more crowded by the minute, a car can be your worst nightmare—you're likely to end up stuck in traffic with lots of aggressive and frustrated drivers, pay upwards of $30 a day to park (plus a whopping new 14% parking lot tax), and spend a good portion of your vacation looking for a parking space. Don't bother. However, if you want to venture outside the city, driving is the best way to go.

Before heading outside the city, especially in winter, call © **800/427-7623** for California road conditions. You can also call © **511** for current traffic information.

CAR RENTALS   All the major rental companies operate in the city and have desks at the airports. When we last checked, you could get a compact car for a week for anywhere from $165 to $315, including all taxes and other charges, but prices change dramatically on a daily basis and depend on which company you rent from.

Some of the national car-rental companies operating in San Francisco include **Alamo** (© **800/327-9633**; www.alamo.com), **Avis** (© **800/331-1212**; www.avis.com), **Budget** (© **800/527-0700**; www.budget.com), **Dollar** (© **800/800-4000**; www.dollar.com), **Enterprise** (© **800/325-8007**; www.enterprise.com), **Hertz** (© **800/654-3131**; www.hertz.com), **National** (© **800/227-7368**; www.nationalcar.com), and **Thrifty** (© **800/367-2277**; www.thrifty.com).

Car-rental rates vary even more than airline fares. A few key questions can save you hundreds of dollars, but you have to ask—reservations agents don't often volunteer money-saving information:

- Are weekend rates lower than weekday rates?
- Does the agency assess a drop-off charge if you don't return the car to the same location where you picked it up?
- Are special promotional rates available?
- Are discounts available for members of AARP, AAA, frequent-flier programs, or trade unions?
- How much tax will be added to the rental bill?
- How much does the rental company charge to refill your gas tank if you return with the tank less than full?

Some companies offer "refueling packages," in which you pay for an entire tank of gas upfront. The cost is usually fairly competitive with local prices, but you don't get credit for any gas remaining in the tank. If a stop at a gas station on

Safe Driving

Keep in mind the following handy driving tips:

o California law requires that drivers and passengers all wear seat belts.

o You can turn right at a red light (unless otherwise indicated), after yielding to traffic and pedestrians, and after coming to a complete stop.

o Cable cars always have the right of way, as do pedestrians at intersections and crosswalks.

o Pay attention to signs and arrows on the streets and roadways, or you might suddenly find yourself in a lane that requires exiting or turning when you want to go straight. What's more, San Francisco's many one-way streets can drive you in circles, but most road maps of the city indicate which way traffic flows.

---

the way to the airport will make you miss your plane, then by all means take advantage of the fuel purchase option. Otherwise, skip it.

Most agencies enforce a minimum-age requirement—usually 25. Some also have a maximum-age limit. If you're concerned that these limits might affect you, ask about rental requirements at the time of booking to avoid problems later.

Make sure you're insured. Hasty assumptions about your personal auto insurance or a rental agency's additional coverage could end up costing you tens of thousands of dollars, even if you are involved in an accident that is clearly the fault of another driver.

If you already have your own car insurance, you are most likely covered in the United States for loss of or damage to a rental car and liability in case of injury to any other party involved in an accident. Be sure to check your policy before you spend extra money (around $10 or more per day) on the collision damage waiver (CDW) offered by all agencies.

Most major credit cards (especially gold and platinum cards) provide some degree of coverage as well—if they were used to pay for the rental. Terms vary widely, however, so be sure to call your credit card company directly before you rent and rely on the card for coverage.

If you're visiting from abroad and plan to rent a car in the United States, keep in mind that foreign driver's licenses are usually recognized in the U.S., but you may want to consider obtaining an international driver's license.

PARKING If you want to have a relaxing vacation, don't even attempt to find street parking on Nob Hill, in North Beach, in Chinatown, by Fisherman's Wharf, or on Telegraph Hill. Park in a garage or take a cab or a bus. If you do find street parking, pay attention to street signs that explain when you can park and for how long. Be especially careful not to park in zones that are tow areas during rush hours. And be forewarned, San Francisco has instituted a 14% parking tax, so don't be surprised by that garage fee!

Curb colors also indicate parking regulations. Red means no stopping or parking, blue is reserved for drivers with disabilities who have a disabled plate or placard, white means there's a 5-minute limit and the driver must stay in the vehicle, green indicates a 10-minute limit, and yellow and yellow-and-black curbs are for stopping to load or unload passengers or luggage only. Also, don't park at a bus stop or in front of a fire hydrant, and watch out for street-cleaning signs. If you violate the law, you might get a hefty ticket or your car might be towed; to get your car back, you'll have to get a release from the nearest district police department and then go to the towing company to pick up the vehicle.

When parking on a hill, apply the hand brake, put the car in gear, and *curb your wheels*—toward the curb when facing downhill, away from the curb when facing uphill. Curbing your wheels not only prevents a possible "runaway" but also keeps you from getting a ticket—an expensive fine that is aggressively enforced.

By Ferry

TO/FROM SAUSALITO, TIBURON, OR LARKSPUR   The Golden Gate Ferry Service fleet (© **415/455-2000;** www.goldengateferry.org) shuttles passengers daily between the San Francisco Ferry Building, at the foot of Market Street, and downtown Sausalito and Larkspur. Service is frequent, departing at reasonable intervals every day of the year except January 1, Thanksgiving Day, and December 25. Phone or check the website for an exact schedule. The ride takes half an hour, and one-way fares are $7.85 for adults, $3.90 for seniors, passengers with disabilities, and youth 6 to 18. Children 5 and under travel free when accompanied by a full-fare paying adult (limit two children per adult). Family rates are available on weekends.

Ferries of the **Blue & Gold Fleet** (© **415/773-1188** for recorded info, or 705-5555 for tickets; www.blueandgoldfleet.com) also provide round-trip service to downtown Sausalito and Tiburon, leaving from Fisherman's Wharf at Pier 41. The one-way cost is $11 for adults, $6.75 for kids 5 to 11. Boats run on a seasonal schedule; phone for departure information. Tickets can be purchased at Pier 41.

[Fast FACTS] SAN FRANCISCO

Area Codes   The area code for San Francisco is **415;** for Oakland, Berkeley, and much of the East Bay, **510;** for the peninsula, generally **650.** Napa and Sonoma are **707.** Most phone numbers in this book are in San Francisco's 415 area code, but there's no need to dial it if you're within the city limits.

ATMs   In the land of shopping malls and immediate gratification, there's an ATM on almost every block—often droves of them. In fact, finding a place to withdraw cash is one of the easiest tasks you'll partake in while visiting San Francisco.

Nationwide, the easiest and best way to get cash away from home is from an ATM (automated teller machine), sometimes referred to as a "cash machine" or "cashpoint." The **Cirrus** (© **800/424-7787;** www.mastercard.com) and PLUS (© **800/843-7587;** www.visa.com) networks span the country; you can find them even in remote regions. Go to your bank card's website to find ATM locations at your destination. Be sure you know your daily withdrawal limit before you depart.

Note: Many banks impose a fee every time you use a card at another bank's ATM, and that fee is often higher for international transactions (up to $5 or more) than for domestic ones (where they're rarely more than $2). In addition, the bank from which you withdraw cash may charge its own fee. To compare banks' ATM fees within the U.S., use www. bankrate.com. Visitors from outside the U.S. should also find out whether their bank assesses a 1% to 3% fee on charges incurred abroad.

Tip: One way around these fees is to ask for cash back at grocery, drug, and convenience stores that accept ATM cards and don't charge usage fees (be sure to ask). Of course, you'll have to purchase something first.

Business Hours   Most banks are open Monday through Friday from 9am to 5pm as well as Saturday mornings. Many banks also have ATMs for 24-hour banking. (See "ATMs," above.) Most stores are open Monday through Saturday from 10 or 11am to at least 6pm, with shorter hours on Sunday. But there are exceptions: Stores in Chinatown, Ghirardelli Square, and Pier 39 stay open much later during the tourist season, and large department stores, including Macy's and Nordstrom, keep late hours. Most restaurants serve lunch from about 11:30am to 2:30pm and dinner from about 5:30 to 10pm. They sometimes serve later on weekends. Nightclubs and bars are usually open daily until 2am, when they are legally bound to stop serving alcohol.

Car Rental   See "By Car," under "Getting Around," earlier.

Cellphones   See "Mobile Phones," below.

Crime   See "Safety," later in this section.

Disabled Travelers   Most disabilities shouldn't stop anyone from traveling. There are more options and resources out there than ever before.

Most of San Francisco's major museums and tourist attractions have wheelchair ramps. Many hotels offer special accommodations and services for wheelchair users and other visitors with disabilities. As well as the ramps, they include extra-large bathrooms and telecommunication devices for hearing-impaired travelers. The Visitor Information Center (p. 404) should have the most up-to-date information.

Travelers in wheelchairs can request special ramped taxis by calling **Yellow Cab** (📞 **415/626-2345**), which charges regular rates for the service. Travelers with disabilities can also get a free copy of the *Muni Access Guide,* published by the San Francisco Municipal Transportation Agency, Accessible Services Program, One South Van Ness, 3rd floor (📞 **415/923-6142**), which is staffed weekdays from 8am to 5pm. Many of the major car-rental companies offer hand-controlled cars for drivers with disabilities. **Alamo** (📞 **800/651-1223**), **Avis** (📞 **800/331-1212,** ext. 7305), and **Budget** (📞 **800/314-3932**) have special hot lines that help provide such a vehicle at any of their U.S. locations with 48 hours' advance notice; **Hertz** (📞 **800/654-3131**) requires between 24 and 72 hours' advance notice at most locations.

Organizations that offer a vast range of resources and assistance to travelers with disabilities include **MossRehab** (📞 **800/CALL-MOSS** [2255-6677]; www.mossresourcenet. org), the **American Foundation for the Blind** (**AFB;** 📞 **800/232-5463;** www.afb.org), and **SATH** (Society for Accessible Travel & Hospitality; 📞 **212/447-7284;** www.sath.org). **AirAmbulanceCard.com** is now partnered with SATH and allows you to preselect top-notch hospitals in case of an emergency.

Access-Able Travel Source (📞 **303/232-2979;** www.access-able.com) offers a comprehensive database on travel agents from around the world with experience in accessible travel, destination-specific access information, and links to such resources as service animals, equipment rentals, and access guides.

Many travel agencies offer customized tours and itineraries for travelers with disabilities. Among them are **Flying Wheels Travel** (✆ **507/451-5005;** www.flyingwheelstravel. com) and **Accessible Journeys** (✆ **800/846-4537** or 610/521-0339; www.disabilitytravel. com).

Flying with Disability (www.flying-with-disability.org) is a comprehensive information source on airplane travel. **Avis Rent A Car** (✆ **888/879-4273**) has an "Avis Access" program that offers services for customers with special travel needs. These include specially outfitted vehicles with swivel seats, spinner knobs, and hand controls; mobility scooter rentals; and accessible bus service. Be sure to reserve well in advance.

Also check out the quarterly magazine *Emerging Horizons* (www.emerginghorizons. com), available by subscription ($17 year U.S.; $22 outside U.S.).

The "Accessible Travel" link at **Mobility-Advisor.com** (www.mobility-advisor.com) offers a variety of travel resources to persons with disabilities.

British travelers should contact **Holiday Care** (✆ **0845-124-9971** in U.K. only; www. holidaycare.org.uk) to access a wide range of travel information and resources for seniors and those with disabilities.

Doctors   See "Hospitals" below.

Drinking Laws   The legal age for purchase and consumption of alcoholic beverages is 21; proof of age is required and often requested at bars, nightclubs, and restaurants, so it's always a good idea to bring ID when you go out. Supermarkets and convenience stores in California sell beer, wine, and liquor. Most restaurants serve alcohol, but some serve only beer and wine. By law, all bars, clubs, restaurants, and stores cannot sell or serve alcohol after 2am, and "last call" tends to start at 1:30am. Do not carry open containers of alcohol in your car or any public area that isn't zoned for alcohol consumption. The police can fine you on the spot. And nothing will ruin your trip faster than getting a citation for DUI (driving under the influence).

Driving Rules   See "Getting Around," earlier in this chapter.

Earthquakes   In the rare event of an earthquake, don't panic. If you're in a tall building, don't run outside; instead, move away from windows and toward the building's center. Crouch under a desk or table, or stand against a wall or under a doorway. If you're in bed, get under the bed, stand in a doorway, or crouch under a sturdy piece of furniture. When exiting the building, use stairwells, not elevators. If you're in your car, pull over to the side of the road and stop, but wait until you're away from bridges or overpasses, as well as telephone or power poles and lines. Stay in your car. If you're outside, stay away from trees, power lines, and the sides of buildings.

Electricity   Like Canada, the United States uses 110–120 volts AC (60 cycles), compared to 220–240 volts AC (50 cycles) in most of Europe, Australia, and New Zealand. Downward converters that change 220–240 volts to 110–120 volts are difficult to find in the United States, so bring one with you.

Embassies & Consulates   All embassies are in the nation's capital, Washington, D.C. Some consulates are in major U.S. cities, and most nations have a mission to the United Nations in New York City. If your country isn't listed below, call for directory information in Washington, D.C. (✆ **202/555-1212**), or check www.embassy.org/embassies.

The embassy of **Australia** is at 1601 Massachusetts Ave. NW, Washington, DC 20036 (✆ **202/797-3000;** www.usa.embassy.gov.au). Consulates are in New York, Honolulu, Houston, Los Angeles, and San Francisco.

The embassy of **Canada** is at 501 Pennsylvania Ave. NW, Washington, DC 20001 (✆ **202/682-1740;** www.canadainternational.gc.ca/washington). Canadian consulates are in Buffalo (New York), Detroit, Los Angeles, New York, and Seattle.

The embassy of **Ireland** is at 2234 Massachusetts Ave. NW, Washington, DC 20008 (✆ **202/462-3939;** www.embassyofireland.org). Irish consulates are in Boston, Chicago, New York, San Francisco, and other cities. See the website for a complete listing.

The embassy of **New Zealand** is at 37 Observatory Circle NW, Washington, DC 20008 (✆ **202/328-4800;** www.nzembassy.com). New Zealand consulates are in Los Angeles, Salt Lake City, San Francisco, and Seattle.

The embassy of the **United Kingdom** is at 3100 Massachusetts Ave. NW, Washington, DC 20008 (✆ **202/588-6500;** http://ukinusa.fco.gov.uk). British consulates are in Atlanta, Boston, Chicago, Cleveland, Houston, Los Angeles, New York, San Francisco, and Seattle.

Emergencies   Call ✆ **911** to report a fire, call the police, or get an ambulance anywhere in the United States. This is a toll-free call. (No coins are required at public telephones.)

Family Travel   If you have enough trouble getting your kids out of the house in the morning, dragging them thousands of miles away may seem like an insurmountable challenge. But family travel can be immensely rewarding, giving you new ways of seeing the world through smaller pairs of eyes.

To make things easier for families vacationing in San Francisco, we include two family-friendly sidebars that highlight the best hotels (p. 86) and attractions (p. 211) for parents and kids.

Recommended family travel websites include **Family Travel Forum** (www.familytravelforum.com), a comprehensive site that offers customized trip planning; **Family Travel Network** (www.familytravelnetwork.com), an online magazine providing travel tips; and **TravelWithYourKids.com** (www.travelwithyourkids.com), a comprehensive site written by parents for parents offering sound advice for long-distance and international travel with children.

To locate accommodations, restaurants, and attractions that are particularly kid friendly, see the "Kids" icon throughout this guide.

Health   If you worry about getting sick away from home, you may want to consider **medical travel insurance.** (See www.frommers.com/planning for detailed information.) In most cases, however, your existing health plan will provide all the coverage you need, but be sure to carry your identification card in your wallet.

If you suffer from a chronic illness, consult your doctor before your departure. Pack **prescription medications** in your carry-on luggage, and carry them in their original containers, with pharmacy labels—otherwise they won't make it through airport security. Visitors from outside the U.S. should carry generic names of prescription drugs. For U.S. travelers, most reliable healthcare plans provide coverage if you get sick away from home. Foreign visitors may have to pay all medical costs upfront and be reimbursed later.

Hospitals   **Saint Francis Memorial Hospital,** 900 Hyde St., between Bush and Pine streets on Nob Hill (✆ **866/240-2087** or 415/353-6000; www.saintfrancismemorial.org), provides emergency service 24 hours a day; no appointment is necessary. The hospital also operates a **physician-referral service** (✆ **800/333-1355** or 415/353-6566).

Insurance   For information on traveler's insurance, trip cancellation insurance, and medical insurance while traveling, please visit www.frommers.com/planning.

Internet & Wi-Fi   San Francisco is totally wired. You'll find that many cafes have wireless access, as do many hotels. Check www.wififreespot.com for a huge list of free Wi-Fi hotspots—including every Peet's coffee shop, Panera, or McDonald's—or stop by one of the following locations around town: **Brainwash,** 1122 Folsom St., between Seventh and Eighth streets (✆ **415/861-FOOD** [3663]; www.brainwash.com); **Quetzal,** 1234 Polk St., at Bush Street (✆ **415/673-4181**); **Copy Central,** 110 Sutter St., at Montgomery Street (✆ **415/392-6470;** www.copycentral.com); **FedEx Office,** 1967 Market St., near Gough Street (✆ **415/252-0864;** www.fedex.com/office). To find a comprehensive list of public Wi-Fi hotspots in San Francisco, go to www.jiwire.com; its Hotspot Finder holds the world's largest directory of public wireless hotspots. To find a list of cybercafes in San Francisco, log onto www.cybercaptive.com or www.cybercafe.com.

   Wherever you go, bring a connection kit of the right power and phone adapters, and a spare Ethernet network cable—or find out whether your hotel supplies them to guests.

Legal Aid   While driving, if you are pulled over for a minor infraction (such as speeding), never attempt to pay the fine directly to a police officer; this could be construed as attempted bribery, a much more serious crime. Pay fines by mail, or directly into the hands of the clerk of the court. If accused of a more serious offense, say and do nothing before consulting a lawyer. In the U.S., the burden is on the state to prove a person's guilt beyond a reasonable doubt, and everyone has the right to remain silent, whether he or she is suspected of a crime or actually arrested. Once arrested, a person can make one telephone call to a party of his or her choice. The international visitor should call his or her embassy or consulate.

LGBT Travelers   Since the 1970s, the Castro has acted as the city's center of gay life and nightlife in the city—though with society's changing norms, gay life has become less centralized (some might say less ghettoized) over the years. For some gay travelers, this is still the Place to Be, especially on a festival weekend, when the streets are filled with out and proud revelry; for other gays, the neighborhood is a quaint relic of the past to be visited occasionally (while shielding their children's eyes from the sex toys in the shop windows). For other San Franciscans and many travelers, it's a fun area with some wonderful shops.

   Gays and lesbians make up a good portion of San Francisco's population, so it's no surprise that clubs and bars all over town cater to them. Although lesbian interests are concentrated primarily in the East Bay (especially Oakland), a significant community resides in the Mission District, around 16th and Valencia streets and in Hayes Valley.

   Several local publications concentrate on in-depth coverage of news, information, and listings of goings-on around town for gays and lesbians. The *Bay Area Reporter* (www.ebar.com) has the most comprehensive listings, including a weekly calendar of events. Distributed free on Thursday, it can be found stacked at the corner of 18th and Castro streets and at Ninth and Harrison streets, as well as in bars, bookshops, and stores around town. It may also be available in gay and lesbian bookstores elsewhere in the country.

   The **International Gay and Lesbian Travel Association (IGLTA;** ✆ **800/448-8550** or 954/776-2626; www.iglta.org) is the trade association for the gay and lesbian travel industry, and offers an online directory of gay- and lesbian-friendly travel businesses and tour operators.

   Many agencies offer tours and travel itineraries specifically for gay and lesbian travelers. **Above and Beyond Tours** (✆ **800/397-2681;** www.abovebeyondtoursllc.com) are gay

Australia tour specialists. San Francisco–based **Now, Voyager** (✆ 800/255-6951; www.nowvoyager.com) offers worldwide trips and cruises, and **Olivia** (✆ 800/631-6277; www.olivia.com) offers lesbian cruises and resort vacations.

Gay.com Travel (✆ 800/929-2268 or 415/644-8044; www.gay.com) also owns *Out Traveler,* now online-only at www.outtraveler.com. Both provide regularly updated information about gay-owned, gay-oriented, and gay-friendly lodging, dining, sightseeing, nightlife, and shopping establishments in every popular destination worldwide. British travelers should click on the "Travel" link at www.gay.co.uk for advice and gay-friendly trip ideas.

The Canadian website **GayTraveler** (www.gaytraveler.ca) offers ideas and advice for gay travel all over the world.

For travel guides, try *Spartacus International Gay Guide* (Bruno Gmünder Verlag; www.spartacusworld.com/gayguide), or the *Damron* guides (www.damron.com), both with separate, annual books for gay men and lesbians. For more gay and lesbian travel resources, visit frommers.com.

Mail   At press time, domestic postage rates were 32¢ for a postcard and 45¢ for a letter. For international mail, a first-class letter of up to 1 ounce costs $1.05 (85¢ to Canada and to Mexico); a first-class postcard costs the same as a letter. For more information go to www.usps.com.

If you aren't sure what your address will be in the United States, mail can be sent to you, in your name, c/o General Delivery at the main post office of the city or region where you expect to be. (Call ✆ 800/275-8777 for information on the nearest post office.) The addressee must pick up mail in person and must produce proof of identity (driver's license, passport, and the like). Most post offices will hold mail for up to 1 month, and are open Monday to Friday from 8am to 6pm, and Saturday from 9am to 3pm.

Always include zip codes when mailing items in the U.S. If you don't know your zip code, visit www.usps.com/zip4.

Medical Requirements   Unless you're arriving from an area known to be suffering from an epidemic (particularly cholera or yellow fever), inoculations or vaccinations are not required for entry into the United States.

Mobile Phones   Just because your cellphone works at home doesn't mean it'll work everywhere in the U.S. (thanks to our nation's fragmented cellphone system). It's a good bet that your phone will work in major cities, but take a look at your wireless company's coverage map on its website before heading out; T-Mobile, Sprint, and Nextel are particularly weak in rural areas. If you need to stay in touch at a destination where you know your phone won't work, rent a phone that does from **InTouch USA** (✆ 800/872-7626; www.intouchglobal.com) or a rental car location, but be aware that you'll pay $1 a minute or more for airtime.

If you're not from the U.S., you'll be appalled at the poor reach of our **GSM** (Global System for Mobile Communications) **wireless network,** which is used by much of the rest of the world. Your phone will probably work in most major U.S. cities; it definitely won't work in many rural areas. To see where GSM phones work in the U.S., check out www.t-mobile.com/coverage/national_popup.asp. And you may or may not be able to send SMS (text messaging) home.

Money & Costs   Frommer's lists exact prices in the local currency. The currency conversions quoted were correct at press time. However, rates fluctuate, so before departing consult a currency exchange website such as www.oanda.com/currency/converter to check up-to-the-minute rates.

THE VALUE OF THE U.S. DOLLAR VS. OTHER POPULAR CURRENCIES

US$	Can$	UK£	Euro (€)	Aus$	NZ$
1	1.026	0.66	0.73	1.094	1.42

It's always advisable to bring money in a variety of forms on a vacation: a mix of cash, credit cards, and ATM cards. You should also have enough petty cash upon arrival to cover airport incidentals, tipping, and transportation to your hotel before you leave home. You can always withdraw money upon arrival at an airport ATM, but you'll still need to make smaller change for tipping.

The most common bills in the U.S. are the $1 (a "buck"), $5, $10, and $20 denominations. There are also $2 bills (seldom encountered), $50 bills, and $100 bills. (The last two are usually not welcome as payment for small purchases.)

Coins come in seven denominations: 1¢ (1 cent, or a penny); 5¢ (5 cents, or a nickel); 10¢ (10 cents, or a dime); 25¢ (25 cents, or a quarter); 50¢ (50 cents, or a half dollar); the gold-colored Sacagawea coin, worth $1; and the rare silver dollar.

Credit cards are the most widely used form of payment in San Francisco: **Visa** (Barclaycard in Britain), **MasterCard** (Eurocard in Europe, Access in Britain, Chargex in Canada), **American Express, Diners Club,** and **Discover.** They also provide a convenient record of all your expenses and offer relatively good exchange rates. You can withdraw cash advances from your credit cards at banks or ATMs, but high fees make credit card cash advances a pricey way to get cash.

It's highly recommended that you travel with at least one major credit card. You must have a credit card to rent a car, and hotels and airlines usually require a credit card imprint as a deposit against expenses.

ATM cards with major credit card backing, known as **"debit cards,"** are now a commonly acceptable form of payment in most stores and restaurants. Debit cards draw money directly from your checking account. Some stores enable you to receive cash back on your debit-card purchases as well. The same is true at most U.S. post offices.

WHAT THINGS COST IN SAN FRANCISCO

	US$
Taxi from SFO to downtown	$40–$50
Inexpensive hotel room, double occupancy	$120–$150
Moderate hotel room, double occupancy	$150–$200
Cup of small coffee (Peets or Starbucks)	$1.75–$1.80
1 gallon of regular gas	$4.09–4.29
Admission to museums	$10–$25
Glass of Napa Valley red wine	$7–$15
Bus or streetcar fare for adults	$2
Cable car fare	$5

Beware of hidden credit card fees while traveling. Check with your credit or debit card issuer to see what fees, if any, will be charged for overseas transactions. Recent reform legislation in the U.S., for example, has curbed some exploitative lending practices. But many banks have responded by increasing fees in other areas, including fees for customers who use credit and debit cards while out of the country—even if those charges were made in U.S. dollars. Fees can amount to 3% or more of the purchase price. Check with your bank before departing to avoid any surprise charges on your statement.

For help with currency conversions, tip calculations, and more, download Frommer's convenient Travel Tools app for your mobile device. Go to www.frommers.com/go/mobile and click on the Travel Tools icon.

Newspapers & Magazines   The city's main daily (and getting thinner and crappier by the week) is the *San Francisco Chronicle* (www.sfgate.com), which is distributed throughout the city. Check out the *Chronicle's* Sunday edition, which includes a pink "Datebook" section—a preview of the week's upcoming events. The free *San Francisco Examiner* (www.sfexaminer.com) is published Monday through Friday with a weekend edition. The free weekly *San Francisco Bay Guardian* (www.sfbg.com) and *San Francisco Weekly* (www.sfweekly.com), tabloids of news and listings, are indispensable for nightlife information; they're widely distributed through street-corner kiosks and at city cafes and restaurants.

Of the many free tourist-oriented publications, the most widely read are *San Francisco Guide* (www.sfguide.com), a handbook-size weekly containing maps and information on current events, and *Where San Francisco* (www.wheremagazine.com), a glossy regular format monthly magazine. You can find them in most hotels, shops, and restaurants in the major tourist areas.

Packing   Dress warm, even in the summer. As the saying goes in San Francisco, if you don't like the weather, wait 5 minutes. Because of offshore breezes, microclimates, and the prevalence of fog in the summer, the temperature changes constantly in San Francisco, particularly if you're on the move. Even if it's sunny and warm at noon, bring a sweater or light jacket just in case—when the fog rolls in its gets chilly fast. For more helpful information on packing for your trip, download our convenient Travel Tools app for your mobile device. Go to www.frommers.com/go/mobile and tap on the Travel Tools icon.

Passports   Virtually every air traveler entering the U.S. is required to show a passport. All persons, including U.S. citizens, traveling by air between the United States and Canada, Mexico, Central and South America, the Caribbean, and Bermuda are required to present a valid passport. *Note:* U.S. and Canadian citizens entering the U. S. at land and sea ports of entry from within the western hemisphere must now also present a passport or other documents compliant with the Western Hemisphere Travel Initiative (WHTI; see www.getyouhome.gov for details). Children 15 and under may continue entering with only a U.S. birth certificate, or other proof of U.S. citizenship.

Australia   **Australian Passport Information Service** (✆ 131-232; www.passports.gov. au).

Canada   **Passport Office,** Department of Foreign Affairs and International Trade, Ottawa, ON K1A 0G3 (✆ 800/567-6868; www.ppt.gc.ca).

Ireland   **Passport Office,** Setanta Centre, Molesworth Street, Dublin 2 (✆ 01/671-1633; www.foreignaffairs.gov.ie).

New Zealand   **Passports Office,** Department of Internal Affairs, 47 Boulcott St., Wellington, 6011 (✆ 0800/225-050 in New Zealand or 04/474-8100; www.passports.govt.nz).

United Kingdom   Visit your nearest passport office, major post office, or travel agency or contact the **Identity and Passport Service (IPS)**, 89 Eccleston Sq., London, SW1V 1PN (📞 **0300/222-0000;** www.ips.gov.uk).

United States   To find your regional passport office, check the U.S. State Department website (travel.state.gov/passport) or call the **National Passport Information Center** (📞 **877/487-2778**) for automated information.

Police   In an emergency, dial 📞 911. For nonemergency police matters, call 📞 415/553-0123.

Safety   For a big city, San Francisco is relatively safe and requires only that you use common sense (for example, don't leave your new video camera on the seat of your parked car). However, in neighborhoods such as Lower Haight, the Mission, the Tenderloin (a few blocks west of Union Square), and Fisherman's Wharf (at night especially), it's a good idea to pay attention to yourself and your surroundings.

Avoid carrying valuables with you on the street, and don't display expensive cameras or electronic equipment. Hold on to your pocketbook, and place your billfold in an inside pocket. In theaters, restaurants, and other public places, keep your possessions in sight.

Remember also that hotels are open to the public, and in a large hotel, security may not be able to screen everyone entering. Always lock your room door—don't assume that inside your hotel you are automatically safe.

Driving safety is important, too. Ask your rental agency about personal safety, and ask for a traveler-safety brochure when you pick up your car. Ask for written directions to your destination or a map with the route clearly marked. (Many agencies offer the option of renting a cellphone for the duration of your car rental; check with the rental agent when you pick up the car.) Try to arrive and depart during daylight hours.

Recently, more crime has involved cars and drivers. If you drive off a highway into a doubtful neighborhood, leave the area as quickly as possible. If you have an accident, even on the highway, stay in your car with the doors locked until you assess the situation or until the police arrive. If you're bumped from behind on the street or are involved in a minor accident with no injuries, and the situation appears to be suspicious, motion to the other driver to follow you. Never get out of your car in such situations. Go directly to the nearest police precinct, well-lit service station, or 24-hour store.

Always try to park in well-lit and well-traveled areas. Never leave any packages or valuables in sight. If someone attempts to rob you or steal your car, don't try to resist the thief or carjacker. Report the incident to the police department immediately by calling 📞 911. This is a free call, even from pay phones.

Senior Travel   Nearly every attraction in San Francisco offers a senior discount; age requirements vary, and specific prices are listed in chapter 6. Public transportation and movie theaters also have reduced rates. Don't be shy about asking for discounts, but always carry some kind of identification, such as a driver's license, that shows your date of birth.

Members of **AARP,** 601 E St. NW, Washington, DC 20049 (📞 **888/687-2277;** www. aarp.org), get discounts on hotels, airfares, and car rentals. AARP offers members a wide range of benefits, including *AARP The Magazine* and a monthly newsletter. Anyone 50 and over can join.

Recommended publications offering travel resources and discounts for seniors include the quarterly magazine *Travel 50 & Beyond* (www.travel50andbeyond.com) and the

Earthquake Advice

Earthquakes are fairly common in California, though most are so minor you won't even notice them. However, in case of a significant shaker, there are a few basic precautionary measures to follow: If you are inside a building, do not run outside into falling debris. Seek cover—stand under a doorway or against a wall, and stay away from windows. If you exit a building after a substantial quake, use stairwells, not elevators. If you're in a car, pull over to the side of the road and stop—but not until you are away from bridges, overpasses, telephone poles, and power lines. Stay in your car. If you're out walking, stay outside and away from trees, power lines, and the sides of buildings. If you're in an area with tall buildings, find a doorway in which to stand. And if you're having cocktails, find a straw.

best-selling paperback *Unbelievably Good Deals and Great Adventures That You Absolutely Can't Get Unless You're Over 50 2005–2006, 16th Edition* (McGraw-Hill), by Joann Rattner Heilman.

Smoking   If San Francisco is California's most European city in looks and style, the comparison stops when it comes to smoking in public. Each year, smoking laws in the city become stricter. Ergo, heavy smokers are in for a tough time in San Francisco. Smoking is illegal in public buildings, sports arenas, elevators, theaters, banks, lobbies, restaurants, offices, stores, bed-and-breakfasts, most small hotels, and bars. That's right: You can't even smoke in California bars unless drinks are served solely by the owner (though you will find that a few neighborhood bars turn a blind eye and pass you an ashtray). Hotels are also increasingly going nonsmoking, though some still offer smoking rooms. City lawmakers are also currently considering bans in outdoor public areas.

Student Travel   A valid student ID will often qualify students for discounts on airfare, accommodations, entry to museums, cultural events, movies, and more in San Francisco. Check out the **International Student Travel Confederation** (ISTC; www.istc.org) website for comprehensive travel services information and details on how to get an **International Student Identity Card (ISIC)**, which qualifies students for substantial savings on rail passes, plane tickets, entrance fees, and more. It also provides students with basic health and life insurance and a 24-hour help line. The card is valid for a maximum of 18 months. You can apply for the card online or in person at **STA Travel** (📞 **800/781-4040** in North America, 132 782 in Australia, or 0871/230-0040 in the U.K.; www.statravel.com), the biggest student travel agency in the world; check out the website to locate STA Travel offices worldwide. If you're no longer a student but are still under 26, you can get an **International Youth Travel Card (IYTC)** from the same people, which entitles you to some discounts. **Travel CUTS** (📞 **800/592-2887**; www.travelcuts.com) offers similar services for both Canadians and U.S. residents. Irish students may prefer to turn to **USIT** (📞 **01/602-1906;** www.usit.ie), an Ireland-based specialist in student, youth, and independent travel.

Taxes   The United States has no value-added tax (VAT) or other indirect tax at the national level. Every state, county, and city may levy its own local tax on all purchases, including hotel and restaurant checks and airline tickets. These taxes will not appear on price tags. Sales tax in San Francisco is 8.5%. Hotel tax is charged on the room tariff only (which is not subject to sales tax) and is set by the city, ranging from 12% to 17% around Northern California.

Telephones   Many convenience groceries and packaging services sell **prepaid calling cards** in denominations up to $50. Many public pay phones at airports now accept

American Express, MasterCard, and Visa. **Local calls** made from most pay phones cost either 25¢ or 35¢. Most long-distance and international calls can be dialed directly from any phone. **To make calls within the United States and to Canada,** dial 1 followed by the area code and the seven-digit number. **For other international calls,** dial 011 followed by the country code, city code, and the number you are calling.

Calls to area codes **800, 888, 877,** and **866** are toll-free. However, calls to area codes **700** and **900** (chat lines, bulletin boards, "dating" services, and so on) can be expensive—charges of 95¢ to $3 or more per minute. Some numbers have minimum charges that can run $15 or more.

For **reversed-charge or collect calls,** and for person-to-person calls, dial the number 0 then the area code and number; an operator will come on the line, and you should specify whether you are calling collect, person-to-person, or both. If your operator-assisted call is international, ask for the overseas operator.

For **directory assistance** ("Information"), dial 411 for local numbers and national numbers in the U.S. and Canada. For dedicated long-distance information, dial 1, then the appropriate area code plus 555-1212.

Time   The continental United States is divided into **four time zones:** Eastern Standard Time (EST), Central Standard Time (CST), Mountain Standard Time (MST), and Pacific Standard Time (PST). Alaska and Hawaii have their own zones. For example, when it's 9am in San Francisco (PST), it's 7am in Honolulu (HST), 10am in Denver (MST), 11am in Chicago (CST), noon in New York City (EST), 5pm in London (GMT), and 2am the next day in Sydney.

Daylight saving time is in effect from 1am on the second Sunday in March to 1am on the first Sunday in November, except in Arizona, Hawaii, the U.S. Virgin Islands, and Puerto Rico. Daylight saving time moves the clock 1 hour ahead of standard time.

For help with time translations, and more, download our convenient Travel Tools app for your mobile device. Go to www.frommers.com/go/mobile and tap on the Travel Tools icon.

Tipping   In hotels, tip **bellhops** at least $1 per bag ($2–$3 if you have a lot of luggage) and tip the **chamber staff** $1 to $2 per day (more if you've left a big mess for him or her to clean up). Tip the **doorman** or **concierge** only if he or she has provided you with some specific service (for example, calling a cab for you or obtaining difficult-to-get theater tickets). Tip the **valet-parking attendant** $1 every time you get your car.

In restaurants, bars, and nightclubs, tip **service staff** and **bartenders** 15% to 20% of the check, tip **checkroom attendants** $1 per garment, and tip **valet-parking attendants** $1 per vehicle.

As for other service personnel, tip **cabdrivers** 15% of the fare, tip **skycaps** at airports at least $1 per bag ($2–$3 if you have a lot of luggage), and tip **hairdressers and barbers** 15% to 20%.

For help with tip calculations, currency conversions, and more, download our convenient Travel Tools app for your mobile device. Go to www.frommers.com/go/mobile and tap on the Travel Tools icon.

Toilets   Those weird, oval-shaped, olive-green kiosks on the sidewalks throughout San Francisco are high-tech self-cleaning public toilets. They've been placed on high-volume streets to provide relief for pedestrians. French potty-maker JCDecaux gave them to the city for free—advertising covers the cost. It costs 25¢ to enter, with no time limit, but we don't recommend using the ones in the sketchier neighborhoods such as the Mission because they're mostly used by crackheads and prostitutes. Toilets can also be found in hotel lobbies, bars, restaurants, museums, department stores, railway and bus stations, and service stations. Large hotels and fast-food restaurants are often the best bet for clean facilities. Restaurants and bars in resorts or heavily visited areas may reserve their restrooms for patrons.

VAT   See "Taxes," above.

Visas   The U.S. State Department has a Visa Waiver Program (VWP) allowing citizens of the following countries to enter the United States without a visa for stays of up to 90 days: Andorra, Australia, Austria, Belgium, Brunei, Czech Republic, Denmark, Estonia, Finland, France, Germany, Greece, Hungary, Iceland, Ireland, Italy, Japan, Latvia, Liechtenstein, Lithuania, Luxembourg, Malta, Monaco, the Netherlands, New Zealand, Norway, Portugal, San Marino, Singapore, Slovakia, Slovenia, South Korea, Spain, Sweden, Switzerland, and the United Kingdom. (**Note:** This list was accurate at press time; for the most up-to-date list of countries in the VWP, consult http://travel.state.gov/visa.) Even though a visa isn't necessary, in an effort to help U.S. officials check travelers against terror watch lists before they arrive at U.S. borders, visitors from VWP countries must register online through the Electronic System for Travel Authorization (ESTA) before boarding a plane or a boat to the U.S. Travelers must complete an electronic application providing basic personal and travel eligibility information. The Department of Homeland Security recommends filling out the form at least 3 days before traveling. Authorizations will be valid for up to 2 years or until the traveler's passport expires, whichever comes first. Currently, there is one US$14 fee for the online application. Existing ESTA registrations remain valid through their expiration dates. **Note:** Any passport issued on or after October 26, 2006, by a VWP country must be an **e-Passport** for VWP travelers to be eligible to enter the U.S. without a visa. Citizens of these nations also need to present a round-trip air or cruise ticket upon arrival. E-Passports contain computer chips capable of storing biometric information, such as the required digital photograph of the holder. If your passport doesn't have this feature, you can still travel without a visa if the valid passport was issued before October 26, 2005, and includes a machine-readable zone; or if the valid passport was issued between October 26, 2005, and October 25, 2006, and includes a digital photograph. For more information, go to http://travel.state.gov/visa. Canadian citizens may enter the United States without visas, but will need to show passports and proof of residence.

Citizens of all other countries must have (1) a valid passport that expires at least 6 months later than the scheduled end of their visit to the U.S.; and (2) a tourist visa.

For information about **U.S. visas,** go to http://travel.state.gov and click on "Visas." Or go to one of the following websites:

Australian citizens can obtain up-to-date visa information from the **U.S. Embassy Canberra,** Moonah Place, Yarralumla, ACT 2600 (✆ **02/6214-5600**), or by checking the U.S. Diplomatic Mission's website at http://canberra.usembassy.gov/visas.html.

British subjects can obtain up-to-date visa information by calling the **U.S. Embassy Visa Information Line** (✆ **09042-450-100** from within the U.K. at £1.20 per minute; or ✆ 866/382-3589 from within the U.S. at a flat rate of $16 payable by credit card only) or by visiting the "Visas to the U.S." section of the American Embassy London's website at http://london.usembassy.gov/visas.html.

Irish citizens can obtain up-to-date visa information through the **U.S. Embassy Dublin,** 42 Elgin Rd., Ballsbridge, Dublin 4 (✆ **1580-47-VISA** [8472] from within the Republic of Ireland at €2.40 per minute; http://dublin.usembassy.gov).

Citizens of **New Zealand** can obtain up-to-date visa information by contacting the **U.S. Embassy New Zealand,** 29 Fitzherbert Terrace, Thorndon, Wellington (✆ **644/462-6000;** http://newzealand.usembassy.gov).

Visitor Information   The **San Francisco Visitor Information Center,** on the lower level of Hallidie Plaza, 900 Market St., at Powell Street (✆ **415/391-2000;** www.onlyinsan francisco.com), is the best source of specialized information about the city. Even if you don't have a specific question, you might want to request the free *Visitors Planning Guide* and the *San Francisco Visitors kit,* which includes a 6-month calendar of events; a city history; shopping and dining information; several good, clear maps; plus lodging information.

For information on the state as a whole, log onto the **California Tourism** website at www.visitcalifornia.com. U.S. and Canadian residents can receive free travel planning information by mail by calling ✆ **800/862-2543.** Most cities and towns also have a tourist bureau or chamber of commerce that distributes information on the area.

Wi-Fi   See "Internet & Wi-Fi," earlier in this section.

Index

Restaurants

RESTAURANT INDEX

PHOTO CREDITS

PHOTO CREDITS